CUSTOM ED
TRIDENT TECHNIC

DISPUTE MORAL ISSUES
A Reader
Third Edition

Mark Timmons

Source material from:
Timmons, *Disputed Moral Issues: A Reader, 3rd edition.*
978-0-19-994679-2

Oxford New York
OXFORD UNIVERSITY PRESS

OXFORD
UNIVERSITY PRESS

Oxford University Press is a department of the University of Oxford. It furthers the University's
objective of excellence in research, scholarship, and education by publishing worldwide.

Oxford   New York
Auckland   Cape Town   Dar es Salaam   Hong Kong   Karachi
Kuala Lumpur   Madrid   Melbourne   Mexico City   Nairobi
New Delhi   Shanghai   Taipei   Toronto

With offices in
Argentina   Austria   Brazil   Chile   Czech Republic   France   Greece
Guatemala   Hungary   Italy   Japan Poland   Portugal   Singapore
South Korea   Switzerland   Thailand   Turkey   Ukraine   Vietnam

Copyright © 2015 by Oxford University Press.

Published by Oxford University Press.
198 Madison Avenue, New York, New York 10016
http://www.oup.com

Oxford is a registered trademark of Oxford University Press.

ISBN 978-0-19-024457-6

Contents

1 } A Moral Theory Primer

In 1998, Dr. Jack Kevorkian helped Thomas Youk end his life by giving him a lethal injection of drugs—an incident that was videotaped and later broadcast on CBS's *60 Minutes.*[1] Youk had been suffering from amyotrophic lateral sclerosis (often called Lou Gehrig's disease), a progressive neurodegenerative disease that attacks nerve cells in the brain and spinal cord, eventually leading to death. In the later stages of the disease, its victims are completely paralyzed, as was Youk at the time of his death.

Kevorkian's killing Youk was a case of euthanasia, which is defined as the act of killing (or allowing to die) on grounds of mercy for the victim. In this case, because Youk consented to his own death and because Kevorkian brought about Youk's death by an act of lethal injection, Kevorkian's action was an instance of voluntary active euthanasia. Kevorkian was eventually tried and convicted of second degree murder for his active role in bringing about Youk's death. But even if Kevorkian did violate the law, was his action morally wrong? Youk's immediate family and many others saw nothing morally wrong with Youk's decision or with Kevorkian's act. They argued, for example, that proper respect for an individual's freedom of choice means that people in Youk's situation have a moral right to choose to die and that, therefore, Kevorkian was not acting immorally in helping Youk end his life. Of course, many others disagreed, arguing, for example, that euthanasia is morally wrong because of its possible bad effects over time on society, including the possibility that the practice of euthanasia could be abused, and vulnerable persons might be put to death without their consent. Which side of this moral dispute is correct? Is euthanasia at least sometimes morally right, or is this practice morally wrong?

Disputes over moral issues are a fact of our social lives. Most people, through television, the Internet, magazines, and conversing with others, are familiar with some of the general contours of such disputes—disputes, for example, over the death penalty, the ethical treatment of animals, human cloning, abortion. The same sort of moral question raised about the actions of Kevorkian can be raised about these and other moral issues. Thinking critically about such moral issues is where philosophy becomes especially important.

A *philosophical* approach to moral issues has as its guiding aim arriving at correct or justified answers to questions about the morality of the death penalty, the ethical treatment of animals, human cloning, abortion, and other issues of moral concern. Given the contested nature of such practices as cloning and abortion, one needs to be able to defend one's position with *reasons.* Just as those who dispute questions about, say, science or history are expected to give reasons for the scientific and historical beliefs they hold, those who seriously dispute moral questions are expected to give reasons for whatever moral position they take on

1

a certain issue. If we examine how philosophers go about providing reasons for the moral positions they take on certain issues, we find that very often they appeal to a **moral theory.** That is, in arguing for a particular position on the topic of, say, euthanasia, philosophers often make their case by applying a moral theory to the practice of euthanasia. Applying moral theory to issues of practical concern—practical issues—is one dominant way in which reasoning in ethics proceeds, and this way of tackling moral issues by applying theory to cases is featured in this book of readings.

But what is a moral theory? What are its guiding aims? What moral theories are there? How is a moral theory used in reasoning about disputed moral issues? These are the main questions of concern in this moral theory primer.

1.   WHAT IS A MORAL THEORY?

According to philosopher John Rawls, "The two main concepts of ethics are those of the right and the good. . . . The structure of an ethical theory is, then, largely determined by how it defines and connects these two basic notions."[2]

In explaining what a moral theory is, then, the place to begin is by clarifying the two main concepts featured in such a theory.

The Main Concepts: The Right and the Good

In ethics, the terms "right" and "wrong" are used primarily to evaluate the morality of actions, and in this chapter we are mainly concerned with moral theories that address the nature of right and wrong action (or right action, for short). Here, talk of right action in contrast to wrong action involves using the term "right" broadly to refer to actions that aren't wrong. Used in this broad sense, to say of an action that it is right is to say that it is "all right" (not wrong) to perform, and we leave open the question of whether the act, in addition to being all right, is an action that we morally ought to perform—an obligation or duty. But we sometimes find "right" being used narrowly to refer to actions that are "the" morally right action for one to perform, and when so used, it refers to actions that are morally required or obligatory (one's obligation or duty). Actions that are all right to perform (right in the sense of merely being not wrong) and that are also not one's moral obligation to perform—actions that are all right to perform and all right not to perform—are morally optional. So, we have three basic categories of moral evaluation into which an action may fall: an action may be morally obligatory (something one morally ought to do, is morally required to do, is one's duty), or morally optional, or morally wrong. To help keep this terminology straight, I have summarized what I have been saying in Figure 1.1.

Again, in ethics, the terms "good" and "bad" are used primarily in assessing the value of persons (their character) as well as experiences, things, and states of affairs. Philosophers distinguish between something's having **intrinsic value** (that is, being intrinsically good or bad) and something's having **extrinsic value** (that is, being extrinsically good or bad). Something has intrinsic value when its value depends on features that are *inherent* to it,

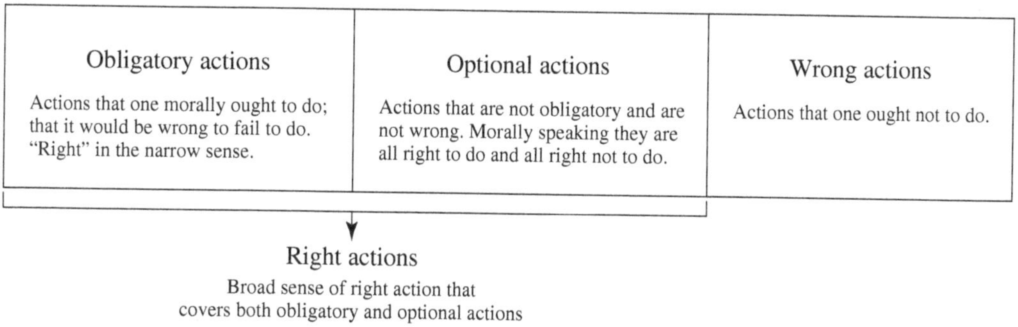

Obligatory actions	Optional actions	Wrong actions
Actions that one morally ought to do; that it would be wrong to fail to do. "Right" in the narrow sense.	Actions that are not obligatory and are not wrong. Morally speaking they are all right to do and all right not to do.	Actions that one ought not to do.

Right actions
Broad sense of right action that
covers both obligatory and optional actions

FIGURE 1.1   Basic Categories of Right Conduct

whereas something is extrinsically good when its goodness is a matter of how it is related to something else that is intrinsically good. For instance, some philosophers maintain that happiness is intrinsically good—its goodness depends on the inherent nature of happiness—and that things like money and power, while not intrinsically good, are nevertheless extrinsically good (valuable) because they can be used to bring about or contribute to happiness. Thus, the notion of intrinsic value is the more basic of the two notions, and so philosophical accounts of value are concerned with the nature of intrinsic value. And here we can recognize three basic value categories: the *intrinsically good,* the *intrinsically bad* (also referred to as the intrinsically *evil*), and what we may call the *intrinsically value-neutral*—that is, the category of all those things that are neither intrinsically good nor bad (though they may have extrinsic value).[3]

A moral theory, then, is a theory about the nature of the right and the good and about the proper method for making correct or justified moral decisions. Accordingly, here are some of the main questions that a moral theory attempts to answer:

1. What *makes* an action right or wrong—what *best explains why* right acts are right and wrong acts are wrong?
2. What *makes* something good or bad—what *best explains why* intrinsically good things are intrinsically good (and similarly for things that are intrinsically bad or evil)?
3. What is the *proper method* (supposing there is one) for reasoning our way to correct or justified moral conclusions about the rightness and wrongness of actions and the goodness and badness of persons, and other items of moral evaluation?

In order to understand more fully what a moral theory is and how it attempts to answer these questions, let us relate what has just been said to the two guiding aims of moral theory.

Two Main Aims of a Moral Theory

Corresponding to the first two questions about the nature of the right and the good is what we may call the theoretical aim of a moral theory:

The **theoretical aim** of a moral theory is to discover those underlying features of actions, persons, and other items of moral evaluation that *make* them right or wrong, good or bad and thus *explain why* such items have the moral properties they have. Features of this sort serve as *moral criteria* of the right and the good.

Our third main question about proper methodology in ethics is the basis for the practical aim of a moral theory:

> The **practical aim** of a moral theory is to offer *practical guidance* for how we might arrive at correct or justified moral verdicts about matters of moral concern—verdicts which we can then use to help guide choice.

Given these aims, we can evaluate a moral theory by seeing how well it satisfies them. We will return to the issue of evaluating moral theories in section 3. For the time being, we can gain a clearer understanding of these aims by considering the role that principles typically play in moral theories.

The Role of Moral Principles

In attempting to satisfy these two aims, philosophers typically propose **moral principles**— very general moral statements that specify conditions under which an action is right (or wrong) and something is intrinsically good (or bad). Principles that state conditions for an action's being right (or wrong) are **principles of right conduct,** and those that specify conditions under which something has intrinsic value are **principles of value.** Here is an example of a principle of right conduct (where "right" is being used in its broad sense to mean "not wrong"):

> P   An action is right if and only if (and because) it would, if performed, likely bring about at least as much overall happiness as would any available alternative action.[4]

This principle, understood as a moral criterion of right action, purports to reveal the underlying nature of right action—what *makes* a right action right. According to P, facts about how much overall happiness an action would bring about were it to be performed are what determine whether it is morally right. Although P addresses the rightness of actions, it has implications for wrongness as well. From P, together with the definitional claim that if an action is not morally right (in the broad sense of the term) then it is morally wrong, we may infer the following:

> P*   An action is wrong if and only if (and because) it would, if performed, likely not bring about at least as much overall happiness as would some available alternative action.

Since, as we have just seen, principles about moral wrongness can be derived from principles of rightness, I shall, in explaining a moral theory's account of right and wrong, simply formulate a theory's principles (there may be more than one) for right action.

In addition to serving as moral criteria, principles like P are typically intended to provide some practical guidance for coming to correct or justified moral verdicts about particular issues, thus addressing the practical aim of moral theory. The idea is that if P is a correct moral principle, then we should be able to use it to guide our moral deliberations in coming to correct conclusions about the rightness of actions, thus serving as a basis for moral decision making. In reasoning our way to moral conclusions about what to do, P has us focus on the consequences of actions and instructs us to consider in particular how much overall happiness actions would likely bring about.

To sum up, a moral theory can be understood as setting forth moral principles of right conduct and value that are supposed to explain what makes an action or other object of evaluation right or wrong, good or bad (thus satisfying the theoretical aim), as well as principles that can be used to guide moral thought in arriving at correct or justified decisions about what to do (thus satisfying the practical aim).

The Structure of a Moral Theory

Finally, what Rawls calls the "structure" of a moral theory is a matter of how a theory connects the right and the good. As we shall see, some theories take the concept of the good to be more basic than the concept of the right and thus define or characterize the rightness of actions in terms of considerations of intrinsic goodness. Call such theories value-based moral theories. **Value-based moral theories** include versions of consequentialism, natural law theory, and virtue ethics. However, some moral theories do not define rightness in terms of goodness. Some theories are **duty-based moral theories**—theories that take the concept of duty to be basic and so define or characterize the rightness of actions independently of considerations of goodness. These theories are often called "deontological" moral theories (from *deon,* the Greek term for duty). The moral theory of Immanuel Kant (see later in this chapter) and theories inspired by Kant (Kantian moral theories) are arguably deontological.[5] And what is called the ethics of prima facie duty, if not a pure deontological theory, contains deontological elements, as we shall see when we discuss this theory later in section 2.

Brief Summary

Now that we have reviewed a few basic elements of moral theory, let us briefly sum up.

- *Main concepts of moral theory.* The two main concepts featured in moral theory are the concepts of the right (and wrong) and the good (and bad).
- *Two aims of moral theory.* A moral theory can be understood as having two central aims. The theoretical aim is to explain the underlying nature of the right and the good—specifying those features of actions or other items of evaluation that *make* an action or whatever right or wrong, good or bad. We call such features "**moral criteria**." The practical aim is to offer practical guidance for how we might arrive at correct or justified moral verdicts about matters of moral concern.
- *The role of moral principles.* A moral theory is typically composed of moral principles (sometimes a single, fundamental principle) that are intended to serve as criteria of the right and the good (thus satisfying the theoretical aim) and are also intended to be useful in guiding moral thinking toward correct, or at least justified conclusions about some moral issue.
- *The structure of a moral theory.* Considerations of structure concern how a moral theory connects the concepts of the right and the good. Value-based theories make the good (intrinsic value) more basic than the right and define or characterize the right in terms of the good. Duty-based theories characterize the right independently of considerations of value.

In the next section, we briefly examine seven moral theories that play a large role in philosophical discussions of disputed moral issues. After presenting these theories, I devote the remaining section and an appendix to questions that are likely to occur to readers. First, there is the question of why studying moral theories is helpful in thinking about disputed moral issues when there is no *one* moral theory that is accepted by all those who study moral theory. Rather, we find a variety of apparently competing moral theories that sometimes yield conflicting moral verdicts about the same issue. So, how can appealing to moral theory really help in trying to think productively about moral issues? This is a fair question that I address in section 3. However, before going on, let me say something about how one might use this chapter in studying the moral issues featured in this book.

User's Guide Interlude

In the "User's Guide," I suggested that although this chapter can be read straight through, readers may want to stop here and go on to one of the following chapters and begin their study of disputed moral issues. In the chapter introductions and the brief article summaries that precede each reading selection, I prompt readers to read (or reread) my presentations of one or more of the moral theories I describe in the next section of this chapter. And, of course, for those who wish to consult primary sources corresponding to the moral theories in question, there are the selections in the next chapter.

As I explained in the user's guide, I like to teach moral theory along with the readings. Seeing how a moral theory applies to a particular moral issue is helpful for understanding an author's position on the issue, which in turn helps readers gain a deeper understanding of and appreciation for moral theory. As for integrating section 3, I recommend consulting this part of the chapter when the questions it addresses are prompted by one's thinking about and discussing the book's readings.

2.   SEVEN ESSENTIAL MORAL THEORIES

Seven types of moral theory are prominently represented in our readings: consequentialism, natural law theory, Kantian moral theory, rights-based moral theory, virtue ethics, the ethics of prima facie duty, and social contract theory. Here, then, is an overview of these various theories that will provide useful background for understanding our readings.

A. Consequentialism

In thinking about moral issues, one obvious thing to do is to consider the consequences or effects of various actions—the consequences or effects on matters that are of concern to us. **Consequentialism** is a type of moral theory according to which consequences of actions are all that matter in determining the rightness and wrongness of actions. Its guiding idea is this:

   C   Right action is to be understood entirely in terms of the overall intrinsic value of the consequences of the action compared to the overall intrinsic value of the consequences associated with alternative actions an agent might perform instead. An action is right if and only if (and because) its consequences would be at least as good as the consequences of any alternative action that the agent might instead perform.

A number of important ideas are packed into C that we need to unpack—ideas that are present in the varieties of consequentialist moral theory presented next. Let us sort them out.

- First, consequentialist moral theory is a *value-based moral theory*: it characterizes or defines right action in terms of intrinsic value.
- Second, this sort of theory involves the fairly intuitive idea of *alternative actions* open to an agent: in circumstances calling for a moral choice, an agent is confronted by a range of alternative actions, any one of which she might choose to perform.
- Third (and relatedly), consequentialism is a *comparative* theory of right action: the rightness (or wrongness) of an action depends on how much intrinsic value it would likely produce (if performed) compared to how much intrinsic value alternative actions would likely produce (if performed).
- Fourth, the consequentialist account of right action is a *maximizing* conception: we are to perform that action, from among the alternatives, whose consequences will have *at least as much* overall value as any other.
- Fifth, and finally, consequentialism is a strongly *impartialist* moral theory in the sense that the rightness or wrongness of an action is made to depend on the values of the consequences for *everyone* who is affected by the action, where everyone affected counts *equally.* (This fifth point will become clearer when we consider particular versions of consequentialism.)

Consequentialism, we have noted, is a *general type* of moral theory that has a variety of species. For instance, consequentialists may differ over the issue of what has intrinsic value. Those versions that take happiness or welfare alone to have intrinsic value are versions of utilitarianism, whereas those that take human perfection to have intrinsic value are versions of perfectionism. Again, consequentialists may differ over the primary focus of consequentialist evaluation. Some versions focus on individual actions, other versions focus on rules. So, we can distinguish four main species of consequentialism. Let us explore further.

Utilitarianism has been perhaps the most prominent form of consequentialism, so let us begin with it.

Utilitarianism

Utilitarianism was originally developed and defended by Jeremy Bentham (1748–1832) and later refined by John Stuart Mill (1806–1873).[6] Their basic idea is that it is *human welfare* or *happiness* that alone is intrinsically valuable and that the rightness or wrongness of actions depends entirely on how they affect human welfare or happiness. As a consequentialist theory, utilitarianism requires that one *maximize* welfare where the welfare of *all* individuals who will be affected by some action counts. We can sharpen our characterization of this theory by introducing the technical term "utility," which refers to the *net value* of the consequences of actions—how much overall welfare or happiness would likely result from an action, taking into account both the short-term and long-term effects of the action on the welfare of all who will be affected. The basic idea is that the moral status of an action—its rightness or wrongness—depends both on how much happiness (if any) it would likely produce for each individual affected were it to be performed, as well as how much unhappiness (if any) it would likely produce for each affected person were it to be performed. For each alternative action, then, we can consider the *net balance* of overall happiness versus unhappiness associated with that action. Call this overall net value the **utility** of an action. We can now formulate a generic statement of the basic utilitarian principle—the **principle of utility:**

> U   An action is right if and only if (and because) it would (if performed) likely produce at least as high a utility (net overall balance of welfare) as would any other alternative action one might perform instead.[7]

Notice that the utility of an action might be negative. That is, all things considered, an action may produce a net balance of unhappiness over happiness were it to be performed. Moreover, since U (like all versions of C) is comparative, it may turn out that the right action in some unfortunate circumstance is the one that would likely bring about the least amount of overall negative utility.

As formulated, U leaves open questions about the nature of happiness and unhappiness about which there are different philosophical theories.[8] Bentham and (apparently) Mill held that happiness is entirely constituted by experiences of pleasure and unhappiness by experiences of displeasure or pain. And so their theory of intrinsic value is called **value hedonism:** *only* states of pleasure have positive intrinsic value and *only* states of pain have intrinsic negative value; anything else of value is of mere extrinsic value. So, for instance, for the value hedonist, any positive value that knowledge may have is extrinsic: it is only of positive value when it contributes to bringing about what has intrinsic value, namely pleasure (or the alleviation of pain). It should be noted that a value hedonist need not (and should not) take an excessively narrow view of pleasure and pain; the hedonist can follow Bentham and Mill in holding that in addition to such bodily pleasures of the sort one gets from eating delicious food or having a massage, there are aesthetic and intellectual pleasures such as appreciating a beautifully written poem. Moreover, the value hedonist will recognize not only passive pleasures of the sort just mentioned, but also active pleasures as when one plays a game or is involved in some creative activity. So value hedonism can recognize a broad range of pleasurable experiences that have positive intrinsic value and a broad range of painful experiences that have negative intrinsic value.

If we now combine the principle of utility (U) with value hedonism, we obtain **hedonistic utilitarianism:**

> HU   An action is right if and only if (and because) it would likely produce (if performed) at least as high a net balance of pleasure (or less pain) as would any other alternative action one might do instead.

But as I hope my presentation has made clear, one need not accept hedonism as a theory of value in order to be a utilitarian. In fact, many contemporary utilitarians reject value hedonism and accept some other conception of happiness or welfare. But, again, what makes a theory a version of utilitarianism is that the theory accepts the basic consequentialist claim, C, together with the idea that it is human happiness or human well-being that has intrinsic value and is to be promoted in what we do.

Perfectionist Consequentialism

But a consequentialist need not be a utilitarian—she might hold that there are items having intrinsic value other than happiness that are important in determining the rightness or wrongness of action. To illustrate, I have chosen what is called **perfectionist consequentialism**—a species of the generic view that accepts a perfectionist theory of value.[9] According to a **value perfectionist,** it is states of human perfection, including knowledge and achievement that have intrinsic value.[10] One might come to have a great deal of knowledge and achievement in one's life, yet not be happy. So a perfectionist theory of the good is not the same as a happiness theory of the good. We might formulate the basic principle of perfectionist consequentialism as follows:

> **PC** An action is right if and only if (and because) it would (if performed) likely bring about a greater net balance of perfectionist goods than would any alternative action one might perform instead.

The distinction between utilitarianism and perfectionist consequentialism has to do with differences over what has intrinsic value for purposes of morally evaluating actions. And notice that the consequentialist principles presented thus far refer to particular concrete actions and their consequences, so the views (expressed in principles U, HU, and PC) are versions of **act consequentialism.** However, as mentioned at the outset, another important division within the ranks of consequentialists is between act and rule versions of the view. So let us turn from act versions to rule versions.

Rule Consequentialism

Moral rules—rules, for example, against lying, theft, and killing—are generally thought to be significant in thinking about particular moral issues. The importance of moral rules is emphasized by rule consequentialists. Whereas act consequentialism is the view that the rightness of a particular, concrete action—an actual or possible doing by a person at a time—depends on the value of its consequences, **rule consequentialism** is the view that the rightness or wrongness of an action depends on whether it is required, permitted, or prohibited by a rule whose consequences are best.[11] So rule consequentialism involves two levels of evaluation: first, rules that require, permit, or prohibit various courses of action are evaluated by reference to the values of their consequences, and second, a particular action is evaluated by determining whether it is required, permitted, or prohibited by a rule whose consequences are best. Let us explore this view a bit further.

The sense in which a rule can have consequences has to do with the fact that were people to accept the rule in question, this would influence what they do. So, we can evaluate a rule by asking what consequences would likely be brought about were it to be generally accepted in society. Call the value associated with rules their **acceptance value.** This idea is familiar. Think of debates in the sporting world about changing the rules of some sport. The focus in such debates is on the likely effects the proposed rule change would have on the game, were it to be accepted.

According to rule consequentialism, then, the morality of a particular action in some situation depends upon the acceptance values of various competing rules that are relevant to the situation in question. We can thus formulate this theory with the following principle of right conduct:

>   **RC** An action is right if and only if (and because) it is permitted by a rule whose associated acceptance value is at least as high as the acceptance value of any other rule applying to the situation.

In order to better understand this principle, let us illustrate its application with a simple example.

Suppose that I have promised to help you move next Friday morning. Friday morning arrives, and many alternative courses of action are open to me. Among them are these:

A1. Keep my promise (and show up at your place),
A2. Break my promise (and do something else).

Corresponding to each of these alternative actions, we have these rules:

R1. Whenever one makes a promise, keep it,
R2. Whenever one makes a promise, break it if one feels like it.

Now consider the acceptance values associated with these rules. I think we can all agree that acceptance value of R1 is far greater than that of R2. So (ignoring for the moment that there may be other competing rules to be considered in this situation) rule consequentialism implies that one ought to keep one's promise.

Finally notice that act and rule consequentialism may diverge in their moral implications. To stick with the previous example, suppose that by breaking my promise and instead hanging out with some friends at the local pool hall will likely produce a greater level of overall intrinsic value than would the backbreaking work of helping you move. Besides, you've lined up plenty of help; I won't be missed that much. Act consequentialism implies that it would be morally permissible to go ahead and break the promise; rule consequentialism by contrast implies that I am morally obliged to keep my promise.

Brief Summary

Let us pause for a moment to summarize (see Fig. 1.2) what we have covered. As we have seen, the basic consequentialist idea (C) can be developed in a variety of ways; we have considered four versions of this generic approach to ethics.

For now, the main idea to take away from this discussion is that for all varieties of consequentialism, the rightness or wrongness of an action depends entirely on the net intrinsic value of the consequences of either individual actions or rules. Consequentialist theories

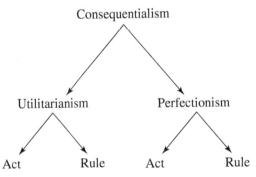

FIGURE 1.2   Some Forms of Consequentialism

(and especially utilitarianism) are often discussed in articles and books about disputed moral issues. Some authors appeal to consequentialism to justify their particular views on some moral issue; other authors will contrast their approach with consequentialism.

Applying Consequentialism

To convey a sense of how one is to go about applying consequentialism to a particular moral issue, let us work with act utilitarianism as expressed earlier in U. And to make things fairly manageable, let us consider a rather simple case.

Suppose that I am in charge of inviting a guest philosopher to speak at my university and that I've narrowed the choices to two. On the one hand, I can invite Dr. Brilliant, a very well-known and innovative philosopher but whose manner of presentation is decidedly dull. The philosophy faculty will no doubt take pleasure in his presentation and will benefit intellectually from what he has to say, but others will be bored stiff and get little out of the talk. On the other hand, I can invite Dr. Flash, who is not nearly as accomplished as Dr. Brilliant but who I know is an extremely engaging speaker. Suppose that five professional philosophers and forty-five students are expected to attend the lecture no matter which of these two philosophers I invite.

Now if I apply U to my situation, it would have me invite the speaker whose talk will produce the greatest amount of overall happiness. A careful application of U would require that I consider each person who will be affected by the lecture of Dr. Brilliant and determine how much happiness (if any) that person would experience as a result of this lecture and then determine how much unhappiness (if any) that person would experience as a result of this lecture. Once I have done this calculation for each person, I then calculate how much total happiness the lecture would cause and how much total unhappiness it would cause in order to arrive at the overall net value associated with Dr. Brilliant's lecture. I do the same for Dr. Flash. The lecture I ought to sponsor and hence the philosopher I ought to invite depends on which talk will result in the greatest amount of intrinsic value.

Obviously, to apply U to one's own choices with any precision would require much factual information: information about one's circumstances, about the various alternative actions one might perform in one's particular circumstances, about the individuals who will be affected either negatively or positively were one to perform a particular action, and about the overall amount of happiness or unhappiness, both short term and long term, that would likely result from each of the various alternative actions. Some critics of consequentialism argue that when it comes to satisfying the practical aim of moral theory—the aim of providing practical guidance for arriving at correct or justified verdicts for the further aim of acting on such verdicts—consequentialism makes implausible demands on what one needs to know in order to apply it to particular cases. Defenders reply that even if *precise* application of this sort of moral theory is not feasible, we can and do make rough estimates of the values of the consequences of various alternative actions, and that in doing so we must realize that the moral verdicts we reach as a result are likely to be highly fallible. But this, say the defenders, is something we just have to live with given our limited information about the effects of our actions.

B. Natural Law Theory

The idea that certain actions or practices are "natural" while others are "unnatural" is commonly offered as a reason why certain "unnatural" actions are wrong and that we ought to do what is natural. Think of popular arguments against homosexuality. This idea of morality being natural is associated with the **natural law theory**.[12]

This type of moral theory is often traced to the thirteenth-century philosopher and theologian St. Thomas Aquinas (1225–1274). It gets its name from the guiding idea that there are objectively true moral principles that are grounded in human nature.[13] Because there are objective facts about human nature that determine what our good consists in, and because moral requirements have to do with maintaining and promoting the human goods, these requirements, unlike the rules of some club or made-up game, are part of the natural order. Because the natural law theory bases right action on considerations of intrinsic value, it is a value-based theory of right conduct, as is consequentialism. However, as we shall see in setting out this theory, natural law theory is opposed to consequentialism—it denies that the *only* considerations that matter when it comes to right action are consequences. So, to understand this theory let us proceed by first presenting its theory of intrinsic value and then presenting its theory of right conduct in two parts: (a) first, the "core" of theory and then (b) the doctrine of double effect.

Theory of Intrinsic Value[14]

According to Aquinas's version of natural law theory, there are four basic intrinsic goods:

- Human life
- Human procreation (which includes raising children)
- Human knowledge
- Human sociability (this value has to do with associations and bonds with others, including friendship, social organizations, and political organizations)

Each of these items, then, has intrinsic value and its destruction is intrinsically bad or evil. These four values are the basis for the core of natural law theory.

The Core

We can state the basic principle of natural law theory roughly as follows:

NLT   An action is right if and only if (and because) in performing the action one does not directly violate any of the basic values.

Thus, killing a human being (with some exceptions explained later) is morally wrong. If we suppose, as many natural law theorists do, that the use of contraceptives thwarts human procreation, then their use is morally wrong. Interfering with the good of knowledge by distorting information or by lying is morally wrong. Destroying legitimate social bonds through the advocacy of anarchy is morally wrong.

But what about hard cases in which no matter what one does, one will violate at least one of the basic values and thus bring about evil through whichever action one chooses? Let us consider a much discussed case involving abortion. Suppose that a pregnant woman has cancer of the uterus and must have a hysterectomy (removal of her uterus) to save her life. Human life is one of the intrinsic goods, so having the operation will have at least one good effect. But suppose (just for the sake of the example) that from conception the fetus counts as a human life and so having the hysterectomy would bring about the death of the unborn human life. This effect, because it involves the destruction of something having intrinsic value—human life—is an evil. And let us suppose that this moral dilemma is unavoidable in this case because there is no way to save the woman's life while also preserving the life of her fetus. How does the natural law theory deal with this kind of case? After all, the core of the theory seems to say that any action that violates one or more of the basic goods is wrong, period. But if it really does say this, then we have to conclude that her having the operation is wrong, but also her not having the operation is wrong (because she will fail to preserve her own life). How can natural law theory deal with this moral dilemma?

If we go back and inspect the basic principle of natural law theory, NLT, we notice that what it prohibits are actions that *directly* violate one or more of the basic goods, thereby bringing about evil. But what counts as a direct violation? Can there be morally permissible "indirect" violations? These questions bring us to the next major component of natural law ethics—the doctrine of double effect.

The Doctrine of Double Effect

In addition to the core principle (NLT), the natural law theory also embraces the following set of provisions that compose the **doctrine of double effect**—so named because it concerns cases in which performing an action would have at least one good effect and one bad effect (where good and bad have to do with the theory's list of intrinsic goods). So this doctrine is meant to address the question of whether it is ever morally permissible to knowingly bring about bad or evil consequences where one's aim in action is to bring about or preserve one or more of the basic human goods. Here, then, is a statement of the various provisions making up the doctrine:

> **DDE**   An action that would bring about at least one evil effect and at least one good effect is morally permissible if (and only if) the following conditions are satisfied:
>
> *Intrinsic permissibility:* The action in question, apart from its effects, is morally permissible;
> *Necessity:* It is not possible to bring about the good effect except by performing an action that will bring about the evil effect in question;
> *Nonintentionality:* The evil effect is not intended—it is neither one's end nor a chosen means for bringing about some intended end;
> *Proportionality:* The evil that will be brought about by the action is not out of proportion to the good being aimed at.

What this principle does is help define the idea of a direct violation of a human good which is the central idea in the core principle, NLT. We shall return to this point in a moment. For the time being, let us explain DDE by showing how it would apply to the case just described.

In applying DDE to our moral dilemma, we must ask whether all four of the doctrine's provisions are satisfied. Let us take them in order. (1) First, since having a hysterectomy is not an intrinsically wrong action, the first requirement is satisfied. (2) Furthermore, given my description of the case, the second requirement of DDE is met because having a hysterectomy is the *only* way to save her life. Were there some other operation or some medication that would both save the woman's life and preserve the life of the fetus, then the necessity condition would not be met and the hysterectomy would be wrong. But we are supposing that there are no such options in this case.

(3) The third requirement rests on the distinction between effects that one intends in action and effects that may be foreseen but are unintended. One intends some consequence or effect when either it is something one is aiming to bring about (an end) or it is one's chosen means for bringing about some desired end. Here is a simple, everyday example. I fire a rifle in order to hit the paper target, but in so doing I know that the noise from the rifle will frighten nearby wildlife. But even though I can foresee that my act of pulling the trigger will frighten those animals, this effect is not intended: it is not my purpose—my purpose is to hit the target, and their being frightened is not a means for achieving my end—the means is taking aim and firing. So the effect of my act of firing—frightening those animals—is not something I intend, rather it is a foreseen but unintended side effect of what I do.

Returning now to our example, we find that this third provision is satisfied because although the death of the unborn child is a foreseen effect of the hysterectomy, its death is not her chief aim or end (saving her own life), and it is not a means by which her life will be saved. After all, were she not pregnant, she would still have the operation to save her life, and so the death of the unborn is a mere unintended and unfortunate side effect of the operation. Removing the cancer is what will save her life.

(4) Finally, the evil that will result from the operation (loss of one innocent human life) is not grossly out of proportion to the good that will result (saving an innocent human life). (When DDE is applied to the morality of war activities, considerations of proportionality of evil to good become especially relevant. See the introduction to chapter 13 and the article in that chapter by Andrew Valls.)

Having explained the DDE, we can now return to the core principle, NLT, and explain how these two elements are related in natural law ethics. The idea is that, according to NLT, we are not to *directly* violate any of the basic human goods. The DDE helps define what counts as a direct violation: direct violations are those that cannot be justified by the doctrine of double effect.

Before going on, it will be useful to pause for a moment to compare the natural law theory with consequentialism. In response to our moral dilemma involving the hysterectomy, an act consequentialist will say that we should consider the value of the consequences of the alternative actions (having a hysterectomy or refraining from this operation) and choose the action with the best consequences. In short, for the act consequentialist good results justify the means. But not for the natural law theorist, because on her theory one may not act in direct violation of the basic goods even if by doing so one would produce better consequences. Good ends do not always justify an action that is a means to those ends. For instance, I am not permitted to intentionally kill one innocent human being (do evil) even if by doing so I can save five others (bring about good). To see how consequentialism and natural law theory yield different verdicts about a difficult moral case, consider the case of a woman who is pregnant, but this time she is suffering from a "tubal" pregnancy, which means that her fetus is lodged in her fallopian tube and thus has not implanted itself into the uterine wall. If nothing is done, both fetus and woman will die. The only thing that can be done to save the woman is to remove the fetus, which will bring about its death. Exercise: Apply act consequentialism and the natural law theory to this case to see whether they differ in their moral implications.

Applying Natural Law Theory

In applying the natural law theory to some case in order to determine whether a particular course of action is morally right, one begins with the core principle, NLT, and asks whether the action in question would violate any of the basic goods. If not, then the action is not wrong. But if it would violate one or more of the basic goods, then one has to determine whether the action would constitute a *direct* violation. And to do that, one makes use of the DDE. If the action satisfies all four provisions of DDE, then the violation is not direct and the action is morally permissible. If the action does not pass DDE, then the action involves a direct violation of one or more of the intrinsic goods and is, therefore, wrong.

Of course, as with all moral theories, applying the natural law theory is not a mechanical process. For one thing, one must address questions about the proper interpretation of the four basic human goods. Surely coming to have knowledge of the basic laws that govern the physical universe is intrinsically valuable, if any knowledge is. But what if, for example, I spend my time counting the number of needles on a cactus plant for no particular reason: is the knowledge I acquire about the number of needles really of any intrinsic value? One can raise similar questions about the other three basic human goods. Furthermore, applying the doctrine of double effect raises questions of interpretation. For instance, the proportionality provision requires that the evil caused by an action not be "out of proportion" to the good effects of that action. But, of course, determining when things are out of proportion requires sensitivity to particular cases and the use of good judgment.

These points about interpretation are not meant as a criticism of natural law theory; rather they call attention to the fact that applying it to particular moral issues requires that we interpret its various elements. As we shall see, a similar point applies to Kantian moral theory.

C. Kantian Moral Theory

Most everyone has come across moral arguments that appeal to the **golden rule**: do unto others as you would have them do unto you. This rule encapsulates a kind of test for thinking about the morality of actions: it asks the individual making a moral choice that will affect others to consider how one would like it were one on the receiving end of the action in question. In the case of Thomas Youk with which we began the chapter, the golden rule would have Kevorkian consider what he would want done to (or for) him were he in Youk's situation. Various objections have been made to the golden rule—for instance, it suggests that the rightness or wrongness of an action depends simply on what one does or would desire. But people can have crazy desires. A masochist who inflicts pain on others might cheerfully say that he would have others do unto him as he is doing to them. Do we want to conclude that his causing others pain is morally right? Perhaps there is some interpretation of the golden rule that does not yield the wrong result in the case of the masochist or other examples that have been used against it. Nevertheless, there is something about the *spirit* of the golden rule that seems right. The idea suggested by this rule is that morality requires that we not treat people unfairly, that we respect other persons by taking them into account in our moral deliberations. This suggestion is quite vague but finds one articulation in Kantian moral theory to which we now turn.

Kantian moral theory derives from the moral writings of the German philosopher Immanuel Kant (1724–1804), which continue to have an enormous influence on contemporary ethics.[15] Central to Kant's moral theory is the idea that moral requirements can be expressed as commands or imperatives that categorically bid us to perform certain actions—requirements that apply to us regardless of what we might happen to want or desire or how such actions bear on the production of our own happiness. Kant thought that specific moral requirements could be derived from a fundamental moral principle that he called the **categorical imperative.** Moreover, Kant offered various alternative formulations of his fundamental moral principle. The two I will consider are the ones that are most often applied to moral issues.

The Humanity Formulation

One of Kant's formulations of his categorical imperative is called the **Humanity formulation:**

> H   An action is right if and only if (and because) the action treats persons (including oneself) as ends in themselves and not merely as a means.

Obviously, to make use of this principle, we need to know what it means to treat someone as an end and what it means to treat someone merely as a means. Space does not permit a thorough discussion of these ideas, so a few illustrations will have to suffice.[16]

Deception and coercion are two ways in which one can treat another person merely as a means—as an object to be manipulated. Deceiving someone in order to get him or her to do something he or she would otherwise not agree to do constitutes using the person as though that person were a mere instrument at one's disposal for promoting one's own ends. Again, many cases of coercing someone by threats involve attempting to manipulate that person for one's own purposes and hence constitute an attempt to use him or her merely as a means to one's own ends.

But Kant's Humanity formulation requires not only that we not treat others merely as means to our own ends (a negative requirement), but also that we treat them as ends in themselves (a positive requirement). For Kant, to say that persons are ends in themselves is to say that they have a special worth or value that demands of us that we have a certain positive regard for them. Kant refers to this special worth as *dignity.*[17] So, for instance, if I fail to help those who need and deserve my help, I don't treat them merely as means, but I do fail to have a positive regard for their welfare and thus fail to properly recognize their worth as persons.

Applying Kant's Humanity Formulation

As just explained, applying the Humanity formulation requires consideration of the dual requirements that we not treat people merely as means and that we also not fail to treat them as ends in themselves—as individuals who have dignity. Interpreting these requirements is where the hard work comes in: what are the boundaries when it comes to treating people *merely* as a means? If, in walking by, I see that you are wearing a watch and ask you for the time, I am using you as a means for finding out what time it is, but I am not thereby using you *merely* as a means to my own ends. We have noted that deception and coercion represent main ways in which one might use someone merely as a means—as something to be manipulated. So we have a good start on interpreting the idea of such treatment. Here is not the place to consider other ways in which our actions might involve treating someone this way. Rather, the point I wish to make is that we have some idea of what it means to treat someone merely as a means, and we must build on this understanding to apply the Humanity formulation to a range of moral issues.

Similar remarks apply to the requirement that we positively treat others as ends in themselves. Here it is interesting to note that Kant argued that in satisfying this requirement, we are obligated to adopt two very general goals—the goal of promoting the (morally permissible) ends of others and the goal of self-perfection. Such wide-open goals allow a person much latitude in deciding in what ways and on what occasions to promote the ends of others and one's own self-perfection. For Kant, then, applying the positive requirement embedded in H is a matter of figuring out how best to integrate the promotion of the well-being of others and one's own self-perfection into a moral life.

The Universal Law Formulation

Kant's other main formulation of the categorical imperative, the **Universal Law formulation**, expresses a test whereby we can determine whether our actions are right or wrong.

> UL   An action is right if and only if one can both (a) consistently conceive of everyone adopting and acting on the general policy (that is, the maxim) of one's action, and also (b) consistently will that everyone act on that maxim.[18]

This formulation will remind readers of the golden rule, though notice that UL does not refer to an agent's wants; rather it represents a kind of consistency test.[19] Unfortunately, interpreting Kant's two-part test requires some explanation. So let me say a bit more about UL and then, using some of Kant's own examples, show how it can be applied.

According to Kant, when we act, we act on a general policy that is called a "maxim." To determine the morality of an action, one formulates the general policy of one's action and asks whether one could consistently both conceive of and will that everyone act on the same policy or, to put it in Kant's terms, one asks whether one could consistently conceive and will that the maxim of one's action become a "universal law" governing everyone's behavior. If so, then the action is right; if not, then the action is wrong. So UL expresses a two-part test one can use to determine the rightness or wrongness of actions. To make Kant's tests more concrete, let us consider a few of Kant's own sample applications of UL.

One of Kant's examples involves making a lying promise—that is, a promise that one has no intention of keeping. Consider a case in which I desperately need money right away and the only way I can get it is by getting a loan which I must promise to repay. I know, however, that I won't be able to repay the loan. The maxim corresponding to the action I am considering is:

> M1   Whenever I need money and can get it only by making a lying promise, I will borrow the money by making a lying promise.

Kant's principle, UL, would have me test the morality of making a lying promise by asking whether I could *consistently conceive* and *will* that everyone act on M1—that everyone who needs money in such circumstances as mine make a lying promise. Let us first ask whether this is something I can consistently conceive. If it isn't, then I certainly can't consistently will that everyone adopt and act on it.

Kant claims that when I think through what would be involved in everyone acting on M1, I realize that I cannot even consistently conceive of a world in which everyone in need of money successfully makes lying promises. After all, a world in which everyone in need of money goes around trying to get the money by making a lying promise is one in which successful promising becomes impossible since, as Kant observes, "no one would believe what was promised him but would laugh at all such expressions as vain pretenses."[20] Thus, trying to even conceive of a world in which everyone in need of money acts on M1 involves an inconsistency: it is a world in which (1) *everyone* in need gets money by making a lying promise; but because of the breakdown in the institution of promising that would result, it is a world in which (2) *not everyone* in need gets money by making a lying promise for the reason Kant gives. But if I can't consistently conceive of everyone acting on M1, then my maxim fails the first test mentioned in UL. And if I can't consistently conceive that everyone act on M1, this shows me that, in making a lying promise, I am acting on an immoral policy and that my action is wrong.

But why is the fact that one cannot consistently conceive that everyone act on one's maxim an indication that the action in question is wrong? Kant's idea here seems to be that in performing an action whose maxim I cannot consistently conceive everyone adopting, I am, in effect, proposing to make an exception of myself—an exception that I cannot justify. In making an exception of myself, I am failing to respect others because I'm taking advantage of the fact that many others do not make lying promises. And so these reflections lead us to conclude that making a lying promise is morally wrong.

Here is another example Kant uses to illustrate the application of UL that has to do with clause (b) of UL. Suppose I am in a position to help someone in need but would rather not be bothered. The maxim Kant has us consider is:

M2   Whenever I am able to help others in need, I will refrain from helping them.

Using UL, I am to consider whether I can consistently conceive of a world in which everyone adopts and acts on this maxim. Is such a world conceivable? It would seem so. Granted, a world in which people in need did not receive help from others would be a very unpleasant place. Perhaps the human race would not survive in such a world. But we can certainly conceive of a world in which the human race ceases to exist. So, M2 passes the first part of Kant's UL test.

But can one *will* that M2 be adopted and acted upon by everyone? Upon reflection I realize that if I will that everyone adopt and act on M2, I am thereby willing that others refuse to help me when I am in need. But willing that others refuse to help me is inconsistent with the fact that as a rational agent I do will that others help me when I am in need. That is, as a rational agent, I embrace the following maxim:

RM   I will that others who are able to do so help me when I am in need.

But an implication of my willing that everyone adopt and act on M2 would be:

IM   I will that others who are able to help me refuse to do so when I am in need.

RM is inconsistent with IM—and IM is an implication of willing that everyone adopt and act on M2. Thus, I cannot consistently will that everyone adopt and act on M2. Since I cannot consistently will that everyone adopt M2, then according to clause (b) of Kant's UL, my action of refusing to help others in need is morally wrong.

What is the point of Kant's UL formulation involving two tests? Kant thought that these two tests could distinguish between what he called "narrow" or "perfect" duty and "wide" or "imperfect" duty: maxims that one cannot consistently conceive as adopted and acted on by everyone involve actions that are contrary to narrow duty, whereas those that can be so conceived but which one cannot consistently will involve actions that are contrary to wide duty. The realm of narrow duty concerns those actions and omissions regarding which one has comparatively little room for when and how one complies with the duty. If I have promised to do something for you on a particular occasion—help you with your taxes—then to fulfill my obligation I must perform some rather specific action (helping you with your taxes) at a certain time. By contrast, a wide duty is one which can be fulfilled in a variety of ways and situations, giving one much leeway in how and when to fulfill the duty. Duties of charity—helping others—are like this.

It is important to notice that in his examples, Kant is not arguing that if everyone went around making lying promises the consequences would be bad and therefore making a lying promise is wrong. Again, he does not argue that the consequences of everyone refusing to help others in need would be bad and therefore refusing help to others is wrong. Such ways of arguing are characteristic of consequentialism, but Kant rejects consequentialism. He has us consider the implications of everyone acting on the general policy behind one's own action because he thinks doing so is a way of revealing any inconsistencies in what one wills, which in turn indicates whether an action fails to respect persons. So the test involved in the categorical imperative is meant to reveal whether one's action shows a proper respect for persons.

Applying the Universal Law Formulation

Since this formulation expresses tests for determining the rightness or wrongness of actions, I have been illustrating how it is to be applied in thinking through moral issues. If we step back from these illustrations, we can summarize the basic procedure to be followed. In applying UL to some actual or contemplated action of yours, here are the basic steps to follow:

- Formulate the maxim on which you are proposing to act, which will have the form "I will ____ whenever ____," where the blanks are filled with a description of your action and circumstances, respectively.
- Next, you consider the possibility of everyone in your circumstances adopting and acting on that same maxim. In particular, you ask yourself whether you can consistently *conceive* of a world in which everyone adopts and acts on the maxim in question. This is the test expressed in clause (a) of UL.
- If you cannot even conceive of such a world, then action on the maxim is morally wrong—a violation of narrow duty. The lying promise example illustrates this result.
- If you can consistently conceive of a world in which everyone adopts and acts on the maxim, then you are to ask yourself whether you could, even so, consistently will that everyone adopt and act on the maxim. This is the test expressed in clause (b) of UL.
- If you cannot consistently will that everyone adopt and act on that maxim, then action on the maxim is wrong—a violation of wide duty. The case of refusing to help others illustrates this result.
- Finally, if your maxim is such that you can both consistently conceive of a world in which everyone adopts and acts on your maxim and consistently will this to be the case—if the maxim passes both tests—then action on the maxim is morally right.

The two main challenges for anyone applying the UL formulation to a particular issue is to correctly formulate one's maxim and then carefully think through Kant's two consistency tests.

How are the two formulations of the categorical imperative—H and UL—related? They are supposed to be alternative formulations of the same basic principle, rather than two entirely distinct principles. One way to see how this might be so is to notice that in cases in which I cannot consistently conceive or will that my maxim be adopted by everyone, I am making an exception of myself, and in doing so either I am treating someone merely as a means or I am failing to treat others as ends in themselves. And, of course, treating others merely as means and failing to treat them as ends in themselves is precisely what the Humanity formulation rules out.

D. Rights-Based Moral Theory

In our brief survey of moral theories up to this point, we have seen how those theories attempt to give accounts of the nature of right (and wrong) action, where "right" is being used in its adjectival sense. Nothing so far has been said about the notion of *a right* or *rights*. However, in moral theory we distinguish between the adjectival use of "right" as in *right action* and its use as a noun as in *a right to life*. One can hold that actions may or may not be right— actions that are either permissible or impermissible to do—without also holding that there are things called rights. Perhaps the most basic idea of a **right** is that of an *entitlement* to be free to engage in some activity, to exercise a certain power, or to be provided with some benefit. One's having such an entitlement typically imposes duties on others (including governments) either to refrain from interfering with one's freedom (or exercise of power) or to provide one with some benefit, depending on the right in question. In explaining the idea of a right and how it figures both in moral theory and in moral controversies, it will be useful to briefly discuss the following topics: (1) some basic elements of a right, (2) categories of rights, (3) rights and moral theory, (4) the idea of a rights-based moral theory, (5) the application of rights-based theories in practice, and (6) so-called rights-focused approaches to moral issues.[21]

Rights: Some Basic Elements

A right has the following characteristics. First, there is the **rights holder**, the party who has or "holds" the right. If you own property, then as a property owner you hold a property right. A rights holder may be an individual or a group. Minority rights are one type of group rights. One of the most important philosophical questions about rights concerns the *scope* of rights holders—those beings that *have* rights. According to some views that would restrict the scope of rights holders, only those creatures that have a developed capacity to reason can be the holders of rights. Less restrictive views would allow that anything having interests, including certain nonhuman animals, can be rights holders. Among those who approach moral issues from the perspective of rights—including the issues of abortion, animals, and the environment—we find important differences in views about the requirements for holding rights and thus differences in views about the scope of rights holders.

A second element of a right is what we might call the **rights addressee**, that is, the individual or group with regard to whom the rights holder is entitled to certain treatment. If I have entered into a contract with you to provide you a service, then I am the addressee of your right; you are entitled to demand that I provide that service. The relationship between a rights holder and the corresponding rights addressee can most often be understood in terms of the idea of a *claim*. For instance, in light of a rights holder being entitled to certain treatment by others, we may say that the former has a valid *claim* on the behavior of the latter. And so, corresponding to a rights holder's claim, the addressee of a right has an obligation or duty to either perform or refrain from performing actions that would affect the rights holder and the treatment to which he or she is entitled. Thus, at least for most rights, there is a correlation between the rights of rights holders and certain duties on the part of addressees.

A third element is the **content** of a right, which refers to whatever action, states, or objects the right concerns. The right to freedom of expression differs in content from the right to life. And, of course, these rights differ in content from property rights, and so on.

Finally, another dimension of rights is that of **strength**. Think of a right as a claim on others that has a certain degree of strength in the sense that the stronger right, the stronger the justification needed to defeat the right in question. For instance, some hold the view that nonhuman animals as well as human beings have a right to life. Suppose this is correct. It may still be the case that the right to life of a human being is stronger than the right to life of, say, a dog or cat. The difference in strength here would be reflected, for example, by the fact that one would be arguably justified in euthanizing a dog or cat if the animal were no longer able to walk, while this same sort of reason would not be strong enough to euthanize a human being.

Related to the fact that rights come in degrees of strength is the fact that in some situations someone might be morally justified in performing an action that "goes against" another person's right. And when this occurs, let us say that the person's right has been infringed. So, for instance, suppose my property rights involve the claim that no one may enter my house and use my property without my consent. Now suppose that my next door neighbor's child has been seriously hurt and needs immediate medical attention, and so calling an ambulance is in order. Suppose also that the closest phone available to my neighbor is the one in my house, but I am not at home. Were the neighbor to break into my house to use my phone, he or she would be infringing upon my property rights. But assuming that the neighbor is morally justified in doing this, we may call this case of "going against" my right, a **rights infringement**. By contrast, **rights violations** involve cases where someone goes against another person's rights but is not morally justified in doing so. Thus, as we are using these terms, rights infringements involve actions that are not morally wrong given the circumstances, while rights violations involve actions that are morally wrong.

Categories of Rights

It is common to recognize both negative and positive rights. A **negative right** is an entitlement of noninterference and thus involves a claim by the rights holder that others refrain from interfering with her or his engaging in some activity. Because such rights require that others *not* act in certain ways, they impose what are called negative duties. Rights that are correlated with negative duties are called negative rights. A right to certain liberties such as free speech is an example of a negative right—a right that imposes a duty on others not to interfere with one's expressing one's ideas. A **positive right**, by contrast, involves the rights holder being entitled to something and thus having a valid claim that some other party do or provide something (some service or some good) to that rights holder. Because the duty in question requires positive action on the part of the addressee, the corresponding right is called a positive right. For instance, Article 25 of the United Nations 1948 *Universal Declaration of Human Rights* states:

> Everyone has a right to a standard of living adequate for the health and well-being of himself and of his family, including food, clothing, housing, and medical care and necessary social services, and the right to security in the event of unemployment, sickness, disability, widowhood, old age, or other lack of livelihood in circumstances beyond his control.

This (alleged) right is supposed to be held by all human beings and presumably it is a right that one be provided certain necessities by one's nation or perhaps other nations in a position to provide such goods.

In addition to the distinction between negative and positive rights, it is also important to distinguish **moral rights** from legal rights. This distinction has to do with the source of a right. A so-called moral right is a right that a being has independently of any legal system or other set of conventions.[22] So, for instance, it is often claimed that all human beings, in virtue of facts about humanity, have certain rights, including the rights to life, liberty, and well-being. Such alleged universal rights of humanity[23] are typically referred to as **human rights**. A **legal right** is something that results or comes into existence as the result of a legal statute or some other form of governmental activity. One reason it is important to distinguish moral from legal rights is that controversies over moral issues are often framed in terms of whether some individual (including nonhumans) or group has certain moral rights—rights that may or may not be recognized by some particular legal system and thus not (at the time in question) count as legal rights within the system in question. So, in debates over the morality of various activities and practices where talk of rights enter the discussion, one is mainly concerned with moral rights.

Another common distinction, often associated with human rights, is the distinction between "basic" and "nonbasic" rights. Roughly speaking, a **basic right** is a universal right that is especially important in the lives of individuals—rights such as the rights to life and to liberty, which arguably must be met in order to live a decent life. One's right to life and freedom from torture is clearly more important compared with one's right to be repaid a sum of money by a borrower. Just how to distinguish basic from nonbasic rights is controversial, and we need not examine various proposals here. It is enough for our purposes to leave the distinction at a more or less intuitive level and recognize that rights differ in their importance and thus in their comparative strengths.

Let us now turn from our general discussion of rights to their place in moral theory and in contemporary debates over particular moral issues.

Rights and Moral Theory

A great deal of contemporary discussion about moral issues is couched in terms of rights. Does a human fetus have a moral right to life? Does a terminally ill patient in severe pain have a moral right to die? Do people have a moral right to reproduce by cloning? Do animals have moral rights? In this subsection and the next, I want to explain how rights figure in moral theories. In doing so, I will make two main points: (1) All of the moral theories we have already surveyed (as well as the two that follow) can recognize moral rights. (2) However, what is distinctive of a rights-based moral theory is that it takes rights to be in some sense more basic than such notions as value (including utility), dignity, and right action (including duty). Let us take these points one by one.

First, a utilitarian who recognizes moral rights will attempt to explain rights on the basis of utility by claiming that a moral right is a kind of entitlement that imposes various claims on addressees justified by the fact that its recognition will contribute to the maximization of overall welfare. This means that for the utilitarian—who, as a consequentialist, embraces a value-based moral theory—rights are derivative rather than basic in her moral theory. Similar remarks apply to the moral theories featured in this chapter. For instance, according to Kantian ethics, all human beings possess moral rights in virtue of having a certain status— being the sort of creature that possesses dignity. Having this sort of status, according to the Kantian, demands that persons be treated in certain ways and thus that they enjoy certain moral rights. Thus, utilitarians and Kantians can agree that persons have moral rights. They disagree in how they explain the basis of such rights. And notice that because utilitarians and Kantians purport to explain moral rights in terms of more basic elements—utility in the case of utilitarianism, the possession of dignity in the case of Kantians—it would be incorrect to think of these theories as rights-based.

Rights-Based Moral Theory

Might there be a **rights-based moral theory**—a moral theory according to which rights are more basic than utility, dignity, and even duty? Unlike the other theories featured in this chapter, rights-based theories are relatively underdeveloped despite the fact that appeals to rights are very common in discussions of moral issues. What we find in the writings of authors who appeal to rights in discussing particular moral issues is that they often fail to indicate the nature of rights—whether they have a consequentialist, natural law, Kantian, or some other basis on one hand, or whether, on the other hand, they are conceived as basic in the theory. So let us consider the idea of a rights-*based* moral theory.

According to such a theory, rights are even more basic than right action and duty. But one might think that duties must be more basic than rights and so there cannot be a rights-based moral theory. After all, as explained above, a typical moral right is a claim one party has against others that they do or refrain from some activity, and it is natural to think of these burdens as duties or obligations that are owed to the rights-holder. If I have a right to free speech, then this seems to entail that others have a duty not to interfere with me in certain ways and thus that the concept of duty must be used to explain what a right is. If so, then duty is more basic than a right and so a rights-based theory is conceptually impossible.

Granted, it is common to explain the idea of a moral right of one party in terms of certain corresponding duties on the part of others. But as J. L. Mackie, a defender of rights-based moral theory explains, instead of thinking of rights in terms of duties, "we could look at it the other way round: what is primary is A's having this right in a sense indicated by the pre-scription 'Let A be able to do X if he chooses,' and the duty of others not to interfere follows from this."[24]

So let us follow Mackie and suppose that there is no conceptual barrier to there being a rights-based theory of right and wrong action. How might it be developed? The idea would be to begin with a list of moral rights, perhaps distinguishing such basic rights, including for instance the rights to life and to liberty, from nonbasic rights. Once one has identified the various moral rights, one could then proceed to define or characterize the concepts of right and wrong action in terms of moral rights. Here, then, is how we might express the basic idea of right conduct for a rights-based theory:

R   An action is right if and only if (and because) in performing it either (a) one does not violate the moral rights of others, or (b) in cases where it is not possible to respect all such rights because they are in conflict, one's action is among the best ways to protect the most important rights in the case at hand.

This principle—it is more of a *scheme*—all by itself is too abstract to be of any practical use. What needs to be added, of course, is a specification of the moral rights that figure in this scheme and their relative importance. Mackie proposes a single basic moral right: the right of persons to "choose how they shall live."[25] But this right to choose is wide open, and to work our way from it to specific moral obligations, we will need to specify what sorts of more specific rights people have in virtue of having this most basic right. Perhaps we can begin by recognizing the Jeffersonian moral rights to life, liberty, and the pursuit of happiness. And then, for each of these general rights, we might specify them further by recognizing a set of specific moral rights including, for example, a right to free speech.

So, specifying a single basic and perhaps very general moral right (or set of them) and working toward a specification of more specific moral rights is one task of a rights-based moral theory. However one works out the details of what the moral rights are, we must keep in mind the obvious fact that in some contexts moral rights will come into conflict. My right of free speech may conflict with the rights that others have to be safe from harm. Suppose, for instance, that on some occasion, my speaking out would seriously jeopardize the personal safety of others. If so, then in such circumstances, it is plausible to suppose that people's right of personal safety overrides a person's right to free speech. How is one to determine whether one right overrides another in cases of conflict? This question brings us to the issue of applying a rights-based theory to moral issues.

Applying a Rights-Based Moral Theory

Principle (or scheme) R purports to explain an action's being morally right (and by implication morally wrong) in terms of respecting fundamental moral rights. Clause (a) of R covers the easy case in which one's action simply does not come into contact with the moral rights of others. I get up in the morning and decide to eat Cheerios for breakfast. Unusual cases aside, this action has nothing to do with the moral rights of others—I'm morally free to eat the Cheerios or not. Clause (b), however, is where a rights-based approach to moral problems is most relevant: one can frame many of the disputed moral issues featured in this book as a conflict of rights: right to life versus right to choice; right to express oneself in speech and writing versus right to public safety, and so on.

So in applying R (supplemented with a theory of rights) to moral issues, the challenge is to find the best way of properly balancing competing rights claims in arriving at a moral verdict about what ought to be done. As I will explain more thoroughly below in connection with the ethics of prima facie duty, it is very doubtful that there is some fixed mechanical procedure that one can use in arriving at a correct or justified moral verdict in particular cases based on a consideration of competing rights. Rather, what one needs is what philosophers call **moral judgment**—roughly, an acquired skill at discerning what matters the most morally speaking and coming to an all-things-considered moral verdict where this skill cannot be entirely captured by a set of rules. The point to stress here is that, as with the other moral theories we are considering, applying a moral theory—its principles—to particular issues is not a mechanical process. But this does not take away from the value of such theories in guiding one's moral deliberations and subsequent choices.

Rights-Focused Approaches to Moral Issues

We have noted that talk of rights is very common in moral thought and discussion. However, we have also noted that in thinking about a moral issue in terms of competing rights claims, one need not accept a rights-based moral theory as just described. As noted earlier, consequentialists, Kantians, and natural law theorists can and do recognize rights—although on these theories rights are not what is most morally basic in the theory. So, because one may appeal to rights in discussing a moral issue without accepting a rights-based moral theory, we must recognize what we may call **rights-focused approaches** to moral issues. To say that an author's approach to a moral issue is rights-focused is simply to say that the author appeals to rights as a basis for taking a stand on the issue at hand—the author may or may not also embrace a rights-based moral theory. In my article introductions, I have chosen to use the term "rights-focused" in summarizing the views of those authors who appeal primarily to rights in their article, unless the author makes it clear that he or she embraces a rights-based moral theory.

E. Virtue Ethics

Sometimes our moral thinking is dominated by thoughts about what sort of person one would be if one were to perform some action. The thought of living up to certain ideals or virtues of what a morally good person is like is crucial here. Being an unselfish person is an ideal that we may use in evaluating some course of action, and sometimes we may think, "Not helping her would be selfish on my part, so I'm going to help." When our moral thinking takes this turn, we are evaluating actions in terms of virtue and vice. The ideas of virtue and vice have played a negligible role in the moral theories we have surveyed (at least as I have presented them).[26] However, inspired primarily by the ethical views of the ancient Greek philosophers Plato and Aristotle, **virtue ethics** makes the concepts of virtue and vice central in moral theory. Such theories, as I will understand them, take the concepts of virtue and vice to be more basic than the concepts of right and wrong, and thus propose to define or characterize the latter in terms of the former.[27]

One might characterize right and wrong in terms of virtue and vice in different ways, but here (roughly) is how Rosalind Hursthouse, whose article on abortion is included in chapter 10, formulates a virtue ethical principle of right action:

> **VE**   An action is right if and only if (and because) it is what a virtuous agent (acting in character) would not avoid doing in the circumstances under consideration.

How are we to understand the concept of a virtuous agent featured in this principle? One straightforward way is to say that the virtuous agent is one who has the virtues. But what is a virtue? And which ones does the virtuous agent have?

A **virtue** is a trait of character or mind that typically involves dispositions to act, feel, and think in certain ways and that is central in the *positive* evaluation of persons. Honesty and loyalty are two commonly recognized virtues. The trait of honesty, for instance, involves at a minimum being disposed to tell the truth and avoid lying, as well as the disposition to have certain feelings about truth telling (positive ones) and about lying (negative ones). Honesty, as a virtue, is a trait that has positive value and contributes to what makes someone a good person. In contrast to a virtue, a **vice** is a trait of character or mind which typically involves dispositions to act, feel, and think in certain ways, and that is central in the *negative* evaluation of persons. So, for instance, opposed to the virtue of honesty is the vice of dishonesty, which may be understood as having inappropriate dispositions of action and feeling regarding truth telling and lying. Furthermore, as a vice, dishonesty has negative value and contributes to what makes someone a morally bad person. So, in general, virtues and vices are character traits that are manifested in having certain dispositions to act and feel in certain ways and that bear on what makes a person morally good or bad. Here, then, is a short (and by no means complete) list of fairly commonly recognized moral virtues and their corresponding vices:[28]

- Honesty/Dishonesty
- Courage/Cowardice
- Justice/Injustice
- Temperance/Intemperance
- Beneficence/Selfishness
- Humility/Arrogance
- Loyalty/Disloyalty
- Gratitude/Ingratitude

Applying Virtue Ethics

To apply VE to a particular case, then, we must first determine which character traits are the virtues that are possessed by the virtuous agent (we may begin with the previous list), and then determine how, on the basis of such traits, this agent would be disposed to act in the circumstances in question. An action that a virtuous agent, acting in character, would not fail to perform in some circumstance is morally required; an action she might or might not do at her discretion is morally optional, and one that she would avoid doing is morally wrong.

Of course, in applying virtue ethics to disputed moral issues, we encounter the fact that more than one virtue is relevant to the case at hand and that one of them—say, honesty—favors telling the truth, whereas one of the others—say, loyalty—favors telling a lie. In such cases of conflict among the virtues, we must examine the particular details of the case at hand and ask such questions as, "What is at stake here?" "How important is telling the truth in this case?" "How important is loyalty to an organization?" It is only by examining the details of such cases of conflict that we can come to an all-things-considered moral evaluation of some particular action based on considerations of virtue. This point is reflected in VE's reference to a virtuous agent *acting in character.* Presumably, such an ideal agent has the sort of practical wisdom or judgment that is required in order for her to discern which virtue consideration, from among the competing virtue considerations in a particular case, has the most weight. As I have been noting all along in presenting the various moral theories—something that we explore a bit further in the next subsection—the application of moral theories to particular issues requires moral judgment.

F. Ethics of Prima Facie Duty

Whereas consequentialism, for instance, features a single moral principle of right conduct, what I am calling the **ethics of prima facie duty** features a plurality of basic moral principles of right conduct. The most famous version of this kind of view was developed by the twentieth-century British philosopher W. D. Ross (1877–1971). To understand the elements of Ross's view, we need to do the following: (1) explain what he means by talk of "prima facie duty"; (2) present his basic principles of prima facie duty; and then (3) explain the role of moral judgment in applying them in practice.

The Concept of a Prima Facie Duty

To say that one has a **prima facie duty** to perform some action is to say that one has *some* moral reason to perform the action, but the reason in question might be *overridden* by some other moral reason that favors not performing the action. The best way to understand the concept is with an example. Suppose I have promised to pick you up on Saturday by 10:00 A.M. so that you can get to a very important job interview (your car is in the shop). Ross would say that because of my having made a promise to you, I have a prima facie duty (of fidelity—see later discussion) to do what I said I would do: pick you up by 10:00 A.M. on Saturday. But now suppose that as I am about to leave to pick you up, my child falls off the roof of my house and needs immediate medical attention. Ross would say that here I have a prima facie duty to take my child to the emergency ward of the hospital. So, I have a prima facie duty to start out for your place and a conflicting prima facie duty to attend to my child: as things have turned out, I am not able to fulfill both prima facie duties. Now the point of calling a duty "prima facie" is that the moral reasons provided by such facts as that I've made a promise or that my child needs my help can be outweighed by other moral reasons that favor doing some other action. Ross puts this point by saying that a prima facie duty can be overridden—beat out—by a competing prima facie duty. In the case I've described, because it is my child and because she needs immediate medical attention, my prima facie duty to help her overrides my prima facie duty to come pick you up. When one prima facie duty prevails in some conflict of duties situation, it becomes one's *all-things-considered duty*—it is what you ought, all things considered, to do in that circumstance. So, for Ross, to say that one has a prima facie duty to perform action *A* on some occasion is to say that one has a moral reason to do *A*, and unless something comes up that is morally more important, one has an all-things-considered duty to do *A* on that occasion.

Ross's theory of right conduct, which is our main concern, is based partly on his theory of intrinsic value to which we now turn.

Ross's Theory of Intrinsic Value

Ross held that there are four basic intrinsic goods:

1. *Virtue.* The disposition to act from certain desires, including the desire to do what is morally right, is intrinsically good.
2. *Pleasure.* States of experiencing pleasure are intrinsically good.
3. *Pleasure in proportion to virtue.* The state of experiencing pleasure in proportion to one's level of virtue is intrinsically good.
4. *Knowledge.* Having knowledge (at least of a nontrivial sort) is intrinsically good.

The items on this list are the basis for some of Ross's basic prima facie duties—call them "value-based" prima facie duties. What Ross calls duties of "special obligation" are not based on his theory of intrinsic value.

Ross's Prima Facie Duties

Here, then, is Ross's list of basic prima facie duties, organized into the two categories just mentioned:

Basic Value-Based Prima Facie Duties

1. Justice: prima facie, one ought to ensure that pleasure is distributed according to merit.
2. Beneficence: prima facie, one ought to help those in need and, in general, increase the virtue, pleasure, and knowledge of others.
3. Self-improvement: prima facie, one ought to improve oneself with respect to one's own virtue and knowledge.
4. Nonmaleficence: prima facie, one ought to refrain from harming others.

Basic Prima Facie Duties of Special Obligation

5. Fidelity: prima facie, one ought to keep one's promises (including the implicit promise to be truthful).
6. Reparation: prima facie, one ought to make amends to others for any past wrongs one has done them.
7. Gratitude: prima facie, one ought to show gratitude toward one's benefactors.

The first four basic prima facie duties, then, make reference to what has intrinsic value according to Ross's theory of value. Ross himself points out that the prima facie duties of justice, beneficence, and self-improvement "come under the general principle that we should produce as much good as possible."[29] This part of Ross's theory fits the characterization of consequentialism.

The duties of special obligation do not make reference to what has intrinsic value: the duties of fidelity, reparation, and gratitude do not depend for their prima facie rightness on the values of the consequences of those actions. This part of Ross's theory is clearly duty-based or deontological. Overall, then, Ross's theory represents a hybrid: part consequentialist, part deontological.

Applying the Ethics of Prima Facie Duties

But how, on Ross's view, does one determine in some particular case that one prima facie duty overrides another, competing prima facie duty? Ross denies that there is any correct super-principle like the principle of utility or Kant's categorical imperative to which one might appeal to determine one's all-things-considered duty in cases of conflict. Nor is there any fixed ranking of the various prima facie duties such that the duty higher up on the list always beats out duties below it. Rather, according to Ross, in determining which prima facie duty is most "stringent" in some particular case and thus represents one's all-things-considered duty, one must examine the details of the case by using one's *judgment* about which of the competing duties is (in that situation) strongest. As mentioned earlier, moral judgment is a matter of discerning the morally important features of a situation and determining what ought or ought not to be done, where doing so cannot be fully captured in a set of rules. Judgment is largely a matter of skill that one may acquire through experience.

One final remark. One need not agree with Ross's own list of basic prima facie duties in order to accept the other tenets of Ross's view. For instance, Robert Audi has recently defended an ethic of prima facie duties that features ten basic prima facie duties.[30] Audi, unlike Ross, distinguishes duties not to lie from duties of fidelity, and he adds two additional duties to Ross's list. So were we to make the additions Audi proposes, we would have the following:

8. Veracity: prima facie, one ought not to lie.
9. Enhancement and preservation of freedom: prima facie, one ought to contribute to increasing or at least preserving the freedom of others with priority given to removing constraints over enhancing opportunities.
10. Respectfulness: prima facie, one ought, in the manner of our relations with other people, treat others respectfully.

The main point I wish to make here is that Ross's version of an ethic of prima facie duties is one version of this general sort of view. Audi's view attempts to build upon and improve Ross's view.

G. Social Contract Theory

The basic idea of **social contract theories of morality** is that correct or justified moral rules or principles are ones that result from some sort of social agreement—whether the agreement is conceived as having actually taken place or (more likely) the agreement in question is hypothetical. Philosophers Thomas Hobbes (1588–1679) and Jean-Jacques Rousseau (1712–1778) developed influential versions of social contract theory. But the view has found its most powerful contemporary development in the writings of John Rawls (*A Theory of Justice*, 1971), David Gauthier (*Morals by Agreement*, 1986), and T. M. Scanlon (*What We Owe to Each Other*, 1998). The selection featured in the next chapter representing this type of theory is an excerpt from Rawls's 1971 book, about which I will say more in a moment. But first I will formulate a representative statement of the theory of right conduct that is characteristic of social contract theory.

Begin with the assumption that parties to the (hypothetical) agreement are conceived to be free and equal and that each is motivated to reach an agreement on the fundamental rules and principles governing conduct. There are various ways of filling in the details that would lead these hypothetical agents to reach such an agreement, and different social contract theorists do so in distinctive and somewhat different ways. And, of course, such details will matter greatly in getting from the idea of individuals involved in the hypothetical agreement to a single set of moral rules and principles that are supposed to emerge from some process involved in reaching an agreement. But putting aside such details for the time being, here is a generic formulation of a social contract theory of right action:

SC An action is morally right if and only if (and because) it is permitted by a set of moral principles that hypothetical agents would agree to under conditions that are ideal for choosing moral principles (the precise characteristics of the hypothetical agents and ideal conditions to be spelled out).

Of course, SC does not say anything substantive about the agents or the conditions that ground the agreement, and so, as stated, it is useless as a criterion of right action until details are provided. And as I've said, there are different ways of filling out the details. To put some flesh on this bare-bones formulation of social contract theory, let us briefly consider the view of Rawls.

As the preceding formula indicates, in order to develop a social contract theory, one must specify the characteristics, including the motivations of the hypothetical agents who are party to the agreement, as well as the ideal conditions under which the agreement is hypothesized to take place. This is the first general task of such theories. The second task is to argue that some determinate set of moral principles would be favored over competing moral principles under the specified ideal conditions. In *A Theory of Justice*, Rawls is primarily interested in a social contract account of the justification of principles of justice governing the basic institutions of a well-ordered society. The gist of Rawls's theory is nicely expressed in the first paragraph of our selection in the next chapter:

> [T]he guiding idea is that the principles of justice for the basic structure of society are the object of an original agreement. They are the principles that free and rational persons concerned to further their own interests would accept in an initial position of equality as defining the fundamental terms of their associations. These principles are to regulate all further agreements that specify the kinds of social cooperation that can be entered into and the forms of government that can be established. This way of regarding the principles of justice I shall call justice as fairness. (Rawls 1971, 11)

Rawls uses the term *original position* to describe the hypothetical situation—the ideal circumstances—in which persons are to decide on basic principles of justice. As hypothetical, it is not presented as an actual historical state of affairs; instead, it is supposed to represent circumstances for choosing moral principles that capture the idea of fair terms of cooperation. The individuals occupying the original position are understood to be free and equal human beings who each have a rational conception of what constitutes his or her own good. But to ensure that the selection process is as unbiased and thus as fair as possible, the occupants are to choose principles of justice under a "veil of ignorance." That is, they are to choose principles without knowing their own place in society, their class or social position, or anything about their natural talents, abilities, and strength. As Rawls observes, "since all are similarly situated and no one is able to design principles to favor his particular condition, the principles of justice are the result of a fair agreement or bargain" (Ibid., 12). Further details about the original position and its rationale are provided in our reading from Rawls.

Once Rawls has described the hypothetical choice situation, the remaining question is, "Which set of principles will be agreed to by those in the original position?" Rawls argues that two lexically ordered principles would likely be chosen.

> *The principle of greatest equal liberty:* Each person is to have an equal right to the most extensive basic liberty compatible with a similar liberty for others.

The basic liberties in question include such political liberties as the right to vote and run for public office, freedom of assembly, and freedom of speech and conscience.

> *The difference principle:* Social and economic inequalities are to be arranged so that they are both (a) reasonably expected to be to everyone's advantage and (b) attached to positions and offices open to all.

This principle, as Rawls explains, applies primarily to the distribution of wealth and income as well as to the design of organizations having to do with differences in authority and responsibility.

Roughly speaking, the lexical ordering of these principles means that the first is prior to the second, and so social and economic inequalities cannot be legitimately obtained at the expense of compromising the equal liberties of individuals. As Rawls remarks, "The distribution of wealth and income, and the hierarchies of authority, must be consistent with both the liberties of equal citizenship and equality of opportunity" (Ibid., 61). More detail about these principles and Rawls's particular version of social contract are provided in our next chapter's reading. Hopefully, enough has been said here to convey the basic idea of Rawls's version of social contract theory.

It is worth noting that Rawls's theory of justice has had an enormous impact on moral and political philosophy. Although most of the articles in this anthology are not about matters of social justice, or at least many of our authors do not approach their topics from this angle, readers will note many references to the work of Rawls in the book's selections.

Applying Social Contract Theory

Rawls uses the label *justice as fairness* for his conception of justice, and though he admits that his theory is not intended as a complete social contract account of morality, he does note, in our selection from his book, that his social contract theory could be extended to provide a general account of morality, a view appropriately labeled *rightness as fairness*. More recently, T. M. Scanlon (1998) developed the social contract account of morality he calls "contractualism," which is intended to provide a general account of interpersonal moral obligation and so represents a view that is not restricted to principles of social justice. Again, the basic idea of right action that such a view is meant to capture is expressed by SC. But, as noted earlier, in order for a social contract principle of right conduct to have any implications for what is right or wrong, one must first specify in sufficient detail the hypothetical choice situation from which moral principles are to be chosen and then use those more specific principles to address particular moral issues. We have one such version, featuring two fundamental principles of justice, in the work of Rawls.

This completes our survey of some of the leading moral theories that figure importantly in many of this book's readings. As mentioned earlier, I recommend using these summaries as an aid in understanding those writings in which an author appeals to one or another moral theory. In the final section of this chapter, we take up the following question:

What is the point of moral theory in thinking about disputed moral issues in light of the existence of a variety of competing moral theories?

3.   COPING WITH MANY MORAL THEORIES

This chapter began with a brief overview of the central concepts and guiding aims of moral theory and then proceeded to survey some types of moral theory. In working through the various moral problems featured in this book, one will find that different moral theories often yield different and conflicting answers to questions about the morality of some action. The natural law theory, for instance, arguably condemns all homosexual behavior as morally wrong; a consequentialist approach does not. So the application of one theory to an issue may yield one moral verdict, while the application of another theory may yield a conflicting moral verdict. What, then, a student may ask, is the point of thinking about disputed moral issues from the perspective of moral theory? It all seems rather arbitrary.

This is a completely understandable question whose answer requires that one move from a focus on particular moral issues to questions about the nature and evaluation of moral theories. It is not possible to fully address such questions in a chapter whose aim is to provide students with a basic understanding of a range of moral theories. But because of its importance, the question does deserve to be addressed, even if briefly. In so doing, I will first offer some remarks about evaluating a moral theory, and then I will suggest a way of looking at the various moral theories for the illumination I think they provide in thinking about moral issues.

Evaluating a Moral Theory

Philosophers who develop a moral theory do not just state some moral principle or other and leave it at that; rather, they *argue* for whatever principles they are proposing. And we can critically evaluate their arguments. So the first point I wish to make is that there can be rational debate about a moral theory—not any old moral theory is as good as any other.

Furthermore, there are standards for evaluating a moral theory—standards that are not arbitrary but rather have to do with the guiding aims of a moral theory that we discussed in section 1 of this chapter. Corresponding to the theoretical aim of moral theory—the aim of explaining what makes something right or wrong, good or bad—is the principle of **explanatory power:**

> A moral theory should feature principles that explain our more specific considered moral beliefs, thus helping us understand *why* actions, persons, and other objects of moral evaluation are right or wrong, good or bad. The better a theory's principles in providing such explanations, the better the theory.

This principle appeals to our "considered" moral beliefs, which may be defined as those moral beliefs that are *deeply held* and *very widely shared.* I hope that everyone reading this text believes that murder is wrong, that rape is wrong, and that child molestation is wrong. The list could be extended. Moreover, such moral beliefs are (for those who have them) very likely deeply held convictions. The principle of explanatory power tells us to evaluate a moral theory by determining whether its principles properly explain why such actions are morally wrong. Similar remarks apply to widely shared and deeply held beliefs about our obligations. So we can help confirm a moral theory by showing that it can properly explain the rightness or wrongness of actions about whose moral status we are virtually certain. Correlatively, we can criticize a moral theory by showing that it does not properly explain the rightness or wrongness of actions about whose moral status we are virtually certain. Applying this principle requires that we can tell what counts as a good explanation of the rightness or wrongness of actions. This is a topic of lively and ongoing philosophical inquiry whose study would take us far beyond the scope of this book. But in thinking about moral issues from the perspective of moral theory, the reader is invited to consider not only what a theory implies about some action or practice, but also what explanation it provides for whatever verdict it reaches about the action or practice under consideration. (I return briefly to this matter toward the end of this section.)

According to the practical aim of moral theory, we want moral principles that will help guide our moral deliberations and subsequent choices. Corresponding to this aim is the principle of **practical guidance:**

> A moral theory should feature principles that are useful in guiding moral deliberation toward correct or justified moral verdicts about particular issues which we can then use to help guide choice. The better a theory's principles are in providing practical guidance, the better the theory.

Any moral theory that would yield inconsistent verdicts about some particular concrete action is obviously of no practical help on the issue at hand. Furthermore, a moral theory whose principles are so vague that it fails to have clear implications for a range of moral issues is again of no help in guiding thought about those issues. Finally, a moral theory whose principles are extremely difficult to apply because, for example, applying them requires a great deal of factual information that is humanly impossible to acquire, is at odds with the principle of practical guidance. These are three measures to consider in evaluating how well a moral theory does in satisfying the principle of practical guidance and thus how well it does in satisfying the practical aim of moral theory.

These brief remarks are only meant to indicate how one can begin to evaluate a moral theory. Hopefully, what I have said is enough to make a start on answering the challenge that began this section. Let us now move on to the second point I wish to make in response to the challenge.

Moral Theory and Moral Illumination[31]

I conclude with a plea for the importance of moral theory, even if there is no one theory that currently commands the allegiance of all philosophers who specialize in ethics. The plea is that moral theory can help focus and sharpen our moral thinking about particular issues, and it can thereby provide a kind of insight and illumination of moral issues that is otherwise easily missed. Let me explain.

No doubt readers of this chapter will have noticed that the various moral theories we have surveyed build on ideas that are very familiar. To see this, let us return to the case of euthanasia with which this chapter began. You may recall that in that case, Dr. Jack Kevorkian brought about the death of his patient Thomas Youk by a lethal injection. We described Kevorkian's action as an instance of voluntary active euthanasia. Now if one pays attention to on-line discussions and newspaper editorials that focus on this moral issue, and listens to the views of politicians and other social activists who discuss it, we find that some arguments appeal to the likely effects or consequences of allowing this practice. And of course, the idea that an action's rightness or wrongness is to be explained by reference to its likely consequences is the main idea of the various varieties of consequentialist moral theory. Similar remarks can be made about the other types of moral theory presented in section 2. Some arguments over euthanasia focus on the intrinsic value of human life—one of the four basic human goods featured in natural law ethics. Related to questions about end-of-life moral decisions, some have argued that providing a terminal patient with painkilling drugs that will knowingly cause the patient to die of liver failure before succumbing to cancer is nevertheless permissible because death in this case is merely a foreseen side effect of the painkilling drug. Here we have a tacit appeal to the doctrine of double effect. Again, we find arguments that appeal to the special dignity and worth of human beings, as well as arguments that appeal to such alleged rights as the right to die or the right to die with dignity—arguments that tacitly appeal, respectively, to elements of Kantian moral theory and to rights-based moral theory (or at least rights-focused approaches to moral issues). Similar points can be made about virtue ethics, the ethics of prima facie duties, and social contract theory.

So the first point I wish to make about studying moral issues from the perspective of moral theory is that one thereby gains greater insight and clarity into the kinds of arguments that one commonly reads and hears (and perhaps is disposed to give) over disputed moral issues. In fact, one may think of the various moral theories we have surveyed as attempts to develop such familiar ideas from moral thought and discourse in a rigorous philosophical manner. To really understand some moral issue for purposes of making up your own mind about it, you first have to understand the issue, which in turn requires that you consider the various reasons that reflective people bring to bear in thinking and debating the issue at hand. Such reasons, as I have just indicated, are often developed systematically in a moral theory. So coming to understand moral theory helps provide a kind of moral illumination or insight into moral issues.

The further point is this. Different moral theories differ partly because of how they propose to *organize* our moral thinking about practical issues. For instance, utilitarianism has us organize our moral thinking about some issue in terms of its likely effects on well-being or happiness. Virtue ethics, by contrast, has us organize our moral thinking around considerations of virtue and vice, asking us, for example, to view a proposed course of action in terms of what it would express about our characters. Rights-based moral theories have us think about an issue in terms of competing moral claims that can be made by various involved parties. Similar remarks apply to Kantian moral theory, natural law theory, the ethics of prima facie duty, and social contract theory. But let us put aside for the moment the fact that the various moral theories in question offer competing answers to questions about the underlying nature of right and wrong, good and bad. If we do, we might then view these theories as providing different ways of diagnosing and thinking about a moral problem, where in some cases the best approach is utilitarian, whereas in others the best approach is from a virtue ethics perspective, and still in others, some other moral theory best gets at what is morally most important to consider. In other words, it strikes me that some practical moral questions are best approached from, say, the perspective of act utilitarianism, others not. Here is an example that comes up in the chapter on war, terrorism, and torture and is discussed in the reading from Alan M. Dershowitz. He considers a "ticking bomb" scenario in which a captured terrorist very likely knows the whereabouts of a powerful explosive set to go off in a heavily populated city. Would it be morally permissible to torture this (uncooperative) individual in an attempt to extract information that might be used to locate and defuse the explosive? Given what is at stake in *this* particular case, I can well understand why one's moral thinking would be guided by essentially act utilitarian reasoning. But in other cases, thinking in these terms seems morally askew. Thomas E. Hill Jr., in his article included in chapter 15, argues that in thinking about how we ought to relate to the environment, utilitarianism fails to properly diagnose what is wrong with certain ways of treating the environment. He also argues that thinking in terms of rights fails to get at what is really morally important about our dealings with the environment. His proposal is to think in terms of virtue—ideals of excellence—rather than in terms of utility or rights. As explained in section 1 of this chapter, a moral theory is partly in the business of providing practical guidance for moral thinking and decision making. My suggestion is that in some contexts it makes sense to think as an act utilitarian, in other contexts it makes most sense to think in terms of rights, and in still other contexts, thinking in terms of virtue and excellence seems most illuminating. The same can be said about the other moral theories we have surveyed. Thinking exclusively about all moral issues in terms of some one particular moral theory assumes a *one-size-fits-all* approach to moral thinking. I am suggesting that this probably isn't the best way to use theory to illuminate practice.[32]

Returning now to the challenge that began this section, I have tried to address it in two ways. First, moral theory is not arbitrary in the sense that you can just pick and choose your favorite or make up your own: there are standards for evaluating moral theories that have to do with the theoretical and practical aims of moral theory. Second, the variety of moral theories on offer can positively aid in one's moral thinking about controversial moral issues in two ways. First, it can do so by providing rigorous articulations of common ideas about morality. And second, it can do so if one views these theories as diagnostic tools for getting to the heart of moral problems. Some tools are better for some jobs than other tools. My suggestion is that a particular moral theory may be a better tool than others when it comes to thinking through some particular issue, though a different theory may be better at helping one think through other issues.

NOTES

1. A few paragraphs of material in this essay are taken from my "Ethics" in *Reflections on Philosophy,* 2nd ed., ed. L. McHenry and T. Yagisowa (New York: Longman's Publishers, 2003), 103–25.
2. John Rawls, *A Theory of Justice* (Cambridge, MA: Harvard University Press, 1971), 24.
3. Given this understanding of the notions of intrinsic and extrinsic value, it is possible for something to have value of both sorts. Suppose, for example, that both happiness and knowledge have intrinsic positive value. Since knowledge can be of use in promoting happiness, knowledge can also have extrinsic value.
4. The "if and only if (and because) . . ." is meant to make clear that what follows the "and because" is meant to be a moral criterion that explains *why* the item being evaluated has whatever moral property (e.g., rightness) is mentioned in the first part of the principle.
5. To categorize Kant's ethical theory as deontological in the sense of being fundamentally duty-based may be inaccurate. Arguably, the notion of dignity—a kind of status that all persons have—is the explanatory basis of duties in Kant's ethical theory. Since dignity is a kind of value, this would make Kant's theory a certain kind of value-based theory, but nevertheless distinct from consequentialist views.
6. See Jeremy Bentham, *An Introduction to the Principles of Morals and Legislation* (New York: Hafner Press, 1948, originally published in 1789), and J. S. Mill, *Utilitarianism* (Indianapolis, IN: Hackett Publishing, 1979, originally published in 1861).
7. Another important distinction within consequentialism is between versions that appeal to the *actual* consequences (and associated value) that would occur were some action to be performed and versions that appeal to the *likely* consequences (and associated value) of actions—those consequences and their associated value that can be reasonably expected to follow from an action were it to be performed. I have chosen to formulate consequentialist principles in terms of likely consequences, since in applying a consequentialist theory to practice, we have to rely on our *estimates* of the consequences and associated value of actions.
8. I have explained utilitarianism in terms of *human* happiness or welfare, but a utilitarian may expand the scope of moral concern to all creatures for whom it makes sense to talk about their happiness or welfare.

9. For a defense of perfectionist consequentialism, see Tom Hurka, *Perfectionism* (Oxford: Oxford University Press, 1993).

10. What I am describing is a pure perfectionist account of value. It is, of course, possible to accept a hybrid view of intrinsic value according to which both happiness and perfectionist goods such as knowledge and achievement have intrinsic value.

11. For a recent defense of rule consequentialism, see Brad Hooker, *Ideal Code, Real World* (Oxford: Oxford University Press, 2000).

12. This is not to say that the best form of the natural law theory embraces the idea that "unnatural" actions are wrong and "natural" actions are right. The version I am about to present does not feature such ideas.

13. For a defense of natural law theory, see John Finnis, *Natural Law and Natural Rights* (Oxford: Oxford University Press, 1980).

14. Here is an appropriate place to clarify what I am calling theories of intrinsic value that figure importantly in those moral theories which feature value-based theories of right conduct. Ideally, a complete theory of intrinsic value would accomplish two related tasks: (1) provide a complete list of those types of things that have intrinsic value and also (2) specify those underlying features of intrinsically good and bad things *in virtue of which* they have whatever intrinsic value they do have. However, since our main concern in this chapter is with that part of a moral theory having to do with right and wrong action, we need only consider how a theory of intrinsic value responds to the first task—a specification of the types of things that have intrinsic value. So, for example, in what immediately follows, I will simply list the most basic types of items that have positive intrinsic value according to the natural law theory.

15. Kant's major writings in ethics include *Groundwork of the Metaphysics of Morals* (1785), *Critique of Practical Reason* (1790), and *The Metaphysics of Morals* (1797). All of these writings are included in Mary E. Gregor, trans., *Kant's Practical Philosophy* (Cambridge: Cambridge University Press, 1997). Page references to Kant's writings are to this edition. For a recent defense of Kantian ethics, see Onora O'Neill, *Towards Justice and Virtue* (Cambridge: Cambridge University Press, 1996).

16. In her article on a Kantian approach to world hunger included in chapter 14, Onora O'Neill develops these ideas in more detail.

17. See *Groundwork of the Metaphysics of Morals,* section II, 84–85.

18. I have left out the "and because" since arguably this formulation does not purport to express a moral criterion of right action—what *makes* an action right for Kant is expressed by the Humanity formulation; a *test* of an action's rightness is provided by the Universal Law formulation. For more on this, see my *Moral Theory: An Introduction,* 2nd ed. (Lanham, MD: Rowman & Littlefield, 2013), chap. 8.

19. In the *Groundwork,* section II, in the footnote on p. 80, Kant raises objections to the golden rule.

20. *Practical Philosophy,* 74.

21. Readers should be aware that the topic of rights is extremely complex and contentious. In what follows, my aim is to introduce readers to some distinctions and to some observations about rights, moral theory, and moral controversies which, although elementary and perhaps contentious, are useful for understanding moral disputes that are framed in terms of rights.

22. Such rights are sometimes referred to as "natural rights."

23. *Universal* human rights are rights that are enjoyed by all human beings regardless of nationality, sex, race, religion, or other such distinctions. Universal rights, as universal, are contrasted with the particular rights of particular individuals, such as the rights that come with owning a house or having a certain occupation.

24. J. L. Mackie, "Can There Be a Rights-Based Moral Theory?" *Midwest Studies in Philosophy* 3 (1978): 351.

25. Mackie, "Rights-Based Moral Theory," 355.
26. This does not mean that such theories have little to say about such matters. For instance, Kant elaborates a theory of virtue in the "Doctrine of Virtue" which makes up part 2 of his 1797 *Metaphysics of Morals.*
27. For a defense of virtue ethics, see Rosalind Hursthouse, *On Virtue Ethics* (Oxford: Oxford University Press, 1999).
28. Defenders of virtue ethics often attempt to explain the basis of the virtues and vices (why some trait is a virtue or a vice) by appealing to the idea of human flourishing. The idea is that a trait of character or mind is a virtue because it contributes to or partly constitutes the flourishing of its possessor. For more on this point, see Hursthouse's "Virtue Theory and Abortion" included in chapter 10.
29. W. D. Ross, *The Right and the Good* (Oxford: Oxford University Press, 1930), 27.
30. See Audi's *The Good in the Right* (Princeton, NJ: Princeton University Press, 2004) for a recent defense of an ethic of prima facie duty that attempts to integrate this sort of view into a basically Kantian framework.
31. Special thanks to Jason Brennan and to Dave Schmidtz for very helpful conversations about moral theory and illumination.
32. These remarks suggest the possibility of combining certain elements from the various theories into one big super-theory featuring a plurality of principles, some having to do with duties, others with virtuous actions, others with rights, others with utility, and perhaps all of them unified by the Kantian idea of respect for persons, animals, and the environment. Doing so would still leave open the question of whether some one element of the theory—duties, virtues, rights, etc.—is most basic in the theory. One possibility (and the one that strikes me as initially plausible) is a theory according to which these notions are "interpenetrating"—a full understanding of any one of them requires appeal to the others.

5 } Drugs and Addiction

In 1973 President Richard M. Nixon appointed Myles Ambrose to head up a new federal agency—the Drug Enforcement Administration (DEA)—which announced a war on drugs. How successful this "war" has been in its forty-year history is a matter of dispute. According to various sources, international trade in illegal drugs is a thriving business with yearly profits in the billions. The war on drugs, which most recently has focused on the production and use of methamphetamine, has brought to public attention various moral and legal questions about drug use, among them the following:

- Is it morally permissible to take drugs?
- In those cases (if any) in which taking drugs is morally wrong, what explains its wrongness?
- Is it morally acceptable for a government to pass laws that make the production and consumption of some drugs illegal?

Our questions refer simply to drugs, but there are all sorts of drugs that can be easily obtained over the counter (aspirin, cold medications, and so on) as well as drugs one can legally obtain by prescription. Moral disputes about drugs have pertained only to certain kinds of drugs. So let us begin by clarifying the sorts of drugs that are at issue.

1. DRUGS

Speaking most generally, a **drug** is any chemical substance that affects the functioning of living things (including the organisms that inhabit living things). *Medical uses* of drugs are for the purposes of prevention and treatment of disease, whereas *nonmedical uses* include uses for religious, aesthetic, political, and recreational purposes.[1] What is often called *drug use* refers to the nonmedical use of so-called **psychotropic drugs** that produce changes in mood, feeling, and perception. Psychotropic drugs (at least those that are the subject of moral and legal scrutiny) are often classified into these groups: opiates, hallucinogens, stimulants, cannabis, and depressants. Figure 5.1 is a chart describing each of these types.

In moral and legal discussions of drugs, drug abuse, and drug addiction, the term "drug" is meant to refer to the kinds of psychotropic drugs listed in Figure 5.1.[2] Because there are

OPIATES	Include opium, heroin, and morphine. Opium, obtained from the seedpods of the poppy plant, has as one of its main constituents morphine, from which heroin was developed. These drugs (also referred to as *narcotics*) are highly effective in reducing or eliminating pain and inducing sleep, but they are also highly addictive and strongly associated with drug abuse.
HALLUCINOGENS	Often referred to as 'psychedelics' and include: LSD, mescaline (the active ingredient in peyote cactus), and psilocybin and psilocin, which come from Mexican mushrooms. One effect of these drugs (for which they are sought) is their capacity to alter perception by inducing illusions and hallucinations.
STIMULANTS	Include cocaine (derived from coca plants), crack (a concentrated form of cocaine), caffeine, nicotine, amphetamines, methamphetamine, and diet pills. When taken in small doses, these stimulants typically produce a sense of well-being, increased mental alertness, and physical strength, but large doses may produce increased excitement and mental confusion.
CANNABIS DRUGS	Derived from a hemp plant (*Cannabis sativa*), include marijuana, hashish, and other related drugs. The effects of this drug vary in strength depending on the preparation, and compare to those associated with hallucinogens.
DEPRESSANTS	Include sedatives, barbiturates, and alcohol, which produce drowsiness and sedation.

FIGURE 5.1   Types of Psychotropic Drugs.

many types of (psychotropic) drugs, it is important to be aware of their differences, which may be important for sorting out the morality and legality of drug use. Heroin, LSD, and cocaine differ in some ways from one another, and as a group they all differ markedly from nicotine. But like the "harder" drugs, nicotine is addictive. So, if one argues for the legal prohibition of hard drugs based on their alleged addictive powers, what about smoking? Should it be illegal too? Before getting to these questions, let us briefly consider the nature of addiction.

2. ADDICTION

Addiction is most closely associated with drug use, but the term is often used very broadly to refer to a type of compulsive behavior involving dependence on some substance or activity which, for whatever reason, is undesirable. Thus, we hear of sexual addiction and gambling addiction, as well as drug addiction. If we concentrate on drug addiction, it is common to distinguish *physical addiction* from *psychological addiction*. Addiction of both sorts involves a dependence on a drug despite its ill effects on one's health, work, activities, and general well-being. Physical addiction is indicated by physical withdrawal symptoms that occur when an individual ceases to use the drug—symptoms that include body aches, constant movement, and fitful sleeping. Psychological dependence involves a strong desire or perceived need to take the drug for its psychological effects (e.g., a sense of well-being), where withdrawal does not produce the physical effects characteristic of physical dependence. As mentioned earlier, opiates are highly physically addictive, whereas marijuana is psychologically addictive.

What is called **drug abuse** is the excessive nonmedical use of a drug that may cause harm to oneself or to others, including, for instance, abuse of alcohol by drinking too much on some one occasion. Here, we are focused on addiction. There are disputes about the nature of drug addiction. On what Daniel Shapiro calls a "standard view," addiction is caused by the pharmacological effects of the drug—the drug itself is the source of the addiction. On a nonstandard view defended by Shapiro, addiction results from the interplay of the drug, a user's personality, and social circumstances.

The dangers of drug addiction are often cited in disputes over the morality of government interference in the use of drugs for nonmedical reasons. So let us turn to questions about drugs and the law.

3. LIBERTY-LIMITING PRINCIPLES

In discussions of the morality of the legal restriction and prohibition of drugs for nonmedical uses, the same liberty-limiting principles that we discussed in the previous chapter on censorship are relevant here. Here, then, is a brief summary of the previous discussion of these principles. (For more detail, see section 2 of the introduction to pornography, hate speech, and censorship.)

A **liberty-limiting principle** purports to set forth conditions under which a government may be morally justified in passing laws that limit the liberty of its citizens. There are four such principles.

The Harm Principle

According to the **harm principle**, a government may justifiably pass laws that interfere with the liberty of individuals in order to *prohibit individuals from causing harm to other individuals or to society.* The harms in question include both serious physical harms (e.g., maiming, killing, inflicting injury) as well as serious psychological and economic harms.

The Offense Principle

According to the **offense principle**, a government may justifiably pass laws that interfere with individual liberty in order to *prohibit individuals from offending others,* where offensive behavior includes causing others shame, embarrassment, or discomfort. Laws against public nudity are often defended by appealing to this principle.

The Principle of Legal Paternalism

According to the principle of **legal paternalism**, a government is morally justified in passing laws in order to *protect individuals from harming themselves.* Motorcycle helmet laws and seat belt laws are often defended on the basis of this principle.

The Principle of Legal Moralism

The principle of **legal moralism** states that a government may justifiably pass laws that interfere with individual liberty in order to *protect common moral standards, independently of whether the activities in question are harmful to others or to oneself.* This principle is often used in the attempt to justify laws against so-called victimless violations of moral standards—violations that are (arguably) harmful neither to self or others and, because they are not done in public, are not offensive to the viewing public.

There are two points about the use of these principles worth noting. First, in order for a government to appeal to one of these principles in an attempt to morally justify laws that interfere with individual liberty of its citizens, two conditions must be met. First, the principle in question must be a correct liberty-limiting principle—it must correctly state a condition under which a government can (really) morally justify limiting the liberty of its citizens. Second, the activity or practice in question must satisfy the condition set forth in the principle. If, for instance, one appeals to the harm principle to prohibit the production and consumption of a type of drug, then one must show that the use of the drug in question does cause harm to other individuals or to society generally. (Additionally, one must show that the level of harm that would be caused by use of the drug under conditions where it is not prohibited by law would be higher than the level of harm that would result from passing and enforcing laws against its use.)

The second general point is that some of these principles are relatively uncontroversial, but others are not. The harm principle is relatively uncontroversial. And perhaps the same can be said of the offense principle. However, the principles of paternalism and legal moralism are quite controversial, particularly in liberal democratic countries such as the United States. In such countries that strongly value individual liberty of choice, it is widely believed that the proper role of government is limited to preventing harm (and perhaps offense) to others.

4. DRUGS, LIBERTY, AND THE LAW

Here it is important to distinguish the issue of **drug prohibition** versus **legalization** from the issue of **drug criminalization** versus **decriminalization**. Peter de Marneffe, in his selection included in this chapter, defines drug prohibition as referring to legal penalties for the manufacture, sale, and distribution of large quantities of drugs. Drug legalization refers to having no such penalties. By contrast, drug criminalization refers to criminal penalties for using drugs and possessing small quantities of drugs, while drug decriminalization refers to the opposite of criminalization. The importance of distinguishing prohibition from criminalization is that it is possible to defend the former but reject the latter (as we shall see in our readings).

In debates over the legalization and the decriminalization of nonmedical uses of drugs, the principles of harm, paternalism, and legal moralism are all relevant. To appeal to the harm principle requires demonstration of harm to others or to society generally caused by the use of the drug in question. It is widely believed that many of the drugs mentioned earlier are addictive and thereby lead to the commission of crimes that cause harm to others and society.

However, as we shall see when we read the article by Daniel Shapiro, there is disagreement about whether drug use is the cause of crimes that are committed owing to addiction. Furthermore, in order to justify a law by the harm principle, one must show that the level of harm that would likely result from not having a law prohibiting use outweighs the level of harm that would likely result from having a law. Again, those in favor of the legalization of drugs often argue that given the crimes that are committed as a result of a black market in the production, distribution, and sale of drugs, existing drug laws ought to be repealed. David Boaz defends this view in the first selection, while Peter de Marneffe opposes legalization of the sale, manufacture and distribution of drugs, though he also argues that it ought not to be against the law for individuals to use drugs or possess small quantities of drugs.

Nicotine is an addictive drug, and so the legality of smoking has recently received some attention from philosophers. In the United States, laws prohibit smoking in certain public places including airports and shopping malls. And some states have laws that prohibit smoking in restaurants. All of these laws can be justified by the harm principle. However, in his article, Robert E. Goodin takes a more radical approach to smoking and the law: he advocates a principle of legal paternalism and explores the implications of this liberty-limiting principle for the activity of smoking.

5. THEORY MEETS PRACTICE

We have already considered arguments regarding the moral permissibility of passing laws that would interfere with an individual's liberty to obtain and use drugs. So let us turn to issues of personal morality and consider the kinds of moral arguments that are grounded in some of the major moral theories.

Consequentialism

For the consequentialist, the morality of an action (or practice) depends on how much overall intrinsic value (or disvalue) it would bring about compared to alternative actions (including the alternative of simply refraining from the action under scrutiny). So this view implies that whether taking a drug is wrong depends on its effects—where we consider the effects both on the individual performing the action and on anyone else affected. Presumably for the consequentialist, the morality of some instance of taking a drug will vary from person to person depending on how much overall value would be brought about.[3] Applying the theory with any degree of accuracy will require some reliable information about one's own personality and circumstances—how taking a drug will likely affect you and others—and so will be no easy task.

Kantian Moral Theory

According to the Humanity formulation of Kant's categorical imperative, an action is morally right if and only if in performing it one does not treat persons merely as means to an end but as ends in themselves. What does this principle imply about the morality of drug use? Again, this will depend on the drug in question as well as the quantity used and the frequency of use. Of course, drug use that harms others constitutes a failure to treat those others as ends in themselves, as would any gratuitous harm. But perhaps the more interesting question from a Kantian perspective is whether drug use represents a violation of one's duty to self. Arguably, if drug use would hinder the development of those important physical, moral, aesthetic, or intellectual capacities that are part of a balanced human existence, then such activities would be wrong—a violation of one's duty to oneself.

Virtue Ethics

Enjoying oneself is certainly part of a flourishing human life, and as long as drug use does not interfere with (or threaten to interfere with) those ingredients of a good life, there is nothing wrong with it and perhaps some reason to use drugs, at least on occasion. If temperance in food and drink and other pleasures is a virtue and intemperance a vice, then the virtuous agent will avoid engaging in any form of drug use that would express intemperance. So if we accept a virtue account of right action according to which an action is morally right or permissible if and only if a virtuous agent (one who has the virtues) may choose to engage in the action, then whether or not the use of some particular drug on some occasion is right will depend on facts about the exercise of temperance by that person on that occasion.

NOTES

1. In 2012 Colorado and Washington became the first U.S. states to legalize the possession and sale of marijuana for recreational use, contrary to federal law. However, in 2009 the government issued new guidelines stating that patients and suppliers in states that legally allow the use of marijuana for medical purposes are not to be prosecuted under federal law for using or supplying this drug. As of 2013, eighteen states and the District of Columbia permit the use of marijuana for medicinal purposes.

2. There are also moral and legal issues about performance-enhancing drugs (anabolic and androgenetic steroids) as well as inhalants and solvents that are often used for nonmedical purposes.

3. This holds for an *act* consequentialist. A *rule* consequentialist (as explained in chap. 1, sec. 2A) will compare the likely effects of a rule prohibiting the use of certain drugs with the likely effects of not having a prohibitive rule as a basis for arriving at a conclusion about the morality of particular acts of drug use.

DAVID BOAZ

Drug-Free America or Free America?

Boaz favors the legalization of marijuana, heroin, and cocaine, arguing that individuals have a natural right to live as they choose so long as they do not violate the equal rights of others. Against those who argue that the right to take drugs is justifiably restricted in order to protect society from certain social harms, Boaz argues that drug prohibition has been a failure, creating greater social ills than would result from legalization.

Recommended Reading: rights-based moral theory, chap. 1, sec. 2D.

INTRODUCTION: THE DRUG PROBLEM

Human beings have used mind-altering substances throughout recorded history. Why? . . . Perhaps because we fail to love one another as we should. Perhaps because of the social pressure for success. Perhaps because—and this is what really irks the prohibitionists—we enjoy drugs' mind-altering effects.

Though the reasons for drug use are numerous, the governmental response has been singular: almost as long as humans have used drugs, governments have tried to stop them. In the sixteenth century the Egyptian government banned coffee. In the seventeenth century the Czar of Russia and the Sultan of the Ottoman Empire executed tobacco smokers. In the eighteenth century England tried to halt gin consumption and China penalized opium sellers with strangulation.

The drug prohibition experiment most familiar to Americans is the prohibition of alcohol in the 1920s. The period has become notorious for the widespread illegal consumption of alcohol and the resultant crime. Movies such as *Some Like It Hot* typify the popular legend of the era. The failure of Prohibition, however, is not just legendary. Consumption of alcohol probably fell slightly at the beginning of Prohibition but then rose steadily throughout the period. Alcohol became more potent, and there were reportedly more illegal speakeasies than there had been legal saloons. More serious for nondrinkers, the per capita murder rate and the assault-by-firearm rate both rose throughout Prohibition.

Most of the same phenomena are occurring with today's prohibition of marijuana, cocaine, and heroin. Use of these drugs has risen and fallen during the seventy-seven years since Congress passed the Harrison Narcotics Act [designed to curb opium trafficking], with little relationship to the level of enforcement. In the past decade, the decade of the "War on Drugs," use of these drugs seems to have declined, but no faster than the decline in the use of the legal drugs, alcohol and tobacco. In the 1980s Americans became more health- and fitness-conscious, and use of all drugs seems to have correspondingly decreased. Drug prohibition, however, has not stopped thirty million people from trying cocaine and sixty million people from trying marijuana. Prohibition also has not stopped the number of heroin users from increasing by one hundred fifty percent and the number of cocaine users from increasing by ten thousand percent. Moreover, prohibition has not kept drugs out of the hands of children: in 1988 fifty-four percent of high school seniors admitted to having tried illicit drugs; eighty-eight percent said it was fairly easy or very easy to obtain marijuana; and fifty-four percent said the same about cocaine.

Although drug prohibition has not curtailed drug use, it has severely limited some fundamental American liberties. Programs such as "Zero Tolerance," which advocates seizing a car or boat on the mere allegation of a law enforcement official that the vehicle contains drugs, ignore the constitutional principle that a person is innocent until proven guilty.

In attempting to fashion a solution to "the drug problem," one first needs to define the problem society is trying to solve. If the problem is the age-old human instinct to use mind-altering substances, then the solution might be God, or evolution, or stronger families, or Alcoholics Anonymous. History suggests, however, that the solution is unlikely to be found in the halls of Congress. If, on the other hand, the problem is the soaring murder rate, the destruction of inner-city communities, the creation of a criminal subculture, and the fear millions of Americans experience on their own streets, then a solution may well be found in Congress—not in the creation of laws but in their repeal.

This article proposes that the repeal of certain laws will force individuals to take responsibility for their actions; the repeal of other laws will provide individuals the right to make important decisions in their lives free from outside interference. Together these changes will create the society in which drugs can, and must, be legalized. Legalization of drugs, in turn, will end the need for the government to make the intrusions into our fundamental rights as it does so often in its War on Drugs.

THE FUTILITY OF PROHIBITION

A. The War on Drugs

Prohibition of drugs is not the solution to the drug problem. [Since 1981] the United States has waged a

"War on Drugs." The goals of this War were simple: prohibit the cultivation or manufacture of drugs, prohibit the import of drugs, and prohibit the use of drugs. As the aforementioned statistics demonstrate, the War has not achieved its goals.

Prohibitionists, however, sometimes claim that the United States has not yet "really fought a drug war." The prohibitionists argue that a "true drug war" would sharply lower drug use. They feel that the government has not fully committed itself to winning this battle. One need only look at the War on Drugs record, however, to see the commitment.

- Congress passed stricter anti-drug laws in 1984, 1986, and 1988. Congress and state legislators steadily increased penalties for drug law violations, mandating jail time even for first offenders, imposing large civil fines, seizing property, denying federal benefits to drug law violators, and evicting tenants from public housing.
- Federal drug war outlays tripled between 1980 and 1988, and the federal government spent more than $20 billion on anti-drug activities during the decade. Adjusted for inflation, the federal government spends ten times as much on drug-law enforcement every year as it spent on Prohibition enforcement throughout the Roaring Twenties.
- Police officers made more than one million drug law arrests in 1989, more than two-thirds of them for drug possession.
- The number of drug busts tripled during the 1980s, and the number of convictions doubled.
- America's prison population more than doubled between 1981 and 1990, from 344,283 to 755,425. Prisons in thirty-five states and the District of Columbia are under court orders because of overcrowding or poor conditions. An increasing percentage of these prisoners are in jail for nonviolent drug law violations.
- The armed services, Coast Guard, and Civil Air Patrol became more active in the drug fight, providing search and pursuit planes, helicopters, ocean interdiction, and radar. Defense Department spending on the War on Drugs rose from $200 million in 1988 to $800 million in 1990.

45

- The Central Intelligence Agency (CIA) and National Security Agency began using spy satellites and communications listening technology as part of the drug war. The CIA also designed a special Counter Narcotics Center.
- The federal government forced drug testing upon public employees and required contractors to establish "drug-free" workplaces. Drug testing has also expanded among private companies.
- Seizures of cocaine rose from 2,000 kilograms in 1981 to 57,000 kilograms in 1988.

Despite this enormous effort, drugs are more readily available than ever before. The War on Drugs has failed to achieve its primary goal of diminishing the availability and use of drugs.

B. Prohibition Creates Financial Incentives

One reason for the failure of the War on Drugs is that it ignores the fact that prohibition sets up tremendous financial incentives for drug dealers to supply the demand. Prohibition, at least initially, reduces the supply of the prohibited substance and thus raises the price. In addition, a large risk premium is added onto the price. One has to pay a painter more to paint the Golden Gate Bridge than to paint a house because of the added danger. Similarly, drug dealers demand more money to sell cocaine than to sell alcohol. Those who are willing to accept the risk of arrest or murder will be handsomely—sometimes unbelievably—rewarded.

Drug dealers, therefore, whatever one may think of them morally, are actually profit-seeking entrepreneurs. Drug researcher James Ostrowski points out that "[t]he public has the false impression that drug enforcers are highly innovative, continually devising new schemes to catch drug dealers. Actually, the reverse is true. The dealers, like successful businessmen, are usually one step ahead of the 'competition.'"[1]

New examples of the drug dealers' entrepreneurial skills appear every day. For example, partly because the Supreme Court upheld surveillance flights over private property to look for marijuana fields, marijuana growers have been moving indoors and underground. The Drug Enforcement Administration seized about 130 indoor marijuana gardens in California in 1989; by November the figure for 1990 was 259.

Overseas exporters have also been showing off their entrepreneurial skills. Some have been sending drugs into the United States in the luggage of children traveling alone, on the assumption that authorities will not suspect children and will go easy on them if they are caught. Others have concealed drugs in anchovy cans, bean-sprout washing machines, fuel tanks, and T-shirts. At least one man surgically implanted a pound of cocaine in his thighs. Some smugglers swallow drugs before getting on international flights. Professor Ethan Nadelmann has explained the spread of overseas exporters as the "push-down/pop-up factor": push down drug production in one country, and it will pop up in another.[2] For example, Nadelmann notes that "Colombian marijuana growers rapidly expanded production following successful eradication efforts in Mexico during the mid-1970s. Today, Mexican growers are rapidly taking advantage of recent Colombian government successes in eradicating marijuana."

Prohibition of drugs creates tremendous profit incentives. In turn, the profit incentives induce drug manufacturers and dealers to creatively stay one step ahead of the drug enforcement officials. The profit incentives show the futility of eradication, interdiction, and enforcement and make one question whether prohibition will ever be successful. . . .

INDIVIDUAL RIGHTS

Many of the drug enforcement ideas the prohibitionists suggest trample upon numerous constitutional and natural rights. In any discussion of government policies, it is necessary to examine the effect on natural rights for one simple reason: Individuals have rights that governments may not violate. In the Declaration of Independence, Thomas Jefferson defined these rights as life, liberty, and the pursuit of happiness. I argue that these inviolable rights can actually be classified as one fundamental right: Individuals have the right to live their lives in any way they choose so long as they do not violate the equal rights of others. To put this idea in the drug context, what right could be more basic, more inherent in human nature, than the right to choose what substances to put in one's own body? Whether it is alcohol, tobacco, laetrile, AZT, saturated fat, or cocaine, this is a decision that the individual should make, not the government. This point seems so obvious to me that it is, to borrow Jefferson's words, self-evident.

The prohibitionists, however, fail to recognize this fundamental freedom. They advance several arguments in an effort to rebut the presumption in favor of liberty. First, they argue, drug users are responsible for the violence of the drug trade and the resulting damage to innocent people. The erstwhile Drug Czar, William Bennett, when asked how his nicotine addiction differed from a drug addiction, responded, "I didn't do any drive-by shootings."[3] Similarly former First Lady Nancy Reagan said, "The casual user may think when he takes a line of cocaine or smokes a joint in the privacy of his nice condo, listening to his expensive stereo, that he's somehow not bothering anyone. But there is a trail of death and destruction that leads directly to his door. I'm saying that if you're a casual drug user, you are an accomplice to murder."[4]

The comments of both Mr. Bennett and Mrs. Reagan, however, display a remarkable ignorance about the illegal-drug business. Drug use does not cause violence. Alcohol did not cause the violence of the 1920s, Prohibition did. Similarly drugs do not cause today's soaring murder rates, drug prohibition does. The chain of events is obvious: drug laws reduce the supply and raise the price of drugs. The high price causes addicts to commit crimes to pay for a habit that would be easily affordable if obtaining drugs was legal. The illegality of the business means that business disputes—between customers and suppliers or between rival suppliers—can be settled only through violence, not through the courts. The violence of the business then draws in those who have a propensity—or what economists call a comparative advantage—for violence. When Congress repealed Prohibition, the violence went out of the liquor business. Similarly, when Congress repeals drug prohibition, the heroin and cocaine trade will cease to be

violent. As columnist Stephen Chapman put it, "the real accomplices to murder" are those responsible for the laws that make the drug business violent.[5]

Another prohibitionist argument against the right to take drugs is that drug use affects others, such as automobile accident victims and crack babies. With regard to the former, certainly good reasons exist to strictly penalize driving (as well as flying or operating machinery) while under the influence of drugs. It hardly seems appropriate, however, to penalize those who use drugs safely in an attempt to stop the unsafe usage. As for harm to babies, this is a heart-rending problem (though perhaps not as large a problem as is sometimes believed). Again, however, it seems unnecessary and unfair to ban a recreational drug just because it should not be used during pregnancy. Moreover, drug-affected babies have one point in common with driving under the influence: misuse of legal drugs (alcohol, tobacco, codeine, caffeine) as well as illegal drugs, contribute to both problems. Thus, if society wants to ban cocaine and marijuana because of these drugs' potential for misuse, society should logically also ban alcohol, tobacco, and similar legal drugs.

The question of an individual right to use drugs comes down to this: If the government can tell us what we can put into our own bodies, what can it not tell us? What limits on government action are there? We would do well to remember Jefferson's advice: "Was the government to prescribe to us our medicine and diet, our bodies would be in such keeping as our souls are now."[6]

THE SOLUTION: RE-ESTABLISH INDIVIDUAL RESPONSIBILITY

For the past several decades a flight from individual responsibility has taken place in the United States. Intellectuals, often government funded, have concocted a whole array of explanations as to why nothing that happens to us is our own fault. These intellectuals tell us that the poor are not responsible for their poverty, the fat are not responsible for their overeating, the alcoholic are not responsible for their drinking. Any attempt to suggest that people are sometimes responsible for their own failures is denounced as "blaming the victim."

These nonresponsibility attitudes are particularly common in discussions of alcohol, tobacco, and other drugs. Development of these attitudes probably began in the 1930s with the formulation of the classic disease theory of alcoholism. The disease theory holds that alcoholism is a disease that the alcoholic cannot control. People have found it easy to apply the theory of addiction to tobacco, cocaine, heroin, even marijuana. In each case, according to the theory, people get "hooked" and simply cannot control their use. Author Herbert Fingarette, however, stated that "*no* leading research authorities accept the classic disease concept [for alcoholism]."[7] Many scientists, though, believe it is appropriate to mislead the public about the nature of alcoholism in order to induce what they see as the right behavior with regard to alcohol.

In the popular press the addiction theory has spread rapidly. Popular magazines declare everything from sex to shopping to video games an addiction that the addicted person has no power to control. As William Wilbanks said, the phrase "I can't help myself" has become the all-purpose excuse of our time.[8]

The addiction theory has also gained prominence in discussions of illegal drugs. Both prohibitionists and legalizers tend to be enamored of the classic notion of addiction. Prohibitionists say that because people cannot help themselves with respect to addictive drugs, society must threaten them with criminal sanctions to protect them from their own failings. Legalizers offer instead a "medical model": treat drug use as a disease, not a crime. The legalizers urge that the billions of dollars currently spent on drug enforcement be transferred to treatment programs so that government can supply "treatment on demand" for drug addicts.

Despite the popular affection for the addiction theory, numerous commentators denounce the theory. For example, addiction researcher Stanton Peele deplores the effects of telling people that addictive behavior is uncontrollable:

[O]ne of the best antidotes to addiction is to teach children responsibility and respect for others and to insist

on ethical standards for everyone—children, adults, addicts. Crosscultural data indicate, for instance, that when an experience is defined as uncontrollable, many people experience such loss of control and use it to justify their transgressions against society. For example, studies find that the "uncontrollable" consequences of alcohol consumption vary from one society to another, depending upon cultural expectations.[9]

. . . The United States requires . . . more reforms—in addition to drug legalization—to create the kind of society in which people accept responsibility for their actions. . . .

Americans might take . . . steps to restore traditional notions of individual responsibility. Laws regarding drugs should only punish persons who violate the rights of others; private actions should go unpunished. Thus, laws should strictly punish those who drive while under the influence of alcohol or other drugs. Intoxication, moreover, should not be a legal defense against charges of theft, violence, or other rights violations, nor should a claim of "shopping addiction" excuse people from having to pay their debts. Physicians, intellectuals, and religious leaders should recognize that the denial of responsibility has gone too far, and they should begin to stress the moral value of individual responsibility, the self-respect such responsibility brings, and the utilitarian benefits of living in a society in which all persons are held responsible for the consequences of their actions.

CONCLUSION

Society cannot really make war on drugs, which are just chemical substances. Society can only wage wars against people, in this case people who use and sell drugs. Before America continues a war that has cost many billions of dollars and many thousands of lives—more than eight thousand lives per year even before the skyrocketing murder rates of the past few years—Americans should be sure that the benefits exceed the costs. Remarkably, all of the high-ranking officers in the Reagan administration's drug war reported in 1988 that they knew of no studies showing that the benefits of prohibition exceeded the costs.

There is a good reason for the lack of such a study. Prohibition is futile. We cannot win the War on Drugs. We cannot even keep drugs out of our prisons. Thus, we could turn the United States into a police state, and we still would not win the War on Drugs. The costs of prohibition, however, are very real: tens of billions of dollars a year, corruption of law enforcement officials, civil liberties abuses, the destruction of inner-city communities, black-market murders, murders incident to street crime by addicts seeking to pay for their habit, and the growing sense that our major cities are places of uncontrollable violence.

Hundreds, perhaps thousands, of years of history teach us that we will never make our society drug-free. In the futile attempt to do so, however, we may well make our society unfree.

NOTES

1. Ostrowski, *Thinking About Drug Legalization*, 121 Pol'y Analysis, May 25, 1989, at 34. . . .

2. Nadelmann, *The Case for Legalization*, 92 Pub. Interest 3, 9 (1988). . . .

3. Isikoff, *Bennett Rebuts Drug Legalization Ideas*, Washington Post, Dec. 12, 1989, at A10, col. 1.

4. Chapman, *Nancy Reagan and the Real Villains in the Drug War*, Chicago Tribune, Mar. 6, 1988, § 4, at 3, col. 1. . . .

5. Chapman, supra note 4.

6. T. Jefferson, *Notes on Virginia*, in The Life and Selected Writings of Thomas Jefferson 187, 275 (1944).

7. H. Fingarette, Heavy Drinking at 3 (1988) (emphasis in original). . . .

8. Wilbanks, *The New Obscenity*, 54 Vital Speeches of the Day 658, 658–59 (1988).

9. See generally S. Peele, *Control Yourself*, Reason, Feb. 1990, at 25.

READING QUESTIONS

1. What reasons does Boaz give for thinking that prohibition of drugs like cocaine and marijuana has restricted liberty?
2. What are the three goals of the war on drugs? How has the government shown its commitment to fighting this war?
3. Why has the war on drugs failed according to Boaz? How, specifically, has the prohibition of certain drugs created financial incentives for dealers of illegal drugs?
4. In what ways does prohibition violate our natural and constitutional rights?
5. Explain Boaz's reasons for saying that drug use does not cause violence in the way suggested by supporters of prohibition and the war on drugs.
6. How does Boaz incorporate the notion of increased responsibility into a possible solution to the problems caused by the sale and use of illegal drugs?

DISCUSSION QUESTIONS

1. Boaz denies the claim that the benefits of the war on drugs has outweighed the costs. Is he right to deny this claim? If so, can you think of any changes to the way the war on drugs is waged that might make it more beneficial?
2. Should drug users be blamed for any of the violence that occurs as a result of their drug use? Try to come up with some examples of cases in which violence is caused by drug users that are either under the influence of a particular drug or otherwise impaired as a result of their involvement with drugs.

49

PETER DE MARNEFFE

Decriminalize, Don't Legalize

De Marneffe defends the decriminalization of drugs but argues that this position is consistent with being against the legalization of such drugs. He bases his case for decriminalization largely on an appeal to respect for the autonomy of individuals, while he bases his case for the legal prohibition of the manufacture and sale of large quantities of drugs on the claim that legalization would likely dramatically increase the incidence of drug abuse, thus bringing about an increase in harm to drug users and society generally. In defending his view, de Marneffe argues that drug prohibition does not violate individual rights, that it does not represent an unacceptable form of paternalism, and that it does not imply that alcohol, fatty foods, or tobacco ought also to be prohibited.

Recommended Reading: Section 3 of this chapter's introduction to liberty-limiting principles. Also relevant are Kantian moral theory, chap. 1, sec. 2C, and consequentialism, chap. 1, sec. 2A.

Drugs should be decriminalized, but not legalized. There should be no criminal penalties for using drugs or for possessing small quantities for personal use, but there should be criminal penalties for the manufacture and sale of drugs and for the possession of large quantities. Isn't this inconsistent? If it is legal to use drugs, shouldn't it also be legal to make and sell them? Here I explain why not.

First, some terminology. Drug prohibition refers to criminal penalties for the manufacture, sale, and possession of large quantities of drugs. Its opposite is drug legalization. Drug criminalization refers to criminal penalties for using drugs and for possessing small quantities of drugs. Its opposite is drug decriminalization. Here I defend drug prohibition, not drug criminalization.

THE BASIC ARGUMENT

The basic argument for drug prohibition is that if drugs are legalized, there will be more drug abuse.

People use drugs because they enjoy them; they find them fun and relaxing. If it is easier, safer, and less expensive to do something fun and relaxing, more people will do it and do it more often. If drugs are legalized, they will be easier to get, safer to use, and less expensive to buy. They will be easier to get because they will be sold at the local drug or liquor store. They will be safer to use because they will be sold in standard doses and will come with safety precautions. They will be less expensive because the supply will increase and the risk of making, transporting, and selling drugs will decrease. So if drugs are legalized, there will be more drug use and consequently more drug abuse.

Evidence comes from the study of drinking. Alcohol abuse declines with alcohol use, which declines with decreased availability and higher prices (Cook 2007). For example, alcohol abuse declined substantially during the early years of Prohibition, when alcohol became less easily available and more expensive (Miron and Zwiebel 1991). Evidence for this is that during Prohibition deaths from cirrhosis of the liver declined by about 50%, and admissions to state hospitals for alcoholic psychosis declined substantially as well (Warburton 1932). The study of alcohol regulation since Prohibition further supports the conclusion that alcohol abuse declines with an increase in price—resulting from excise taxes, for example—and that alcohol abuse also declines with availability—when, for example, the law restricts the times when alcohol can be legally sold and when it prohibits those under twenty-one from purchasing alcohol (Cook 2007). Another commonly cited piece of evidence that drug use declines with availability is that heroin use was much higher among army personnel in Vietnam where it was easily available than it was among veterans who returned to the U.S., where it was much less available (Robins, Davis, and Goodwin 1974). Another piece of evidence is that the percentage of physicians who use psychoactive drugs is much higher than the general population, which can be attributed to the fact that drugs are more available to doctors (Vaillant, Brighton, and McArthur 1970).

Critics of drug prohibition commonly argue that it does no good because there is still so much drug use even though drugs are illegal. This is a bad argument. It is true there is a lot of drug use in the U.S., but this is no reason to conclude that drug laws do no good or that drugs should be legalized. There is also a lot of theft in the U.S. and it doesn't follow that laws against larceny do no good or that theft should be decriminalized. This is because, although many things are now stolen, it is likely that many more things would be stolen if theft were decriminalized.

In fact almost everyone who studies the question agrees that drug abuse will probably increase if drugs are legalized. Where there is disagreement is on how much it will increase. Those who defend drug legalization believe that although drug abuse will probably increase with legalization, it will not increase by very much, and a moderate increase is justified by the benefits of drug legalization. What are these benefits? If drugs are legalized, the argument goes, there will no longer be a black market for drugs, and so the associated violence and police corruption will cease. There will be fewer drug overdoses because drugs will be safer, because they will be sold in standard, regulated doses. Drugs will also be cheaper, so drug addicts will not need to steal to support their habits. Finally,

if drugs are legalized the government can tax drugs the way it taxes alcohol and tobacco and thereby raise needed revenue. These benefits are so great, the defender of drug legalization maintains, that they justify the cost of a moderate increase in drug abuse that will probably accompany drug legalization.

The defender of drug prohibition has a different view. He believes that if drugs are legalized there will be a dramatic increase in drug abuse. He then argues that the risks of violence to innocent bystanders caused by the illegal drug trade can be reduced to acceptable levels by adequate community policing; that police corruption can be adequately controlled by proper police training, monitoring, and compensation; that there will not be significantly fewer overdoses with legalization because drug abuse will increase dramatically as a result and because heavy drug use is inherently dangerous and often reckless; that although drugs will be cheaper with legalization, there will be more drug addicts as a result, some of whom will stop working to concentrate on drug use, and so who will steal to support their habits; and that the social cost of a dramatic increase in drug abuse is much greater than anything that could be paid for by taxing legalized drugs. The probable costs of legalizing drugs therefore outweigh any probable benefit, the argument for prohibition goes, and the costs of prohibiting drugs can be reduced by wise policies of enforcement, by enough so that drug prohibition can be justified by its benefit in reducing drug abuse.

Who is right? No one is justified in feeling certain, but here I assume that the defenders of prohibition are right, partly because this is what I believe, but mostly because I want to explain how, on this assumption, it makes sense to support drug prohibition and not drug criminalization. Some people think that drug criminalization is wrong because it violates our rights to liberty. From this they naturally conclude that drugs should be legalized. This, however, is a non sequitur, because it makes perfect sense to hold that although drug criminalization violates our rights, drug prohibition does not, as I now explain.

The basic argument for drug prohibition is that drug abuse will increase substantially if drugs are legalized. By *drug abuse* I mean drug use that harms the user or others or that creates a significant risk of harm. The term "drug abuse" is sometimes used more broadly than this, to include the recreational use of any illegal drug. Since the drug is illegal, its use is abuse. This characterization is misleading, however, because recreational drug use, in itself, is not harmful, and does not always create a significant risk of harm. Usually nothing bad occurs when someone smokes marijuana, or snorts cocaine, or ingests a tablet of LSD. Only very rarely is the user harmed by a moderate dose of these drugs, and others are harmed even less often. Heavy drug use, in contrast, can have lasting negative effects on a person's life and on the lives of those who depend on him. If, for example, a young person uses heroin heavily, he is less likely to do his school work and finish high school. If a parent uses heroin heavily, he is more likely to neglect his children, and less likely to take care of his health and to meet other important obligations, such as showing up for work. When a child's parents neglect him due to heavy drug use or when a young person neglects his own education and career, this can have lasting bad consequences on his life. So it makes sense to want there to be less drug abuse of this kind.

It is natural to think that if this argument justifies drug prohibition, it also justifies drug criminalization. After all, if drug use is decriminalized, surely the amount of drug abuse will also increase. Isn't it inconsistent, then, to hold that drugs should be prohibited but not criminalized? No, because there are important differences between prohibition and criminalization.

One important difference is that whereas drug criminalization prohibits individuals from having certain experiences that are enjoyable and illuminating, drug prohibition does not do this. Drug prohibition is similar to alcohol prohibition of the 1920s, which prohibited the manufacture, sale, and transportation of alcohol for commercial purposes, but did not prohibit drinking or the making of alcoholic beverages for personal use. Likewise, drug prohibition prohibits the manufacture, sale and possession of large quantities, but it does not prohibit drug use or making drugs for personal use. Drug criminalization, in contrast, does prohibit this. It thus prohibits people from using their own minds and their own bodies for certain kinds of pleasure and adventure. It prohibits people from regulating their moods in certain ways.

This seems overly intrusive. As adults we are entitled to determine what happens in our minds and to our bodies, unless our decisions pose a serious risk of harm to others or to ourselves. Because drug use in itself does not pose a serious risk of harm to anyone, respect for persons, as independent beings who are properly sovereign over their own minds and bodies, seems incompatible with drug criminalization.

Drug prohibition, in contrast, is compatible with respect for persons. Drug prohibition makes it illegal to operate a certain kind of business; but it does not prohibit anyone from experimenting with drugs or from regulating their moods in the ways that illegal drugs provide. It does not deprive anyone of control over their own minds and bodies. Where will people get drugs if others are not permitted to manufacture and sell them? In some cases they can safely make them on their own. In other cases they can receive them as a gift from friends who are good at chemistry, and, of course, people can still buy drugs illegally even if they are prohibited. What's the point of drug prohibition if people still buy drugs anyway? Well, what's the point of murder laws if people are still murdered? Presumably murder laws reduce the number of murders by enough to justify the costs of enforcement and the risks of wrongful conviction. If drug prohibition significantly reduces the amount of drugs that are made and sold and thereby reduces drug abuse, it can likewise be justified as *reducing* drug abuse even if it does not *eliminate* it.

To the self-sovereignty argument against criminalization, we should add that adults have important interests in the freedom necessary to lead a life that seems worthwhile to them, a life that makes sense to them as the right sort of life for them to lead, provided that in doing so they do not seriously harm others or themselves or pose a serious risk of harm. Each of us has one earthly life to lead, and it is important that we determine how we lead this life, what experiences we have, what goals we pursue, what kinds of relationships we have, and what kinds of people we become. For some, drug use is an important part of the kind of life that makes most sense to them. This is true not only of those who use drugs in religious ceremonies. It is also true of those who orient their lives around certain kinds of social and aesthetic experiences. "Dead heads" used to orient their lives around attending Grateful Dead concerts, smoking marijuana, and sharing this experience with others. Assuming the use of marijuana does not pose a serious risk of harm to the user or others, the fact that marijuana played a central role in this kind of life is a strong argument against criminalizing its use.

It is not, however, a strong argument for *legalizing* marijuana. After all, a person who wants to orient his life in this way can do this perfectly well even if it is illegal to manufacture and sell marijuana for profit. He can grow his own or share with friends. No doubt some will want to live the life of a drug dealer; this is the kind of life they want to lead. What is distinctive, however, about the life of a drug dealer is a function of its illegality. Hence this career aspiration does not provide a compelling argument for legalization. If anything, it is a reason to prohibit drugs, because if drugs are legalized, those who value dealing drugs as part of an outlaw lifestyle will no longer have the opportunity to lead an outlaw life in this way. Nor is the loss of the opportunity to sell drugs legally a serious loss, because under drug prohibition similar job opportunities will continue to exist, such as the opportunity to legally sell pharmaceuticals and alcoholic beverages. (If you are tempted to argue that the opportunity to sell alcoholic beverages and pharmaceuticals is not in fact available to most of those who sell drugs now, you should understand that this counts in favor of drug prohibition, not legalization, since only prohibition offers this kind of business opportunity to those who otherwise have little chance of entering the corporate world.)

Drug criminalization threatens personal autonomy in a way that drug prohibition does not. This is the main point so far. The claim, however, that drug criminalization threatens autonomy might be jarring. Aren't some drugs highly addictive, and isn't drug addiction inconsistent with autonomy? Doesn't concern for autonomy therefore warrant the criminalization of drugs? No. For one thing, laws that criminalize drugs deprive people of the legal discretion to use drugs, whether for good reasons or bad, and so deprive them of a kind of personal authority, which is a form of personal autonomy. For another, only a small proportion of those who use drugs are addicts.

This is true even of those who use heroin, cocaine, and methamphetamine (Goode 1999). For this reason, respect for the autonomy of the vast majority of drug users provides a strong reason against criminalization. Furthermore, the claim that drug addiction is incompatible with autonomy is based on a misunderstanding of what addiction is. In the imagination of some philosophers, an addict is like a zombie who has lost the capacity to choose or to act in accordance with his own judgment of what is best. This is not an accurate picture of any real drug addict. We call people drug addicts for one or more of the following reasons. (1) They use a drug to relieve a craving. (2) They use a drug even though they obviously shouldn't, because of the harm their drug use is likely to do them or others. (3) Although they believe they should use this drug at the moment they choose to use it, at other times when their judgment is more reliable and less distorted by temptation, they sincerely believe they should not use this drug any more. Even when all these things are true of a person, it is an error to characterize him as a zombie who has lost his power of choice. The addict is still someone who chooses, and chooses on the basis of his own judgment of what is best, just like the rest of us. If the drug addict were someone whose real self has decided not to use drugs, but who is then attacked by an alien desire that takes over his body and forces him to use drugs against his will, and if a person is less likely to be attacked in this way if drugs are criminalized, there might be a sense in which drug criminalization promotes the autonomy of addicts. But drug addiction is nothing like this. The addict's desire to use drugs is just as much a part of his real self as any desire he might have to stop. It's not an alien desire that forces him to do something against his will. It arises from his own sincere belief that the pleasure or relief of using this drug is a good reason to use it. So it is a mistake to suppose that drug use, even heavy drug use, is not autonomous.

Autonomy means different things and one thing it means is independence. In this sense a person might be less autonomous due to drug abuse. If a person drops out of high school due to drug abuse, he may be less intellectually and emotionally mature as a result and less capable of supporting himself. A person who abuses drugs may also be less capable of holding a job. So a person who abuses drugs may be less intellectually, emotionally, and financially independent as a result. If drug laws reduce this kind of drug abuse, there is therefore a sense in which they promote autonomy. This is not because drug abuse itself is not autonomous or because addicts are zombies who have lost the capacity for choice. It is because drug abuse is often infantilizing.

In evaluating drug laws, we must therefore consider whether the way in which they promote autonomy justifies the way in which they limit it. Because most drug users are not addicts and because even addicts use drugs as a matter of choice, respect for autonomy seems incompatible with a blanket prohibition of drug use. But drug prohibition does not threaten personal autonomy in the same way. To this we should add that those at risk of being harmed by drug abuse have a stronger complaint against those who manufacture and sell drugs than they do against those who use them privately or make them for their own use. When a person grows marijuana and smokes it by himself or with friends, he does little to significantly increase anyone else's risk of harm. In contrast, when a businessman sets up a lab to make heroin and then distributes this product to retailers who sell it to any willing buyer, this businessman increases others' risk of harm significantly. Others therefore have a stronger complaint against his activities. Because those at risk of harm from drug abuse have a stronger complaint against drug manufacturers and dealers than they have against private users, and because there are weighty reasons of personal autonomy against drug criminalization, but not against drug prohibition, it makes sense to make a distinction between these policies, and *to* support one and not the other.

DOES DRUG PROHIBITION VIOLATE INDIVIDUAL RIGHTS?

Even so, prohibition might violate our rights. I have suggested that if the benefits of prohibition outweigh the costs, then this policy is justifiable. But a policy can violate a person's rights even if its aggregated benefits outweigh its aggregated costs. "Each person," writes John Rawls, "possesses an inviolability founded on justice that even the welfare of society as a whole cannot override" (Rawls 1971, 3). Utilitarianism, which Rawls rejects, directs the government to adopt whatever policies will result in the most happiness, summed over individuals, and this principle may warrant policies that violate our moral rights. Because it is wrong for a government to sacrifice the individual in this way, a defender of drug prohibition must therefore explain why this policy violates no one's rights.

Part of the explanation has already been given: unlike drug criminalization, drug prohibition does not pose a serious threat to personal autonomy. Recognizing the value of autonomy, however, is not all there is to taking rights seriously. Taking rights seriously also involves commitment to *individualism*, according to which we may not evaluate government policies solely by subtracting aggregated costs from aggregated benefits, but must also make one-to-one comparisons of the burdens that individuals bear under these policies. In this way we take seriously the separateness of persons. It is possible, although unlikely, that a system of slavery could be justified by utilitarian reasoning, because, although a few are harmed by this system, so many benefit from it. To understand what would be wrong with this, we must make one-to-one comparisons and recognize that the worst burden imposed on the individual slave is substantially worse than the worst burden anyone would bear if this system were rejected or abolished.

Sometimes, however, it is permissible for the government to limit the liberty of the few for the benefit of the many. It is permissible, for example, for the government to imprison some people to protect society as a whole. To apply individualism to the assessment of government policies, we must therefore find a way of evaluating whether a government policy objectionably sacrifices an individual for the benefit of society. I offer the following hypothesis: the government *objectionably* sacrifices a person in limiting her liberty if and only if it violates the *burdens principle*. This principle is that the government may not limit a person's liberty in ways that impose a burden on her that is substantially worse than the worst burden anyone would bear in the absence of this policy. When the government violates this principle in adopting policies for the good of society, it objectionably sacrifices someone for the benefit of society; it fails to respect her inviolability; it violates her rights. To illustrate, even if a system of slavery maximizes economic productivity, it imposes a burden on the individual slave that is substantially worse than the worst burden anyone would bear if the government were not to maintain this system. So the government violates the burdens principle in maintaining this system, and consequently violates the rights of those enslaved.

Does the burdens principle prove too much? Consider the following objection. Surely it is worse to be in jail than to have something stolen from a store one owns, works at, or shops at. Don't laws prohibiting shoplifting therefore violate the burdens principle? Doesn't this show that this principle is invalid? This challenge can be addressed once we understand how burdens are to be compared. The relative weight of burdens is to be assessed by the relative weight of reasons that individuals have to want or want not to be in the relevant situations. The reasons there are for us to want to be free to take whatever we want from a store without paying are not very weighty. Consequently, our reasons are not very weighty to want to avoid a situation in which we must either pay for what we take or risk criminal penalties. On the other hand, there are good reasons for each of us to want the government to enforce a rule prohibiting shoplifting, grounded partly in the fact that without this policy the availability of retail goods will decline sharply over time. A law that prohibits shoplifting therefore does not violate the burdens principle, provided this law is administered fairly, harsh penalties are avoided, and necessity is accepted as an excuse.

I now assume that the burdens principle provides the correct basis for assessing whether the government in limiting a person's liberty objectionably sacrifices her for the benefit of society as a whole. If so, a defender of drug prohibition should be able to explain why this policy does not violate this principle. Suppose, then, that if drugs are legalized, drug abuse by young people and parents will increase

dramatically. Suppose, too, that drug abuse by young people commonly damages their future prospects, because it results in a failure to perform important tasks, such as finishing school, and to develop important habits, such as being a reliable employee, and that these failures early on have a lasting negative impact on a person's life. Suppose, too, that drug abuse by parents commonly damages the future prospects of their children because it results in serious forms of child neglect. On these assumptions, there are good reasons for some people to prefer their situations when drugs are less easily available. Some people will therefore bear a significant burden as a result of drug legalization: those who will be at a substantially higher risk of harm from drug abuse if drugs are legalized. These burdens appear to be at least as great as the burden that drug prohibition imposes on businessmen in prohibiting them from manufacturing and selling drugs. The burden on businessmen is equivalent to the choice of not going into the drug business or risking legal penalties. This is not a heavy burden because there are alternative business opportunities under drug prohibition that are similar to those that would exist in the drug trade if drugs were legalized. Hence drug prohibition does not objectionably sacrifice the liberty of businessmen for the benefit of society as a whole, and so does not violate their rights.

If the burdens principle is valid as a constraint on government policies that limit individual liberty, then someone who defends drug prohibition but not drug criminalization must defend one of the following positions: (1) Although drug criminalization violates the burdens principle, drug prohibition does not. (2) Although neither drug criminalization nor drug prohibition violates the burdens principle, drug prohibition can be justified by a cost–benefit analysis whereas drug criminalization cannot. Note here that although the burdens principle imposes an individualistic constraint on the justification of liberty-limiting government policies, it allows a policy to be justified by a cost–benefit analysis provided that this policy does not violate the burdens principle. If the worst burden that a policy imposes on someone is not substantially worse than the worst burden someone would bear in the absence of this policy, then this policy does not violate the burdens principle, and it can be justified provided that its benefits outweigh its costs, however this is properly determined.

Given the important differences between drug criminalization and drug prohibition identified above, it makes sense to argue that whereas drug criminalization violates the burdens principle, drug prohibition does not. But even if drug criminalization does not violate the burdens principle, it makes sense to defend drug prohibition and not drug criminalization. Suppose for the sake of argument that the burden that drug criminalization imposes on drug users, although significant, is not substantially worse than the worst burden someone would bear as the result of drug decriminalization. Perhaps some young people will be at a significantly higher risk of self-destructive drug abuse or drug-induced parental neglect if drugs are decriminalized than they are when drugs are criminalized. Perhaps this burden is comparable to the burden that drug users bear when drugs are criminalized. (Bear in mind that drug criminalization might be justified even if harsh penalties for drug possession are not.) It is still arguable that whereas the costs of criminalization outweigh the benefits, this is not true of drug prohibition. Perhaps the aggregate costs in restricting personal autonomy and in prohibiting a form of adventure and mood control outweigh the aggregate costs of increased risk of drug abuse that would result from decriminalization, even though the aggregated costs of increased drug abuse that would result from drug legalization outweigh its aggregated costs.

COMMON OBJECTIONS

1. Paternalism

Sometimes the government violates a person's rights even when it does not sacrifice him for the benefit of society as a whole. Sometimes it violates a person's rights when it limits his liberty for his own benefit. A common objection to drug laws is that they are paternalistic: they limit people's liberty for their own good.

Because drug prohibition does not prohibit anyone from buying drugs for personal use, it does not limit the liberty of drug users in this way for their own good. Assuming, though, that this policy is effective, it does limit a drug user's opportunity to buy drugs. So if this policy is justified by the assumption that it is bad for some people to have these opportunities, there is arguably a sense in which this policy is paternalistic.

This kind of paternalism, however, is not the kind that defenders of individual liberty have found most objectionable. The most objectionable forms of paternalism are those that satisfy the following description: the policy prohibits a mature adult from doing what he sincerely and consistently believes it is best for him to do; this person is mentally competent and adequately informed about the possible negative consequences; this policy limits an important liberty of this person, such as religious or sexual freedom; this policy limits this liberty by imposing criminal penalties; this policy cannot be justified except as benefitting this person, by deterring him from doing something presumed by others to be unwise. Policies that satisfy this description seem to involve an unjustifiable restriction of personal autonomy. Drug prohibition, however, does not satisfy this description. For one thing, drug prohibition limits the liberty of businessmen for the benefit of others—those who would otherwise be at a higher risk of being harmed by drug abuse. It does not limit the liberty of businessmen for *their* own good. Furthermore, the primary intended beneficiaries of drug prohibition are young people—those who would otherwise be at a higher risk of self-destructive drug abuse and parental neglect—and not mature adults who enjoy using drugs and so would like to have a legal supply. Moreover, drug prohibition does not prohibit anyone from using drugs. So even granting, what might be questioned, that the freedom to use drugs is an important liberty, like religious and sexual freedom, drug prohibition does not restrict this liberty, since it does not prohibit anyone from using drugs. Finally, drug prohibition does not impose criminal penalties on anyone for drug use. One can therefore agree that any policy that satisfies the above description is objectionably paternalistic, and yet consistently defend drug prohibition, since this policy does not involve this kind of paternalism.

2. Prohibition and Harsh Penalties

Another common objection to drug laws is that it is terrible that so many people are in prison on drug offenses. This is terrible. It is important, however, to distinguish the question of drug prohibition from the question of penalties. It is possible that, although some drugs should be prohibited, our current penalties for drug dealing are too harsh. A defender of prohibition can hold that although there should be penalties of some sort for the manufacture and sale of drugs, the penalties for first offenses should be mild, and should increase only gradually, with stiffer penalties only for repeat offenses. Moreover, a defender of drug prohibition can consistently oppose any penalties for simple drug possession, which are the penalties most strongly protested by critics of U.S. drug laws. Observe, too, that someone who opposes the legalization of all drugs might nonetheless support the legalization of some. For example, someone who supports the prohibition of heroin, cocaine, and methamphetamine might nonetheless consistently support the legalization of marijuana and some hallucinogenic drugs, such as LSD, mescaline, peyote, and MDMA (Ecstasy). This makes sense because some drugs are more harmful than others.

3. Alcohol Prohibition?

Another common objection to drug laws is that it makes no sense to defend drug prohibition and not alcohol prohibition. After all, alcohol abuse is much more harmful than drug abuse, much more highly associated with violence, property crime, accidental injury and death. So if the government is justified in prohibiting drugs, it must also be justified in prohibiting the manufacture and sale of alcohol. Assuming that alcohol prohibition is unjustifiable, drug prohibition must be unjustifiable too.

One possible response is to hold, contrary to popular belief, that alcohol prohibition is justifiable.

In fact, general opposition to alcohol prohibition is based on false beliefs about its effects, such as that it does nothing to reduce alcohol abuse and that it necessarily results in a huge increase in crime and corruption (Moore 1989). But it is not necessary to endorse alcohol prohibition in order to defend drug prohibition. One can argue instead that, although drinking is more harmful than drug use, the costs of now instituting alcohol prohibition would outweigh the benefits, whereas this is not true of continuing the policy of drug prohibition. A policy that reduces the availability of a socially stigmatized drug is likely to do more to reduce its abuse than a policy that reduces the availability of a socially accepted drug. Drinking is socially accepted and fully integrated into normal social life. This is not true of heroin, cocaine, and methamphetamine, which are widely regarded as evil. For this reason drug prohibition might be much more effective at reducing drug abuse than alcohol prohibition would now be at reducing alcohol abuse. It is also true that if alcohol prohibition is adopted now, many people who have built their livelihood around manufacturing, selling, and serving alcohol would be adversely affected. These are people who made certain decisions, for example, to open a restaurant, based on the assumption that it will be legal to sell alcohol. This is not true of continuing the policy of drug prohibition. Taking these and other considerations into account, it is arguable that whereas the benefits of continuing drug prohibition outweigh the costs, the costs of now instituting alcohol prohibition outweigh the benefits, even though alcohol abuse is generally more destructive than the abuse of other drugs.

4. Fatty Foods and Tobacco Prohibition?

A related objection is that the consumption of other goods is at least as harmful as drug use and we do not think that these other goods should be prohibited. For example, obesity and smoking cause far more deaths than drug use does, and we don't think that the manufacture and sale of fatty foods or cigarettes should be prohibited. Isn't this inconsistent? No, because one can reasonably argue that whereas the benefits of continuing to prohibit the manufacture and sale of drugs outweigh the costs, this is not true of now prohibiting these other products. Food production and the food service industry is a large sector of our economy, and the production, sale, and preparation of fatty foods is a large part of this sector. If the government were now to prohibit the manufacture and sale of all fatty foods this would have a huge negative impact on our economy, our way of life, and our habits of socializing. The same cannot be said for continuing (and properly modifying) drug prohibition. Tobacco prohibition is a harder case, but even here there are important differences between the case for drug prohibition and for laws prohibiting the manufacture and sale of cigarettes. A central concern in defending drug laws is the damage that drug abuse does to young people in limiting their future prospects, by causing the loss of important opportunities that will be difficult to recover. If a young person neglects his schoolwork and employment as a result of drug abuse, this is likely to have a lasting negative impact on his life. If a child is neglected by her parents due to drug abuse, this will increase her risk of serious injury and may have a lasting negative impact on her emotional and intellectual development. The availability of cigarettes does not have this same kind of negative impact. When a young person smokes, she increases her risk of certain serious diseases as an adult. Smoking, however, does not interfere with a person's intellectual and emotional development in the way that drug abuse and parental neglect do. Furthermore, the risks created by smoking as teenager can be effectively reduced later in life, by quitting as an adult. A similar point may be made about obesity. Finally, although cigarette smoking and obesity may be more likely to shorten a person's life, the kind of drug abuse that results in parental neglect or dropping out of school may have a greater negative impact on the overall quality of a person's life. The risk to a young person of being in an environment where drugs are easily available is thus different, and in some ways significantly worse, than being in an environment where cigarettes or fatty foods are easily available. Consequently there is no inconsistency in accepting this argument for drug prohibition and

rejecting corresponding arguments for prohibiting cigarettes and fatty foods.

CONCLUSION

To conclude, support for drug prohibition is consistent with opposing drug criminalization; it is consistent with respect for personal autonomy; it is consistent with the principle that each person possesses an inviolability founded on justice that even the welfare of society as a whole cannot override; it is consistent with opposing the kind of paternalism that defenders of individual liberty have found most appalling; it is consistent with not supporting alcohol prohibition; it is consistent with not supporting cigarette and fatty food prohibition.

It remains an open question whether the benefits of drug prohibition really justify its costs. One cost I haven't considered is the negative impact that drug prohibition has on the political cultures of drug producing countries, such as Mexico, Colombia and Afghanistan. Because drugs are illegal in Europe and North America, drug wholesalers in drug producing countries can make huge profits by selling drugs to drug retailers in rich countries, which the drug wholesalers then use to bribe and intimidate local police, judges, and politicians, fostering government corruption. It is also true that because drugs are illegal in these countries those in the drug trade must settle their disputes with violence and intimidation, and that innocent bystanders in these countries are sometimes harmed as a result. So it is arguable that drug prohibition harms the citizens of drug producing countries too much to be justified by the goal of reducing drug abuse in rich countries, even granting that drug abuse in rich countries would soar if drugs were legalized there.

This is a serious objection. Whether it is decisive depends on how much less corrupt the governments of drug producing nations would be and how much safer their citizens would be without drug prohibition. It depends, too, on how much drug abuse would increase in drug producing countries if drugs were legalized there. One of the most serious worries about legalizing drugs is the expected increase in drug abuse by relatively disadvantaged youth who already lack good educational and employment opportunities, and the expected increase in drug abuse by their parents. If there is reason to worry about the impact of drug legalization on the disadvantaged youth of rich countries, there is also reason to worry about the impact of drug legalization on the disadvantaged youth of drug producing nations, which are relatively poorer. When we consider the negative impact of drug prohibition on these countries, we must therefore also consider the likely negative impact of drug legalization. If drug abuse among young people and their parents in drug producing countries would increase dramatically with drug legalization, and if drug prohibition is not the primary cause of government corruption in these countries, and is not a major cause of violence to innocent bystanders, then it makes sense to believe that the overall benefits of drug prohibition to everyone outweigh the costs, and so to oppose drug legalization on this ground.

REFERENCES

Cook, Philip J. *Paying the Tab.* (Princeton: Princeton University Press, 2007).

Goode, Erich. *Drugs in American Society*, 5th ed. (New York: McGraw–Hill, 1999).

Miron, Jeffrey A. and Jeffrey Zwiebel. "Alcohol Consumption During Prohibition." *American Economic Review* 81 (1991): 242–47.

Moore, Mark. "Actually, Prohibition Was a Success." *New York Times*, October 16 (1989): A21.

Rawls, John. *A Theory of Justice.* (Cambridge, MA: Harvard University Press, 1971).

Robins, Lee N., Darlene H. Davis, and Donald Goodwin. "Drug Use by U.S. Army Enlisted Men in Vietnam: A Follow-Up on Their Return Home." *American Journal of Epidemiology* 99 (1974): 235–49.

Vaillant, George E., Jane R. Brighton, and Charles McArthur. "Physicians' Use of Mood-Altering Drugs." *The New England Journal of Medicine* 282 (1970): 365–70.

Warburton, Clark. *The Economic Results of Prohibition.* (New York: Columbia University Press, 1932).

READING QUESTIONS

1. According to de Marneffe, drug criminalization is incompatible with personal autonomy, but drug prohibition is not. How does de Marneffe argue for these claims?
2. In discussing drug prohibition and individual rights, de Marneffe invokes what he calls the "burdens principle." What is this principle and how does de Marneffe use it in defending his claim that drug prohibition is consistent with respecting individual rights?
3. What reasons does de Marneffe give for claiming that his position on drug prohibition does not automatically imply that prohibitions on alcohol, fatty foods and tobacco would be justified?

DISCUSSION QUESTIONS

1. Do you agree with de Marneffe that the legalization of drugs will result in a dramatic increase in serious and harmful drug abuse? Why or why not?
2. In the concluding section of his article, de Marneffe raises a potential objection to his view on drug prohibition, namely, that the benefits of prohibition are outweighed by the costs. What costs does de Marneffe mention? Do you think the costs in question are enough to outweigh the benefits of prohibition? (In thinking about this question, readers are advised to consult Web resources to gather information about drug-related violence and drug abuse.)

ROBERT E. GOODIN

Permissible Paternalism:
Saving Smokers from Themselves

Contrary to the widely shared assumption that legal paternalism is at odds with the proper practices of liberal democracies, Goodin argues that some forms of control and interference may be morally justified on paternalist grounds. In defending legal paternalism, Goodin focuses on smoking, arguing that there may be good reasons, consistent with liberal democracy, for public officials to pass laws that would interfere with this activity. Goodin does recognize a presumption against paternalistic interference by government, and claims that public officials should refrain from paternalistic intervention in the lives of its citizens regarding any type of activity when they are convinced that persons engaging in that activity are acting on preferences that are *relevant, settled, preferred*, and perhaps *their own*. Using the case of Rose Cipollone (a smoker who successfully won a court case against a tobacco company) as an example, Goodin explains how the "manifest preferences" of smokers are often not relevant, not settled, not preferred, and not their own. Goodin concludes by considering the kinds of governmental regulation of smoking that might be paternalistically justified.

Recommended Reading: Section 3 of this chapter's introduction to liberty-limiting principles. Also relevant, chap. 1, sec. 2D, on rights.

Paternalism is desperately out of fashion. Nowadays notions of "children's rights" severely limit what even parents may do to their own offspring, in their children's interests but against their will. What public officials may properly do to adult citizens, in their interests but against their will, is presumably even more tightly circumscribed. So the project I have set for myself—carving out a substantial sphere of morally permissible paternalism—might seem simply preposterous in present political and philosophical circumstances.

Here I shall say no more about the paternalism of parents toward their own children. My focus will instead be upon ways in which certain public policies designed to promote people's interests might be morally justifiable even if those people were themselves opposed to such policies.

Neither shall I say much more about notions of rights. But in focusing upon people's interests rather than their rights, I shall arguably be sticking closely to the sorts of concerns that motivate rights theorists. Of course, what it is to have a right is itself philosophically disputed; and on at least one account (the so-called "interest theory") to have a right is nothing more than to have a legally protected interest. But on the rival account (the so-called "choice theory") the whole point of rights is to have a legally protected choice. There, the point of having a right is that your choice in the matter will be respected, even if that choice actually runs contrary to your own best interests.

It is that understanding of rights which leads us to suppose that paternalism and rights are necessarily at odds, and there are strict limits in the extent to which we might reconcile the two positions. Still, there is some substantial scope for compromise between the two positions.

Those theorists who see rights as protecting people's choices rather than promoting their interests would be most at odds with paternalists who were proposing to impose upon people what is judged to be *objectively* good for them. That is to say, they would be most at odds if paternalists were proposing to impose upon people outcomes which are judged to be good for those people, whether or not there were any grounds for that conclusion in those people's own subjective judgments of their own good.

Rights theorists and paternalists would still be at odds, but less at odds, if paternalists refrained from talking about interests in so starkly objective a way. Then, just as rights command respect for people's choices, so too would paternalists be insisting that we respect choices that people themselves have or would have made. The two are not quite the same, to be sure, but they are much more nearly the same than the ordinary contrast between paternalists and rights theorists would seem to suggest.

That is precisely the sort of conciliatory gesture that I shall here be proposing. In paternalistically justifying some course of action on the grounds that it is in someone's interests, I shall always be searching for some warrant in that person's own value judgments for saying that it is in that person's interests.

"Some warrant" is a loose constraint, to be sure. Occasionally will we find genuine cases of what philosophers call "weakness of will": people being possessed of a powerful, conscious present desire to do something that they nonetheless just cannot bring themselves to do. Then public policy forcing them to realize their own desire, though arguably paternalistic, is transparently justifiable even in terms of people's own subjective values. More often, though, the subjective value to which we are appealing is one which is present only in an inchoate form, or will only arise later, or can be appreciated only in retrospect.

Paternalism is clearly paternalistic in imposing those more weakly-held subjective values upon people in preference to their more strongly held ones. But, equally clearly, it is less offensively paternalistic thanks to this crucial fact: at least it deals strictly in terms of values that are or will be subjectively present, at some point or another and to some extent or another, in the person concerned.

I. THE SCOPE OF PATERNALISM

When we are talking about public policies (and maybe even when we are talking of private, familial relations), paternalism surely can only be justified for the "big decisions" in people's lives. No one, except possibly parents and perhaps not even they, would propose to stop you from buying candy bars on a whim, under the influence of seductive advertising and at some marginal cost to your dental health.

So far as public policy is concerned, certainly, to be a fitting subject for public paternalism a decision must first of all involve high stakes. Life-and-death issues most conspicuously qualify. But so do those that substantially shape your subsequent life prospects. Decisions to drop out of school or to begin taking drugs involve high stakes of roughly that sort. If the decision is also substantially irreversible—returning to school is unlikely, the drug is addictive—then that further bolsters the case for paternalistic intervention.

The point in both cases is that people would not have a chance to benefit by learning from their mistakes. If the stakes are so high that losing the gamble once will kill you, then there is no opportunity for subsequent learning. Similarly, if the decision is irreversible, you might know better next time but be unable to benefit from your new wisdom.

II. EVALUATING PREFERENCES

The case for paternalism, as I have cast it, is that the public officials might better respect your own preferences than you would have done through your own actions. That is to say that public officials are engaged in evaluating your (surface) preferences, judging them according to some standard of your own (deeper) preferences. Public officials should refrain from paternalistic interference, and allow you to act without state interference, only if they are convinced that you are acting on:

- *relevant* preferences;
- *settled* preferences;
- *preferred* preferences; and, perhaps,
- *your own* preferences.

In what follows, I shall consider each of those requirements in turn. My running example will be the problem of smoking and policies to control it. Nothing turns on the peculiarities of that example, though. There are many others like it in relevant respects.

It often helps, in arguments like this, to apply generalities to particular cases. So, in what follows, I shall further focus in on the case of one particular smoker, Rose Cipollone. Her situation is nowise unique—in all the respects that matter here, she might be considered the prototypical smoker. All that makes her case special is that she (or more precisely her heir) was the first to win a court case against the tobacco companies whose products killed her.

In summarizing the evidence presented at that trial, the judge described the facts of the case as follows.

> Rose...Cipollone...began to smoke at age 16,...while she was still in high school. She testified that she began to smoke because she saw people smoking in the movies, in advertisements, and looked upon it as something "cool, glamorous and grown-up" to do. She began smoking Chesterfields...primarily because of advertising of "pretty girls and movie stars," and because Chesterfields were described as "mild."...
>
> Mrs. Cipollone attempted to quit smoking while pregnant with her first child..., but even then she would sneak cigarettes. While she was in labor she smoked an entire pack of cigarettes, provided to her at her request by her doctor, and after the birth...she resumed smoking. She smoked a minimum of a pack a day and as much as two packs a day.
>
> In 1955, she switched...to L&M cigarettes... because...she believed that the filter would trap whatever was "bad" for her in cigarette smoking. She relied upon advertisements which supported that contention.

> She...switched to Virginia Slims...because the cigarettes were glamorous and long, and were associated with beautiful women—and the liberated woman....
>
> Because she developed a smoker's cough and heard reports that smoking caused cancer, she tried to cut down her smoking. These attempts were unsuccessful....
>
> Mrs. Cipollone switched to lower tar and nicotine cigarettes based upon advertising from which she concluded that those cigarettes were safe or safer...[and] upon the recommendation of her family physician. In 1981 her cancer was diagnosed, and even though her doctors advised her to stop she was unable to do so. She even told her doctors and her husband that she had quit when she had not, and she continued to smoke until June of 1982 when her lung was removed. Even thereafter she smoked occasionally—in hiding. She stopped smoking in 1983 when her cancer had metastasized and she was diagnosed as fatally ill.

This sad history contains many of the features that I shall be arguing make paternalism most permissible.

Relevant Preferences

The case against paternalism consists in the simple proposition that, morally, we ought to respect people's own choices in matters that affect themselves and by-and-large only themselves. But there are many questions we first might legitimately ask about those preferences, without in any way questioning this fundamental principle of respecting people's autonomy.

One is simply whether the preferences in play are genuinely *relevant* to the decision at hand. Often they are not. Laymen often make purely factual mistakes in their means-ends reasoning. They think—or indeed, as in the case of Rose Cipollone, are led by false advertising to suppose—that an activity is safe when it is not. They think that an activity like smoking is glamorous, when the true facts of the matter are that smoking may well cause circulatory problems requiring the distinctly unglamorous amputation of an arm or leg.

When people make purely factual mistakes like that, we might legitimately override their surface preferences (the preference to smoke) in the name of their own deeper preferences (to stay alive and bodily intact). Public policies designed to prevent youngsters from taking up smoking when they want to, or to make it harder (more expensive or inconvenient) for existing smokers to continue smoking when they want to, may be paternalistic in the sense of running contrary to people's own manifest choices in the matter. But this overriding of their choices is grounded in their own deeper preferences, so such paternalism would be minimally offensive from a moral point of view.

Settled Preferences

We might ask, further, whether the preferences being manifested are "settled" preferences or whether they are merely transitory phases people are going through. It may be morally permissible to let people commit euthanasia voluntarily, if we are sure they really want to die. But if we think that they may subsequently change their minds, then we have good grounds for supposing that we should stop them.

The same may well be true with smoking policy. While Rose Cipollone herself thought smoking was both glamorous and safe, youngsters beginning to smoke today typically know better. But many of them still say that they would prefer a shorter but more glamorous life, and that they are therefore more than happy to accept the risks that smoking entails. Say what they may at age sixteen, though, we cannot help supposing that they will think differently when pigeons eventually come home to roost. The risk-courting preferences of youth are a characteristic product of a peculiarly dare-devil phase that virtually all of them will, like their predecessors, certainly grow out of.

Insofar as people's preferences are not settled—insofar as they choose one option now, yet at some later time may wish that they had chosen another—we have another ground for permissible paternalism. Policymakers dedicated to respecting people's own choices have, in effect, two of the person's own choices to choose between. How such conflicts should be settled is hard to say. We might weigh the strength or duration of the preferences, how well they fit with the person's other preferences, and so on.

Whatever else we do, though, we clearly ought not privilege one preference over another just because it got there first. Morally, it is permissible for policymakers to ignore one of a person's present preferences (to smoke, for example) in deference to another that is virtually certain later to emerge (as was Rose Cipollone's wish to live, once she had cancer).

Preferred Preferences

A third case for permissible paternalism turns on the observation that people have not only multiple and conflicting preferences but also preferences for preferences. Rose Cipollone wanted to smoke. But, judging from her frequent (albeit failed) attempts to quit, she also wanted *not to want* to smoke.

In this respect, it might be said, Rose Cipollone's history is representative of smokers more generally. The US Surgeon General reports that some 90 percent of regular smokers have tried and failed to quit. That recidivism rate has led the World Health Organization to rank nicotine as an addictive substance on a par with heroin itself.

That classification is richly confirmed by the stories that smokers themselves tell about their failed attempts to quit. Rose Cipollone tried to quit while pregnant, only to end up smoking an entire pack in the delivery room. She tried to quit once her cancer was diagnosed, and once again after her lung was taken out, even then only to end up sneaking an occasional smoke.

In cases like this—where people want to stop some activity, try to stop it but find that they cannot stop—public policy that helps them do so can hardly be said to be paternalistic in any morally offensive respect. It overrides people's preferences, to be sure. But the preferences which it overrides are ones which people themselves wish they did not have.

The preferences which it respects—the preferences to stop smoking (like preferences of reformed alcoholics to stay off drink, or of the obese to lose weight)—are, in contrast, preferences that the people concerned themselves prefer. They would themselves rank those preferences above their own occasional inclinations to backslide. In helping them to implement their own preferred preferences, we are only respecting people's own priorities.

Your Own Preferences

Finally, before automatically respecting people's choices, we ought to make sure that they are really their *own* choices. We respect people's choices because in that way we manifest respect for them as persons. But if the choices in question were literally someone else's—the results of a post-hypnotic suggestion, for example—then clearly there that logic would provide no reason for our respecting those preferences.

Some people say that the effects of advertising are rather like that. No doubt there is a certain informational content to advertising. But that is not all there is in it. When Rose Cipollone read the tar and nicotine content in advertisments, what she was getting was information. What she was getting when looking at the accompanying pictures of movie stars and glamorous, liberated women was something else altogether.

Using the power of subliminal suggestion, advertising implants preferences in people in a way that largely or wholly bypasses their judgment. Insofar as it does so, the resulting preferences are not authentically that person's own. And those implanted preferences are not entitled to the respect that is rightly reserved for a person's authentic preferences, in consequence.

Such thoughts might lead some to say that we should therefore ignore altogether advertising-induced preferences in framing our public policy. I demur. There is just too much force in the rejoinder that, "Wherever those preferences came from in the first instance, they are mine now." If we want our policies to respect people by (among other things) respecting their preferences, then we will have to respect all of those preferences with which people now associate themselves.

Even admitting the force of that rejoinder, though, there is much that still might be done to curb the preference-shaping activities of, for example, the tobacco industry. Even those who say "they're my preferences now" would presumably have preferred, ahead of time, to make up their own minds in the matter. So there we have a case, couched in terms of people's own (past) preferences, for severely restricting the advertising and promotion of products—especially ones which people will later regret having grown to like, but which they will later be unable to resist.

III. CONCLUSIONS

What, in practical policy terms, follows from all that? Well, in the case of smoking, which has served as my running example, we might ban the sale of tobacco altogether or turn it into a drug available only on prescription to registered users. Or, less dramatically, we might make cigarettes difficult and expensive to obtain—especially for youngsters, whose purchases are particularly price-sensitive. We might ban all promotional advertising of tobacco products, designed as it is to attract new users. We might prohibit smoking in all offices, restaurants, and other public places, thus making it harder for smokers to find a place to partake and providing a further inducement for them to quit.

All of those policies would be good for smokers themselves. They would enjoy a longer life expectancy and a higher quality of life if they stopped smoking. But that is to talk the language of interests rather than of rights and choices. In those latter terms, all those policies clearly go against smokers' manifest preferences, in one sense or another. Smokers want to keep smoking. They do not want to pay more or drive further to get their cigarettes. They want to be able to take comfort in advertisements constantly telling them how glamorous their smoking is.

In other more important senses, though, such policies can be justified even in terms of the preferences of smokers themselves. They do not want to die, as a quarter of them eventually will (and ten to fifteen years before their time) of smoking-related diseases; it is only false beliefs or wishful thinking that make smokers think that continued smoking is consistent with that desire not to avoid a premature death. At the moment they may think that the benefits of smoking outweigh the costs, but they will almost certainly revise that view once those costs are eventually sheeted home. The vast majority of smokers would like to stop smoking but, being addicted, find it very hard now to do so.

Like Rose Cipollone, certainly in her dying days and intermittently even from her early adulthood, most smokers themselves would say that they would have been better off never starting. Many even agree that they would welcome anything (like a workplace ban on smoking) that might now make them stop. Given the internally conflicting preferences here in play, smokers also harbor at one and the same time preferences pointing in the opposite direction; that is what might make helping them to stop seem unacceptably paternalistic. But in terms of other of their preferences—and ones that deserve clear precedence, at that—doing so is perfectly well warranted.

Smoking is unusual, perhaps, in presenting a case for permissible paternalism on all four of the fronts here canvassed. Most activities might qualify under only one or two of the headings. However, that may well be enough. My point here is not that paternalism is always permissible but merely that it may always be.

In the discourse of liberal democracies, the charge of paternalism is typically taken to be a knock-down objection to any policy. If I am right, that knee-jerk response is wrong. When confronted with the charge of paternalism, it should always be open to us to say, "Sure, this proposal is paternalistic—but is the paternalism in view permissible or impermissible, good or bad?" More often than not, I think we will find, paternalism might prove perfectly defensible along the lines sketched here.

READING QUESTIONS

1. What should the scope of paternalism be according to Goodin?
2. When should public officials refrain from paternalistic interference according to Goodin?
3. Explain the case of Rose Cipollone and the differences among relevant, settled, preferred, and one's own preferences.
4. What are some of the public policies that Goodin thinks might be justified in the light of his considerations about the interests and preferences of smokers?

DISCUSSION QUESTION

1. Kant and many other philosophers hold that one has duties to oneself, including a duty to refrain from harmful activities. Can there be duties that one owes to oneself? If not, why not? If so, is refraining from smoking one of them?

DANIEL SHAPIRO

Addiction and Drug Policy

According to the "standard view" of addiction, certain drugs are highly addictive largely because of their pharmacological effects—effects on the brain owing to the chemical constitution of the drug. This kind of pharmacological explanation plays a significant role in some arguments in favor of legal bans on certain drugs, especially "hard drugs." Shapiro challenges the standard view, arguing that factors such as an individual's mind-set as well as an individual's social and cultural setting importantly contribute to drug addiction. According to Shapiro, then, cravings, increased drug tolerance, and withdrawal symptoms cannot explain drug addiction. He bolsters his case against the standard view by examining nicotine addiction.

Most people think that illegal drugs, such as cocaine and heroin, are highly addictive. Usually their addictiveness is explained by pharmacology: their chemical composition and its effects on the brain are such that, after a while, it's hard to stop using them. This view of drug addiction—I call it the standard view—underlies most opposition to legalizing cocaine and heroin. James Wilson's (1990) arguments are typical: legalization increases access, and increased access to addictive drugs increases addiction. The standard view also underlies the increasingly popular opinion, given a philosophical defense by Robert Goodin (1989), that cigarette smokers are addicts in the grip of a powerful drug.

However, the standard view is false: pharmacology, I shall argue, does not by itself do much to explain drug addiction. I will offer a different explanation of drug addiction and discuss its implications for the debate about drug legalization.

PROBLEMS WITH THE STANDARD VIEW

We label someone as a drug addict because of his behavior. A drug addict uses drugs repeatedly, compulsively, and wants to stop or cut back on his use but finds it's difficult to do so; at its worst, drug addiction dominates or crowds out other activities and concerns. The standard view attempts to explain this compulsive behavior by the drug's effects on the brain. Repeated use of an addictive drug induces cravings and the user comes to need a substantial amount to get the effect she wants, i.e., develops tolerance. If the user tries to stop, she then suffers very disagreeable effects, called withdrawal symptoms. (For more detail on the standard view, see American Psychiatric Association 1994, 176–81.)

Cravings, tolerance, and withdrawal symptoms: do these explain drug addiction? A craving or strong desire to do something doesn't *make* one do something: one can act on a desire or ignore it *or* attempt to extinguish it. Tolerance explains why the user increases her intake to get the effect she wants, but that doesn't explain why she would find it difficult to *stop wanting* this effect. Thus, the key idea in the standard view is really withdrawal symptoms, because that is needed to explain the difficulty in extinguishing the desire to take the drug or to stop wanting the effects the drug produces. However, for this explanation to work, these symptoms have to be really bad, for if they aren't, why not just put up with them as a small price to pay for getting free of the drug? However, withdrawal symptoms aren't *that* bad. Heroin is considered terribly addictive, yet pharmacologists describe its withdrawal symptoms as like having a bad flu for about a week: typical withdrawal symptoms include fever, diarrhea, sneezing, muscle cramps, and vomiting (Kaplan 1983, 15, 19, 35). While a bad flu is quite unpleasant, it's not so bad that one has little choice but to take heroin rather than experience it. Indeed, most withdrawal symptoms for any drug cease within a few weeks, yet most heavy users who relapse do so after that period and few drug addicts report withdrawal symptoms as the reason for their relapse (Peele 1985, 19–20, 67; Schacter 1982, 436–44; Waldorf, Reinarman, and Murphy 1991, 241).

Thus, cravings, tolerance, and withdrawal symptoms cannot explain addiction. An additional problem for the standard view is that most drug users, whether they use legal or illegal drugs, do not become addicts, and few addicts remain so permanently. (Cigarette smokers are a partial exception, which I discuss later.) Anonymous surveys of drug users by the Substance Abuse and Mental Health Services Administration (2002) indicate that less than 10 percent of those who have tried powder cocaine use it monthly (National Household Survey of Drug Abuse 2001, tables H1 and H2). Furthermore, most monthly users are not addicts; a survey of young adults, for example (Johnston, O'Malley, and Bachman for the National Institute on Drug Abuse 1996, 84–5), found that less than 10 percent of monthly cocaine users used it daily. (Even a daily user need not be an addict; someone who drinks daily is not thereby an alcoholic.) The figures are not appreciably different for crack cocaine (Erickson, Smart, and Murray 1994, 167–74, 231–32, Morgan and Zimmer 1997, 142–44) and only slightly higher for heroin (Husak 1992, 125; Sullum 2003, 228). These surveys have been confirmed by longitudinal studies—studies of a set of users over time—which indicate that moderate and/or controlled use of these drugs is the norm, not the exception, and that even heavy users do not inevitably march to addiction, let alone remain permanent addicts (Waldorf, Reinarman, and Murphy 1991, Erickson, Smart, and Murray 1994; Zinberg 1984, 111–34, 152–71). The standard view has to explain the preeminence of controlled use by arguing that drug laws reduce access to illegal drugs. However, I argue below that even with easy access to drugs most people use them responsibly, and so something other than the law and pharmacology must explain patterns of drug use.

AN ALTERNATIVE VIEW

I will defend a view of addiction summed up by Norman Zinberg's book, *Drug, Set, and Setting* (1984). "Drug" means pharmacology; "set" means the individual's mindset, his personality, values, and expectations; and "setting" means the cultural or social surroundings of drug use. This should sound like common sense. Humans are interpretative animals, and so what results from drug use depends not just on the experience or effects produced by the drug but *also* on the interpretation of that experience or effects. And how one interprets or understands the experience depends on one's individuality and the cultural or social setting. I begin with setting. Hospital patients that get continuous and massive doses of narcotics rarely get addicted or crave the drugs after release from the hospital (Peele 1985, 17; Falk 1996, 9). The quantity and duration of their drug use pales in significance compared with the setting of their drug consumption: subsequent ill effects from the drug are rarely interpreted in terms of addiction. A study of Vietnam veterans, the largest study of untreated heroin users ever conducted, provides more dramatic evidence of the role of setting. Three-quarters of Vietnam vets who used heroin in Vietnam became addicted, but after coming home, only half of heroin users in Vietnam continued to use, and of those only 12 percent were addicts (Robins, Heltzer, Hesselbrock, and Wish 1980). Wilson also mentions this study and says that the change was because heroin is illegal in the U.S. (1990, 22), and while this undoubtedly played a role, so did the difference in social setting: Vietnam, with its absence of work and family, as well as loneliness and fear of death, helped to promote acceptance of heavy drug use.

Along the same lines, consider the effects of alcohol in different cultures. In Finland, for example, violence and alcohol are linked, for sometimes heavy drinkers end up in fights; in Greece, Italy, and other Mediterranean countries, however, where almost all drinking is moderate and controlled, there is no violence-alcohol link (Peele 1985, 25). Why the differences? Humans are social or cultural animals, not just products of their biochemistry, and this means, in part, that social norms or rules play a significant role in influencing behavior. In cultures where potentially intoxicating drugs such as alcohol are viewed as supplements or accompaniments to life, moderate and controlled use will be the norm—hence, even though Mediterranean cultures typically consume large amounts of alcohol, there is little alcoholism—while in cultures where alcohol is also viewed as a way of escaping one's problems, alcoholism will be more prevalent, which may explain the problem in Finland and some other Scandinavian cultures. In addition to cultural influences, most people learn to use alcohol responsibly by observing their parents. They see their parents drink at a ball game or to celebrate special occasions or with food at a meal, but rarely on an empty stomach; they learn it's wrong to be drunk at work, to drink and drive; they learn that uncontrolled behavior with alcohol is generally frowned upon; they absorb certain norms and values such as "know your limit," "don't drink alone,"

"don't drink in the morning," and so forth. They learn about rituals which reinforce moderation, such as the phrase "let's have a drink." These informal rules and rituals teach most people how to use alchohol responsibly (Zinberg 1987, 258–62).

While social controls are harder to develop with illicit drugs—accurate information is pretty scarce, and parents feel uncomfortable teaching their children about controlled use—even here sanctions and rituals promoting moderate use exist. For example, in a study of an eleven-year follow-up of an informal network of middle-class cocaine users largely connected through ties of friendship, most of whom were moderate users, the authors concluded that:

> Rather than cocaine overpowering user concerns with family, health, and career, we found that the high value most of our users placed upon family, health, and career achievement . . . mitigated against abuse and addiction. Such group norms and the informal social controls that seemed to stem from them (e.g., expressions of concern, warning about risks, the use of pejorative names like "coke hog," refusal to share with abusers) mediated the force of pharmacological, physiological, and psychological factors which can lead to addiction (Murphy et al. 1989: 435).

Even many heavy cocaine users are able to prevent their use from becoming out of control (or out of control for significant periods of time) by regulating the time and circumstances of use (not using during work, never using too late at night, limiting use on weekdays), using with friends rather than alone, employing fixed rules (paying bills before spending money on cocaine), etc. (Waldorf, Reinarman, and Murphy 1991). Unsurprisingly, these studies of controlled cocaine use generally focus on middle-class users: their income and the psychological support of friends and family put them at less of a risk of ruining their lives by drug use than those with little income or hope (Peele 1991, 159–60).

I now examine the effects of set on drug use, that is, the effect of expectations, personality, and values. Expectations are important because drug use occurs in a pattern of ongoing activity, and one's interpretation of the drug's effects depends upon expectations of how those effects will fit into or alter those activities. Expectations explain the well-known placebo effect: if people consume something they mistakenly believe will stop or alleviate their pain, it often does. Along the same lines, in experiments with American college-age men, aggression and sexual arousal increased when these men were told they were drinking liquor, even though they were drinking 0 proof, while when drinking liquor and told they were not, they acted normally (Peele 1985, 17). The role of expectations also explains why many users of heroin, cocaine, and other psychoactive drugs do not like or even recognize the effects when they first take it and have to be taught to or learn how to appreciate the effects (Peele 1985, 13–14; Waldorf, Reinarman, and Murphy 1991, 264; Zinberg 1984, 117). The importance of expectations means that those users who view the drug as overpowering them will tend to find their lives dominated by the drug, while those who view it as an enhancement or a complement to certain experiences or activities will tend not to let drugs dominate or overpower their other interests (Peele 1991, 156–58, 169–70).

As for the individual's personality and values, the predictions of common sense are pretty much accurate. Psychologically healthy people are likely to engage in controlled, moderate drug use, or if they find themselves progressing to uncontrolled use, they tend to cut back. On other hand, drug addicts of all kinds tend to have more psychological problems before they started using illicit drugs (Peele 1991, 153–54, 157; Zinberg 1984, 74–76). People who are motivated to control their own lives will tend to make drug use an accompaniment or an ingredient in their lives, not the dominant factor. Those who place a high value on responsibility, work, family, productivity, etc., will tend to fit drug use into their lives rather than letting it run their lives (Waldorf, Reinarman, and Murphy 1991, 267; Peele 1991, 160–66). That's why drug use of all kinds, licit or illicit, tends to taper off with age: keeping a job, raising a family, and so forth leave limited time or motivation for uncontrolled or near continuous drug use (Peele 1985, 15). And it's why it's not uncommon for addicts to explain their addiction by saying that they drifted into the addict's life; with little to compete with their drug use, or lacking motivation to substitute other activities or interests, drug use comes to dominate their lives (DeGrandpre

and White 1996, 44–46). Those with richer lives, or who are motivated on an individual and/or cultural level to get richer lives, are less likely to succumb to addiction. To summarize: even with easy access to intoxicating drugs, most drug users don't become addicts, or if they do, don't remain addicts for that long, because most people have and are motivated to find better things to do with their lives. These better things result from their individual personality and values and their social or cultural setting.

CIGARETTE SMOKING AND THE ROLE OF PHARMACOLOGY

I've discussed how set and setting influence drug use, but where does pharmacology fit in? Its role is revealed by examining why it is much harder to stop smoking cigarettes—only half of smokers that try to stop smoking succeed in quitting—than to stop using other substances. (For more detail in what follows, see Shapiro 1994 and the references cited therein.)

Smokers smoke to relax; to concentrate; to handle anxiety, stress, and difficult interpersonal situations; as a way of taking a break during the day; as a social lubricant; as a means of oral gratification—and this is a partial list. Since smoking is a means to or part of so many activities, situations, and moods, stopping smoking is a major life change and major life changes do not come easily. Part of the reason smoking is so integrated into people's lives is pharmacological. Nicotine's effects on the brain are mild and subtle: it doesn't disrupt your life. While addicts or heavy users of other drugs such as cocaine, heroin, or alcohol *also* use their drugs as a means to or part of a variety of activities, situations, and moods, most users of these drugs are not lifelong addicts or heavy users, because these drugs are not so mild and heavy use has a stronger tendency over time to disrupt people's lives.

The pharmacology of smoking, however, cannot be separated from its social setting. Smoking doesn't disrupt people's lives in part because it is legal. Even with increasing regulations, smokers still can smoke in a variety of situations (driving, walking on public streets, etc.), while one cannot use illegal drugs except in a furtive and secretive manner. Furthermore, the mild effects of nicotine are due to its mild potency—smokers can carefully control their nicotine intake, getting small doses throughout the day—and its mild potency is due partly to smoking being legal. Legal drugs tend to have milder potencies than illegal ones for two reasons. First, illegal markets create incentives for stronger potencies, as sellers will favor concentrated forms of a drug that can be easily concealed and give a big bang for the buck. Second, in legal markets different potencies of the same drug openly compete, and over time the weaker ones come to be preferred—consider the popularity of low tar/nicotine cigarettes and wine and beer over hard liquor.

Thus, pharmacology and setting interact: smoking is well integrated into people's lives because the nicotine in cigarettes has mild pharmacological effects and because smoking is legal, and nicotine has those mild effects in part because smoking is legal. Pharmacology also interacts with what I've been calling set. The harms of smoking are slow to occur, are cumulative, and largely affect one's health, not one's ability to perform normal activities (at least prior to getting seriously ill). Furthermore, to eliminate these harms requires complete smoking cessation; cutting back rarely suffices (even light smokers increase their chances of getting lung cancer, emphysema, and heart disease). Thus, quitting smoking requires strong motivation, since its bad effects are not immediate and it does not disrupt one's life. Add to this what I noted earlier, that stopping smoking means changing one's life, and it's unsurprising that many find it difficult to stop.

Thus, it is a mistake to argue, as Goodin did, that the difficulty in quitting is mainly explicable by the effects of nicotine. Smokers are addicted to smoking, an *activity*, and their being addicted to it is not reducible to their being addicted to a *drug*. If my explanation of the relative difficulty of quitting smoking is correct, then the standard view of an addictive drug is quite suspect. That view suggests that knowledge of a drug's pharmacology provides a basis for making reasonable predictions about a drug's addictiveness. However, understanding nicotine's effects upon the brain (which is what Goodin

stressed in his explanation of smokers' addiction) does not tell us that it's hard to stop smoking; we only know that once we add information about set and setting. Generalizing from the case of smoking, all we can say is:

> The milder the effects upon the brain, the easier for adults to purchase, the more easily integrated into one's life, and the more the bad effects are cumulative, slow-acting and only reversible upon complete cessation, the more addictive the drug. (Goodin 1989)

Besides being a mouthful, this understanding of drug addiction requires introducing the *interaction* of set and setting with pharmacology to explain the addictiveness potential of various drugs. It is simpler and less misleading to say that people tend to *addict themselves* to various substances (and activities), this tendency varying with various cultural and individual influences.

CONCLUSION

My argument undercuts the worry that legalizing cocaine and heroin will produce an explosion of addiction because people will have access to inherently and powerfully addictive drugs. The standard view that cocaine and heroin are *inherently* addictive is false, because no drug is inherently addictive. The desire of most people to lead responsible and productive lives in a social setting that rewards such desires is what controls and limits most drug use. Ironically, if cocaine and heroin in a legal market would be as disruptive as many drug prohibitionists fear, then that is an excellent reason why addiction would not explode under legalization—drug use that tends to thrive is drug use that is woven into, rather than disrupts, responsible people's lives.

ADDENDUM

After I wrote this article, some of my students raised the following objection. I argue that drug addiction that disrupts people's lives would not thrive under legalization because most people's desire and ability to lead responsible lives would break or prevent such addiction. However, suppose that legalization of cocaine and heroin makes the use of those drugs similar to the use of cigarettes—small, mild doses throughout the day which are well integrated into people's lives. If legalization brings it about that those who addict themselves to these drugs are like those who addict themselves to smoking—their addiction does not disrupt their lives, but is integrated into it—wouldn't that mean that addiction to these drugs would become as prevalent as cigarette addiction?

It is possible that legalizing heroin and cocaine would make its use similar to the current use of cigarettes. However, if this happened, the main worry about heroin and cocaine addiction would be gone. We would not have a problem of a large increase in the number of people throwing away or messing up their lives. At worst, if legalizing cocaine and heroin produced as bad health effects as cigarette smoking does (which is dubious—see Carnwath and Smith 2002, 137–39; Morgan and Zimmer 1997, 131, 136, 141), then we would have a new health problem. Of course, someone might argue that one should not legalize a drug which could worsen the health of a significant percentage of its users, even if that use does not mess up most of its users' lives. It is beyond the scope of this paper to evaluate such arguments (however, see Shapiro 1994), but notice that the implications of my essay cut against the claim that these health risks were not voluntarily incurred. Since one's drug use partly depends on one's values and personality, then to the extent that one can be said to be responsible for the choices influenced by one's values and personality, then to that extent those who addict themselves to a certain drug can be said to have voluntarily incurred the risks involved in that drug use.

REFERENCES

American Psychiatric Association. 1994. *Diagnostic and Statistical Manual of Mental Disorders.* 4th ed. Washington, D.C.: American Psychiatric Association.

Carnwath, T., and I. Smith. 2002. *Heroin Century.* London: Routledge.

DeGrandpre, R., and E. White. 1996. "Drugs: In Care of the Self." *Common Knowledge* 3: 27–48.

Erickson, P., E. Edward, R. Smart, and G. Murray. 1994. *The Steel Drug: Crack and Cocaine in Perspective.* 2nd ed. New York: MacMillan.

Falk, J. 1996. "Environmental Factors in the Instigation and Maintenance of Drug Abuse." In W. Bickel and R. DeGrandpre, eds., *Drug Policy and Human Nature.* New York: Plenum Press.

Goodin, R. 1989. "The Ethics of Smoking." *Ethics* 99: 574–624.

Husak, D. 1992. *Drugs and Rights.* New York: Cambridge University Press.

Johnston, L. D., P. M. O'Malley, and J. G. Bachman. 1996. *Monitoring the Future Study, 1975–1994: National Survey Results on Drug Use.* Volume II: *College Students and Young Adults.* Rockville, Md.: National Institute on Drug Abuse.

Kaplan, J. 1983. *The Hardest Drug: Heroin and Public Policy.* Chicago: University of Chicago Press.

Morgan, J., and L. Zimmer. 1997. "The Social Pharmacology of Smokeable Cocaine: Not All It's Cracked Up to Be." In C. Reinarman and H. Levine, eds., *Crack in America: Demon Drugs and Social Justice.* Berkeley: University of California Press.

Murphy, S., C. Reinarman, and D. Waldorf. 1989. "An 11 Year Follow-Up of a Network of Cocaine Users." *British Journal of Addiction* 84: 427–36.

Peele, S. 1985. *The Meaning of Addiction: Compulsive Experience and Its Interpretation.* Lexington, Mass.: D.C. Heath and Company.

Peele, S. 1991. *The Diseasing of America: Addiction Treatment Out of Control.* Boston: Houghton Mifflin Company.

Robins, L., J. Helzer, M. Hesselbrock, and E. Wish. 1980. "Vietnam Veterans Three Years After Vietnam: How Our Study Changed Our View of Heroin." In L. Brill and C. Winick, eds., *The Yearbook of Substance Use and Abuse.* Vol. 2. New York: Human Sciences Press.

Schacter, S. 1982. "Recidivism and Self-Cure of Smoking and Obesity." *American Psychologist* 37: 436–44.

Shapiro, D. 1994. "Smoking Tobacco: Irrationality, Addiction and Paternalism." *Public Affairs Quarterly* 8: 187–203.

Substance Abuse and Mental Health Services Administration. 2002. *Tables from the 2001 National Household Survey on Drug Abuse,* Department of Health and Human Services, available online at http://www.sam-hsa.gov/oas/NHSDA/2klNHSDA/vol2/appendixh_1.htm.

Sullum, J. 2003. *Saying Yes: In Defense of Drug Use.* New York: Tarcher/Putnam.

Waldorf, D., C. Reinarman, and S. Murphy. 1991. *Cocaine Changes: The Experience of Using and Quitting.* Philadelphia: Temple University Press.

Wilson, J. 1990. "Against the Legalization of Drugs." *Commentary* 89: 21–28.

Zinberg, N. 1984. *Drug, Set, and Setting.* New Haven, Conn.: Yale University Press.

Zinberg, N. 1987. "The Use and Misuse of Intoxicants." In R. Hamowy, ed., *Dealing with Drugs.* Lexington, Mass.: D. C. Heath and Company.

READING QUESTIONS

1. How does Shapiro characterize the "standard view" of addiction as it relates to drugs like heroin and cocaine?
2. Explain the problems with the standard view according to Shapiro.
3. What is the alternative view of addiction suggested by Shapiro? What is meant by the terms "drug," "set," and "setting" in the context of this view?
4. How does Shapiro contrast the case of cigarette smoking with the cases of addiction predicted by the standard view?

DISCUSSION QUESTIONS

1. Are there any remaining merits of the standard view of addiction rejected by Shapiro?
2. Do you think that Shapiro overestimates the positive influences of social and individual controls on the use of illicit drugs like heroin and cocaine?
3. Are there any downsides to the legalization of illicit drugs that Shapiro fails to consider?

ADDITIONAL RESOURCES

Web Resources

U.S. Drug Enforcement Administration (DEA), <www.usdoj.gov/dea>. Provides information on drugs, drug laws, as well as prevention of drug abuse.

National Institute on Drug Abuse (NIDA), <www.nida.gov>. NIDA's main objective is to bring to bear on drug abuse the results of scientific inquiry. The agency also provides detailed information about specific drugs and about prevention of drug abuse.

National Organization for the Reform of Marijuana Laws (NORML), <www.norml.org>. A site with information about marijuana and dedicated to its legalization.

Authored Books and Articles

Butler, Keith, "The Moral Status of Smoking," *Social Theory and Practice* 19 (1993): 1–26. Argues that smoking routinely violates the harm principle.

de Marneffe, Peter, "Do We Have a Right to Use Drugs?" *Public Affairs Quarterly* 10 (1996): 229–47. De Marneffe argues that democratic countries are justified in passing some laws against the sale and use of certain drugs.

Husak, Douglas N., *Drugs and Rights* (New York: Cambridge University Press, 1992). Husak argues that the "war on drugs" violates basic human rights to take drugs for recreational purposes.

Husak, Douglas and Peter De Marneffe, *The Legalization of Drugs: For and Against* (Cambridge: Cambridge University Press, 2005). Husak defends the 'for' position while DeMarneffe defends the 'against' position in this very readable and highly recommended book.

Miron, Jeffrey A. and Jeffrey Zwiebel, "The Economic Case Against Drug Prohibition," *Journal of Economic Perspectives* 9 (1995): 175–192. Authors argue that a free market in drugs is preferable to the current policy of drug prohibition.

Shapiro, Daniel, "Smoking Tobacco," *Public Affairs Quarterly* 8 (1994): 187–203. Critical of Goodin's case in favor of paternalistic laws aimed at regulating smoking.

Slone, Frank A., J. Ostermann, G. Picone, C. Conover, and D. H. Taylor Jr., *The Price of Smoking* (Boston: The MIT Press, 2006). Discussion of the social effects of smoking.

Wilson, James Q., "Against the Legalization of Drugs," *Commentary* 89 (1990): 21–28. Wilson presents arguments against legalization that appeal to both the harm principle and the principle of legal moralism.

Edited Collections

Belenko, Steven R. (ed.), *Drugs and Drug Policy in America* (Westport, CT: Greenwood Press, 2000). A collection of over 250 primary documents including Court cases, speeches, laws, and opinion pieces that usefully trace the history of drugs and drug policy in America from the nineteenth century to the present.

Schaler, Jeffrey A. (ed.), *Shall We Legalize, Decriminalize, or Regulate?* (Buffalo, NY: Prometheus Books, 1998). Twenty nine essays divided into eight parts: 1. Those Who Cannot Remember the Past, 2. A War on Drugs or a War on People? 3. Just Say 'No' to Drug Legalization, 4. Medical Marijuana: What Counts as Medicine? 5. Drug War Metaphors and Additions: Drugs are Property, 6. Addiction Is a Behavior: The Myth of Loss of Control, 7. Do Drugs Cause Crime? 8. State-Supported and Court-Ordered Treatment for Addiction Is Unconstitutional.

8 } Euthanasia and Physician-Assisted Suicide

The sad case of Terri Schiavo was intermittently in the news for a number of years. Schiavo suffered severe brain damage in 1990 owing to cardiac arrest. She was diagnosed by many physicians as being in a "persistent vegetative state," in which the individual is arguably not consciously experiencing anything, but unlike being in a coma, the individual undergoes periods of wakefulness. Schiavo's case was the subject of an intense public debate after her feeding tube was removed on March 18, 2005, at the request of her husband and after many legal battles with the parents of Schiavo. On March 21, 2005, Congress passed special legislation that would allow the parents of Schiavo to seek a review of their case in federal court to have a feeding tube reinserted, legislation that was signed that same day by President George W. Bush. Various federal courts turned down the appeal from Schiavo's parents to have the case reviewed further. Terri Schiavo died from dehydration on March 31, 2005.

As we shall see shortly, the decision to remove Schiavo's feeding tube, thus allowing her to die of dehydration, is a case of passive euthanasia. A number of legal and constitutional issues are raised by the Schiavo case, but no doubt what stirred such intense public interest in this case are the moral issues concerning euthanasia and suicide. Some of the most basic questions are these:

- Is euthanasia or suicide ever morally permissible?
- In those cases in which either of these activities is wrong, what best explains their wrongness?

Here, as with the issue of abortion, we (unfortunately) find parties to the debate being labeled as pro-life or pro-choice, which, of course, frames the issue as though one must (or should) respond to the first question with a simple yes or a simple no. But, as with most all controversial moral issues, there is a range of possible views, including moderate views which, in the case of euthanasia (and suicide), would reject simple answers and insist that details of specific cases do matter morally. In order to make progress in our understanding of the moral disputes over euthanasia and suicide, let us first explain what practices and types of action are the subject of these disputes, and then we will be prepared to understand how various ethical theories approach the moral questions just mentioned.

1. EUTHANASIA

Euthanasia is typically defined as the act or practice of killing or allowing someone to die on grounds of mercy. Because this definition covers a number of importantly different types of activity that may differ in their moral status, let us begin by calling attention to these types. There are two dimensions, so to speak, to be considered. First there is what we may call the "mode of death" dimension, which has to do with whether the death results from actively intervening to bring about the death of the patient or whether the death results from (or is hastened by) withholding some form of treatment which, had it been administered, would likely have prolonged the life of the patient. The former type of case is one of **active euthanasia,** whereas the latter type is often called **passive euthanasia.**

The other dimension has to do with matters concerning the consent or nonconsent of the patient. And here we need to distinguish three importantly different cases. Cases of **voluntary euthanasia** are those in which the patient has consented to the active bringing about of her death or to some means of passively allowing her to die. There are various ways in which a patient might consent, including the making of a living will in which the person specifies how he is to be treated under conditions in which his consent in that situation is not possible. Cases of **nonvoluntary euthanasia** are those in which the patient has not given his consent to be subject to euthanasia because the patient has not expressed a view about what others may do in case, for example, he goes into a persistent vegetative state. Cases of **involuntary euthanasia** are those in which the patient expresses (or may be presumed to have) a desire not to be the subject of euthanasia.

Although these distinctions are commonly made in the literature on euthanasia, the active/passive distinction, as I've explained it, seems to leave out, or at least does not clearly include, cases like that of Terri Schiavo in which treatment (the feeding tube) is withdrawn. On one hand, withdrawing treatment is doing something active, but on the other hand, in withdrawing treatment one is allowing nature to take its course, and so rather than actively bringing about the death, one is passively allowing it to come about. Because space does not allow us to pursue this matter in any detail, I propose that because there does seem to be an important moral difference between clear cases of actively bringing about the death of a patient (e.g., by way of lethal injection) on one hand, and cases of withholding and withdrawing treatment on the other, we ought to classify cases of withdrawing treatment as a type of passive euthanasia, making sure that within that category we recognize the two cases in question.

If we now combine the various modes of death with the various modes bearing on consent, we have nine distinct types of euthanasia. On the next page, is a visual aid that charts the types of cases just explained (Fig. 8.1).

In light of this taxonomy, we can now formulate moral questions about euthanasia more precisely by asking, for each type of euthanasia (e.g., nonvoluntary passive withholding), whether it is ever morally permissible and if so under what conditions. Clearly, whether or not someone has given their consent to be a subject of euthanasia has an important bearing on the morality of euthanasia.

But what about the distinction between active and passive euthanasia: Does this distinction mark a morally relevant difference? One might suppose that it does because it

Mode of Death

	Active	Passive	
		Withdrawing	Withholding
Voluntary	Lethal injection with patient's consent	Disconnecting patient from life support with patient's	Refraining from administering a life-extending drug with patient's consent
Nonvoluntary	Lethal injection without patient's consent	Disconnecting patient from life support without patient's consent	Refraining from administering a life-extending drug without patient's consent
Involuntary	Lethal injection against patient's consent	Disconnecting patient from life support against patient's consent	Refraining from administering a life-extending drug against patient's consent

Mode of Consent (label at left)

FIGURE 8.1   Types of Euthanasia

might seem that *all else equal,* actively killing someone is morally worse than allowing someone to die. This supposition is challenged by James Rachels in his contribution to this chapter, while Philippa Foot in her reply to Rachels defends the moral relevance of the distinction between actively killing and allowing someone to die. So, one interesting theoretical question in ethics entails the moral relevance of the killing/letting die distinction, and thus over the moral relevance of the active/passive distinction in connection with euthanasia.

2. SUICIDE

Whereas euthanasia, by definition, involves the termination of someone's life by someone else, **suicide** involves intentionally and thus voluntarily ending one's own life. This definition, then, rules out the possibility of there being nonvoluntary or involuntary cases of suicide. But this definition does not rule out the possibility of passive suicide—suicide in which one either withdraws some means of life support or refrains from intervening to save oneself from death. However, most discussion of the morality of suicide is focused on cases of active suicide.

Assisted suicides are those cases in which another person is involved to some degree in assisting an individual to commit suicide. Much recent discussion on this topic has focused on the role of physicians in helping a patient to commit suicide. Of particular interest is the dispute in the United States over Death with Dignity laws.

3. DEATH WITH DIGNITY LAWS

In 1997 the Death with Dignity Act took effect in the state of Oregon; this legislation residents of that state who are diagnosed as terminally ill to request medication that will end their lives.[1] "Terminal illness" is defined in the act as "an incurable and irreversible disease that has been medically confirmed and will, within reasonable medical judgment, produce death within six months." Various safeguards are part of the act, including (1) the patient must make two written requests of his or her attending physician fifteen days apart, (2) the patient must sign a consent form in front of two witnesses, at least one of whom is not related to the patient, and (3) the attending physician's diagnosis of the patient must be confirmed by a second physician. In 2008 voters in Washington State approved a death with dignity act. However, in the general election of 2012 a ballot initiative in Massachusetts failed to pass, even though the Western New England Polling Institute showed that 60 percent of the residents of that state were in favor of allowing patients to end their lives by legally obtaining life-ending drugs. Nine hundred patients in Oregon have received life-ending drugs legally since 1997, and more than six hundred did take the prescribed drugs and die. In Washington State roughly 135 patients have died from taking a legally prescribed life-ending drug.

It is notable that the American Medical Association opposes the Death with Dignity Act, citing the AMA Code of Medical Ethics, which states: "Physician-assisted suicide is fundamentally incompatible with the physician's role as a healer." Whether physician-assisted suicide is truly incompatible with the role of physicians is contentious. Michael B. Gill discusses this question in his article about the Oregon law, included here.

4. THEORY MEETS PRACTICE

Let us turn to four theoretical approaches to the topics of euthanasia and suicide: Kantian moral theory, consequentialism, natural law theory, and the ethics of prima facie duty, some of them featured in this chapter's selections.

Kantian Moral Theory

Kant argued that suicide is morally wrong because it violates the dignity of the human being who commits it. The problem with his argument is that he assumes that suicide in all (or most) cases represents a violation of human dignity, but this assumption needs defense—more than Kant provides. If my life is close to an end and I am in excruciating pain about which physicians can do nothing, is it a violation of my dignity if I end my life rather than pointlessly live on for a month or two? Perhaps so, but the case needs to be argued. The same general point holds in any attempt to apply Kant's Humanity formulation of the categorical imperative to cases of euthanasia: whether any such case fails to treat the patient as an end in herself requires supporting argument.

Consequentialism

Many discussions of euthanasia and suicide focus exclusively on the likely consequences of these practices, thus appealing, at least implicitly, to consequentialist moral theory. And here, as with many other issues featured in this book, worries about slippery slopes are raised. A slippery slope argument may take various forms, but behind all such arguments is the idea that if we allow some action or practice *P*, then we will open the door to other similar actions and practices that will eventually lead us down a slope to disastrous results. So, the argument concludes, *P* should not be permitted. Any such argument, in order to be good, must meet two requirements. First, it must be true that the envisioned results really are bad. But second, the central idea of the argument—that allowing one action or practice will likely lead us down a path to disaster—must be plausible. If either of these conditions is not met, the argument is said to commit the "slippery slope *fallacy.*"

Used in connection with euthanasia and assisted suicide, one common slippery slope worry is that if we allow voluntary euthanasia, we will put ourselves on the road to permitting (or encouraging) *in*voluntary euthanasia—cases of murder. This particular slippery slope argument apparently meets the first condition of any good slippery slope argument, but does it meet the second? And if so, will the same worries apply to assisted suicide? These are difficult questions because to answer them, we must rely on predictions about the likely effects (within a culture over a particular span of time) of engaging in, say, voluntary euthanasia. And for predictions to be reliable (and not just a prejudice based on one's antecedent views about the morality of these practices), we need solid empirical evidence—evidence that we probably lack at this time. Many opponents of euthanasia will, at this point, appeal to what we may call the "moral safety" argument, according to which when we are in doubt about such matters, it is better to play it safe and not start out on a road that *may* lead to disaster. As with any consequentialist approach to moral issues, the crucial factor in determining the rightness or wrongness of some action or practice depends on how much net intrinsic value the action or practice will likely bring about compared to alternative actions and practices. Consequentialist defenders of euthanasia (and/or assisted suicide) will stress the great benefits of such practices in relation to relieving great human suffering. And, of course, consequentialists might be opposed to some forms of euthanasia but in favor of some forms of assisted suicide.

Natural Law Theory

Part of the traditional natural law approach to matters of life and death rests on the distinction between intentionally bringing about the death of someone and unintentionally but foreseeably doing so. (This distinction is central in the doctrine of double effect explained in chapter 1, section 2B.) According to the natural law theory, intentionally taking innocent human life is always wrong; if certain conditions are met, however, one may be justified in foreseeably bringing about the death of an innocent person unintentionally, where, roughly, this means that the person's death is not one's aim in action, nor is it a means to achieving some further end. Thus, according to natural law thinking, any form of euthanasia that involves intentionally bringing about the death of a patient, even for reasons of mercy, is morally forbidden. A critical evaluation of the use of the doctrine of double effect by those who oppose physician-assisted suicide is to be found in Michael B. Gill's selection included in this chapter.

Ethics of Prima Facie Duty

Finally, one might approach the moral issues of euthanasia and suicide from the perspective of an ethic of prima facie duties. Both W. D. Ross and Robert Audi, defenders of this sort of moral theory, hold that we have a prima facie duty to avoid harming ourselves and others, and they both recognize a prima facie duty of self-improvement, which, as formulated by Audi, involves the prima facie duty to sustain, as well as develop, our distinctively human capacities.[2] If euthanasia and suicide count as harms, then one has a prima facie obligation to not engage in such actions. Additionally, since being alive is a necessary condition for sustaining our distinctively human capacities, one may conclude we have a prima facie duty of self-improvement to not participate in euthanasia or commit suicide. From these two basic prima facie duties we may derive a further prima facie duty—the prima facie duty to not engage in euthanasia or in suicide.

But as we learned in the moral theory primer, the very idea of prima facie duty allows that in a particular case it can be overridden by some other, more stringent prima facie duty that also applies to the case. So the fundamental moral question for this theoretical approach to these topics is whether there are cases in which the prima facie duty prohibiting euthanasia and suicide is overridden. If we recognize that we have a prima facie duty to relieve horrible suffering in the world, then we have a basis for arguing that there may be morally permissible cases of euthanasia and suicide. One might do so by arguing that the only way of relieving the horrible suffering of certain patients—perhaps patients who are terminally ill—is to bring about their death mercifully. If one adds that we also have a prima facie duty to respect the autonomy of patients, we can build a case for the claim that some cases of voluntary euthanasia are morally permissible because the duty of relieving suffering out-weighs the prima facie duty prohibiting euthanasia and suicide. But the validity of appealing to autonomy to support euthanasia and suicide is controversial and a topic of dispute that is debated in the selections by Daniel Callahan and Michael B. Gill.

NOTES

1. In 1997, the state of Oregon enacted the Death with Dignity Act, the first physician-assisted suicide law in the United States. In 2001, U.S. attorney general John D. Ashcroft issued a directive that stated that the use of controlled substances to assist suicides violates the Federal Controlled Substances Act. One aim of Ashcroft's directive was to allow the federal government to try as criminals physicians in Oregon who assisted in suicides. After legal battles between Ashcroft and lower courts, the case made it all the way to the U.S. Supreme Court. In 2006, in the case *Gonzales v. State of Oregon* (No. 04-623), the Court upheld Oregon's law allowing physician-assisted suicide.

2. See Robert Audi, *The Good in the Right* (Princeton, NJ: Princeton University Press, 2004), 193–94.

JAMES RACHELS

Active and Passive Euthanasia

James Rachels is critical of the 1973 American Medical Association (AMA) policy regarding euthanasia, which he understands as forbidding all mercy killing but permitting some cases of allowing a patient to die. Rachels argues that this policy would force physicians to sometimes engage in the inhumane treatment of patients and that it would allow life-and-death decisions to be made on morally irrelevant grounds. He then proceeds to argue that the policy is based on the false assumption that killing is intrinsically morally worse than letting someone die.

Recommended Reading: natural law theory, esp. doctrine of double effect, chap. 1, sec. 2B. Rachels does not mention this doctrine, but it is relevant for thinking about the AMA's policy that he criticizes.

The distinction between active and passive euthanasia is thought to be crucial for medical ethics. The idea is that it is permissible, at least in some cases, to withhold treatment and allow a patient to die, but it is never permissible to take any direct action designed to kill the patient. This doctrine seems to be accepted by most doctors, and it is endorsed in a statement adopted by the House of Delegates of the American Medical Association on December 4, 1973:

> The intentional termination of the life of one human being by another—mercy killing—is contrary to that for which the medical profession stands and is contrary to the policy of the American Medical Association.
>
> The cessation of the employment of extraordinary means to prolong the life of the body when there is irrefutable evidence that biological death is imminent is the decision of the patient and/or his immediate family. The advice and judgment of the physician should be freely available to the patient and/or his immediate family.

However, a strong case can be made against this doctrine. In what follows, I will set out some of the relevant arguments, and urge doctors to reconsider their views on this matter.

To begin with a familiar type of situation, a patient who is dying of incurable cancer of the throat is in terrible pain, which can no longer be satisfactorily alleviated. He is certain to die within a few days, even if present treatment is continued, but he does not want to go on living for those days since the pain is unbearable. So he asks the doctor for an end to it, and his family joins in the request.

Suppose the doctor agrees to withhold treatment, as the conventional doctrine says he may. The justification for his doing so is that the patient is in terrible agony, and since he is going to die anyway, it would be wrong to prolong his suffering needlessly. But now notice this. If one simply withholds treatment, it may take the patient longer to die, and so he may suffer more than he would if more direct action were taken and a lethal injection given. This fact provides strong reason for thinking that, once the initial decision not to prolong his agony has been made, active euthanasia is actually preferable to passive euthanasia, rather than the reverse. To say otherwise is to endorse the option that leads to more suffering rather than less, and is contrary to the humanitarian impulse

From James Rachels, "Active and Passive Euthanasia," *New England Journal of Medicine* 292 (1975): 78–80.

that prompts the decision not to prolong his life in the first place.

Part of my point is that the process of being "allowed to die" can be relatively slow and painful, whereas being given a lethal injection is relatively quick and painless. Let me give a different sort of example. In the United States about one in 600 babies is born with Down's syndrome. Most of these babies are otherwise healthy—that is, with only the usual pediatric care, they will proceed to an otherwise normal infancy. Some, however, are born with congenital defects such as intestinal obstructions that require operations if they are to live. Sometimes, the parents and the doctor will decide not to operate, and let the infant die. Anthony Shaw describes what happens then:

> . . . When surgery is denied [the doctor] must try to keep the infant from suffering while natural forces sap the baby's life away. As a surgeon whose natural inclination is to use the scalpel to fight off death, standing by and watching a salvageable baby die is the most emotionally exhausting experience I know. It is easy at a conference, in a theoretical discussion, to decide that such infants should be allowed to die. It is altogether different to stand by in the nursery and watch as dehydration and infection wither a tiny being over hours and days. This is a terrible ordeal for me and the hospital staff—much more so than for the parents who never set foot in the nursery.[1]

I can understand why some people are opposed to all euthanasia, and insist that such infants must be allowed to live. I think I can also understand why other people favor destroying these babies quickly and painlessly. But why should anyone favor letting "dehydration and infection wither a tiny being over hours and days"? The doctrine that says that a baby may be allowed to dehydrate and wither, but may not be given an injection that would end its life without suffering, seems so patently cruel as to require no further refutation. The strong language is not intended to offend, but only to put the point in the clearest possible way.

My second argument is that the conventional doctrine leads to decisions concerning life and death made on irrelevant grounds.

Consider again the case of the infants with Down's syndrome who need operations for congenital defects

unrelated to the syndrome to live. Sometimes, there is no operation, and the baby dies, but when there is no such defect, the baby lives on. Now, an operation such as that to remove an intestinal obstruction is not prohibitively difficult. The reason why such operations are not performed in these cases is, clearly, that the child has Down's syndrome and the parents and doctor judge that because of that fact it is better for the child to die.

But notice that this situation is absurd, no matter what view one takes of the lives and potentials of such babies. If the life of such an infant is worth preserving, what does it matter if it needs a simple operation? Or, if one thinks it better that such a baby should not live on, what difference does it make that it happens to have an unobstructed intestinal tract? In either case, the matter of life and death is being decided on irrelevant grounds. It is the Down's syndrome, and not the intestines, that is the issue. The matter should be decided, if at all, on that basis, and not be allowed to depend on the essentially irrelevant question of whether the intestinal tract is blocked.

What makes this situation possible, of course, is the idea that when there is an intestinal blockage, one can "let the baby die," but when there is no such defect there is nothing that can be done, for one must not "kill" it. The fact that this idea leads to such results as deciding life or death on irrelevant grounds is another good reason why the doctrine should be rejected.

One reason why so many people think that there is an important moral difference between active and passive euthanasia is that they think killing someone is morally worse than letting someone die. But is it? Is killing, in itself, worse than letting die? To investigate this issue, two cases may be considered that are exactly alike except that one involves killing whereas the other involves letting someone die. Then, it can be asked whether this difference makes any difference to the moral assessments. It is important that the cases be exactly alike, except for this one difference, since otherwise one cannot be confident that it is this difference and not some other that accounts for any variation in the assessments of the two cases. So, let us consider this pair of cases:

In the first, Smith stands to gain a large inheritance if anything should happen to his six-year-old cousin. One evening while the child is taking his bath, Smith sneaks into the bathroom and drowns the child, and then arranges things so that it will look like an accident.

In the second, Jones also stands to gain if anything should happen to his six-year-old cousin. Like Smith, Jones sneaks in planning to drown the child in his bath. However, just as he enters the bathroom Jones sees the child slip and hit his head, and fall face down in the water. Jones is delighted; he stands by, ready to push the child's head back under if it is necessary, but it is not necessary. With only a little thrashing about the child drowns all by himself, "accidentally," as Jones watches and does nothing.

Now Smith killed the child, whereas Jones "merely" let the child die. That is the only difference between them. Did either man behave better, from a moral point of view? If the difference between killing and letting die were in itself a morally important matter, one should say that Jones's behavior was less reprehensible than Smith's. But does one really want to say that? I think not. In the first place, both men acted from the same motive, personal gain, and both had exactly the same end in view when they acted. It may be inferred from Smith's conduct that he is a bad man, although that judgment may be withdrawn or modified if certain further facts are learned about him—for example, that he is mentally deranged. But would not the very same thing be inferred about Jones from his conduct? And would not the same further considerations also be relevant to any modification of this judgment? Moreover, suppose Jones pleaded, in his own defense, "After all, I didn't do anything except just stand there and watch the child drown. I didn't kill him; I only let him die." Again, if letting die were in itself less bad than killing, this defense should have at least some weight. But it does not. Such a "defense" can only be regarded as a grotesque perversion of moral reasoning. Morally speaking, it is no defense at all.

Now, it may be pointed out, quite properly, that the cases of euthanasia with which doctors are concerned are not like this at all. They do not involve personal gain or the destruction of normally healthy children. Doctors are concerned only with cases in which the patient's life is of no further use to him, or

in which the patient's life has become or will soon become a terrible burden. However, the point is the same in these cases: the bare difference between killing and letting die does not, in itself, make a moral difference. If a doctor lets a patient die, for humane reasons, he is in the same moral position as if he had given the patient a lethal injection for humane reasons. If his decision was wrong—if, for example, the patient's illness was in fact curable—the decision would be equally regrettable no matter which method was used to carry it out. And if the doctor's decision was the right one, the method used is not in itself important.

The AMA policy statement isolates the crucial issue very well; the crucial issue is "the intentional termination of the life of one human being by another." But after identifying this issue, and forbidding "mercy killing," the statement goes on to deny that the cessation of treatment is the intentional termination of a life. This is where the mistake comes in, for what is the cessation of treatment, in these circumstances, if it is not "the intentional termination of the life of one human being by another?" Of course, it is exactly that, and if it were not, there would be no point to it.

Many people will find this judgment hard to accept. One reason, I think, is that it is very easy to conflate the question of whether killing is, in itself, worse than letting die, with the very different question of whether most actual cases of killing are more reprehensible than most actual cases of letting die. Most actual cases of killing are clearly terrible (think, for example, of all the murders reported in the newspapers), and one hears of such cases every day. On the other hand, one hardly ever hears of a case of letting die, except for the actions of doctors who are motivated by humanitarian reasons. So one learns to think of killing in a much worse light than of letting die. But this does not mean that there is something about killing that makes it in itself worse than letting die, for it is not the bare difference between killing and letting die that makes the difference in these cases. Rather, the other factors—the murderer's motive of personal gain, for example, contrasted with the doctor's humanitarian motivation—account for different reactions to the different cases.

I have argued that killing is not in itself any worse than letting die; if my contention is right, it follows that active euthanasia is not any worse than passive euthanasia. What arguments can be given on the other side? The most common, I believe, is the following:

"The important difference between active and passive euthanasia is that, in passive euthanasia, the doctor does not do anything to bring about the patient's death. The doctor does nothing, and the patient dies of whatever ills already afflict him. In active euthanasia, however, the doctor does something to bring about the patient's death: he kills him. The doctor who gives the patient with cancer a lethal injection has himself caused his patient's death; whereas if he merely ceases treatment, the cancer is the cause of the death."

A number of points need to be made here. The first is that it is not exactly correct to say that in passive euthanasia the doctor does nothing, for he does do one thing that is very important: he lets the patient die. "Letting someone die" is certainly different, in some respects, from other types of action—mainly in that it is a kind of action that one may perform by way of not performing certain other actions. For example, one may let a patient die by way of not giving medication, just as one may insult someone by way of not shaking his hand. But for any purpose of moral assessment, it is a type of action nonetheless. The decision to let a patient die is subject to moral appraisal in the same way that a decision to kill him would be subject to moral appraisal: it may be assessed as wise or unwise, compassionate or sadistic, right or wrong. If a doctor deliberately let a patient die who was suffering from a routinely curable illness, the doctor would certainly be to blame for what he had done, just as he would be to blame if he had needlessly killed the patient. Charges against him would then be appropriate. If so, it would be no defense at all for him to insist that he didn't "do anything." He would have done something very serious indeed, for he let his patient die.

Fixing the cause of death may be very important from a legal point of view, for it may determine whether criminal charges are brought against the doctor. But I do not think that this notion can be used to show a moral difference between active and passive euthanasia. The reason why it is considered bad to be the cause of someone's death is that death is regarded as a great evil—and so it is. However, if it has been decided that euthanasia—even passive euthanasia—is desirable in a given case, it has also been decided that in this instance death is no greater an evil than the patient's continued existence. And if this is true, the usual reason for not wanting to be the cause of someone's death simply does not apply.

Finally, doctors may think that all of this is only of academic interest—the sort of thing that philosophers may worry about but that has no practical bearing on their own work. After all, doctors must be concerned about the legal consequences of what they do, and active euthanasia is clearly forbidden by the law. But even so, doctors should also be concerned with the fact that the law is forcing upon them a moral doctrine that may well be indefensible, and has a considerable effect on their practices. Of course, most doctors are not now in the position of being coerced in this matter, for they do not regard themselves as merely going along with what the law requires. Rather, in statements such as the AMA policy statement that I have quoted, they are endorsing this doctrine as a central point of medical ethics. In that statement, active euthanasia is condemned not merely as illegal but as "contrary to that for which the medical profession stands," whereas passive euthanasia is approved. However, the preceding considerations suggest that there is really no moral difference between the two, considered in themselves (there may be important moral differences in some cases in their *consequences,* but, as I pointed out, these differences may make active euthanasia, and not passive euthanasia, the morally preferable option). So, whereas doctors may have to discriminate between active and passive euthanasia to satisfy the law, they should not do any more than that. In particular, they should not give the distinction any added authority and weight by writing it into official statements of medical ethics.

NOTE

1. A. Shaw: "Doctor, Do We Have a Choice?" *The New York Times Magazine,* Jan. 30, 1972, p. 54.

READING QUESTIONS

1. What is the AMA's 1973 policy regarding euthanasia? What are some of the differences between passive and active forms of euthanasia according to Rachels? Describe some cases of allowing a patient to die and killing a patient directly.
2. What is Rachels's main concern with allowing a patient to die? How does direct action by a doctor differ from cases where treatment is withheld from a patient?
3. Explain Rachels's argument for the claim that decisions to let patients die are made on morally irrelevant grounds. What objections are raised against this view, and how does Rachels respond?
4. Why does Rachels think that doctors accepted the AMA's policy? How does he think that doctors should act with respect to policy and the law?

DISCUSSION QUESTIONS

1. Rachels presents hypothetical cases of individuals drowning to illustrate the difference between killing and letting die. Are there any reasons to think that an individual who allows another to drown while looking on is not like the case of a doctor who allows a patient to die by withholding treatment? Consider the morally relevant features of such situations which incline us to make the evaluations that we do.
2. What are the morally relevant differences between allowing someone to die and killing someone directly? Is allowing someone to die always a slow and painful process as Rachels suggests? Is taking direct action in order to kill someone always quick and painless?

PHILIPPA FOOT

Killing and Letting Die

Philippa Foot's essay is a reply to Rachels's claim that there is no morally relevant difference per se between killing someone and letting the person die. Foot makes her case in two steps. First, she provides examples (Rescue I and Rescue II) in which she thinks readers will agree that there is a morally relevant difference between killing and letting die—cases in which one holds fixed the motives of the agent and the outcomes of the two rescue cases. The essential element in cases of killing that distinguished them from cases of letting die is one's agency

From Philippa Foot, "Killing and Letting Die," in J. L. Garfield and P. Hennessy, *Abortion: Moral and Legal Perspectives*. Amherst: The University of Massachusetts Press, 1984. Reprinted with permission of the University of Massachusetts Press.

in initiating the death. Second, she proposes an explanation of *why* this distinction is at least in some cases morally relevant. Her explanation is in terms of two classes of rights: rights to noninterference and rights to goods and services.

Recommended Reading: rights-focused approach to moral issues, chap. 1, sec. 2D.

Is there a morally relevant distinction between killing and allowing to die? Many philosophers say that there is not, and further insist that there is no other closely related difference, as for instance that which divides act from omission, whichever plays a part in determining the moral character of an action. James Rachels has argued this case in his well-known article on active and passive euthanasia, Michael Tooley has argued it in his writings on abortion, and Jonathan Bennett argued it in the Tanner Lectures given in Oxford in 1980.[1] I believe that these people re mistaken, and this is what I shall try to show in this essay. . . .

The question with which we are concerned has been dramatically posed by asking whether we are as equally to blame for allowing people in Third World countries to starve to death as we would be for killing them by sending poisoned food? In each case it is true that if we acted differently—by sending good food or by not sending poisoned food—those who are going to die because we do not send the good food or do send the poisoned food would not die after all. Our agency plays a part in what happens whichever way they die. Philosophers such as Rachels, Tooley, and Bennett consider this to be all that matters in determining our guilt or innocence. Or rather they say that although related things are morally relevant, such as our reasons for acting as we do and the cost of acting otherwise, these are only contingently related to the distinction between doing and allowing. If we hold *them* steady and vary only the way in which our agency enters into the matter, no moral differences will be found. It is of no significance, they say, whether we kill others or let them die, or whether they die by our act or our omission. Whereas these latter differences may at first seem to affect the morality of action, we shall always find on further enquiry that some other difference—such as a difference of motive or cost—has crept in.

Now this, on the face of it, is extremely implausible. We are not inclined to think that it would be no worse to murder to get money for some comfort such as a nice winter coat than it is to keep the money back before sending a donation to Oxfam or Care. We do not think that we might just as well be called murderers for one as for the other. And there are a host of other examples which seem to make the same point. We may have to allow one person to die if saving him would mean that we could not save five others, as for instance when a drug is in short supply and he needs five times as much as each of them, but that does not mean that we could carve up one patient to get "spare parts" for five.

These moral intuitions stand clearly before us, but I do not think it would be right to conclude from the fact that these examples all seem to hang on the contrast between killing and allowing to die that this is precisely the distinction that is important from the moral point of view. For example, having someone killed is not strictly *killing* him, but seems just the same morally speaking; and on the other hand, turning off a respirator might be called killing, although it seems morally indistinguishable from allowing to die. Nor does it seem that the difference between 'act' and 'omission' is quite what we want, in that a respirator that had to be turned on each morning would not change the moral problems that arise with the ones we have now. Perhaps there is no locution in the language which exactly serves our purposes and we should therefore invent our own vocabulary. Let us mark the distinction we are after by saying that one person may or may not be 'the agent' of harm that befalls someone else.

When is one person 'the agent' in this special sense of someone else's death, or of some harm other than death that befalls him? This idea can easily be described in a general way. If there are difficulties when it comes to detail, some of these ideas may be best left unsolved, for there may be an area of indefiniteness reflecting the uncertainty that belongs to our moral judgments in some complex and perhaps infrequently encountered situations. The idea of agency, in the sense that we want, seems to be composed of two subsidiary ideas. First, we think of particular effects as the result of particular sequences, as when a certain fatal sequence leads to someone's death. This idea is implied in coroners' verdicts telling us what someone died of, and this concept is not made suspect by the fact that it is sometimes impossible to pick out a single fatal sequence—as in the lawyers' example of the man journeying into the desert who had two enemies, one of whom bored a hole in his water barrel while another filled it with brine. Suppose such complications absent. Then we can pick out the fatal sequence and go on to ask who initiated it. If the subject died by poisoning and it was I who put the poison into his drink, then I am the agent of his death; likewise if I shot him and he died of a bullet wound. Of course there are problems about fatal sequences which would have been harmless but for special circumstances, and those which although threatening would have run out harmlessly but for something that somebody did. But we can easily understand the idea that a death comes about through our agency if we send someone poisoned food or cut him up for spare parts, but not (ordinarily) if we fail to save him when he is threatened by accident or disease. Our examples are not problem cases from *this* point of view.

Nor is it difficult to find more examples to drive our original point home, and show that it is sometimes permissible to allow a certain harm to befall someone, although it would have been wrong to bring this harm on him by one's own agency, i.e., by originating or sustaining the sequence which brings the harm. Let us consider, for instance, a pair of cases which I shall call Rescue I and Rescue II. In the first Rescue story we are hurrying in our jeep to save some people—let there be five of them—who are imminently threatened by the ocean tide. We have not a moment to spare, so when we hear of a single person who also needs rescuing from some other disaster we say regretfully that we cannot rescue him, but must leave him to die. To most of us this seems clear, and I shall take it as clear. . . . This is

Rescue I and with it I contrast Rescue II. In this second story we are again hurrying to the place where the tide is coming in in order to rescue the party of people, but this time it is relevant that the road is narrow and rocky. In this version the lone individual is trapped (do not ask me how) on the path. If we are to rescue the five we would have to drive over him. But can we do so? If we stop he will be all right eventually: he is in no danger unless from us. But of course all five of the others will be drowned. As in the first story our choice is between a course of action which will leave one man dead and five alive at the end of the day and a course of action which will have the opposite result. And yet we surely feel that in one case we can rescue the five men and in the other we cannot. We can allow someone to die of whatever disaster threatens him if the cost of saving him is failing to save five; we cannot, however, drive over *him* in order to get to *them*. We cannot originate a fatal sequence, although we can allow one to run its course. Similarly, in the pair of examples mentioned earlier, we find a contrast between on the one hand refusing to give to one man the whole supply of a scarce drug, because we can use portions of it to save five, and on the other, cutting him up for spare parts. And we notice that we may not originate a fatal sequence even if the resulting death is in no sense our object. We could not knowingly subject one person to deadly fumes in the process of manufacturing some substance that would save many, even if the poisoning were a mere side effect of the process that saves lives.

Considering these examples, it is hard to resist the conclusion that it makes all the difference whether those who are going to die if we act a certain way will die as a result of a sequence that we originate or of one that we allow to continue, it being of course something that did not *start* by our agency. So let us ask how this could be? If the distinction—which is roughly that between killing and allowing to die—*is* morally relevant, because it sometimes makes the difference between what is right and what is wrong, how does this work? After all, it cannot be a magical difference, and it does not satisfy anyone to hear that what we have is just an ultimate moral fact. Moreover, those who deny the relevance can point to cases in which it seems to make no difference to the goodness or badness of an action having a certain result, as, for example, that some innocent person dies, whether due to a sequence we originate or because of one we merely allow. And if the way the result comes about *sometimes* makes no difference, how can it ever do so? If it sometimes makes an action bad that harm came to someone else as a result of a sequence we *originated,* must this not always contribute some element of badness? How can a consideration be a reason for saying that an action is bad in one place without being at least a reason for saying the same elsewhere?

Let us address these questions. As to the route by which considerations of agency enter the process of moral judgment, it seems to be through its connection with different types of rights. For there are rights to noninterference, which form one class of rights; and there are also rights to goods or services, which are different. And corresponding to these two types of rights are, on the one hand, the duty not to interfere, called a 'negative duty,' and on the other the duty to provide the goods or services, called a 'positive duty.' These rights may in certain circumstances be overridden, and this can in principle happen to rights of either kind. So, for instance, in the matter of property rights, others have in ordinary circumstances a duty not to interfere with our property, though in exceptional circumstances the right is overridden, as in Elizabeth Anscombe's example of destroying someone's house to stop the spread of a fire.[2] And a right to goods or services depending, for example, on a promise will quite often be overridden in the same kind of case. There is, however, no guarantee that the special circumstances that allow one kind of right to be overridden will always allow the overriding of the other. Typically, it takes more to justify an interference than to justify the withholding of goods or services; and it is, of course, possible to think that nothing whatsoever will justify, for example, the infliction of torture or the deliberate killing of the innocent. It is not hard to find how all this connects with the morality of killing and allowing to die—and in general with harm which an agent allows to happen and harm coming about through his agency, in

my special sense having to do with originating or sustaining harmful sequences. For the violation of a right to noninterference consists in interference, which implies breaking into an existing sequence and initiating a new one. It is not usually possible, for instance, to violate that right to noninterference, which is at least part of what is meant by 'the right to life' by failing to save someone from death. So if, in any circumstances, the right to noninterference is the only right that exists, or if it is the only right special circumstances have not overridden, then it may not be permissible to initiate a fatal sequence, but it *may* be permissible to with-hold aid.

The question now is whether we ever find cases in which the right to noninterference exists and is not overridden, but where the right to goods or services either does not exist or *is* here overridden. The answer is, of course, that this is quite a common case. It often happens that whereas someone's rights stand in the way of our interference, we owe him no *service* in relation to that which he would lose if we interfered. We may not deprive him of his property, though we do not have to help him secure his hold on it, in spite of the fact that the balance of good and evil in the outcome (counting his loss or gain and the cost to us) will be the same regardless of how they come about. Similarly, where the issue is one of life and death, it is often impermissible to kill someone—although special circumstances having to do with the good of others make it permissible, or even required, that we do not spend the time or resources needed to save his life, as for instance, in the story of Rescue I, or in that of the scarce drug.

It seems clear, therefore, that there are circumstances in which it makes all the difference, morally speaking, whether a given balance of good and evil came about through our agency (in our sense), or whether it was rather something we had the ability to prevent but, for good reasons, did not prevent. Of course, we often have a strict duty to prevent harm to others, or to ameliorate their condition. And even where they do not, strictly speaking, have a *right* to our goods or services, we should often be failing (and sometimes grossly failing) in charity if we did not help them. But, to reiterate, it may be right to allow one person to die in order to save five, although it would not be right to kill him to bring the same good to them.

How is it, then, that anyone has ever denied this conclusion, so sympathetic to our everyday moral intuitions and apparently so well grounded in a very generally recognized distinction between different types of rights? We must now turn to an argument first *given,* by James Rachels, and more or less followed by others who think as he does. Rachels told a gruesome story of a child drowned in a bathtub in two different ways: in one case someone pushed the child's head under water, and in the other he found the child drowning and did not pull him out. Rachels says that we should judge one way of acting as bad as the other, so we have an example in which killing is as bad as allowing to die. But how, he asks, can the distinction ever be relevant if it is not relevant here?[3]

Based on what has been said earlier, the answer to Rachels should be obvious. The reason why it is, in ordinary circumstance, "no worse" to leave a child drowning in a bathtub than to push it under, is that both charity and the special duty of care that we owe to children give us a positive obligation to save them, and we have no particular reason to say that it is "less bad" to fail in this than it is to be in dereliction of the negative duty by being the agent of harm. The level of badness is, we may suppose, the same, but because a different kind of bad action has been done, there is no reason to suppose that the two ways of acting will always give this same result. In other circumstances one might be worse than the other, or only one might be bad. And this last result is exactly what we find in circumstances that allow a positive but not a negative duty to be overridden. Thus, it could be right to leave someone to die by the roadside in the story of Rescue I, though wrong to run over him in the story of Rescue II; and it could be right to act correspondingly in the cases of the scarce drug and the "spare parts."

Let me now consider an objection to the thesis I have been defending. It may be said that I shall have difficulty explaining a certain range of examples in which it seems permissible, and even obligatory, to make an intervention which jeopardizes people not already in danger in order to save others who are.

The following case has been discussed. Suppose a runaway trolley is heading toward a track on which five people are standing, and that there is someone who can possibly switch the points, thereby diverting the trolley onto a track on which there is only one person. It seems that he should do this, just as the pilot whose plane is going to crash has a duty to steer, if he can, toward a less crowded street than the one he sees below. But the railway man then puts the one man newly in danger, instead of allowing the five to be killed. Why does not the one man's right to noninterference stand in his way, as one person's right to noninterference impeded the manufacture of poisonous fumes when this was necessary to save five?

The answer seems to be that this is a special case, in that we have here the *diverting* of a fatal sequence and not the starting of a new one. So we could not start a flood to stop a fire, even when the fire would kill more than the flood, but we could divert a flood to an area in which fewer people would be drowned.

A second and much more important difficulty involves cases in which it seems that the distinction between agency and allowing is inexplicably irrelevant. Why, I shall be asked, is it not morally permissible to allow someone to die deliberately in order to use his body for a medical procedure that would save many lives? It might be suggested that the distinction between agency and allowing is relevant when what is allowed to happen is itself aimed at. Yet this is not quite right, because there are cases in which it does make a difference whether one originates a sequence or only allows it to continue, although the allowing is with deliberate intent. Thus, for instance, it may not be permissible to deprive someone of a possession which only harms him, but it may be reasonable to refuse to get it back for him if it is already slipping from his grasp.[4] And it is arguable that nonvoluntary passive euthanasia is sometimes justifiable although nonvoluntary active euthanasia is not. What these examples have in common is that *harm* is not in question, which suggests that the 'direct', i.e., deliberate, intention of *evil* is what makes it morally objectionable to allow the beggar to die. When this element is present it is impossible to justify an action by indicating that no *origination* of evil is involved. But this special case leaves no doubt about the relevance of distinguishing between originating an evil and allowing it to occur. It was never suggested that there will *always and everywhere* be a difference of permissibility between the two. . . .

NOTES

1. James Rachels, "Active and Passive Euthanasia," *New England Journal of Medicine* 292 (January 9, 1975):

78–80; Michael Tooley, "Abortion and Infanticide," *Philosophy and Public Affairs* 2, no. 1 (Fall 1972); Jonathan Bennett, "Morality and Consequences," in *The Tanner Lectures on Human Values,* vol. 2, ed. Sterling McMurrin (Cambridge: Cambridge University Press, 1981).

2. G. E. M. Anscombe, "Modern Moral Philosophy," *Philosophy* 33 (1958): 1–19.

3. Rachels, "Active and Passive Euthanasia."

4. Cf. Philippa Foot, "Killing, Letting Die, and Euthanasia: A Reply to Holly Smith Goldman," *Analysis* 41, no. 4 (June 1981).

READING QUESTIONS

1. Crucial to Foot's case is her account of a person who is 'the agent' of someone's death. Explain her notion of being the agent in this special sense.
2. Describe Foot's two rescue cases. How does her special sense of being an agent figure in these examples to explain one's moral intuitions about the two cases?
3. What is Foot's example of a case in which a duty of noninterference can be legitimately overridden by a duty to provide goods or services?
4. What explanation does Foot give for why Rachels denies the moral significance of the distinction between killing and letting die?

DISCUSSION QUESTIONS

1. Suppose Foot is right in thinking that there are cases in which there is a morally relevant distinction between killing and letting die. What implications does this distinction have for cases of both active and passive euthanasia? (Keep in mind the distinctions between voluntary, involuntary, and nonvoluntary cases.)
2. In one of the many trolley examples that figure in discussions of killing and letting die, one is standing on a bridge that goes over the trolley tracks next to a large individual wearing a backpack. By pushing the large individual onto the tracks, one could stop the trolley before it ran over five trapped workers who otherwise would be run over and killed. Of course the backpacker will be killed if he is pushed onto the tracks and the trolley smashes into him. Would pushing the backpacker to his death be morally permissible on Foot's account? Why or why not?
3. Now consider a variant of the case described in question 2. The backpacker, in trying to walk across the tracks, trips, and one foot is caught in the tracks, he can't get the foot loose, and the trolley is fast approaching. You are nearby and can pull him to safety. Of course, if you do not intervene in the unfolding events, the backpacker will be killed, but the five trapped workers will be saved. What would Foot say about pulling the backpacker to safety? Are you obligated to intervene and save his life?

DANIEL CALLAHAN

A Case against Euthanasia

Daniel Callahan considers euthanasia to be a form of suicide. He begins by noting that suicide is comparatively rare among people who face debilitating pain or incapacitating diseases, and that it is common for people to look upon suicide with sadness and perhaps revulsion. These facts do not serve as an argument against the moral permissibility of suicide, but Callahan does think making sense of such reactions offers a perspective on human life that can reveal why euthanasia and suicide generally are morally problematic. After arguing that three prominent arguments in favor of suicide are flawed, he turns critical attention to the issue of legalization of euthanasia and physician-assisted suicide of the sort found in Dutch law and in the Oregon Death with Dignity Act. Here the focus is on the small minority who choose euthanasia (including physician-assisted suicide) and the potential abuse of such laws.

Consider what I take to be a mystery. Life presents all of us with many miseries, sick or well. Why is it then that so few people choose to end their, own lives in response to them? Why is it that when someone does commit suicide—even for reasons that seem understandable—the common reaction (at least in my experience) is one of sorrow, a feeling of pity that someone was driven to such a desperate extreme, particularly when most others in a similar situation do not do likewise? I ask these questions because, behind the movement and arguments in favor of euthanasia or physician-assisted suicide (PAS)—and I consider euthanasia a form of suicide—lies an effort to make the deliberate ending of one's life something morally acceptable and justifiable; and which looks as well to the help of government and the medical profession to move that cause along.[1]

It goes against the grain, I believe, of reason, emotion, and tradition, and all at the same time. If not utterly irrational, it is at least unreasonable—that is, it is not a sensible way to deal with the tribulations of life, of which a poor death is only one of life's horrible possibilities. Suicide generally provokes a negative emotional response in people, even if they can grasp the motive behind it. That response does not prove it is wrong, but it is an important signal of a moral problem. As for tradition, the doctor is being asked by a patient to go against the deep historical convictions of his discipline, to use his or her skills to take life rather than to preserve it, and to lend to the practice of euthanasia the blessing of the medical profession. I understand all of this to be opening the door to new forms of killing in our society, not a good development.

There have been, in Western culture, only three generally accepted reasons for taking the life of another, which is what euthanasia amounts to: self-defense when one's life is threatened, warfare when the cause is serious and just, and capital punishment, the ultimate sanction against the worst crimes. The movement to empower physicians legally to take the life of a patient, or help the patient take his own life,

From "A Case Against Euthanasia" by Daniel Callahan, in *Contemporary Debates in Applied Ethics*, edited by Andrew I. Cohen and Christopher Heath Wellman, Blackwell Publishing Co., 2005, pp. 179–190.

would then legitimate a form of suicide, but would also add still another reason by calling on medical skills to end a person's life.

SUICIDE: THE WAY (RARELY) TAKEN

Let me return to the first of my two questions. Why do comparatively few people turn to suicide as a way of dealing with awful lives? People die miserable deaths all the time, from a wide range of lethal diseases and other causes. While it may cross their minds from time to time, few seem to want euthanasia or physician-assisted suicide as a way out. Millions of people have been brutally treated in concentration camps, with many of them ultimately to die—and yet suicide has never been common in such camps. Many millions of others have undergone all kinds of personal tragedy—the death of children or a spouse, the end of marriage or a deep romance, failures in their work or profession—but most of them do not turn to suicide either. The disabled have been long known to have a lower suicide rate than able-bodied people.

Euthanasia is often presented as a "rational" choice for someone in great pain and whose prospects are hopeless. And yet rationality implies some predictability of behavior, that is, some reasonable certainty that people will act in a consistent and foreseeable way under certain familiar circumstances. Yet it is almost impossible, save for severe depression, to predict whether someone suffering from a lethal illness is likely to turn to suicide. It is far more predictable that, when faced with even the worst horrors of life, most people will *not* turn to suicide. It is no less predictable that, when gripped by pain and suffering, they will want relief, but not to the extent of ending their lives to get it.

We may of course say that people fear ending their own lives, lacking the nerve to do so, or that religious beliefs have made suicide a taboo, or that it has hitherto been difficult to find expert assistance in ending one's life. Those are possible explanations, but since some people do in fact commit suicide, we know that it is hardly impossible to overcome those deterrents.

Moreover, to say that most of the great religions and moral traditions of the world have condemned suicide does not in the end explain much at all. *Why* have they done so, even when at the same time they usually do not condemn laying down one's life to save another? In the same vein, why has the Western medical tradition for some 2,500 years, going back to Hippocrates, prohibited physicians from helping patients to commit suicide?

My guess is that the answer to the first of those two questions is that suicide is seen as a particularly bad way to handle misery and suffering, even when they are overwhelming—and the behavior of most people in turning away from suicide suggests they share that perception. It is bad because human life is better, even nobler, when we human beings put up with the pain and travail that come our way. Life is full of pain, stress, tragedy, and travail, and we ought not to want to tempt others to see suicide as a way of dealing with it. We would fail ourselves and, by our witness, our neighbor as well, who will know what we did and be led to do so themselves some day.

I began by asking at the outset why most suicides are treated as unhappy events, even when they obviously relieved someone's misery, which we would ordinarily consider valuable. Those readers who have been to the funerals of suicides will know how rarely those at such funerals feel relief that the misery of the life leading up to them has now been relieved. They almost always wish the life could have ended differently, that the suffering could have been borne. My surmise is that those of us who are bystanders or spectators to such deaths know that a fundamental kind of taboo of a rational kind has been broken, some deep commitment to life violated, and that no relief of pain and suffering can justify that. To say this is by no means to condemn those who do so. We can often well enough comprehend why they were driven to that extreme. Nor do I want to imply that they must have been clinically depressed. I am only saying that it is very hard to feel good about suicide or to rejoice that it was the way chosen to get out of a burdensome life.

I present these considerations about suicide as speculations only, not as some kind of decisive arguments against euthanasia. But I think it important to see what sense can be made of a common revulsion against suicide, and sadness when it happens, that has marked generations of people in most parts of the world. Moreover, as I will develop more fully below, it turns out that the experience with the Dutch euthanasia laws and practice, as well as with the Oregon experience with physician-assisted suicide, indicates that it is not misery, pain, and suffering in any ordinary sense that are the motivation for the desire to put an end to one's life. It is instead in great part a function of a certain kind of patient with a certain kind of personality and outlook upon the world.

It is, I believe, important that we try to make sense of these background experiences and reactions. They tell us something about ourselves, our traditions, and our human nature. They offer an enriched perspective when considering the most common arguments in favor of euthanasia. On the surface those arguments are meant to seem timely, in tune with our mainstream values, commonsensical and compassionate, and of no potential harm to our medical practice or our civic lives together. I would like to show that they are indeed in tune with many of our mainstream values, but that they are misapplied in this case, harmful to ourselves and others if we accept them.

THREE ARGUMENTS IN FAVOR OF EUTHANASIA

I want now to turn to the main arguments in favor of euthanasia, and to indicate why I think they are weak and unpersuasive. I will follow that with a discussion of the legal problem of euthanasia and physician-assisted suicide, and conclude with some comments on the experience with euthanasia and physician-assisted suicide in the Netherlands and the state of Oregon.

Three moral arguments have been most prominent in the national debate. One of them is that we ought, if we are competent, to have the right to control our body as we see fit and to end our life if we choose to do so. This is often called the right of self-determination. Another is that we owe it to each other, in the

name of beneficence or charity, to relieve suffering when we can do so. Still another is that there is no serious or logical difference between terminating the treatment of a dying patient, allowing the patient to die, and directly killing a patient by euthanasia. I will look at each of these arguments in turn.

If there is any fundamental American value, it is that of freedom and particularly the freedom to live our own lives in light of our own values. The only limit to that value is that, in the name of freedom, we may not do harm to others. At least a hundred years ago the value of freedom was extended to the inviolability of our bodies – that is, our right not to have our bodies invaded, abused, or used without our consent. Even to put our hands on another without their permission can lead to our being charged with assault and battery. That principle was extended to participation in medical research and the notion of informed consent: no individual can use your body for medical research without your specific informed consent granting them permission to do so. In later years, many construed earlier bans on abortion as an interference with the right of a woman to make her own choices about her body and the continuance of a pregnancy.

It seemed, then, only a small and logical step to extend the concept of freedom and self-determination to the end of our life. If you believe that your pain and suffering are insupportable, and if there is no hope that medicine can cure you of a fatal disease, why should you not have the right to ask a physician directly to end your life (euthanasia) or to provide you with the means of doing so (physician-assisted suicide)? After all, it is your body, your suffering, and if there is no reason to believe others will be harmed by your desire to see your life come to an end, what grounds are there for denying you that final act of self-determination? As I suggested above, it is precisely because the claim of self-determination in this context seems so much in tune with our traditional value of liberty that it seems hard to find a reason to reject it.

But we should reject it, and for a variety of considerations, three of which seem most important. The first is that euthanasia is mistakenly understood as a personal and private matter only of self-determination. Suicide, once a punishable crime, was removed from the law some decades ago in this country. But it is one thing not to prosecute a person for attempting suicide and quite another to think that euthanasia is a private act, impacting on no other lives. On the contrary, with euthanasia as its means, it becomes a social act by virtue of calling upon the physician to take part in it. Legalizing it would also provide an important social sanction and legitimation of those practices. They would require regulation and legal oversight.

Most critically, it would add to the acceptable range of killing in our society, noted above, one more occasion for the taking of life. To do so would be to reverse the long-developing trend to limit the occasions of socially sanctioned killing, too often marked by abuse. Euthanasia would also reinstate what I would call "private killing," by which I mean a situation where the agreement of one person to kill another is ratified in private by the individuals themselves, not by public authorities (even if it is made legal and supposed safeguards put in place). Dueling as a way of settling differences was once accepted, a form of private killing, something between the duelists only. But it was finally rejected as socially harmful and is nowhere now accepted in civilized society. The contention that it was *their* bodies at stake, *their* private lives, was rejected as a good moral reason to legally accept dueling.

EUTHANASIA AS A SOCIAL, NOT PRIVATE, ACT

A closely related objection is that what makes euthanasia and physician-assisted suicide social, and not individual, matters is that, by definition, they require the assistance of a physician. Two points are worth considering here. The first is whether we want to sanction the private killing that is euthanasia by allowing physicians to be one of the parties to euthanasia agreements. Since the doctor-patient relationship is protected by the long-standing principle of confidentiality—what goes on between doctor and patient may not be legally revealed to any third party—that gives doctors enormous power over patients.

Whatever the law might be, there will be no way of knowing whether doctors are obeying regulations allowing for euthanasia or physician-assisted suicide, no way of knowing whether they are influencing patient decisions in wrongful ways, no way of knowing whether they are acting with professional integrity. As Sir Charles Allbutt, a British physician, nicely put the problem a century ago:

> If all professions have their safeguards they also have their temptations, and ours is no exception. . . . Unfortunately the game of medicine is played with the cards under the table . . . who is there to note the significant glance, the shrug, the hardly expressed innuendo of our brethren. . . . Thus we work not in the light of public opinion but in the secrecy of the chamber. (Cited in Scarlett, 1991: 24–5)

To give physicians the power to kill patients, or assist in their suicide, when their actions are clothed in confidentiality is to run a considerable risk, one hard to spot and one hard to act upon. As will be noted below, the Dutch experience with euthanasia makes clear how easy it was for doctors to violate the court-established rules for euthanasia and to do so with impunity. There is just no way, in the end, for outsiders to know exactly what doctors do behind the veil of confidentiality; that in itself is a threat.

The second consideration is that the tradition of medicine has, for centuries, opposed the use of medical knowledge and skill to end life. Every important Western medical code of ethics has rejected euthanasia—and rejected it even in those eras when there were many fewer ways of relieving pain than are now available. That could hardly have been because earlier generations of doctors knew less about, or were more indifferent to, pain and suffering. Their relief was at the very heart of the doctor's professional obligation.

There was surely another reason. The medical tradition knew something of great importance: doctors are all too skilled in knowing how to kill to be entrusted with the power to deliberately use that skill. This is not to say that physicians are corrupt, prone to misuse their power; not at all. It is only to say, on the one hand, that the very nature of their profession is to save and protect life, not end it; and that they also, on the other hand, become inured much more than the rest of us to death. Ordinary prudence suggests that the temptation to take life should be kept from them as far as possible. To move in any other direction is to risk the corruption of medicine and to threaten the doctor-patient relationship.

But what of the duty to relieve suffering, to act out of compassion for another? Did the moral strictures against euthanasia and physician-assisted suicide in effect simply forget about, or ignore, that duty? Not at all, but the duty to relieve suffering has never been an absolute duty, overriding all moral objections. No country now allows, or has ever allowed, euthanasia without patient consent even if the patient is incompetent and obviously suffering. Nor are patients' families authorized to request euthanasia under those circumstances. Moreover, as time has gone on, the ability of physicians to relieve patients of just about all pain and suffering through good palliative care has shown that most suffering can be relieved without the ultimate solution of killing the patient. In any event, any alleged duty to relieve suffering has historically always given way to the considerations, noted above, about the nature of medicine as a profession whose principal duty is construed as the saving not the taking of life, and not even when the life cannot medically be saved.

The third argument against euthanasia I want to consider is based on the belief that there is no inherent moral difference between killing a patient directly by euthanasia and allowing a patient to die by deliberately terminating a patient's life-supporting treatment (by turning off a ventilator, for example). Since physicians are allowed to do the latter, it is said that they should be allowed to do the former as well—and indeed that it may be more merciful to carry out euthanasia than to stop treatment, perhaps increasing and prolonging the suffering before the patient actually dies. In effect, the argument goes, terminating treatment will foreseeably end the life of the patient, a death hastened by the physician's act; and that is no different, in its logic or outcome, from killing the patient directly by euthanasia (Rachels, 1975).

There are some mistakes in this argument. One of them is a failure to remember that patients with truly lethal, fatal diseases cannot be saved in the long run. The most that can be accomplished is, by aggressive

treatment, to delay their death. At some point, typically, a physician will legitimately decide that treatment cannot bring the patient back to good health and cannot reverse the downhill course of the illness. The disease is in control at that point and, when the physician stops treatment, the disease takes over and kills the patient. It has been long accepted that, in cases of that kind, the cause of death is the disease, not the physician's action.

Moreover, how can it be said that a physician has "hastened" a patient's death by ending life-saving treatment? After all, but for the doctor's action in keeping the patient alive in the first place and then continuing the life-sustaining treatment, the patient would have died much earlier. Put another way, the doctor saves the patient's life at one point in time, sustains the patient's life through a passage of time, and then allows the patient to die at still another time. Since no physician has the power to stay indefinitely the hand of death, at some point or other, in any case, the physician's patient will be irreversibly on the way to death; that is, at some point, life-sustaining treatment will be futile. To think that doctors "kill" patients by terminating treatment is tantamount at that point to saying that doctors have abolished lethal disease and that they now die only because of a physician's actions. It would be lovely if doctors have achieved that kind of power over nature, with death solely in their hands. It has not happened, and is not likely ever to happen. To say this is not to deny that physicians can misuse their power to terminate treatment wrongly: they can stop treatment when it could still do some good, or when a competent patient wants it continued. In that case, however, the physician is blameworthy. It is still the underlying disease that does the killing, but the physician is culpable for allowing that to happen when it ought not to have happened.

EUTHANASIA AND THE LAW

I have provided some reasons why, ethically speaking, euthanasia and physician-assisted suicide cannot be well defended. But what of the law? If we claim to live in a free country, and believe in pluralism, should not the law leave it up to us as individuals to decide how our lives should end? Many people will reject my arguments against euthanasia, and public opinion polls have consistently shown a majority of Americans to be in favor of it. A law that simply allowed those practices, but coerces no one to embrace them, would seem the most reasonable position.

Not necessarily. I noted earlier that the moral acceptance of euthanasia would have the effect of legitimating the role of the physician as someone now empowered to end life. It would also bring an enormous change in the role of the physician, changing the very notion of what it means to be one (Kass, 2002). Seen in that light, a law permitting euthanasia would have social implications far beyond simply giving patients the right to choose how their lives end. As in so many other matters, what on the surface looks like a narrowly private decision turns out, with legalization, to send much wider ripples through society in general and the practice of medicine in particular. It has been said that, in addition to its regulatory functions, the law is a teacher, providing a picture of the way we think people should live together. Legalized euthanasia would teach the wrong kind of lesson.

The actual enforcement of a law on euthanasia would be enormously difficult to carry out. The privacy of the doctor-patient relationship means that there is an area that the law cannot enter. Whatever conditions the law might set for legal euthanasia, there is in the end no good way to know whether it is being obeyed. Short of having a policeman sitting in on every encounter between a doctor and a patient, what they agree to will remain unavailable to the rest of us. All laws are subject to abuse, particularly when they are controversial in the first place. Not everyone will agree with the law as written, and we can be sure that some will bend it or ignore it if they can get away with it. But in most cases it is possible to detect the violation. We know when our goods have been stolen, just as we can know when someone has been brutally beaten.

It would be far more difficult to detect abuses with euthanasia. For one thing, two of the main reasons offered in favor of euthanasia—self-determination

and the relief of suffering—do not readily lend themselves to the limits of law. Why should a right of self-determination be limited to those in a terminal state, which is what is commonly proposed and is required in Holland and Belgium? The Dutch law, which does not require a terminal illness, but only unbearable suffering, is in that respect much more perceptive about the logical and legal implications of the usual moral arguments in favor of euthanasia, which is why it rejected a terminal illness requirement.

The Dutch realized that the open-ended logic of the moral reasons behind euthanasia do not lend themselves well to artificial, legal barriers. Impending death is not the only horrible thing in life and, if an individual's body is her own, why should any interference with her choice be tolerated? The requirement of an impending death seems arbitrary in the extreme. As for the relief of suffering, why should someone have to be competent and able to give consent, as if the suffering of those lacking such capacities counts for less? In short, the main reasons given for the legalization of euthanasia seem, logically, to resist the kinds of limit built into the Oregon and Belgian laws. That reality opens the way to abuse of the law. All it requires is a physician who finds the law too narrow, the deed too easy, and a desperate patient all too eager to die.

THE DUTCH EXPERIENCE

This is not speculation. The Netherlands offers a case study of how it happens. For many decades, until a formal change in the law only recently, the Dutch courts had permitted euthanasia if certain conditions were met: a free choice, a considered and persistent request, unacceptable suffering, consultation with another physician, and accurate reporting on the cause of death. Throughout the 1970s and 1980s euthanasia (and occasionally physician-assisted suicide) was carried out, with many assurances that the conditions were being met. But, curious to find out about the actual practice, the Dutch government established a Commission on Euthanasia in 1990 to carry out an anonymous survey of Dutch physicians (Van der Maas, 1992).

The survey encompassed a sample of 406 physicians, and two other studies, which, taken together, were eye-opening. The official results showed that, based on their sample, out of a total of 129,000 deaths there were some 2,300 cases of voluntary ("free choice") euthanasia and 400 cases of assisted suicide. In addition, most strikingly, there were some 1,000 cases of intentional termination of life without explicit request, what the Dutch called "non-voluntary euthanasia." In sum, out of 3,300 euthanasia deaths, nearly one-third were non-voluntary. Less than 50 percent of the euthanasia cases were reported as euthanasia: another violation of the court rules. Worst of all, some 10 percent of the non-voluntary cases were instances of euthanasia with competent patients who were not asked for their consent.

None of that was supposed to be happening—a clear abuse of the court-established rules. A number of doctors had obviously taken it upon themselves to unilaterally end the lives of many patients. If that could happen there, it could happen here. Since that time, the Dutch have officially established a legal right to euthanasia (replacing the early court-established guidelines), but the government there has recently found that only 50 percent of the physicians who carry it out report doing so, and that there continue to be 400 cases a year of voluntary euthanasia (Sheldon, 2003).

The American state of Oregon, which legalized physician-assisted suicide in 1994, but whose actual implementation was delayed until 1997 by a number of court challenges, offers a variety of further insights into the practice. To the surprise of many, the actual number of people to take advantage of the new law has been small. The number of prescriptions for physician-assisted suicide, written for the first four years, beginning in 1998, has been 24 (1998), 33 (1999), 39 (2000) and 44 (2001)—and the thing seems to depend on individual differences in values, not in bodily responses to pain or impending death. In reporting on the first year of the Oregon law, the state Oregon Health Commission noted that a majority of the 16 reported cases involved people with a particular fear of a "loss of control or the fear

of loss of general control, and a loss of bodily function" (Chin et al., 1999: 580, 582). It was not the unbearable and unrelievable physical pain so often and luridly emphasized in the efforts to legalize PAS, or a fear of abandonment, or dependency on others (though some mentioned that), or a feeling of meaninglessness in suffering.

Worry about such a loss represents a particular set of personal (and idiosyncratic) values, by no means a widely distributed set. This was well brought out in the official state report. What the state officials did was to match those who received PAS (called the "case" group) with a group (called the "control" group) of patients with "similar underlying illnesses," and matched as well for age and date of death (Chin et al., 1999: 578). Their findings were striking: the PAS group was much more concerned about autonomy and control than the other group. Even more provocative was the fact that the PAS group was far more able to function physically than the control group: "21 percent of the case patients, as compared with 84 percent of the control patients . . . were completely disabled" (Chin et al., 1999: 580). In other words, the PAS group was far better off physically than the control group. It was their personal values that led them in one direction rather than another, not the objective intensity of their incapacities. Or to put it in terms we used earlier, PAS represents a legitimation of suicide for those who have a particular conception of the optimum life and its management, one of complete control.

CATERING TO A SMALL MINORITY

If it turns out, then, that PAS heavily attracts a particular kind of person, one very different from most terminally ill people, then much of the public policy argument on its behalf fails. It is not a general problem requiring drastic changes in law, tradition, and medical practice. Just as suicide in general, whatever the level of misery, is not the way most people seek to deal with it, so also are euthanasia and PAS the desire of a tiny minority. These results, it should be added, are much the same as those found in the Netherlands. At a 1991 conference there with the leaders of the Dutch euthanasia movement, I asked the physicians how it was possible reliably to diagnose "unbearable" or "untreatable" suffering as a medical condition and thus suitable for their euthanasia or PAS ministrations. They conceded that there is no reliable medical diagnosis, no way of really knowing what was going on within the mind and emotions of the patient, and—consistent with the findings of the Oregon state study—no correlation *whatever* between a patient's actual medical condition and the reported suffering.

Perhaps euthanasia is not, as many would like to put it, simply a logical extension of the physician's duty to relieve pain and suffering, an old obligation in a new garment. Perhaps it is just part of the drift toward the medicalization of the woes of life, particularly that version of life that regards the loss of control as the greatest of human indignities. Not only that, but even the fear of a loss of control is for many tantamount to its actual loss. I wonder if the voters of Oregon, and all of those who believe euthanasia a needed progressive move, mean to empower unto death that special, and small, subclass of patients uncommonly bent on the control of their lives and eager to have the help of doctors to do so. Somehow I doubt it, but it looks as if that may be what they got.

Underlying much of what I have written here are two assumptions, which need some defense. One of them is that good palliative care, a rapidly growing medical specialty, can relieve most pain and suffering. Some cases, I readily concede, may not be helped, or not enough, by even the best palliative care, but the overwhelming majority can be. My second assumption is this: it is bad public policy to abandon long-standing legal prohibitions, with important reasons and traditions behind them, for the sake of a very small minority, and particularly when the consequences open the way for abuse and a fundamental change in medical values. The fact, for so it seems, that the small minority reflects not some general human response to pain and suffering but a personal, and generally idiosyncratic, view of suffering is all the more reason to hesitate before legally blessing

euthanasia. Human beings, in their lives and in their deaths, have long been able to see their lives come to an end without feeling some special necessity to have it ended of them, directly by euthanasia or self-inflicted by physician-assisted suicide.

What about the notion of "death with dignity," a phrase much used by euthanasia supporters? It is a misleading, obfuscating phrase. Death is no indignity, even if accompanied by pain and a loss of control. Death is a fundamental fact of human biology, as fundamental as any other part of human life. If that human life has dignity as human life, it cannot be lost because death brings it to an end, even if in a disorderly, unpleasant fashion. It takes more than that to erase our dignity. Human beings in concentration camps did not lose their essential human value and dignity by being tortured, humiliated, and degraded. Euthanasia confers no dignity on the process of dying; it only creates the illusion of dignity for those who, mistakenly, believe a loss of control is not to be endured. It can be, and most human beings have endured it. No one would say that the newborn baby, unable to talk, incontinent, utterly unable to control her situation, and unable to interact with others, lacks dignity. Neither does the dying older person, even if displaying exactly the same traits. Dignity is not so easily taken from human beings. Nor can euthanasia confer it on someone.

NOTES

1. Unless there is a need to deal with the difference between euthanasia and physician-assisted suicide, I will hereafter refer only to euthanasia. By euthanasia I mean the direct killing of a patient by a doctor, ordinarily by means of a lethal injection. By physician-assisted suicide I mean the act of killing oneself by means of lethal drugs provided by a physician.

REFERENCES

Chin, Arthur E., Hedberg, Katrina, Higginson, Grant K., and Fleming, David W. (1999). "Legalized physician-assisted suicide in Oregon—the first year's experience." *The New England Journal of Medicine,* 340: 577–83.

Kass, Leon Richard (2002). "'I will give no deadly drugs': why doctors must not kill." In K. Foley and H. Hendin (eds.), *The Case against Assisted Suicide: For the Right to End-of-life Care.* Baltimore, MD: Johns Hopkins University Press.

Oregon Death with Dignity Legal Defense and Education Center (2000). *Oregon Death with Dignity.* Portland, OR: Oregon Death with Dignity Legal Defense and Education Center.

Rachels, James (1975). "Active and passive euthanasia." *The New England Journal of Medicine,* 292: 78–80.

Scarlett, Earle (1991). "What is a profession?" In B. R. Reynolds and J. Stone (eds.), *On Doctoring: Stories, Poems, Essays* (pp. 124–5). New York: Simon & Schuster.

Sheldon, Tony (2003). "Only half of Dutch doctors report euthanasia." *British Medical Journal,* 326: 1164.

Van der Maas, Paul J. (1992). *Euthanasia and other Decisions at the End of Life.* Amsterdam: Elsevier.

READING QUESTIONS

1. What reasons does Callahan give for asserting that relief of pain and suffering cannot justify suicide? Does he think this is a position based merely on tradition and religion, or are there reasons based in rationality alone?
2. How does Callahan describe 'private killing'? Why would euthanasia be a form of private killing, and what, according to Callahan, is wrong with it as such?
3. Explain the argument given by Callahan's opponents that there is no moral difference between killing a patient directly and allowing a patient to die by withholding or withdrawing treatment. Include an explanation of the causal difference between the two, according to Callahan.
4. Why does Callahan think that legalized euthanasia would teach the wrong kind of lesson to society?
5. What difference does Callahan note between the Dutch laws surrounding euthanasia and the Oregon Death with Dignity Act?

DISCUSSION QUESTIONS

1. Do you agree with Callahan that a negative emotional response to suicide is an important signal of a moral problem with PAS?
2. Callahan worries that legalized PAS gives physicians too much power to kill patients, including influencing patient decisions in wrongful ways. What reasons can you think of that a physician might have for doing this? Do you think it is plausible that this could be a widespread concern?
3. Discuss the tension created by having both a duty to relieve suffering and a duty to save life, given that the two are incompatible in some cases. How would you respond if you were a physician in such cases?
4. Callahan argues that in the case of withdrawing treatment from a dying patient, the disease causes death, unlike cases of euthanasia whereby the physician causes the death. Do you agree that there is a causal difference, and if so, do you think it matters morally? Why or why not?
5. Do you agree with Callahan that fear of losing control and autonomy over one's own life is not a reason to hasten death, since this is an eventuality faced by most of us anyway? Is relief of pain and suffering a stronger reason? Why or why not?

MICHAEL B. GILL

A Moral Defense of Oregon's Physician-Assisted Suicide Law

Michael Gill considers two main lines of moral argument against Oregon's physician-assisted suicide law: (1) that for reasons grounded in a person's autonomy, suicide is intrinsically wrong and (2) that given the moral foundations of the medical profession, it is wrong for a physician to assist in a patient's suicide. The second of these arguments leads Gill to a critical discussion of the principle of double effect, which is sometimes invoked in objecting to physician-assisted suicide.

Recommended reading: natural law theory, especially the principle of double effect, chap. 1, Sec. 2B.

INTRODUCTION

Since 1998, physician-assisted suicide (PAS) has been legal in the state of Oregon. If an Oregon resident has less than six months to live and is mentally competent, she can request that a physician prescribe her drugs that will cause a quick and painless death.

Most of the objections to the Oregon law fall into one of three categories. In the first category is the claim that it is intrinsically wrong for someone to kill herself. In the second category is the claim that it is intrinsically wrong for physicians to assist someone in killing herself. In the third category is the claim that legalizing PAS will lead to very bad consequences for the sick, the elderly and other vulnerable elements of our population.

In this article, I address the first and second categories of objections. In the first part of the article, I try to show that it is not intrinsically wrong for someone with a terminal disease to kill herself. In the second part, I try to show that it is not intrinsically wrong for physicians to assist someone with a terminal disease who has reasonable grounds for wanting to kill herself.

I do not discuss the consequentialist arguments that occupy the third category of objections to the Oregon law. These consequentialist arguments are important, and they need to be addressed. But they fall outside my current purview.

Let me also mention another important aspect of my position. I do not argue that anyone has a constitutionally protected *right* to assisted suicide. Laws prohibiting PAS and laws allowing PAS may both be equally consistent with the US Constitution. I try to give reasons for thinking that we ought to support the Oregon law, but I do not try to show that the Constitution demands that we make PAS available. I try to show that there may be good moral reasons for implementing a law allowing PAS, even if there is no basis for anyone to claim that she has a constitutionally protected right to assistance in suicide.

From "A Moral Defense of Oregon's Physician-Assisted Suicide Law" by Michael B. Gill, *Mortality*, Feb. 2005; 10 (2), pp. 53–67.

WHY IT IS NOT INTRINSICALLY WRONG FOR A TERMINAL PATIENT TO COMMIT SUICIDE

Arguments against the Autonomy-Based Justification for Allowing Suicide

Leon Kass has provided one of the most influential statements of the belief that someone using the Oregon law to kill herself is doing something intrinsically wrong. Kass uses the concept of tragedy to frame his opposition. Something is tragic, Kass tells us, if it is necessarily self-contradictory. "In tragedy the failure is imbedded in the hero's success, the defeats in his victories, the miseries in his glory" (Kass, 2002a: 48). Kass claims that many of the recent developments in health care are tragic in the way that he defines it, or necessarily self-contradictory. PAS under the Oregon law is one of his prime examples. PAS, Kass argues, inevitably destroys the thing of value that it is intended to promote.

The value the Oregon law is intended to promote is the autonomy of human beings. In the following, I say more about how we ought to conceive of what is valuable about autonomy, but for now we can think of it simply as a person's ability to make decisions for herself, to decide for herself what will happen to her own body. According to its proponents, the Oregon law promotes autonomy because it expands the range of decisions a person can make. When PAS is legal, a person has the choice of deciding whether or not to end her life by taking a pill. But when PAS is illegal, a person does not have that choice. And a state of affairs that gives a person more choices is, from the standpoint of trying to promote autonomy, better than a state of affairs that offers a person fewer choices.

According to Kass, however, this way of thinking is tragically simplistic, shallow and short-sighted. For in fact the legalization of PAS does not promote autonomy but encourages its destruction. Far from giving people more choices, PAS brings about a state of affairs in which a person has lost the ability to make choices altogether. For the person who engages in PAS will, obviously, be dead, and someone who is dead can no longer exercise her autonomy. It is thus *self-contradictory* to argue for PAS by claiming that it promotes autonomy, as PAS destroys a person's ability to make decisions. As Kass puts it, there can be "no ground at all" for claiming that "autonomy licenses an act that puts our autonomy permanently out of business" (Kass, 2002a: 217–218).

Opponents of PAS often color in this charge of self-contradiction by contending that the autonomy-based justification of PAS leads to obvious absurdities (Callahan, 2002: 61–63). One such absurdity is the legalization of a certain kind of slavery. It is illegal to sell yourself into slavery. Even if you want to contract with someone to become her slave, you are not allowed to do so. The contract would be null and void. According to PAS opponents, however, the autonomy-based justification of PAS implies that forbidding someone from selling herself into slavery restricts her range of self-determining choices, and that as a result we should give everyone the option of deciding whether or not to become a slave. So the autonomy-based justification of PAS implies that we should legalize self-slavery contracts. But the idea of legalizing slavery of any kind is absurd. And so, PAS opponents conclude, the autonomy-based justification of PAS is fundamentally flawed.

Another absurdity PAS opponents try to foist on the attempted justification of the Oregon law is the legalization of PAS for people who are healthy and non-terminal. Oregon's law allows PAS only for people who have six months or less to live. But the autonomy-based justification of PAS implies that we ought to expand the range of self-regarding decisions every competent individual can make. The autonomy-based justification implies, then, that we should give even healthy and non-terminal people the option of deciding whether or not to commit suicide. But, opponents of PAS argue, the idea of legalizing PAS for healthy and non-terminal people is absurd. So we have, once again, a clear reason to reject the autonomy-based justification for PAS.

Defense of the Oregon Law's Autonomy-Based Justification for Allowing Suicide

Proponents of PAS can respond to these criticisms of their autonomy-based justification in one of two ways. First, they can take the hard-line libertarian route, which consists of biting the bullet and embracing the implications that PAS opponents say are absurd. Hard-line libertarian supporters of PAS will agree that their justification of PAS implies that we should legalize self-slavery and assisted suicide for healthy, non-terminal individuals, but then go on to argue that people *should* be allowed to sell themselves into slavery if they freely choose to do so, and that healthy, non-terminal individuals should be allowed to seek assisted suicide. According to this hard-line libertarian approach, everyone really should be given the legal option to make whatever self-regarding decisions she wants. Whether we think a decision is moral or immoral is legally irrelevant. As long as no one else is harmed, the moral status of a person's justificatory principles is none of the law's business. So even if we come to believe that there is some kind of "self-contradiction" involved in a person's choosing to undertake some course of action, that would not justify using the law to prevent a person from undertaking that course of action, so long as no other person is hurt. This hard-line libertarian position has an internal consistency that shields it from any quick and simple refutation. A full treatment of this position would, however, involve us in a large-scale critique of the American legal system, and would thus take us far afield from the Oregon law, which is in fact in conflict with the hard-line libertarian position. I think, consequently, that we would do best to leave to one side the libertarian defense of assisted suicide. It's a topic for a different discussion.

The reason the Oregon law conflicts with the hard-line libertarian position is that it does not allow healthy, non-terminal individuals to choose PAS. And this feature of the Oregon law points towards the second way in which one can try to defend the autonomy-based justification of PAS against the charge of self-contradiction. Those proposing this second kind of defense will agree that self-slavery and assisted suicide for healthy, non-terminal individuals ought to remain illegal, but then go on to argue that their autonomy-based justification of the Oregon law does not imply that those other things ought to be legal. They will argue, rather, that there is a clear and morally significant difference between what the Oregon law provides for, on the one hand, and self-slavery and assisted suicide for healthy, non-terminal individuals, on the other. So while it would be wrong to legalize self-slavery and assisted suicide for healthy, non-terminal individuals, the autonomy-based defense of the Oregon law does not commit one to holding that those other things should be legal. The self-contradiction that afflicts those other things does not afflict the kind of assisted suicide that the Oregon law allows.

The Oregon law has provisions to ensure that the people who engage in PAS are competent, and that their decision to commit suicide is a result of autonomous decision making. But, crucially, it also has provisions to ensure that the people who engage in PAS have terminal illnesses. Specifically, the Oregon law allows a person to receive lethal drugs only if two doctors have verified that she has six months or less to live. And what defenders of the Oregon law can argue is that the suicide of a person who is about to die does not violate the value of autonomy because the person's decision-making ability is going to disappear whether she commits suicide or not. The person with a terminal disease who decides to commit suicide is not changing the universe from a place in which she would have been able to exercise her autonomy in the future into a place in which she will not be able to exercise her autonomy in the future. For she will not be able to exercise her autonomy in the future no matter what she does. Hers is not a decision to prevent herself from being able to make future decisions, because future decisions will not be hers to make regardless. The ending of her decision-making ability is a foregone conclusion. She is simply choosing that it end in one way rather than another. The person who commits suicide under the Oregon law should be compared to someone who blows out a candle that has used up all its wax and is now nothing but a sputtering wick that is just about to go out on its own. She should not be compared to someone who snuffs out the bright, strong flame of a new candle.

This autonomy-based defense of the Oregon law gains strength through a consideration of how the final stages of a terminal disease can corrode a person's autonomous nature. Progressive bodily deterioration can limit and ultimately eliminate one's ability to undertake physical action, and mental deterioration can limit and ultimately eliminate one's ability to make any kind of decision at all. In the end, one may be barely conscious and maintained by machines, bereft of the autonomous nature that gives human beings dignity and inestimable moral worth. It is this lingering half-life that persons who use the Oregon law may seek to prevent. And such a decision does not necessarily contradict the value of autonomy because during such a half-life autonomy does not exist anyway. Indeed, defenders of the Oregon law can argue that the decision to commit suicide in the final stages of a terminal illness can proceed from a great respect for autonomy, as such a decision can reveal that what a person values about herself is not simply her physical existence but the ability to decide what happens to her.

The fact that the Oregon law allows only terminal patients to commit suicide also gives PAS proponents the conceptual resources for repelling the absurd consequences PAS opponents try to foist on them. Opponents, recall, claimed that the autonomy-based justification of PAS implied that we should legalize self-slavery and assisted suicide for healthy, non-terminal individuals. But PAS proponents can point to a clear moral difference between the suicides allowed under the Oregon law, on the one hand, and self-slavery and the assisted suicide of healthy, non-terminal individuals, on the other. Someone who makes herself into a slave or commits suicide while healthy is throwing away the capacity for self-determination. If she does not make herself a slave or commit suicide, she will be able to make her own decisions for years to come; but if she does either of those things, she will not be able to make her own future decisions. But a person who is about to die is not going to be able to make decisions for years to come, whether she commits suicide or not. She is not throwing away her ability to determine her future

because that ability no longer exists. So the autonomy-based justification of assisted suicide for terminal individuals is completely compatible with the prohibitions on self-slavery and assisted suicide for healthy, non-terminal individuals. PAS proponents can consistently condemn actions that destroy the ability to make future decisions, because the suicide of a terminal individual is not a case of such destruction.

Opponents of PAS will respond, however, by claiming that the suicide of a person with a terminal disease *is* a case of the destruction of the ability to make future decisions. For a person who has six months to live has, after all, six months to live. And while she may be unconscious and unable to make her own decisions for part of that time, she will be conscious and able to make her own decisions for the other part. It might be true that her ability to make decisions will persist for only a few weeks or months. But, according to this way of criticizing the Oregon law, that ability is still of ultimate value, even if its temporal reach is relatively short. Earlier, I compared a terminal individual who commits suicide to someone who blows out a dying candle. There is a difference, however, between extinguishing a candle that is almost burned out but still providing light, and letting the candle burn itself out. A person who blows out a candle, even one that is almost finished, is undertaking a course of action that extinguishes light. As a result of her action, darkness comes sooner than it otherwise would have. Similarly, allowing a person to kill herself is allowing her to destroy the ability to make decisions, and that remains true even if the person would die of natural causes in a few months time anyway.

Opponents of PAS could try to put the point of the previous paragraph in terms of a nasty dilemma for proponents. If proponents of PAS really do base their position on the value of autonomy, opponents might argue, then they must be opposed both to the killing of a person who is incompetent to make her own decisions (which the Oregon law does in fact prohibit) and to the suicide of someone who will be able to make her own decisions in the future (no matter how short that future may be). But everyone falls into one of those two categories. Everyone is either incompetent to make her own decisions or will be able to make her own decisions in the (immediate) future. So the value of autonomy implies the moral legitimacy of the suicide of no one.

Autonomy as the Ability to Make "Big Decisions"

Does this criticism defeat the autonomy-based justification of PAS? Does the fact that even a terminal patient still possesses decision-making ability show that the value of autonomy cannot be used to support the Oregon law? I don't think so. I think, rather, that the goal of promoting autonomy is consistent with PAS in general and the Oregon law in particular, and that the criticism described in the previous two paragraphs is mistaken. In order to explain what is wrong with the criticism, however, we need to say a bit more about the value of autonomy.

Many ethical discussions that invoke the value of autonomy equate autonomy with the ability to make one's own decisions. To this point, I too have accepted this equation. But if we want to be clear about what the value of autonomy in end-of-life issues really involves, we need to draw a distinction between the kinds of decisions a person may make. The distinction I want to draw is between what I will call "big decisions" and "little decisions."

Big decisions are decisions that shape your destiny and determine the course of your life. Big decisions call on you to make a choice in light of things that matter most to you, in light of the things that give your life whatever meaning it has. Big decisions proceed from your deepest values. Little decisions, by contrast, concern matters that are momentary or insignificant. They do not proceed from your deepest values, but draw only on preferences that rest on the surface of your character. Big decisions are momentous, in that making one big decision rather than another will change in some non-negligible way the course of your life. But little decisions don't matter that much. Regardless of whether you make one little decision or another, your life will continue in much the same way. Little decisions don't shape your destiny. So an example of a big decision would be deciding to get married, while an example of a

little decision would be deciding to eat the blue jello instead of the red jello.[1]

I maintain that to respect autonomy is, first and foremost, to respect a person's ability to make big decisions. It is to respect a person's ability to determine her own fate, to shape her own life. The capacity to make little decisions matters less. That's not to say that the freedom to make little decisions doesn't matter at all. We should let people make as many of the little decisions that affect them as is possible. But it is the ability to make big decisions that is of inestimable value. That is where the great moral weight of the value of autonomy lies.

A person who meets the Oregon law's criteria of competence and terminality will probably have the capacity to make little decisions for weeks or months to come. She will, that is, probably be able to continue to make decisions about many of the details of her daily routine. But she may very well not have the same ability to make big decisions. Her ability to determine her own destiny, to shape her own life, may be all but gone. There are two reasons for this. First, the limited amount of time a person with a terminal disease has left to live eliminates many of the options that constitute big decision making. Long-range planning of a life is impossible when the life will end in a few months. Second, the nature of many terminal diseases can preclude big decision making in a manner that is distinct even from the amount of time a person has left to live. Terminal diseases can consume the mind as well as the body. And all too often, the only decisions a person ends up making at the end-stage are those that concern pain management and the most basic of bodily functions. The kinds of concerns that involve big decision making, the kind that call on one's deepest values and create the opportunity to shape a life, are crowded out by the immediacy of disease.

There is, however, one big decision a person who meets Oregon's criteria will still be able to make, one choice about her destiny that will still be open to her. She can still decide how and when to die. She can still choose the shape of the end of her life, the concluding words of her final chapter. This may, in fact, be the only big decision that her limited time left affords her. Thus, giving a person with a terminal disease the option of PAS can promote the thing of value that we have in mind when we talk of respect of autonomy. For the option of PAS can enhance such a person's ability to make a big decision for herself. When, by contrast, we make it more difficult for a person with a terminal disease to commit suicide, we restrict her ability to make a big decision. And this restriction cannot be justified by claiming that we are respecting her autonomy, unless what we mean by autonomy is simply the capacity to make little decisions for a few more weeks or months. For besides the choice of how she wants her life to end, ever littler decisions may be all that such a person has any prospect of making.

Once again, then, we can see the clear difference between PAS for people with terminal diseases, on the one hand, and the suicide of healthy people, on the other. A typical healthy person possesses the ability to make big decisions in the future. Such a person, typically, can control her own destiny and shape her own life for years to come. So by killing herself, a healthy person does violate what is most important about autonomy: she has before her the choice between a future in which she can make big decisions and a future in which she cannot make big decisions, and she opts for the latter. But a person with a terminal disease may not be able to make big decisions in the future, no matter what decision she makes now. So it is not necessarily the case that a person with a terminal disease will be choosing between a future in which she can make big decisions and a future in which she cannot make big decisions. It may be the case, rather, that such a person's ability to make big decisions will be nonexistent in all the futures between which she must choose.

The difference between PAS for people with diseases and self-slavery is even more clear and instructive. A slave may very well be able to make numerous little decisions throughout her life. She may be in control of the details of fulfilling her basic bodily needs, and she could have some degree of choice about how to go about completing her assigned tasks. But even if a slave possesses the capacity to make little decisions, we will still believe that her slavery violates autonomy in a fundamental way. And that is because the slave lacks the ability to make big decisions. She lacks the ability to control her own destiny, to shape her own life. It is the ability to make big decisions that is of profound moral importance. The fact that the slave may be able to make little decisions is, by comparison, morally insignificant. It is the ability to make big decisions that ought not to be tossed away. But a person with a terminal disease who chooses PAS will not necessarily be tossing away her ability to make big decisions; she may, rather, be exercising it in the only way she can. For the ability of such a person to make big decisions may already be all but gone, the only big decision left to her being that of deciding how her life will end. Now it is true that a person with a terminal disease who chooses PAS will be tossing away a few weeks or months of little decision making. But as the case of the slave illustrates, the ability to make little decisions is relatively unimportant.

Opponents of PAS may object that I have underestimated the extent to which a person with a terminal disease can be able to make big decisions. They may argue that even a person whose physical abilities are severely limited and who will die within a few months may still be able to do many things to affect the shape of her life. Such a person may, for instance, use the time she has left to change her will or to make vital arrangements for the care of her loved ones. She may reconcile with people from whom she has long been estranged. Through the experience of suffering and dying, she may learn profound truths about herself and the human condition. She may forge a new relationship with God. All of these things are of the utmost importance to the shape of a life. None of them is little or insignificant. But by availing herself of PAS, a person destroys her ability to do any of these things.

In response to this objection, let me say first of all that it is true that *some* people may have profound, life-changing experiences at the very end of life. The very end of life may be the time when *some* people achieve a new awareness or forge new relationships that cast all their previous years in an entirely different light. What is crucial to realize, however, is that this may not be true for *all* people. There may also be people who have settled all their worldly and spiritual affairs a month or two before they are expected to die. Some people may have no need to make financial arrangements or pursue any sort of interpersonal reconciliation in the final months of life because they may already have done all the work on their wills and their relationships that they believe they need to do. Some people may not need to experience any more suffering and dying because they may believe that they have learned all the lessons about themselves and the human condition that they are ever going to learn. Some people may have already achieved exactly the relationship with God to which they aspire. So while PAS may be the wrong thing for *some* people, it is not necessarily the wrong thing for *all* people. Proponents of the Oregon law do not claim, of course, that everyone with a terminal disease should commit suicide. They claim, rather, that because suicide may be right for some people, it should be an option. It should be available to all people who are terminal and competent to make their own decisions.

Opponents of PAS seem to believe, however, that it is wrong for *anyone* with a terminal disease to commit suicide. They seem to believe that there are morally significant reasons against suicide in every situation, that everyone should live for as long as she can so that she can learn for herself, and teach others, profound lessons about the meaning of life. Thus, Kass maintains that "what humanity needs most" are people who "continue to live and work and love as much as they can for as long as they can," and that such people are worthy of admiration in a way that suicides are not (Kass, 2002b: 39). And Callahan implies that people who live for as long as they can in the face of suffering and a lack of control are more "noble and heroic" than those who choose suicide (Callahan, 2002: 57), that the former fulfill the "duty to bear suffering as a form of mutual human support" in a way that the latter do not (Callahan, 2002: 66).

But some people may believe that the very end of their lives will *not* produce any profound and meaningful insights, for them or anyone else, into "the point or purpose or end of human existence" (Callahan, 2002: 58). And this belief of theirs may follow from their own fundamental values. It may proceed from their own deepest views of what is profound and meaningful about life. To respect autonomy is to promote their ability to act on these fundamental values. Suicide may be an unreasonable end to the lives of some people with terminal diseases. But it may not be an unreasonable end for the lives of others. And everyone should be allowed to decide for herself whether she is the first sort of person or the second. It is a big decision, deciding what sort of ending is for you the fundamentally right one, maybe one of the biggest decisions of all. That is why everyone whose end is imminent should be allowed to make it for herself.

WHY IT IS NOT INTRINSICALLY WRONG FOR A PHYSICIAN TO PARTICIPATE IN PAS

Physicians and the Decision of Whether Life Is Worth Living

Let us now turn to the second objection to PAS as it occurs under the Oregon law. This objection is based on the role of a physician. Even if it is in some cases morally acceptable for a person to commit suicide, PAS opponents maintain, it still will always be wrong for a physician to assist her. Those who defend PAS "misunderstand the moral foundations of medical practice," failing to appreciate that medicine "is intrinsically a moral profession, with *its own* immanent principles and standards of conduct that set limits on what physicians may properly do" (Kass, 2002b: 19).

Now it is worth noting, first, that even if physicians' special moral position makes it wrong for them to assist in suicide, that does not mean that it is wrong for *anyone* to assist in suicide.[2] Perhaps we should allow members of some other profession—such as lawyers—to provide lethal drugs to competent people with terminal diseases (see Sade & Marshall, 1996). Indeed, the more the argument against PAS depends upon principles that are special to the medical profession, the less applicable it will be to other professions' assistance in suicide.

But of course the Oregon law does allow physicians to prescribe lethal drugs. So in the interests of defending the Oregon law, let me now address the charge that assisting in suicide violates the essential moral duty of the medical profession.

Opponents of the Oregon law contend that, in requesting PAS, a person is asking her physician to make a decision that is inappropriate for a physician to make. This is because a physician who must decide whether to assist in a person's suicide is forced to make a judgment about moral and spiritual matters that have nothing to do with medicine. Thus Kass contends that to comply with a request for PAS, "the physician must, willy-nilly, play the part of judge, and his judgments will be decidedly nonmedical and nonprofessional, based on personal standards" (Kass, 2002b: 29–30). And Pellegrino maintains that in prescribing a lethal dose a physician is making the nonmedical judgment that her patient's "life is unworthy of living" (Pellegrino, 2002: 51). Callahan makes the same point when he writes, "The purpose of medicine is not to relieve all the problems of human mortality, the most central and difficult of which is why we have to die at all or die in ways that seem pointless to us . . . This is not the role of medicine because it has no competence to manage the meaning of life and death, only the physical and psychological manifestations of those problems. Medicine's role must be limited to what it can appropriately do, and it has neither the expertise nor the wisdom necessary to respond to the deepest and oldest human questions" (Callahan, 2002: 59).

This criticism seems to me to miss entirely the provisions of the Oregon law. For the Oregon law makes very clear the role physicians are to play in requests for PAS. It says that physicians are to determine if the patient requesting PAS has a terminal disease and if the patient is competent. These are both medical judgments. In order to make them, a physician does not need to make any judgments about "fundamental philosophical and religious matters" pertaining to the meaning of life. The physician is not asked to decide for the patient whether or not life is worth living. The patient makes that decision for herself. Indeed, it is Kass, Pellegrino and Callahan who would take the decision about whether life is worth living out of the hands of the patient. For they are the ones who contend that suicide is always the morally inferior option. It is their view that passes a substantive "philosophical and religious" judgment on how one should cope with terminal disease. The Oregon law, by contrast, asks physicians to make two medical judgments, and then (if the patient meets the relevant criteria) to assist the patient in doing whatever the patient herself has decided about how best to cope with suffering and loss of control at the end of life.[3]

Of course, there may be some physicians who are personally morally opposed to all forms of suicide (just as there are some physicians who are personally morally opposed to abortion), and such physicians should have the option of refusing to participate in any requests for PAS. But there may also be some physicians who believe that an individual should be allowed to make up her own mind about how she wants her life to end, and those physicians' participation in requests for PAS will consist entirely of their making medical judgments about individuals' mental competence and life expectancy, and then facilitating the patient's own decision.

The Duty to Promote Health and the Duty to Reduce Suffering

Kass, Pellegrino and Callahan go on to argue, however, that so long as the physician is knowingly involved in a process that leads to suicide, she is doing something wrong. For, according to Kass, Pellegrino and Callahan, to participate in such a process is to violate the essential moral duty of the medical profession: it is to violate the medical duty to promote health (Callahan, 2002: 58; Kass, 2002b: 20–21).

Kass, Pellegrino and Callahan are certainly correct in saying that physicians have a moral duty to promote health. But there is an obvious problem with claiming that trying to make patients healthy is a physician's *only* moral duty. The problem is that people with terminal diseases cannot be made healthy. A physician cannot heal someone whose disease is lethal and untreatable. So if trying to make patients healthy were their *only* duty, physicians would have no role to play in the care of dying patients. It is clear, however, that physicians do have a role to play in the care of the dying. No one advocates that physicians are obligated by their professional ethic to abandon their patients upon making a terminal diagnosis. On the contrary, it is well recognized that physicians have especially pressing obligations to such patients' care.

In caring for dying patients, one of a physician's principal roles is to reduce suffering. When healing is no longer possible, the reduction of suffering takes center stage.

This duty to reduce the suffering of dying patients is limited in at least one crucial respect. If the dying patient is competent, then physicians should reduce her suffering only in ways to which the patient consents. This limitation on the duty to reduce suffering also applies to the physician's duty to promote health. It is just as wrong for a physician to try to cure a competent patient by undertaking a course of action to which the patient does not agree as it is for a physician to try to reduce the suffering of a competent patient by undertaking a course of action to which the patient does not agree.

Kass, Pellegrino and Callahan acknowledge this role of the physician. They agree that a physician has a moral duty to help to reduce the suffering of a patient with a terminal disease. I presume they would also agree with the limitation on the duty to reduce pain that I have described—that is, that they would agree that physicians should undertake courses of action to reduce the suffering of competent patients with terminal diseases only if the patients have consented to those courses of action. But Kass, Pellegrino and Callahan place another limitation on this duty as well. They argue that a physician's duty to reduce the suffering of patients with terminal diseases can never include assistance in suicide.

So while the Oregon law implies that a physician's duty to reduce the pain of competent patients with terminal diseases should be limited by the patient's own wishes, Kass, Pellegrino and Callahan believe that this duty should also be limited by a prohibition on assisting in suicide. But why do they believe the additional limitation is warranted? Why do they believe that if a patient is competent and

dying, her physician should not be allowed to help her reduce her suffering by suicide, if that is what she requests?

Kass argues that the second limitation on the duty to reduce suffering is warranted because it is impossible to benefit a patient by helping to bring about her death. Thus, the idea that we can make a patient better off by helping to kill must be morally incoherent. As Kass puts it, " 'Better off dead' is logical nonsense—unless, of course, death is not death indeed but instead a gateway to a new and better life beyond. Despite loose talk to the contrary, it is in fact impossible to compare the goodness or badness of one's existence with the goodness or badness of one's 'nonexistence,' because it nonsensically requires treating 'nonexistence' as a condition one is nonetheless able to experience and enjoy . . . [T]o intend and to act for someone's good requires that person's continued existence for the benefit to be received . . . This must be the starting point in discussing all medical benefits: no benefit without a beneficiary" (Kass, 2002b: 34).

Kass claims, then, that it is logically impossible and morally incoherent to try to justify assisted suicide by saying that a person may be better off dead than alive. And perhaps there is some peculiarly literal reading of the words "person" and "better off" that makes Kass's claim true. But there is nothing at all incoherent about a person's preferring a state of affairs in which she is dead to a state of affairs in which she is alive. Throughout human history, many people have believed death is preferable to life under intolerable conditions. And some of the people who have acted on those preferences—people who have sacrificed their lives—have been deemed morally heroic. Even if we refrain from saying that these people are "better off" dead, we can still make perfect sense of the idea that they had morally impeccable reasons for their actions. But what of others who assisted those who sacrificed their lives? What should we say about those who have helped another person undertake a course of action that leads to her death? Again, we might refrain from saying that these others made the person who sacrificed her life "better off." But that does not mean that what those others did is morally incoherent. If a person has morally impeccable reasons to sacrifice her life, then a person who helps her may have reasons that are equally morally impeccable. Just as assisting someone in carrying out the ultimate sacrifice can be morally coherent, so too may helping a dying patient carry out suicide be morally coherent. There is no logical barrier to justifying these courses of action in terms of the wishes and suffering of the person who will die as a result of them. A person who is dying may reasonably prefer to be dead rather than alive. Helping that person take a course of action that leads to her death can accord with the duty to respect the person's autonomy and to reduce her suffering. The fact that the person will not be able to "experience and enjoy" the results of this course of action does not vitiate any attempted justification to help her. Indeed, Kass's own attitude towards certain kinds of care at the end of life reveals that he himself believes that it may be right to help someone undertake a course of action even if she will not able to "experience and enjoy" the results of it. For Kass believes that a physician may be right to undertake courses of action that will increase the likelihood of death (Kass, 2002b: 22 and 37).

But perhaps what Kass means to argue is that participating in PAS violates physicians' first duty of promoting health. It is not clear, however, that that duty *can* be violated when a patient has an incurable, terminal disease. If it is impossible to heal someone, it is difficult to see how the duty to heal her even applies. Physicians have the duty to try to heal patients who can be healed (and who want to be healed). But when a patient cannot be healed, the duty to reduce suffering (in concert with the patient's wishes) takes center stage. The duty to heal no longer seems to be in the picture.

The Principle of Double Effect

Kass, Pellegrino and Callahan would probably object at this point that my conception of the duty to heal is illegitimately attenuated and isolated. That duty, Kass, Pellegrino and Callahan might say, stems from an even more fundamental duty—the duty to life itself. It is life itself to which physicians must always remain devoted. And this devotion must

take precedence over all other considerations, even the attempt to reduce pain or accede to patients' requests.

The idea that physicians must always place morally conclusive value on life itself fits well with Kass, Pellegrino and Callahan's suggestion that all people ought "to live . . . for as long as they can." But this devotion to life seems *not* to fit with a practice that is common to the medical profession today—the practice of participating in the withdrawal of life-sustaining treatment, including food and water, which Kass, Pellegrino and Callahan all explicitly endorse (Kass, 2002b: 22; Pellegrino, 2002: 50–51; Callahan, 2002: 54). A physician who participates in the withdrawal of life-sustaining treatment undertakes a course of action that does not promote life itself. Such a physician is participating in a course of action that will lead to less life rather than more. So how do Kass, Pellegrino and Callahan justify physician participation in the withdrawal of life-sustaining treatment without committing themselves to the justifiability of assisted suicide? How do they fit the withdrawal of life-sustaining treatment into their conception of the moral role of physicians while at the same time keeping PAS out? They do so by deploying the principle of double effect. As Kass explains, "The well-established rule of medical ethics that governs this practice is known as the principle of double effect . . . It is morally licit to embrace a course of action that intends and serves a worthy goal (like relieving suffering), employing means that may have, as an unintended and undesired consequences, some harm or evil for the patient. Such cases are distinguished from the morally illicit efforts that indirectly 'relieve suffering' by deliberately providing a lethal dose of a drug and thus eliminating the sufferer" (Kass, 2002b: 37).

So the argument that the Oregon law conflicts with physicians' moral duty presupposes the principle of double effect. Indeed, the principle of double effects seems to be doing more work in this argument than the duty to heal or promote life. For Kass, Pellegrino and Callahan's endorsement of the withdrawal of life-sustaining treatment shows that they accept physician participation in courses of action that are intended neither to heal nor to promote life, which seems to imply (in contrast to some of their other comments) that they do not take the duty to heal or promote life to be always applicable to medical practice.

Now the principle of double effect is a general moral principle. It is not unique to the world of medical ethics. This is worth noting because opponents of the Oregon law sometimes contend that their arguments against PAS are based on the special moral status of physicians. Callahan, for instance, often relies on claims about the "purpose of medicine" or "medicine's role" (Callahan, 2002: 59) and Kass maintains that his "argument rests on understanding the special moral character of the medical profession and the ethical obligations it entails" (Kass, 2002b: 17). If a person really understands the intrinsic moral character of medicine, opponents of the Oregon law suggest, she will never accept PAS. We now find, however, that their arguments against PAS depend on the principle of double effect. And a defense of that principle cannot be grounded in the "special moral character of the medical profession." The anti-PAS position is based, in other words, not on the unique moral role of medicine but on a contentious non-medical moral principle.

This raises the question of whether there are in fact decisive grounds for accepting the principle of double effect. I myself think that the principle is extremely problematic. It relies on the drawing of a very sharp distinction between, on the one hand, the intentions and goals of all the physicians who engage in terminal sedation or withdraw food and water and, on the other hand, the intentions and goals of all the physicians who would prescribe a lethal dose of drugs. It seems to me, however, that there is no principled way of distinguishing the morally relevant features of the intentions and goals of these two groups of physicians, no non-question-begging reason to think that there is some feature of the actions of all those who would prescribe lethal doses that is inconsistent with the practice of medicine but is also absent from the actions of all those who engage in terminal sedation or withdraw food and water. Unfortunately, an extensive treatment of the principle of double effect is beyond the scope of this article. Note, however, that even if the principle is generally defensible, that on its own will not vindicate Kass, Pellegrino and Callahan's argument against the Oregon law. For not

all defensible moral principles ought to be enforced by law. Some moral questions are so difficult, profound or personal that the law rightly allows each person the opportunity to answer them for herself. If reasonable people can disagree about the soundness of a moral principle, the best public policy might be one that is neutral between a person's living in accord with it or not. And it seems that the principle of double effect is something with which reasonable people can disagree. Indeed, the traditionally most influential defenses of the principle are based on religio-theological commitments. But such religio-theological commitments are not shared by every reasonable person, and they are not typically thought of as the basis for public policy in a secular society. At the very least, the opponents of PAS must give us reasons for believing not merely that the principle of double effect is philosophically defensible but also that it ought to shape our legislation concerning end-of-life decisions.

Kass's claim that the principle of double effect is a "well-established rule of medical ethics" does not help to make the case. For not all medical ethicists or physicians agree that the essential moral duty of physicians implies that the principle of double effect should be used to forbid PAS. Miller, Brody and Quill, for instance, have argued that assisting in suicide can be entirely consistent with the integrity of the medical profession (see Quill, 1991; Miller & Brody, 1995; Quill *et al.,* 1997).

Moreover, when the principle of double effect is invoked in medical ethics, it is usually done so in the context of explaining the prohibition on PAS. To say that the principle of double effect is a "well-established rule of medical ethics" is to say little more than that physicians have traditionally been prohibited from assisting in suicide. But the pressing question is whether physicians *should* be prohibited from assisting in suicide. The fact that PAS has been prohibited in the past does not constitute an argument for continuing to prohibit it in the future.

But the greatest weakness of the attempt to use the principle of double effect to defeat the Oregon law is that the principle will imply the wrongness of PAS only on the assumption that it is bad that a person with a terminal disease die sooner rather than later. The only business the principle of double effect is in is telling us when it is permissible to perform an action that has foreseeable bad consequences and when it is impermissible. If an action's consequences are not bad, the principle is completely inapplicable. Now the opponents of PAS believe that it is bad if a terminal patient dies sooner rather than later, and it is on the basis of the badness of such a death that they deploy the principle of double effect. But many proponents of PAS disagree, holding that in certain circumstances it is not bad if a terminal patient dies sooner rather than later. Of course, there is a great deal of dispute about which side is correct—about whether it is necessarily bad that a terminal patient dies sooner rather than later (this was one of the topics of the first part of this article). But unless that issue is resolved in their favor, opponents of PAS cannot use the principle of double effect to argue against the Oregon law. Even if the principle is generally philosophically defensible, and even if it should be enshrined in law (two big ifs), we still will not have reason to prohibit PAS unless there are also independent grounds for thinking that it is always bad for a terminal, competent patient to die sooner rather than later. The principle of double effect is downstream of the central justificatory question of whether it is bad that a terminal, competent patient commits suicide.

The final point I want to make about the principle of double effect is that it cannot be used to bolster another significant criticism of PAS that Kass, Pellegrino and Callahan present. This other criticism is that although it may seem as though the Oregon law leaves the decision of whether or not to request PAS entirely up to the patient, in fact the law leads her physician to make that decision for her. In theory, the Oregon law restricts the physician's role simply to medical judgments. But in practice (according to Kass, Pellegrino and Callahan's criticism), the physician's own values will pressure the patient into whatever decision finally gets made. The patient's thinking will be "easily and subtly manipulated" by the physician (Kass, 2002b: 24). The physician will exercise "subtle coercion" that will undermine "the patient autonomy that assisted suicide and euthanasia presume to protect" (Pellegrino, 2002: 48).

Now in claiming that the legalization of PAS will increase the chance of manipulation and coercion,

Kass, Pellegrino and Callahan are making an essentially consequentialist argument.[4] They are contending not that PAS is intrinsically morally wrong but that it will lead to morally unacceptable consequences. This consequentialist argument against PAS has to be taken very seriously. If it turns out that the Oregon law increases manipulation and coercion, then there will be at least one consequentialist but still extremely important reason to reject the law.

It seems to me, however, that the fact that physicians can ethically participate in the withdrawal of life-sustaining treatment gives us at least some reason for doubting that the legalization of PAS will necessarily lead to increased manipulation and coercion. For if allowing physicians to participate in the withdrawal of food and water does not necessarily increase manipulation and coercion, why think that allowing physicians to participate in PAS will do so? If it is possible for the option of withdrawing life-sustaining treatment to exist without an increase in manipulation and coercion, why should it not also be possible for the option of PAS to exist with an increase in manipulation and coercion?

We have seen, of course, that opponents of the Oregon law believe that there is an intrinsic moral difference between assisting in suicide and withdrawing life-support, a difference explained by the principle of double effect. But they cannot rely on that putative intrinsic difference when they are making the consequentialist argument that the Oregon law will lead physicians to manipulate and coerce patients into choosing PAS. For this consequentialist argument is based on claims about the real-world effects of the Oregon law. And we cannot determine what those effects will be simply through an examination of the morally contentious principle of double effect.

CONCLUSION

I have presented reasons for thinking that there is nothing intrinsically morally wrong with PAS as it is currently practiced in Oregon. In the first part of this article, I have tried to show that there are morally reasonable grounds to restrict PAS to individuals who are competent and have less than six months to live. In the second part, I have tried to show that participation in PAS does not necessarily violate physicians' professional integrity. The value of autonomy and physicians' duty to reduce the suffering of dying patients together imply that PAS can sometimes be a morally acceptable option.

NOTES

1. Of course this distinction is far from sharp. For one thing, the combination of all of your little decisions does affect in a non-negligible way the shape of your overall life. For another thing, there are many decisions that fall somewhere between the big and the little, decisions that are not as momentous as deciding to get married but are nonetheless more important than deciding to eat the blue jello. There is a continuum between big decisions and little ones, not an absolute cut-off. Still, some decisions are clearly closer to one end of the continuum rather than the other, and we often find it natural and easy enough to draw such a distinction.

2. Showing that it might be morally acceptable for a person to commit suicide does not on its own show that it might be morally acceptable for someone else to assist in the suicide. There can be goals that are morally acceptable for me to pursue but that nonetheless it would morally unacceptable for others to help me pursue. It is, for instance, morally acceptable for me to try to win a competitive sporting event but it is morally unacceptable for a referee to try to help me win. I believe, however, that the burden of proof lies with those who would argue that assistance is morally unacceptable. If a course of action is morally acceptable for me to pursue, then generally there will be no absolute moral reasons forbidding anyone else from helping me to pursue it (which is not to say that I necessarily have the *right* to demand assistance in the pursuit of my morally acceptable goal). Those who contend that it is morally unacceptable to assist someone in performing a morally acceptable act will need to explain the added moral feature that makes assistance unacceptable in that particular circumstance. In the case of a competitive sporting event, it is morally unacceptable for a referee to try to help me win because (as competitive sporting events are zero-sum games) it is unfair to the side against which I am competing.

3. So I disagree with Callahan in that I hold that allowing PAS is "socially neutral" on the question of whether "some suffering is meaningless and unnecessary"

(Callahan, 2002: 57). A society that allows PAS, it seems to me, does not take a position on whether it is better or worse for a dying, competent person to commit suicide; such a society facilitates each person's making that decision for herself. Callahan, in contrast, bases his opposition to society's allowing PAS on a non-neutral view of the positive value of suffering (Callahan, 2002: 58–59).

4. Perhaps Kass, Pellegrino and Callahan would argue that it is misleading to say that worries about physician manipulation and coercion are entirely "consequentialist." For they may contend that the role physicians play in patient decision making would make it impossible for them *not* to exert undue pressure on patients for whom PAS is an option. But the claim that it would be impossible for physicians not to exert undue pressure depends upon a certain view of what is essential to the role of physicians, a view others might not share (see, for example, Miller & Brody, 1995). That claim also seems to me to be contradicted by the fact that the possibility of the withdrawal of life-sustaining treatment does not necessarily produce undue pressure on patients.

REFERENCES

Callahan, D. (2002). Reason, self-determination, and physician-assisted suicide. In K. Foley & H. Hendin (Eds), *The case against assisted suicide.* Baltimore and London: Johns Hopkins University Press.

Kass, L. (2002a). *Life, liberty and the defense of dignity.* San Francisco: Encounter Books.

Kass, L. (2002b). 'I will give no deadly drug': Why doctors must not kill. In K. Foley & H. Hendin (Eds), *The case against assisted suicide.* Baltimore and London: Johns Hopkins University Press.

Miller, F. G., & Brody, H. (1995). Professional integrity and physician-assisted death. *Hastings Center Report, 25,* 8–17.

Pellegrino, E. (2002). Compassion is not enough. In K. Foley & H. Hendin (Eds), *The case against assisted suicide.* Baltimore and London: Johns Hopkins University Press.

Quill, T. E. (1991). Death and dignity: A case of individualized decision making. *New England Journal of Medicine, 324,* 691–694.

Quill, T. E., Dresser, R., & Brock, D. W. (1997). The rule of double effect—A critique of its role in end-of-life decision making. *The New England Journal of Medicine, 337,* 1768–1771.

Sade, R. M., & Marshall, M. F. (1996). Legistrothanatry: a new specialty for assisting in death. *Perspectives in Biology and Medicine, 39,* 222–224.

READING QUESTIONS

1. Gill first suggests that we can think of the value of autonomy as simply a person's ability to make decisions for herself. But Kass—a PAS opponent—thinks PAS is tragically self-contradictory with regard to autonomy. What does Kass mean by this?

2. Explain the hardline libertarian response to opponents of PAS who claim it leads to absurd permissible outcomes such as selling oneself into slavery or electing PAS when fully healthy.

3. How does Gill argue for the claim that PAS of a terminal individual is not a case of destroying the ability to make future decisions? How do his opponents respond?

4. Gill argues that terminally ill patients have few opportunities left to make big decisions. How does Gill reply to the objection that a terminally ill patient may, in fact, have profoundly important decisions yet to make?

5. How does Gill describe the role of the physician under the Oregon law, and how is this different from the view taken by PAS opponents?

6. Gill claims that opponents of PAS must rely on the general principle of double effect to support their position, rather than an appeal to the 'special moral character of the medical profession' to promote life. What reasons does he give for this claim?

7. Why does Gill maintain that we must first determine whether it is bad that a terminal patient dies sooner rather than later before we can use the principle of double effect to argue against the Oregon law?

DISCUSSION QUESTIONS

1. Should we agree with Gill's candle analogy? What is his point, and what are the morally significant differences, if any, between the dying candle and the dying patient?

2. Gill gives his 'big decisions' argument to refute the claim by PAS opponents that the value of autonomy cannot be used to support Oregon law. Discuss the big decision argument and the extent to which it succeeds in meeting the PAS opponents' claim.

3. Discuss the logical point made by some opponents of PAS that it is impossible to be better off dead than alive. Even if the logical argument were sound, are there other reasons to claim that suicide for a terminally ill patient is morally justified?

4. Do you agree with Gill that the general principle of double effect is extremely problematic? Identify his reasons for this claim and discuss to what extent you think his argument succeeds or not. How does this argument support Gill's view that public policy ought to remain neutral with respect to PAS?

ADDITIONAL RESOURCES

Web Resources

Pew Research Center, <http://pewresearch.org/>. A nonpartisan site that conducts public opinion polls on public policy issues. One can find numerous links from this site to articles about attitudes toward physician-assisted suicide.

Young, Robert, "Voluntary Euthanasia," <http://plato.stanford.edu/entries/voluntary-euthanasia/>. An overview of the debate over voluntary euthanasia.

Authored Books

Dworkin, Gerald, R. G. Frey, and Sissela Bok (eds.) *Euthanasia and Physician Assisted Suicide: For and Against* (Cambridge: Cambridge University Press, 1998). In this two-part book Dworkin and Frey defend the practices of euthanasia and physician-assisted suicide, and Bok argues against these practices.

Keown, John, *Euthanasia, Ethics and Public Policy: An Argument Against Legalisation* (Cambridge: Cambridge University Press, 2002). As the title indicates, Keown makes a case for not legalizing euthanasia and assisted suicide.

Orfali, Robert, *Death with Dignity: The Case for Legalizing Physician-Assisted Dying and Euthanasia* (Minneapolis, MN: Mill City Press, 2011). Employing recent data from Oregon and the Netherlands, Orfali defends the legalization of physician-assisted suicide, answering critics who oppose PAS by appealing to considerations of the integrity of medicine, the sanctity of life, and slippery slopes.

Edited Collections and Articles

Battin, Margaret P., Rosamond Rhodes, and Anita Silvers (eds.), *Physician Assisted Suicide: Expanding the Debate* (New York: Routledge, 1998). This collection features 23 essays, mostly by philosophers, debating the moral, social, and legal implications of physician-assisted suicide. The essays are organized into five parts: (1) Conceptual Issues, (2) Considering Those at Risk, (3) Considering the Practice of Medicine, (4) Considering the Impact of Legalization, and (5) Considering Religious Perspectives.

Birnbacher, Dieter and Edgar Dahl (eds.), *Giving Death a Helping Hand: Physician-Assisted Suicide and Public Policy: An International Perspective*. International Library of Ethics, Law, and the New Medicine. (New York: Springer, 2008). This anthology includes 13 essays by a broad array of authors, including academics and health care practitioners, and incorporates various international perspectives on physician-assisted suicide.

Foley, K. M. and H. Hendin (eds.), *The Case against Assisted Suicide: For the Right to End-of-Life Care* (Baltimore: Johns Hopkins University Press, 2002). Fourteen essays by professionals in law, medicine, and bioethics arguing against the legalization of physician-assisted suicide.

Hastings Center Report, vol. 22, March–April, 1992. This issue of HCR includes the entire version of Dan Brock's defense of voluntary active euthanasia. Brock's position is opposed in an essay by Daniel Callahan in that same issue.

Moreno, Jonathan D. (ed.), *Arguing Euthanasia: The Controversy Over Mercy Killing, Assisted Suicide, And The "Right To Die"* (New York: Touchstone, 1995). This collection features both outspoken advocates and critics debating the moral and social implications of euthanasia and assisted suicide.

9 } The Ethical Treatment of Animals

Nonhuman animals are used by humans as sources of food, clothing, entertainment, experimentation, and companionship. Most everyone thinks that there are moral limits to how we use animals, that cruelty to animals is morally wrong. For example, in 2004, California governor Arnold Schwarzenegger signed into law a bill which, when it took effect in 2012, banned completely the production and sale of foie gras in California. Considered a gourmet delicacy, foie gras (French for "fatty liver") is produced by force-feeding ducks or geese so that their livers enlarge up to ten times their normal size. In the process, these animals experience ruptured necks as well as painful enlargement and rupturing of internal organs owing to the intense pressure caused by the forced feeding. Other cases are more difficult. In 2008 U.S. military researchers dressed pigs in armor and subjected them to various explosions in order to study the link between roadside bombs and brain damage. The point of the study, of course, was to help benefit U.S. soldiers fighting in Iraq and Afghanistan. Pigs were selected because their brains, hearts, and lungs are similar to those of humans. Are such experiments aimed at benefiting humans morally justified? Furthermore, what about the many other uses humans have for (nonhuman) animals, uses that do not necessarily inflict extreme pain on animals? Is there anything wrong with, say, painlessly killing and eating an animal for the taste of the meat?

In order to properly focus the ethical dispute over the use of animals, let us consider these two questions:

- Do any animals have direct moral standing?
- If so, what does this imply about various practices such as eating meat and using animals as subjects for experimentation?

In order to introduce the readings in this chapter, let us first explain what is meant in the first question by talk of "direct moral standing."

1. DIRECT MORAL STANDING

For purposes of introducing the selections both in this chapter and in the next, let us distinguish between two types of moral standing: *direct* and *indirect*. Roughly, for something to have **direct moral standing** is for it, independently of its relation to other things or creatures, to possess features in virtue of which it deserves to be given moral consideration by agents who are capable of making moral choices. Different moral theories represent direct moral standing in different ways. To claim that a creature has rights is one way of explaining how it is that it has direct moral standing. So is the claim that something has intrinsic or inherent value. And to claim that we have duties *to* something and not just duties *with regard* to it is yet another way of representing the idea that the item in question has direct moral standing. Of course, if something has direct moral standing—whether because it has rights, intrinsic value, or is something toward which we have duties—there must be some features or properties of the item in question in virtue of which it has such standing. Just what those features are is what is most philosophically contentious in debates about the ethical treatment of animals. As we shall see in the next chapter, this same general issue arises in the controversy over abortion.

Direct moral standing contrasts with indirect moral standing. For something to have mere **indirect moral standing** is for it to deserve moral consideration only because it is related to something with direct moral standing. Such items, including most obviously one's material possessions, do not themselves have features that would make taking, changing, or destroying them a wrong that is done *to or against* them. Rather, whatever moral requirements we have *with regard to* our treatment of material possessions is dependent upon their relation to beings that have direct moral standing.

As mentioned at the outset of this chapter, most everyone agrees that animals ought not to be treated cruelly. But being against the cruel treatment of animals does not require one to think that they have direct moral standing. The real philosophical dispute, then, which is reflected in the first question listed earlier, is whether any of them have what we are calling direct moral standing. If they do, then presumably it will be possible to launch arguments against various forms of treatment including killing and eating them and using them for certain sorts of experimentation.[1] But do they?

2. SPECIESISM?

Racism and sexism are familiar forms of morally unjustified prejudice. These practices involve the systematic discrimination against the interests of members of some racial groups because of their race in the case of racism and against the members of one sex because of their sex in the case of sexism, respectively. Because people of all races and both men and women have direct moral standing, the sort of discrimination characteristic of racism and sexism is morally unjustified. These types of discrimination are the subject of chapter 6.

The basic idea of systematic discrimination against the interests of members of some group has been extended by some philosophers to the treatment of animals. **Speciesism**, then, refers to the systematic discrimination against the members of some species by the members of another species. And certainly such discrimination goes on today. But whether such discrimination is morally wrong depends upon such questions as whether any of the nonhuman animals who are the victims of discrimination have direct moral standing. The articles included in this chapter are focused on this central issue.

3. THEORY MEETS PRACTICE

In our chapter's readings, we find appeals to consequentialism, rights, the ethics of prima facie duty, and virtue ethics prominent in debates about the ethical treatment of animals. Let us briefly consider each of these approaches.

Consequentialism

Utilitarianism is the most familiar form of consequentialism that has played an important role in arguments over the ethical treatment of animals. According to one standard version of the principle of utility, an action is wrong just in case (and because) performing it will likely fail to maximize happiness impartially considered. Moreover, for traditional utilitarians, happiness (and unhappiness) over a period of time in a creature's life is a matter of its experiences of pleasure and experiences of displeasure or pain. Further, since many nonhuman animals can experience pleasure and pain, these utilitarians conclude that they have direct moral standing and must be factored into our decision making. Utilitarian arguments, of course, depend heavily on factual claims about the overall comparative effects of contemplated courses of action. Gaverick Matheny argues on utilitarian grounds that when we estimate overall net happiness for all sentient creatures, we ought to conclude that many of our present practices involving the use of animals are morally wrong. Critics of this line of argument, whether or not they share a commitment to utilitarianism, challenge the utility calculation. In our readings, Tom Regan and Jordan Curnutt raise this calculation worry. And, of course, there are those who reject a strictly utilitarian approach to moral issues.

Rights Approaches

According to a rights-focused approach that would accord animals direct moral standing, the nonhuman animals in question possess the relevant characteristics that qualify them for having rights, including a right to life, to some kinds of liberty, and perhaps to whatever kind of life would allow them some measure of happiness. This approach is famously defended by Tom Regan, but its plausibility requires a defense of the nature of rights, their content, and their relative strengths—topics that are controversial. Carl Cohen argues that Regan's defense fails and that moral rights remain exclusively within the human realm. Mary Ann Warren attempts to answer various questions about rights, arguing that although animals do have rights and thus have direct moral standing, their rights are generally weaker than the corresponding rights of human beings. Nevertheless, disputes over basic questions about rights are often taken as a sticking point for rights-based approaches to the ethical treatment of animals.

Ethics of Prima Facie Duty

One might attempt to dodge the worries just raised against utilitarian and rights approaches by working with an ethic of prima facie duty. Certainly, if there are prima facie duties, one of them is the duty not to cause harm. And in our readings, Jordan Curnutt appeals to this duty in his defense of vegetarianism. His argument, then, requires defending certain factual claims about animals (they can be harmed), as well as claims about their treatment in meat production. Furthermore, since the whole point of a duty's being prima facie is that it can be overridden, Curnutt's argument requires defense of the claim (which he offers) that the prima facie duty not to harm, as applied to animals, is not overridden by various competing concerns.

Virtue Ethics

Although none of the readings in this chapter appeal to a virtue-based moral theory and its application to the ethical treatment of animals, the article by Thomas E. Hill Jr. in the final chapter, on the environment, does take a virtue approach to environmental issues. His approach, which appeals specifically to vices that represent a lack of the virtue of humility, could easily be extended to the case of animals.

NOTE

1. Although, even if some animals do have direct moral standing, it does not automatically follow that using them for such things as food and experimentation is wrong. For instance, direct moral standing may come in degrees so that the members of some species only have it to some small degree, in which case perhaps their use by humans under certain circumstances is not, all things considered, morally wrong.

GAVERICK MATHENY

Utilitarianism and Animals

Matheny defends what he calls a "strong principle of equal consideration of interests" according to which, in making correct moral decisions, one must give equal weight to the like interests of all creatures who will be affected by one's actions. Given that many nonhuman animals have interests, it follows from the principle just mentioned that they deserve to have their interests in being free from pain and suffering count as much as the like interests of human beings. Matheny proceeds to explain what implications his principle has for such practices as meat eating, experimental use of animal subjects, and our treatment of wildlife.

Recommended Reading: consequentialism, chap. 1, sec. 2A.

From Gaverick Matheny, "Utilitarianism and Animals," in Peter Singer, ed., *In Defense of Animals: The Second Wave* (Oxford: Blackwell Publishing, 2006).

In North America and Europe, around 17 billion land animals were raised and killed during 2001 to feed us. Somewhere between 50 and 100 million other animals were killed in laboratories, while another 30 million were killed in fur farms. The vast majority of these animals were forced to live and die in conditions most of us would find morally repugnant. Yet their use—and the use of comparable numbers of animals every year—has been justified by the belief that nonhuman animals do not deserve significant moral consideration. Several plausible ethical theories argue that this belief is mistaken. Utilitarianism is one such theory that condemns much of our present use of animals. If this theory is reasonable, then most of us should change the way we live.

ETHICS

There is broad consensus within both religious and secular ethics that an ethical life respects virtues like fairness, justice, and benevolence. At the heart of these virtues lies a more basic principle: I cannot reasonably claim that my interests matter more than yours simply because my interests are *mine*. My interests may matter more to *me*, but I cannot claim they matter more in any objective sense. From the ethical point of view, everyone's interests deserve equal consideration.

In the Judeo-Christian tradition, this sentiment is embodied in "The Golden Rule" attributed to Moses: "Love your neighbor as you love yourself" (Matthew 22:39) and in the Talmud, "What is hateful to you, do not to your fellow men" (Shabbat 31a). In the secular tradition, this sentiment is embodied in the "principle of equal consideration of interests": "Act in such a way that the like interests of everyone affected by your action are given equal weight." This phrase may lack the elegance of Scripture but conveys the same general idea. The principle of equal consideration of interests asks that we put ourselves in the shoes of each person affected by an action and compare the strengths of her or his interests to those of our own—regardless of *whose* interests they are. To be

fair, just, and benevolent, any ethical rule we adopt should respect this principle.

UTILITARIANISM

Utilitarianism is an ethical theory with the rule, "act in such a way as to maximize the expected satisfaction of interests in the world, equally considered." This rule is a logical extension of the principle of equal consideration of interests in that it says I should sum up the interests of all the parties affected by all my possible actions and choose the action that results in the greatest net satisfaction of interests. Another way of thinking about this is to imagine which actions I would choose if I had to live the lives of all those affected by me. Because the rule of utilitarianism represents a simple operation upon a principle of equality, it is perhaps the most minimal ethical rule we could derive. Utilitarianism is said to be universalist, welfarist, consequentialist, and aggregative. Each of these properties needs some explanation.

Utilitarianism is *universalist* because it takes into account the interests of all those who are affected by an action, regardless of their nationality, gender, race, or other traits that we find, upon reflection, are not morally relevant. The rule "act in such a way as to maximize the expected satisfaction of interests" is one we would be willing to have everyone adopt. Some writers have even claimed, forcefully, this is the only such rule.

Utilitarianism is *welfarist* because it defines what is ethically "good" in terms of people's welfare, which we can understand as the satisfaction (or dissatisfaction) of people's interests. Most of us are interested in good health, a good job, and our friends and family, among other things. We could reduce many if not all of these interests to something more general, such as an interest in a happy, pleasurable, relatively painless life. I will use the word "interests" to describe whatever it is that we value here—all those things that matter to us. We can safely say we all have an interest, at a minimum, in a pleasurable life, relatively free of pain. And from experience, we know when our happiness is decreased, as when we suffer acute pain, any other interests we may have tend to recede into the background. That being so, utilitarianism promotes an ethical rule that seeks to satisfy our interests, particularly those in a pleasurable, relatively painless life.

Utilitarianism is *consequentialist* because it evaluates the rightness or wrongness of an action by that action's expected consequences: the degree to which an action satisfies interests. These consequences can often be predicted and compared accurately with little more than common sense.

Finally, utilitarianism is said to be *aggregative* because it adds up the interests of all those affected by an action. To make a decision, I need to weigh the intensity, duration, and number of interests affected by all of my possible actions. I choose the action that results in the greatest net satisfaction of interests—"the greatest good for the greatest number." Utilitarian decisions thus involve a kind of accounting ledger, with our like interests serving as a common currency. This is no easy exercise. But, as we'll see, in many of our most important moral judgments, even a rough comparison of interests is enough to make a wise decision.

THE ADVANTAGES OF UTILITARIANISM

Utilitarianism has several advantages over other ethical theories. First, its consequentialism encourages us to make full use of information about the world as it is. If you have access to the same information as I do, you can argue with me about how I ought to act. This lends utilitarianism a greater degree of empirical objectivity than most ethical theories enjoy.

Some ethical theories hold less regard for consequences than does utilitarianism and address their ethical rules either to actions themselves or to the motivations prompting them. These rules would often lead to misery if they were followed without exception. For instance, we would not have praised Miep Gies, the woman who hid Anne Frank and

her family from the Nazis, had she followed the rule "never tell a lie" and turned the Franks over to the Nazis. Most of us believe the kind of deception Gies engaged in was justified, even heroic. So when should you tell a lie? When the consequences of not telling the lie are worse than the consequences of telling it. To decide otherwise would be to engage in a kind of rule worship at the expense of other people's interests. Because we are often forced to choose between the lesser of two evils, any rule about particular actions—lying, promising, killing, and so on—can lead to terrible results.

At the same time, it would be foolhardy to live without any general principles. I would not be an efficient utilitarian if, every time I approached a stoplight, I weighed the consequences of respecting traffic laws. This would waste time and regularly lead to poor results. It would be best if I adopted "rules of thumb" that, in general, promote the greatest satisfaction of interests by guiding my actions in ordinary situations. Such rules of thumb would likely include most of our common views about right and wrong. However, in extraordinary situations, these rules of thumb should be overridden, as in the case of Miep Gies. In this way, utilitarianism supports most of our common moral intuitions while, at the same time, overriding them in important cases where following them could be catastrophic.

Utilitarianism's aggregative properties offer additional advantages. Our moral decisions regularly benefit one individual at the expense or neglect of another. For instance, in North America and Europe, some citizens are taxed in order to provide financial support to the disabled, among others. Is it ethical to benefit one group with this tax while another suffers some expense? While such conflicts arise regularly in public policy, they also arise in our personal choices. In deciding to spend $1,000 on a piece of artwork instead of on a donation to a charity, I know a charity now has less money with which to help those in need than it would had I given it my $1,000. Is it ethical to have benefited myself while neglecting others? Utilitarianism, in allowing some exchange of costs and benefits, can help us answer questions like these, whereas many other ethical theories cannot.

Many of the moral stances implied by utilitarianism are familiar and widely accepted. Historically, utilitarians were among the most outpoken opponents of slavery and the strongest proponents of women's suffrage, public education, public health, and other social democratic institutions. In recent years, utilitarians have advanced some of the strongest moral arguments for charity to the poor and sick. At the same time, however, utilitarianism leads us to moral views many of us do not already accept. Prominent among these are moral views regarding nonhuman animals.

DO ANY NONHUMANS HAVE INTERESTS?

By the principle of equal consideration of interests, interests matter, regardless of *whose* interests they are. We can agree that we all have an interest, at a minimum, in a pleasurable life, relatively free of pain. Pleasure and pain *matter* to all of us who feel them. As such, it follows that we are obliged to consider, at a minimum, the interests of all those who are capable of feeling pleasure and pain—that is, all those who are sentient. We can then say that sentience is a sufficient condition for having interests and having those interests considered equally.

Are any nonhuman animals sentient? That is, are any nonhumans biologically capable of feeling pleasure and pain? There are few people today, including biologists, who seriously doubt the answer is yes. For most of us, our common sense and experience with animals, especially dogs and cats, are sufficient to let us answer affirmatively. However, our common sense and experience cannot always be trusted, and so we should look for further evidence that animals other than ourselves are sentient.

How do we know that other *human beings* are sentient? We cannot know for certain. My friend who shrieks after burning himself on the stove could be a very sophisticated robot, programmed to respond to certain kinds of stimuli with a shriek. But, because my friend is biologically similar to me, his awareness of pain would offer a biological advantage, his behavior is similar to my own when I am in pain, and his behavior is associated with a stimulus that would be painful for me, I have good reason to believe my friend feels pain.

We have similar reasons for believing that many nonhuman animals feel pain. Human beings evolved from other species. Those parts of the brain involved in sensing pleasure and pain are older than human beings and common to mammals and birds, and probably also to fish, reptiles, and amphibians. For most of these animals, awareness of pain would serve important functions, including learning from past mistakes.

Like my potentially robotic friend, these animals also respond to noxious stimuli much the same way we do. They avoid these stimuli and shriek, cry, or jerk when they can't escape them. The stimuli that cause these behaviors are ones we associate with pain, such as extreme pressure, heat, and tissue damage. These biological and behavioral indications do not guarantee sentience, but they are about as good as those that we have for my human friend.

Whether invertebrates such as insects feel pain is far less certain, as these animals do not possess the same equipment to feel pain and pleasure that we have; and, by their having short life-cycles in stereotyped environments, the biological advantages of being sentient are less obvious.

That some nonhuman animals feel pain needn't imply that their *interests* in not feeling pain are as intense as our own. It's possible that ordinary, adult humans are capable of feeling more intense pain than some nonhumans because we are self-conscious and can anticipate or remember pain with greater fidelity than can other animals. It could also be argued, however, that our rationality allows us to distance ourselves from pain or give pain a purpose (at the dentist's office, for instance) in ways that are not available to other animals. Moreover, even if other animals' interests in not feeling pain are less intense than our own, the sum of a larger number of interests of lesser intensity (such as 100,000 people's interests in $1 each) can still outweigh the sum of a smaller number of interests of greater intensity (such as my interest in $100,000).

So it is possible, even in those cases where significant human interests are at stake, for the interests of animals, considered equally, to outweigh our own. As we will see, however, in most cases involving animals, there are no significant human interests at stake, and the right course of action is easy to judge.

SOME REBUTTALS

Philosophers have never been immune to the prejudices of their day. In the past, some advanced elaborate arguments against civil rights, religious tolerance, and the abolition of slavery. Similarly, some philosophers today seek to justify our current prejudices against nonhuman animals, typically not by challenging the claim that some nonhumans are sentient, but rather by arguing that sentience is not a sufficient condition for moral consideration. Common to their arguments is the notion that moral consideration should be extended only to those individuals who also possess certain levels of rationality, intelligence, or language, or to those capable of reciprocating moral agreements, which likewise implies a certain level of rationality, intelligence, or language.

It is not clear how these arguments could succeed. First, why would an animal's lack of normal human levels of rationality, intelligence, or language give us license to ignore her or his pain? Second, if rationality, intelligence, or language were necessary conditions for moral consideration, why could we not give moral preference to humans who are more rational, intelligent, or verbose than other humans? Third, many adult mammals and birds exhibit greater rationality and intelligence than do human infants. Some nonhuman animals, such as apes, possess language, while some humans do not. Should human infants, along with severely retarded and brain-damaged humans, be excluded from moral consideration, while apes, dolphins, dogs, pigs, parrots, and other nonhumans are included? Efforts to limit moral consideration to human beings based on the possession of certain

traits succeed neither in including all humans nor in excluding all nonhuman animals.

The most obvious property shared among all human beings that excludes all nonhuman animals is our membership of a particular biological group: the species *Homo sapiens*. What is significant about species membership that could justify broad differences in moral consideration? Why is the line drawn at species, rather than genus, subspecies, or some other biological division? There have been no convincing answers to these questions. If species membership is a justification for excluding sentient animals from moral consideration, then why not race or gender? Why could one not argue that an individual's membership of the biological group "human female" excludes that individual from moral consideration? One of the triumphs of modern ethics has been recognizing that an individual's membership of a group, alone, is not morally relevant. The cases against racism and sexism depended upon this point, as the case against speciesism does now.

If a nonhuman animal can feel pleasure and pain, then that animal possesses interests. To think otherwise is to pervert the sense in which we understand pleasure and pain, feelings that matter to us and to others who experience them. At a minimum, a sentient animal has an interest in a painless, pleasurable life. And if he or she possesses this interest, then he or she deserves no less consideration of his or her interests than we give to our own. This view, while modern in its popularity, is not new. The utilitarian Jeremy Bentham held it at a time when black slaves were treated much as we now treat nonhuman animals:

> The day may come when the rest of the animal creation may acquire those rights which never could have been witholden from them but by the hand of tyranny. The French have already discovered that the blackness of the skin is no reason why a human being should be abandoned without redress to the caprice of a tormentor. It may one day come to be recognized that the number of the legs, the villosity of the skin, or the termination of the *os sacrum*, are reasons equally insufficient for abandoning a sensitive being to the same fate. What else is it that should trace the insuperable line? Is it the faculty of reason, or perhaps the faculty

of discourse? But a full-grown horse or dog is beyond comparison a more rational, as well as a more conversable animal, than an infant of a day, or a week, or even a month, old. But suppose they were otherwise, what would it avail? The question is not, Can they reason? nor Can they talk? but, Can they suffer? (1988 [1823]: 1988: 310–11)

The principle of equal consideration of interests requires we count the interests of any individual equally with the like interests of any other. The racist violates this rule by giving greater weight to the interests of members of her own race. The sexist violates this rule by giving greater weight to the interests of members of his own sex. Similarly, the speciesist violates this rule by giving greater weight to the interests of members of his own species.

If an animal is sentient and if sentience is a sufficient condition for having interests, then we should consider that animal's interests equal to our own when making ethical decisions.... Animals are used in a wide range of human activities, including agriculture, product testing, medical and scientific research, entertainment, hunting and fishing, the manufacture of clothing, and as our pets. In most of these activities, we treat animals in ways that do not show proper regard for their interests and thereby are unethical. I will limit discussion here to our treatment of animals in agriculture, laboratories, and the wild.

FOOD

It is difficult...to convey factory farming practices in print, so I encourage you either to visit a factory farm or to watch video footage from these facilities at the website listed at the end of this essay. Factory farm conditions are believed by many to be so inhumane that it would be better if animals living in these facilities had not existed. Deciding what makes a life worth living is no simple matter, but we can think how we consider whether or not to euthanize a hopelessly sick dog or cat.

The pain experienced by animals in factory farms is likely greater than that experienced by many of those sick dogs and cats we choose to euthanize, as factory-farmed animals often experience an entire lifetime of pain, compared with a few weeks or months. If, for instance, we knew that our dog or cat would have no choice but to be confined in a cage so restrictive that turning around or freely stretching limbs is difficult if not impossible; live in his own excrement; be castrated or have her teeth, tail, or toes sliced off without anesthesia, I suspect most of us would believe that euthanizing the animal is the humane choice. It would be better, then, if farmed animals who endure these conditions did not exist.

One is hard-pressed to find, even among philosophers, any attempt to justify these conditions or the practice of eating factory-farmed animals. We have no nutritional need for animal products. In fact, vegetarians are, on average, healthier than those who eat meat. The overriding interest we have in eating animals is the pleasure we get from the taste of their flesh. However, there are a variety of vegetarian foods available, including ones that taste like animal products, from meat to eggs to milk, cheese, and yogurt. So, in order to justify eating animals, we would have to show that the pleasure gained from consuming them *minus* the pleasure gained from eating a vegetarian meal is greater than the pain caused by eating animals.

Whatever pleasure we gain from eating animals cannot be discounted. However, equal consideration of interests requires that we put ourselves in the place of a farmed animal as well as in the place of a meat-eater. Does the pleasure we enjoy from eating a chicken outweigh the pain we would endure were we to be raised and killed for that meal? We would probably conclude that our substantial interest in not being raised in a factory farm and slaughtered is stronger than our trivial interest in eating a chicken instead of chickpeas. There is, after all, no shortage of foods that we can eat that don't require an animal to suffer in a factory farm or slaughterhouse. That our trivial interest in the taste of meat now trumps the pain endured by 17 *billion* farmed animals may be some measure of how far we are from considering their interests equally.

Accordingly, equal consideration of interests requires that we abstain, at a minimum, from eating factory-farmed products—particularly poultry and eggs, products that seem to cause the most pain per unit of food. Ideally, we should not consume products from any animal that we believe is sentient. This is the least we can do to have any real regard for the pain felt by other animals. Eating animals is a habit for most of us and, like other habits, can be challenging to break. But millions of people have made the switch to a vegetarian diet and, as a result, have enjoyed better health and a clearer conscience.

The use of animals for food is by far the largest direct cause of animal abuse in North America and Europe; and our consumption of animal flesh, eggs, and milk probably causes more pain than any other action for which each of us is responsible. The average North American or European eats somewhere between 1,500 and 2,500 factory-farmed animals in his or her lifetime. If we ended our discussion here and all became vegans, we would effectively abolish 99 percent of the present use of animals. Still, there are other ways in which animals are abused that deserve discussion. The use of animals in laboratories, in particular, provides a testing ground for the principle of equal consideration of interests.

LABORATORIES

Somewhere between 50 and 100 million animals are killed each year in North American and European laboratories. As Richard Ryder (2006) describes, these include animals used in testing new products, formulations, and drugs as well as those used in medical and scientific research. U.S. law does not require research or testing facilities to report numbers of most of these animals—primarily rats, mice, and birds—so there is considerable uncertainty about the statistics.

There are potentially non-trivial benefits to human beings and other animals in using nonhuman animals for testing and in medical and veterinary research. That being so, utilitarianism cannot provide as simple an objection to the use of animals in experiments as it did to the use of animals for food. It can, however, provide a yardstick by which to judge whether a particular experiment is ethical.

We should first ask whether the experiment is worth conducting. Most product tests on animals involve household or personal care products that are only superficially different from existing products. How many different formulations of laundry detergent or shampoo does the world need? And much basic research involving animals may answer intellectually interesting questions but promise few benefits to either human or nonhuman animals. Do we need to know what happens to kittens after their eyes are removed at birth, or to monkeys when deprived of all maternal contact from infancy? In every case, we should ask if the pain prevented by an experiment is greater than the pain caused by that experiment. As experiments routinely involve thousands of animals with an uncertain benefit to any human or nonhuman animal, in most cases these experiments are not justified. It is difficult to imagine that the pain experienced by 100 million animals each year is *averting* an equivalent amount of pain.

However, if we believe that an experiment is justified on utilitarian grounds, there is another question we should ask to check our prejudices. Most adult mammals used in lab research—dogs, cats, mice, rabbits, rats, and primates—are more aware of what is happening to them than and at least as sensitive to pain as any human infant. Would researchers contemplating an animal experiment be willing, then, to place an orphaned human infant in the animal's place? If they are not, then their use of an animal is simple discrimination on the basis of species, which, as we found above, is morally unjustifiable. If the researchers are willing to place an infant in the animal's place, then they are at least morally consistent. Perhaps there are cases in which researchers believe an experiment is so valuable as to be worth an infant's life, but I doubt that many would make this claim.

WILDLIFE

Except for those hunted and fished, wild animals are often ignored in discussions of animal protection and seen as the domain of environmental protection.

Part of this neglect is probably justified. I would certainly choose to be an animal in the wild over being an animal in a factory farm. Nevertheless, animals in the wild deserve as much moral consideration as do those animals in farms or laboratories. Likewise, wild animals raise important questions for those interested, as we are, in the proper moral consideration of animals' interests.

There are few human activities that do not affect the welfare of wild animals. Particularly in developed countries, humans consume a tremendous amount of energy, water, land, timber, minerals, and other resources whose extraction or use damages natural habitats—killing or preventing from existing untold billions of wild animals. Many of these activities may well be justified. Nevertheless, most of us can take steps to reduce the impact we have on wild animals without sacrificing anything of comparable moral significance.

Most of these steps are familiar ones encouraged by environmental protection groups. We should drive less, use public transit more, adopt a vegetarian or preferably vegan diet, reduce our purchases of luxury goods, buy used rather than new items, and so on. For decades, environmentalists in Europe and North America have also encouraged couples to have smaller families. In Europe, it is not uncommon to find one-child families, and the same is beginning to be true in North America. Smaller families not only carry many social and economic advantages to parents and nations, they also significantly reduce the resources used and the number of animals threatened by human consumption. Of course, most of these measures help humans, too. Investments in family planning, for instance, are probably the most cost-effective measures to reduce global warming.

CONCLUSIONS

I have argued that utilitarianism is a reasonable ethical theory, that this theory includes animals in its moral consideration, and that it obliges us to make dramatic changes in our institutions and habits—most immediately, that we become vegetarian or preferably vegan. While my aim here has been to present a *utilitarian* argument, similar arguments regarding our mistreatment of animals have been put forward on the basis of all of the major secular and religious ethical theories.... But even less ambitious ethical arguments should convince us that much of our present treatment of animals is unethical.

Take, for instance, what I will call the "weak principle" of equal consideration of interests. Under the weak principle, we will consider the interests of nonhuman animals to be equal *only* to the like interests of other nonhuman animals. I don't believe there is any good reason to adopt the weak principle in place of the strong one discussed earlier. But, even if we were to adopt the weak principle, we would reach many of the same conclusions.

Almost all of us agree that we should treat dogs and cats humanely. There are few opponents, for instance, of current anti-cruelty laws aimed at protecting pets from abuse, neglect, or sport fighting. And therein lies a bizarre contradiction. For if these anti-cruelty laws applied to animals in factory farms or laboratories, the ways in which these animals are treated would be illegal throughout North America and Europe. Do we believe dogs and cats are so different from apes, pigs, cows, chickens, and rabbits that one group of animals—pets—deserve legal protection from human abuse, while the other group—animals in factory farms and in labs—deserve to have their abuse institutionalized? We cannot justify this contradiction by claiming that the abuse of farmed animals, for example, serves a purpose, whereas the abuse of pets does not. Arguably, the satisfaction enjoyed by someone who fights or otherwise abuses dogs and cats is just as great as that enjoyed by someone who eats meat.

What separates pets from the animals we abuse in factory farms and in labs is physical proximity. Our disregard for "food" or "lab" animals persists because we don't see them. Few people are aware of the ways in which they are mistreated and even fewer actually see the abuse. When people become aware, they are typically appalled—not because they have adopted a new ethical theory, but because they believe animals feel pain and they believe morally decent people should want to prevent pain whenever possible. The utilitarian argument for considering animals helps us to return to this common-sense view.

There are remarkably few contemporary defenses of our traditional treatment of animals. This may suggest that the principal obstacles to improving the treatment of animals are not philosophical uncertainties about their proper treatment but, rather, our ignorance about their current abuse and our reluctance to change deeply ingrained habits. Even the most reasonable among us is not invulnerable to the pressures of habit. Many moral philosophers who believe that eating animals is unethical continue to eat meat. This reflects the limits of reasoned argument in changing behavior. While I can't overcome those limits here, I encourage you, as you read this [chapter], to replace in your mind the animals being discussed with an animal familiar to you, such as a dog or cat, or, better yet, a human infant. If you do this, you are taking to heart the principle of equal consideration of interests and giving animals the consideration they deserve.

REFERENCES

Bentham, Jeremy (1988 [1828]) *The Principles of Morals and Legislation*, Amherst, N.Y.: Prometheus.

Ryder, Richard D. (2006) "Speciesism in the Laboratory," in *In Defense of Animals: The Second Wave*, P. Singer, ed., Oxford: Blackwell Publishing.

RECOMMENDATION

The reader is encouraged to watch video footage from factory farms such as *Meet Your Meat*. www.goveg.com/meetmeat.html.

READING QUESTIONS

1. Explain the basic ethical principle that Matheny focuses on in this article. What are some of the variations of this principle? Explain in particular the secular principle of equal consideration of interests.
2. How does Matheny define utilitarianism? Explain the four different properties of utilitarianism. What are the advantages of utilitarianism according to Matheny?
3. How does Matheny argue for the view that nonhuman animals have interests? What objections does he consider against his view and how does he respond to each objection?
4. What are some of the ways that we use and treat animals? Which of these are unethical according to Matheny? What arguments does he give to support his view that some of these practices are unethical?
5. Explain the utilitarian assessment offered by Matheny for whether experiments on nonhuman animals are worth conducting.

DISCUSSION QUESTIONS

1. Do any of the suggested advantages of utilitarianism introduce potential disadvantages for the view, especially as it relates to the treatment of nonhuman animals?
2. To what extent should the interests of nonhuman animals be taken into consideration in order to answer questions about how we ought to treat them? Should we adopt a strong or a weak principle of equal consideration of interests with respect to nonhuman animals?

Tom Regan

Are Zoos Morally Defensible?

Regan considers both utilitarian and rights approaches to the title question. He argues that because the utilitarian approach to the moral question about zoos requires far more information about the good and bad effects of zoos than can possibly be acquired, the view does not yield a determinate answer to the question. Regan favors the rights view according to which animals do have rights and therefore leads to the conclusion that zoos are not morally defensible.

Recommended Reading: rights-focused approach to moral issues, chap. 1, sec. 2D.

A great deal of recent work by moral philosophers—much of it in environmental ethics, for example, but much of it also in reference to questions about obligations to future generations and international justice—is directly relevant to the moral assessment of zoos. (Here and throughout I use the word "zoo" to refer to a professionally managed zoological institution accredited by the AZA and having a collection of live animals used for conservation, scientific studies, public education, and public display.) Yet most of this work has been overlooked by advocates of zoological parks. Why this is so is unclear, but certainly the responsibility for this lack of communication needs to be shared. Like all other specialists, moral philosophers have a tendency to converse only among themselves, just as, like others with a shared, crowded agenda, zoo professionals have limited discretionary time, thus little time to explore current tendencies in academic disciplines like moral philosophy. The present essay attempts to take some modest steps in the direction of better communication between the two professions....

CHANGING TIMES

Time was when philosophers had little good to say about animals other than human beings. "Nature's automata," writes Descartes (Regan and Singer 1976, 60). Morally considered, animals are in the same category as "sticks and stones," opines the early twentieth-century Jesuit Joseph Rickaby (179). True, there have been notable exceptions, throughout history, who celebrated the intelligence, beauty, and dignity of animals: Pythagoras, Cicero, Epicurus, Herodotus, Horace, Ovid, Plutarch, Seneca, Virgil—hardly a group of ancient-world animal crazies. By and large, however, a dismissive sentence or two sufficed or, when one's corpus took on grave proportions, a few paragraphs or pages. Thus we find Immanuel Kant, for example, by all accounts one of the most influential philosophers in the history of ideas, devoting almost two full pages to the question of our duties to nonhuman animals, while Saint Thomas Aquinas, easily the most important philosopher-theologian in the Roman Catholic tradition, bequeaths perhaps ten pages to this topic.

Times change. Today even a modest bibliography of the past decade's work by philosophers on the moral status of nonhuman animals (Magel 1989) would easily equal the length of Kant's and Aquinas's treatments combined (Regan and Singer 1976, 122–124, 56–60, 118–122), a quantitative symbol of the changes that have taken place, and continue to take place, in philosophy's attempt to excise the cancerous prejudices lodged in the anthropocentric belly of Western thought.

With relatively few speaking to the contrary (Saint Francis always comes to mind in this context), theists and humanists, rowdy bedfellows in most quarters, have gotten along amicably when discussing questions about the moral center of the terrestrial universe: human interests form the center of this universe. Let the theist look hopefully beyond the harsh edge of bodily death, let the humanist denounce, in Freud's terms, this "infantile view of the world," at least the two could agree that the moral universe revolves around us humans—our desires, our needs, our goals, our preferences, our love for one another. An intense dialectic now characterizes philosophy's assaults on the traditions of humanism and theism, assaults aimed not only at the traditional account of the moral status of nonhuman animals but also at the foundations of our moral dealings with the natural environment, with Nature generally. These assaults should not be viewed as local skirmishes between obscure academicians each bent on occupying a deserted fortress. At issue are the validity of alternative visions of the scheme of things and our place in it. The growing philosophical debate over our treatment of the planet and the other animals with whom we share it is both a symptom and a cause of a culture's attempt to come to critical terms with its past as it attempts to shape its future.

At present moral philosophers are raising a number of major challenges against moral anthropocentrism. I shall consider two. The first comes from utilitarians, the second from proponents of animal rights…. This essay offers a brief summary of each position with special reference to how it answers our central question—the question, again, Are zoos morally defensible?

UTILITARIANISM

The first fairly recent spark of revolt against moral anthropocentrism comes, as do other recent protests against institutionalized prejudice, from the pens of the nineteenth-century utilitarians Jeremy Bentham and John Stuart Mill. In an oft-quoted passage Bentham enfranchises sentient animals in the utilitarian moral community by declaring, "The question is not, Can they talk?, or Can they reason?, but, Can they suffer?" (Regan and Singer 1976, 130). Mill goes even further, writing that utilitarians "are perfectly willing to stake the whole question on this one issue. Granted that any practice causes more pain to animals than it gives pleasure to man: is that practice moral or immoral? And if, exactly in proportion as human beings raise their heads out of the slough of selfishness, they do not with one voice answer 'immoral' let the morality of the principle of utility be forever condemned" (132). Some of our duties are direct duties to other animals, not indirect duties to humanity. For utilitarians, these animals are themselves involved in the moral game.

Viewed against this historical backdrop, the position of the influential contemporary moral philosopher Peter Singer can be seen to be an extension of the utilitarian critique of moral anthropocentrism (Singer 1990). In Singer's hands utilitarianism requires that we consider the interests of everyone affected by what we do, and also that we weigh equal interests equally. We must not refuse to consider the interests of some people because they are Catholic, or female, or black, for example. Everyone's interests must be considered. And we must not discount the importance of equal interests because of whose interests they are. Everyone's interests must be weighed equitably. Now, to ignore or discount the importance of a woman's interests because she is a woman is an obvious example of the moral prejudice we call sexism, just as to ignore or discount the importance of the interests of African or Native Americans, Hispanics, etc. is an obvious form of racism. It remained for Singer to argue, which he does with great vigor, passion, and skill, that a similar moral prejudice lies at the heart of moral anthropocentrism, a prejudice that Singer,

127

borrowing a term coined by the English author and animal activist Richard Ryder, denominates speciesism (Ryder 1975).

Like Bentham and Mill before him, therefore, Singer denies that humans are obliged to treat other animals equitably in the name of the betterment of humanity and also denies that acting dutifully toward these animals is a warm-up for the real moral game played between humans or, as theists would add, between humans and God. We owe it to those animals who have interests to take their interests into account, just as we also owe it to them to count their interests equitably. In these respects we have direct duties to them, not indirect duties to humanity. To think otherwise is to give sorry testimony to the very prejudice—speciesism—Singer is intent upon silencing.

UTILITARIANISM AND THE MORAL ASSESSMENT OF ZOOS

From a utilitarian perspective, then, the interests of animals must figure in the moral assessment of zoos. These interests include a variety of needs, desires, and preferences, including, for example, the interest wild animals have in freedom of movement, as well as adequate nutrition and an appropriate environment. Even zoos' most severe critics must acknowledge that in many of the most important respects, contemporary zoos have made important advances in meeting at least some of the most important interests of wild animals in captivity.

From a utilitarian perspective, however, there are additional questions that need to be answered before we are justified in answering our central question. For not only must we insist that the interests of captive animals be taken into account and be counted equitably, but we must also do the same for all those people whose interests are affected by having zoos—and this involves a very large number of people indeed, including those who work at zoos, those who visit them, and those (for example, people in the hotel and restaurant business, as well as local and state governments) whose business or tax base benefits from having zoos in their region. To make an informed moral assessment of zoos, given utilitarian theory, in short, we need to consider a great deal more than the interests of those wild animals exhibited in zoos (though we certainly need to consider their interests). Since everyone's interests count, we need to consider everyone's interests, at least insofar as these interests are affected by having zoos—or by not having them.

Now, utilitarians are an optimistic, hearty breed, and what for many (myself included) seems to be an impossible task, to them appears merely difficult. The task is simple enough to state—namely, to determine how the many, the varied, and the competing interests of everyone affected by having zoos (or by not having them) are or will be affected by having (or not having) them. That, as I say, is the easy part. The hard (or impossible) part is actually to carry out this project. Granted, a number of story lines are possible (for example, stories about how much people really learn by going to zoos in comparison with how much they could learn by watching National Geographic specials). But many of these story lines will be in the nature of speculation rather than of fact, others will be empirical sketches rather than detailed studies, and the vital interests of some individuals (for example, the interests people have in having a job, medical benefits, a retirement plan) will tend not to be considered at all or to be greatly undervalued.

Moreover, the utilitarian moral assessment of zoos requires that we know a good deal more before we can make an informed assessment. Not only must we canvass all the interests of all those individuals who are affected, but we must also add up all the interests that are satisfied as well as all the interests that are frustrated, given the various options (for example, keeping zoos as they are, changing them in various ways, or abolishing them altogether). Then, having added all the pluses and minuses—and only then—are we in a position to say which of the options is the best one.

But (to put the point as mildly as possible) how we rationally are to carry out this part of the project (for example, how we rationally determine what an equitable trade-off is between, say, a wild animals' interest in roaming free and a tram operator's interest in a steady job) is far from clear. And yet unless we have comprehensible, comprehensive, and intellectually reliable instructions regarding how we are to do this, we will lack the very knowledge that, given utilitarian theory, we must have before we can make an informed moral assessment of zoos. The suspicion is, at least among utilitarianism's critics, the theory requires knowledge that far exceeds what we humans are capable of acquiring. In the particular case before us, then, it is arguable that utilitarian theory, conscientiously applied, would lead to moral skepticism—would lead, that is, to the conclusion that we just don't know whether or not zoos are morally defensible. At least for many people, myself included, this is a conclusion we would wish to avoid.

In addition to problems of this kind, utilitarianism also seems open to a variety of damaging moral criticisms, among which the following is representative. The theory commits us to withholding our moral assessment of actions or practices until everyone's interests have been taken into account and treated equitably. Thus the theory implies that before we can judge, say, whether the sexual abuse of very young children is morally wrong, we need to consider the interests of everyone involved—the very young child certainly, but also those of the abuser. But this seems morally outrageous. For what one wants to say, it seems to me, is that the sexual abuse of children is wrong independently of the interests of abusers, that their interests should play absolutely no role whatsoever in our judgment that their abuse is morally wrong, so that any theory that implies that their interests should play a role in our judgment must be mistaken. Thus, because utilitarianism does imply this, it must be mistaken.

Suppose this line of criticism is sound. Then it follows that we should not make our moral assessment of anything, whether the sexual abuse of children or the practice of keeping and exhibiting wild animals in zoos, in the way this theory recommends. If the theory is irredeemably flawed—and that it is, is what the example of child abuse is supposed to illustrate—then its answer to any moral question, including in particular our question about the defensibility of zoos, should carry no moral weight, one

way or the other (that is, whether the theory would justify zoos or find them indefensible). Despite its historic importance and continued influence, we are, I think, well advised to look elsewhere for an answer to our question.

THE RIGHTS VIEW

An alternative to the utilitarian attack on anthropocentrism is the rights view. Those who accept this view hold that (1) the moral assessment of zoos must be carried out against the backdrop of the rights of animals and that (2) when we make this assessment against this backdrop, zoos, as they presently exist, are not morally defensible. How might one defend what to many people will seem to be such extreme views? This is not a simple question by any means, but something by way of a sketch of this position needs to be presented here (Regan 1983).

The rights view rests on a number of factual beliefs about those animals humans eat, hunt, and trap, as well as those relevantly similar animals humans use in scientific research and exhibit in zoos. Included among these factual beliefs are the following: These animals are not only in the world, but they are also aware of it—and of what happens to them. And what happens to them matters to them. Each has a life that fares experientially better or worse for the one whose life it is. As such, all have lives of their own that are of importance to them apart from their utility to us. Like us, they bring a unified psychological presence to the world. Like us, they are somebodies, not somethings. They are not our tools, not our models, not our resources, not our commodities.

The lives that are theirs include a variety of biological, psychological, and social needs. The satisfaction of these needs is a source of pleasure, their frustration or abuse, a source of pain. The untimely death of the one whose life it is, whether this be painless or otherwise, is the greatest of harms since it is the greatest of losses: the loss of one's life itself. In these fundamental ways these nonhuman animals are the same as human beings. And so it is that according to the rights view, the ethics of our dealings with them and with one another must rest on the same fundamental moral principles.

At its deepest level an enlightened human ethic, according to the rights view, is based on the independent value of the individual: the moral worth of any one human being is not to be measured by how useful that person is in advancing the interests of other human beings. To treat human beings in ways that do not honor their independent value—to treat them as tools or models or commodities, for example—is to violate that most basic of human rights: the right of each of us to be treated with respect.

As viewed by its advocates, the philosophy of animal rights demands only that logic be respected. For any argument that plausibly explains the independent value of human beings, they claim, implies that other animals have this same value, and have it equally. Any argument that plausibly explains the right of humans to be treated with respect, it is further alleged, also implies that these other animals have this same right, and have it equally, too.

Those who accept the philosophy of animal rights, then, believe that women do not exist to serve men, blacks to serve whites, the rich to serve the poor, or the weak to serve the strong. The philosophy of animal rights not only accepts these truths, its advocates maintain, but also insists upon and justifies them. But this philosophy goes further. By insisting upon the independent value and rights of other animals, it attempts to give scientifically informed and morally impartial reasons for denying that these animals exist to serve us. Just as there is no master sex and no master race, so (animal rights advocates maintain) there is no master species.

ANIMAL RIGHTS AND THE MORAL ASSESSMENT OF ZOOS

To view nonhuman animals after the fashion of the philosophy of animal rights makes a truly profound difference to our understanding of what we may do to them. Because other animals have a moral right to respectful treatment, we ought not reduce their moral status to that of being useful means to our ends. That being so, the rights view excludes from consideration many of those factors that are relevant to the utilitarian moral assessment of zoos. As explained earlier, conscientious utilitarians need to ask how having zoos affects the interests people have in being gainfully employed, how the tourist trade and the local and state tax base are impacted, and how much people really learn from visiting zoos. All these questions, however, are irrelevant if those wild animals confined in zoos are not being treated with appropriate respect. If they are not, then, given the rights view, keeping these animals in zoos is wrong, and it is wrong independently of how the interests of others are affected.

Thus, the central question: Are animals in zoos treated with appropriate respect? To answer this question, we begin with an obvious fact—namely, the freedom of these animals is compromised, to varying degrees, by the conditions of their captivity. The rights view recognizes the justification of limiting another's freedom but only in a narrow range of cases. The most obvious relevant case would be one in which it is in the best interests of a particular animal to keep that animal in confinement. In principle, therefore, confining wild animals in zoos can be justified, according to the rights view, but only if it can be shown that it is in their best interests to do so. That being so, it is morally irrelevant to insist that zoos provide important educational and recreational opportunities for humans, or that captive animals serve as useful models in important scientific research, or that regions in which zoos are located benefit economically, or that zoo programs offer the opportunity for protecting rare or endangered species, or that variations on these programs insure genetic stock, or that any other consequence arises from keeping wild animals in captivity that forwards the interests of other individuals, whether humans or nonhumans.

Now, one can imagine circumstances in which such captivity might be defensible. For example, if the life of a wild animal could be saved only by temporarily removing the animal from the threat of human predation, and if, after this threat had abated, the animal was reintroduced into the wild, then this temporary confinement arguably is not disrespectful and thus might be justified. Perhaps there are other circumstances in which a wild animal's liberty could be limited temporarily, for that animal's own good. Obviously, however, there will be comparatively few such cases, and no less obviously, those cases that satisfy the requirements of the rights view are significantly different from the vast majority of cases in which wild animals are today confined in zoos, for these animals are confined and exhibited not because temporary captivity is in their best interests but because their captivity serves some purpose useful to others. As such, the rights view must take a very dim view of zoos, both as we know them now and as they are likely to be in the future. In answer to our central question—Are zoos morally defensible?—the rights view's answer, not surprisingly, is No, they are not....

REFERENCES

Magel, C. 1989. *Keyguide to Information Sources in Animal Rights.* London: Mansell.

Regan, T. 1983. *The Case for Animal Rights.* Berkeley: University of California Press.

Regan, T., and P. Singer, eds. 1976. *Animal Rights and Human Obligations.* Englewood Cliffs, N.J.: Prentice-Hall.

Ryder, R. 1975. *Victims of Science.* London: Davis-Poynter.

Singer, P. 1990. *Animal Liberation.* 2d ed. New York: Random House.

READING QUESTIONS

1. How does Regan define a "zoo"?
2. How would a utilitarian provide a moral assessment of zoos according to Regan? What are his objections to the utilitarian task in this particular case? What other criticisms does he raise against the utilitarian view generally?
3. What defense does Regan offer for the claim that zoos are not morally defensible according to the right's view?
4. In what cases does Regan claim that captivity of a nonhuman animal would be morally defensible?
5. Provide examples of the interests of nonhuman animals according to Regan.

DISCUSSION QUESTIONS

1. Should we reject utilitarianism as a way to assess the morality of zoos as Regan suggests? How might a utilitarian respond to the criticisms he raises?
2. Suppose that nonhuman animals have rights. Should nonhuman animal rights be respected as equal to those of humans? Describe cases where the rights of humans might trump the rights of nonhuman animals.

CARL COHEN

Do Animals Have Rights?

Cohen's negative answer to his title question involves two parts. First, he explains why non-human animals lack moral rights, even though humans have moral obligations with regard to them. Second, he critically evaluates Tom Regan's argument (from his 1983 book, *The Case for Animal Rights*) for the claim that nonhuman animals have rights. Regan's argument depends crucially on the claim that nonhuman animals, like human beings, have inherent value, and that therefore they have moral rights. Cohen argues that Regan's argument commits the fallacy of equivocation owing to multiple meanings of the term "inherent value."

    Recommended Reading: rights-focused approaches, chap. 1, sec. 2D.

Whether animals have rights is a question of great importance because if they do, those rights must be respected, even at the cost of great burdens for human beings. A right (unlike an interest) is a valid claim, or potential claim, made by a moral agent, under principles that govern both the claimant and the target of the claim. Rights are precious; they are dispositive; they count.

You have a right to the return of money you lent me; we both understand that. It may be very convenient for me to keep the money, and you may have no need of it whatever; but my convenience and your needs are not to the point. You have a *right* to it, and we have courts of law partly to ensure that such rights will be respected.

If you make me a promise, I have a moral right to its fulfillment—even though there may be no law to enforce my right. It may be very much in your interest to break that promise, but your great interests and the silence of the law cut no mustard when your solemn promise—which we both well understood—had been given. Likewise, those holding power may have a great and benevolent interest in denying my rights to travel or to speak freely—but their interests are overridden by my rights.

A great deal was learned about hypothermia by some Nazi doctors who advanced their learning by soaking Jews in cold water and putting them in refrigerators to learn how hypothermia proceeds. We have no difficulty in seeing that they may not advance medicine in that way; the subjects of those atrocious experiments had rights that demanded respect. For those who ignored their rights we have nothing but moral loathing.

Some persons believe that animals have rights as surely as those Jews had rights, and they therefore look on the uses of animals in medical investigations just as we look at the Nazi use of the Jews, with moral loathing. They are consistent in doing so. If animals have rights they certainly have the right not to be killed, even to advance our important interests.

Some may say, "Well, they have rights, but we have rights too, and our rights override theirs." That may be true in some cases, but it will not solve the problem because, although we may have a weighty *interest* in learning, say, how to vaccinate against polio or other diseases, we do not have a *right* to learn such things. Nor could we honestly claim that we kill research animals in self-defense; they did not attack us. If animals have rights, they certainly have

Reprinted from *Ethics and Behavior*, 1997, vol. 7, no. 2, pp. 91–102.

the right not to be killed to advance the interests of others, whatever rights those others may have.

In 1952 there were about 58,000 cases of polio reported in the United States, and 3,000 polio deaths; my parents, parents everywhere, trembled in fear for their children at camp or away from home. Polio vaccination became routine in 1955, and cases dropped to about a dozen a year; today polio has been eradicated completely from the Western Hemisphere. The vaccine that achieved this, partly developed and tested only blocks from where I live in Ann Arbor, could have been developed *only* with the substantial use of animals. Polio vaccines had been tried many times earlier, but from those earlier vaccines children had contracted the disease; investigators had become, understandably, exceedingly cautious.

The killer disease for which a vaccine now is needed most desperately is malaria, which kills about 2 million people each year, most of them children. Many vaccines have been tried—not on children, thank God—and have failed. But very recently, after decades of effort, we learned how to make a vaccine that does, with complete success, inoculate mice against malaria. A safe vaccine for humans we do not yet have—but soon we will have it, thanks to the use of those mice, many of whom will have died in the process. To test that vaccine first on children would be an outrage, as it would have been an outrage to do so with the Salk and Sabin polio vaccines years ago. We use mice or monkeys *because there is no other way*. And there never will be another way because untested vaccines are very dangerous; their first use on a living organism is inescapably experimental; there is and will be no way to determine the reliability and safety of new vaccines without repeated tests on live organisms. Therefore, because we certainly may not use human children to test them, we will use mice (or as we develop an AIDS vaccine, primates) *or we will never have such vaccines*.

But if those animals we use in such tests have rights as human children do, what we did and are doing to them is as profoundly wrong as what the Nazis did to those Jews not long ago. Defenders of animal rights need not hold that medical scientists are vicious; they simply believe that what medical investigators are doing with animals is morally wrong.

Most biomedical investigations involving animal subjects use rodents: mice and rats. The rat is the animal appropriately considered (and used by the critic) as the exemplar whose moral stature is in dispute here. Tom Regan is a leading defender of the view that rats do have such rights, and may not be used in biomedical investigations. He is an honest man. He sees the consequences of his view and accepts them forthrightly. In *The Case for Animal Rights* (Regan, 1983) he wrote,

> The harms others might face as a result of the dissolution of [some] practice or institution is no defense of allowing it to continue....No one has a right to be protected against being harmed if the protection in question involves violating the rights of others....No one has a right to be protected by the continuation of an unjust practice, one that violates the rights of others....Justice *must* be done, though the...heavens fall. (pp. 346–347)

That last line echoes Kant, who borrowed it from an older tradition. Believing that rats have rights as humans do, Regan (1983) was convinced that killing them in medical research was morally intolerable. He wrote,

> On the rights view, [he means, of course, the Regan rights view] we cannot justify harming a single rat *merely* by aggregating "the many human and humane benefits" that flow from doing it....Not even a single rat is to be treated as if that animal's value were reducible to his *possible utility* relative to the interests of others. (p. 384)

If there are some things that we cannot learn because animals have rights, well, as Regan (1983) put it, so be it.

This is the conclusion to which one certainly is driven if one holds that animals have rights. If Regan is correct about the moral standing of rats, we humans can have no right, ever, to kill them—unless perchance a rat attacks a person or a human baby, as rats sometimes do; then our right of self-defense may enter, I suppose. But medical investigations cannot honestly be described as self-defense, and medical investigations commonly require that many mice and rats be killed. Therefore, all medical investigations relying on them, or any other animal subjects—which includes most studies and all the most important studies of certain kinds—will have to stop. Bear in mind that the replacement of animal subjects by computer simulations, or tissue samples, and so on, is in most research a phantasm, a fantasy. Biomedical investigations using animal subjects (and of course all uses of animals as food) will have to stop.

This extraordinary consequence has no argumentative force for Regan and his followers; they are not consequentialists. For Regan the interests of humans, their desire to be freed of disease or relieved of pain, simply cannot outweigh the rights of a single rat. For him the issue is one of justice, and the use of animals in medical experiments (he believes) is simply not just. But the consequences of his view will give most of us, I submit, good reason to weigh very carefully the arguments he offers to support such far-reaching claims. Do you believe that the work of Drs. Salk and Sabin was morally right? Would you support it now, or support work just like it saving tens of thousands of human children from diphtheria, hepatitis, measles, rabies, rubella, and tetanus (all of which relied essentially on animal subjects)—as well as, now, AIDS, Lyme disease, and malaria? I surely do. If you would join me in this support we must conclude that the defense of animal rights is a gigantic mistake. I next aim to explain why animals cannot possess rights.

WHY ANIMALS DO NOT HAVE RIGHTS

Many obligations are owed by humans to animals; few will deny that. But it certainly does not follow from this that animals have rights because it is certainly not true that every obligation of ours arises from the rights of another. Not at all. We need to be clear and careful here. Rights entail obligations. If you have a right to the return of the money I borrowed, I have an obligation to repay it. No issue. If we have the right to speak freely on public policy matters, the community has the obligation to respect our right to do so. But

the proposition *all rights entail obligations* does not convert simply, as the logicians say. From the true proposition that all trees are plants, it does not follow that all plants are trees. Similarly, not all obligations are entailed by rights. Some obligations, like mine to repay the money I borrowed from you, do arise out of rights. But many obligations are owed to persons or other beings who have no rights whatever in the matter.

Obligations may arise from commitments freely made: As a college professor I accept the obligation to comment at length on the papers my students submit, and I do so; but they have not the right to *demand* that I do so. Civil servants and elected officials surely ought to be courteous to members of the public, but that obligation certainly is not grounded in citizens' rights.

Special relations often give rise to obligations: Hosts have the obligation to be cordial to their guests, but the guest has not the right to demand cordiality. Shepherds have obligations to their dogs, and cowboys to their horses, which do not flow from the rights of those dogs or horses. My son, now 5, may someday wish to study veterinary medicine as my father did; I will then have the obligation to help him as I can, and with pride I shall—but he has not the authority to demand such help as a matter of right. My dog has no right to daily exercise and veterinary care, but I do have the obligation to provide those things for her.

One may be obliged to another for a special act of kindness done; one may be obliged to put an animal out of its misery in view of its condition—but neither the beneficiary of that kindness nor that dying animal may have had a claim of right.

Beauchamp and Childress (1994) addressed what they called the "correlativity of rights and obligations" and wrote that they would defend an "untidy" (pp. 73–75) variety of that principle. It would be very untidy indeed. Some of our most important obligations—to members of our family, to the needy, to neighbors, and to sentient creatures of every sort—have no foundation in rights at all. Correlativity appears critical from the perspective of one who holds a right; your right correlates with my obligation to respect it. But the claim that rights and obligations are reciprocals, that every obligation flows from another's right, is false, plainly inconsistent with our general understanding of the differences between what we think we ought to do, and what others can justly *demand* that we do.

I emphasize this because, although animals have no rights, it surely does not follow from this that one is free to treat them with callous disregard. Animals are not stones; they feel. A rat may suffer; surely we have the obligation not to torture it gratuitously, even though it be true that the concept of a right could not possibly apply to it. We humans are obliged to act humanely, that is, being aware of their sentience, to apply to animals the moral principles that govern us regarding the gratuitous imposition of pain and suffering; which is not, of course, to treat animals as the possessors of rights.

Animals cannot be the bearers of rights because the concept of rights is essentially *human*; it is rooted in, and has force within, a human moral world. Humans must deal with rats—all too frequently in some parts of the world—and must be moral in their dealing with them; but a rat can no more be said to have rights than a table can be said to have ambition. To say of a rat that it has rights is to confuse categories, to apply to its world a moral category that has content only in the human moral world.

Try this thought experiment. Imagine, on the Serengeti Plain in East Africa, a lioness hunting for her cubs. A baby zebra, momentarily left unattended by its mother, is the prey; the lioness snatches it, rips open its throat, tears out chunks of its flesh, and departs. The mother zebra is driven nearly out of her wits when she cannot locate her baby; finding its carcass she will not even leave the remains for days. The scene may be thought unpleasant, but it is entirely natural, of course, and extremely common. If the zebra has a right to live, if the prey is just but the predator unjust, we ought to intervene, if we can, on behalf of right. But we do not intervene, of course—as we surely would intervene if we saw the lioness about to attack an unprotected human baby or you. What accounts for the moral difference? We justify different responses to humans and to zebras on the ground (implicit or explicit) that their moral stature is very different. The human has a right not

to be eaten alive; it is, after all, a human being. Do you believe the baby zebra has the right not to be slaughtered by that lioness? That the lioness has the *right* to kill that baby zebra for her cubs? If you are inclined to say, confronted by such natural rapacity—duplicated with untold variety millions of times each day on planet earth—that neither is right or wrong, that neither has a *right* against the other, I am on your side. Rights are of the highest moral consequence, yes; but zebras and lions and rats are totally amoral; there is no morality for them; they do no wrong, ever. In their world there are no rights.

A contemporary philosopher who has thought a good deal about animals, referring to them as "moral patients," put it this way:

> A moral patient lacks the ability to formulate, let alone bring to bear, moral principles in deliberating about which one among a number of possible acts it would be right or proper to perform. Moral patients, in a word, cannot do what is right, nor can they do what is wrong....Even when a moral patient causes significant harm to another, the moral patient has not done what is wrong. Only moral agents can do what is wrong. (Regan, 1983, pp. 152–153)

Just so. The concepts of wrong and right are totally foreign to animals, not conceivably within their ken or applicable to them, as the author of that passage clearly understands.

When using animals in our research, therefore, we ought indeed be humane—but we can never violate the rights of those animals because, to be blunt, they have none. Rights do not *apply* to them.

But humans do have rights. Where do our rights come from? Why are we not crudely natural creatures like rats and zebras? This question philosophers have struggled to answer from earliest times. A definitive account of the human moral condition I cannot here present, of course. But reflect for a moment on the kinds of answers that have been widely given:

- Some think our moral understanding, with its attendant duties, to be a divine gift. So St. Thomas said: The moral law is binding, and humans have the power, given by God, to grasp its binding character, and must therefore respect the rights that other humans possess. God makes us (Saint Augustine said before him) in his own image, and therefore with a will that is free, and gives us the power to recognize that, and therefore, unlike other creatures, we must choose between good and evil, between right and wrong.

• Many philosophers, distrusting theological justifications of rights and duties, sought the ground of human morality in the membership, by all humans, in a moral community. The English idealist, Bradley, called it an organic moral community; the German idealist, Hegel, called it an objective ethical order. These and like accounts commonly center on human inter-relations, on a moral *fabric* within which human agents always act, and within which animals never act and never can possibly act.

• The highly abstract reasoning from which such views emerge has dissatisfied many; you may find more nearly true the convictions of ethical intuitionists and realists who said, as H. A. Prichard, Sir David Ross, and my friend and teacher C. D. Broad, of happy memory, used to say, that there is a direct, underivative, intuitive cognition of rights as possessed by other humans, but not by animals.

• Or perhaps in the end we will return to Kant, and say with him that critical reason reveals at the core of human action a uniquely moral will, and the unique ability to grasp and to lay down moral laws for oneself and for others—an ability that is not conceivably within the capacity of any nonhuman animal whatever.

To be a moral agent (on this view) is to be able to grasp the generality of moral restrictions on our will. Humans understand that some things, which may be in our interest, *must not be willed*; we lay down moral laws for ourselves, and thus exhibit, as no other animal can exhibit, moral autonomy. My dog knows that there are certain things she must not do—but she knows this only as the outcome of her learning about her interests, the pains she may suffer if she does what had been taught forbidden. She does not know, cannot know (as Regan agrees) that any conduct is wrong. The proposition *It would be highly advantageous to act in such-and-such a way, but I may not because it would be wrong* is one that no dog or mouse or rabbit, however sweet and endearing, however loyal or attentive to its young, can ever entertain, or intend, or begin to grasp. Right is not in their world. But right and wrong are the very stuff of human moral life, the ever-present awareness of human beings who can do wrong, and who by seeking (often) to avoid wrong conduct prove themselves members of a moral community in which rights may be exercised and must be respected.

Some respond by saying, "This can't be correct, for human infants (and the comatose and senile, etc.) surely have rights, but they make no moral claims or judgments and can make none—and any view entailing that children can have no rights must be absurd." Objections of this kind miss the point badly. It is not individual persons who qualify (or are disqualified) for the possession of rights because of the presence or absence in them of some special capacity, thus resulting in the award of rights to some but not to others. Rights are universally human; they arise in a *human moral world*, in a moral *sphere*. In the human world moral judgments are pervasive; it is the fact that all humans including infants and the senile are members of that moral community—not the fact that as individuals they have or do not have certain special capacities, or merits—that makes humans bearers of rights. Therefore, it is beside the point to insist that animals have remarkable capacities, that they really have a consciousness of self, or of the future, or make plans, and so on. And the tired response that because infants plainly cannot make moral claims they must have no rights at all, or rats must have them too, we ought forever put aside. Responses like these arise out of a misconception of right itself. They mistakenly suppose that rights are tied to some identifiable individual abilities or sensibilities, and they fail to see that rights arise only in a community of moral beings, and that therefore there are spheres in which rights do apply and spheres in which they do not.

Rationality is not at issue; the capacity to communicate is not at issue. My dog can reason, if rather weakly, and she certainly can communicate. Cognitive criteria for the possession of rights,...are morally perilous. Indeed they are. Nor is the capacity to suffer here at issue. And, if *autonomy* be understood only as the capacity to choose this course rather than that, autonomy is not to the point either. But *moral autonomy*—that is, *moral self-legislation*—is to the point, because moral autonomy is uniquely human and is for animals out of the question, as we have seen, and as Regan and I agree. In talking about autonomy, therefore, we must be careful and precise.

Because humans do have rights, and these rights can be violated by other humans, we say that some humans commit *crimes*. But whether a crime has been committed depends utterly on the moral state of mind of the actor. If I take your coat, or your book, honestly thinking it was mine, I do not steal it. The *actus reus* (the guilty deed) must be accompanied, in a genuine crime, by a guilty mind, a *mens rea*. That recognition, not just of possible punishment for an act, but of moral duties that govern us, no rat or cow ever can possess. In primitive times humans did sometimes bring cows and horses to the bar of human justice. We chuckle at that practice now, realizing that accusing cows of crimes marks the primitive moral view as inane. Animals never can be criminals because they have no moral state of mind....

WHY ANIMALS ARE MISTAKENLY BELIEVED TO HAVE RIGHTS

From the foregoing discussion it follows that, if some philosophers believe that they have proved that animals have rights, they must have erred in the alleged proof. Regan is a leader among those who claim to *argue* in defense of the rights of rats; he contends that the best arguments are on his side. I aim next to show how he and others with like views go astray....

[Regan's] case is built entirely on the principle that allegedly *carries over* almost everything earlier claimed about human rights to rats and other animals. What principle is that? It is the principle, put in italics but given no name, that equates moral agents with moral patients:

The validity of the claim to respectful treatment, and thus the case for the recognition of the right to such

treatment, cannot be any stronger or weaker in the case of moral patients than it is in the case of moral agents. (Regan, p. 279)

But hold on. Why in the world should anyone think this principle to be true? Back in Section 5.2, where Regan first recounted his view of moral patients, he allowed that some of them are, although capable of experiencing pleasure and pain, lacking in other capacities. But he is interested, he told us there, in those moral patients—those animals—that are like humans in having *inherent value*. This is the key to the argument for animal rights, the possession of inherent value. How that concept functions in the argument becomes absolutely critical. I will say first briefly what will be shown more carefully later: *Inherent value* is an expression used by Regan (and many like him) with two very different senses—in one of which it is reasonable to conclude that those who have inherent value have rights, and in another sense in which that inference is wholly unwarranted. But the phrase, *inherent value* has some plausibility in both contexts, and thus by sliding from one sense of inherent value to the other Regan appears to succeed, in two pages, in making the case for animal rights.

The concept of inherent value first entered the discussion in the seventh chapter of Regan's (1983) book, at which point his principal object is to fault and defeat utilitarian arguments. It is not (he argued there) the pleasures or pains that go "into the cup" of humanity that give value, but the "cups" themselves; humans are equal in value because they are humans, having inherent value. So we are, all of us, equal—equal in being moral agents who have this inherent value. This approach to the moral stature of humans is likely to be found quite plausible. Regan called it the "postulate of inherent value"; all humans, "The lonely, forsaken, unwanted, and unloved are no more nor less inherently valuable than those who enjoy a more hospitable relationship with others" (p. 237). And Regan went on to argue for the proposition that all moral agents are "equal in inherent value." Holding some such views we are likely to say, with Kant, that all humans are beyond price. Their inherent value gives them moral dignity, a unique role in the moral world, as agents having the capacity to act morally and make moral judgments. This is inherent value in Sense 1.

The expression *inherent value* has another sense, however, also common and also plausible. My dog has inherent value, and so does every wild animal, every lion and zebra, which is why the senseless killing of animals is so repugnant. Each animal is unique, not replaceable in itself by another animal or by any rocks or clay. Animals, like humans, are not just things; they live, and as unique living creatures they have inherent value. This is an important point, and again likely to be thought plausible; but here, in Sense 2, the phrase *inherent value* means something quite distinct from what was meant in its earlier uses.

Inherent value in Sense 1, possessed by all humans but not by all animals, which warrants the claim of human rights, is very different from inherent value in Sense 2, which warrants no such claim. The uniqueness of animals, their intrinsic worthiness as individual living things, does not ground the possession of rights, has nothing to do with the moral condition in which rights arise. Regan's argument reached its critical objective with almost magical speed because, having argued that beings with inherent value (Sense 1) have rights that must be respected, he quickly asserted (putting it in italics lest the reader be inclined to express doubt) that rats and rabbits also have rights because they, too, have inherent value (Sense 2).

This is an egregious example of the fallacy of equivocation: the informal fallacy in which two or more meanings of the same word or phrase have been confused in the several premises of an argument (Cohen & Copi, 1994, pp. 143–144). Why is this slippage not seen at once? Partly because we know the phrase inherent value often is used loosely, so the reader is not prone to quibble about its introduction; partly because the two uses of the phrase relied on are both common, so neither signals danger; partly because inherent value in Sense 2 is indeed shared by those who have it in Sense 1; and partly because the phrase *inherent value* is woven into accounts of what Regan (1983) elsewhere called the *subject-of-a-life criterion*, a phrase of his own devising for which he can stipulate any meaning he pleases, of course, and which also slides back and forth between the sphere of genuine moral agency and the sphere of animal experience. But perhaps the chief reason the equivocation between these two uses of the phrase *inherent value* is obscured (from the author, I believe, as well as from the reader) is the fact that the assertion that animals have rights appears only indirectly, as the outcome of the application of the principle that moral patients are entitled to the same respect as moral agents—a principle introduced at a point in the book long after the important moral differences between moral patients and moral agents have been recognized, with a good deal of tangled philosophical argument having been injected in between....

Animals do not have rights. Right does not apply in their world. We do have many obligations to animals, of course, and I honor Regan's appreciation of their sensitivities. I also honor his seriousness of purpose, and his always civil and always rational spirit. But he is, I submit, profoundly mistaken. I conclude with the observation that, had his mistaken views about the rights of animals long been accepted, most successful medical therapies recently devised—antibiotics, vaccines, prosthetic devices, and other compounds and instruments on which we now rely for saving and improving human lives and for the protection of our children—could not have been developed; and were his views to become general now (an outcome that is unlikely but possible) the consequences for medical science and for human well-being in the years ahead would be nothing less than catastrophic.

Advances in medicine absolutely require experiments, many of which are dangerous. Dangerous experiments absolutely require living organisms as subjects. Those living organisms (we now agree) certainly may not be human beings. Therefore, most advances in medicine will continue to rely on the use of nonhuman animals, or they will stop. Regan is free to say in response, as he does, "so be it." The rest of us must ask if the argument he presents is so compelling as to force us to accept that dreadful result.

REFERENCES

Beauchamp, T.L., & Childress, J.F. (1994). *Principles of biomedical ethics* (4th ed.). New York: Oxford University Press.

Cohen, C., & Copi, I. M. (1994). *Introduction to logic* (9th ed.). New York: Macmillan.

Regan, T. (1983). *The case for animal rights*. Berkeley: University of California Press.

READING QUESTIONS

1. Explain Cohen's distinction between interests and rights, giving examples of each.
2. Cohen claims that although rights entail obligations, the converse obligations entail rights is not true. Give your own example to support Cohen's negative claim.
3. What are the ways in which obligations arise according to Cohen?
4. Describe the four different views about where human rights come from according to Cohen.
5. What is Cohen's response to those who argue that humans such as infants have rights but can't make moral judgments?
6. What reasons does Cohen give for claiming that nonhuman animals lack moral rights?
7. Explain the particular fallacy of equivocation that Cohen claims Regan's argument for animal rights commits.

DISCUSSION QUESTIONS

1. Suppose that Cohen is correct in claiming that Regan's argument commits the fallacy of equivocation. Can you think of another argument for the claim that nonhuman animals have rights?
2. Suppose nonhuman animals do have some rights. How do they compare in content and strength to the basic rights of typical human beings?
3. Cohen admits that human beings do have obligations toward nonhuman animals even if those animals do not have rights. What sorts of obligations do we have toward nonhuman animals? Do these obligations differ in any significant ways from the obligations we have toward other human beings?
4. Cohen argues that human beings are the only kind of thing for which morality is an issue and that nonhuman animals are essentially amoral. What evidence do we have, if any, that nonhuman animals understand the difference between right and wrong? Is their understanding any different from our own?

Mary Anne Warren

Human and Animal Rights Compared

Warren distinguishes between the *content* of a right (the sphere of activity the right protects) and their *strength* (the strength of reasons required for it to be legitimately overridden). The content of the rights of members of a species depends on what its members require to pursue the needs and satisfactions of a life that is natural to its species. Thus, sentient nonhuman animals, according to Warren, have some rights to life, liberty (including freedom of movement), and happiness. However, she further argues that (1) because humans desire liberty and life more strongly than do nonhuman animals and (2) because humans possess moral autonomy whereas nonhuman animals do not, the rights of animals are weaker than the corresponding rights of humans. If moral autonomy is a basis for assigning stronger rights to typical human beings, what about nonparadigm humans including infants, small children, and those who are severely brain damaged? Warren answers that (1) the potential (of infants) and partial autonomy (of children) is a proper basis for assigning strong moral rights to them and that (2) the fact that typical humans place a very high value on nonparadigm humans is itself a further reason for assigning strong moral rights to nonparadigm humans.

Recommended Reading: rights-focused approach to moral issues, chap. 1, sec. 2D.

None of the animal liberationists have thus far provided a clear explanation of how and why the moral status of (most) animals differs from that of (most) human beings; and this is a point which must be clarified if their position is to be made fully persuasive. That there is such a difference seems to follow from some very strong moral intuitions which most of us share. A man who shoots squirrels for sport may or may not be acting reprehensibly; but it is difficult to believe that his actions should be placed in *exactly* the same moral category as those of a man who shoots women, or black children, for sport. So too it is doubtful that the Japanese fishermen who slaughtered dolphins because the latter were thought to be depleting the local fish populations were acting quite *as* wrongly as if they had slaughtered an equal number of their human neighbours for the same reason. . . . There are two dimensions in which we may find differences between the rights of human beings and those of animals. The first involves the *content* of those rights, while the second involves their strength; that is, the strength of the reasons which are required to override them.

Consider, for instance, the right to liberty. The *human* right to liberty precludes imprisonment without due process of law, even if the prison is spacious and the conditions of confinement cause no obvious physical suffering. But it is not so obviously wrong to imprison animals, especially when the area to which they are confined provides a fair approximation of the conditions of their natural habitat, and a reasonable opportunity to pursue the satisfactions natural to their kind. Such conditions, which often result in an increased lifespan, and which may exist in wildlife sanctuaries or even well-designed zoos, need not frustrate the needs or interests of animals in any significant way, and thus do not clearly violate their rights. Similarly treated human beings, on the other hand (e.g., native peoples confined to prison-like reservations), do tend to suffer from their loss of freedom. Human dignity and the fulfillment of the sorts of plans, hopes and desires which appear (thus far) to be uniquely human, require a more extensive freedom of movement than is the case with at least many nonhuman animals. Furthermore, there are aspects of human freedom, such as freedom of thought, freedom of speech and freedom of political association, which simply do not apply in the case of animals.

Thus, it seems that the human right to freedom is more extensive; that is, it precludes a wider range of specific ways of treating human beings than does the corresponding right on the part of animals. The argument cuts both ways, of course. *Some* animals, for example, great whales and migratory birds, may require at least as much physical freedom as do human beings if they are to pursue the satisfactions natural to their kind, and this fact provides a moral argument against keeping such creatures imprisoned. And even chickens may suffer from the extreme and unnatural confinement to which they are subjected on modern "factory farms." Yet it seems unnecessary to claim for *most* animals a right to a freedom quite as broad as that which we claim for ourselves.

Similar points may be made with respect to the right to life. Animals, it may be argued, lack the cognitive equipment to value their lives in the way that human beings do. Ruth Cigman argues that animals have *no* right to life because death is no misfortune for them.[1] In her view, the death of an animal is not a misfortune, because animals have no desires which are *categorical;* that is which do not "merely presuppose being alive (like the desire to eat when one is hungry), but rather answer the question whether one wants to remain alive."[2] In other words, animals appear to lack the sorts of long-range hopes, plans, ambitions and the like, which give human beings such a powerful interest in continued life. Animals, it seems, take life as it comes and do not specifically desire that it go on. True, squirrels store nuts for the winter and deer run from wolves; but these may be seen as instinctive or conditioned responses to present circumstances, rather than evidence that they value life as such.

These reflections probably help to explain why the death of a sparrow seems less tragic than that of a human being. Human lives, one might say, have greater intrinsic value, because they are worth more *to their possessors.* But this does not demonstrate that no nonhuman animal has *any* right to life. Premature death may be a less *severe* misfortune for sentient nonhuman animals than for human beings, but it is a misfortune nevertheless. In the first place, it is a misfortune in that it deprives them of whatever pleasures the future might have held for them, regardless of whether or not they ever *consciously anticipated* those pleasures. The fact that they are not here afterwards, to *experience* their loss, no more shows that they have not lost anything than it does in the case of humans. In the second place, it is (possibly) a misfortune in that it frustrates whatever future-oriented desires animals *may* have, unbeknownst to us. Even now, in an age in which apes have been taught to use simplified human languages and attempts have been made to communicate with dolphins and whales, we still know very little about the operation of nonhuman minds. We know much too little to assume that nonhuman animals never consciously pursue relatively distant future goals. To the extent that they do, the question of whether such desires provide them with *reasons for living* or merely *presuppose* continued life, has no satisfactory answer, since they cannot contemplate these alternatives—or, if they can, we have no way of knowing what their conclusions are. All we know is that the more intelligent and psychologically complex an animal is, the more *likely* it is that it possesses specifically future-oriented desires, which would be frustrated even by *painless* death.

For these reasons, it is premature to conclude from the apparent intellectual inferiority of nonhuman animals that they have no right to life. A more plausible conclusion is that animals do have a right to life but that it is generally somewhat weaker than that of human beings. It is, perhaps, weak enough to enable us to justify killing animals when we have no other ways of achieving such vital goals as feeding or clothing ourselves, or obtaining knowledge which is necessary to save human lives. Weakening their right to life in this way does not render meaningless the assertion that they have such a right. For the point remains that *some* serious justification for the killing of sentient nonhuman animals is always necessary; they may not be killed merely to provide amusement or minor gains in convenience.

If animals' rights to liberty and life are somewhat weaker than those of human beings, may we say the same about their right to *happiness;* that is, their right not to be made to suffer needlessly or to be deprived of the pleasures natural to their kind? If so, it is not immediately clear why. There is little reason to suppose that pain or suffering are any less unpleasant for the higher animals (at least) than they are for us. Our large brains *may* cause us to experience pain more intensely than do most animals, and *probably* cause us to suffer more from the anticipation or remembrance of pain. These facts might tend to suggest that pain is, on the whole, a worse experience for us than for them. But it may also be argued that pain may be *worse* in some respects for nonhuman animals, who are presumably less able to distract themselves from it by thinking of something else, or to comfort themselves with the knowledge that it is temporary. Brigid Brophy points out that "pain is likely to fill the sheep's whole capacity for experience in a way it seldom does in us, whose intellect and imagination can create breaks for us in the immediacy of our sensations."[3]

The net result of such contrasting considerations is that we cannot possibly claim to know whether pain is, on the whole, worse for us than for animals, or whether their pleasures are any more or any less intense than ours. Thus, while we may justify assigning them a somewhat weaker right to life or liberty, on the grounds that they desire these goods less intensely than we do, we cannot discount their rights to freedom from needlessly inflicted pain or unnatural frustration on the same basis. There may, however, be *other* reasons for regarding all of the moral rights of animals as somewhat less stringent than the corresponding human rights.

A number of philosophers who deny that animals have moral rights point to the fact that nonhuman animals evidently lack the capacity for moral autonomy. Moral autonomy is the ability to act as a moral agent; that is, to act on the basis of an understanding of, and adherence to, moral rules or principles. H. J. McCloskey, for example, holds that "it is the capacity for moral autonomy . . . that is basic to the possibility of possessing a right."[4] McCloskey argues that it is inappropriate to ascribe moral rights to any entity which is not a moral agent, or *potentially* a moral agent, because a right is essentially an entitlement granted to a moral agent, licensing him or her to *act* in certain ways and to *demand* that other moral agents refrain from interference. For this reason, he says, "Where there is no possibility of [morally autonomous] action, potentially or actually . . . and where the being is not a member of a kind which is normally capable of [such] action, we withhold talk of rights."[5]

If moral autonomy—or being *potentially* autonomous, or a member of a kind which is *normally* capable of autonomy—is a necessary condition for having moral rights, then probably no nonhuman animal can qualify. For moral autonomy requires such probably uniquely human traits as "the capacity to be critically self-aware, manipulate concepts, use a sophisticated language, reflect, plan, deliberate, choose, and accept responsibility for acting."[6]

But why, we must ask, should the capacity for autonomy be regarded as a precondition for possessing moral rights? Autonomy is clearly crucial for the *exercise* of many human moral or legal rights, such as the right to vote or to run for public office. It is less clearly relevant, however, to the more basic human rights, such as the right to life or to freedom from unnecessary suffering. The fact that animals, like many human beings, cannot *demand* their moral rights (at least not in the words of any conventional human language) seems irrelevant. For, as Joel Feinberg points out, the interests of non-morally autonomous human beings may be defended by others, for example, in legal proceedings; and it is not clear why the interests of animals might not be represented in a similar fashion.[7]

It is implausible, therefore, to conclude that because animals lack moral autonomy they should be accorded *no moral rights whatsoever.* Nevertheless, it may be argued that the moral autonomy of (most) human beings provides a second reason, in addition to their more extensive interests and desires, for according somewhat *stronger* moral rights to human beings. The fundamental insight behind contractualist theories of morality is that, for morally autonomous beings such as ourselves, there is enormous mutual advantage in the adoption of a moral system designed to protect each of us from the harms that might otherwise be visited upon us by others. Each of us ought to accept and promote such a system because, to the extent that others also accept it, we will all be safer from attack by our fellows, more likely to receive assistance when we need it, and freer to engage in individual as well as cooperative endeavours of all kinds.

Thus, it is the possibility of *reciprocity* which motivates moral agents to extend *full and equal* moral rights, in the first instance, only to other moral agents. I respect your rights to life, liberty and the pursuit of happiness in part because you are a sentient being, whose interests have intrinsic moral significance. But I respect them as *fully equal to my own* because I hope and expect that you will do the same for me. Animals, insofar as they lack the degree of rationality necessary for moral autonomy, cannot agree to respect our interests as equal in moral importance to their own, and neither do they expect or demand such respect from us. Of course, domestic animals may expect to be fed, etc. But they do not, and cannot, expect to be treated as moral equals, for they do not understand that moral concept or what it implies. Consequently, it is neither pragmatically feasible nor morally obligatory to extend to them the same *full and equal* rights which we extend to human beings.

Is this a speciesist conclusion? Defenders of a more extreme animal-rights position may point out that this argument, from the lack of moral autonomy, has exactly the same form as that which has been used for thousands of years to rationalize denying equal moral rights to women and members of "inferior" races. Aristotle, for example, argued that women and slaves are naturally subordinate beings, because they lack the capacity for moral autonomy and self-direction,[8] and contemporary versions of this argument, used to support racist or sexist conclusions, are easy to find. Are we simply repeating Aristotle's mistake, in a different context?

The reply to this objection is very simple: animals, unlike women and slaves, really *are* incapable of moral autonomy, at least to the best of our knowledge. Aristotle certainly *ought* to have known that women and slaves are capable of morally autonomous action; their capacity to use moral language alone ought to have alerted him to this likelihood. If comparable evidence exists that (some) nonhuman animals are moral agents we have not yet found it. The fact that some apes (and, possibly, some cetaceans, are capable of learning radically simplified human languages, the terms of which refer primarily to objects and events in their immediate environment, in no way demonstrates that they can understand abstract moral concepts, rules or principles, or use this understanding to regulate their own behaviour.

On the other hand, this argument implies that if we *do* discover that certain nonhuman animals are capable of moral autonomy (which is certainly not impossible), then we ought to extend full and equal moral rights to those animals. Furthermore, if we someday encounter extraterrestrial beings, or build robots, androids or supercomputers which function as self-aware moral agents, then we must extend full and equal moral rights to these as well. Being a member of the human species is not a necessary condition for the possession of full "human" rights. Whether it is nevertheless a *sufficient* condition is the question to which we now turn.

THE MORAL RIGHTS OF NONPARADIGM HUMANS

If we are justified in ascribing somewhat different, and also somewhat stronger, moral rights to human beings than to sentient but non-morally autonomous animals, then what are we to say of the rights of human beings who happen not to be capable of moral autonomy, perhaps not even potentially? Both Singer and Regan have argued that if any of the superior intellectual capacities of normal and mature human beings are used to support a distinction between the moral status of *typical,* or paradigm, human beings, and that of animals, then consistency will require us to place certain "nonparadigm" humans, such as infants, small children and the severely retarded or incurably brain damaged, in the same inferior moral category.[9] Such a result is, of course, highly counterintuitive.

Fortunately, no such conclusion follows from the autonomy argument. There are many reasons for extending strong moral rights to nonparadigm humans; reasons which do not apply to most nonhuman animals. Infants and small children are granted strong moral rights in part because of their *potential* autonomy. But *potential* autonomy, as I have argued elsewhere,[10] is not in itself a sufficient reason for the ascription of full moral rights; if it were, then not only human foetuses (from conception onwards) but even ununited human sperm-egg pairs would have to be regarded as entities with a right to life the equivalent of our own—thus making not only abortion, but any intentional failure to procreate, the moral equivalent of murder. Those who do not find this extreme conclusion acceptable must appeal to reasons other than the *potential* moral autonomy of infants and small children to explain the strength of the latter's moral rights.

One reason for assigning strong moral rights to infants and children is that they possess not just *potential* but *partial* autonomy, and it is not clear how much of it they have at any given moment. The fact that, unlike baby chimpanzees, they are already learning the things which will enable them to *become* morally autonomous, makes it likely that their minds have more subtleties than their speech (or the lack of it) proclaims. Another reason is simply that most of us tend to place a very high value on the lives and well-being of infants. Perhaps we are to some degree "programmed" by nature to love and protect them; perhaps our reasons are somewhat egocentric; or perhaps we value them for their potential. Whatever the explanation, the fact that we do feel this way about them is in itself a valid reason for extending to them stronger moral and legal protections than we extend to nonhuman animals, even those which may have just as well or better-developed psychological capacities. A third, and perhaps the most important, reason is that if we did *not* extend strong moral rights to infants, far too few of them would ever *become* responsible, morally autonomous adults; too many would be treated "like animals" (i.e., in ways that it is generally wrong to treat even animals), and would consequently become socially crippled, antisocial or just very unhappy people. If any part of our moral code is to remain intact, it seems that infants and small children *must* be protected and cared for.

Analogous arguments explain why strong moral rights should also be accorded to other nonparadigm humans. The severely retarded or incurably senile, for instance, may have no potential for moral autonomy, but there are apt to be friends, relatives or other people who care what happens to them. Like children, such individuals may have more mental capacities than are readily apparent. Like children, they are more apt to achieve, or return to moral autonomy if they are valued and well cared for. Furthermore, any one of us may someday become mentally incapacitated to one degree or another, and we would all have reason to be anxious about our own futures if such incapacitation were made the basis for denying strong moral rights.

There are, then, sound reasons for assigning strong moral rights even to human beings who lack the mental capacities which justify the general distinction between human and animal rights. Their rights are based not only on the value which they themselves place upon their lives and well-being, but also on the value which other human beings place upon them.

But is this a valid basis for the assignment of moral rights? . . . Regan argues that we cannot justify the ascription of stronger rights to nonparadigm humans than to nonhuman animals in the way suggested, because "what underlies the ascription of rights to any given X is that X has value independently of anyone's valuing X."[11] After all, we do not speak of expensive paintings or gemstones as having rights, although many people value them and have good reasons for wanting them protected.

There is, however, a crucial difference between a rare painting and a severely retarded or senile human being; the latter not only has (or may have) value for other human beings but *also* has his or her own needs and interests. It may be this which leads us to say that such individuals have intrinsic value. The sentience of nonparadigm humans, like that of sentient nonhuman animals, gives them a place in the sphere of rights holders. So long as the moral rights of all sentient beings are given due recognition, there should be no objection to providing some of them with *additional* protections, on the basis of our interests as well as their own. Some philosophers speak of such additional protections, which are accorded to X on the basis of interests other than X's own, as *conferred* rights, in contrast to *natural* rights, which are entirely based upon the properties of X itself. But such "conferred" rights are not necessarily any weaker or less binding upon moral agents than are "natural" rights. Infants, and most other nonparadigm humans have the *same* basic moral rights that the rest of us do, even though the reasons for ascribing those rights are somewhat different in the two cases. . . .

NOTES

1. Ruth Cigman, "Death, Misfortune, and Species Inequality," *Philosophy and Public Affairs* 10, no. 1 (Winter 1981): p. 48.

2. Ibid., pp. 57–58. The concept of a categorical desire is introduced by Bernard Williams, "The Makropoulous Case," in his *Problems of the Self* (Cambridge: Cambridge University Press), 1973.

3. Brigid Brophy, "In Pursuit of a Fantasy," in *Animals, Men and Morals,* ed. Stanley and Rosalind Godlovitch (New York: Taplinger Publishing Co., 1972), p. 129.

4. H. J. McCloskey, "Moral Rights and Animals," *Inquiry* 22, nos. 1–2 (1979): 31.

5. Ibid., p. 29.

6. Michael Fox, "Animal Liberation: A Critique," *Ethics* 88, no. 2 (January 1978): 111.

7. Joel Feinberg, "The Rights of Animals and Unborn Generations," in *Philosophy and Environmental Crisis,* ed. William T. Blackstone (Athens, Ga.: University of Georgia Press), 1974, pp. 46–47.

8. Aristotle, *Politics* I. 1254, 1260, and 1264.

9. Peter Singer, *Animal Liberation: A New Ethics for Our Treatment of Animals* (New York: Avon, 1975), pp. 75–76; Tom Regan, "One Argument Concerning Animal Rights," *Inquiry* 22, nos. 1–2 (1979): 189–217.

10. Mary Anne Warren, "Do Potential People Have Moral Rights?" *Canadian Journal of Philosophy* 7, no. 2 (June 1977): 275–89.

11. Regan, "One Argument Concerning Animal Rights," p. 189.

READING QUESTIONS

1. Explain the difference between the content and strength of rights according to Warren.
2. Why does Warren believe that nonhuman animals lack a strong right to life? Why might death be a more severe misfortune for a human being than a nonhuman animal?
3. What is Warren's argument against the view that moral autonomy is required in order to possess certain rights? How does she argue for the view that nonhuman animals possess weaker rights than humans? What is Warren's response to the objection that her view is speciesist?
4. What is a nonparadigm human according to Warren? What reasons does she give for thinking that we should grant full moral rights to nonparadigm humans?

DISCUSSION QUESTIONS

1. Suppose that Warren is right to claim that nonparadigm humans should have full moral rights. What reasons could be given in favor of the view that nonhuman animals should have full moral rights as well? Consider some possible objections to Warren's argument for the view that nonparadigm humans should have full moral rights.
2. How relevant should moral autonomy be in the discussion of moral rights? Discuss whether autonomy is ever irrelevant to the ascription of an individual's standing in the moral community.

Jordan Curnutt

A New Argument for Vegetarianism

Curnutt argues that attempts by utilitarians and rights-based moral theorists to defend vegetarianism fail. He defends a new argument for vegetarianism based on the prima facie duty against inflicting harm. In outline, his argument goes as follows. Since many nonhuman animals are harmed by the practice of killing and eating them, such treatment is prima facie morally wrong. Moreover, other considerations including those of cultural practices, aesthetic preferences, convenience, and nutrition do not provide reasons that override this prima facie duty. Thus, killing and eating animals is all-things-considered wrong (in most cases), and thus being a vegetarian is morally required.

Recommended Reading: ethics of prima facie duty, chap. 1, sec. 2F.

Philosophical discussion of vegetarianism has been steadily decreasing over the last ten years or so. This follows a prolific period in the 1970s and 1980s when a veritable flood of books and journal articles appeared, devoted wholly or in part to various defenses and rejections of vegetarianism. What has happened? Have the relevant problems been solved? Have philosophers simply lost interest in the topic? I don't think so. My hypothesis is that the major theoretical approaches to the issue which have been most rigorously pursued have produced a stalemate: appeal to some form of utilitarian theory, or to rights-based theories, or to pain and suffering, have not proved fruitful for resolving the problems.

I would like to present an alternative to these traditional approaches. This alternative avoids the difficulties which result in the stalemate, successfully eludes subsequent objections, and justifies a moral requirement to refrain from eating animals. I will first briefly explain why the old arguments have not been helpful. The remainder of the paper is devoted to the explanation and defense of a new argument for vegetarianism, one which does not depend on calculations of utility, any particular conception of rights, or the imposition of pain and suffering.

OLD ARGUMENTS FOR VEGETARIANISM

Peter Singer has been the leading utilitarian defender of vegetarianism for more than twenty years.[1] He has often cited the vast amounts of pain and suffering experienced by domesticated animals "down on the factory farm" as they await and inevitably succumb to their fate as food for human consumption.[2] A utilitarian of any species is required to produce that state of affairs in which aggregations of certain positive and negative mental states exceed (or at least equal) such aggregations of any alternative state of affairs. Singer has argued that factory farming woefully fails to meet this standard. Vegetarianism is morally obligatory simply because it maximizes utility, precisely what utilitarians say we are supposed to do.

From Jordan Curnutt, "A New Argument for Vegetarianism," *Journal of Social Philosophy* 28 (1997). Reprinted by permission of *Journal of Social Philosophy*.

Animal-eating promotes disutility, precisely what we are supposed to avoid.

But several philosophers have urged that utilitarianism is a perilous ally for the vegetarian. One major problem is that the end of animal-eating produces disutilities which must be accounted for in the utilitarian ledger. When that is done, animal-eating may not emerge as morally wrong after all. For example, R. G. Frey has claimed that the demise of the meat industry and its satellites which would attend a wholesale conversion to vegetarianism would be catastrophic to human welfare, and so could not be given a utilitarian justification.[3] Frey lists fourteen different ways in which rampant vegetarianism would deleteriously affect human affairs, mainly in the form of economic losses for those employed in the industry. In the face of this, his utilitarian calculation yields the result that we are permitted to eat animals at will, but we must strive to reduce the amount of suffering they experience.[4]

Not only does vegetarianism produce disutilities, but animal-eating can actually maximize utility: utilitarianism may *require* animal-eating. Roger Crisp contends that this theory leads to what he calls the "Compromise Requirement view."[5] According to Crisp, "nonintensively-reared animals lead worthwhile lives: and humans derive gustatory pleasure, satisfaction, or some other positive mental state from eating them. Vegetarianism would put an end to these two sources of utility. Thus, given the requirement to maximize utility, raising and eating animals in these circumstances becomes a utilitarian obligation.[6]

These philosophers, among others, have pinpointed why the utilitarian case for vegetarianism is a shaky one. Like any other utilitarian calculation, the issue here is an empirical and hence contingent one: vegetarianism is at the mercy of such capricious factors as the number of humans who eat meat relative to the number of animals eaten, and the negative and positive mental states attendant on a wide variety of animal husbandry situations and human living conditions. A similar contingency concerning methods of livestock-rearing also obtains for any argument premised on the pain and suffering caused to the animals eaten, whether or not these experiences are deployed

in a utilitarian schema. Moreover, this theory requires summing and comparing the positive and negative mental states of *billions* of individuals of several different species. That prospect alone certainly makes it appear as though the problem is an intractable one. The lesson to be learned is that a successful argument for vegetarianism must be independent of any current or possible method of livestock-rearing and must appeal to factors which are fairly clear and manageable.

The leading contender to utilitarian theory in this area has been the rights-based perspective of Tom Regan. His dedication to defending animals in general and vegetarianism in particular nearly matches Singer's in duration and production.[7] In brief, Regan's position is that mammals of at least one year old are "subjects-of-a-life": they are conscious beings with a wide variety of mental states, such as preferences, beliefs, sensations, a sense of self and of the future. These features identify animals as rightsholders and possessors of "inherent" value. One implication of this view is that killing animals for food, whether or not this is done painlessly and independently of the quality of the animals' life, is a violation of their right to respectful treatment, since it uses them as a means to our own ends. Hence, vegetarianism is morally required.

Regan is one of many philosophers who advocate the view that nonpersons in general or animals in particular (or both) qualify as moral rightsholders. These philosophers tend to identify rightsholders according to their possession of certain affective capacities, such as interests or desires, and a number of them argue that animals do have these capacities. On the other hand, many other philosophers prefer cognitive criteria, confining rightsholders to beings with certain more advanced mental capacities—rationality and autonomy are the favorites—and explicitly or by implication disqualifying animals from this category.

The Case for Animal Rights represents the *opus classicus* of the deontological approach to animal issues. Through more than four hundred pages of dense and tightly argued text, Regan has canvassed the philosophical problems of human-animal relationships more thoroughly than anyone has ever done. Even so, his view has been subjected to some quite damaging criticisms, ranging from concern over the mysterious and controversial nature of "inherent value" to charges of inconsistency and implausibility when the rights of humans and those of animals come into conflict.[8] This fact, along with the formidable arguments marshaled by those who champion cognitive requirements for rights-holding, suggest that basing a case for vegetarianism upon the foundation of moral rights is an onerous task. The major problem is that the topic is exceedingly complex. A study of rights must address such daunting question as: What are rights? Are they real independently existing entities (natural rights) or human inventions (political, legal) or both? What is needed to qualify as a rights-holder? Exactly what rights are held by whom and why? How are conflicts among rights settled?

Thus, we have a very complicated theoretical endeavor marked by profound differences, yielding an area of philosophical debate which is highly unsettled. This tells us that a new argument for vegetarianism should traverse a relatively uncontroversial theoretical region which is stable and fixed.

A NEW ARGUMENT FOR VEGETARIANISM (NEW)

NEW makes no appeal to utility, rights, or pain and suffering:

[1] Causing harm is prima facie morally wrong.
[2] Killing animals causes them harm.
[3] Therefore, killing animals is prima facie morally wrong.
[4] Extensive animal-eating requires the killing of animals.
[5] Therefore, animal-eating is prima facie morally wrong.
[6] The wrongness of animal-eating is not overridden.
[7] Therefore, animal-eating is ultima facie morally wrong.

Premise [1] is an assumption: harming is wrong, not because it violates some right or because it fails to maximize utility, but simply because it is wrong. As "prima facie," however, the wrongness may be overridden in certain cases. I discuss premise [6] in the last section of the paper, and there I argue that the wrongness of the harm which eating animals causes them is not overridden, that it is "all things considered" or ultima facie wrong.

The term "extensive" in premise [4] indicates that the target of NEW is the industrialized practice of killing billions of animals as food for hundreds of millions of people, what has been referred to as "factory farming." NEW allows small-scale subsistence hunting, and eating animals who died due to accidents, natural causes, or other sources which do not involve the deliberate actions of moral agents.

The term "animal" used here and throughout this paper refers to any vertebrate species. For reasons I will make clear, NEW is more tentative with regard to invertebrate species. NEW is concerned with the harm caused by the killing and eating of animals, so it does not prohibit uses of animals which do not directly result in their deaths, in particular, those characteristic of the egg and dairy industries. Thus, the argument claims that "ovolacto vegetarianism" is not morally required.

I now proceed to defend the remainder of NEW: how killing animals causes them harm (premise [2]); why the prima facie wrongness of killing animals (conclusion [3]) means that eating animals is also prima facie wrong (conclusion [5]); and why the wrongness is not overridden (premise [6]).

KILLING AND HARM

The claim that killing animals causes them harm might seem too obvious to warrant much discussion. However, its importance here is to distance NEW more clearly from other defenses of vegetarianism. As we will see, killing is harmful—and therefore morally wrong—whether or not any rights are violated, and whether or not any pain or suffering occurs or some other conception of utility fails to be maximized.

Joel Feinberg's analysis of harm is especially useful here. To harm a being is to do something which adversely affects that individual's *interests*. According to Feinberg, harming amounts to "the thwarting, setting back, or defeating of an interest."[9] Interests are not univocal. Some interests are more important than others depending on their function in maintaining the basic well-being or welfare of the individual concerned. The most critical and essential interests that anyone can have are what Feinberg calls "welfare interests":

> In this category are the interests in the continuance for a foreseeable interval of one's life, the interests in one's own physical health and vigor, the integrity and normal functioning of one's body, the absence of absorbing pain and suffering . . . , emotional stability, the absence of groundless anxieties and resentments, the capacity to engage normally in social intercourse . . . , a tolerable social and physical environment, and a certain amount of freedom from interference and coercion.[10]

Welfare interests are "the very most important interests . . . cry[ing] out for protection" not only because they are definitive of basic well-being, but also because their realization is necessary before one can satisfy virtually any other interest or do much of anything with one's life. We cannot achieve our (ulterior) interests in a career or personal relationships or material goods if we are unhealthy, in chronic pain, emotionally unstable, living in an intolerable social and physical environment, and are constantly interfered with and coerced by others. Feinberg concludes that when welfare interests are defeated, a very serious harm indeed has been done to the possessor of those interests.[11]

What does it take to have an interest? Feinberg points out that there is a close connection between interests and desires: if A does in fact have an interest in x, we would typically not deny that A wants x.[12] However, we do speak of x *being in* A's interest, whether A wants x or not; this seems to be especially so when we are considering the welfare interests described above. We believe that normally an individual's life, physical and mental health, and personal freedom are in his or her interest even if these things are not wanted by that individual. This suggests to Feinberg that interests of this kind obtain independently of and are not derived from desires.[13]

We have here all that is needed to defend the claim that killing an animal causes it harm and is therefore (by the moral principle assumed in premise [1]) morally wrong. Moreover, killing is perhaps the most serious sort of harm that can be inflicted upon an animal by a moral agent; this is so not only because of the defeat of an animal's welfare interests—in life, health, and bodily integrity—but also because these are likely the only kind of interests animals have. One understanding of such interests appeals to the desire the animal has to live in a healthy, normal state of well-being. On Feinberg's analysis, another understanding of these interests makes no appeal to any such desire. This implies that killing defeats welfare interests independently of whether or not animals have a desire for life and well-being. They have an interest in this which is defeated when agents cause their deaths.

Some might object here that this is much too fast. Although it is true that x can be in A's interest even when A does not desire x, still x cannot be in A's interest if A has no desires whatever. Otherwise, we would be allowing that plants have interests, and that, some might think, is clearly absurd. Therefore, in order for this analysis of harm to be applicable to animals, it must be shown that they have some desires, preferably desires for that which agents are defeating.

DESIRE

Let us agree that the morally relevant sense of interest we want here is one constituted by certain desires. So why would anyone think that animals do not have desires? We attribute desires to animals routinely on much the same basis that we attribute desires to other people: as an explanation of their behavior. To say that some animal A wants x, uttered because A is doing something, is an extremely common locution for those who are in contact with animals everyday and seems to cause no problem for those who rarely ever encounter an animal. This creates a strong presumption in favor of animal desire. Since nobody denies that humans have desires, what do we have which animals do not have?

An answer that has been given, and perhaps the only answer available, is that animals do not have language. R. G. Frey holds this view that it is linguistic ability which makes desires possible. He maintains that for A to desire x, A must believe that something about x obtains.[14] However, "in expressions of the form '[A] believes that . . .' what follows the 'that' is a sentence, and what [A] believes is that the sentence is true."[15] Since animals do not have a language, they cannot believe that any sentence is true. It follows that animals have neither beliefs nor desires.

This argument has serious defects. Consider first: Frey does not give us any reason to accept the implication that belief is a necessary condition for desire. This is not obvious: the relationship between belief and desire is a complex one which has not been thoroughly investigated by philosophers. Some have held that the relation is one of correlativity, while others argue against it. And what can be called "primitive" desires do not seem to be attended by any particular beliefs: if I desire food or drink or sex or sleep, just what is it that I believe? That I am hungry, thirsty, aroused, or tired? But are these distinguishable from the desires themselves? I might believe that satisfying the desire will bring pleasure or satiation. But I might not. It is by no means clear that there must be some belief lurking about in order to genuinely have a desire.

Consider next Frey's claim that when A believes something, what A believes is that a certain sentence is true. So, for example, Harry's belief that the Chicago Cubs will win the pennant is his believing that the sentence "The Cubs will win the pennant" is true. But in that case, his belief that this sentence is true must itself be the belief that some other sentence is true, namely, the sentence "The sentence 'The Cubs will win the pennant' is true" is true. But then if Harry believes *that* sentence is true, he has to believe another sentence about this sentence about a

sentence is true, and so on. What Frey needs is some way to stop this regress.

Assume there is some nonarbitrary and convincing way to stop the regress; the belief under consideration is Harry's believing that the sentence "The Cubs will win the pennant" is true. But this is not what Harry believes. What he believes is *the Cubs will win the pennant,* that is, he believes that a group of men playing baseball will win more games than any team in their division over the course of the entire season, and then beat the winner of the other division four times in a playoff series. Harry's belief is about certain states of affairs in the world involving complex sets of persons, objects, and events, extended over a significant amount of time. His belief is clearly not about the truth value of a sentence.

So Frey has not shown that belief is a necessary condition for desire, and his argument that animals do not have desires fails. The next move would be to attack the specific desire in question. I have argued that killing an animal is morally wrong because of the harm the killing does; this harm is constituted by the defeat of welfare interests, and this interest is primarily a desire to live. One could then deny that animals have *this* desire. Ruth Cigman takes this approach when she denies that animals have "categorical desires," these being required to genuinely suffer death as a harm or "misfortune":

> to discover whether [death] is a misfortune for an animal, we must ask whether, or in what sense, animals don't want to die. . . . [A categorical desire] . . . answers the question whether one wants to remain alive . . . I reject the suggestion that a categorical desire is attributable to animals [because] . . . animals would have to possess essentially the same conceptions of life and death as persons do [and] . . . understand death as a condition which closes a possible future forever. . . .[16]

Cigman is denying that animals have this desire because it requires understanding certain *concepts:* life, death, the future, the value of life, and others.

The difficulties with Frey's argument suggest that concepts, or language generally, are not required in order to have desires (or beliefs), but these "categorical" kind are presumably supposed to be very special and hard to obtain. Let us assume that there really are these sorts of desires and they are as Cigman has described them. The question is: Why does a being need "categorical desires" in order to have a desire to live?

Cigman does not say. She simply notes that Bernard Williams says the desire to remain alive is a categorical desire and then proceeds to detail what such a desire involves in a way which excludes animals. She has given us no argument for the view that the observations we make of animal activities are not enough to attribute a desire to live to them: fleeing from predators and enemies, seeking cover from severe weather, tending to injuries (such as they can), struggling to extricate themselves from potentially fatal situations, and exhibiting palpable fear in the face of threats to their lives are just the sorts of behaviors which exhibit this desire. Cigman might respond here that such actions only show that animals are "blindly clinging on to life"[17] rather than manifesting a genuine desire to live; it is instinct or some automatic response, not intentional action. But these activities are not blind clutchings, they are purposive and deliberate with a particular point to them, namely, to maintain that life. We would make precisely the same attributions to humans who acted in this way, without pausing to consider whether or not they had the concepts Cigman asserts are requisite. And if we were to learn that these humans did not have these concepts, we would not and should not withdraw our judgment and chalk it all up to instinct. . . .

RECAPITULATION AND ELABORATION

At this point in the defense of NEW, we have firmly established the following:

[1] Causing harm is prima facie morally wrong.
[2] Killing animals causes them harm.
[3] Therefore, killing animals is prima facie morally wrong.

We have seen why killing animals harms them, and we have successfully countered challenges to the analysis of animal harms. We understand why this is one of the worst harms an animal can undergo, which indicates that this is a very serious (though prima facie) wrong when perpetrated by a moral agent. We can also now see the advantages of NEW over the old arguments for vegetarianism. NEW is not contingent upon any current or possible methods of raising animals for humans to eat: no matter how it is done, supplying food for millions of animal-eaters means the defeat of animal welfare interests. NEW does not employ any theoretical constructs which are unsettled and divisive: the analysis of harm in terms of interests and desires which are exhibited by certain behaviors is widely accepted and intuitively appealing. NEW does not introduce any indeterminacy or unwieldy ratiocination into the discussion: the desires and interests of animals, and the wrongness of defeating them, are plainly evident for all those who would simply look and see.

We can also now understand two further aspects of the vegetarianism required by NEW. Killing any creature with certain desires defeats its welfare interests, and is therefore harmful, but not all living things have such desires and interests. The judgment that some being has the requisite mental states must be formed on the basis of behavior and physiological evidence. Since invertebrates and plants either do not exhibit the appropriate behavior or they do not possess the appropriate physiological equipment (or both), consuming them is permitted. Although I do not hold that "interest-less" forms of life have no moral status whatever, I cannot here develop the notion of degrees of moral value or consider what else besides interests would qualify an entity for a moral status. It will have to suffice to say that beings with certain mental states are of greater moral worth than those without them, from the moral point of view it is better (ceteris paribus) to kill and eat a plant than an animal. Moreover, much vegetable matter can be eaten without killing anything: most vegetarian fare consists of the fruits and flowers of plants which are not killed or are harvested at the end of annual life cycles.

THE MORAL WRONGNESS OF EATING ANIMALS

The next step is to link the wrongness of *killing* animals with the wrongness of *eating* them:

[3] Therefore, killing animals is prima facie morally wrong.

[4] Animal-eating requires the killing of animals.

[5] Therefore, animal-eating is prima facie morally wrong.

Many might regard this step as especially problematic. All that has been shown so far is that moral agents who kill animals are engaged in actions which are prima facie wrong; how can it follow from this that different actions, done by different agents, are also prima facie wrong? After all, very few of those who consume animal flesh have personally killed the animals they eat. Those who actually do the killing—slaughterhouse workers—act impermissibly, while those who merely eat the body parts of dead animals supplied by those workers do not. How could the wrongness of one set of agents and actions *transfer* to an entirely different set?

One response would point out that purchasing and consuming the products of "factory farming" contributes to a morally abhorrent practice and thus perpetuates future wrongdoing. So although it is the killing which constitutes what is wrong with the practice of animal-eating, and conceding that very few animal-eaters actually kill what they eat, this contribution to and perpetuation of the killing should prompt us to act *as if* eating the animals is itself wrong. . . .

[But] we must not make this concession. Animal-eating is itself wrong, but this is not due to any "transference" of wrongness from the act of killing to the act of purchasing and eating animal flesh. The purchasing and consuming are two parts of the same wrong.

To see this, consider this [argument]:

This is a lovely lamp. You say its base is made from the bones and its shade from the skin of Jews killed in concentration camps? Well, so what? I didn't kill them.

Of course what the Nazis did was wrong, a very great moral evil. But my not buying the lamp is obviously not going to bring any of them back. Nor will it prevent any future harm: this sort of thing doesn't even occur any more, so there is no future wrongdoing to prevent even if my refusal to buy were effective in this way, which of course it wouldn't be. So what's wrong with buying and using the lamp?

. . . We do not need to find some way to understand this activity which will allow it to be construed "as if" it were wrong (but really isn't). Animal-eating is wrong for much the same reason that purchasing and using the products of a concentration camp or those of slave labor generally is wrong; it is wrong for the same reason that buying stolen property or accepting any of the ill-gotten gains of another is wrong: a person who eats animals, or buys and uses lamps from Auschwitz or cotton clothing from the antebellum South, or a hot stereo from a hoodlum is profiting from, benefiting from a morally nefarious practice. Doing so, and especially doing so when morally innocuous alternatives are readily available, not only indicates support for and the endorsement of moral evil, it is also to participate in that evil. It is an act of complicity, partaking in condemnable exploitation, reaping personal advantages at a significant cost to others. This is so whether or not an individual's abstinence from the practice has any effect whatsoever on its perpetuation. It strikes me as quite uncontroversial to say that one who concurs and cooperates with wrongdoing, who garners benefits through the defeat of the basic welfare interests of others, is himself doing something which is seriously morally wrong.

OVERRIDING THE MORAL WRONGNESS OF EATING ANIMALS

The final step in the defense of NEW is to support premise [6]: the prima facie wrongness of animal-eating is not defeated by additional factors which serve as overriding reasons; from this it will follow that animal-eating is ultima facie morally wrong (the conclusion [7]). There are at least four grounds for overriding this wrong: [1] traditional-cultural; [2] esthetic; [3] convenience; [4] nutrition. Do any of these supply an overriding reason which would morally justify the very serious harm that killing animals for food causes them?

[1] People eat animals because they have been raised on that diet, as have their parents and grandparents and on back through the generations. Animal-eating is a social practice which is deeply embedded into modern culture. Slavery, the oppression of women, and institutionalized racism also once had this status; however, few if any suppose that this status is what makes practices morally right or wrong. Slavery, for example, is wrong because it requires the persistent exploitation, coercion, and degradation of innocent people, not because it happens to be extinct in our society. The fact that a practice has the weight of tradition on its side and a prominent place in a given culture does not in itself carry any moral weight.[18]

[2] Animal flesh is regarded by most people as esthetically pleasing. Animal body parts are prepared for consumption in hundreds of different ways, employing many cooking techniques, spices, and accompaniments. Yet the esthetic attractions of other practices are regarded as irrelevant to their moral appraisal. Heliogabalus had masses of people gathered in fields, only to be mercilessly slaughtered solely for the pleasing effect he found in the sign of red blood on green grass.[19] Or consider "snuff films" whose "plot" is centered around the filming of an actual murder of a person apparently chosen at random. Who would not condemn such cinema in the strongest possible terms, even if it were directed by Orson Welles or Martin Scorcese and starred Dustin Hoffman or Meryl Streep? Yet one has only to enter the nearest slaughterhouse with a video camera on any given day of the week to produce a movie every bit as horrific as the most polished "snuff film."

[3] The convenience of animal-eating is largely a function of the other two factors. The pervasiveness of the desire to eat animals and its prominence within a variety of social functions naturally provokes free market economies to supply meat relatively cheaply and easily. Again, this seems to say nothing about whether or not animal-eating is morally permissible. It is often quite inconvenient and very difficult to keep a promise or discharge a parental duty or make a sacrifice for a stranger—or a friend; it is often quite convenient and very easy to conceal the trust or pocket merchandise without paying or take advantage of powerless persons. Few of us believe that convenience and ease have much of anything to do with whether these actions are morally right or wrong. Why should it be any different when it comes to killing animals for food?

It might be said that the difference is that human interests in convenience, in tradition, and esthetic pleasure override animal interests in life and well-being. This is because the defeat of an *animal* welfare interest, though morally wrong, is not a serious moral wrong. But what is it about humans which gives these nonbasic interests a moral priority over the most basic and important interests an animal can have? And what is it about animals which prevents a severe harm to them from being a serious moral problem? Certainly the nonbasic interests of some humans do not have a moral priority over the welfare interests of other humans, and there is no question that the gravity of a wrong increases with the severity of harm caused to humans. So in order to sustain the objection, some feature, unique to our species, must be identified which accounts for the disparity between human and animal harms and wrongs. Two such distinguishing features, already encountered, immediately present themselves as possibilities: rationality and language. However, appeal to one or both of these capacities raises two immediate problems. First, neither feature is uniquely absent in animal species. No one would seriously contend that a taste for human baby flesh morally overrides anything, nor would anyone claim that the defeat of a child's welfare interest was not a serious moral wrong. Second, why does the proposed feature make such an enormous moral difference? The suggestion is that rationality or language justifies a gap in treatment so vast that it means utmost respect and consideration for humans but allows killing animals out of habit and pleasure. This seems very implausible. The lack of the requisite capacities might reasonably justify *some* difference in treatment, but not a difference which requires a dignified life for those who are favored and permits an ignominious death for those who are not.

[4] Nutrition. Most recent debate about vegetarianism has focused on the question of the adequacy of a meatless diet for human nutrition. This could provide the best reason for overriding the wrongness of killing animals. Let us assume as a fundamental principle that no moral agent can be required to destroy his or her own health and basic welfare for the sake of others; therefore, a diet having this consequence is not morally justified. Does vegetarianism seriously endanger an individual's health and well-being?

Kathryn Paxton George has argued that a vegetarian diet would make large numbers of humans worse off than they would otherwise be if they ate animals. She lists seven groups of people for whom such abstinence possess a significant risk to personal health.[20] Evelyn Pluhar has disputed many of George's findings, especially those regarding the benefits of iron and the threat of osteoporosis. Supported by numerous nutrition studies, she argues that vitamin and mineral supplementation, as well as the utilization of appropriate plant sources, will alleviate any deficiencies; furthermore, Pluhar contends that the correlation between consuming animal products and meeting certain health requirements is a dubious one.[21] George responded that Pluhar had either misinterpreted or willfully ignored certain facts of the studies she had herself cited.[22] The exchange continues; a journal has devoted an entire issue to their disagreement.[23]

Fortunately, we need not enter this particular debate; George's target is what she calls "strict vegetarianism," the vegan diet totally devoid of any animal product. Both George and Pluhar admit that eggs and dairy products, which are allowed by NEW, would fulfill all or most of the required protein, vitamin, and mineral intake. I am not aware of any humans who, as a matter of basic welfare, must consume animal flesh in addition to eggs and dairy products, but if there are any such people, NEW would allow them to eat animals: we are under no moral requirement to significantly harm ourselves so that others, human or non-human, may benefit. . . .

I conclude that none of [1]–[4] serve as a sufficiently compelling reason to override the wrongness of harming the animals eaten. If there are any

individuals who must eat animal flesh (rather than just eggs and dairy products) in order to avoid a pronounced deterioration of their health, they are not prohibited from doing so by NEW. This possible case notwithstanding, the eating of animal flesh is ultima facie morally wrong.

The success of NEW indicates the direction in which future philosophical discussion of vegetarianism ought to proceed. That path avoids the intractable, contingent, and highly controversial nature of rights-based theories and utilitarianism, focusing instead on the more manageable and less contentious areas of the wrongness of harming as a basic moral principle, the analysis of harm as a defeat of interests, and the understanding of interests in terms of certain desires. Much work remains to be done: the philosophy of mind which accounts plausibly for attributions of the appropriate mental states to animals needs to be specified; a fuller analysis of moral status (especially regarding the status of plant life) and the respective natures of basic and nonbasic interests will go a long way toward explaining the conditions under which various moral judgments are overridden; that project will lead to a certain ontological understanding of moral value and the general metaethical underpinnings of the normative ethic employed here. For now, the failure of arguments intended to deny animals the requisite interests and desires, and the failure of those intended to undermine NEW by appeal to overriding reasons and the wrong done by the consumer of animal flesh, means that vegetarianism emerges as a moral requirement as compelling as many of those that are more readily acknowledged and more assiduously practiced.

NOTES

1. In many works, but most notably *Animal Liberation*, Avon, 1st ed., 1975, 2nd ed., 1990; and *Practical Ethics*, Cambridge, 1st ed., 1979, 2nd ed., 1993.

2. For example, *Animal Liberation*, chap. 3. See also *Animal Factories*, Harmony Books, rev. ed., 1990, coauthored with Jim Mason.

3. *Rights, Killing, and Suffering*, Basil Blackwell, 1983.

4. Frey: 197–202.

5. "Utilitarianism and Vegetarianism," *International Journal of Applied Philosophy* 4 (1988): 41–49.

6. Crisp: 44. However, utility is not maximized by eating the products of factory farming. Crisp argues against Frey, that utilitarian considerations do not permit us to eat "intensively-reared" animals. But Frey asserts that "millions upon millions" of animals are not intensively-reared anyway (pp. 33–34).

7. Principally in a series of papers beginning with "The Moral Basis of Vegetarianism," *Canadian Journal of Philosophy* 5 (1975): 181–214, and culminating in *The Case for Animal Rights,* University of California Press, 1983.

8. For example: Paul Taylor, "Inherent Value and Moral Rights," and Jan Narveson, "On a Case for Animal Rights," both in *The Monist* 70 (1987): 15–49; David Ost, "The Case Against Animal Rights," *The Southern Journal of Philosophy* 24 (1986): 365–73; Mary Anne Warren, "Difficulties with the Strong Animal Rights Position," *Between the Species* 2 (1987): 163–73; and J. Baird Callicott, "Review of Tom Regan, *The Case For Animal Rights:* repr. in *In Defense of the Land Ethic,* State University of New York Press, 1989: 39–47.

9. *Harm to Others,* Oxford University Press, 1984: 33.

10. Feinberg: 37. Welfare interests are contrasted with "ulterior interests," which presuppose but also require as a necessary condition that certain welfare interests are satisfied. Feinberg lists raising a family, building a dream house, advancing a social cause, and others as examples of ulterior interests.

11. Ibid.

12. Ibid.: 38.

13. Ibid.: 42.

14. *Interests and Rights,* Clarendon, 1980: 72. Actually, Frey holds that desiring x requires that "I believe that I am deficient in respect of" x. This is too strong. I have amended the belief statement to a weaker claim, leaving it open what exactly A believes about x.

15. Frey: 87.

16. "Death, Misfortune, and Species Inequality," *Philosophy and Public Affairs* 10 (1980): 57–58. The concept of a "categorical desire" is adopted from Bernard Williams. I am taking "misfortune" and "harm" as synonymous, though Cigman herself never equates the two.

17. Cigman: 57.

18. A point forcefully made by means of a macabre device in the classic short story by Shirley Jackson, "The Lottery."

19. As reported by R. M. Hare in *Freedom and Reason,* Clarendon Press, 1963: 161.

20. "So Animal a Human . . . , or the Moral Relevance of Being An Omnivore," *Journal of Agricultural Ethics* 3 (1990): 172–186. Her list (pp. 175–78) includes children, pregnant and lactating women, the elderly, the poor, and the "undereducated."

21. "Who Can be Morally Obligated to be a Vegetarian?" *Journal of Agricultural and Environmental Ethics* 5 (1992): 189–215.

22. "The Use and Abuse of Scientific Studies," *Journal of Agricultural and Environmental Ethics* 5 (1992): 217–33.

23. *Journal of Agricultural and Environmental Ethics* 7 (1994).

READING QUESTIONS

1. Explain the old arguments for vegetarianism according to Curnutt. What are the problems he raises for Peter Singer and Tom Regan's arguments?
2. What is Curnutt's new argument? What does this argument not appeal to according to Curnutt? Why is the first premise problematic?
3. Explain the objection to the view that nonhuman animals have interests of a certain kind. How are interests and desires related according to Curnutt? What reasons does he consider for the view that nonhuman animals lack certain desires that humans have?
4. What are the four considerations that could potentially override the view that it is morally wrong to eat nonhuman animals? How does Curnutt respond to the problems raised by each consideration?

DISCUSSION QUESTIONS

1. Is Curnutt's argument an improvement over the arguments offered by Peter Singer and Tom Regan? Why or why not? What reasons might we have for thinking that Curnutt's new argument does appeal to utility, rights, or pain and suffering?

2. Consider whether there are any morally relevant differences between killing or harming animals and the act of eating them. Could eating animals be morally permitted even though killing and harming them is impermissible?

ADDITIONAL RESOURCES

Web Resources

People for the Ethical Treatment of Animals, <http://www.peta.org/>. Site of one of the most prominent animal advocacy organizations.

Gruen, Lori, "The Moral Status of Animals," <http://plato.stanford.edu/entries/moral-animal/>. An overview of the debate over the moral standing of nonhuman animals.

Authored Books

Francione, Gary L. and Robert Garner, *The Animal Rights Debate: Abolition or Regulation?* (New York: Columbia University Press, 2010). The authors engage in a lively debate over different approaches to the protection of nonhuman animals.

Gruen, Lori, *Ethics and Animals: An Introduction* (Cambridge: Cambridge University Press, 2011). A clear, concise, and balanced overview of the major issues regarding the ethical treatment of animals.

Regan, Tom, *The Case for Animal Rights*, 2nd ed. (Berkeley: University of California Press, 2004). An elaboration and defense of the view presented in his article in this chapter.

Singer, Peter, *Animal Liberation*, 2nd ed. (New York: Harper Perennial, 2002). Citing a wealth of empirical information, Singer's classic book (first published in 1975) defends the equal treatment of all sentient creatures.

Scully, Matthew, *Dominion: The Power of Man, the Suffering of Animals, and the Call to Mercy* (New York: St. Martin's Griffin, 2003). Journalist and former speechwriter for President George W. Bush, Scully argues against affording rights to animals and instead holds that the same goals of those who advocate animal rights can be obtained by appealing to the proper respect we ought to have toward animals.

Edited Collections

Armstrong, Susan J. and Richard G. Botzler (eds.), *The Animal Ethics Reader* (London: Routledge, 2003). An encyclopedic anthology covering all facets of the ethical treatment of animals, including for example, articles on animal experimentation, animals and entertainment, and animals and biotechnology.

Baird, Robert M. and Stuart E. Rosenbaum (eds.), *Animal Experimentation: The Moral Issues* (Amherst, N.Y.: Prometheus Books, 1991). A collection of sixteen essays including articles about the utilitarian and rights approaches to the issues.

Singer, Peter, (ed.), *In Defense of Animals: The Second Wave* (Oxford: Blackwell, 2006). A collection of eighteen essays, most of them appearing here for the first time, representing the most recent wave of thinking about the ethical treatment of animals.

Sunstein, Cass R. and Martha C. Nussbaum (eds.), *Animal Rights: Current Debates and New Directions* (Oxford: Oxford University Press, 2004). A collection of essays addressing ethical questions about ownership, protection against unjustified suffering, and the ability of animals to make their own choices free from human control.

11) Cloning and Genetic Enhancement

Reproductive technology has made significant advances in the past forty years. For instance, **in vitro** ("under glass") **fertilization** (IVF) through which a sperm fertilizes an egg in a petri dish and, after a few days of growth, is then implanted in a woman's uterus, is available to otherwise infertile couples. In 1978, Louise Brown, the first "test tube" baby, was born using in vitro fertilization, and since then over three million children have been born using this procedure. And just as this procedure was subject to intense moral scrutiny when it came on the scene, so also have cloning and the prospect of genetic enhancement, the subjects of this chapter. In order to gain a basic understanding of what is at stake in the moral controversy over these developments, let us focus first on the issue of cloning—what it is and the moral controversy it has caused—and then turn briefly to the ethics of genetic enhancement.

In 1997, a research team, led by Dr. Ian Wilmut of the Roslin Institute in Scotland, produced a cloned sheep named Dolly. The significance of Dolly is that she was the first mammal ever cloned, making it very probable that cloning other mammals, including humans, is possible. The apparently real prospect of cloning a human being—**reproductive cloning**—has generated much recent scientific and ethical debate. And so has **therapeutic cloning**, whose purpose is the production of embryos for use in medical research. If we turn our attention to *human* reproductive and therapeutic cloning, the central moral questions are the following:

- Is either type of human cloning (therapeutic or reproductive) ever morally permissible?
- If not, what best explains why such activities are morally wrong?

In order to appreciate the significance of these questions, we will need to review some very elementary scientific facts about the two types of cloning in question. After we understand what cloning is, we will proceed to recount recent attempts to ban this type of biotechnology and then return to the ethical issues just raised.

1. WHAT IS CLONING?

If we consider **cloning** an organism as an activity that we may choose to perform, then we can say that it involves the process of "asexually" producing a biological organism that is virtually genetically identical to another organism.[1] (The terms "asexual" and "sexual" have technical scientific meanings that are explained later.) The process in question involves **somatic cell**[2] **nuclear transfer** (SCNT for short), and the basic idea here is easy to understand. So, let us begin with what we are calling reproductive cloning and then turn to therapeutic cloning.

In sexual reproduction an unfertilized egg (called an **oocyte**, pronounced, oh-oh-site) is fertilized by a sperm resulting in what is called a **zygote**—a one-cell organism whose nucleus contains genetic information contributed by the individual who produced the egg and by the individual who produced the sperm. A one-cell zygote then undergoes cellular division, and many cells later we have what is commonly called an **embryo**. As the embryo develops, its cells begin to differentiate, forming cells with different functions—nerve cells, blood cells, fat cells, and so on. A complex organism is the eventual result.[3] Here is it important to notice that the process just described refers to cases in which reproduction takes place entirely in a woman's reproductive system *and* to cases in which fertilization is made to occur *in vitro*. Both count as "sexual" in the technical sense of the term, because both involve the genetic contribution from two individuals.

Cloning involves asexual reproduction in which (1) the nucleus of an unfertilized egg is removed and (2) the nucleus of another cell—the "donor" nucleus—is removed and then (3) inserted into the "hollow" unfertilized egg, (4) which is then implanted in a female's uterus. In this process, incidentally, the unfertilized egg and the donor nucleus may be contributed by different individuals, neither of whom may be the individual in whom the embryo is implanted. The resulting individual will be virtually genetically identical—will have nearly the same genetic makeup—as the individual from whom the donor nucleus was taken.[4] The crucial difference between sexual and asexual reproduction, then, is that in the former, the genetic makeup of the zygote and the resulting offspring are the direct result of the genetic contributions of two individuals—the produced offspring is not genetically identical to either of the other two individuals. However, individuals produced asexually by the process of nuclear transfer are virtually genetically identical to the nuclear donor. Let us call the offspring produced by what we are calling reproductive cloning **SCNT individuals**.

We now turn from reproductive cloning to therapeutic cloning. They differ mainly in the purposes for which the process of nuclear transfer is being used. But to understand the therapeutic use of cloning, we need to explain the nature and importance of **stem cells**. Stem cells are found throughout the body and are significant because they have the capability of developing into various kinds of cells or tissues in the body. Stem cells have three general properties: (1) Unlike muscle cells, blood cells, and nerve cells, stem cells have the capacity to renew themselves for long periods of time. (2) Stem cells are "undifferentiated" in that they do not have a specific function as do, for instance, red blood cells whose job is to carry oxygen through the bloodstream. (3) Stem cells can result in specialized cells through a process called differentiation. There are two main types of stem cells that we need to distinguish.

Adult stem cells are undifferentiated cells found among differentiated cells in a tissue or organ. Adult stem cells function to help maintain and repair damaged differentiated cells of the same organ or tissue type in which they are found. This would appear to limit their therapeutic use, since, for example, a heart adult stem cell could only be used to generate heart cells and thus not cells of any other type.[5]

Embryonic stem cells are found in embryos and are "pluripotent," that is, they can become any cell type found in the body. The use of embryonic stem cells, derived from human embryos created by *in vitro* fertilization, has generated moral controversy because extracting these pluripotent cells from embryos inevitably resulted in the destruction of the embryos. However, the use of embryonic stem cells, given that they can be manipulated to become a particular body cell type, makes them particularly valuable for treating disease and other medical conditions. Indeed, cloning makes it possible for a patient who, let us say, is suffering from heart disease, to have the nucleus of one of her body cells injected into an enucleated egg, which could then be induced to multiply, thereby producing an embryo. From the embryo, stem cells could be extracted and used for purposes of producing heart cells that would be used to treat one's heart disease. Because the embryonic stem cells produced in this way match your genetic makeup, there is reduced risk of tissue rejection and thus greater chance of success.

Until recently, use of embryonic stem cells for purposes of research required the destruction of the embryos from which these stem cells were derived. And the destruction of embryos has been a basis of moral objection to such research by those who consider the embryo to have direct moral standing. However, in 2006, scientists developed a technique for extracting embryonic stem cells without destroying the embryos. This breakthrough was greeted by some as removing any serious moral objections to the use of such cells in research.[6]

So, although both types of human cloning—reproductive and therapeutic—involve the process of nuclear transfer, the former has as its aim the bringing about of a child, while the latter aims only at producing a human embryo, stem cells from which might then be used for medical purposes. And, as we have just seen, although there have been moral objections to therapeutic cloning of the sort that involves the destruction of embryos, with new advances in the extraction of stem cells from human embryos that do not destroy the embryo, therapeutic cloning promises to become less morally problematic. In any case, it is the issue of reproductive cloning that has stirred most of the recent moral controversy over cloning and is the topic of concern in our selections dealing with cloning.

2. THE MOVE TO BAN CLONING

In the United States, one immediate response to the announcement of Dolly (the cloned sheep mentioned earlier) was the creation by President William Clinton of the National Bioethics Advisory Council (NBAC), whose task it was to investigate American public policy on the topic of cloning. After conducting hearings during which religious and secular moral arguments were presented and discussed, the NBAC called on Congress to pass laws that would make reproductive cloning a federal crime. To date, Congress has not been able to pass any such law.

On August 9, 2001, President George W. Bush announced that federal funding for stem cell research would be restricted to stem cell lines already in existence on the date of his announcement. This was generally seen as a compromise between factions that oppose therapeutic cloning and those in favor of it. On March 9, 2009, President Barack Obama

159

issued an executive order ("Removing Barriers to Responsible Research Involving Human Stem Cells") that lifted the funding restrictions that President Bush's directive prohibited. Obama's order lifted the ban on the use of federal funding for research on stem cells created with private money, but did not address the ban on the use of federal funds to develop new stem cell lines.

As of January 2008, fifteen U.S. states have passed laws to ban reproductive cloning of humans, while six states also ban human therapeutic cloning.[7] According to the Center for Genetics and Society based in California, as of December of 2009 approximately fifty countries had passed laws banning reproductive cloning.

3. GENETIC ENHANCEMENT

Our developed capacity to manipulate human genetic material not only promises to provide ways to treat disease and other human maladies, but also may enable us to enhance our bodies and our minds. **Genetic enhancement** differs from cloning in that the latter is a form of asexual reproduction as explained earlier, whereas (human) genetic enhancement refers to manipulating genetic material in order to "improve" the talents and capacities of living humans or to produce offspring with certain desirable traits. For instance, the Genetics and IVF Institute in Fairfax, Virginia, already offers a process of sperm separation through which the sex of offspring can be selected. Creating "designer babies," as they are often called, is now an option for those who can afford it. There are further implications. For instance, **eugenics,** the project of "improving" humanity by bringing about genetic changes in future generations, is now very much a possibility.

Let us suppose that therapeutic (medical) genetic manipulation is at least sometimes morally permissible. So the controversy that has generated much recent discussion concerns these questions:

- Is genetic manipulation *for purposes of enhancement* ever morally permissible?
- If they are not, why is such manipulation for such purposes morally impermissible?

4. THEORY MEETS PRACTICE

Let us now turn to some of the moral arguments about cloning and genetic enhancement that are grounded in various moral theories.

Natural Law Theory

One kind of natural law argument against reproductive cloning begins with the thought that cloning (and other forms of assisted reproduction such as in vitro fertilization), because they are asexual, break the natural connection between sex and reproduction—they represent "unnatural" activities. If one then thinks that "unnatural" activities are morally wrong, one will conclude that cloning is morally wrong.[8] (For a critical assessment of arguments that appeal to the idea of "unnaturalness," see the article in chapter 3 by John Corvino.)

But a natural law approach need not appeal to the alleged unnaturalness of actions. Instead, natural law theorists often take reproduction to be intrinsically good and thus something that we are morally obliged to preserve and protect. Our moral obligations regarding reproduction are also taken to include proper child rearing—child rearing that fully respects the dignity of the child. Worries about respecting the worth of the child are a basis for natural law objections to cloning. And here is one place where natural law theory and Kantian ethics coincide in their moral concern about cloning. Let us pursue this line of thought further by turning to the Kantian perspective on this issue.

Kantian Moral Theory

The idea that morality requires that we respect the humanity in both ourselves and others is a guiding idea of the Kantian approach to moral issues. One of the most commonly voiced arguments against reproductive cloning is that it violates the dignity of the SCNT individual—it involves treating the individual as a mere means to some end. The specific manner in which this form of argument is expressed may differ from author to author, but we find a representative example of it in the article from Leon R. Kass included in this chapter.

The plausibility of this line of argument depends on the crucial claim that cloning represents or necessarily involves treating someone merely as a means. But this claim is contested by those who otherwise accept a Kantian approach. For instance, one might argue that there is nothing about cloning that necessarily involves treating anyone merely as a means.[9] Rather, so the argument might continue, whether a child is treated merely as a means and is thus treated immorally depends on the details of how he or she is treated, regardless of how that child was produced.

Consequentialism

Consequentialist thinking about ethical issues is guided by judgments about the likely consequences of actions and practices. Those who oppose cloning point to what they think are likely negative consequences of cloning including, in particular, physical and psychological harms they think are likely to be to be suffered by SCNT individuals.

One particular consequentialist argument is called the "slippery slope." A slippery slope argument may take various forms, but behind all such arguments is the idea that if we allow some action or practice *P*, then we will open the door to other similar actions and practices that will eventually lead us down a slope to disastrous results. So, the argument concludes, we morally ought not to allow *P*. Any such argument, in order to be good, must meet two requirements. First, it must be true that the envisioned results really are bad. But second, the central idea of the argument—that allowing one action or practice will be likely to lead us down a path to disaster—must be plausible. If either of these conditions is not met, the argument is said to commit the slippery slope *fallacy*.

With regard to cloning, the argument is that if we allow certain forms of reproductive cloning for what may seem like acceptable reasons, this will open the door to further and further cases of cloning, leading eventually to its abuse and thus to disaster.[10] Perhaps the most vivid portrayal of what might happen is to be found in Aldous Huxley's 1932 novel, *Brave New World,* in which cloning is the chief means of reproduction through which the majority of humans in that world are genetically engineered for various purposes. Huxley's novel portrays a world in which cloning plays a central role in the loss of human dignity and individuality. In light of the recent advances in biotechnology and the very real possibility of reproductive cloning, Francis Fukuyama writes that "Huxley was right, that the most significant threat posed by contemporary biotechnology is the possibility that it will alter human nature and thereby move us into a 'posthuman' stage in history."[11] Voicing similar worries, Leon R. Kass, in an article included in this chapter, explicitly raises the specter of *Brave New World* in his opposition to cloning.

How forceful are such consequentialist arguments? Their plausibility depends crucially on the estimates of the likely consequences of cloning. Gregory Pence, in one of the selections included in this chapter, attempts to rebut the claims of the anticloning consequentialists. Still, many people who oppose reproductive cloning seem to base their opposition at least partly on what they take to be its likely consequences. Notice that those whose opposition to cloning depends *entirely* on an appeal to consequences will have to retract their moral stance on this topic if we have good reason (now or in the future) to believe that the effects of cloning are no more disastrous than, say, IVF.

Peter Singer raises consequentialist concerns about the ethics of allowing a "genetic supermarket" in which prospective parents can pay to have an embryo genetically modified with the aim of producing a child whose abilities are likely to be superior to a child they would have otherwise had. Singer's "Parental Choice and Human Improvement" is the final selection in this chapter.

Rights Approaches

Approaching the moral issues of both therapeutic and reproductive cloning from the perspective of rights has led to various opposing conclusions about such practices. For instance, some argue that various forms of assisted reproduction are plausibly included within a general right to reproductive liberty.[12] On this basis, one might argue that cloning should be regarded as something we may choose and which is presumptively morally permissible, unless there are compelling reasons against exercising this form of reproductive liberty. Thus, unlike many writers on the ethics of cloning who think that the burden of moral justification rests with those who favor cloning, one might appeal to rights of reproduction and claim that the burden of moral justification rests with those who think that there is something morally wrong with the practice.

But rights are often center stage in arguments that oppose therapeutic as well as reproductive cloning. A main ethical objection to therapeutic cloning is based on the fact that extracting stem cells from a human embryo inevitably destroys the embryo. Those who think that a human embryo has a right to life are against therapeutic cloning for the same reason they are against abortion—such activities involve the killing of an innocent human being with a right to life. Of course, whether this argument is sound depends on the crucial moral claim that a human embryo has a right to life, an issue discussed in the chapter on abortion.

Virtue Ethics

The ethical issues that genetic enhancement raises are much like the ones implicated in the debate over cloning. Consequentialist worries about the likely negative effects of this practice, Kantian worries about whether it is somehow dehumanizing, and natural law questions about its "naturalness" are all represented in the literature on the ethics of enhancement. In addition, ethical concerns that focus on the dispositions and attitudes that would be expressed through engaging in or condoning genetic enhancement—concerns that focus on virtue, vice, and the morality of character—have been raised by some critics of the practice. Michael J. Sandel, whose essay is included here, is one such critic whose approach to the ethics of enhancement is perhaps best viewed as an example of applied virtue ethics. Sandel's position is subjected to critical scrutiny by Frances M. Kamm in her essay included in this chapter.

NOTES

1. Strictly speaking "cloning" refers very generally to the process of duplicating genetic material. There are different types of cloning: DNA cloning, reproductive cloning, and therapeutic cloning. The Human Genome Project has information on types of cloning. See Additional Resources for reference.

2. A **somatic cell** is any cell in the body other than an egg or sperm (gametes).

3. For more detail about human fetal development, see the introduction to the chapter on abortion.

4. The clone's chromosomal or nuclear DNA is the same as the donor's. Some of the clone's genetic material is contributed by the mitochondrial DNA in the cytoplasm of the enucleated egg, hence the claim that clones are "nearly" genetically identical to the cell donor.

5. Through a process of what is called "transdifferentiation" it may be possible for an adult stem cell to differentiate into a different cell type. For example, an adult brain stem cell might differentiate into a blood cell. However, whether this process does actually occur in humans is controversial.

6. Very recently scientists have been able to "reprogram" adult somatic cells so that they come to be like embryonic stem cells—cells that can become differentiated cells of most any type. Such genetically reprogrammed cells are called **induced pluripotent stem (iPS) cells**. If adult cells can be used for the same purposes of embryonic stem cells, then there is no need to engage in the process of cloning to produce an embryo from which embryonic stem cells are then extracted. For more information about iPS cells, consult "Stem Cell Information" to be found on the National Institutes of Health website mentioned in Additional Resources for this chapter.

7. This statistic is reported by the National Conference of State Legislatures (NCSL). See <http://www.ncsl.org/issuesresearch/health/humancloninglaws/tabid/14284/default.aspx>

8. This form of argument can be found in Leon Kass's "The Wisdom of Repugnance," *The New Republic* 216: 22, June 1997. Notice that this argument, if sound, would also show that IVF is morally wrong, since sexual intercourse is not involved in the process. One might respond to this argument by pointing out that although there is a "natural" connection between eating and nutrition, breaking this connection by intravenous feeding would not be morally wrong. Thus, the mere breaking of a "natural" connection cannot make an action morally wrong. See also the Vatican declaration pertaining to bio-ethical issues mentioned in Additional Resources for this chapter under Congregation for the Doctrine of the Faith.

9. This argument is to be found in Philip Kitcher's *The Lives to Come* mentioned in Additional Resources for this chapter.

10. This same slippery slope argument is often used to oppose therapeutic cloning. What forms of cloning might be understood as at least initially acceptable? There is some dispute over whether there are such cases.

11. Francis Fukuyama, *Our Posthuman Future* (New York: Farrar, Straus and Giroux, 2002), 7.

12. See, for instance, John Robertson, "Liberty, Identity, and Human Cloning," *Texas Law Review* 1371, 1998.

Leon R. Kass

Preventing Brave New World

Kass has been a vocal and longtime opponent of cloning. In the selection that follows, he begins by describing the dystopian world envisioned in Aldous Huxley's 1932 *Brave New World* and then proceeds to raise four moral arguments against reproductive cloning. In addition to objections based on likely bad consequences of cloning, Kass argues that cloning is "unethical in itself" because in various ways it represents a degradation of our human nature and thus is not in accord with respect for humanity—this latter sort of reasoning representative of Kantian and natural law ethics. Kass concludes by raising a slippery slope objection to defenders of cloning who, like John Robertson, base their defense on "reproductive liberty."

Recommended Reading: Kantian moral theory, chap. 1, sec. 2C, particularly the Humanity formulation of Kant's categorical imperative. Also relevant is natural law theory, chap. 1, sec. 2B.

I

The urgency of the great political struggles of the twentieth century, successfully waged against totalitarianisms first right and then left, seems to have blinded many people to a deeper and ultimately darker truth about the present age: all contemporary societies are travelling briskly in the same utopian direction. All are wedded to the modern technological project; all march eagerly to the drums of progress and fly proudly the banner of modern science; all sing loudly the Baconian anthem, "Conquer nature, relieve man's estate." Leading the triumphal procession is modern medicine, which is daily becoming ever more powerful in its battle against disease, decay, and death, thanks especially to astonishing achievements in biomedical science and technology—achievements for which we must surely be grateful.

Yet contemplating present and projected advances in genetic and reproductive technologies, in neuroscience and psychopharmacology, and in the development of artificial organs and computer-chip implants for human brains, we now clearly recognize new uses for biotechnical power that soar beyond the traditional medical goals of healing disease and relieving suffering. Human nature itself lies on the operating table, ready for alteration, for eugenic and psychic "enhancement," for wholesale re-design. In leading laboratories, academic and industrial, new creators are confidently amassing their powers and quietly honing their skills, while on the street their evangelists are zealously prophesying a post-human future. For anyone who cares about preserving our humanity, the time has come to pay attention.

Some transforming powers are already here. The Pill. In vitro fertilization. Bottled embryos. Surrogate wombs. Cloning. Genetic screening.

Genetic manipulation. Organ harvesting. Mechanical spare parts. Chimeras. Brain implants. Ritalin for the young, Viagra for the old, Prozac for everyone. And, to leave this vale of tears, a little extra morphine accompanied by Muzak.

Years ago Aldous Huxley saw it coming. In his charming but disturbing novel, *Brave New World* (it appeared in 1932 and is more powerful on each re-reading), he made its meaning strikingly visible for all to see. Unlike other frightening futuristic novels of the past century, such as Orwell's already dated *Nineteen Eighty-Four,* Huxley shows us a dystopia that goes with, rather than against, the human grain. Indeed, it is animated by our own most humane and progressive aspirations. Following those aspirations to their ultimate realization, Huxley enables us to recognize those less obvious but often more pernicious evils that are inextricably linked to the successful attainment of partial goods.

Huxley depicts human life seven centuries hence, living under the gentle hand of humanitarianism rendered fully competent by genetic manipulation, psychoactive drugs, hypnopaedia, and high-tech amusements. At long last, mankind has succeeded in eliminating disease, aggression, war, anxiety, suffering, guilt, envy, and grief. But this victory comes at the heavy price of homogenization, mediocrity, trivial pursuits, shallow attachments, debased tastes, spurious contentment, and souls without loves or longings. The Brave New World has achieved prosperity, community, stability and nigh-universal contentment, only to be peopled by creatures of human shape but stunted humanity. They consume, fornicate, take "soma," enjoy "centrifugal bumble-puppy," and operate the machinery that makes it all possible. They do not read, write, think, love, or govern themselves. Art and science, virtue and religion, family and friendship are all passé. What matters most is bodily health and immediate gratification: "Never put off till tomorrow the fun you can have today." Brave New Man is so dehumanized that he does not even recognize what has been lost.

Huxley's novel, of course, is science fiction. Prozac is not yet Huxley's "soma"; cloning by nuclear transfer or splitting embryos is not exactly "Bokanovskification"; MTV and virtual-reality parlors are not quite the "feelies"; and our current safe and consequenceless sexual practices are not universally as loveless or as empty as those in the novel. But the kinships are disquieting, all the more so since our technologies of bio-psycho-engineering are still in their infancy, and in ways that make all too clear what they might look like in their full maturity. Moreover, the cultural changes that technology has already wrought among us should make us even more worried than Huxley would have us be.

In Huxley's novel, everything proceeds under the direction of an omnipotent—albeit benevolent—world state. Yet the dehumanization that he portrays does not really require despotism or external control. To the contrary, precisely because the society of the future will deliver exactly what we most want—health, safety, comfort, plenty, pleasure, peace of mind and length of days—we can reach the same humanly debased condition solely on the basis of free human choice. No need for World Controllers. Just give us the technological imperative, liberal democratic society, compassionate humanitarianism, moral pluralism, and free markets, and we can take ourselves to a Brave New World all by ourselves—and without even deliberately deciding to go. In case you had not noticed, the train has already left the station and is gathering speed, but no one seems to be in charge.

Some among us are delighted, of course, by this state of affairs: some scientists and biotechnologists, their entrepreneurial backers, and a cheering claque of sci-fi enthusiasts, futurologists, and libertarians. There are dreams to be realized, powers to be exercised, honors to be won, and money—big money—to be made. But many of us are worried, and not, as the proponents of the revolution self-servingly claim, because we are either ignorant of science or afraid of the unknown. To the contrary, we can see all too clearly where the train is headed, and we do not like the destination. We can distinguish cleverness about means from wisdom about ends, and we are loath to entrust the future of the race to those who cannot tell the difference. No friend of humanity cheers for a post-human future.

Yet for all our disquiet, we have until now done nothing to prevent it. We hide our heads in the sand because we enjoy the blessings that medicine keeps supplying, or we rationalize our inaction by declaring that human engineering is inevitable and we can do nothing about it. In either case, we are complicit in preparing for our own degradation, in some respects more to blame than the bio-zealots who, however misguided, are putting their money where their mouth is. Denial and despair, unattractive outlooks in any situation, become morally reprehensible when circumstances summon us to keep the world safe for human flourishing. Our immediate ancestors, taking up the challenge of their time, rose to the occasion and rescued the human future from the cruel dehumanizations of Nazi and Soviet tyranny. It is our more difficult task to find ways to preserve it from the soft dehumanizations of well-meaning but hubristic biotechnical "re-creationism"—and to do it without undermining biomedical science or rejecting its genuine contributions to human welfare. . . .

Not the least of our difficulties in trying to exercise control over where biology is taking us is the fact that we do not get to decide, once and for all, for or against the destination of a post-human world. The scientific discoveries and the technical powers that will take us there come to us piecemeal, one at a time and seemingly independent from one another, each often attractively introduced as a measure that will "help [us] not to be sick." But sometimes we come to a clear fork in the road where decision is possible, and where we know that our decision will make a world of difference—indeed, it will make a permanently different world. Fortunately, we stand now at the point of such a momentous decision. Events have conspired to provide us with a perfect opportunity to seize the initiative and to gain some control of the biotechnical project. I refer to the prospect of human cloning, a practice absolutely central to Huxley's fictional world. Indeed, creating and manipulating life in the laboratory is the gateway to a Brave New World, not only in fiction but also in fact.

"To clone or not to clone a human being" is no longer a fanciful question. Success in cloning sheep, and also cows, mice, pigs, and goats, makes it perfectly clear that a fateful decision is now at hand: whether we should welcome or even tolerate the cloning of human beings. If recent newspaper reports are to be believed, reputable scientists and physicians have announced their intention to produce the first human clone in the coming year. Their efforts may already be under way. . . .

But we dare not be complacent about what is at issue, for the stakes are very high. Human cloning, though partly continuous with previous reproductive technologies, is also something radically new in itself and in its easily foreseeable consequences—especially when coupled with powers for genetic "enhancement" and germline genetic modification that may soon become available, owing to the recently completed Human Genome Project. I exaggerate somewhat, but in the direction of the truth: we are compelled to decide nothing less than whether human procreation is going to remain human, whether children are going to be made to order rather than begotten, and whether we wish to say yes in principle to the road that leads to the dehumanized hell of *Brave New World*.

[W]e have here a golden opportunity to exercise some control over where biology is taking us. The technology of cloning is discrete and well defined, and it requires considerable technical know-how and dexterity; we can therefore know by name many of the likely practitioners. The public demand for cloning is extremely low, and most people are decidedly against it. Nothing scientifically or medically important would be lost by banning clonal reproduction; alternative and non-objectionable means are available to obtain some of the most important medical benefits claimed for (nonreproductive) human cloning. The commercial interests in human cloning are, for now, quite limited; and the nations of the world are actively seeking to prevent it. Now may be as good a chance as we will ever have to get our hands on the wheel of the runaway train now headed for a post-human world and to steer it toward a more dignified human future.

II

What is cloning? Cloning, or asexual reproduction, is the production of individuals who are genetically identical to an already existing individual. The procedure's name is fancy—"somatic cell nuclear transfer"—but its concept is simple. Take a mature but unfertilized egg; remove or deactivate its nucleus; introduce a nucleus obtained from a specialized (somatic) cell of an adult organism. Once the egg begins to divide, transfer the little embryo to a woman's uterus to initiate a pregnancy. Since almost all the hereditary material of a cell is contained within its nucleus, the re-nucleated egg and the individual into which it develops are genetically identical to the organism that was the source of the transferred nucleus.

An unlimited number of genetically identical individuals—the group, as well as each of its members, is called "a clone"—could be produced by nuclear transfer. In principle, any person, male or female, newborn or adult, could be cloned, and in any quantity; and because stored cells can outlive their sources, one may even clone the dead. Since cloning requires no personal involvement on the part of the person whose genetic material is used, it could easily be used to reproduce living or deceased persons without their consent—a threat to reproductive freedom that has received relatively little attention.

Some possible misconceptions need to be avoided. Cloning is not Xeroxing: the clone of Bill Clinton, though his genetic double, would enter the world hairless, toothless, and peeing in his diapers, like any other human infant. But neither is cloning just like natural twinning: the cloned twin will be identical to an older, existing adult; and it will arise not by chance but by deliberate design; and its entire genetic makeup will be preselected by its parents and/or scientists. Moreover, the success rate of cloning, at least at first, will probably not be very high: the Scots transferred two hundred seventy-seven adult nuclei into sheep eggs, implanted twenty-nine clonal embryos, and achieved the birth of only one live lamb clone.

For this reason, among others, it is unlikely that, at least for now, the practice would be very popular; and there is little immediate worry of mass-scale production of multicopies. Still, for the tens of thousands of people who sustain more than three hundred assisted-reproduction clinics in the United States and already avail themselves of in vitro fertilization and other techniques, cloning would be an option with virtually no added fuss. Panos Zavos, the Kentucky

reproduction specialist who has announced his plans to clone a child, claims that he has already received thousands of e-mailed requests from people eager to clone, despite the known risks of failure and damaged offspring. Should commercial interests develop in "nucleus-banking," as they have in sperm-banking and egg-harvesting; should famous athletes or other celebrities decide to market their DNA the way they now market their autographs and nearly everything else; should techniques of embryo and germline genetic testing and manipulation arrive as anticipated, increasing the use of laboratory assistance in order to obtain "better" babies—should all this come to pass, cloning, if it is permitted, could become more than a marginal practice simply on the basis of free reproductive choice.

What are we to think about this prospect? Nothing good. Indeed, most people are repelled by nearly all aspects of human cloning: the possibility of mass production of human beings, with large clones of look-alikes, compromised in their individuality; the idea of father-son or mother-daughter "twins"; the bizarre prospect of a woman bearing and rearing a genetic copy of herself, her spouse, or even her deceased father or mother; the grotesqueness of conceiving a child as an exact "replacement" for another who has died; the utilitarian creation of embryonic duplicates of oneself, to be frozen away or created when needed to provide homologous tissues or organs for transplantation; the narcissism of those who would clone themselves, and the arrogance of others who think they know who deserves to be cloned; the Frankensteinian hubris to create a human life and increasingly to control its destiny; men playing at being God. Almost no one finds any of the suggested reasons for human cloning compelling, and almost everyone anticipates its possible misuses and abuses. And the popular belief that human cloning cannot be prevented makes the prospect all the more revolting.

Revulsion is not an argument; and some of yesterday's repugnances are today calmly accepted—not always for the better. In some crucial cases, however, repugnance is the emotional expression of deep wisdom, beyond reason's power completely to articulate it. Can anyone really give an argument fully adequate to the horror that is father-daughter incest (even with consent), or bestiality, or the mutilation of a corpse, or the eating of human flesh, or the rape or murder of another human being? Would anybody's failure to give full rational justification for his revulsion at those practices make that revulsion ethically suspect?

I suggest that our repugnance at human cloning belongs in this category. We are repelled by the prospect of cloning human beings not because of the strangeness or the novelty of the undertaking, but because we intuit and we feel, immediately and without argument, the violation of things that we rightfully hold dear. We sense that cloning represents a profound defilement of our given nature as procreative beings, and of the social relations built on this natural ground. We also sense that cloning is a radical form of child abuse. In this age in which everything is held to be permissible so long as it is freely done, and in which our bodies are regarded as mere instruments of our autonomous rational will, repugnance may be the only voice left that speaks up to defend the central core of our humanity. Shallow are the souls that have forgotten how to shudder.

III

Yet repugnance need not stand naked before the bar of reason. The wisdom of our horror at human cloning can be at least partially articulated, even if this is finally one of those instances about which the heart has its reasons that reason cannot entirely know. I offer four objections to human cloning: that it constitutes unethical experimentation; that it threatens identity and individuality; that it turns procreation into manufacture (especially when understood as the harbinger of manipulations to come); and that it means despotism over children and perversion of parenthood. Please note: I speak only about so-called reproductive cloning, not about the creation of cloned embryos for research. The objections that may be raised against creating (or using) embryos for research are entirely independent of whether the research embryos are produced by cloning. What is radically distinct and radically new is reproductive cloning.

Any attempt to clone a human being would constitute an unethical experiment upon the resulting child-to-be. In all the animal experiments, fewer than two to three percent of all cloning attempts succeeded. Not only are there fetal deaths and stillborn infants, but many of the so-called "successes" are in fact failures. As has only recently become clear, there is a very high incidence of major disabilities and deformities in cloned animals that attain live birth. Cloned cows often have heart and lung problems; cloned mice later develop pathological obesity; other live-born cloned animals fail to reach normal developmental milestones.

The problem, scientists suggest, may lie in the fact that an egg with a new somatic nucleus must re-program itself in a matter of minutes or hours (whereas the nucleus of an unaltered egg has been prepared over months and years). There is thus a greatly increased likelihood of error in translating the genetic instructions, leading to developmental defects some of which will show themselves only much later. (Note also that these induced abnormalities may also affect the stem cells that scientists hope to harvest from cloned embryos. Lousy embryos, lousy stem cells.) Nearly all scientists now agree that attempts to clone human beings carry massive risks of producing unhealthy, abnormal, and malformed children. What are we to do with them? Shall we just discard the ones that fall short of expectations? Considered opinion is today nearly unanimous, even among scientists: attempts at human cloning are irresponsible and unethical. We cannot ethically even get to know whether or not human cloning is feasible.

If it were successful, cloning would create serious issues of identity and individuality. The clone may experience concerns about his distinctive identity not only because he will be, in genotype and in appearance, identical to another human being, but because he may also be twin to the person who is his "father" or his "mother"—if one can still call them that. Unaccountably, people treat as innocent the homey case of intra-familial cloning—the cloning of husband or wife (or single mother). They forget about the unique dangers of mixing the twin relation with the parent-child relation. (For this situation, the relation of contemporaneous twins is no precedent; yet even this less problematic situation teaches us how difficult it is to wrest independence from the being for whom one has the most powerful affinity.) Virtually no parent is going to be able to treat a clone of himself or herself as one treats a child generated by the lottery of sex. What will happen when the adolescent clone of Mommy becomes the spitting image of the woman with whom Daddy once fell in love? In case of divorce, will Mommy still love the clone of Daddy, even though she can no longer stand the sight of Daddy himself?

Most people think about cloning from the point of view of adults choosing to clone. Almost nobody thinks about what it would be like to be the cloned child. Surely his or her new life would constantly be scrutinized in relation to that of the older version. Even in the absence of unusual parental expectations for the clone—say, to live the same life, only without its errors—the child is likely to be ever a curiosity, ever a potential source of déjà vu. Unlike "normal" identical twins, a cloned individual—copied from whomever—will be saddled with a genotype that has already lived. He will not be fully a surprise to the world: people are likely always to compare his doings in life with those of his alter ego, especially if he is a clone of someone gifted or famous. True, his nurture and his circumstance will be different; genotype is not exactly destiny. But one must also expect parental efforts to shape this new life after the original—or at least to view the child with the original version always firmly in mind. For why else did they clone from the star basketball player, the mathematician, or the beauty queen—or even dear old Dad—in the first place?

Human cloning would also represent a giant step toward the transformation of begetting into making, of procreation into manufacture (literally, "hand-made"), a process that has already begun with in vitro fertilization and genetic testing of embryos. With cloning, not only is the process in hand, but the total genetic blueprint of the cloned individual is selected and determined by the human artisans. To be sure, subsequent development is still according to natural processes; and the resulting children will be recognizably human. But we would be taking a major step into making man himself simply another one of the man-made things.

How does begetting differ from making? In natural procreation, human beings come together to give existence to another being that is formed exactly as we were, by what we are—living, hence perishable, hence aspiringly erotic, hence procreative human beings. But in clonal reproduction, and in the more advanced forms of manufacture to which it will lead, we give existence to a being not by what we are but by what we intend and design.

Let me be clear. The problem is not the mere intervention of technique, and the point is not that "nature knows best." The problem is that any child whose being, character, and capacities exist owing to human design does not stand on the same plane as its makers. As with any product of our making, no matter how excellent, the artificer stands above it, not as an equal but as a superior, transcending it by his will and creative prowess. In human cloning, scientists and prospective "parents" adopt a technocratic attitude toward human children: human children become their artifacts. Such an arrangement is profoundly dehumanizing, no matter how good the product.

Procreation dehumanized into manufacture is further degraded by commodification, a virtually inescapable result of allowing baby-making to proceed under the banner of commerce. Genetic and reproductive biotechnology companies are already growth industries, but they will soon go into commercial orbit now that the Human Genome Project has been completed. "Human eggs for sale" is already a big business, masquerading under the pretense of "donation." Newspaper advertisements on elite college campuses offer up to $50,000 for an egg "donor" tall enough to play women's basketball and with SAT scores high enough for admission to Stanford; and to nobody's surprise, at such prices there are many young coeds eager to help shoppers obtain the finest babies money can buy. (The egg and womb-renting entrepreneurs shamelessly proceed on the ancient, disgusting, misogynist premise that most women will give you access to their bodies, if the price is right.) Even before the capacity for human cloning is perfected, established companies will have invested in the harvesting of eggs from ovaries obtained at autopsy or through ovarian surgery, practiced embryonic genetic alteration, and initiated the stockpiling of prospective donor tissues. Through the rental of surrogate-womb services, and through the buying and selling of tissues and embryos priced according to the merit of the donor, the commodification of nascent human life will be unstoppable.

Finally, the practice of human cloning by nuclear transfer—like other anticipated forms of genetically engineering the next generation—would enshrine and aggravate a profound misunderstanding of the meaning of having children and of the parent-child relationship. When a couple normally chooses to procreate, the partners are saying yes to the emergence of new life in its novelty—are saying yes not only to having a child, but also to having whatever child this child turns out to be. In accepting our finitude, in opening ourselves to our replacement, we tacitly confess the limits of our control.

Embracing the future by procreating means precisely that we are relinquishing our grip in the very activity of taking up our own share in what we hope will be the immortality of human life and the human species. This means that our children are not our children: they are not our property, they are not our possessions. Neither are they supposed to live our lives for us, or to live anyone's life but their own. Their genetic distinctiveness and independence are the natural foreshadowing of the deep truth that they have their own, never-before-enacted life to live. Though sprung from a past, they take an uncharted course into the future.

Much mischief is already done by parents who try to live vicariously through their children. Children are sometimes compelled to fulfill the broken dreams of unhappy parents. But whereas most parents normally have hopes for their children, cloning parents will have expectations. In cloning, such overbearing parents will have taken at the start a decisive step that contradicts the entire meaning of the open and forward-looking nature of parent-child relations. The child is given a genotype that has already lived, with full expectation that this blueprint of a past life ought to be controlling the life that is to come. A wanted child now means a child who exists precisely to fulfill parental wants. Like all the more precise eugenic manipulations that will follow in its wake, cloning is thus inherently despotic, for it seeks to make one's children after one's own image (or an image of one's choosing) and their future according to one's will.

Is this hyperbolic? Consider concretely the new realities of responsibility and guilt in the households of the cloned. No longer only the sins of the parents, but also the genetic choices of the parents, will be visited on the children—and beyond the third and fourth generation; and everyone will know who is responsible. No parent will be able to blame nature or the lottery of sex for an unhappy adolescent's big nose, dull wit, musical ineptitude, nervous disposition, or anything else that he hates about himself. Fairly or not, children will hold their cloners responsible for everything, for nature as well as for nurture. And parents, especially the better ones, will be limitlessly liable to guilt. Only the truly despotic souls will sleep the sleep of the innocent.

IV

The defenders of cloning are not wittingly friends of despotism. Quite the contrary. Deaf to most other considerations, they regard themselves mainly as friends of freedom: the freedom of individuals to reproduce, the freedom of scientists and inventors to discover and to devise and to foster "progress" in genetic knowledge and technique, the freedom of entrepreneurs to profit in the market. They want large-scale cloning only for animals, but they wish to preserve cloning as a human option for exercising our "right to reproduce"—our right to have children, and children with "desirable genes." As some point out, under our "right to reproduce" we already practice early forms of unnatural, artificial, and extra-marital reproduction, and we already practice early forms of eugenic choice. For that reason, they argue, cloning is no big deal.

We have here a perfect example of the logic of the slippery slope. The principle of reproductive freedom currently enunciated by the proponents of cloning logically embraces the ethical acceptability of sliding all the way down: to producing children wholly in the laboratory from sperm to term (should it become feasible), and to producing children whose entire genetic makeup will be the product of parental eugenic planning and choice. If reproductive freedom means the right to have a child of one's own choosing by whatever means, then reproductive freedom knows and accepts no limits.

Proponents want us to believe that there are legitimate uses of cloning that can be distinguished from illegitimate uses, but by their own principles no such limits can be found. (Nor could any such limits be enforced in practice: once cloning is permitted, no one ever need discover whom one is cloning and why.) Reproductive freedom, as they understand it, is governed solely by the subjective wishes of the parents-to-be. The sentimentally appealing case of the childless married couple is, on these grounds, indistinguishable from the case of an individual (married or not) who would like to clone someone famous or talented, living or dead. And the principle here endorsed justifies not only cloning but also all future artificial attempts to create (manufacture) "better" or "perfect" babies. . . .

If you think that such scenarios require outside coercion or governmental tyranny, you are mistaken. Once it becomes possible, with the aid of human genomics, to produce or to select for what some regard as "better babies"—smarter, prettier, healthier, more athletic—parents will leap at the opportunity to "improve" their offspring. Indeed, not to do so will be socially regarded as a form of child neglect. Those who would ordinarily be opposed to such tinkering will be under enormous pressure to compete on behalf of their as yet unborn children—just as some now plan almost from their children's birth how to get them into Harvard. Never mind that, lacking a standard of "good" or "better," no one can really know whether any such changes will truly be improvements.

Proponents of cloning urge us to forget about the science-fiction scenarios of laboratory manufacture or multiple-copy clones, and to focus only on the sympathetic cases of infertile couples exercising their reproductive rights. But why, if the single cases are so innocent, should multiplying their performance be so off-putting? (Similarly, why do others object to people's making money from that practice if the practice itself is perfectly acceptable?) The so-called science-fiction cases—say, Brave New World—make vivid the meaning of what looks to us, mistakenly, to be benign. They reveal that what looks like compassionate humanitarianism is, in the end, crushing dehumanization.

V

Whether or not they share my reasons, most people, I think, share my conclusion: that human cloning is unethical in itself and dangerous in its likely consequences, which include the precedent that it will establish for designing our children. Some reach this conclusion for their own good reasons, different from my own: concerns about distributive justice in access to eugenic cloning; worries about the genetic effects of asexual "in-breeding"; aversion to the implicit premise of genetic determinism; objections to the embryonic and fetal wastage that must necessarily accompany the efforts; religious opposition to "man playing God." But never mind why: the overwhelming majority of our fellow Americans remain firmly opposed to cloning human beings. . . .

READING QUESTIONS

1. According to Kass, What significance does a person's feeling of repugnanace at the thought of reproductive cloning have for questions about the morality of this practice?
2. According to Kass, why would reproductive cloning involve unethical experimentation?
3. According to Kass, why would reproductive cloning "create serious issues for identity and individuality"?
4. Kass claims that reproductive cloning would represent "a giant step toward transformation of begetting into making." What does he mean in saying this? What reasons does he give in support of this claim?
5. According to Kass, why is reproductive cloning "inherently despotic"?

171

DISCUSSION QUESTIONS

1. Consider how a critic might respond to each of Kass's four objections to reproductive cloning.
2. How would Kass respond to Robertson's appeal to reproductive liberty in defense of reproductive cloning?

GREGORY E. PENCE

Will Cloning Harm People?

Many object to reproductive cloning on consequentialist grounds—they claim that this sort of cloning will have bad or even disastrous effects on the individuals who are cloned and on society generally. Pence argues that such objections are often a combination of ignorance about, and unwarranted fear of, the realities of cloning. Of particular interest here are the claims about predicted psychological harm to cloned children. For instance, some worry that reproductive cloning will severely limit the cloned individual's future, since in the process of cloning some decision is made about the clone's genotype. Wouldn't choosing a genotype limit a child's future, genetically determining her or his future life? Pence argues that this sort of reasoning is based on the false view of "genetic determinism" and thus fails to consider the fact that differences in gestation, parents, and environment importantly contribute to the personality, interests, and future prospects of any child. Pence's article thus represents a rebuttal of consequentialist arguments against reproductive cloning, including the various objections brought up in the previous article by Leon Kass.
Recommended Reading: consequentialism, chap. 1, sec. 2A.

The most important moral objection to originating a human by cloning is the claim that the resulting person may be unnecessarily harmed, either by something in the process of cloning or by the unique expectations placed upon the resulting child. This essay considers this kind of objection.

By now the word "cloning" has so many bad associations from science fiction and political demagoguery that there is no longer any good reason to continue to use it. A more neutral phrase, meaning the same thing, is "somatic cell nuclear transfer" (SCNT), which refers to the process by which the

From "Will Cloning Harm People?" Gregory E. Pence, *Flesh of My Flesh: The Ethics of Cloning Humans*, G. E. Pence (Lanham, MD: Rowman and Littlefield, 1998).

genotype of an adult, differentiated cell can be used to create a new human embryo by transferring its nucleus to an enucleated human egg. The resulting embryo can then be gestated to create a baby who will be a delayed twin of its genetic ancestor.

For purposes of clarity and focus, I will only discuss the simple case where a couple wants to originate a single child by SCNT and not the cases of multiple origination of the same genotype. I will also not discuss questions of who would regulate reproduction of genotypes and processes of getting consent to reproduce genotypes.

PARALLELS WITH IN VITRO FERTILIZATION: REPEATING HISTORY?

Any time a new method of human reproduction may occur, critics try to prevent it by citing possible harm to children. The implicit premise: before it is allowed, any new method must prove that only healthy children will be created. Without such proof, the new method amounts to "unconsented to" experimentation on the unborn. So argued the late conservative, Christian bioethicist Paul Ramsey in the early 1970s about in vitro fertilization (IVF).[1]

Of course, ordinary sexual reproduction does not guarantee healthy children every time. Nor can a person consent until he is born. Nor can he really consent until he is old enough to understand consent. The requirement of "consent to be born" is silly.

Jeremy Rifkin, another critic of IVF in the early 1970s, seemed to demand that new forms of human reproduction be risk-free.[2] Twenty years later, Rifkin predictably bolted out the gate to condemn human cloning, demanding its world-wide ban, with penalties for transgressions as severe as those for rape and murder: "It's a horrendous crime to make a Xerox of someone," he declared ominously. "You're putting a human into a genetic straitjacket. For the first time, we've taken the principles of industrial design—quality control, predictability—and applied them to a human being."[3]

Daniel Callahan, a philosopher who had worked in the Catholic tradition and who founded the Hastings Center for research in medical ethics, argued in 1978 that the first case of IVF was "probably unethical" because there was no possible guarantee that Louise Brown would be normal.[4] Callahan added that many medical breakthroughs are unethical because we cannot know (using the philosopher's strong sense of "know") that the first patient will not be harmed. Two decades later, he implied that human cloning would also be unethical: "We live in a culture that likes science and technology very much. If someone wants something, and the rest of us can't prove they are going to do devastating harm, they are going to do it."[5]

Leon Kass, a social conservative and biologist-turned-bioethicist, argued strenuously in 1971 that babies created by artificial fertilization might be deformed: "It doesn't matter how many times the baby is tested while in the mother's womb," he averred, "they will never be certain the baby won't be born without defect."[6]

What these critics overlooked is that no reasonable approach to life avoids all risks. Nothing in life is risk-free, including having children. Even if babies are born healthy, they do not always turn out as hoped. Taking such chances is part of becoming a parent.

Without some risk, there is no progress, no advance. Without risk, pioneers don't cross prairies, astronauts don't walk on the moon, and Freedom Riders don't take buses to integrate the South. The past critics of assisted reproduction demonstrated a psychologically normal but nevertheless unreasonable tendency to magnify the risk of a harmful but unlikely result. Such a result—even if very bad—still represents a very small risk. A baby born with a lethal genetic disease is an extremely bad but unlikely result; nevertheless, the risk shouldn't deter people from having children.

HUMANITY WILL NOT BE HARMED

Human SCNT is even more new and strange-sounding than in vitro fertilization (IVF). All that means is that it will take longer to get used to. Scaremongers have predicted terrible harm if children are born by SCNT, but in fact very little will change. Why is that?

First, to create a child by SCNT, a couple must use IVF, which is an expensive process, costing about $8,000 per attempt [in 1998]. Most American states do not require insurance companies to cover IVF, so IVF is mostly a cash-and-carry operation. Second, most IVF attempts are unsuccessful. The chances of any couple taking home a baby is quite low—only about 15%.

Only about 40,000 IVF babies have been born in America since the early 1980s. Suppose 50,000 such babies are born over the next decade. How many of these couples would want to originate a child by SCNT? Very few—at most, perhaps, a few hundred.

These figures are important because they tamp down many fears. As things now stand, originating humans by SCNT will never be common. Neither evolution nor old-fashioned human sex is in any way threatened. Nor is the family or human society. Most fears about human cloning stem from ignorance.

Similar fears linking cloning to dictatorship or the subjugation of women are equally ignorant. There are no artificial wombs (predictions, yes; realities, no-otherwise we could save premature babies born before 20 weeks). A healthy woman must agree to gestate any SCNT baby and such a woman will retain her right to abort. Women's rights to abortion are checks on evil uses of any new reproductive technology.

NEW THINGS MAKE US FEAR HARMS IRRATIONALLY

SCNT isn't really so new or different. Consider some cases on a continuum. In the first, the human embryo naturally splits in the process of twinning and produces two genetically-identical twins. Mothers have been conceiving and gestating human twins for all of human history. Call the children who result from this process Rebecca and Susan.

In the second case a technique is used where a human embryo is deliberately twinned in order to create more embryos for implantation in a woman

who has been infertile with her mate. Instead of a random quirk in the uterus, now a physician and an infertile couple use a tiny electric current to split the embryo. Two identical embryos are created. All embryos are implanted and, as sometimes happens, rather than no embryo implanting successfully or only one, both embryos implant. Again, Rebecca and Susan are born.

In the third case, one of the twinned embryos is frozen (Susan) along with other embryos from the couple and the other embryo is implanted. In this case, although several embryos were implanted, only the one destined to be Rebecca is successful. Again, Rebecca is born.

Two years pass, and the couple desires another child. Some of their frozen embryos are thawed and implanted in the mother. The couple knows that one of the implanted embryos is the twin of Rebecca. In this second round of reproductive assistance, the embryo destined to be Susan successfully implants and a twin is born. Now Susan and Rebecca exist as twins, but born two years apart. Susan is the delayed twin of Rebecca. (Rumors abound that such births have already occurred in American infertility clinics.)

Suppose now that the "embryo that could become Susan" was twinned, and the "non-Susan" embryo is frozen. The rest of the details are then the same as the last scenario, but now two more years pass and the previously-frozen embryo is now implanted, gestated, and born. Susan and Rebecca now have another identical sister, Samantha. They would be identical triplets, born two and four years apart. In contrast to SCNT, where the mother's contribution of mitochondrial genes introduces small variations in nearly-identical genotypes, these embryos would have identical genomes.

Next, suppose that the embryo that could have been Rebecca miscarried and never became a child. The twinned embryo that could become Susan still exists. So the parents implant this embryo and Susan is born. Query to National Bioethics Advisory Commission: have the parents done something illegal? A child has been born who was originated by reproducing an embryo with a unique genotype. Remember, the embryo-that-could-become Rebecca existed first. So Susan only exists as a "clone" of the non-existent Rebecca.

Now, as bioethicist Leroy Walters emphasizes, let us consider an even thornier but more probable scenario.[7] Suppose we took the embryo-that-could-become Susan and transferred its nucleus to an enucleated egg of Susan's mother. Call the person who will emerge from this embryo "Suzette," because she is like Susan but different, because of her new mitochondrial DNA. Although the "Susan" embryo was created sexually, Suzette's origins are through somatic cell nuclear transfer. It is not clear that this process is illegal. The NBAC *Report* avoids taking a stand on this kind of case.[8]

Now compare all the above cases to originating Susan asexually by SCNT from the genotype of the adult Rebecca. Susan would again have a nearly-identical genome with Rebecca (identical except for mitochondrial DNA contributed by the gestating woman). Here we have nearly identical female genotypes, separated in time, created by choice. But how is this so different from choosing to have a delayed twin-child? Originating a child by SCNT is not a breakthrough in kind but a matter of degree along a continuum invoking twins and a special kind of reproductive choice.

COMPARING THE HARMS OF HUMAN REPRODUCTION

The question of multiple copies of one genome and its special issues of harm are ones that will not be discussed in this essay, but one asymmetry in our moral intuitions should be noticed.

The increasing use of fertility drugs has expanded many times the number of humans born who are twins, triplets, quadruplets, quintuplets, sextuplets, and even (in November of 1997 to the McCaugheys of Iowa) septuplets. If an entire country can rejoice about seven humans who are gestated in the same womb, raised by the same parents, and simultaneously created randomly from the same two sets of chromosomes, why should the same country fear deliberately originating copies of the same genome, either at once or over time? Our intuitions are even more skewed when we rejoice in the statistically-unlikely case of the seven healthy McCaughey children and ignore the far more likely cases where several of the multiply-gestated fetuses are disabled or dead.

People exaggerate the fears of the unknown and downplay the very real dangers of the familiar. In a very important sense, driving a car each day is far more dangerous to children than the new form of human reproduction under discussion here. Many, many people are hurt and killed every day in automobile wrecks, yet few people consider not driving.

In SCNT, there are possible dangers of telomere shortening, inheritance of environmental effects on adult cells passed to embryonic cells, and possible unknown dangers. Mammalian animal studies must determine if such dangers will occur in human SCNT origination. Once such studies prove that there are no special dangers of SCNT, the crucial question will arise: how safe must we expect human SCNT to be before we allow it?

In answering this question, it is very important to ask about the baseline of comparison. How safe is ordinary, human sexual reproduction? How safe is assisted reproduction? Who or what counts as a subject of a safety calculation about SCNT?

At least 40% of human embryos fail to implant in normal sexual reproduction.[9] Although this fact is not widely known, it is important because some discussions tend to assume that every human embryo becomes a human baby unless some extraordinary event occurs such as abortion. But this is not true. Nature seems to have a genetic filter, such that malformed embryos do not implant. About 50% of the rejected embryos are chromosomally abnormal, meaning that if they were somehow brought to term, the resulting children would be mutants or suffer genetic dysfunction.

A widely-reported but misleading aspect of Ian Wilmut's work was that it took 277 embryos to produce one live lamb. In fact, Wilmut started with 277 eggs, fused nuclei with them to create embryos, and then allowed them to become the best 29 embryos, which were allowed to gestate further. He had three lambs almost live, with one true success, Dolly. Subsequent work may easily bring the efficiency rate to 25%. When the calves "Charlie" and "George" were born in 1998, four live-born calves were created from an initial batch of only 50 embryos.[10]

Wilmut's embryo-to-birth ratio only seems inefficient or unsafe because the real inefficiency fate of accepted forms of human assisted reproduction is so little known. In in vitro fertilization, a woman is given drugs to stimulate superovulation so that physicians can remove as many eggs as possible. At each cycle of attempted in vitro fertilization, three or four embryos are implanted. Most couples make several attempts, so as many as nine to twelve embryos are involved for each couple. As noted, only about 15–20% of couples undergoing such attempts ever take home a baby.

Consider what these numbers mean when writ large. Take a hundred couples attempting assisted reproduction, each undergoing (on average) three attempts. Suppose there are unusually good results and that 20% of these couples eventually take home a baby. Because more than one embryo may implant, assume that among these 20 couples, half have non-identical twins. But what is the efficiency rate here? Assuming a low number of three embryos implanted each time for the 300 attempts, it will take 900 embryos to produce 30 babies, for an efficiency rate of 1 in 30.

Nor is it true that all the loss of human potential occurred at the embryonic stage. Unfortunately, some of these pregnancies will end in miscarriages of fetuses, some well along in the second trimester.

Nevertheless, such loss of embryos and fetuses is almost universally accepted as morally permissible. Why is that? Because the infertile parents are trying to conceive their own children, because everyone thinks that is a good motive, and because few people object to the loss of embryos and fetuses *in this context of trying to conceive babies.* Seen in this light, what Wilmut did, starting out with a large number of embryos to get one successful lamb at birth, is not so novel or different from what now occurs in human assisted reproduction.

SUBJECTS AND NONSUBJECTS
OF HARM

One premise that seems to figure in discussions of the safety of SCNT and other forms of assisted reproduction is that loss of human embryos morally matters. That premise should be rejected.

As the above discussion shows, loss of human embryos is a normal part of human conception and, without this process, humanity might suffer much more genetic disease. This process essentially involves the loss of human embryos as part of the natural state of things. Indeed, some researchers believe that for every human baby successfully born, there has been at least one human embryo lost along the way.

In vitro fertilization is widely-accepted as a great success in modern medicine. As said, over 40,000 American babies have been born this way. But calculations indicate that as many as a million human embryos may have been used in creating such successes.

Researchers often create embryos for subsequent cycles of implantation, only to learn that a pregnancy has been achieved and that such stored embryos are no longer needed. Thousands of such embryos can be stored indefinitely in liquid nitrogen. No one feels any great urgency about them and, indeed, many couples decline to pay fees to preserve their embryos.

The above considerations point to the obvious philosophical point that embryos are not persons with rights to life. Like an acorn, their value is all potential, little actual. Faced with a choice between paying a thousand dollars to keep two thousand embryos alive for a year in storage, or paying for an operation to keep a family pet alive for another year, no one will choose to pay for the embryos. How people actually act says much about their real values.

Thus an embryo cannot be harmed by being brought into existence and then being taken out of existence. An embryo is generally considered such until nine weeks after conception, when it is called a "fetus" (when it is born, it is called a "baby"). Embryos are not sentient and cannot experience pain. They are thus not the kind of subjects that can be harmed or benefitted.

As such, whether it takes one embryo to create a human baby or a hundred does not matter morally. It may matter aesthetically, financially, emotionally, or in time spent trying to reproduce, but it does not matter morally. As such, new forms of human reproduction such as IVF and SCNT that involve significant loss of embryos cannot be morally criticized on this charge.

Finally, because embryos don't count morally, they could be tested in various ways to eliminate defects in development or genetic mishaps. Certainly, if four or five SCNT embryos were implanted, only the healthiest one should be brought to term. As such, the risk of abnormal SCNT babies could be minimized.

SETTING THE STANDARD ABOUT THE RISK OF HARM

Animal tests have not yet shown that SCNT is safe enough to try in humans, and extensive animal testing should be done over the next few years. That means that, before we attempt SCNT in humans, we will need to be able to routinely produce healthy offspring by SCNT in lambs, cattle, and especially, nonhuman primates. After this testing is done, the time will come when a crucial question must be answered: how safe must human SCNT be before it is allowed? This is probably the most important, practical question before us now.

Should we have a very high standard, such that we take virtually no risk with a SCNT child? Daniel Callahan and Paul Ramsey, past critics of IVF, implied that unless a healthy baby could be guaranteed the first time, it was unethical to try to produce babies in a new way. At the other extreme, a low standard would allow great risks.

What is the appropriate standard? How high should be the bar over which scientists must be made to jump before they are allowed to try to originate a SCNT child? In my opinion, the standard of Callahan and Ramsey is too high. In reality, only God can meet that Olympian standard. It is also too high for those physicians trying to help infertile couples. If this high standard had been imposed on these people in the past, no form of assisted reproduction—including in vitro fertilization—would ever have been allowed.

On the other end of the scale, one could look at the very worst conditions for human gestation, where mothers are drug-dependent during pregnancy or exposed to dangerous chemicals. Such worst-case conditions include parents with a 50% chance of passing on a lethal genetic disease. The lowest standard of harm allows human reproduction even if there is such a high risk of harm ("harm" in the sense that the child would likely have a sub-normal future). One could argue that since society allows such mothers and couples to reproduce sexually, it could do no worse by allowing a child to be originated by SCNT.

I believe that the low standard is inappropriate to use with human SCNT. There is no reason to justify down to the very worst conditions under which society now tolerates humans being born. If the best we can do by SCNT is to produce children as good as those born with fetal-maternal alcohol syndrome, we shouldn't originate children this way.

Between these standards, there is the normal range of risk that is accepted by ordinary people in sexual reproduction. Human SCNT should be allowed when the predicted risk from animal studies falls within this range. "Ordinary people" refers to those who are neither alcoholic nor dependent on an illegal drug and where neither member of the couple knowingly passes on a high risk for a serious genetic disease.

This standard seems reasonable. It does not require a guarantee of a perfect baby, but it also rejects the "anything goes" view. For example, if the rate of serious deformities in normal human reproduction is 1%, and if the rate of chimpanzee SCNT reproduction were brought down to this rate, and if there were no reason to think that SCNT in human primates would he any higher, it should be permissible to attempt human SCNT. . . .

PSYCHOLOGICAL HARM TO THE CHILD

Another concern is about psychological harm to a child originated by SCNT. According to this objection, choosing to have a child is not like choosing a car or house. It is a moral decision because another being is affected. Having a child should be a careful, responsible choice and focused on what's best for the child. Having a child originated by SCNT is not morally permissible because it is not best for the child.

The problem with this argument is the last six words of the last sentence, which assumes bad motives on the part of parents. Unfortunately, SCNT is associated with bad motives in science fiction, but until we have evidence that it will be used this way, why assume the worst about people?

Certainly, if someone deliberately brought a child into the world with the intention of causing him harm, that would be immoral. Unfortunately, the concept of harm is a continuum and some people have very high standards, such that not providing a child a stay-at-home parent constitutes harming the child. But there is nothing about SCNT per se that is necessarily linked to bad motives. True, people would have certain expectations of a child created by SCNT, but parents-to-be already have certain expectations about children.

Too many parents are fatalistic and just accept whatever life throws at them. The very fact of being a parent for many people is something they must accept (because abortion was not a real option). Part of this acceptance is to just accept whatever genetic combination comes at birth from the random assortment of genes.

But why is such acceptance a good thing? It is a defeatist attitude in medicine against disease; it is a defeatist attitude toward survival when one's culture or country is under attack; and it is a defeatist attitude toward life in general. "The expectations of parents will be too high!" critics repeat. "Better to leave parents in ignorance and to leave their children as randomness decrees." The silliness of that view is apparent as soon as it is made explicit.

If we are thinking about harm to the child, an objection that comes up repeatedly might be called the argument for an open future. "In the case of cloning," it is objected, "the expectations are very specifically tied to the life of another person. So in a sense, the child's future is denied to him because he will be expected to be like his ancestor. But part of the wonder of having children is surprise at how they turn out. As such, some indeterminacy should remain

a part of childhood. Human SCNT deprives a person of an open future because when we know how his previous twin lived, we will know how the new child will live."

It is true that the adults choosing this genotype rather than that one must have some expectations. There has to be some reason for choosing one genotype over another. But these expectations are only half based in fact. As we know, no person originated by SCNT will be identical to his ancestor because of mitochondrial DNA, because of his different gestation, because of his different parents, because of his different time in history, and perhaps, because of his different country and culture. Several famous pairs of conjoined twins, such as Eng and Chang, with both identical genotypes and identical uterine/childhood environments, have still had different personalities.[11] To assume that a SCNT child's future is not open is to assume genetic reductionism.

Moreover, insofar as parents have specific expectations about children created by SCNT, such expectations will likely be no better or worse than the normal expectations by parents of children created sexually. As said, there is nothing about SCNT per se that necessitates bad motives on the part of parents.

Notice that most of the expected harm to the child stems *from the predicted, prejudicial attitudes of other people to the SCNT child.* ("Would you want to be a cloned child? Can you imagine being called a freak and having only one genetic parent?") As such, it is important to remember that social expectations are *merely* social expectations. They are malleable and can change quickly. True, parents might initially have expectations that are too high and other people might regard such children with prejudice. But just as such inappropriate attitudes faded after the first cases of in vitro fertilization, they will fade here too.

Ron James, the Scottish millionaire who funded much of Ian Wilmut's research, points out that social attitudes change fast. Before the announcement of Dolly, polls showed that people thought that cloning animals and gene transfer to animals were "morally problematic," whereas germ-line gene therapy fell in the category of "just wrong." Two months after the announcement of Dolly, and after much discussion of human cloning, people's attitudes had shifted to accepting animal cloning and gene transfer to humans as "morally permissible," whereas germ-line gene therapy had shifted to being merely "morally problematic."[12]

James Watson, the co-discoverer of the double helix, once opposed in vitro fertilization by claiming that prejudicial attitudes of other people would harm children created this way. . . .[13] In that piece, the prejudice was really in Watson, because the way that he was stirring up fear was doing more to create the prejudice than any normal human reaction. Similarly, Leon Kass's recent long essay in *The New Republic* . . . where he calls human asexual reproduction "repugnant" and a "horror," creates exactly the kind of prejudiced reaction that he predicts.[14] Rather than make a priori, self-fulfilling prophecies, wouldn't it be better to be empirical about such matters? To be more optimistic about the reactions of ordinary parents?

Children created by SCNT would not *look* any different from other children. Nobody at age two looks like he does at age 45 and, except for his parents, nobody knows what the 45-year-old man looked liked at age two. And since ordinary children often look like their parents, no one would be able to tell a SCNT child from others until he had lived a decade.

Kass claims that a child originated by SCNT will have "a troubled psychic identity" because he or she will be "utterly" confused about his social, genetic, and kinship ties.[15] At worst, this child will be like a child of "incest" and may, if originated as a male from the father, have the same sexual feelings towards the wife as the father. An older male might in turn have strong sexual feelings toward a young female with his wife's genome.

Yet if this were so, any husband of any married twin might have an equally troubled psychic identity because he might have the same sexual feelings toward the twin as his wife. Instead, those in relationships with twins claim that the individuals are very different.

Much of the above line of criticism simply begs the question and assumes that humans created by SCNT will be greeted by stigma or experience confusion. It is hard to understand why, once one gets beyond the novelty, because a child created asexually would know *exactly* who his ancestor was. No confusion there. True, prejudicial expectations could damage children, but why make public policy based on that?

Besides, isn't this kind of argument hypocritical in our present society? Where no one is making any serious effort to ban divorce, despite the overwhelming evidence that divorce seriously damages children, even teenage children. It is always far easier to concentrate on the dramatic, far-off harm than the ones close-at-hand. When we are really concerned about minimizing harm to children, we will pass laws requiring all parents wanting to divorce to go through counseling sessions or to wait a year. We will pass a federal law compelling child-support from fathers who flee to other states, and make it impossible to renew a professional license or get paid in a public institution in another state until all child-support is paid. After that is done, then we can non-hypocritically talk about how much our society cares about not harming children who may be originated in new ways.

In conclusion, the predicted harms of SCNT to humans are wildly exaggerated, lack a comparative baseline, stem from irrational fears of the unknown, overlook greater dangers of familiar things, and are often based on the armchair psychological speculation of amateurs. Once studies prove SCNT as safe as normal sexual reproduction in non-human mammals, the harm objection will disappear. Given other arguments that SCNT could substantially benefit many children, the argument that SCNT would harm children is a weak one that needs to be weighed against its many potential benefits.[16]

NOTES

1. Paul Ramsey, *Fabricated Man: The Ethics of Genetic Control* (New Haven, Conn.: Yale University Press, 1970).

2. "What are the psychological implications of growing up as a specimen, sheltered not by a warm womb but by steel and glass, belonging to no one but the lab technician who joined together sperm and egg? In a world already populated with people with identity crises, what's

the personal identity of a test-tube baby?" J. Rifkin and T. Howard, *Who Shall Play God?* (New York: Dell, 1977), 15.

3. Quoted in Ehsan Masood, "Cloning Technique 'Reveals Legal Loophole'," *Nature* 38, 27 February 1987.

4. *New York Times,* 27 July 1978, A16.

5. Knight-Ridder newspapers, 10 March 1997.

6. Leon Kass, "The New Biology: What Price Relieving Man's Estate?" *Journal of the American Medical Association,* vol. 174, 19 November 1971, 779–788.

7. Leroy Walters, "Biomedical Ethics and Their Role in Mammalian Cloning," Conference on Mammalian Cloning: Implications for Science and Society, 27 June 1997, Crystal City Marriott, Crystal City, Virginia.

8. National Bioethics Advisory Commission (NBAC), *Cloning Human Beings: Report and Recommendations of the National Bioethics Advisory Commission,* Rockville, Md., June 1997.

9. A. Wilcox et al., "Incidence of Early Loss of Pregnancy," *New England Journal of Medicine* 319, no. 4, 28 July 1988, 189–194. See also J. Grudzinskas and A. Nysenbaum, "Failure of Human Pregnancy after Implantation," *Annals of New York Academy of Sciences*

442, 1985, 39–44; J. Muller et al., "Fetal Loss after Implantation," *Lancet* 2, 1980, 554–556.

10. Rick Weiss, "Genetically Engineered Calves Cloned," 21 January 1998, *Washington Post,* A3.

11. David R. Collins, *Eng and Chang: The Original Siamese Twins* (New York: Dillon Press, 1994). Elaine Landau, *Joined at Birth: The Lives of Conjoined Twins* (New York: Grolier Publishing, 1997). See also Geoffrey A. Machin, "Conjoined Twins: Implications for Blastogenesis," *Birth Defects: Original Articles Series* 20, no. 1, 1993, March of Dimes Foundation, 142.

12. Ron James, Managing Director, PPL Therapeutics, "Industry Perspective: The Promise and Practical Applications," Conference on Mammalian Cloning: Implications for Science and Society, 27 June 1997, Crystal City Marriott, Crystal City, Virginia.

13. James D. Watson, "Moving Towards the Clonal Man," *Atlantic,* May 1971, 50–53.

14. Leon Kass, "The Wisdom of Repugnance," *The New Republic,* 2 June 1997.

15. Kass, "The Wisdom of Repugnance," 22–23.

16. Thanks to Mary Litch for comments on this essay.

READING QUESTIONS

1. What is the primary aim of Pence's article?
2. Why does Pence think that reproductive cloning will not harm humanity?
3. How does Pence defend the claim that an embryo cannot be the subject of harm?
4. One argument against reproductive cloning is that individuals who are brought about by this method will lack an "open future." Explain this argument. How does Pence criticize the argument?
5. How does Pence criticize Kass's "troubled psychic identity" objection to reproductive cloning?

DISCUSSION QUESTIONS

1. Pence claims that objections to reproductive cloning based on alleged psychological harms to cloned individuals are not good objections. Should we agree with him about this matter?
2. Given that infertile couples can try to have children by means of IVF (in vitro fertilization), can you think of any situations in which someone has good reason to prefer reproductive cloning to IVF as a method of assisted reproduction?

MICHAEL J. SANDEL

The Case against Perfection

Sandel's article is concerned with the ethics of genetic engineering and, in particular, with the prospect of enhancing human beings through such processes as sex selection; in short, it is concerned with the "ethics of enhancement," including eugenics. Sandel argues that such enhancement is morally questionable, not because of its likely consequences but because of the attitudes toward human beings that it expresses and promotes. As Sandel puts it, "The deepest moral objection to enhancement lies less in the perfection it seeks than in the human disposition it expresses and promotes." Enhancement, claims Sandel, devalues the moral significance of what he calls "giftedness," which "honors the cultivation and display of natural talents." From a religious perspective, enhancement devalues natural gifts because by allowing our talents and powers to be subject to human design, we "confuse our role with God's." From a secular perspective, if we come to see our talents as up to us, we damage the virtues of humility, responsibility, and solidarity. He explains why this is so in his discussion of eugenics.

Sandel's moral case against genetic engineering can be viewed as grounded in considerations of virtue and hence a virtue ethics approach to this issue. Here, it is important to recall from the moral theory primer that some consequentialists in ethics (perfectionists) make considerations of human perfection the basis of their theory of right conduct. Morally right actions are ones that best promote such human perfections as knowledge and achievement. This is not Sandel's approach to the ethics of enhancement. Rather, he stresses the kinds of dispositions of character and associated attitudes toward human life that loss of a sense of giftedness would bring in its wake.

Recommended Reading: virtue ethics, chap. 1, sec. 2E. Also relevant is consequentialism, chap. 1, sec. 2A.

Breakthroughs in genetics present us with a promise and a predicament. The promise is that we may soon be able to treat and prevent a host of debilitating diseases. The predicament is that our newfound genetic knowledge may also enable us to manipulate our own nature—to enhance our muscles, memories, and moods; to choose the sex, height, and other genetic traits of our children; to make ourselves "better than well." When science moves faster than moral understanding, as it does today, men and women struggle to articulate their unease. In liberal societies they reach first for the language of autonomy, fairness, and individual rights. But this part of our moral vocabulary is ill equipped to address the hardest questions posed by genetic engineering. The genomic revolution has induced a kind of moral vertigo.

Consider cloning. The birth of Dolly the cloned sheep, in 1997, brought a torrent of concern about

From Michael J. Sandel, "The Case Against Perfection: What's Wrong with Designer Children, Bionic Athletes, and Genetic Engineering?" *Atlantic Monthly*, April 2004.

the prospect of cloned human beings. There are good medical reasons to worry. Most scientists agree that cloning is unsafe, likely to produce offspring with serious abnormalities. (Dolly recently died a premature death.) But suppose technology improved to the point where clones were at no greater risk than naturally conceived offspring. Would human cloning still be objectionable? Should our hesitation be moral as well as medical? What, exactly, is wrong with creating a child who is a genetic twin of one parent, or of an older sibling who has tragically died—or, for that matter, of an admired scientist, sports star, or celebrity?

Some say cloning is wrong because it violates the right to autonomy: by choosing a child's genetic makeup in advance, parents deny the child's right to an open future. A similar objection can be raised against any form of bioengineering that allows parents to select or reject genetic characteristics. According to this argument, genetic enhancements for musical talent, say, or athletic prowess, would point children toward particular choices, and so designer children would never be fully free.

At first glance the autonomy argument seems to capture what is troubling about human cloning and other forms of genetic engineering. It is not persuasive, for two reasons. First, it wrongly implies that absent a designing parent, children are free to choose their characteristics for themselves. But none of us chooses his genetic inheritance. The alternative to a cloned or genetically enhanced child is not one whose future is unbound by particular talents but one at the mercy of the genetic lottery.

Second, even if a concern for autonomy explains some of our worries about made-to-order children, it cannot explain our moral hesitation about people who seek genetic remedies or enhancements for themselves. Gene therapy on somatic (that is, nonreproductive) cells, such as muscle cells and brain cells, repairs or replaces defective genes. The moral quandary arises when people use such therapy not to cure a disease but to reach beyond health, to enhance their physical or cognitive capacities, to lift themselves above the norm.

Like cosmetic surgery, genetic enhancement employs medical means for nonmedical ends—ends unrelated to curing or preventing disease or repairing injury. But unlike cosmetic surgery, genetic enhancement is more than skin-deep. If we are ambivalent about surgery or Botox injections for sagging chins and furrowed brows, we are all the more troubled by genetic engineering for stronger bodies, sharper memories, greater intelligence, and happier moods. The question is whether we are right to be troubled, and if so, on what grounds.

In order to grapple with the ethics of enhancement, we need to confront questions largely lost from view—questions about the moral status of nature, and about the proper stance of human beings toward the given world. Since these questions verge on theology, modern philosophers and political theorists tend to shrink from them. But our new powers of biotechnology make them unavoidable. To see why this is so, consider four examples already on the horizon: muscle enhancement, memory enhancement, growth-hormone treatment, and reproductive technologies that enable parents to choose the sex and some genetic traits of their children. In each case what began as an attempt to treat a disease or prevent a genetic disorder now beckons as an instrument of improvement and consumer choice.

Muscles

Everyone would welcome a gene therapy to alleviate muscular dystrophy and to reverse the debilitating muscle loss that comes with old age. But what if the same therapy were used to improve athletic performance? Researchers have developed a synthetic gene that, when injected into the muscle cells of mice, prevents and even reverses natural muscle deterioration. The gene not only repairs wasted or injured muscles but also strengthens healthy ones. This success bodes well for human applications. H. Lee Sweeney, of the University of Pennsylvania, who leads the research, hopes his discovery will cure the immobility that afflicts the elderly. But Sweeney's bulked-up mice have already attracted the attention of athletes seeking a competitive edge. Although the therapy is not yet approved for human use, the prospect of genetically enhanced weight lifters, home-run sluggers, linebackers, and sprinters is easy to imagine. The widespread use of steroids and other performance-improving drugs in professional sports suggests that many athletes will be eager to avail themselves of genetic enhancement.

Suppose for the sake of argument that muscle-enhancing gene therapy, unlike steroids, turned out to be safe—or at least no riskier than a rigorous weight-training regimen. Would there be a reason to ban its use in sports? There is something unsettling about the image of genetically altered athletes lifting SUVs or hitting 650-foot home runs or running a three-minute mile. But what, exactly, is troubling about it? Is it simply that we find such superhuman spectacles too bizarre to contemplate? Or does our unease point to something of ethical significance?

It might be argued that a genetically enhanced athlete, like a drug-enhanced athlete, would have an unfair advantage over his unenhanced competitors. But the fairness argument against enhancement has a fatal flaw: it has always been the case that some athletes are better endowed genetically than others, and yet we do not consider this to undermine the fairness of competitive sports. From the standpoint of fairness, enhanced genetic differences would be no worse than natural ones, assuming they were safe and made available to all. If genetic enhancement in sports is morally objectionable, it must be for reasons other than fairness.

Memory

Genetic enhancement is possible for brains as well as brawn. In the mid-1990s scientists managed to manipulate a memory-linked gene in fruit flies, creating flies with photographic memories. More recently researchers have produced smart mice by inserting extra copies of a memory-related gene into mouse embryos. The altered mice learn more quickly and remember things longer than normal mice. The extra copies were programmed to remain active even in old age, and the improvement was passed on to offspring.

Human memory is more complicated, but biotech companies, including Memory Pharmaceuticals, are in hot pursuit of memory-enhancing drugs, or "cognition enhancers," for human beings. The obvious

market for such drugs consists of those who suffer from Alzheimer's and other serious memory disorders. The companies also have their sights on a bigger market: the 81 million Americans over fifty, who are beginning to encounter the memory loss that comes naturally with age. A drug that reversed age-related memory loss would be a bonanza for the pharmaceutical industry: a Viagra for the brain. Such use would straddle the line between remedy and enhancement. Unlike a treatment for Alzheimer's, it would cure no disease; but insofar as it restored capacities a person once possessed, it would have a remedial aspect. It could also have purely nonmedical uses: for example, by a lawyer cramming to memorize facts for an upcoming trial, or by a business executive eager to learn Mandarin on the eve of his departure for Shanghai.

Some who worry about the ethics of cognitive enhancement point to the danger of creating two classes of human beings: those with access to enhancement technologies, and those who must make do with their natural capacities. And if the enhancements could be passed down the generations, the two classes might eventually become subspecies—the enhanced and the merely natural. But worry about access ignores the moral status of enhancement itself. Is the scenario troubling because the unenhanced poor would be denied the benefits of bioengineering, or because the enhanced affluent would somehow be dehumanized? As with muscles, so with memory: the fundamental question is not how to ensure equal access to enhancement but whether we should aspire to it in the first place.

Height

Pediatricians already struggle with the ethics of enhancement when confronted by parents who want to make their children taller. Since the 1980s human growth hormone has been approved for children with a hormone deficiency that makes them much shorter than average. But the treatment also increases the height of healthy children. Some parents of healthy children who are unhappy with their stature (typically boys) ask why it should make a difference whether a child is short because of a hormone deficiency or because his parents happen to be short. Whatever the cause, the social consequences are the same.

In the face of this argument some doctors began prescribing hormone treatments for children whose short stature was unrelated to any medical problem. By 1996 such "off-label" use accounted for 40 percent of human-growth-hormone prescriptions. Although it is legal to prescribe drugs for purposes not approved by the Food and Drug Administration, pharmaceutical companies cannot promote such use. Seeking to expand its market, Eli Lilly & Co. recently persuaded the FDA to approve its human growth hormone for healthy children whose projected adult height is in the bottom one percentile—under five feet three inches for boys and four feet eleven inches for girls. This concession raises a large question about the ethics of enhancement: If hormone treatments need not be limited to those with hormone deficiencies, why should they be available only to very short children? Why shouldn't all shorter-than-average children be able to seek treatment? And what about a child of average height who wants to be taller so that he can make the basketball team?

Some oppose height enhancement on the grounds that it is collectively self-defeating; as some become taller, others become shorter relative to the norm. Except in Lake Wobegon, not every child can be above average. As the unenhanced began to feel shorter, they, too, might seek treatment, leading to a hormonal arms race that left everyone worse off, especially those who couldn't afford to buy their way up from shortness.

But the arms-race objection is not decisive on its own. Like the fairness objection to bioengineered muscles and memory, it leaves unexamined the attitudes and dispositions that prompt the drive for enhancement. If we were bothered only by the injustice of adding shortness to the problems of the poor, we could remedy that unfairness by publicly subsidizing height enhancements. As for the relative height deprivation suffered by innocent bystanders, we could compensate them by taxing those who buy their way to greater height. The real question is whether we want to live in a society where parents feel compelled to spend a fortune to make perfectly healthy kids a few inches taller.

Sex Selection

Perhaps the most inevitable nonmedical use of bioengineering is sex selection. For centuries parents have been trying to choose the sex of their children. Today biotech succeeds where folk remedies failed.

One technique for sex selection arose with prenatal tests using amniocentesis and ultrasound. These medical technologies were developed to detect genetic abnormalities such as spina bifida and Down syndrome. But they can also reveal the sex of the fetus—allowing for the abortion of a fetus of an undesired sex. Even among those who favor abortion rights, few advocate abortion simply because the parents do not want a girl. Nevertheless, in traditional societies with a powerful cultural preference for boys, this practice has become widespread.

Sex selection need not involve abortion, however. For couples undergoing in vitro fertilization (IVF), it is possible to choose the sex of the child before the fertilized egg is implanted in the womb. One method makes use of preimplantation genetic diagnosis (PGD), a procedure developed to screen for genetic diseases. Several eggs are fertilized in a petri dish and grown to the eight-cell stage (about three days). At that point the embryos are tested to determine their sex. Those of the desired sex are implanted; the others are typically discarded. Although few couples are likely to undergo the difficulty and expense of IVF simply to choose the sex of their child, embryo screening is a highly reliable means of sex selection. And as our genetic knowledge increases, it may be possible to use PGD to cull embryos carrying undesired genes, such as those associated with obesity, height, and skin color. The science-fiction movie *Gattaca* depicts a future in which parents routinely screen embryos for sex, height, immunity to disease, and even IQ. There is something troubling about the *Gattaca* scenario, but it is not easy to identify what exactly is wrong with screening embryos to choose the sex of our children.

One line of objection draws on arguments familiar from the abortion debate. Those who believe that an embryo is a person reject embryo screening for the same reasons they reject abortion. If an eight-cell embryo growing in a petri dish is morally equivalent to a fully developed human being, then discarding it is no better than aborting a fetus, and both practices are equivalent to infanticide. Whatever its merits, however, this "pro-life" objection is not an argument against sex selection as such.

The latest technology poses the question of sex selection unclouded by the matter of an embryo's moral status. The Genetics & IVF Institute, a for-profit infertility clinic in Fairfax, Virginia, now offers a sperm-sorting technique that makes it possible to choose the sex of one's child before it is conceived. X-bearing sperm, which produce girls, carry more DNA than Y-bearing sperm, which produce boys; a device called a flow cytometer can separate them. The process, called MicroSort, has a high rate of success.

If sex selection by sperm sorting is objectionable, it must be for reasons that go beyond the debate about the moral status of the embryo. One such reason is that sex selection is an instrument of sex discrimination—typically against girls, as illustrated by the chilling sex ratios in India and China. Some speculate that societies with substantially more men than women will be less stable, more violent, and more prone to crime or war. These are legitimate worries—but the sperm-sorting company has a clever way of addressing them. It offers MicroSort only to couples who want to choose the sex of a child for purposes of "family balancing." Those with more sons than daughters may choose a girl, and vice versa. But customers may not use the technology to stock up on children of the same sex, or even to choose the sex of their firstborn child. (So far the majority of MicroSort clients have chosen girls.) Under restrictions of this kind, do any ethical issues remain that should give us pause?

The case of MicroSort helps us isolate the moral objections that would persist if muscle-enhancement, memory-enhancement, and height-enhancement technologies were safe and available to all.

It is commonly said that genetic enhancements undermine our humanity by threatening our capacity to act freely, to succeed by our own efforts, and to consider ourselves responsible—worthy of praise or blame—for the things we do and for the way we are. It is one thing to hit seventy home runs as the result

of disciplined training and effort, and something else, something less, to hit them with the help of steroids or genetically enhanced muscles. Of course, the roles of effort and enhancement will be a matter of degree. But as the role of enhancement increases, our admiration for the achievement fades—or, rather, our admiration for the achievement shifts from the player to his pharmacist. This suggests that our moral response to enhancement is a response to the diminished agency of the person whose achievement is enhanced.

Though there is much to be said for this argument, I do not think the main problem with enhancement and genetic engineering is that they undermine effort and erode human agency. The deeper danger is that they represent a kind of hyperagency—a Promethean aspiration to remake nature, including human nature, to serve our purposes and satisfy our desires. The problem is not the drift to mechanism but the drive to mastery. And what the drive to mastery misses and may even destroy is an appreciation of the gifted character of human powers and achievements.

To acknowledge the giftedness of life is to recognize that our talents and powers are not wholly our own doing, despite the effort we expend to develop and to exercise them. It is also to recognize that not everything in the world is open to whatever use we may desire or devise. Appreciating the gifted quality of life constrains the Promethean project and conduces to a certain humility. It is in part a religious sensibility. But its resonance reaches beyond religion.

It is difficult to account for what we admire about human activity and achievement without drawing upon some version of this idea. Consider two types of athletic achievement. We appreciate players like Pete Rose, who are not blessed with great natural gifts but who manage, through striving, grit, and determination, to excel in their sport. But we also admire players like Joe DiMaggio, who display natural gifts with grace and effortlessness. Now, suppose we learned that both players took performance-enhancing drugs. Whose turn to drugs would we find more deeply disillusioning? Which aspect of the athletic ideal—effort or gift—would be more deeply offended?

Some might say effort: the problem with drugs is that they provide a shortcut, a way to win without striving. But striving is not the point of sports; excellence is. And excellence consists at least partly in the display of natural talents and gifts that are no doing of the athlete who possesses them. This is an uncomfortable fact for democratic societies. We want to believe that success, in sports and in life, is something we earn, not something we inherit. Natural gifts, and the admiration they inspire, embarrass the meritocratic faith; they cast doubt on the conviction that praise and rewards flow from effort alone. In the face of this embarrassment we inflate the moral significance of striving, and depreciate giftedness. This distortion can be seen, for example, in network-television coverage of the Olympics, which focuses less on the feats the athletes perform than on heartrending stories of the hardships they have overcome and the struggles they have waged to triumph over an injury or a difficult upbringing or political turmoil in their native land.

But effort isn't everything. No one believes that a mediocre basketball player who works and trains even harder than Michael Jordan deserves greater acclaim or a bigger contract. The real problem with genetically altered athletes is that they corrupt athletic competition as a human activity that honors the cultivation and display of natural talents. From this standpoint, enhancement can be seen as the ultimate expression of the ethic of effort and willfulness—a kind of high-tech striving. The ethic of willfulness and the biotechnological powers it now enlists are arrayed against the claims of giftedness.

The ethic of giftedness, under siege in sports, persists in the practice of parenting. But here, too, bio-engineering and genetic enhancement threaten to dislodge it. To appreciate children as gifts is to accept them as they come, not as objects of our design or products of our will or instruments of our ambition. Parental love is not contingent on the talents and attributes a child happens to have. We choose our friends and spouses at least partly on the basis of qualities we find attractive. But we do not choose our children. Their qualities are unpredictable, and even the most conscientious parents cannot be held wholly responsible for the kind of children they have. That is why parenthood, more than other human relationships, teaches what the theologian William F. May calls an "openness to the unbidden."

May's resonant phrase helps us see that the deepest moral objection to enhancement lies less in the perfection it seeks than in the human disposition it expresses and promotes. The problem is not that parents usurp the autonomy of a child they design. The problem lies in the hubris of the designing parents, in their drive to master the mystery of birth. Even if this disposition did not make parents tyrants to their children, it would disfigure the relation between parent and child, and deprive the parent of the humility and enlarged human sympathies that an openness to the unbidden can cultivate. . . .

The mandate to mold our children, to cultivate and improve them, complicates the case against enhancement. We usually admire parents who seek the best for their children, who spare no effort to help them achieve happiness and success. Some parents confer advantages on their children by enrolling them in expensive schools, hiring private tutors, sending them to tennis camp, providing them with piano lessons, ballet lessons, swimming lessons, SAT-prep courses, and so on. If it is permissible and even admirable for parents to help their children in these ways, why isn't it equally admirable for parents to use whatever genetic technologies may emerge (provided they are safe) to enhance their children's intelligence, musical ability, or athletic prowess?

The defenders of enhancement are right to this extent: improving children through genetic engineering is similar in spirit to the heavily managed, high-pressure child-rearing that is now common. But this similarity does not vindicate genetic enhancement. On the contrary, it highlights a problem with the trend toward hyperparenting. One conspicuous example of this trend is sports-crazed parents bent on making champions of their children. Another is the frenzied drive of overbearing parents to mold and manage their children's academic careers.

As the pressure for performance increases, so does the need to help distractible children concentrate on the task at hand. This may be why diagnoses of attention deficit and hyperactivity disorder have increased so sharply. Lawrence Diller, a pediatrician and the author of *Running on Ritalin*, estimates that five to six percent of American children under eighteen (a total of four to five million kids) are currently prescribed Ritalin,

Adderall, and other stimulants, the treatment of choice for ADHD. (Stimulants counteract hyperactivity by making it easier to focus and sustain attention.) The number of Ritalin prescriptions for children and adolescents has tripled over the past decade, but not all users suffer from attention disorders or hyperactivity. High school and college students have learned that prescription stimulants improve concentration for those with normal attention spans, and some buy or borrow their classmates' drugs to enhance their performance on the SAT or other exams. Since stimulants work for both medical and nonmedical purposes, they raise the same moral questions posed by other technologies of enhancement. . . .

This demand for performance and perfection animates the impulse to rail against the given. It is the deepest source of the moral trouble with enhancement.

Some see a clear line between genetic enhancement and other ways that people seek improvement in their children and themselves. Genetic manipulation seems somehow worse—more intrusive, more sinister—than other ways of enhancing performance and seeking success. But morally speaking, the difference is less significant than it seems. Bioengineering gives us reason to question the low-tech, high-pressure child-rearing practices we commonly accept. The hyperparenting familiar in our time represents an anxious excess of mastery and dominion that misses the sense of life as a gift. . . .

Why not shake off our unease about genetic enhancement as so much superstition? What would be lost if biotechnology dissolved our sense of giftedness?

From a religious standpoint the answer is clear: To believe that our talents and powers are wholly our own doing is to misunderstand our place in creation, to confuse our role with God's. Religion is not the only source of reasons to care about giftedness, however. The moral stakes can also be described in secular terms. If bioengineering made the myth of the "self-made man" come true, it would be difficult to view our talents as gifts for which we are indebted, rather than as achievements for which we are responsible. This would transform three key features of our moral landscape: humility, responsibility, and solidarity.

In a social world that prizes mastery and control, parenthood is a school for humility. That we care deeply about our children and yet cannot choose the kind we want teaches parents to be open to the unbidden. Such openness is a disposition worth affirming, not only within families but in the wider world as well. It invites us to abide the unexpected, to live with dissonance, to rein in the impulse to control. A *Gattaca*-like world in which parents became accustomed to specifying the sex and genetic traits of their children would be a world inhospitable to the unbidden, a gated community writ large. The awareness that our talents and abilities are not wholly our own doing restrains our tendency toward hubris.

Though some maintain that genetic enhancement erodes human agency by overriding effort, the real problem is the explosion, not the erosion, of responsibility. As humility gives way, responsibility expands to daunting proportions. We attribute less to chance and more to choice. Parents become responsible for choosing, or failing to choose, the right traits for their children. Athletes become responsible for acquiring, or failing to acquire, the talents that will help their teams win.

One of the blessings of seeing ourselves as creatures of nature, God, or fortune is that we are not wholly responsible for the way we are. The more we become masters of our genetic endowments, the greater the burden we bear for the talents we have and the way we perform. Today when a basketball player misses a rebound, his coach can blame him for being out of position. Tomorrow the coach may blame him for being too short. Even now the use of performance-enhancing drugs in professional sports is subtly transforming the expectations players have for one another; on some teams players who take the field free from amphetamines or other stimulants are criticized for "playing naked."

The more alive we are to the chanced nature of our lot, the more reason we have to share our fate with others. Consider insurance. Since people do not know whether or when various ills will befall them, they pool their risk by buying health insurance and life insurance. As life plays itself out, the healthy wind up subsidizing the unhealthy, and those who live to a ripe old age wind up subsidizing the families of those who die before their time. Even without a sense of mutual obligation, people pool their risks and resources and share one another's fate.

But insurance markets mimic solidarity only insofar as people do not know or control their own risk factors. Suppose genetic testing advanced to the point where it could reliably predict each person's medical future and life expectancy. Those confident of good health and long life would opt out of the pool, causing other people's premiums to skyrocket. The solidarity of insurance would disappear as those with good genes fled the actuarial company of those with bad ones.

The fear that insurance companies would use genetic data to assess risks and set premiums recently led the Senate to vote to prohibit genetic discrimination in health insurance. But the bigger danger, admittedly more speculative, is that genetic enhancement, if routinely practiced, would make it harder to foster the moral sentiments that social solidarity requires.

Why, after all, do the successful owe anything to the least-advantaged members of society? The best answer to this question leans heavily on the notion of giftedness. The natural talents that enable the successful to flourish are not their own doing but, rather, their good fortune—a result of the genetic lottery. If our genetic endowments are gifts, rather than achievements for which we can claim credit, it is a mistake and a conceit to assume that we are entitled to die full measure of the bounty they reap in a market economy. We therefore have an obligation to share this bounty with those who, through no fault of their own, lack comparable gifts.

A lively sense of the contingency of our gifts—a consciousness that none of us is wholly responsible for his or her success—saves a meritocratic society from sliding into the smug assumption that the rich are rich because they are more deserving than the poor. Without this, the successful would become even more likely than they are now to view themselves as self-made and self-sufficient, and hence wholly responsible for their success. Those at the bottom of society would be viewed not as disadvantaged, and thus worthy of a measure of compensation, but as simply unfit, and thus worthy of eugenic repair. The meritocracy, less chastened by chance, would become harder, less forgiving. As perfect genetic knowledge would end the simulacrum of solidarity in insurance markets, so perfect genetic control would erode the actual solidarity that arises when men and women reflect on the contingency of their talents and fortunes. . . .

It is often assumed that the powers of enhancement we now possess arose as an inadvertent by-product of biomedical progress—the genetic revolution came, so to speak, to cure disease, and stayed to tempt us with the prospect of enhancing our performance, designing our children, and perfecting our nature. That may have the story backwards. It is more plausible to view genetic engineering as the ultimate expression of our resolve to see ourselves astride the world, the masters of our nature. But that promise of mastery is flawed. It threatens to banish our appreciation of life as a gift, and to leave us with nothing to affirm or behold outside our own will.

READING QUESTIONS

1. Why does Sandel claim that the main ethical problem with genetic enhancement does not have to do with human autonomy?
2. In his discussion of various types of enhancement (muscles, memory, and height) Sandel asks readers to set aside questions about fairness and equal access to the means of such enhancements in reflecting on the morality of genetic enhancement. Why does he do this?
3. What is the difference between what Sandel calls the "ethic of giftedness" and the "ethic of willfulness"?
4. According to Sandel, what is the main moral objection to human genetic enhancement?

DISCUSSION QUESTIONS

1. Should we agree with Sandel that among the likely effects of human genetic enhancement will be a diminished sense of humility and solidarity?
2. Are there reasons, besides the ones that Sandel gives, for thinking that human genetic enhancement is morally wrong?

FRANCES M. KAMM

Is There a Problem with Enhancement?

This selection by Frances M. Kamm is a reply to the preceding essay by Michael Sandel. Her essay is divided into four sections and a conclusion. In section I she briefly summarizes Sandel's main objections to human enhancement, which include considerations having to do with (1) a designer's desire for mastery, (2) treatment versus enhancement, (3) parent-child relationships, and (4) social justice. In the three sections that follow, Kamm takes up (in order) these objections, arguing that they fail to be convincing. In her concluding section, Kamm briefly considers what she calls the "lack of imagination" objection to enhancement (not given by Sandel) which she takes seriously as a worry about some forms of enhancement.

Recommended Reading: Kantian moral theory; in particular, the discussion of the Humanity formulation of the categorical imperative, chap. 1, sec. 2C. Relevant to Kamm's discussion of enhancement and social justice is Rawls's social contract account of distributive justice, chap. 1, sec. 2G.

Should we enhance human performance? There are at least two types of enhancement. In the first, we increase above the norm so that more people are above the norm in ways that many people are already quite naturally. For example, we might increase intelligence so that people who would otherwise be only normally intelligent function as well as those few who are geniuses. In the second form of enhancement, we introduce improvements that no human being has yet evidenced—for example, living to be two hundred years old and healthy. The question of whether we should engage in either type of enhancement has arisen recently within the context of human genetics. Here one generation would probably modify the next. However, enhancement can also occur by way of drugs or intensive training and be done by a person to himself or to another.

Michael Sandel has recently argued that there is a moral problem with both types of enhancements

From Frances M. Kamm, "Is There a Problem With Enhancement?" *The American Journal of Bioethics* 5 (2005): 5–14.

regardless of the way in which they would be brought about, even if there were agreement (which there often is not) that the changes would be improvements, that they were safe, and they were fairly distributed among socioeconomic groups (Sandel 2004). Sandel's discussion is worth significant attention both because he is a member of the President's Council on Bioethics and because it expresses in compact form, readily available to the general public, some of the themes of the longer work on this subject produced by the President's Council. In this essay, I will present what seem to me to be the important components of Sandel's argument and then evaluate it.

I. SANDEL'S VIEWS

Sandel thinks that the deepest objection to enhancement is the desire for mastery that it expresses. He focuses especially (but not exclusively) on the attempt of parents to enhance their children, whether by genetic manipulation, drugs, or extensive training. He says:

> the deepest moral objection to enhancement lies less in the perfection it seeks than the human disposition it expresses and promotes. The problem is not that parents usurp the autonomy of a child they design. The problem is in the hubris of the designing parents, in their drive to master the mystery of birth . . . it would disfigure the relation between parent and child, and deprive the parent of the humility and enlarged human sympathies that an openness to the unbidden can cultivate. (Sandel 2004, 57)

And he thinks:

> . . . the promise of mastery is flawed. It threatens to banish our appreciation of life as a gift, and to leave us with nothing to affirm or behold outside our own will. (62)

However, he believes this objection is consistent with the permissibility and even the obligation to treat illnesses by genetic modification, drugs, or training. He is, therefore, arguing for a moral distinction between treatment and enhancement. He says,

(Sandel 2004, 57): "Medical intervention to cure or prevent illness or restore the injured to health does not desecrate nature but honors it." He also thinks parents must "shape and direct the development of their children . . . ," but he thinks there must be an equilibrium between "accepting love" and "transforming love."

Among the bad effects of mastery, he identifies the increasing responsibility that we must bear for the presence or absence of characteristics in ourselves and others and the effects this may have on human solidarity. The first point is concerned with the fact that we will no longer be able to say that our lacking a perfection is a matter of luck, something outside our control. We might be blamed for not improving ourselves or others. The second point is (supposedly) related to this. Sandel believes that the more our characteristics are a matter of chance rather than choice, "the more reason we have to share our fate with others" (Sandel 2004, 60). He goes on:

> Consider insurance. Since people do no know whether or when various ills will befall them, they pool their risk . . . insurance markets mimic solidarity only insofar as people do not know or control their own risk factors. . . . Why, after all, do the successful owe anything to the least-advantaged members of society? The best answer to this leans heavily on the idea of giftedness. . . . A lively sense . . . that none of us is wholly responsible for his or her success makes us willing to share the fruits of our talents with the less successful. (Sandel 2004, 60)

II. DESIRE FOR MASTERY

Let us clarify the nature of Sandel's objections to enhancement based on the desire for mastery over process. First, note that it implies that if (both types of) enhancements were occurring quire naturally, without our intervention, Sanddel's objection to enhancement would not be pertinent. Indeed, interfering with the natural enhancing changes would itself require mastery over life process, and so Sandel's objectiom might pertain to this. It is also important to keep in mind several distinctions. Actual mastery is different from the desire for it. We could achieve and exercise mastery over nature as a side effect of doing other things, without desiring it. This might be acceptable to Sandel. Suppose we did desire mastery, however. We could desire it as a means to some other end (e.g., achieving such good aims as health, beauty, virtue) or we could desire it as an end in itself. So long as we esire it as a means to other things considered good, it is clearly wrong for Sandel to conclude that desire for mastery will "leave us with nothing to affirm or behold outside our own will" (Sandel 2004, 62). Even if mastery were desired as an end in itself, this need not mean that it is our only end, and so we could still continue to affirm other good aims (such as virtue, health, etc.) as ends. I shall assume that if we desire mastery, it is as a means to good ends, as this seems most reasonable.

Such a desire for mastery is not inconsistent with an openness to the unbidden that Sandel emphasizes (Sandel 2004, 56), if the unbidden means just "those things that come without our deliberately calling for or causing them."[1] For if many good things were to come without our deliberately intervening to bring them about, presumably we would be happy to have them and not regret that they did not come about just because we deliberately brought them about. Such a form of openness to the unbidden does not, however, necessarily imply a willingness to accept whatever comes even if it is bad. Sometimes people are also unwilling to accept things that merely differ from their preferences, though the things are not necessarily bad. One or both of the latter forms of being closed to the unbidden may be what Sandel is concerned with, as he speaks of enlarged human sympathies resulting from an openness to the unbidden.

So far, I have been distinguishing various attitudes and states of mind that might be involved in a desire for mastery. Suppose some form of the desire for mastery and nonopenness to the unbidden is bad. The further question is whether there is any relation between having even a bad attitude and the impermissibility of enhancing conduct. As noted above, even Sandel supports the efforts to find certain treatments for illnesses. But seeking treatments for illnesses by manipulating the genome typically involves desiring mastery as a means, not being open to all things unbidden, and attempting to master the mystery of birth. Hence, Sandel may think that while there is something bad per se about desiring mastery even as a means, not being open to the unbidden, and attempting to master the mystery of birth, these bad aims can be outweighed by the good of curing diseases (if not by the pursuit of enhancements). Alternatively, he may believe that when the unbidden is very horrible—not a gift, even in disguise—not being open to the unbidden is not bad at all. If he believes these things, the question becomes why enhancements cannot outweigh or transform what Sandel believes are bads in the same way he thinks that treatments outweigh or transform them.[2]

There is a further, deeper problem about the relation between having bad dispositions and the impermissibility of conduct. For suppose that desiring mastery as one's sole end in life is a bad desire to have. Suppose a scientist who works on finding a cure for congenital blindness is motivated only by such a bad desire for mastery. Does this make his conduct impermissible? Presumably not. The good of treating diseases still justifies the work of the scientist even when his primary aim is not that there be no disease, but rather to achieve mastery. This is a case where there may be a duty to do the work. However, even when the act we would do would produce a good it is not our duty to produce, I think the act can be permissible independent of our intentions or disposition in doing it. So suppose several people could be saved only if you do an act that has a high probability of killing you. It is not typically your duty to do such an act, though it could be morally outstanding to do it. If the only reason you do it is to make those who care about you worry, this alone will not make saving the people impermissible. More generally, it has been argued, the intentions and attitudes of an agent reflect on the agent's character but not on the permissibility of his act (Scanlon 2002; Thomson 1990).[3]

Perhaps, however, this is not true. Sometimes we think an act is permissible only if it is satisfying a certain desire in an agent who does the act. For example, suppose we set aside scarce resources for a musical performance in order that those who desire pleasure from music shall have some. If someone's only aim in going to a concert is to mingle with other people, this is an indication he has no desire for music per se. Hence, it is an indication that an end which justified the use of scarce resources for musical performances will not be achieved. Hence, this agent should not go to the concert not because of his intention per se, but only because it is an indication that some justifying effect will not come about. Now, suppose someone has a bad aim (e.g., to show off) in doing something otherwise permissible, such as chewing gum. It might be appropriate for him to, in a sense, be punished for the bad aim with which he would chew the gum, by making it impermissible for him to chew the gum. This, of course, is not just any punishment. It specifically makes it the case that his bad aim is not efficacious. But if the achievement of an important good for others or the performance of a dutiful act (e.g., not harming someone) is at stake and this can justify the act, it would not be appropriate to require someone to forgo an act as a way of making his bad aim inefficacious. That would be to punish others for the agent's bad attitude.

It seems, then, that if Sandel is right and "the deepest moral problem with enhancement . . . " is "the human disposition it expresses," then thedeepest moral problem may provide no grounds at all for thinking that acts seeking enhancement are morally impermissible (Sandel 2004, 57). We will have to decide whether particular changes are permissible independently of the aims, attitudes, and dispositions of agents who act. Among the factors we might consider are the good ends to be brought about and the bad effects that might also occur. It is true that if the good outweighs the bad, then it is possible for a rational agent to have as his aim the pursuit of the good, rather than the (supposedly) bad aim of seeking mastery above all else. But it is the evaluation of objective goods and bads, rather than the agent's aims or desires that play a role in accounting for the permissibility of acting. If the only possible aim of a rational agent in seeking a particular change were to seek mastery as an end in itself, then presumably the good ends achieved in the change would not themselves be able to justify the act. But we need not be restricted to a consequentialist weighing of goods and bads in accounting for the permissibility of an

act. Individual rights may be at stake. Furthermore, the causal role of bad effects (e.g., whether they are side effects or necessary means to good aims) can be crucial in a nonconsequentialist analysis of permissibility, even if agent's intention and disposition are not.

In connection with the effects of enhancing, there is a further point that Sandel makes, for he is concerned not only with the disposition that enhancement expresses but with "the human disposition it . . . promotes." Promoting that disposition to seek mastery could be an effect of seeking enhancements, and we have said that the effects of acts can be relevant to their permissibility even if the attitudes of agents who perform the acts are not. Indeed, considering the disposition as an effect helps us understand that when Sandel says that "the deepest moral problem with enhancement is the human disposition it expresses," he is not so much giving an explanation of the wrongness of acts of enhancement, as simply focusing on the bad type of people we will be if we seek mastery.[4] But should we condemn a disposition even if it never leads to any impermissible acts and the disposition always leads people to act for the sake of the very properties that make the acts permissible because they make it permissible? (This is unlike the disposition of the scientist described above, yet it too is ruled out by Sandel's view). Is it inappropriate to be the sort of people who will be disposed to master nature as a means because the goods to be achieved outweigh the bads and no further nonconsequentialist objections are relevant?

Perhaps such a disposition could still be bad to have, if it leads us to focus on these types of acts to the exclusion of other worthwhile activities. Consider an artist who is always seeking to improve her paintings. She never rests content with just appreciating her own and other people's great works. Other people may have a better appreciation of great masters that she lacks. But it is not clear to me that her way of responding to value—by trying to create more of it—is inferior to the admittedly good alternative way of responding to value. And in some people these two approaches to value may be combined to one degree or another. Similarly for the dispositions to enhance and to appreciate goods already present.

III. TREATMENT VERSUS ENHANCEMENT

One conclusion so far is that we must look to such things as the properties of our acts and their effects, rights involved, and the required causal role of bad effects in producing the good, rather than to the dispositions of agents, to decide whether acts of enhancement are wrong. Hence, the disposition that Sandel identifies as a primary moral problem with enhancement has nothing to do with whether producing enhancements is right or wrong. However, one might rephrase an objection bearing on the permissibility of such acts. One might argue that the goods achievable by enhancement do not merit a causal role for the bads of people's uncovering mysteries of birth or mastering nature (whether they desire these or not), rather than letting nature give us whatever gifts it will.

There are two problems with rephrasing in this way. First, it may not be true that people's mastering nature, uncovering the secrets of life, and trying to improve what comes in life are bad in and of themselves. If they are not bad in themselves—but even good in themselves—then we do not have to show that there are great goods at stake that outweigh using the bads, in order to permissibly engage in these activities. Second, if they are bad, one would have to show not only that the good ends of enhancement are not as important as the goods of treatment but that they are not great enough to outweigh or transform the bads.

There are several possible routes to showing that the goods of enhancement are not as important as the goods of treatment. One is the idea of diminishing marginal utility, according to which the benefit someone gets out of a given improvement in his condition decreases the better off he is. Hence, we do more good if we help those who are worse off than if we help those who are already better off. A second route is the view that there is greater moral value in helping people the worse off they are in absolute terms, even if we produce a smaller benefit to them than we could to people who are better off. This is known as prioritarianism. A possible third route is to distinguish qualitatively between what some call harmed states and merely not being as well off as one might be but not badly off in

absolute terms (Shiffrin 1999). None of these routes to comparing the good ends of enhancement and treatment, however, shows that enhancements are not in themselves great enough goods to justify mastery as a means. They also do not rule out that providing enhancements might itself permissibly be a means to achieving the treatments. That is, suppose it is only if we are much smarter than we currently are that we will find a cure for terrible illnesses quickly. Then the importance of finding treatments could be transmitted to the enhancement of intelligence. (Of course, not all means are permitted to even justified ends. So if enhancements were sufficiently intrinsically objectionable, it might not be permissible to use the only available means to acquire treatments.)

At one point, Sandel tries to draw the distinction between treatment and enhancement by claiming that "medical intervention to cure or prevent illness . . . does not desecrate nature but honors it. Healing sickness or injury does not override a child's natural capacities but permits them to flourish" (Sandel 2004, 57). The assumption behind the first sentence is that nature is sacred and should be honored. But why should we believe this? Cancer cells, AIDS, tornadoes, and poisons are all parts of nature. Are they sacred and to be honored? The natural and the good are distinct conceptual categories and the two can diverge: the natural can fail to be good and the good can be unnatural (e.g., art, dams, etc.).[5] Suppose nature was sacred and to be honored. We would clearly be overriding its dictates by making people able to resist (by immunization) illnesses that they could not naturally resist. Is doing this impermissible because it does not honor nature? Surely not.

Sandel's view may better be expressed as the view that we may permissibly override and not honor nature when we get rid of the things in nature that interfere with the other parts of nature that are its gifts (i.e. good things). But if this is so, then Sandel's position does not rule out dramatically lengthening the human life span and preventing the interference of the aging process with the exercise of natural gifts that we have had all our lives. Most people would consider this a radical enhancement.

When Sandel claims that curing and preventing illness does not desecrate nature, he implies that enhancement is a problem because of the sort of relation we should have to nature. Emphasizing that healing allows a child's capacities to flourish, may seem to suggest that enhancement (but not treatment) is a problem because of its effects on our relations to other persons. But while Sandel does move on to the latter issue (and I will discuss his views on it below), he is here still focused on whether we are interfering with nature and the capacities (gifts) that nature has given someone when we enhance rather than cure. Hence, it is pertinent to ask, what if a child's natural capacities are those of a Down's Syndrome child and we seek to supplement these and provide greater gifts than nature provided by changing the child's genome? This would change or add to natural capacities, not merely permit them to flourish. Yet, presumably, Sandel would want to classify this with allowable treatment rather than enhancement. This form of treatment, which involves supplementing nature's gifts with new one's raises the more general question of why appreciation of nature's gifts requires limiting ourselves to them. We can appreciate what is given and yet supplement it with something new.

There are three primary conclusions of this section. First, Sandel's attempt to draw a distinction between treatment and enhancement does not seem successful. Second, given the way he draws the treatment/enhancement distinction. Sandel's objection to enhancement does not rule out maintaining natural gifts (that would otherwise wither) throughout a greatly extended human life span. Third, we would need much more argument to show that there is some duty owed to nature that we offend against when we change natural capacities, and that it is our relation to nature rather than to persons that should be a primary source of concern with enhancement.

IV. PARENTAL AND SOCIAL RELATIONS

In this section I will examine Sandel's views on how enhancement may negatively affect our relations to persons, ourselves or others.

A. One's Children

As noted above, Sandel paints with a broad brush in condemning enhancements due not only to genomic changes but to drugs and training. However, he also realizes that much of ordinary good parenting consists of what might ordinarily be called enhancement. Hence, he says the crucial point is to balance accepting love and transformative love. (Perhaps Sandel would want to apply this idea to changes adults seek to make to themselves as well.) He also seems to think of transformative love as concerned with helping natural gifts be fulfilled, framing and molding them so that they shine forth. (Similarly, in sport, he thinks that good running shoes help bring out a natural gift by comparison to drugs that would change a gift into something else.)

Let us first deal with the issue of balance. For all Sandel says, it remains possible that many more enhancements than he considers appropriate are ones that satisfy the balance between accepting and transformative love. This would most clearly be true if transformation were not merely a matter of molding nature's gifts, but of adding new ones. Furthermore, it is not clear what falls under "balancing." For example, suppose my child already has an IQ of 160. Might balancing the two types of love in her case imply that I may (if this will be good for her) increase her IQ another 10 but not 20 points, even though a parent whose child has an IQ of 80 should not change her child as much as to also give her a 170 IQ, for this would err on the side of too much transformation?

An alternative to such a balancing view might be called Sufficientarianism. It could imply that there is no need at all to increase the first child's IQ and that in the second child's case much more transformation (in the sense of adding to natural gifts) than acceptance is appropriate in order to reach a sufficient level. Sufficientarians are not interested in perfection, though they want enough mastery as a means to getting sufficient goods.

Let us now restrict ourselves to Sandel's sense of transformation—bringing out natural gifts—and consider the ways in which this may be done. To the extent to which Sandel allows training and appliances to be used to transform gifts, should he not also allow genetic manipulation that does exactly the same thing? So suppose that a certain amount of voice training is permitted to strengthen vocal chords. Would a drug or genetic manipulation that could strengthen vocal chords to the same degree also be permissible? If the argument Sandel gives does not rule out training, it alone will not rule out transformation by drugs or genetic means, because a gift is transformed to the same degree by each method. (If appliances such as running shoes are allowed, why not genetically transformed feet that function in the same way?) A different type of argument, based on the possible moral difference in using different means would be necessary to rule out the genetic means, but Sandel does not provide it. Rather, as we have noted, he treats training, drugs, and genetic manipulation on a par.

Hence, while he rightly condemns excessive pressure to transform oneself and one's children in a competitive, meritocratic society, especially if it is governed by shallow values, he does nor condemn moderate training for worthwhile transformation.[6] Unless he emphasizes a difference in means used, he should then permit moderate, worthwhile genetic transformations, even if not excessive ones driven by competitive pressures and/or governed by shallow values.

Now consider one way in which Sandel may be wrong not to distinguish different ways of transforming or bringing about more radical enhancement. Perhaps we should separate how we treat changes that are made before a child exists (what I will call *ex ante changes*) from those that are made once a child exists (what I will call *ex post changes*). The former are primarily genetic, while the latter will include drugs and training. Love, it has been said, is for a particular. Consider love for an adult. Before we love someone, we may be interested in meeting a person who has various properties, such as kindness, intelligence, artistic ability, a good sense of humor, etc. When we meet such a person we may be interested in him rather than someone else because he has these properties. However, though it is through these properties that we may be led to love this particular person, it is the particular person that we wind

up loving, not his set of properties. For if another person appears with the same set of properties, that does not mean that we could as easily substitute him for the person we already love. Even if the person we love loses some of the properties through which we were originally led to love him (e.g., his beauty) and another person has more of the good properties that originally interested us, we would not necessarily stop loving the particular person we love (Nozick 1977).

It seems then that when we love a particular person, this involves much of what Sandel calls *accepting* love. If we do seek transformation in the properties of the person we love, this may be because of moral requirements or because we want what is good for him. By contrast, before a particular person whom we love exists (just as before we find someone to love), it is permissible to think more broadly in terms of the characteristics we would like to have in a person and that we think it is best for a person to have, at least so long as these characteristics would not be bad for the person who will have them and are consistent with respect for persons. (The latter constraint could conflict with merely doing what is best for someone. For example, suppose peace of mind and equanimity are goods for a person. Nevertheless, insuring their presence by modifying someone so that she is self-deceived about awful truths would be inconsistent with taking seriously that one is creating a person, an entity worthy of respect. Sandel says, "Not everything in the world is open to whatever use we may desire or devise" (Sandel 2004, 54). This is certainly true of persons, even when we desire their good.)

Before the existence of a person, there is no person yet with certain characteristics that we have to accept if we love him and do not want to impose undue burdens necessary for changes. Hence, not accepting whatever characteristics nature will bring but altering them ex ante does not show lack of love. Nor can it insult or psychologically pressure a person the way ex post changes might, as no conscious being yet exists. Importantly, it is (somewhat paradoxically) rational and acceptable to seek good characteristics in a new person, even though we know that when the child comes to be and we love him or her, many of these characteristics may come and go and we will continue to love the particular person. This is an instance of what I call the distinction between "caring to have" and "caring about." That is, one can know that one will care about someone just as much whether or not she has certain traits and yet care to have someone that has, rather than lacks, these traits (Kamm 2004).[7] Sandel says that 'parental love is not contingent on talents and attributes a child happens to have" (Sandel 2004, 55). This is true. But I have tried to show this is consistent with seeking better attributes.

Applying what I have said to the issue of enhancement suggests that even if transformative and enhancing projects should be based primarily on what is best for the child, this is consistent with trying to achieve ex ante a child with traits that will be desirable per se, so long as they will not be bad for the child and are not inconsistent with respect for persons. Ex ante enhancement will primarily be through genetic alteration. By contrast ex post enhancement may have to be more constrained for it could involve psychological pressure on the child and lead to fear of rejection. (Altering a fetus or early infant will be somewhere in between.)

Drawing a distinction between the methods of ex ante and ex post "designing" does not, however, put to rest different sorts of objections to even ex ante transformations. First, Sandel thinks that people are not products to be designed. I agree that people are not products in the sense that they are not commodities, but rather beings worthy of concern and respect in their own right. But I do not think this implies that it is morally wrong to design them. Consider first if it would be acceptable to redesign oneself. We are accustomed to people having replacement parts, such as knees, hips, and transplants. Suppose when our parts wore out, we were offered alternatives among the new ones. For example, teeth of various colors, joints that were more or less flexible, limbs that were longer or shorter. It might well make sense to make selections that involved redesigning our bodies. Similarly, if we could replace brain cells, it might make sense to choose ones that gave us new abilities. This would be redesigning ourselves.

Now consider creating new people. We already have much greater control over the timing of pregnancy and, via artificial reproduction, over whether someone can conceive at all. Rather than humility, we have justifiable pride in these accomplishments. Now suppose we each had been designed in detail by other persons. Presumably, we would still be beings of worth and entitled to respect. In this sense, designing persons is not inconsistent with their personhood. But might it be chat although a being retains its high status despite such an origin, it is inconsistent with respect for persons to choose such an origin for them? (Analogously, a person retains his status as a rights bearer even when his rights are violated, but it is not, therefore, appropriate to violate his rights.) But suppose that the natural way of reproducing required that properties be selected for offspring, otherwise they would be mere lumps of flesh. Surely selecting properties would be permissible. Would we be obligated, out of respect for persons, to search for a way to alter this (imagined) natural way for definite properties to come about when it is going well, so that they would happen by chance? I do not think so. Hence, I conclude, designing of persons is not per se inconsistent with respect for persons.[8]

A second objection asks, if someone wants to have a child, should they not focus only on the most basic goods, such as having a normal child to love? If so, then if they focus on achieving many superior qualities, does that not show they are interested in the wrong things in having a child? To answer this worry, consider an analogy. If the primary concern for a philosopher in getting a job should be that she be able to do philosophy, does that mean that it is wrong to choose between possible jobs equally satisfying that characteristic on the basis of other desirable properties such as higher salary or better location? If not, why is the search for properties other than the basic ones in a child wrong, when the basic ones are not thereby put in jeopardy? (Of course, in the case of the child-to-be, unlike the job, the enhanced properties are usually to be for its benefit, not only for those doing the selecting.)

Furthermore, searching for more than the basics does not by itself imply that if one could not achieve those enhancements, one would not still happily have a child who had only the basics. (And even while someone who would refuse to have a child without enhancements might thereby show that he did not care very much about the core reasons for having a child, this does not show he is unfit to be a parent. For he could still come to love the child if he actually has it, through attachment to it as a particular, as described above.)

A third concern is that in the relation of parent to child, a parent will simply have greater control over the child's nature, whether she seeks it or not. (This does not mean that the child has less control, for it is chance, not the child, that will determine things, if persons, such as parents, do not. Nor does it mean that the issues of "designing" children and parental control are not separable in principle. For if someone other than the parent designed the child, relative to the parent the child would still be part of the unbidden). But in numerous areas of life, persons now stand in relations of control over other people where once chance ruled. The important thing is that this be done justly, benevolently, and wisely. Furthermore, if we choose certain characteristics in offspring, the balance of control over the child's life may shift to the child rather than the parent. What I have in mind is that if we could ensure that a child has such enhancing traits as self control and good judgment, the child would be less, not more, likely to be subject to parental control after birth. This is most important.

A fourth concern is that if each parent individually tries to do what is best for its child, all parents will end up making the situation worse for all their children. To avoid this prisoner's dilemma situation, some rule that coordinates the choices of parents seems called for.[9]

B. Social Justice

Finally we come to Sandel's views on the connection between enhancement and the twin issues of the burdens of responsibility and distributive justice. If people are able to enhance themselves or others, can they not be held responsible in the sense of being blamed for not giving themselves or others desirable characteristics? Not necessarily, for one does not have a duty to do everything that could make oneself or someone else better, and if one has no duty, then one is not at fault in not enhancing and so not to be blamed. Even if one has certain duties, for example, to be the best doctor one can be, and taking certain drugs would help one to perform better, it is not necessarily one's duty to take the drugs. Hence, one need not even be at fault if one does not do what will help one perform one's duties better. But one could retain a right not to alter one's body in order to better fulfill one's duties as a physician, without making such alterations impermissible for anyone who wants them. Of course, if the characteristics one will have must be decided by others (for example, one's parents), then one could not be held morally accountable for causing or not causing certain traits, as one could not direct one's parents' behavior.

What about cases in which one can be blamed for a choice not to enhance? Thomas Scanlon has emphasized that one can hold someone responsible for an outcome in the sense of blaming him for it without thereby thinking that it is also his responsibility to bear the costs of his choice (Scanlon unpublished). These are conceptually two separate issues. For example, suppose someone is at fault for acting carelessly in using his hairdryer. If he suffers severe damage and will die without medical treatment, his being at fault in a minor way does not mean that he forfeits a claim on others he otherwise had to free medical care.

Sandel thinks the issue of responsibility for choosing to have or to lack certain characteristics is intimately related to how much of a claim we have against others for aid. However, he is not always clear in distinguishing the role of choice from the role of mere knowledge of one's characteristics. For example, in discussing why we have insurance schemes, he seems to imply that even if we had no control over our traits but only knew what they were (for example, via genetic testing), we would lose a claim against others to share our fate. For if they knew they were not at risk, people would not enter into insurance schemes that mimic solidarity. This is an argument against knowledge as well as against control. But those who urge us to use a veil of ignorance in deciding about what allocation of resources is just are, in effect, saying that even if we have knowledge of each other's traits, there are moral reasons for behaving as though we lack the knowledge.

Let us put aside the issue of blameworthiness for, and the effect of mere knowledge of, one's traits. How should the possibility of making choices that determine one's traits affect responsibility for bearing costs for the outcome of choices. Sandel seems to share with some philosophers (known as luck egalitarians) the view (roughly) that if we have not chosen to have traits but have them as a matter of luck (or other people's choices), the costs of having them should be shared. However, if we choose the traits (by act or by omitting to change them if we can), then even if we do not in any deep sense deserve to have made this choice, there is no reason for the costs of having the traits to be shared. (We may, however, choose to buy insurance that will protect us against bad choices.) Sandel says he cannot think of any better reason for the well-off to help those who are not well-off except that each is not fully responsible for his situation. (Many, however, do not find this a compelling reason for sharing with others. Robert Nozick, for example, argued that one could be entitled to what followed from the exercise of traits that one was not responsible for having[10]).

But it seems that often we want to give people new options without taking away from them help they would have gotten from others when they had no control over their fates. One example given above involved someone whose choice to use a hairdryer should not lead to his forfeiting aid to avert a major disaster. Similarly, if someone for reasons of conscience refuses to take advantage of the option to abort a difficult pregnancy, we do not think that she should forfeit medical care simply because she could have avoided the need for it. In many cases, arguments for the duty to aid others seem to have more to do with respect and concern for the value of other persons than with whether they have or have not gotten themselves into whatever situation they are in. Of course, in cases I have been considering, someone chooses in a way that leads to a bad outcome he does not per se choose. But recall that Kant thought we had a duty to help people pursue even the ends they themselves had deliberately chosen because people

matter in their own right, rather than because they could not be held responsible for their choices or because it was only the unwilled consequences of choices with which we were asked to help.

Finally, suppose it were true that to some degree as we increase the range of individual choice, we limit the claim of a person to the assistance of others. (For example, choosing to be paralyzed because one preferred that sort of life might be considered an "expensive taste," and public assistance for it might be denied). It is still true that, if having the option to enhance leads many people to improve themselves or others, there will be fewer instances of people who are badly off (because they lack good traits) and, hence, fewer who require the assistance of others. For example, rather than redistributing wealth that only the talented can produce in a certain environment, each person would have a talent and so have the opportunity to be more productive in that environment. Furthermore, each person would not only have the material benefits that can be redistributed from some to others. Each person could have the abilities and talents whose intrinsic rewards (that come just from their exercise) cannot be redistributed.

The primary conclusions of this section are that Sandel does not successfully show that we should limit options to enhance ourselves or others as a way of ensuring a right to social assistance. He also does not show that seeking to enhance children, especially ex ante, is inconsistent with a proper balance between accepting and transforming love.

V. CONCLUSION

Sandel focuses on the desire for mastery and the unwillingness to live with what we do not control as objections to enhancement. (He also focuses on the more contingent issue of the misuse of the ability to enhance ourselves and others that is likely to occur in a competitive environment, especially governed by shallow values.) I have argued that what is most troubling about enhancement is neither that there will be people who desire to have control over nature, offspring, and themselves, nor the unwillingness to accept what comes unbidden. However, I do think there are major problems with enhancement. Some are the ones Sandel puts to one side. Namely, could we really safely alter people, not making disastrous mistakes? And given our scarce resources, should enhancement be at the top of the list of things to which we should be attending?

A deeper issue, I think, is our lack of imagination as designers. That is, most people's conception of the varieties of goods is very limited, and if they designed people their improvements would likely conform to limited, predictable types. But we should know that we are constantly surprised at the great range of good traits in people, and even more the incredible range of combinations of traits that turn out to produce "flavors" in people that are, to our surprise, good. For example, could we predict that a very particular degree of irony combined with a certain degree of diffidence would constitute an interesting type of personality? In section IV A, I mentioned the view that potential parents should focus on having children with basic good properties rather than seek improvements beyond this. Oddly, the "lack of imagination" objection to enhancement I am now voicing is based on a concern that in seeking enhancements people will focus on too simple and basic a set of goods.

How does the lack of imagination objection relate to Sandel's view that an openness to the unbidden extends the range of our sympathies? One construal of his point is that if we have no control, we are forced to understand and care about people, as we should, even when they are difficult and nonideal. (Even if we have some control but lack complete control, we would, I think, have to cultivate such a virtue). By contrast, the lack of imagination objection emphasizes that when creatures of limited imagination do not design themselves and others, they are likely to extend the range of their appreciation of goods because the range of goods is likely to be larger. A parent who might have designed his child to have the good trait of composing classical music, could not have conceived that it would be good to have a child who turns out to be one of the Beatles. (To have conceived it, would have involved creating the style before the Beatles did.) The lack

of imagination objection is concerned that too much control will limit the number and combination of goods from what is possible. Hence, at least in those cases where enhancement—greater goods—is more likely to come about if chance rather than unimaginative choice is in control, the desire for enhancement will militate against control.

Finally, if the controlled selection of enhanced properties is a morally acceptable means, at least sometimes, what are the good ends to which it could safely be used? Presumably, it would be a safe end to enhance our capacities to recognize and fulfill our moral duties (or recognize when these are overridden). Recognizing and fulfilling moral duties (or recognizing when it is morally permissible for these to be overridden) is a side constraint on the exercise of any other capacities and the pursuit of any ends. There is no point in worrying about the risk that having such moral capacities will interfere with other unimagined goods. This is because if such moral capacities interfere with other goods, this just means that those other goods are not morally permissible options for us.

NOTES

1. Notice that not deliberately causing something is not the same as not causing it. For example, a parent may cause his child's IQ to move down from 160 to 140 by inadvertently eating improperly during pregnancy. This reduction is unbidden, though caused by the parent. It is in part because we might be causally responsible for making things worse than they could naturally be, that some may think that we have a duty to achieve at least the knowledge of life processes that prevents our interfering with naturally occurring goods.

2. I shall return to this point below.

3. Judith Thomson (1990, 1999) has argued that intention never matters to the permissibility of action. Thomas Scanlon (2000) makes a somewhat more limited claim.

4. As emphasized by Paul Litton and Larry Temkin.

5. Similarly, the human and the good are distinct conceptual categories. Human traits (such as arrogance) could be bad, and inhuman altruism could be good.

6. Hilary Bok emphasized this point.

7. I previously argued for this distinction when discussing the compatibility of (a) a disabled person caring about his life as much as non-disabled person cares about

his life and (b) a disabled person caring to have a non-disabled life rather than a disabled one.

8. Notice also that designing the gene pool so that only enhanced options are available is compatible with chance determination of any given individual.

9. Larry Temkin emphasized this point.

10. See his *Anarchy, State, and Utopia*.

REFERENCES

Kamm, F. 2004. Deciding whom to help, health-adjusted life years, and disabilities. In *Public health, ethics, and equity,* ed. S. Anand, F. Peters, and A. Sen, 225–242. Oxford, UK: Oxford University Press.

Nozick, R. 1977. *Anarchy, state and utopia.* New York: Basic Books.

Sandel, M. 2004. The case against perfection. *The Atlantic Monthly* 293(3): 51–62.

Scanlon, T. 2000. Intention and permissibility I. *Proceedings of the Aristotelian Society* Suppl. 74:301–317.

Scanlon, T. *Blame.* Unpublished article.

Shiffrin, S. 1999. Wrongful life, procreative responsibility, and the significance of harm. *Legal Theory* 5(2): 117–148.

Thomson, J. J. 1990. *The realm of rights.* Cambridge, MA: Harvard University Press.

Thomson, J. J. 1999. Physician-assisted suicide: Two moral arguments. *Ethics* 109(3): 497–518.

READING QUESTIONS

1. Kamm offers an analysis of Sandel's notion of mastery. What is Kamm's distinction between actual mastery and desire for mastery? Why does she think that having a desire for mastery is not inconsistent with an "openness to the unbidden"?

2. What is Kamm's painter analogy—and the painter's way of responding to value—supposed to show with respect to enhancement?

3. Kamm does not think that we should determine whether acts of enhancement are wrong by looking to the disposition of agents. What sorts of things should we look to instead, according to Kamm?

4. What does Kamm suggest as the three possible routes for showing that the goods of enhancement are not as important as the goods of treatment? How does she respond to each?

5. What is Sandel's concept of the balance between "accepting love" and "transformative love"?

6. What does Kamm think the relation is between responsibility for one's choices and rights to social assistance? How does this bear on the issue of self-enhancement and genetic selection for one's children?

DISCUSSION QUESTIONS

1. Sandel does not distinguish between genetic manipulation, drugs, or extensive training as forms of enhancement. All are attempts at mastery, and as such, morally wrong. Do you agree? Why or why not?

2. Discuss the many different ways in which humans "interfere" with nature. Do you think a standard (or standards) can be established to determine which interventions are morally permissible and which are not? Are there some interventions that are morally obligatory? Give examples and reasons for your view.

3. Kamm worries that one of the bigger concerns of genetic enhancement (and what Sandel ignores) is our lack of imagination as designers, which could limit the number and combination of goods possible. How plausible is this idea? Can you think of other contexts in which imaginative enhancement is used to increase the number and combinations of goods? How does this differ, if at all, from the context of genetic enhancement?

PETER SINGER

Parental Choice and Human Improvement[1]

Peter Singer frames his discussion of genetic engineering by considering the idea of a genetic supermarket where prospective parents can (within certain moral limits) pay to have a child that is likely genetically superior to a child they would have had without engineering. Singer's discussion explores the following three possible negative social consequences of a genetic supermarket and how they might be remedied: (1) possible loss of human diversity, (2) the possible negative effects of engineering children to have so-called positional goods, and (3) the possible negative effects on equality of opportunity. Singer argues that addressing such questions and, in particular, the second and third, raises important questions about what goods a society ought to promote and thus basic questions about value.

Recommended Reading: consequentialism, chap. 1, sec. 2A.

Consider . . . the issue of genetic engineering. Many biologists tend to think the problem is one of design, of specifying the best types of persons so that biologists can proceed to produce them. Thus they worry over what sort(s) of person there is to be and who will control this process. They do not tend to think, perhaps because it diminishes the importance of their role, of a system in which they run a "genetic supermarket," meeting the individual specifications (within certain moral limits) of prospective parents. . . . This supermarket system has the great virtue that it involves no centralized decision fixing the future of human type(s).

—*Robert Nozick,* Anarchy, State and Utopia
(New York: Basic Books) 1974, 315n.

BUYING YOURSELF A TALL, BRAINY CHILD

Advertisements in newspapers in some of America's most prestigious universities commonly offer sub-

stantial sums to egg donors who are tall, athletic, and have scored extremely well in scholastic aptitude tests. The fees offered range up to $50,000. Actual sums paid are said to be closer to $10,000, but that is still substantial, and indicates the willingness of some couples to pay for the chance—and by this method it is only a chance—of having a child with above average scholastic aptitude, height, and athletic ability.[2]

Our rapidly increasing knowledge of human genetics already makes it possible for some couples to have children who are genetically superior to the children they would be likely to produce if they left it to the random process of normal reproduction. At present, this is done by prenatal, and sometimes pre-implantation, diagnosis of embryos and fetuses. These techniques are becoming increasingly sophisticated and will in future be able to detect more and more genetically-influenced traits. Later, it will most likely be possible to insert new genetic material safely into the *in vitro* embryo. Both of these techniques will enable couples to have a child whose abilities are likely to be superior to those offered by the natural

From Peter Singer, "Parental Choice and Human Improvement" in Julian Savulescu and Nick Bostrom, eds., *Human Enhancement* (2009). By permission of Oxford University Press.

lottery but who will be "theirs" in the sense of having their genes, not the genes of only one of them (as in cloning), or the genes of a third person (as when an egg is purchased).

Many people say that they accept selection against serious diseases and disabilities, but not for enhancement beyond what is normal. There is, however, no bright line between selection against disabilities and selection for positive characteristics. From selecting against Huntington's Disease it is no great step to selecting against genes that carry a significantly elevated risk of breast or colon cancer, and from there it is easy to move to giving one's child a better than average genetic health profile.

In any case, even if it is possible to distinguish between selection for disabilities and selection for enhancement, it would need further argument to show that this distinction is morally significant. If, as surveys in most developed countries show, at least 85 per cent of couples are willing to abort a fetus that has Down's syndrome, most of them will also be willing to abort one with genes that indicate other intellectual limitations, for example genes that correlate with IQ scores below 80. But why stop at 80? Why not select for at least average IQ? Or, since genetics is only one factor in the determination of IQ, select for genes that make an above average IQ likely, just in case the environmental factors don't work out so well? The existing market in human eggs suggests that some people will also select for height, which in turn correlates to some extent with income. Nor will we spurn the opportunity to ensure that our children are beautiful, to the extent that that is under genetic control.

How should we react to these likely developments? Do they point to a nightmarish future in which children are made to order, and wanted for their specifications, not loved for themselves, however they may turn out? Or should we welcome the prospect of healthier, more intelligent, happier, and perhaps even more ethical children? Do the likely benefits outweigh the costs?

First we need to ask what exactly the costs are going to be. This is itself highly controversial. Is it a problem if, as Michael Sandel has suggested may happen, genetic enhancement will "banish our appreciation of life as a gift, and to leave us with nothing to affirm or behold outside our own will."[3] I hope that human beings will continue to leave some natural ecosystems intact, so that we can always affirm and behold things that are outside our own will. Beyond that, I'm not sure that the idea of life as a "gift" makes much sense independently of belief in God. If there is no God, life can only be a gift from one's parents. And if that is the case, wouldn't we all prefer parents who try to make the gift as good as possible, rather than leaving everything to chance? Indeed, even Sandel does not think parents should leave everything to chance. He opposes "perfectionism", but not current practices of prenatal diagnosis that are aimed at eliminating serious genetic diseases and disabilities. The argument for taking life as a gift clearly has limits. If it is outweighed by the importance of avoiding children with serious diseases or disabilities, it may also be outweighed by the positive characteristics that genetic selection could bring.

Is this weighing of positive and negative aspects of genetic selection an issue for the legislature to resolve for all of us? Nozick's words cited at the head of this paper suggest a different approach: it is not up to government, he argued, to judge whether the outcome of this process will be better or worse. In a free society, all we can legitimately do is make sure that the process consists of freely chosen individual transactions. Let the genetic supermarket rule—and not only the market, but also altruistic individuals, or voluntary organizations, anyone who wishes, for whatever reason, to offer genetic services to anyone who wants them and is willing to accept them on the terms on which they are offered. Similarly, those who wish to preserve the idea that their child's life, with all his or her inherited characteristics, is a gift, may do so, and hence avoid genetic selection or enhancement. Others for whom that idea makes little sense, or is unimportant, may choose to make use of the technologies available to give their child a better chance of having the characteristics that they favor.

That the United States should allow a market in eggs and sperm which goes some way towards fulfilling Nozick's prophecy is no accident. In other countries a practice that threatens to turn the child of a marriage into an item of commerce would meet powerful opposition from both conservative "family values" politics and from left of center groups horrified at the idea of leaving to the market something as socially momentous as the way in which future generations are conceived. In the United States, however, that leftist attitude is restricted to groups on the margins of political life, and the conservatives who dominate Congress show their support for family values merely by preventing the use of federal funds for ends that they dislike; in other respects, they allow their belief that the market always knows best to override their support for traditional family values.

There are strong arguments against state interference in reproductive decisions, at least when those decisions are made by competent adults. If we follow Mill's principle that the state is justified in interfering with its citizens only to prevent harm to others, we could see such decisions as private ones, harming no one, and therefore properly left to the private realm.[4] For who is harmed by the genetic supermarket? The parents are not harmed by having the healthier, handsomer and more intelligent children that they want. Are the children harmed? In an article on the practice of buying eggs from women with specific desired characteristics like height and intelligence, George Annas has commented:

> What's troubling is this commodification, this treating kids like products. Ordering children to specification can't be good for the children. It may be good for adults in the short run, but it's not good for kids to be thought of that way.[5]

But to say that this is "not good" for these children forces us to ask the question: not good compared with *what*? The children for whom this is supposed not to be good could not have existed by any other means. If the egg had not been purchased, to be fertilized with the husband's sperm, that child would not have been alive. Is life going to be so bad for this child that he or she will wish never to have been born? That hardly seems likely. So on one reading of what the standard of comparison should be, it is clearly false that the purchase of these eggs is not good for the kids.[6]

Suppose that we read "not good for kids" as meaning "not the best thing for the next child of this couple". Then whether the purchase of the egg is or

is not good for the kid will depend on a comparison with other ways in which the couple could have had a child. Suppose, to make the comparison easier, they are not infertile—they bought an egg only in order to increase their chances of having a tall, athletic child who would get into a very good university. If they had not done so, they would have had a child in the normal way, who would have been their genetic child. Was it bad for their child to buy the egg? Their child may have a more difficult life because he or she was "made to order", and perhaps will disappoint his or her parents. But perhaps their own child would have disappointed them even more, by being less likely to be any of the things that they wanted their child to be. I don't see how we can know which of these outcomes is more likely. So I do not think we have grounds for concluding that a genetic supermarket would harm either those who choose to shop there, or those who are created from the materials they purchase.

If we switch from an individualist perspective to a broader social one, however, the negative aspects of a genetic supermarket become more serious. Even if we make the optimistic assumption that parents will select only genes that are of benefit to their children, there are at least three separate grounds for thinking that this may have adverse social consequences. The first is that a genetic supermarket would mean less diversity among human beings. Not all forms of diversity are good. Diversity in longevity is greater when there are more people with genes that doom them to an early death. The loss of this diversity is welcome. But what about the loss of the merely unusual, or eccentric? Antony Rao, a specialist in behavioral therapy in children, finds that many middle and upper class parents come to him when their children behave in unusual ways, wanting them to be medicated, because "they fear that any deviation from the norm may cripple their child's future."[7] If this is true of behavioral abnormalities that for many children are merely a passing phase, it is likely to be even more true of genetic abnormalities. It is easy to imagine genetic screening reports that indicate that the child's genes are unusual, although the significance of the abnormality is not well understood (usually medical shorthand for "We don't have a clue"). Would many parents decide to terminate the pregnancy in those circumstances, and if so, would there be a loss of diversity that would leave human society a less rich place?

I am more concerned about a second problem: many of the advantages people will seek to ensure for their children will be advantageous for them only in comparative, not absolute terms. Consider the difference between being tall, and living longer. Living longer than today's average lifespan today is something most of us would want, and the extent to which we want it is not, by and large, affected by whether everyone achieves this good, and so the average lifespan increases. For the purposes of this chapter, I'll call this kind of good an intrinsic good (ignoring the fact that most of us don't really think living longer is intrinsically good, since we would not want to live longer if we were in a coma for all of the additional years). Being taller than a specified height, however, is not something most of us would want for its own sake. True, being above average height correlates significantly with having above average income, and with being able to see over the heads of the crowd, but to gain these advantages we must be taller than the average in our society. To increase one's childrens' height, therefore, is beneficial only if it also moves them up relative to the height of others in their society. There would be no advantage in being 6'3" if the average height is 6'6". I will call this a positional good.

If everyone gains a positional good, no one is better off. They may all be worse off. In the case of height, arguably, it would be better if everyone were shorter, because we would require less food to sustain us, could live in smaller houses, drive smaller, less powerful cars, and reduce our impact on the environment. Thus being able to select for height—something couples are already doing, on a small scale, by offering more for the eggs of tall women—could start the human equivalent of the peacock's tail—an escalating "height race" in which the height that distinguishes "tall" people from those who are "normal" increases year by year, to no one's benefit, at considerable environmental cost, and perhaps eventually even at some health cost to the children themselves.[8] Genetic enhancement could lead to a collective action problem, in which the rational pursuit of individual self-interest makes us all worse off.

A third significant ground for objecting to a genetic supermarket is its threat to the ideal of equality of opportunity. It is, of course, something of a myth to believe that equality of opportunity prevails in the United States or anywhere else, because everywhere wealthy parents already give their children enormous advantages in the race for success. Nevertheless, a future in which the rich have beautiful, brainy, healthy children, while the poor, stuck with the old genetic lottery, fall further and further behind, is not a pleasing prospect. Inequalities of wealth will be turned into genetic inequalities, and the clock will be turned back on centuries of struggle to overcome the privileges of aristocracy. Instead the present generation of wealthy people will have the opportunity to embed their advantages in the genes of their offspring. These offspring will then have not only the abundant advantages that the rich already give their children, but also whatever additional advantages the latest development in genetics can bestow on them. They will most probably therefore continue to be wealthier, longer-lived and more successful than the children of the poor, and will in turn pass these advantages on to their children, who will take advantage of the ever more sophisticated genetic techniques available to them. Will this lead to a *Gattaca* society in which "Invalids" clean toilets while "Valids" run the show and get all the interesting jobs?[9] Lee Silver has pictured a USA a millenium hence in which the separation between "Gene-enriched" humans and "Naturals" has solidified into separate species.[10] That is too far in the future to speculate about, but Maxwell Mehlman and Jeffrey Botkin may well be right when they predict that a free market in genetic enhancement will widen the gap between the top and bottom strata of our society, undermine belief in equality of opportunity, and close the "safety valve" of upward mobility.[11]

How might we respond to these three problems? I think the solution to the first problem is easy. We would face a serious loss of genetic diversity only if the genetic supermarket was very widely used for a long time in a way that tended to focus on a small number of genotypes. Before this had had any real impact, we could observe what is happening, and stop the social experiment. I therefore do not see this as a decisive objection to opening the genetic supermarket.

The other two problems, of the pursuit of positional goods, and of making genetic inequality more rigidly structured than it is now, are more serious. What choices do we have? We might try to ban all uses of genetic selection and genetic engineering that go beyond the elimination of what are clearly defects. There are some obvious difficulties with this course of action:

1. Who will decide what is clearly a defect? Presumably, a government panel will be assigned the task of keeping abreast with relevant genetic techniques, and deciding which are lawful and which are not. This allows the government a role in reproductive decisions, which some may see as even more dangerous than the alternative of leaving them to the market.

2. There are serious questions about whether a ban on genetic selection and engineering for enhancement purposes could be made to work across the United States, given that matters regulating conception and birth are in the hands of the states, rather than the federal government. In the case of infertile couples seeking to pay a woman to bear a child for them, attempts by various U.S. states to make the practice illegal, or to declare surrogacy contracts void, have had little effect because a few states are more friendly to surrogacy. Couples seeking a surrogate to bear a child for them are prepared to travel to achieve what they want. As Lee Silver remarks: "What the brief history of surrogacy tells us is that Americans will not be hindered by ethical uncertainty, state-specific injunctions, or high costs in their drive to gain access to any technology that they feel will help them achieve their reproductive goals."[12]

3. Assume that one nation, for example the United States, decides that genetic selection is not a good thing, and Congress bans genetic selection and engineering when used for enhancement. Suppose also that this ban can be enforced effectively within the nation's boundaries. We

would still have to deal with the fact that we now live in a global economy. An effective global ban seems very unlikely. A small nation might be tempted to allow enhancement genetics, thus setting up a niche industry serving wealthy couples from those nations that have banned enhancement. Moreover, in view of the competitive nature of the global economy, it may pay industrialized nations to encourage enhancement genetics, thus giving them an edge on those that do not. Singapore's former Prime Minister, Lee Kuan Yew, used to speak about the heritability of intelligence, and its importance for Singapore's future. His government introduced measures explicitly designed to encourage university graduates to have more children.[13] Had genetic enhancement been available to Lee Kuan Yew at the time, he might well have preferred it to the government-sponsored computer dating services and financial incentives on which he was then forced to rely. It might appeal to Singapore's present Prime Minister, who is, not coincidentally, Lee Kuan Yew's son.

If a ban in one country turns out to be unattainable, ineffective, or contrary to the vital interests of that country in a competitive global economy, and a global ban is not feasible, a bolder strategy could be tried. Assuming that the objective is to avoid a society divided in two along genetic lines, genetic enhancement services could be subsidized, so that everyone can afford them. But could society afford to provide everyone with the services that otherwise only the rich could afford? Mehlman and Botkin propose an ingenious solution: the state should run a lottery in which the prize is the same package of genetic services that the rich commonly buy for themselves. Tickets in the lottery would not be sold; instead every adult citizen would be given one. The number of prizes would relate to how many of these packages society could afford to pay for, and thus would vary with the costs of the genetic services, as well as with the resources available to provide them. To avoid placing a financial burden on the state, Mehlman and Botkin suggest, the use of genetic technologies could be taxed, with the revenue going to fund the lottery.[14] Clearly universal coverage would be preferable, but the use of a lottery would at least ensure that everyone has some hope that their children will join ranks of the elite, and taxing those who are, by their use of genetic enhancement for their own children, changing the meaning of human reproduction seems a fair way to provide funds for it.

If we are serious about equality of opportunity then, instead of providing genetic enhancement for everyone, we could use our new techniques to provide genetic enhancement for those at the bottom, and restrict enhancement for those at the top.[15] That's a possible strategy, for those who consider equality of opportunity so important a value that it should override the benefits achieved by providing enhancement for those at the top. If, however, equality of opportunity is embraced for consequentialist reasons, rather than its intrinsic value, that is a dubious judgment. Unless we take a gloomy view of human nature, there seems a fair chance that enhancement for all, including those at the top, will eventually improve the situation of everyone, including the worst-off.

There is still a further problem that state provision of genetic enhancement to all citizens does not solve. If the rich nations were to act on this, it would still leave those living in poor countries without enhancement. So the divide that we feared would open up within a society would instead open up between societies. Unless we argue for an obligation for the rich nations to provide genetic enhancement for people living in countries unable to provide similar services, it is difficult to see any way of overcoming this problem.[16]

There is therefore a strong argument that the state should be directly involved in promoting genetic enhancement. But this takes us back to the question of which enhancement services the state should fund, and so we come back to the issue of positional goods. One proposal would be that the state should fund genetic enhancement that provides intrinsic goods, but not genetic enhancement that provides positional goods. For what would be the point of funding everyone to improve their positional goods? It would be as if the authorities dealt with drugs in sport by handing out equal doses of performance enhancing drugs to all athletes. If the drugs pose even small risks to

athletes, no one could sensibly favor such a proposal. But now we need a government committee to decide which forms of genetic enhancement confer intrinsic goods, and which confer positional goods. Suppose, for example, that we can find genes that correlate with doing well on IQ tests and scholastic aptitude tests used as part of the admission process by elite universities. Doing well on university admission tests is obviously a positional good. If everyone does better, the scores needed to get in will rise. If the tests are well designed, however, a good score presumably indicates an ability to learn, or to solve problems, or to write clearly and well. That sounds more like an intrinsic good, and an important one.

Bizarre as it may seem, there are some who might deny that the ability to learn or solve problems is an intrinsic good. Suppose that it is shown that scores on scholastic aptitude tests correlate inversely with the belief that God has an important role to play in one's life—not a far-fetched hypothesis, since we know that educational level does correlate inversely with this belief.[17] Those who think that belief in God is necessary for personal salvation, and that nothing can be more important than salvation, might then deny that scholastic aptitude is good at all.

Recent research on voles—small mouse-like rodents—has suggested that a characteristic more likely to appeal to Christians may be influenced by genetic modification. There are different kinds of voles, and they show different forms of mating behavior. Prairie voles tend to be monogamous, whereas meadow voles are more promiscuous. Researchers noticed that variations in a single gene—the arginine vasopressin receptor gene, which determines the way the brain responds to the hormone vasopressin—correlate with this difference in mating behavior. By manipulating the gene, the behavior of the normally promiscuous meadow voles was altered, so that they became as monogamous as prairie voles. If something similar can be shown for human behavior, would parents who place a high value on sexual fidelity wish to select or modify their children so that they would be more likely to be faithful to their sexual partners? Instead of exchanging promises and rings will people want their potential partners to make a different kind of commitment. Will they ever say: "If you really loved me, you'd get your vasopressin receptors enhanced, so you wouldn't be tempted to stray!" Or is there, as Immanuel Kant might have held, greater moral worth in being faithful *despite* have a genetic tendency to stray?[18] Does making it easier for humans to be faithful somehow reduce the value of faithfulness? Is the only moral virtue worth having that which is achieved through an act of will, rather than with the assistance of genetic modification? But what if having strength of will is itself something that is subject to genetic influence?

CONCLUSION

As these examples show, judgments about what goods we ought to promote will raise fundamental value questions that will not be easy to resolve.

In addition to distinguishing intrinsic and positional goods, each nation will have to consider whether to promote forms of genetic enhancement that have social benefits. Just as societies now spend money on education, especially in science and technology, in the hope of gaining an economic edge by having better-educated people than other nations, so too some nations will seize on genetic enhancement as a way of achieving the same goal. We may therefore have no choice but to allow it, and indeed encourage it, if we want our economy to remain strong.

In the case of promoting scholastic aptitude, the interests of the nation, of the person who is selected for the enhanced characteristics, and of the parents, may all coincide. But that will not always be the case. Some advocates of genetic enhancement hold out the prospect of improving human nature by selecting for children who are less aggressive, or more altruistic. In this way, they suggest, we can hope one day to live in peace, free of war and violence. The regulated and subsidized form of parental choice that I am suggesting might not lead to that happy outcome. There is a collective action problem here, the reverse of that we found with positional goods. We would all be better off if we each selected children who will be less aggressive and more altruistic, but unless the culture changes significantly, our own children may be

better off—at least by conventional measures of what counts as "better off"—if we do not select them in this way. The only way we could get the desired outcome would be to use coercion. Moreover if the desired end is world peace, and not merely a better, more compassionate society in our own country, this coercion would have to be carried out globally, perhaps by each government agreeing to enforce it on its own citizens. Politically, for the foreseeable future, this is fantasy. Genetic enhancement may have benefits, but it doesn't look as if world peace will be one of them.

NOTES

1. This is a substantially revised version of an essay that previously appeared in John Rasko, Gabrielle O'Sullivan, and Rachel Ankeny (eds), *The Ethics of Inheritable Genetic Modification* (Cambridge: Cambridge University Press), 2006.

2. Gina Kolata, "$50,000 Offered to Tall, Smart Egg Donor," *The New York Times,* March 3, 1999, A10; the suggestion that the amount paid is usually significantly less comes from Gregory Stock, personal communication.

3. See Michael Sandel, "The Case Against Perfection," *Atlantic Monthly,* April 2004, 51–62.

4. J. S. Mill, *On Liberty,* first published 1859, available at www.utilitarianism.com/ol/one.html

5. Lisa Gerson, "Human Harvest," *Boston Magazine,* May 1999, www.bostonmagazine.com/highlights/human-harvest.shtml

6. On the difficult issue of whether we can benefit a child by bringing it into existence, see Derek Parfit, *Reasons and Persons* (Oxford: Clarendon Press), 1984, 367, and Peter Singer, *Practical Ethics* (Cambridge: University Press), 2nd edn., 1993, 123–5.

7. Jerome Groopman, "The Doubting Disease," *New Yorker,* April 10, 2000, 55.

8. Helena Cronin, *The Ant and the Peacock* (Cambridge: Cambridge University Press), 1991, ch. 5.

9. *Gattaca,* written and directed by Andrew Niccol, 1997.

10. Lee Silver, *Remaking Eden* (New York: Avon), 1998, 282.

11. Maxwell Mehlman and Jeffrey Botkin, *Access to the Genome: The Challenge to Equality* (Washington, DC: Georgetown University Press), 1998, ch. 6.

12. *Remaking Eden,* 177.

13. Chan Chee Khoon and Chee Heng Leng, "Singapore 1984: Breeding for Big Brother," in Chan Chee Khoon

and Chee Heng Leng, *Designer Genes: I.Q., Ideology and Biology,* Institute for Social Analysis (Insan), Selangor, Malaysia, 1984, 4–13.

14. Mehlman and Botkin, op. cit., 126–8.

15. Dan Brock made this point in discussion, although without endorsing the view that we should give this much weight to equality of opportunity.

16. I owe this point to Art Caplan.

17. Gallup International Millennium Survey, 1999. Available at http://www.gallup-international.com/ContentFiles/millennium15.asp

18. Immanuel Kant, *Groundwork of the Metaphysics of Morals,* trans. Mary Gregor (Cambridge: University Press), 1997.

READING QUESTIONS

1. How does Singer dismiss the "life as a gift" argument against genetic enhancement?
2. Why does Singer object to a completely free-market "genetic supermarket"?
3. Explain Singer's "collective action problem" claim that if everyone gains a positional good, no one is better off. How does this differ from gaining an intrinsic good?
4. What three difficulties does Singer foresee in connection with attempts to ban all uses of genetic selection and engineering that go beyond elimination of defects?
5. In what ways does Singer speculate about the relation of genetic enhancement to national and global economy?
6. Explain Singer's proposal that the state should subsidize and regulate genetic enhancement.

DISCUSSION QUESTIONS

1. Singer does not agree with the claim that the genetic supermarket would be bad for the child who is a product of genetic selection. What reasons (other than the "disappointment" reason) can be given in support of the claim that it would be bad for the child?
2. Singer argues that not all forms of diversity are good. What examples does he give? Discuss forms of diversity that, by contrast, are good.
3. Singer's argument is clearly utilitarian, and he concludes that there are more benefits than harms to regulated genetic enhancement. But is there an opposing argument according to which genetic selection is morally wrong even if there are more benefits than harms?

ADDITIONAL RESOURCES

Web Resources

Note: the first three of the following Web resources were selected mainly for their information about genetics, cloning, and stem cell research.

Center for Genetics and Society, <www.geneticsandsociety.org>. A nonprofit organization that disseminates information about reproductive technologies. According to its site, "The Center supports benign and beneficent medical applications of the new human genetic and reproductive technologies, and opposes those applications that objectify and commodify human life and threaten to divide human society."

Genomics.Energy.Gov, <http://genomics.energy.gov>. Site of the genome programs of the U.S. Department of Energy Office of Science. Includes information about cloning.

The National Institutes of Health, <www.nih.gov>. Includes information about stem cells, stem cell research, ethical issues raised by such research, and information on U.S. policy regarding the use of stem cells in research.

Devolder, Katrien, "Cloning," <http://plato.stanford.edu/entries/cloning>. An overview of the ethical dispute over therapeutic and reproductive cloning, including some discussion of religious perspectives.

Siegel, Andrew, "The Ethics of Stem Cell Research," <http://plato.stanford.edu/entries/stem-cells>. An overview of the ethical controversy over use of stem cells for therapeutic and reproductive purposes.

Authored Books

Agar, Nicholas, *Liberal Eugenics: In Defense of Human Enhancement* (Oxford: Blackwell, 2004). As the title indicates, Agar defends the morality of human enhancement employing what he calls the "method of moral images" that appeals to the idea of treating like cases alike.

Congregation for the Doctrine of the Faith, *Instruction* Dignitas Personae *on Certain Bioethical Questions*, 2008. An update of the Vatican's stance on biomedical issues in which it condemns *in vitro* fertilization, human cloning, genetic testing on embryos, embryonic stem cell research (that involves destruction of the embryos), and use of the RU-486 pill.

Kass, Leon R., *Human Cloning and Human Dignity: The Report of the President's Council on Bioethics* (New York: PublicAffairs Reports, 2002). A report from President George W. Bush's bioethics council with Kass as its chairman in which the ethical issues raised by cloning and matters of public policy are discussed.

Kitcher, Philip, *The Lives to Come: The Genetic Revolution and Human Possibilities* (New York: Simon & Schuster, 1997). A guide to advances in biomedical research including discussion of important moral and political questions such research raises.

Mehlman, Maxwell J., *Transhumanist Dreams and Dystopian Nightmares: The Promise and Peril of Genetic Engineering*. (Baltimore, MD: The Johns Hopkins Press, 2012). The author explores scientific and ethical questions raised by the prospect of human genetic engineering.

Pence, Gregory E., *Flesh of My Flesh: The Ethics of Cloning Humans* (Lanham, MD: Rowman & Littlefield, 1998). An examination of the ethical arguments over cloning and a qualified defense of the practice.

Pence, Gregory E., *Cloning After Dolly: Who's Still Afraid?* (Lanham, MD: Rowman & Littlefield, 2005). A follow up to his 1998 book, extending his case in favor of cloning.

Stock, Gregory, *Redesigning Humans: Our Inevitable Genetic Future* (New York: Houghton Mifflin Co, 2002). Examines the emerging reproductive technologies for selection and alteration of human embryos. Stock argues that ethical objections to such selection and alteration are much like the objections formerly raised against in vitro fertilization.

Wilkinson, Stephen, *Choosing Tomorrow's Children* (New York: Oxford University Press, 2010). An examination of the moral issues raised by the prospects of selective reproduction.

Edited Collections

Klotzko, Arlene Judith (ed.), *The Cloning Sourcebook* (Oxford: Oxford University Press, 2001). Twenty-eight essays divided into four parts: (1) The Science of Cloning, (2) The Context of Cloning, (3) Cloning: The Ethical Issues, and (4) Cloning and Germ-Line Intervention: Policy Issues.

McGee, Glenn (ed.), *The Human Cloning Debate* (Berkeley, CA: Berkeley Hills Books, 2002). This anthology has nineteen selections debating the morality of cloning and includes five articles representing various religious (Jewish, Catholic, Protestant, Buddhist, and Islamic) perspectives on the issue.

Nussbaum, Martha C. and Cass R. Sunstein (eds.), *Clones and Clones: Facts and Fantasies about Human Cloning* (New York: W. W. Norton, 1998). A collection of twenty-four contributions organized into five sections: (1) Science, (2) Commentary, (3) Ethics and Religion, (4) Law and Public Policy, and (5) Fiction and Fantasy.

Rantala, M. L. and Arthur J Milgram (eds.), *Cloning: For and Against* (Chicago: Open Court, 1999). A wide-ranging collection of fifty-four essays by scientists, journalists, philosophers, religious leaders, and legal experts debating the ethical issues and matters of public policy regarding the prospect of cloning.

Ruse, Michael and Christopher A. Pynes (eds.), *The Stem Cell Controversy*, 2nd ed. (Amherst, NY: Prometheus Books, 2006). Twenty-eight essays organized into five parts: (1) The Science of Stem Cells, (2) Medical Cures and Promises, (3) Moral Issues, (4) Religious Issues, and (5) Policy Issues.

Savulescu, Julian and Nick Bostrom, (eds.), *Human Enhancement* (Oxford: Oxford University Press, 2009). Eighteen essays debating the general topic of human enhancement as well as specific applications including, for example, the issue of selection of children and the use of enhancements to improve athletic performance.

12) The Death Penalty

As of 2012, the death penalty was legal in thirty-three U.S. states. In what is often called "the modern era" of the death penalty in the United States from 1976—when the 1972 moratorium on the death penalty was lifted by the U.S. Supreme Court—over 1,200 individuals have been executed in the United States.[1] Although traditionally there has been wide support among U.S. citizens for the death penalty, this support has been declining in recent years. A Gallup Poll conducted in 1988 indicated that 79% of U.S. citizens favored the death penalty for the crime of murder. A 2011 Gallup Poll indicated that 61% of U.S. citizens support the death penalty for the crime of murder, while 35% are opposed. Another Gallup Poll conducted in 2006 is perhaps more revealing. This poll indicated that when presented with the option of sentencing someone to life in prison *without parole* for the crime of murder or sentencing that person to die, only 47% favored the death penalty, 48% favored life without parole, and 5% had no opinion.[2] At least in the United States, the death penalty continues to be a source of moral controversy.[3]

This controversy was fueled in 2009 by the case of Cameron Todd Willingham, who in 2004 was executed in the state of Texas for setting fire to his house in 1991, an act that had killed his three children. Willingham denied setting the fire and refused to enter a plea of guilty in exchange for a life sentence. In 2004 and after a detailed arson report concluded that the evidence against Willingham was "flimsy and inconclusive," Texas governor Rick Perry nevertheless denied a reprieve and Willingham was executed. In 2009, the Forensic Fire Commission hired an arson expert to review the evidence in the Willingham case. The expert, Craig L. Beyler, reported that the evidence in the case did not support the claim that the fire was a case of arson. In October of 2009, Beyler was set to testify before the Texas Forensic Science Commission, but two days before the commission was to hear this testimony, Governor Perry replaced the head and two other members of the commission. The newly appointed head, John M. Bradley, then canceled the meeting. The matter is still under consideration by the commission. Many are convinced that Texas executed an innocent man, and in his article, "Trial by Fire," about the Willingham case published in the *The New Yorker*, David Grann notes that Texas may be the first state forced to acknowledge that it carried out the execution of an innocent person.[4] Perhaps the most forceful moral argument against the death penalty is based on the claim that some people innocent of the crimes for which they are sentenced to die (Willingham may have been such a person) have been and likely will continue to be wrongly put to death. In recent years the use of DNA testing has also played a large role in exonerating some death row convicts and thus calling into question the death penalty. According to the *Innocence Project*, 245 individuals convicted of crimes have been exonerated by the use of DNA testing, 18 of whom were at one time sentenced to death.[5]

In addition to questions about the morality of the death penalty, there are also questions about its legality. The Eighth Amendment to the U.S. Constitution forbids "cruel and unusual" punishment, and some argue that the death penalty, because it is cruel and unusual, is unconstitutional and hence ought to be made illegal. This question of the constitutionality of the death penalty is the leading *general* question about its legality; but there are also *specific* legal questions about its use. For instance, in March 2005, the U.S. Supreme Court ruled it unconstitutional to execute juveniles—those under the age of eighteen who commit murder—a decision[6] in which the Court stressed the importance of appealing to "the evolving standards of decency that mark the progress of a maturing society" in determining which punishments are cruel and unusual.

But our concern here is with the *morality* of the death penalty, and the main questions are these:

- Is the death penalty ever a morally permissible form of punishment?
- If it is ever morally permitted, what best explains why such killing is permissible?

Those who answer the first question negatively are often referred to as **abolitionists,** and those who think that the death penalty is (or could be) morally justified (or perhaps even required) are often referred to as **retentionists.**[7] Of course, a retentionist need not and typically will not think that use of the death penalty is morally justified under *all* conditions. And so anyone who answers the first question affirmatively must address the second question.

In the remainder of this introduction, we shall consider important theoretical background that one must understand to be in a position to follow the moral controversy over the death penalty. We begin with some remarks about the idea of legal punishment and then proceed to outline two general approaches to the morality of punishment that influence moral discussion and debate over the specific punishment of execution.

1. LEGAL PUNISHMENT

The focus of this chapter is **legal punishment**—punishment administered by a legal authority. So, it is important at the outset to begin with a working definition of legal punishment, which will enable us to clarify the moral issues connected with legal punishment generally and the death penalty in particular.

Obviously, legal punishment presupposes a legal system, involving a set of laws and some mechanism of enforcement of those laws. Here, then, is a list of requirements that serve to define the very idea of a legal punishment.[8]

1. It must involve pain or other consequences normally considered unpleasant;
2. It must be for an offense against legal rules;
3. It must be of an actual or supposed offender for his or her offense;
4. It must be intentionally administered by human beings other than the offender;
5. It must be imposed and administered by an authority constituted by a legal system against which the offense is committed.

Because there is a moral presumption against the intentional infliction of pain or other unpleasant consequences on human beings, the practice of legal punishment calls for a moral justification. This moral question is addressed by theories about the morality of punishment.

2. THEORY MEETS PRACTICE

Two theories about the morality of punishment inform much of the debate over the death penalty. One theory is the **retributive theory of punishment**, which is basically Kantian in flavor; the other is the **consequentialist theory of punishment**. These theories attempt to answer two basic questions about the morality of punishment:

- What (if anything) morally justifies the practice of punishment?
- How much and what kinds of punishment are morally justified for various legal offenses?

The retributive and consequentialist theories provide competing answers to these two questions.

The Retributive Theory

The retributive theory in effect looks to the deeds of wrongdoers—both the fact that such deeds break laws and the specific nature of the deeds performed—in order to answer the two questions. So, the retributivist answer to the first question is

R1   What morally justifies punishment of wrongdoers is that those who break the law (and are properly judged to have done so) *deserve* to be punished.

A sense of fairness or justice prevails here. Wrongdoers are viewed as attempting to take unfair advantage of others and law-governed society generally, and the idea behind R1 is simply that justice demands that in response to crime, the wrongdoer suffer some sort of deprivation.

The retributivist response to the second question is

R2   The punishment for a particular offense against the law should "fit" the crime.

The task for the retentionist who accepts the retributive theory is to show that the death penalty is either required by, or at least consistent with, these two basic retributive principles (properly interpreted); opponents of the death penalty who accept the retributive theory must show that there is something about the death penalty that violates one or both of these principles (properly interpreted).

It is clear that R1 is neutral with regard to the moral justification of the death penalty—both retentionists and abolitionists, who otherwise accept the retributivist theory, can agree that punishment in general is justified because the wrongdoer deserves it. So the main focus of the retentionist's strategy in arguing about the death penalty will be R2. And here we find a variety

213

of interpretations of R2, owing to the fact that there is more than one way of understanding the idea of a punishment *fitting* the crime. I will briefly mention two of them.

According to the principle expressed by **lex talionis** (law of retribution), making the punishment fit the crime is a matter of doing to the wrongdoer the *same kind of action* that he or she did to his or her victim(s). This "eye for an eye" principle implies that the appropriate punishment for the crime of murder is the death penalty.

An alternative interpretation of what it means to make the punishment fit the crime is the **principle of proportionality**, according to which the appropriate moral measure of specific punishments requires that they be in "proportion" to the crime: that the severity of the punishment should "be commensurate" with the gravity of the offense.

Thus, the task of the retributivist who wants to defend the death penalty is to provide an interpretation of R2 that (1) represents a philosophically defensible principle of punishment *and* that (2) implies or at least is consistent with having the death penalty. This challenge is discussed by Stephen Nathanson in one of the readings in this chapter, and he argues that it cannot plausibly be met.

Although Kant famously defends the death penalty by appealing to retributivist ideas about the morality of punishment, some abolitionists appeal (rather ironically) to Kant's Humanity formulation of the categorical imperative: *an action is right if and only if (and because) it is consistent with treating human beings as ends in themselves—as beings with an inherent worth or dignity.* Nathanson, for instance, appeals to Kant's principle in arguing against the morality of the death penalty, claiming that execution fails to comport with what he calls "personal desert" grounded in one's innate dignity as a human being.

The Consequentialist Theory

The consequentialist theory of the morality of punishment follows fairly directly from the basic idea of the consequentialist moral theory of right conduct that was presented in chapter 1: *an action or practice is right if and only if (and because) the overall value of the consequences of the action or practice would be at least as great as the overall value of the consequences of alternative actions and practices.* If we now appeal to this basic principle in responding to the two questions about the morality of punishment, we have

C1 Punishment as a response to crime is morally justified if and only if this practice, compared to any other response to crime, will likely produce as much overall intrinsic value as would any other response.

C2 A specific punishment for a certain crime is morally justified if and only if it would likely produce at least as much overall intrinsic value as would any other alternative punishment.

Consequentialist thinking about the death penalty focuses on C2 and thus on an assessment of the values of the consequences that are likely to result from having the death penalty compared to the values of the consequences that are likely to result from eliminating the death penalty. (Again, in cases in which a society does not currently have the death penalty, the comparison will be between instituting this punishment and not instituting it.)

Three things should be kept in mind about consequentialism as it bears on the morality of the death penalty. First, those who accept the consequentialist approach to the morality of punishment may or may not be committed thereby to the claim that the death penalty is morally justified—it all depends on what the values of the likely consequences of having the death penalty are compared with not having it. Second, this issue about values of the likely consequences is partly a moral issue but also partly a complicated empirical issue. The moral issue is this. What sorts of states of affairs (that might be consequences of some action or practice) have positive value, and what sorts have negative value? As we noted in the general introduction to this book, some consequentialists are utilitarians who think that happiness (welfare) is what has positive intrinsic value. But other consequentialists are perfectionists who hold that in addition to human happiness, such items as knowledge and achievement are intrinsically good. However, all parties to the dispute over the death penalty can agree that preserving human life—at least innocent human life, because it is necessary for achieving anything of intrinsic value—has a very high value, that the loss of human life is intrinsically bad or evil. If we agree, then, to focus on the value of human life when it comes to assessing the rightness of the death penalty, there is still the complicated empirical issue of determining whether employing this form of punishment will produce overall good enough consequences for society. This is an issue that criminologists and social scientists have studied and that is still being disputed.[9]

The third observation is that for purposes of evaluating the morality of some action or practice in terms of the values of its likely consequences, it is important to keep in mind that in so doing, one must consider not only the possible positive effects of the death penalty but also any negative effects that are likely to occur in allowing the death penalty. The same point applies when considering the possibility of abolishing the death penalty. So if we are to compare having the death penalty with not having it on strictly consequentialist grounds, then we have to consider the pluses and minuses of both options before we can move to a moral verdict about the morality of the death penalty.

Among the possible positive effects of having the death penalty are the following:

- **Deterrence:** Someone is *deterred* from committing murder by the threat of the death penalty only if his recognition of the death penalty as a possible consequence of committing murder explains why he doesn't commit it. Those who defend the death penalty on deterrence grounds argue that this punishment is *uniquely* effective in its deterrence effects in that there are some people who would be (or are) deterred by the threat of the death penalty, but would not be (or are not) deterred by a lesser punishment such as life without parole.
- **Prevention:** Someone is *prevented* by execution from committing a murder only if *had he not been executed, he would have gone ahead and committed the murder.* The point to be made about prevention and the death penalty is that even though someone's death prevents him from any further activity, it does not follow that he has thereby been prevented from performing certain specific acts. If, had he lived on, he would not have performed some action (for example, running for a seat in Congress), then it is not strictly correct to say that his death prevented him from running for a seat in Congress.

Among the possible negative consequences of having the death penalty are the following:

- Executing the innocent: The risk of executing innocent individuals owing to errors in the legal process that lead to conviction and "capital" (death penalty) sentencing.

215

- Incitement effect: Some argue that the death penalty may actually incite murder.[10]
- Financial cost: The death penalty cases cost more than other cases, and imposing the death penalty generally costs more than a sentence of life imprisonment without parole.[11]

These considerations about the consequences of the death penalty are taken up in the articles by Ernest van den Haag, Jeffrey H. Reiman, and the authors of the report on the evidence of errors in capital sentencing. Van den Haag defends the retentionist position on both retributivist and consequentialist grounds. Reiman is critical of the so-called common sense argument for the claim that the death penalty is a crime deterrent, an argument advanced by van den Haag. The final selection in this chapter is a report of an empirical study which, according to the authors, provides evidence of a significant error rate in the sentencing in death penalty cases.

NOTES

1. In the 1972 landmark decision *Furman v. Georgia* (408 U.S. 238), the U.S. Supreme Court ruled that the death penalty was unconstitutional *as then administered* because state statutes failed to provide guidelines for its use that would guard against its being imposed in an arbitrary and capricious manner. As a result of the Court's 1972 decision, states wanting to impose the death penalty worked to devise standards for its use that would provide safeguards against arbitrariness. In the 1976 case *Gregg v. Georgia* (428 U.S. 153), the Court approved Georgia's revised statutes governing the death penalty, thus lifting the moratorium.

2. The statistics just cited are taken from the website Death Penalty Information Center, www. deathpenaltyinfo.org.

3. According to *Amnesty International* (http://web.amnesty.org/pages/deathpenalty-countries-eng), as of 2012 more than two-thirds of the world's countries have abolished the death penalty either by law or by practice.

4. Grann's article was published in the September 7, 2009, edition. It can be found online at http://www.newyorker.com.

5. The *Innocence Project*, established in 1992, is devoted to "exonerating wrongfully convicted people through DNA testing and reforming the criminal justice system to prevent future injustice." <innocenceproject.org>.

6. *Roper v. Simmons,* No. 03-633.

7. Of course, this terminology is apt only if we are considering the morality of the death penalty in a country or state that currently allows it. Otherwise, those who are pro–death penalty are in favor of instituting it where it does not exist, and those against it are against its being instituted.

8. This list is taken from H. L. A. Hart, "Prolegomenon to the Principles of Punishment," in *Punishment and Responsibility* (Oxford: Oxford University Press, 1968).

9. See, for example, Richard A. Berk, "New Claims about Executions and General Deterrence: Déjà Vu All Over Again?" *Journal of Empirical Legal Studies* (July 19, 2004). Available at http://preprints.stat.ucla.edu/396/JELS.pap.pdf.

10. See for example, Mark Costonzo, *Just Revenge* (New York: St. Martin's Press, 1997).

11. See Richard C. Dieter, "Millions Misspent," in *The Death Penalty in America,* ed. Hugo Adam Bedau (Oxford: Oxford University Press, 1997).

STEPHEN NATHANSON

An Eye for an Eye?

Stephen Nathanson is critical of attempts to defend the morality of the death penalty on retributivist grounds. Focusing on the retributivist idea that a morally justified punishment must "fit" the crime, he considers two versions of what he calls the "equality" interpretation of this idea—a strict version of *lex talionis* and a version that would require that we make the punishment equivalent in the harm it brings to the wrongdoer as was done to the wrongdoer's victims. Against both versions of the equality interpretation Nathanson raises moral and practical objections. Nathanson then argues that the proportionality interpretation of "fit" also cannot be used to morally justify the death penalty. In the final section of his paper, Nathanson presents two arguments against the death penalty.

Recommended Reading: Kantian moral theory, chap. 1, sec. 2C.

AN EYE FOR AN EYE?

Suppose we . . . try to determine what people deserve from a strictly moral point of view. How shall we proceed?

The most usual suggestion is that we look at a person's actions because what someone deserves would appear to depend on what he or she does. A person's actions, it seems, provide not only a basis for a moral appraisal of the person but also a guide to how he should be treated. According to the *lex talionis* or principle of "an eye for an eye," we ought to treat people as they have treated others. What people deserve as recipients of rewards or punishments is determined by what they do as agents.

This is a powerful and attractive view, one that appears to be backed not only by moral common sense but also by tradition and philosophical thought. The most famous statement of philosophical support for this view comes from Immanuel Kant, who linked it directly with an argument for the death penalty. Discussing the problem of punishment, Kant writes,

> What kind and what degree of punishment does legal justice adopt as its principle and standard? None other than the principle of equality . . . the principle of not treating one side more favorably than the other. Accordingly, any undeserved evil that you inflict on someone else among the people is one that you do to yourself. If you vilify, you vilify yourself: if you steal from him, you steal from yourself; if you kill him, you kill yourself. Only the law of retribution (*jus talionis*) can determine exactly the kind and degree of punishment.[1]

Kant's view is attractive for a number of reasons. First, it accords with our belief that what a person deserves is related to what he does. Second, it appeals to a moral standard and does not seem to rely on any particular legal or political institutions. Third, it seems to provide a measure of appropriate punishment that can be used as a guide to creating laws and instituting punishments. It tells us that the punishment is to be identical with the crime. Whatever the criminal did to the victim is to be done in turn to the criminal.

From Stephen Nathanson, *An Eye for an Eye?* 2nd ed. (Lanham, MD: Rowman and Littlefield, 2001). Reprinted by permission.

In spite of the attractions of Kant's view, it is deeply flawed. When we see why, it will be clear that the whole "eye for an eye" perspective must be rejected.

PROBLEMS WITH THE EQUAL PUNISHMENT PRINCIPLE

There are two main problems with this view. First, appearances to the contrary, it does not actually provide a measure of moral desert. Second, it does not provide an adequate criterion for determining appropriate levels of punishment.

Let us begin with the second criticism, the claim that Kant's view fails to tell us how much punishment is appropriate for particular crimes. We can see this, first, by noting that for certain crimes, Kant's view recommends punishments that are not morally acceptable. Applied strictly, it would require that we rape rapists, torture torturers, and burn arsonists whose acts have led to deaths. In general, where a particular crime involves barbaric and inhuman treatment, Kant's principle tells us to act barbarically and inhumanly in return. So, in some cases, the principle generates unacceptable answers to the question of what constitutes appropriate punishment.

This is not its only defect. In many other cases, the principle tells us nothing at all about how to punish. While Kant thought it obvious how to apply his principle in the case of murder, his principle cannot serve as a general rule because it does not tell us how to punish many crimes. Using the Kantian version or the more common "eye for an eye" standard, what would we decide to do to embezzlers, spies, drunken drivers, airline hijackers, drug users, prostitutes, air polluters, or persons who practice medicine without a license? If one reflects on this question, it becomes clear that there is simply no answer to it. We could not in fact design a system of punishment simply on the basis of the "eye for an eye" principle.

In order to justify using the "eye for an eye" principle to answer our question about murder and the death penalty, we would first have to show that it worked for a whole range of cases, giving acceptable answers to questions about amounts of punishment. Then, having established it as a satisfactory general principle, we could apply it to the case of murder. It turns out, however, that when we try to apply the principle generally, we find that it either gives wrong answers or no answers at all. Indeed, I suspect that the principle of "an eye for an eye" is no longer even a principle. Instead, it is simply a metaphorical disguise for expressing belief in the death penalty. People who cite it do not take it seriously. They do not believe in a kidnapping for a kidnapping, a theft for a theft, and so on. Perhaps "an eye for an eye" once was a genuine principle, but now it is merely a slogan. Therefore, it gives us no guidance in deciding whether murderers deserve to die.

In reply to these objections, one might defend the principle by saying that it does not require that punishments be strictly identical with crimes. Rather, it requires only that a punishment produce an amount of suffering in the criminal which is equal to the amount suffered by the victim. Thus, we don't have to hijack airplanes belonging to airline hijackers, spy on spies, etc. We simply have to reproduce in them the harm done to others.

Unfortunately, this reply really does not solve the problem. It provides no answer to the first objection, since it would still require us to behave barbarically in our treatment of those who are guilty of barbaric crimes. Even if we do not reproduce their actions exactly, any action which caused equal suffering would itself be barbaric. Second, in trying to produce equal amounts of suffering, we run into many problems. Just how much suffering is produced by an airline hijacker or a spy? And how do we apply this principle to prostitutes or drug users, who may not produce any suffering at all? We have rough ideas about how serious various crimes are, but this may not correlate with any clear sense of just how much harm is done.

Furthermore, the same problem arises in determining how much suffering a particular punishment would produce for a particular criminal. People vary in their tolerance of pain and in the amount of unhappiness that a fine or a jail sentence would cause them. Recluses will be less disturbed by banishment than extroverts. Nature lovers will suffer more in prison than people who are indifferent to natural beauty. A literal application of the principle would require that we tailor punishments to individual sensitivities, yet this is at best impractical. To a large extent, the legal system must work with standardized and rather crude estimates of the negative impact that punishments have on people.

The move from calling for a punishment that is identical to the crime to favoring one that is equal in the harm done is no help to us or to the defense of the principle. "An eye for an eye" tells us neither what people deserve nor how we should treat them when they have done wrong.

PROPORTIONAL RETRIBUTIVISM

The view we have been considering can be called "equality retributivism," since it proposes that we repay criminals with punishments equal to their crimes. In the light of problems like those I have cited, some people have proposed a variation on this view, calling not for equal punishments but rather for punishments which are proportional to the crime. In defending such a view as a guide for setting criminal punishments, Andrew von Hirsch writes:

> If one asks how severely a wrongdoer deserves to be punished, a familiar principle comes to mind: Severity of punishment should be commensurate with the seriousness of the wrong. Only grave wrongs merit severe penalties; minor misdeeds deserve lenient punishments. Disproportionate penalties are undeserved— severe sanctions for minor wrongs or vice versa. This principle has variously been called a principle of "proportionality" or "just deserts"; we call it commensurate deserts.[2]

Like Kant, von Hirsch makes the punishment which a person deserves depend on that person's actions, but he departs from Kant in substituting proportionality for equality as the criterion for setting the amount of punishment.

In implementing a punishment system based on the proportionality view, one would first make a list of crimes, ranking them in order of seriousness. At one end would be quite trivial offenses like parking meter violations, while very serious crimes such as murder would occupy the other. In between, other crimes would be ranked according to their relative gravity. Then a corresponding scale of punishments would be constructed, and the two would be correlated. Punishments would be proportionate to crimes so long as we could say that the more serious the crime was, the higher on the punishment scale was the punishment administered.

This system does not have the defects of equality retributivism. It does not require that we treat those guilty of barbaric crimes barbarically. This is because we can set the upper limit of the punishment scale so as to exclude truly barbaric punishments. Second, unlike the equality principle, the proportionality view is genuinely general, providing a way of handling all crimes. Finally, it does justice to our ordinary belief that certain punishments are unjust because they are too severe or too lenient for the crime committed.

The proportionality principle does, I think, play a legitimate role in our thinking about punishments. Nonetheless, it is no help to death penalty advocates, because it does not require that murderers be executed. All that it requires is that if murder is the most serious crime, then murder should be punished by the most severe punishment on the scale. The principle does not tell us what this punishment should be, however, and it is quite compatible with the view that the most severe punishment should be a long prison term.

This failure of the theory to provide a basis for supporting the death penalty reveals an important gap in proportional retributivism. It shows that while the theory is general in scope, it does not yield any *specific* recommendations regarding punishment. It tells us, for example, that armed robbery should be punished more severely than embezzling and less severely than murder, but it does not tell us how much to punish any of these. This weakness is, in effect, conceded by von Hirsch, who admits that if we want to implement the "commensurate deserts" principle, we must supplement it with information about what level of punishment is needed to deter crimes.[3] In a later discussion of how to "anchor" the punishment system, he deals with this problem in more depth, but the factors he cites as relevant to making specific judgments (such as available prison space) have nothing to do with what people deserve. He also seems to suggest that a range of punishments may be appropriate for a particular crime. This runs counter to the death penalty supporter's sense that death alone is appropriate for some murderers.[4]

Neither of these retributive views, then, provides support for the death penalty. The equality principle fails because it is not in general true that the appropriate punishment for a crime is to do to the criminal what he has done to others. In some cases this is immoral, while in others it is impossible. The proportionality principle may be correct, but by itself it cannot determine specific punishments for specific crimes. Because of its flexibility and open-endedness, it is compatible with a great range of different punishments for murder.[5] . . .

THE SYMBOLISM OF ABOLISHING THE DEATH PENALTY

What is the symbolic message that we would convey by deciding to renounce the death penalty and to abolish its use?

I think that there are two primary messages. The first is the most frequently emphasized and is usually expressed in terms of the sanctity of human life, although I think we could better express it in terms of respect for human dignity. One way we express our respect for the dignity of human beings is by abstaining from depriving them of their lives, even if they have done terrible deeds. In defense of human well-being, we may punish people, for their crimes, but we ought not to deprive them of everything, which is what the death penalty does.

If we take the life of a criminal, we convey the idea that by his deeds he has made himself worthless and totally without human value. I do not believe that we are in a position to affirm that of anyone. We may hate such a person and feel the deepest anger against him, but when he no longer poses a threat to anyone, we ought not to take his life.

But, one might ask, hasn't the murderer forfeited whatever rights he might have had to our respect? Hasn't he, by his deeds, given up any rights that he had to decent treatment? Aren't we morally free to kill him if we wish?

These questions express important doubts about the obligation to accord any respect to those who have acted so deplorably, but I do not think that they prove that any such forfeiture has occurred. Certainly, when people murder or commit other crimes, they do forfeit some of the rights that are possessed by the law-abiding. They lose a certain right to be left alone. It becomes permissible to bring them to trial and, if they are convicted, to impose an appropriate—even a dreadful—punishment on them.

Nonetheless, they do not forfeit all their rights. It does not follow from the vileness of their actions that we can do anything whatsoever to them. This is part of the moral meaning of the constitutional ban on cruel and unusual punishments. No matter how terrible a person's deeds, we may not punish him in a cruel and unusual way. We may not torture him, for example. His right not to be tortured has not been forfeited. Why do these limits hold? Because this person remains a human being, and we think that there is something in him that we must continue to respect in spite of his terrible acts.

One way of seeing why those who murder still deserve some consideration and respect is by reflecting again on the idea of what it is to deserve something. In most contexts, we think that what people deserve depends on what they have done, intended, or tried to do. It depends on features that are qualities of individuals. The best person for the job deserves to be hired. The person who worked especially hard deserves our gratitude. We can call the concept that applies in these cases *personal* desert.

There is another kind of desert, however, that belongs to people by virtue of their humanity itself and does not depend on their individual efforts or achievements. I will call this impersonal kind of desert *human* desert. We appeal to this concept when we think that everyone deserves a certain level of treatment no matter what their individual qualities are. When the signers of the Declaration of Independence affirmed that people had inalienable rights to "life, liberty, and the pursuit of happiness," they were, appealing to such an idea. These rights do not have to be earned by people. They are possessed "naturally," and everyone is bound to respect them.

According to the view that I am defending, people do not lose all of their rights when they commit terrible crimes. They still deserve some level of decent treatment simply because they remain living, functioning human beings. This level of moral desert need not be earned, and it cannot be forfeited. This view may sound controversial, but in fact everyone who believes that cruel and unusual punishment should be forbidden implicitly agrees with it. That is, they agree that even after someone has committed a terrible crime, we do not have the right to do anything whatsoever to him.

What I am suggesting is that by renouncing the use of death as a punishment, we express and reaffirm our belief in the inalienable, unforfeitable core of human dignity.

Why is this a worthwhile message to convey? It is worth conveying because this belief is both important and precarious. Throughout history, people have found innumerable reasons to degrade the humanity of one another. They have found qualities in others that they hated or feared, and even when they were not threatened by these people, they have sought to harm them, deprive them of their liberty, or take their lives from them. They have often felt that they had good reasons to do these things, and they have invoked divine commands, racial purity, and state security to support their deeds.

These actions and attitudes are not relics of the past. They remain an awful feature of the contemporary world. By renouncing the death penalty, we show our determination to accord at least minimal respect even to those whom we believe to be personally vile or morally vicious. This is, perhaps, why we speak of the *sanctity* of human life rather than its value or worth. That which is sacred remains, in some sense, untouchable, and its value is not dependent on its worth or usefulness to us. Kant expressed this ideal of respect in the famous second version of the Categorical Imperative: "So act as to treat humanity, whether in thine own person or in that of any

other, in every case as an end withal, never as a means only."[6] . . .

THE MORALITY OF RESTRAINT

I have argued that the first symbolic meaning conveyed by a renunciation of the death penalty is that human dignity must be respected in every person. To execute a person for murder is to treat that person as if he were nothing but a murderer and to deprive him of everything that he has. Therefore, if we want to convey the appropriate message about human dignity, we will renounce the death penalty.

One might object that, in making this point, I am contradicting the claim that killing in defense of oneself or others can be morally justified. If it is wrong to execute a person because this violates his dignity as a human being and deprives him of everything, it would seem to be equally wrong to kill this person as a means of defense. Defensive killing seems to violate these ideals in the same way that I claim punishing by death does. Isn't this inconsistent? Mustn't I either retreat to the absolute pacifist view or else allow that the death penalty is permissible?

. . . What I need to do now is to show that defensive killing is compatible with respect for human dignity. We can easily see that it is by recalling the central fact about killing to ward off an assault on one's own life. In this circumstance, someone will die. The only question open is whether it will be the attacker or the intended victim. We cannot act in any way that shows the very same respect and concern for both the attacker and the intended victim. Although we have no wish to harm the attacker, this is the only way to save the innocent person who is being attacked. In this situation, assuming that there are no alternative means of preventing the attack from succeeding, it is permissible to kill the attacker.

What is crucial here is that the choice is forced on us. If we do not act, then one person will be destroyed. There is no way of showing equal concern for both attacker and victim, so we give preference to the intended victim and accept the morality of killing the attacker.

The case of punishing by death is entirely different. If this punishment will neither save the life of the victim nor prevent the deaths of other potential victims, then the decision to kill the murderer is avoidable. We can restrain ourselves without sacrificing the life or well-being of other people who are equally deserving of respect and consideration. In this situation, the restrained reaction is the morally right one.

In addition to providing an answer to the objection, this point provides us with the second important message conveyed by the renunciation of punishing by death. When we restrain ourselves and do not take the lives of those who kill, we communicate the importance of minimizing killing and other acts of violence. We reinforce the idea that violence is morally legitimate only as a defensive measure and should be curbed whenever possible. . . .

When the state has a murderer in its power and could execute him but does not, this conveys the idea that even though this person has done wrong and even though we may be angry, outraged, and indignant with him, we will nonetheless control ourselves in a way that he did not. We will not kill him, even though we could do so and even though we are angry and indignant. We will exercise restraint, sanctioning killing only when it serves a protective function.

Why should we do this? Partly out of a respect for human dignity. But also because we want the state to set an example of proper behavior. We do not want to encourage people to resort to violence to settle conflicts when there are other ways available. We want to avoid the cycle of violence that can come from retaliation and counter-retaliation. Violence is a contagion that arouses hatred and anger, and if unchecked, it simply leads to still more violence.

The state can convey the message that the contagion must be stopped, and the most effective principle for stopping it is the idea that only defensive violence is justifiable. Since the death penalty is not an instance of defensive violence, it ought to be renounced.

We show our respect for life best by restraining ourselves and allowing murderers to live, rather than by following a policy of a life for a life. Respect for life and restraint of violence are aspects of the same ideal. The renunciation of the death penalty would symbolize our support of that ideal.

NOTES

1. Kant, *Metaphysical Elements of Justice,* translated by John Ladd (Indianapolis: Bobbs-Merrill, 1965), 101.

2. *Doing Justice* (New York: Hill & Wang, 1976), 66; reprinted in *Sentencing,* edited by H. Gross and A. von Hirsch (Oxford University Press, 1981), 243. For a more recent discussion and further defense by von Hirsch, see his *Past or Future Crimes* (New Brunswick, N.J.: Rutgers University Press, 1985).

3. von Hirsch, *Doing Justice,* 93–94. My criticisms of proportional retributivism are not novel. For helpful discussions of the view, see Hugo Bedau, "Concessions to Retribution in Punishment," in *Justice and Punishment,* edited by J. Cederblom and W. Blizek (Cambridge, Mass.: Bellinger, 1977), and M. Golding, *Philosophy of Law* (Englewood Cliffs, N.J.: Prentice Hall, 1975), 98–99.

4. See von Hirsch, *Past and Future Crimes,* ch. 8.

5. For more positive assessments of these theories, see Jeffrey Reiman, "Justice, Civilization, and the Death Penalty," *Philosophy and Public Affairs* 14 (1985): 115–48; and Michael Davis, "How to Make the Punishment Fit the Crime," *Ethics* 93 (1983).

6. *Fundamental Principles of the Metaphysics of Morals,* translated by T. Abbott (New York: Liberal Arts Press, 1949), 46.

READING QUESTIONS

1. Why is an eye for an eye an attractive view according to Nathanson? What are the two main problems he raises for this view, and what are the possible replies an advocate of such a view might make?

2. What is proportional retributivism and how does it differ from an eye for an eye?

3. What are the two messages that would be sent by abolishing the death penalty according to Nathanson? How does he reply to the objection that murderers forfeit their right to be respected as human beings?

4. How does Nathanson argue that killing in self defense is compatible with respect for the dignity of human life?

DISCUSSION QUESTIONS

1. Consider whether proportional retributivism is really an improvement on the view of an eye for an eye. How could an advocate of an eye for an eye respond to the claim that equality retributivism provides an adequate criterion for determining appropriate levels of punishment? Are there any other objections to the view that Nathanson fails to consider?
2. Would abolishing the death penalty send the messages that Nathanson suggests? What other messages, positive or negative, might the abolition of the death penalty send? What messages should be sent and how could we ensure that the right messages are sent?

ERNEST VAN DEN HAAG

A Defense of the Death Penalty

In response to various abolitionist arguments of the sort featured in the articles by Nathanson and Bedau, van den Haag defends the morality of the death penalty. In particular, he responds to these objections to the death penalty: (1) that it is unfairly administered, (2) that it is irreversible, (3) that it does not deter, (4) that its financial costs are prohibitive, (5) that it endorses and perhaps encourages unlawful killing, and (6) that it is degrading. Van den Haag then argues that the death penalty can be justified from both consequentialist and retributivist perspectives.

Recommended Reading: consequentialism, chap. 1, sec. 2A.

In an average year about 20,000 homicides occur in the United States. Fewer than 300 convicted murderers are sentenced to death. But because no more than 30 murderers have been executed in any recent year, most convicts sentenced to death are likely to die of old age. Nonetheless, the death penalty looms large in discussions: it raises important moral questions independent of the number of executions.

The death penalty is our harshest punishment. It is irrevocable: it ends the existence of those punished,

From Ernest van den Haag, "The Ultimate Punishment: A Defense," *Harvard Law Review* 99 (1986): 1662–69. Reprinted by permission of the author.

instead of temporarily imprisoning them. Further, although not intended to cause physical pain, execution is the only corporal punishment still applied to adults. These singular characteristics contribute to the perennial, impassioned controversy about capital punishment.

DISTRIBUTION

Consideration of the justice, morality, or usefulness, of capital punishment is often conflated with objections to its alleged discriminatory or capricious distribution among the guilty. Wrongly so. If capital punishment is immoral *in se*, no distribution among the guilty could make it moral. If capital punishment is moral, no distribution would make it immoral. Improper distribution cannot affect the quality of what is distributed, be it punishments or rewards. Discriminatory or capricious distribution thus could not justify abolition of the death penalty. Further, maldistribution inheres no more in capital punishment than in any other punishment.

Maldistribution between the guilty and the innocent is, by definition, unjust. But the injustice does not lie in the nature of the punishment. Because of the finality of the death penalty, the most grievous maldistribution occurs when it is imposed upon the innocent. However, the frequent allegations of discrimination and capriciousness refer to maldistribution among the guilty and not to the punishment of the innocent.

Maldistribution of any punishment among those who deserve it is irrelevant to its justice or morality. Even if poor or black convicts guilty of capital offenses suffer capital punishment, and other convicts equally guilty of the same crimes do not, a more equal distribution, however desirable, would merely be more equal. It would not be more just to the convicts under sentence of death.

Punishments are imposed on persons, not on racial or economic groups. Guilt is personal. The only relevant question is: does the person to be executed deserve the punishment? Whether or not others who deserved the same punishment, whatever their economic or racial group, have avoided execution is irrelevant. If they have, the guilt of the executed convicts would not be diminished, nor would their punishment be less deserved. To put the issue starkly, if the death penalty were imposed on guilty blacks, but not on guilty whites, or, if it were imposed by a lottery among the guilty, this irrationally discriminatory or capricious distribution would neither make the penalty unjust, nor cause anyone to be unjustly punished, despite the undue impunity bestowed on others.

Equality, in short, seems morally less important than justice. And justice is independent of distributional inequalities. The ideal of equal justice demands that justice be equally distributed, not that it be replaced by equality. Justice requires that as many of the guilty as possible be punished, regardless of whether others have avoided punishment. To let these others escape the deserved punishment does not do justice to them, or to society. But it is not unjust to those who could not escape.

These moral considerations are not meant to deny that irrational discrimination, or capriciousness, would be inconsistent with constitutional requirements. But I am satisfied that the Supreme Court has in fact provided for adherence to the constitutional requirement of equality as much as is possible. Some inequality is indeed unavoidable as a practical matter in any system. But, *ultra posse nemo obligatur.* (Nobody is bound beyond ability.)

Recent data reveal little direct racial discrimination in the sentencing of those arrested and convicted of murder. The abrogation of the death penalty for rape has eliminated a major source of racial discrimination. Concededly, some discrimination based on the race of murder victims may exist; yet, this discrimination affects criminal victimizers in an unexpected way. Murderers of whites are thought more likely to be executed than murderers of blacks. Black victims, then, are less fully vindicated than white ones. However, because most black murderers kill blacks, black murderers are spared the death penalty more often than are white murderers. They fare better than most white murderers. The motivation behind unequal distribution of the death penalty may well have been to discriminate against blacks, but the result has favored them. Maldistribution is thus a straw man for empirical as well as analytical reasons.

MISCARRIAGES OF JUSTICE

In a recent survey Professors Hugo Adam Bedau and Michael Radelet found that 7,000 persons were executed in the United States between 1900 and 1985 and that 25 were innocent of capital crimes. Among the innocents they list Sacco and Vanzetti as well as Ethel and Julius Rosenberg. Although their data may be questionable, I do not doubt that, over a long enough period, miscarriages of justice will occur even in capital cases.

Despite precautions, nearly all human activities, such as trucking, lighting, or construction, cost the lives of some innocent bystanders. We do not give up these activities, because the advantages, moral or material, outweigh the unintended losses. Analogously, for those who think the death penalty just, miscarriages of justice are offset by the moral benefits and the usefulness of doing justice. For those who think the death penalty unjust even when it does not miscarry, miscarriages can hardly be decisive.

DETERRENCE

Despite much recent work, there has been no conclusive statistical demonstration that the death penalty is a better deterrent than are alternative punishments. However, deterrence is less than decisive for either side. Most abolitionists acknowledge that they would continue to favor abolition even if the death penalty were shown to deter more murders than alternatives could deter. Abolitionists appear to value the life of a convicted murderer or, at least, his non-execution, more highly than they value the lives of the innocent victims who might be spared by deterring prospective murderers.

Deterrence is not altogether decisive for me either. I would favor retention of the death penalty as retribution even if it were shown that the threat of execution could not deter prospective murderers not already deterred by the threat of imprisonment. Still, I believe the death penalty, because of its finality, is more feared than imprisonment, and deters some prospective murderers not deterred by the threat of imprisonment. Sparing the lives of even a few prospective victims by deterring their murderers is more important than preserving the lives of convicted murderers because of the possibility, or even the probability, that executing them would not deter others. Whereas the lives of the victims who might be saved are valuable, that of the murderer has only negative value, because of his crime. Surely the criminal law is meant to protect the lives of potential victims in preference to those of actual murderers.

Murder rates are determined by many factors; neither the severity nor the probability of the threatened sanction is always decisive. However, for the long run, I share the view of Sir James Fitzjames Stephen: "Some men, probably, abstain from murder because they fear that if they committed murder they would be hanged. Hundreds of thousands abstain from it because they regard it with horror. One great reason why they regard it with horror is that murderers are hanged." Penal sanctions are useful in the long run for the formation of the internal restraints so necessary to control crime. The severity and finality of the death penalty is appropriate to the seriousness and the finality of murder.

INCIDENTAL ISSUES: COST, RELATIVE SUFFERING, BRUTALIZATION

Many nondecisive issues are associated with capital punishment. Some believe that the monetary cost of appealing a capital sentence is excessive. Yet most comparisons of the cost of life imprisonment with the cost of execution, apart from their dubious relevance, are flawed at least by the implied assumption that life prisoners will generate no judicial costs during their imprisonment. At any rate, the actual monetary costs are trumped by the importance of doing justice.

Others insist that a person sentenced to death suffers more than his victim suffered, and that this (excess) suffering is undue according to the *lex talionis* (rule of retaliation). We cannot know whether the murderer on death row suffers more than his victim suffered; however, unlike the murderer, the victim deserved none of the suffering inflicted. Further, the limitations of the *lex talionis* were meant to restrain private vengeance, not the social retribution that has taken its place. Punishment—regardless of the motivation—is not intended to revenge, offset, or compensate for the victim's suffering, or to be measured by it. Punishment is to vindicate the law and the social order undermined by the crime. This is why a kidnapper's penal confinement is not limited to the period for which he imprisoned his victim; nor is a burglar's confinement meant merely to offset the suffering or the harm he caused his victim; nor is it meant only to offset the advantage he gained.

Another argument heard at least since Beccaria is that, by killing a murderer, we encourage, endorse, or legitimize unlawful killing. Yet, although all punishments are meant to be unpleasant, it is seldom argued that they legitimize the unlawful imposition of identical unpleasantness. Imprisonment is not thought to legitimize kidnapping; neither are fines thought to legitimize robbery. The difference between murder and execution, or between kidnapping and imprisonment, is that the first is unlawful and undeserved, the second a lawful and deserved punishment for an unlawful act. The physical similarities of the punishment to the crime are irrelevant. The relevant difference is not physical, but social.

JUSTICE, EXCESS, DEGRADATION

We threaten punishments in order to deter crime. We impose them not only to make the threats credible but also as retribution (justice) for the crimes that were not deterred. Threats and punishments are necessary to deter and deterrence is a sufficient practical justification for them. Retribution is an independent moral justification. Although penalties can be unwise, repulsive, or inappropriate, and those punished can be pitiable, in a sense the infliction of legal punishment on a guilty person cannot be unjust. By committing the crime, the criminal volunteered to assume the risk of receiving a legal punishment that he could have avoided by not committing the crime. The punishment he suffers is the punishment he voluntarily risked suffering and, therefore, it is no more unjust to him than any other event for which one knowingly volunteers to assume the risk. Thus, the death penalty cannot be unjust to the guilty criminal.

There remain, however, two moral objections. The penalty may be regarded as always excessive as retribution and always morally degrading. To regard the death penalty as always excessive, one must believe that no crime—no matter how heinous—could possibly justify capital punishment. Such a belief can be neither corroborated nor refuted; it is an article of faith.

Alternatively, or concurrently, one may believe that everybody, the murderer no less than the victim, has an imprescriptible (natural?) right to life. The law therefore should not deprive anyone of life. I share Jeremy Bentham's view that any such "natural and imprescriptible rights" are "nonsense upon stilts."

Justice Brennan has insisted that the death penalty is "uncivilized," "inhuman," inconsistent with "human dignity" and with "the sanctity of life," that it "treats members of the human race as nonhumans, as objects to be toyed with and discarded," that it is "uniquely degrading to human dignity" and "by its very nature, [involves] a denial of the executed person's humanity." Justice Brennan does not say why he thinks execution "uncivilized." Hitherto most civilizations have had the death penalty, although it has been discarded in Western Europe, where it is currently unfashionable probably because of its abuse by totalitarian regimes.

By "degrading," Justice Brennan seems to mean that execution degrades the executed convicts. Yet philosophers, such as Immanuel Kant and G. W. F. Hegel, have insisted that, when deserved, execution, far from degrading the executed convict, affirms his humanity by affirming his rationality and his responsibility for his actions. They thought that execution, when deserved, is required for the sake of the convict's dignity. (Does not life imprisonment violate human dignity more than execution, by keeping alive a prisoner deprived of all autonomy?)

Common sense indicates that it cannot be death—our common fate—that is inhuman. Therefore, Justice Brennan must mean that death degrades when it comes not as a natural or accidental event, but as a deliberate social imposition. The murderer learns through his punishment that his fellow men have found him unworthy of living; that because he has murdered, he is being expelled from the community of the living. This degradation is self-inflicted. By murdering, the murderer has so dehumanized himself that he cannot remain among the living. The social recognition of his self-degradation is the punitive essence of execution. To believe, as Justice Brennan appears to, that the degradation is inflicted by the execution reverses the direction of causality.

Execution of those who have committed heinous murders may deter only one murder per year. If it does, it seems quite warranted. It is also the only fitting retribution for murder I can think of.

READING QUESTIONS

1. Why does van den Haag think that equality of distribution would not make the death penalty any more just to convicts?
2. What reasons does van den Haag give for thinking that miscarriages of justice are not enough to justify the claim that the death penalty is an unjust practice?
3. Why is deterrence not a decisive factor in the debate about the morality of the death penalty according to van den Haag?
4. How does van den Haag respond to the objections that the penalty of death is always excessive and always morally degrading?

DISCUSSION QUESTIONS

1. Should we agree with van den Haag's claims regarding the death penalty and miscarriages of justice? How many miscarriages of this kind do you believe would have to occur before they would fail to be offset by the moral benefit of the death penalty?
2. Van den Haag claims that "if execution deters only one murderer a year, it is still warranted." He also claims that the death penalty is the only fitting retribution for murder. Does he provide sufficient reasons to accept each of these claims? Why or why not? If not, consider cases in which the death penalty would be warranted or what might be a fitting retribution for murder instead of the death penalty.

JEFFREY H. REIMAN

Civilization, Safety, and Deterrence

Some defenders of the death penalty, including Ernest van den Haag, argue that even if we currently lack good scientific evidence that the death penalty is a uniquely effective deterrent, common sense tells us that this penalty is a crime deterrent. Against this common sense argument, Reiman raises four objections.

Recommended Reading: consequentialism, chap. 1, sec. 2A.

Were the death penalty clearly proven a better deterrent to the murder of innocent people than life in prison, we might have to admit that we had not yet reached a level of civilization at which we could protect ourselves without imposing this horrible fate on murderers, and thus we might have to grant the necessity of instituting the death penalty. But this is far from proven. The available research by no means clearly indicates that the death penalty reduces the incidence of homicide more than life imprisonment does. Even the econometric studies of Isaac Ehrlich, which purport to show that each execution saves seven or eight potential murder victims, have not changed this fact, as is testified to by the controversy and objections from equally respected statisticians that Ehrlich's work has provoked.[1]

Conceding that it has not been proven that the death penalty deters more murders than life imprisonment, van den Haag has argued that neither has it been proven that the death penalty does *not* deter more murders, and thus we must follow common sense which teaches that the higher the cost of something, the fewer people will choose it, and therefore at least some potential murderers who would not be deterred by life imprisonment will be deterred by the death penalty. Van den Haag writes:

...our experience shows that the greater the threatened penalty, the more it deters.

...Life in prison is still life, however unpleasant. In contrast, the death penalty does not just threaten to make life unpleasant—it threatens to take life altogether. This difference is perceived by those affected. We find that when they have the choice between life in prison and execution, 99% of all prisoners under sentence of death prefer life in prison....

From this unquestioned fact a reasonable conclusion can be drawn in favor of the superior deterrent effect of the death penalty. Those who have the choice in practice...fear death more than they fear life in prison....If they do, it follows that the threat of the death penalty, all other things equal, is likely to deter more than the threat of life in prison. One is most deterred by what one fears most. From which it follows that whatever statistics fail, or do not fail, to show, the death penalty is likely to be more deterrent than any other.[2]

Those of us who recognize how common-sensical it was, and still is, to believe that the sun moves around the earth, will be less willing than Professor van den Haag to follow common sense here, especially when it comes to doing something awful to our fellows. Moreover, there are good reasons for doubting common sense on this matter. Here are four:

1. From the fact that one penalty is more feared than another, it does not follow that the more feared penalty will deter more than the less feared, unless we know that the less feared penalty is not fearful enough to deter everyone who can

From Jeffrey H. Reiman, "Justice, Civilization, and the Death Penalty: Answering van den Haag," *Philosophy and Public Affairs* 14 (1985), pp. 115–48.

be deterred—and this is just what we don't know with regard to the death penalty. Though I fear the death penalty more than life in prison, I can't think of any act that the death penalty would deter me from that an equal likelihood of spending my life in prison wouldn't deter me from as well. Since it seems to me that whoever would be deterred by a given likelihood of death would be deterred by an *equal* likelihood of life behind bars, I suspect that the common-sense argument only seems plausible because we evaluate it unconsciously assuming that potential criminals will face larger likelihoods of death sentences than of life sentences. If the likelihoods were equal, it seems to me that where life imprisonment was improbable enough to make it too distant a possibility to worry much about, a similar low probability of death would have the same effect. After all, we are undeterred by small likelihoods of death every time we walk the streets. And if life imprisonment were sufficiently probable to pose a real deterrent threat, it would pose as much of a deterrent threat as death. And this is just what most of the research we have on the comparative deterrent impact of execution versus life imprisonment suggests.

2. In light of the fact that roughly 500 to 700 suspected felons are killed by the police in the line of duty every year, and the fact that the number of privately owned guns in America is substantially larger than the number of households in America, it must be granted that anyone contemplating committing a crime *already* faces a substantial risk of ending up dead as a result.[3] It's hard to see why anyone *who is not already deterred by this* would be deterred by the addition of the more distant risk of death after apprehension, conviction, and appeal. Indeed, this suggests that people consider risks in a much cruder way than van den Haag's appeal to common sense suggests—which should be evident to anyone who contemplates how few people use seatbelts (14% of drivers, on some estimates), when it is widely known that wearing them can spell the difference between life (outside prison) and death.[4]

3. Van den Haag has maintained that deterrence doesn't work only by means of cost–benefit calculations made by potential criminals. It works also by

the lesson about the wrongfulness of murder that is slowly learned in a society that subjects murderers to the ultimate punishment. But if I am correct in claiming that the refusal to execute even those who deserve it has a civilizing effect, then the refusal to execute also teaches a lesson about the wrongfulness of murder. My claim here is admittedly speculative, but no more so than van den Haag's to the contrary. And my view has the added virtue of accounting for the failure of research to show an increased deterrent effect from executions *without having to deny the plausibility of van den Haag's common-sense argument that at least some additional potential murderers will be deterred by the prospect of the death penalty*. If there is a deterrent effect from *not executing*, then it is understandable that while executions will deter some murderers, this effect will be balanced out by the weakening of the deterrent effect of not executing, such that no net reduction in murders will result.[5] And this, by the way, also disposes of van den Haag's argument that, in the absence of knowledge one way or the other on the deterrent effect of executions, we should execute murderers rather than risk the lives of innocent people whose murders might have been deterred if we had. If there is a deterrent effect of not executing, it follows that we risk innocent lives either way. And if this is so, it seems that the only reasonable course of action is to refrain from imposing what we know is a horrible fate.[6]

4. Those who still think that van den Haag's common-sense argument for executing murderers is valid will find that the argument proves more than they bargained for. Van den Haag maintains that, in the absence of conclusive evidence on the relative deterrent impact of the death penalty versus life imprisonment, we must follow common sense and assume that if one punishment is more fearful than another, it will deter some potential criminals not deterred by the less fearful punishment. Since people sentenced to death will almost universally try to get their sentences changed to life in prison, it follows that death is more fearful than life imprisonment, and thus that it will deter some additional murderers. Consequently, we should institute the death penalty to save the lives these additional murderers would have taken. But, since people

sentenced to be tortured to death would surely try to get their sentences changed to simple execution, the same argument proves that death-by-torture will deter still more potential murderers. Consequently, we should institute death-by-torture to save the lives these additional murderers would have taken. Anyone who accepts van den Haag's argument is then confronted with a dilemma: Until we have conclusive evidence that capital punishment is a greater deterrent to murder than life imprisonment, he must grant *either* that we should not follow common sense and not impose the death penalty; *or* we should follow common sense and torture murderers to death. In short, either we must abolish the electric chair or reinstitute the rack. Surely, this is the *reductio ad absurdum* of van den Haag's common-sense argument.

NOTES

1. Isaac Ehrlich, "The Deterrent Effect of Capital Punishment: A Question of Life or Death," *American Economic Review* 65 (June 1975):397–417. For reactions to Ehrlich's work, see Alfred Blumstein, Jacqueline Cohen, and Daniel Nagin, eds., *Deterrence and Incapacitation: Estimating the Effects of Criminal Sanctions on Crime Rates* (Washington, D.C.: National Academy of Sciences, 1978), esp. pp. 59–63 and 336–60; Brian E. Forst, "The Deterrent Effect on Capital Punishment: A Cross-State Analysis," *Minnesota Law Review 61* (May 1977):743–67, Deryck Beyleveld, "Ehrlich's Analysis of Deterrence," *British Journal of Criminology 22* (April 1982):101–23, and Isaac Ehrlich, "On Positive Methodology, Ethics and Polemics in Deterrence Research," *British Journal of Criminology 22* (April 1982):124–39.

2. Ernest van den Haag and John P. Conrad, *The Death Penalty: A Debate* (New York: Plenum Press, 1983), 68, 69.

3. On the number of people killed by the police, see Lawrence W. Sherman and Robert H. Langworthy, "Measuring Homicide by Police Officers," *Journal of Criminal Law and Criminology 70*, no. 4 (Winter 1979):546–60; on the number of privately owned guns, see Franklin Zimring, *Firearms and Violence in American Life* (Washington, D.C.: U.S. Government Printing Office, 1968), pp. 6–7.

4. *AAA World* (Potomac ed.) 4, no. 3 (May–June 1984), pp. 18c and 18i.

5. A related claim has been made by those who defend the so-called brutalization hypothesis by presenting evidence to show that murders *increase* following an execution. See, for example, William J. Bowers and Glenn L. Pierce, "Deterrence or Brutalization: What is the Effect of Executions?" *Crime & Delinquency 26*, no. 4 (October 1980):453–84. They conclude that each execution gives rise to two additional homicides in the month following, and that these are real additions, not just a change in timing of the homicides (ibid., p. 481). My claim, it should be noted, is not identical to this, since, as I indicate in the text, what I call "the deterrence effect of not executing" is not something whose impact is to be seen immediately following executions but over the long haul, and, further, my claim is compatible with finding no net increase in murders due to executions. Nonetheless, should the brutalization hypothesis be borne out by further studies, it would certainly lend support to the notion that there is a deterrent effect of not executing.

6. Van den Haag writes: "If we were quite ignorant about the marginal deterrent effects of execution, we would have to choose—like it or not—between the certainty of the convicted murderer's death by execution and the likelihood of the survival of future victims of other murderers on the one hand, and on the other his certain survival and the likelihood of the death of new victims. I'd rather execute a man convicted of having murdered others than put the lives of innocents at risk. I find it hard to understand the opposite choice" (p. 69). Conway was able to counter this argument earlier by pointing out that the research on the marginal deterrent effects of execution was not *inconclusive* in the sense of *tending to point both ways*, but rather in the sense of *giving us no reason to believe that capital punishment saves more lives than life imprisonment.* He could then answer van den Haag by saying that the choice is not between risking the lives of murderers and risking the lives of innocents, but between killing a murderer with no reason to believe lives will be saved, and sparing a murderer with no reason to believe lives will be lost (David A. Conway, "Capital Punishment and Deterrence: Some Considerations in Dialogue Form," *Philosophy & Public Affairs,* 3 (1974), pp. 442–43). This, of course, makes the choice to spare the murderer more understandable than van den Haag allows. Events, however, have overtaken Conway's argument. The advent of Ehrlich's research, contested though it may be, leaves us in fact with research that tends to point both ways.

230

READING QUESTIONS

1. How does Reiman characterize van den Haag's argument for the death penalty?
2. What are the four reasons Reiman offers for thinking that we should doubt some of our common sense intuitions about the nature of the death penalty as a deterrent?
3. Explain in detail why Reiman thinks that the refusal to execute has a civilizing effect and that it teaches the wrongfulness of murder. Explain also why he believes that van den Haag's argument proves more than it might seem to.

DISCUSSION QUESTIONS

1. Is Reiman right to claim that the refusal to execute individuals would have a civilizing effect? Why or why not? What reasons could we offer for thinking that refusing to execute murderers does not teach the wrongfulness of murder?
2. To what extent do you think criminals take the consequences of their actions into consideration, especially in the case of murder? Discuss how the answers to this question could affect the debate about the moral status of capital punishment.

JAMES S. LIEBMAN, JEFFREY FAGAN, VALERIE WEST, AND JONATHAN LLOYD

Capital Attrition: Error Rates in Capital Cases, 1973–1995

The authors of this report studied the error rate in U.S. cases from 1975 to 1995 involving "capital sentences" (cases in which the sentence was the death penalty). One of the central findings of this research is that in 68 percent of capital cases that underwent judicial review, the death sentences were overturned owing to various errors including incompetent legal representation of the accused and suppression by the prosecution of evidence that the accused was in fact innocent of the crime in question. One implication that the authors draw from this research is that the public's awareness of such error rates would lower the public's confidence in the credibility of the death penalty.

Capital Attrition: Error Rates in Capital Cases, 1973–1995. Reprinted with permission from *Texas Law Review*, 1839 (2000).

I. INTRODUCTION

Americans seem to be of two minds about the death penalty. In the last several years, the overall number of executions has risen steeply, reaching a fifty-year high this year. Although two-thirds of the public support the penalty, this figure represents a sharp decline from the four-fifths of the population that endorsed the death penalty only six years ago, leaving support for capital punishment at a twenty-year low. When life without parole is offered as an alternative, support for the penalty drops even more—often below a majority. Grants of executive clemency reached a twenty-year high in 1999.

In 1999 and 2000, governors, attorneys general, and legislators in Alabama, Arizona, Florida, and Tennessee fought high-profile campaigns to increase the speed and number of executions. In the same period, however:

- The Republican Governor of Illinois, with support from a majority of the electorate, declared a moratorium on executions in that state.
- The Nebraska Legislature attempted to enact a similar moratorium. Although the Governor vetoed the legislation, the legislature appropriated money for a comprehensive study of the even-handedness of the state's exercise of capital punishment.
- Similar studies have been ordered in Illinois by the Chief Justice, task forces of both houses of the state legislature, and the governor. Indiana, Maryland, and the Attorney General of the United States have followed suit.
- Serious campaigns to abolish the death penalty are under way in New Hampshire and (with the support of the governor and a popular former Republican senator) in Oregon.
- The Florida Supreme Court and Mississippi Legislature recently acted to improve the quality of counsel in capital cases, and bills with bipartisan sponsorship aiming to do the same and to improve capital prisoners' access to DNA evidence have been introduced in both houses of the United States Congress.

Observers in the *Wall Street Journal*, *New York Times Magazine*, *Salon*, and on *ABC This Week*
see "a tectonic shift in the politics of the death penalty."

In April 2000 alone, George Will and Reverend Pat Robertson—both strong death penalty supporters—expressed doubts about the manner in which government officials carry out the penalty in the United States, and Robertson subsequently advocated a moratorium on *Meet the Press*. In response, Reverend Jerry Falwell called for continued—even swifter—execution of death sentences.

Fueling these competing initiatives are two beliefs about the death penalty: One is that death sentences move too slowly from imposition to execution, undermining deterrence and retribution, subjecting our criminal laws and courts to ridicule, and increasing the agony of victims. The other is that death sentences are fraught with error, causing justice too often to miscarry, and subjecting innocent and other undeserving defendants—mainly, racial minorities and the poor—to execution.

Some observers attribute these seemingly conflicting events and opinions to "America's own schizophrenia. . . . We believe in the death penalty, but shrink from it as applied." These views may not conflict, however, and Americans who hold *both* may not be irrational. It may be that capital sentences spend too much time under review *and* that they are fraught with disturbing amounts of error. Indeed, it may be that capital sentences spend so much time under judicial review precisely *because* they are persistently and systematically fraught with alarming amounts of error, and that the expanding production of death sentences may compound the production of error. We are led to this conclusion by a study of all 4,578 capital sentences that were finally reviewed by stale direct appeal courts and all 599 capital sentences that were finally reviewed by federal habeas corpus courts between 1973 and 1995.

II. SUMMARY OF CENTRAL FINDINGS

In *Furman v. Georgia* in 1972, the Supreme Court reversed all existing capital statutes and death sentences. The modern death-sentencing era began the next year with the implementation of new capital statutes designed to satisfy *Furman.* In order to collect information about capital sentences imposed and reviewed after 1973 (no central repository exists), we conducted a painstaking search, beginning in 1995, of all published state and federal judicial opinions in the United States conducting direct and habeas review of capital judgments, and many of the available opinions conducting state post-conviction review of those judgments. We then (1) checked and catalogued all cases the opinions revealed, (2) collected hundreds of items of information about each case from the published decisions and the NAACP Legal Defense Fund's quarterly death row census, (3) tabulated the results, and (4) (still in progress) conducted multivariate statistical analyses to identify factors that may contribute to those results.

Six years in the making, our central findings thus far are these:

- Between 1973 and 1995, approximately 5,760 death sentences were imposed in the United States. Only 313 (5.4 percent; one in 19) of those resulted in an execution during the period.

- Of the 5,760 death sentences imposed in the study period, 4,578 (79 percent) were finally reviewed on "direct appeal" by a state high court. Of those, 1,885 (41 percent) were thrown out on the basis of "serious error" (error that substantially undermines the reliability of the outcome).

- Most of the remainder of the death sentences were then inspected by state post-conviction courts. Although incomplete, our data (reported in *A Broken System*[1]) reveal that state post-conviction review is an important source of review in some states, including Florida, Georgia, Indiana, Maryland, Mississippi, and North Carolina. In Maryland, for example, at least 52 percent of capital judgments reviewed in state post-conviction proceedings during the study period were overturned due to serious error; the same was true for at least 25 percent of the capital judgments that were similarly reviewed in Indiana, and at least 20 percent of those reviewed in Mississippi.

- Of the death sentences that survived state direct and post-conviction review, 599 were finally reviewed on a first habeas corpus petition during the 23-year study period. Of those 599, 237 (40 percent) were overturned due to serious error.

- The "overall success rate" of capital judgments undergoing judicial inspection, and its converse, the "overall error-rate," are crucial factors in assessing the efficiency of our capital punishment system. The "overall *success* rate" is the proportion of capital judgments that underwent, and *passed,* the three-stage judicial inspection process during the study period. The "overall *error* rate" is the frequency with which capital judgments that underwent full inspection were *overturned* at one of the three stages due to serious error. Nationally, over the entire 1973–1995 period, the overall error-rate in our capital punishment system was 68 percent.

- Because "serious error" is error that substantially undermines the reliability of the guilt finding or death sentence imposed at trial, each instance of that error warrants public concern. The most common errors found at the state post-conviction stage (where our data are most complete) are (1) egregiously incompetent defense lawyering (accounting for 37 percent of the state post-conviction reversals), and (2) prosecutorial suppression of evidence that the defendant is innocent or does not deserve the death penalty (accounting for another 16 percent—or 19 percent, when all forms of law enforcement misconduct are considered). These two violations count as "serious," and thus warrant reversal, *only* when there is a "reasonable probability" that, but for the responsible lawyer's miscues, the outcome of the trial would have been different.

The result of very high rates of serious, reversible error among capital convictions and sentences, and very low rates of capital reconviction and resentencing, is the severe attrition of capital judgments. Figure 12.1 illustrates the sources of attrition, and the eventual disposition of cases where death sentences were reversed.

For every 100 death sentences imposed and reviewed during the study period, 41 were turned

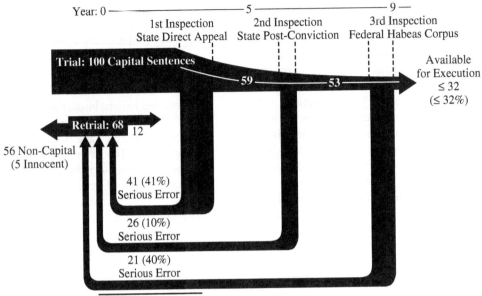

FIGURE 12.1   The Attrition of Capital Judgments

back at the state direct appeal phase because of serious error. Of the 59 that got through that phase to the second, state post-conviction stage, at least 10 percent—six more of the original 100—were turned back due to serious flaws. And, of the 53 that got through that stage to the third, federal habeas checkpoint, 40 percent—an additional 21 of the original 100—were turned back because of serious error. Overall, at least 68 of the original 100 were thrown out because of serious flaws, compared to only 32 (or less) that were found to have passed muster—after an average of nine to ten years had passed.

And for each such 68 individuals whose death sentences were overturned for serious error, 82 percent (56) were found on retrial *not* to have deserved the death penalty, including 7 percent (5) who were *cleared of the capital offense.*

- The seriousness of these errors is also revealed by what happens on retrial when the errors are supposed to be cured. In our state post-conviction sub-study where the post-reversal outcome is known, over four-fifths (56 out of 68) of the capital judgments that were reversed were replaced

on retrial with a sentence less than death, or no sentence at all. In the latter regard, fully 7 percent of the reversals for serious error resulted in a determination on retrial that the defendant was *not guilty* of the offense for which he previously was sentenced to die.

- High error rates pervade American capital-sentencing jurisdictions, and are geographically dispersed. Among the twenty-six death-sentencing jurisdictions in which at least one case has been reviewed in both the state and federal courts and in which information about all three judicial inspection stages is available:

1. 24 (92 percent) have overall error rates of 52 percent or higher;
2. 22 (85 percent) have overall error rates of 60 percent or higher;
3. 15 (61 percent) have overall error rates of 70 percent or higher;
4. Among other states, Georgia, Alabama, Mississippi, Indiana, Oklahoma, Wyoming, Montana, Arizona, and California have overall error rates of 75 percent or higher.

It is sometimes suggested that Illinois, whose governor declared a moratorium on executions in January 2000 because of the spate of death row exonerations there, generates less reliable death sentences than other states. Our data do not support this hypothesis: The overall rate of error found to infect Illinois capital sentences (66 percent) is slightly *lower* than the rate in capital-sentencing states as a whole (68 percent).

- High error rates have persisted for decades. More than 50 percent of all cases reviewed were found seriously flawed in twenty of the twenty-three study years, including in seventeen of the last nineteen years. In half of the years studied, the error rate was over 60 percent. Although error rates detected on state direct appeal and federal habeas corpus dropped modestly in the early 1990s, they went back up in 1995. The amount of error detected on state post-conviction has risen sharply throughout the 1990s.

- The 68 percent rate of *capital* error found by the three stage inspection process is much higher than the <15 percent rate of error those same three inspections evidently discover in *noncapital* criminal cases.

- Appointed federal judges are sometimes thought to be more likely to overturn capital sentences than elected state judges. In fact, state judges are the first and most important line of defense against erroneous death sentences. Elected state judges found serious error in and reversed 90 percent (2,133 of 2,370) of the capital sentences that were overturned during the study period.

- Under current state and federal law, capital prisoners have a legal right to one round of direct appellate, state post-conviction, and federal habeas corpus review. The high rates of error found at *each* stage, and at the *last* stage, and the persistence of high error rates over time and across the nation, confirm the need for multiple judicial inspections. Without compensating changes at the front-end of the process, the contrary policy of cutting back on judicial inspection would seem to make no more sense than responding to the impending insolvency of the Social Security System by forbidding it to be audited.

- Finding this much error takes time. Calculating the amount of time using information in published decisions is difficult. Only a small percentage of direct appeals decisions report the sentence date. By the end of the habeas stage, however, a much larger proportion of sentencing dates is reported in some decision in the case. It accordingly is possible to get an accurate sense of timing for the 599 cases that were finally reviewed on habeas corpus. Among those cases:

1. It took an average of 7.6 years after the defendant was sentenced to die to complete federal habeas corpus consideration in the 40 percent of habeas cases in which reversible error was found.

2. In the cases in which no error was detected at the third inspection stage and an execution occurred, the average time between sentence and execution was nine years.

As Figure 12.2 reveals, high rates of error frustrate the goals of the death penalty system. Figure 12.2 compares the overall rates of error detected during the state direct appeal and federal inspection process in the twenty-eight states with at least one capital judgment that has completed that process, to the percentage of death sentences imposed by each state that it has carried out by execution. In general, where the overall error rate reaches 55 percent or above (as is true for the vast majority of the states), the percentage of death sentences carried out drops below 7 percent.

Figure 12.2 illustrates another finding of interest: The pattern of capital outcomes for the State of Virginia is clearly an outlier—the State's high execution rate is nearly *double* that of the next nearest state and *five times* the national average, and its low rate of capital reversals is nearly *half* that of the next nearest state and less than *one-fourth* the national average. A sharp discrepancy between Virginia and other capital-sentencing jurisdictions characterizes most of our analyses. That discrepancy presents an important question for further study: Are Virginia capital judgments in fact half as prone to serious error as the next lowest state and four times less than the national average? Or, on the other hand, are its courts more

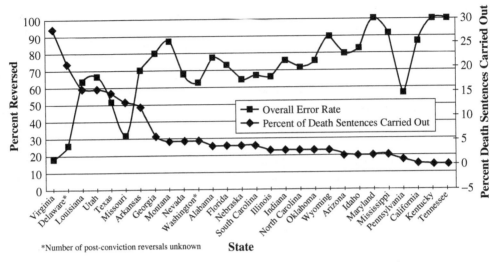

FIGURE 12.2   Overall Error Rate and Percent of Death Sentences Carried Out, 1973–1995

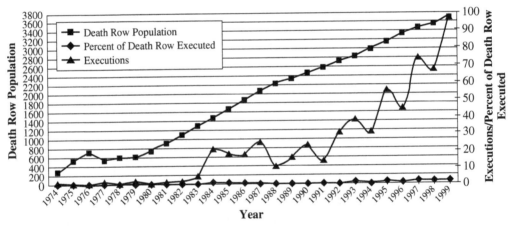

FIGURE 12.3   Persons on Death Row and Percent and Number Executed, 1976–1999

tolerant of serious error? Or, have Virginia's legislature and courts censored opportunities to inspect verdicts and detect error by procedurally constraining the definition of error and the time within which errors can be identified? We will address this issue below and in a subsequent report.

The rising number of executions nationally does not render these patterns obsolete. Instead of indicating improvement in the *quality* of death sentences under review, the rising number of executions may simply reflect how many *more* sentences have piled up awaiting review. If the error-induced pile-up of cases on death row is the *cause* of rising executions, their rise provides no proof that a cure has been found for disturbingly high and persistent error rates. The rising execution rate and the persistent error rate increase the likelihood of an increase in the incidence of wrongful executions. To see why this is true, consider a factory that produced 100 toasters in a year, only 32 of which worked. The factory's production problem would not be deemed fixed if the company simply raised its production run to 200 the next year in order to double the number of working toasters to 66. Thus, the real question isn't the *number* of death sentences carried out each year, but the *proportion.*

Figure 12.3 shows that in contrast to the annual *number* of executions (the middle line in the chart), the *proportion* of death row inmates executed each year (the bottom line in the chart) has remained remarkably stable—and extremely low. Since post-*Furman* executions began in earnest in 1984, the nation has executed only an average of about 1.3 percent of its death row inmates each year; in no year has it carried out more than 2.6 percent—or one in thirty-nine—of death sentences exposed to full review.

Figure 12.3 suggests that the rising number of executions (the middle line) is *not* caused by any improvement in the quality of capital judgments, but instead by the inexorable pile-up of people on death row (the top line in the chart) as judges struggle to exercise a degree of quality control over decade upon decade of error-prone capital judgments.

III. CONFIRMATION FROM A PARALLEL STUDY

Results from a parallel study by the U.S. Department of Justice suggest that our 32 percent figure for valid death sentences actually overstates the chance of execution. The 1998 Justice Department study includes a report showing the outcome of the 263 death sentences imposed in 1989. A final disposition of only 103 of the 263 death sentences had been reached nine years later. Of those 103, 78 (76 percent) had been overturned by a state or federal court. Only thirteen death sentences had been carried out. So, for every one member of the death row class of 1989 whose case was finally reviewed and who was executed as of 1998, six members of the class had their cases overturned in the courts. Because of the intensive review needed to catch so much error, 160 (61 percent) of

the 263 death sentences imposed in 1989 were still under scrutiny nine years later.

The approximately 3,500 people on death row today have been waiting an average of 7.4 years for a final declaration that their capital verdict is error-free—or, far more probably, that it is the product of serious error. Of the 6,700 people sentenced to die between 1973 and 1999, only 598—less than one in eleven—were executed. About three times as many had their capital judgments overturned or gained clemency.

IV. IMPLICATIONS OF CENTRAL FINDINGS

To help appreciate these findings, consider a scenario that might unfold any of the nearly 300 times a year that a death sentence is imposed in the United States. Suppose the defendant, or a relative of the victim, asks a lawyer or the judge, "What now?" Based on almost a quarter century of experience in thousands of cases in twenty-eight death-sentencing states in the United States between 1973 and 1995, a responsible answer would be: "The capital conviction or sentence will probably be overturned due to serious error. It'll take about nine years to find out, given how many other capital cases being reviewed for likely error are lined up ahead of this one. If the judgment is overturned, a lesser conviction or sentence will probably be imposed."

As any person hearing this statement would likely conclude as a matter of common sense, these reversals due to serious error, and the time it takes to expose them, are costly. Capital trials and sentences cost more than noncapital ones. Each time they have to be done over—as happens 68 percent of the time—some or all of that difference is doubled. The error-detection system all this capital error requires is itself a huge expense—evidently *millions of dollars* per case.

When retrial demonstrates that nearly four-fifths of the capital judgments in which serious error is found are more appropriately handled as non-capital cases (and in a sizable number of instances, as non-murder or even *non-criminal* cases), it is hard to escape the conclusion that most of the resources the capital system currently consumes are not buying the public, or victims, the valid death sentences for egregious offenses that a majority support. Rather, those resources are being wasted on the trial and review of cases that for the most part are not capital and are seriously flawed.

Public faith in the courts and the criminal justice system is another casualty of high capital error rates. When the vast majority of capital sentencing jurisdictions carry out fewer than 6 percent of the death sentences they impose, and when the nation as a whole never executes more than 3 percent of its death population in a year, the retributive and deterrent credibility of the death penalty is low.

When condemned inmates turn out to be *innocent,* the error is different in its consequences, but *not* evidently different in its causes, from the other serious error discussed here. There is no accounting for this cost: to the wrongly convicted; to the family of the victim, whose search for justice and closure has been in vain; to later victims whose lives are threatened—and even taken—because the real killers remain at large; and to the wrongly *executed,* should justice miscarry at trial, and should reviewing judges, harried by the amount of capital error they are asked to catch, miss one.

If the issue was the fabrication of toasters (to return to our prior example), or the licensing of automobile drivers, or the conduct of any other private- or public-sector activity, neither the consuming public nor managers and investors would tolerate the error rates and attendant costs that dozens of states and the nation as a whole have tolerated in their capital punishment systems over the course of decades. Any system with this much error and expense would be halted immediately, examined, and either reformed or scrapped. We ask taxpayers, public managers, and policymakers whether that same response is warranted here, when the issue is not the content and quality of tomorrow's breakfast but whether society has a swift and sure response to murder and whether thousands of men and women condemned for that crime in fact deserve to die.

NOTE

1. For a fuller description of the findings presented in this article, see "A Broken System: The Persistent Patterns of Reversals of Death Sentences in the United States," by Andrew Gelman, James S. Liebman, Valerie West, and Alexander Kiss, *Journal of Empirical Legal Studies* 1 (July 2004), pp. 209–61.

READING QUESTIONS

1. How do the authors define overall success and failure rates? What were the overall success and error rates of convictions for capital murder? Cite some of the other relevant statistics mentioned by the authors regarding the error rates in capital cases.
2. What are the three stages of judicial review the cases in consideration can undergo? How do the authors define "serious error"? What are the two most common types of error found in capital murder cases?
3. Explain what the authors discovered about the average time involved in the review of capital cases. What effect does the length of the review process have on the criminal justice system?
4. What are some of the implications of these findings according to the authors? Why do the authors think that public faith in the courts is a casualty of these findings?

DISCUSSION QUESTIONS

1. Are the authors right to assume that knowledge of information regarding the overall success and failure rates of capital cases would undermine the public's faith in the court system? Why or why not? What other responses might the public have to this information?

2. What do the authors' findings suggest about the moral status of the death penalty? Consider and discuss whether the death penalty could be morally permissible even if there are serious errors made in capital cases.

ADDITIONAL RESOURCES

Web Resources

Amnesty International, <http://web.amnesty.org/pages/deathpenalty>. Pro-abolitionist site that reports data regarding the death penalty and its use worldwide.

Death Penalty Information Center, <http://www.deathpenaltyinfo.org/>. Pro-abolitionist forum.

The Pew Forum on Religion & Public Life, <http://pewforum.org/docs/>. An excellent, non-partisan resource for learning about the history of the death penalty in the United States and the current debate over its moral status.

Pro-Death Penalty.Com, <http://www.prodeathpenalty.com/>. A retentionist forum.

Bedau, Hugo Adam, "Punishment," <http://plato.stanford.edu/entries/punishment>. An overview of theories about the ethical justification of punishment.

Authored Books

Costanzo, Mark, *Just Revenge: Costs and Consequences of the Death Penalty* (New York: St. Martin's Press, 1997). An accessible, short book with emphasis on the social scientific research relevant to the death penalty.

Hanks, Gardner C., *Against the Death Penalty: Christian and Secular Arguments against the Death Penalty* (Scottdale, PA: Herald Press, 1997). A survey and defense of Christian and secular arguments against the death penalty.

Pojman, Louis and Jeffrey Reiman, *The Death Penalty* (Lanham, MD: Rowman & Littlefield, 1997). A debate between Pojman, a retentionist, and Rieman, an abolitionist.

Van den Haag, Ernest, and Conrad, John P., *The Death Penalty: A Debate* (New York: Plenum Books, 1983). van den Haag defends the retentionist view and Conrad defends the abolitionist position.

Edited Collections

Baird, Robert M. and Stuart E. Rosenbaum (eds.), *Death Penalty: Debating the Moral, Legal, and Political Issues* (Amherst, NY: Prometheus Books, 2010). A collection of essays by leading experts, including articles that address the impact of new advances in DNA technology on the moral, political, and legal questions about the death penalty.

Bedau, Hugo Adam (ed.), *The Death Penalty in America: Current Controversies* (Oxford: Oxford University Press, 1997). A comprehensive anthology with thirty-three articles ranging over issues about the constitutionality, racial bias, public support, and morality of the death penalty in the United States.

Bedau, Hugo Adam and Paul G. Cassell (eds.), *Debating the Death Penalty: Should America Have Capital Punishment? The Experts on Both Sides Make Their Case* (Oxford: Oxford University Press, 2005). A collection of seven essays by a range of experts—judges, lawyers, prosecutors, and philosophers—debating the death penalty.

13 } War, Terrorism, and Torture

The contemporary world is besieged by acts of war, terrorism, and torture. The 9/11 destruction of the World Trade Center in New York and the coordinated attack on the Pentagon, as well as the terrorist bombings in Madrid (2004), London (2005), Mumbai (2006, 2009), and Boston (2013) have ignited intense worldwide debate over the nature, causes, and morality of war and terrorism. This debate has been further intensified, particularly in the United States, as a result of the U.S. wars in Iraq and Afghanistan. Also, the deplorable abuse of prisoners by U.S. military personnel at the Abu Ghraib prison near the Iraqi capital of Baghdad, as well as so-called enhanced interrogation techniques including waterboarding, has sparked not only worldwide outrage, but also debate over the nature and morality of torture. Many people believe that at least some wars are, or could be, morally justifiable, even if many past and present wars are not justifiable. Terrorism and torture are widely condemned as morally wrong. The central moral questions these practices raise are these:

- Is (war), (terrorism), (torture) ever morally permissible?
- If any of these activities are ever morally permissible, what best explains why this is so?

I have inserted parentheses in the first question to indicate that for each of the three activities, we can raise the moral questions just mentioned, and so we should not just assume that their moral status—whether they are ever permissible and, if so, why—is the same. It may turn out, as some have argued, that, for instance, war is sometimes permissible but terrorism and torture never are.

In order to begin thinking about these moral issues, let us first consider questions and issues about the morality of war, and then turn to terrorism and torture in order.

1. WAR

As with all disputed moral issues, we must begin by specifying the subject of dispute—war. The *Merriam-Webster Online Dictionary* has this entry:

War

(1): a state of usually open and declared armed hostile conflict between states or nations;
(2): a period of such armed conflict[1]

There are also entries for both "hot" and "cold" wars. A **hot war** is defined as "a conflict involving actual fighting," whereas a **cold war** is described as "a conflict over ideological differences carried on by methods short of sustained overt military action and usually without breaking off diplomatic relations." The focus in this chapter is on so-called hot wars—which, in the twentieth century, include World Wars I and II, the Korean War, the Vietnam War, and the Gulf War—and are often the focus of contemporary moral discussions.

One particularly contentious moral question about war concerns the conditions under which a state is morally justified in going to war. Many would readily agree that if attacked first, a state has a right of self-defense to fight back. However, the U.S. initiation of the recent U.S–Iraq war continues to be a subject of dispute, both on moral and legal grounds, given that Iraq did not pose a clear imminent threat to the United States or her allies—the kind of the threat that might justify a preemptive strike, thus launching a **preemptive war**. Rather, the United States engaged in what is properly referred to as a **preventive war**, which as David Rodin characterizes as "a first strike against a potential future aggressor who does not yet pose an imminent threat." (See the selection from Rodin from which this quote is taken.) Assuming that a preemptive war can sometimes be morally justified on grounds of self-defense (a controversial assumption): Could there be circumstances in which a preventive war is morally justified? This question is debated in our selections from Rodin and Walter Sinnott-Armstrong.

Preventive military strikes are also a topic of concern over the use of drones—remotely controlled aircraft that the United States has used extensively in recent years to target leaders of terrorist organizations. Moral and legal controversy over the use of drones has been cast in terms of the legitimacy of employing preventive strikes. Robert Shane, in a front-page story in *The New York Times* (Nov. 25, 2012) wrote the following:

> Facing the possibility that President Obama might not win a second term, his administration accelerated work in the weeks before the election to develop explicit rules for the targeted killing of terrorists by unmanned drones, so that a new president would inherit standards and procedures. . . . Mr. Obama and his advisors are still debating whether remote-control killing should be a measure of last resort against imminent threats to the United States, or a more flexible tool, available to help allied governments attack their enemies or to prevent militants from controlling territory.

Here, again, the contrast between using drones strictly as a preemptive measure ("of last resort against imminent threats") or more liberally as a preventive measure is the focus of attention.

2. TERRORISM

As with moral questions about war, a discussion of the morality of terrorism must begin with a working definition of terrorism. Here we immediately run into controversy, partly because some individuals make the moral wrongness of the violence associated with terrorism part of terrorism's very definition so that by definition terrorism is morally wrong. Such "question-begging" definitions—definitions that merely assume something controversial about what is being defined—are to be avoided here because for one thing, they inhibit asking legitimate moral questions about the sort of violent activity carried on in the name of some cause that we want to be able to ask. For another thing, merely defining terrorism as morally wrong will not solve any moral issues about this kind of violence. After all, those who might think that some forms of violence—for, say, political causes—are morally justified (or might be) can simply grant the morally loaded use of the term "terrorism" and call the kind of violence they might defend by some other name—"freedom fighting," for example. Again, mere verbal stipulation will not settle legitimate moral questions about various forms of violence carried out in the name of various causes.

One definition that avoids the sort question-begging just mentioned and that seems to capture what most people mean when speaking of terrorism is offered by James P. Sterba:

> **Terrorism** is the use or threat of violence against innocent people to elicit terror in them, or in some other group of people, in order to further a political objective.[2]

There are three elements of this definition worth noting. First, terrorism on Sterba's definition is not confined to nonstate groups and individuals; rather, it allows that states can engage in terrorism. In this way, Sterba's definition is broader than the one embraced by the U.S. Department of State, which restricts terrorist activity to "subnational groups or clandestine agents." Second, Sterba's definition restricts the targets of terrorist activity to "innocent people," and similar definitions restrict targets to "noncombatants." But we find other definitions that are not as restrictive in this way. For instance, Tomis Kapitan defines terrorism as being directed upon "civilians," leaving open the matter of whether civilians are innocent.[3] Third, many, if not most definitions of terrorism, like Sterba's, mention *political* goals and objectives as part of what terrorism is. This seems to be entirely in keeping with how the term is typically used. However, we do find definitions that are not restrictive in this way. For instance, Haig Khatchadourian defines terrorism as involving "acts of coercion or of actual use of force, aiming at monetary gain (predatory terrorism), revenge (retaliatory terrorism), a political end (political terrorism), or a putative moral/religious end (moralistic/religious terrorism)."[4] One implication of this definition is that acts of bank robbery for monetary gain, for example, count as acts of terrorism, thus greatly widening the scope of what is to count as terrorism. In any case, the important point here is that in reading about terrorism one must keep an eye on how the term is being defined. Issues about the definition of terrorism are discussed by Andrew Valls in the selection included here, "Can Terrorism Be Justified?"

3. TORTURE

The main focus of discussion about the morality of torture is whether it is absolutely morally wrong or whether in certain "necessity" cases—often illustrated by "ticking bomb" cases— the use of torture to extract potentially life-saving information is morally permissible. Of course, we have to begin with the question "What is torture?"

According to article 1 of the 1984 United Nations Convention against Torture and Other Cruel, Inhuman or Degrading Treatment or Punishment:

> "**Torture**" means any act by which severe pain or suffering, whether physical or mental, is intentionally inflicted on a person for such purposes as [1] obtaining from him or a third person information or a confession, [2] punishing him for an act he or a third person has committed or is suspected of

having committed, or [3] intimidating or coercing him or a third person, or [4] for any reason based on discrimination of any kind, when such pain or suffering is inflicted by or at the instigation of or with the consent or acquiescence of a public official or other person acting in an official capacity.[5]

Three observations about this definition are worth making here. First, the bracketed numbers (which I have inserted) indicate the various purposes or aims of acts of torture. Taking note of these various possible purposes is important because if torture is ever morally permissible, its permissibility will certainly depend in large measure upon the purposes of the torturer. For instance, it is common to distinguish between **terrorist torture** (which would presumably include acts of torture motivated by the sorts of purposes mentioned in 2, 3, and 4 in the previous definition) and **interrogational torture,** done for the purpose (mentioned in 1) of obtaining information from the victim in order, for example, to prevent or avert some impending terrorist attack.

Second, the UN convention also distinguishes torture from what it refers to as "acts of cruel, inhuman, or degrading treatment or punishment which do not amount to torture as defined in article 1." This raises the obvious problem of distinguishing acts of torture from acts of cruel, inhumane, or degrading treatment. Here is not the place to delve into this difficult matter. Rather, for present purposes, it will suffice to list a few acts of what are widely taken to be torture: severe beatings, being made to stand for hours or days at a time, extended sleep deprivation, withholding food or water, being buried alive, electric shocks, having one's head forced underwater until nearly asphyxiated, rape, threatened rape, and threatened death. Such activities as slaps in the face that fall short of severe beatings, shouting obscenities at prisoners, and making prisoners engage in sexual acts are clearly instances of inhuman and degrading treatment, but they seem to fall short of torture.[6]

The third observation about the previous UN convention definition is that to count as torture, the act must be performed by, initiated by, or consented to by a public official or someone acting in an official capacity. This rules out cases that we might ordinarily consider as torture, as when an individual, acting alone and for reasons of personal revenge, kidnaps and inflicts severe pain and suffering on his victim over an extended period of time. But this restriction is perfectly reasonable, given that the aim of the convention was to establish international law.

With a basic understanding of the concepts of war, terrorism, and torture now before us, let us turn to moral issues.

4. THEORY MEETS PRACTICE

Let us begin by distinguishing two sorts of questions we may ask about the morality of war. First, when (if ever) is a state or nation morally justified in going to war against another state or nation? Second, which sorts of military activities are morally permissible within war? In relation to both questions, we find what we may nonprejudicially refer to as extreme positions: moral nihilism and moral pacifism. Let us consider each of these in order, after which we will proceed to consider other, less "extreme," moral perspectives on war.

In discussions about the morality of war, **moral nihilism** is the view that moral considerations do not apply to war, that questions of moral right and wrong, good and bad do not apply because war creates a context in which "anything goes." Thus, to the question "Is war

FIGURE 13.1   Just-War Theory

ever morally justified?" the nihilist in effect refuses to answer the question, claiming that questions about morality do not arise in connection with war. Of course, since there are two general sorts of questions about the morality of war—going to war and conduct within war—one might hold the view that although morality does apply to the decision to go to war and thus claim that some wars are morally justified and others are not, one might also hold that within war, anything goes morally speaking.

At the other end of the moral spectrum is **antiwar pacifism,** according to which wars are always (or at least nearly always) morally wrong.[7] One basis for such a view is the idea that all intentional killing of human beings is morally wrong. But many individuals, including many moral philosophers, hold that some cases of intentionally killing human beings are morally justified—cases of self-defense being the most widely accepted. In the context of war, this would mean that wars of self-defense might sometimes be justified. But there is far more to the moral positions of those who would defend the morality of at least some wars, and here we find that perhaps the most prominent moral approach to war (or at least the most widely discussed) is **just-war theory,** to which we now turn.

Natural Law and Just-War Theory

Just-war theory is perhaps best understood as an extension of natural law ethics applied to the issue of war. One need not embrace natural law theory in order to accept the moral provisions of just-war theory, but in outlining this approach to the morality of war (and terrorism), appealing to some ideas from natural law theory—particularly the doctrine of double effect—is useful.[8]

Just-war theory makes the common distinction between questions about the morality of going to war, **jus ad bellum,** and about the morality of activities within a war, **jus in bello.** Each of these two parts is made up of various moral provisions. Figure 13.1 offers a visual aid.

In what immediately follows, I will briefly state each of these provisions, at least as they are often understood.

Jus ad Bellum

Here, then, is a statement of the five principles composing this part of just-war theory:[9]

Legitimate authority: War must be declared by a legitimate authority—typically understood as the officials of a recognized government. This condition is often understood as a requirement for violence or force to be considered war. So, for instance, spontaneous uprisings that result in violence do not count as wars.

Just cause: There must be a just cause for going to war. A very restrictive interpretation of this provision would require that the war be one of self-defense, in which a government is responding to violent aggression or is attempting to prevent imminent violent aggression by another state. This restrictive interpretation rules out any "aggressive" war that would, for example, forcefully interfere with the internal affairs of some state for "humanitarian" purposes.

Last resort: All reasonable alternatives to going to war must be exhausted. What counts as a "reasonable alternative" is left open to interpretation. Certainly, nonviolent diplomatic solutions are to be sought before going to war.

Prospect of success: In going to war, there must be a reasonable prospect of success. Again, what counts as reasonable is left open, as is the question of what counts as success. Clearly, winning a war counts as success, but in some cases a futile struggle to the death might be justified if the alternative is enslavement or extermination by a nation's opponent.

Political proportionality: The violence of war must be proportional to the wrong being resisted. Both here and in the provisions of jus in bello, considerations of consequences are relevant, though, unlike a pure consequentialist approach, this provision is but one requirement of the just-war approach to the morality of war.

Let us now turn to the provisions of jus in bello. Here my plan is to relate them to the **doctrine of double effect (DDE)**, which was presented in the moral theory primer (chapter 1) as part of natural law ethics. This doctrine is meant to address the question of whether it is ever morally permissible to knowingly bring about evil consequences in the pursuit of some good. According to DDE, in cases in which an action would produce (or likely produce) at least some good effects but at least one bad effect (where for present purposes we can restrict good and bad to the preservation and loss of human life respectively), the action in question is morally permitted only if all of the following conditions are met:

Intrinsic permissibility: The action, apart from its effects, must be morally permissible;

Necessity: The bad effect is unavoidable, and thus the action is necessary if the good effect is to be brought about;

Nonintentionality: The bad effect is not intended—it is neither one's end nor a means to one's end; and

Proportionality: The badness of the bad effect is not grossly out of proportion to the goodness of the good effect being sought.

The latter three principles, reformulated so that they each address aggression in war, yield the following provisions that compose jus in bello:

Jus in Bello

Military necessity: The military activity in question (e.g., the bombing of a military installation) must be judged to be *necessary* in order to bring about some justifiable military end.

Discrimination: The deaths of innocent noncombatants must not be directly intended either as an end of the military action or as a means to some further military purpose. Talk of innocent noncombatants here is meant to refer in particular to citizens of a state who are not actively engaged in that state's war efforts. Clearly, an unarmed young child counts as an innocent noncombatant, whereas armed soldiers do not. Other individuals—for example, those forced to work in a munitions plant—present hard cases requiring that this provision be more finely interpreted.

Military proportionality: Whatever good end the military action in question is supposed to serve, the likely evil that results from that activity (e.g., deaths and loss of property) must not be grossly out of proportion to the intended good ends of that activity.

To understand these provisions, consider cases of "tactical bombing," in which the aim of the mission is to destroy an enemy military base; however, in so doing, it is predictable (given the base's location) that a number of innocent noncombatants will be killed by the bombing. If the conditions of necessity and proportionality are met in a particular case of tactical bombing, then because the deaths of innocent civilians is not intended (either as an end or as a means to the tactical mission), this kind of activity would be morally permitted by just-war theory. Readers can contrast such tactical cases with cases of "terrorist bombing," in which the immediate aim is to kill innocent civilians in an effort to weaken enemy morale.

Finally, it is worth emphasizing that these provisions, as I have indicated in my presentation, require a good deal of interpretation in applying them to concrete cases. But, of course, this is true of all general moral principles.

Turning for a moment to our readings, Michael Walzer begins with the premise that terrorism is always wrong and proceeds to examine various "excuses" that have been offered in defense of terrorist acts. He argues that none of them are morally legitimate. Andrew Valls argues that if the provisions of just-war theory can morally justify some wars, they can also morally justify some acts of terrorism. He thus opposes Walzer's claim the all instances of terrorism are, by definition, morally wrong. With regard to the moral justification for going to war, the "just cause" provision of just-war theory limits going to war to cases of self-defense which, as earlier presented, does not include preventive wars. But Walter Sinnott-Armstrong is critical of standard interpretations of the just-cause provision that are taken to rule out all preventive wars.

Rights Approaches

As explained in chapter 1, section 2D, a rights-based moral theory takes the notion of moral rights as basic in approaching moral issues. Different rights-based theories disagree over which rights are fundamental. David Rodin defends a rights-based theory of self-defense and argues that preventive wars cannot be morally justified on any plausible interpretation of this sort of theory.

Kantian Theory

None of the selections that follow take a Kantian approach to one or another of the chapter's various topics. But Kant's Humanity formulation of the categorical imperative, which requires that one treat others not merely as means to one's own ends but as ends in themselves, sometimes figures in discussions of the morality of war, terrorism, and torture. This principle is often used to evaluate acts of terrorist torture that involve harming individuals as a means of intimidating others—a reasonably clear case of using someone *merely* as a means.

Consequentialism

Consequentialist approaches to torture (as with any moral issue) may take either an act or a rule form. You may recall from chapter 1, section 2A, that act consequentialism focuses on the specific, concrete action being morally evaluated and considers the net intrinsic value of the consequences that would likely be caused by the action and compares them to the net intrinsic value of the likely consequences of some alternative action open to the agent at the time. By contrast, rule consequentialism considers not the values of the likely consequences of the specific, concrete actions under scrutiny, but rather the values of the likely consequences of the general acceptance of various alternative rules under which the action and its alternatives fall. On this version of consequentialism, a concrete action is permitted in a certain set of circumstances if a rule permitting acts of that type in the circumstances in question has at least as high an **acceptance value** as any other alternative rule for those circumstances.[10] So a specific, concrete act of torture would be wrong from a rule consequentialist perspective if a rule prohibiting torture in those circumstances would, if widely accepted, result in a greater level of net intrinsic value than would a rule permitting torture in those circumstances.

Walter Sinnott-Armstrong approaches the issue of preventive war from an act consequentialist perspective, arguing (as one would expect) that whether such wars can be morally justified depends on the actual consequences of engaging in wars for preventive purposes. Alan M. Dershowitz in "Should the Ticking Bomb Terrorist Be Tortured?" also embraces an act consequentialist (he calls it a "case utilitarian") approach in addressing questions about the permissibility of torture. The case of the ticking bomb terrorist is often brought up as a reasonably clear case in which most will agree that torture would be morally permissible; the view defended by Dershowitz. However, such cases are hypothetical, and one might ask, as Marcia Baron does in her essay included here, whether this particular hypothetical case is unacceptably artificial in light of real-world circumstances. She argues that it is, and so should not be used to compromise an absolute prohibition on torture.

NOTES

1. As a third item, this dictionary includes "state of war," which is then linked to further definitions of this expression.

2. James P. Sterba, "Terrorism and International Justice," in James P. Sterba, ed., *Terrorism and International Justice* (New York: Oxford University Press, 2003).

3. Tomis Kapitan, "The Terrorism of 'Terrorism,'" in *Terrorism and International Justice*, ed. James P. Sterba (New York: Oxford University Press, 2003).

4. Haig Khatchadourian, *The Morality of Terrorism* (New York: Peter Lang, 1998).

5. A full text of this convention is available online at www.hrweb.org/legal/cat.html. This document goes on to state that "no exceptional circumstances whatsoever, whether a state of war or a threat of war, internal political instability or any other public emergency" would justify the use of torture: torture, according to this declaration, is *absolutely* prohibited. See article 16. It also prohibits the practice of "rendition" (article 3), whereby one country sends its prisoners to another country—often to a country known for harsh treatment of its prisoners. In 1994, the United States ratified the UN convention, though in so doing it adopted a more restrictive definition of torture requiring that in order to be torture, the act "must be *specifically intended* to inflict *severe* physical or mental pain or suffering." For a useful discussion of the definition of torture generally as well as torture under U.S. law, see John T. Parry, "Escalation and Necessity: Defining Torture at Home and Abroad," in *Torture: A Collection,* ed. Sanford Levinson (New York: Oxford University Press, 2004).

6. In the wake of the Abu Ghraib prison scandal, U.S. senator (and former Vietnam War POW) John McCain proposed an amendment (attached to a defense spending bill) that protects anyone in U.S. custody from "cruel, inhuman, or degrading treatment." On December 15, 2005, the President George W. Bush-led U.S. White House, under pressure from members of both Republican and Democratic parties, agreed to the language of McCain's amendment.

7. There are other more restrictive forms of pacifism, including, for example, nonviolent pacifism, which maintains that any form of violence against human beings is wrong.

8. For instance, Michael Walzer in *Just and Unjust Wars,* 2nd ed. (New York: Basic Books, 1992) defends a version of just-war approach to the morality of war, but he is not a natural law theorist.

9. In presenting the provisions of jus ad bellum, I am following C. A. J. Coady's presentation of it in his "War and Terrorism," in *A Companion to Applied Ethics,* ed. R. G. Frey and Christopher Heath Wellman (Oxford: Blackwell Publishing, 2003).

10. The "acceptance value" of rule (in relation to some group) is defined as the net intrinsic value that would result were the rule accepted by a significant proportion of the members of the group in question.

DAVID RODIN

The Problem with Prevention[1]

After distinguishing preventive from preemptive wars, Rodin argues that consequentialist attempts to address the issue of preventive war (whether act or rule version) are unacceptable because, lacking relevant empirical knowledge about likely outcomes of such wars, they are useless in practice. He then considers arguments that appeal to the right of self-defense in attempting to justify preventive wars and finds that on any plausible interpretation of this right, such arguments fail.

Recommended Reading: consequentialism chap. 1, sec. 2A; rights theory, chap. 1, sec. 2D.

In September 2002, one year after the terrorist attacks on Washington and New York, the Bush administration released its 'National Security Strategy of the United States of America', the blueprint for the development of US military and security policy. This document contained a radical innovation in the grounds for waging war. It proclaimed a readiness to fight preventive wars against 'emerging threats before they are fully formed.'[2] Just over a year later, the United States, together with Britain and a number of other allies, put the policy of preventive war to dramatic effect by invading, defeating, and occupying Iraq in a matter of weeks.[3] The doctrine of preventive war and its implementation in Iraq caused consternation among many long-standing American allies, particularly in Europe. For its critics, the policy is a dangerous and misguided challenge to the legal and moral international order. For its advocates, the policy is a morally and strategically justified response to new forms of security threat.

In this chapter, I argue that there are profound moral problems with the doctrine of preventive war. The argument is structured in two parts. In the first part, I examine consequentialist approaches to preventive war. The case both for and against preventive

war is often made in consequentialist terms. This seems to me a mistake. Consequentialism suffers from debilitating epistemological problems that renders it effectively useless as a moral theory of war. Consequentialism would require historical judgments about the long term overall effects of war that are intrinsically indeterminate and unknowable. Moreover rule-consequentialist assessment of the laws of war suffers from what I call the impasse problem: the persistent presence of equally plausible rule-consequentialist arguments for countervailing conclusions. Much of this part of the discussion uses as its foil a recent and significant contribution to the debate on prevention by David Luban, which provides a vigorous defense of the consequentialist approach to war.[4]

In the second part of the chapter, I examine whether preventive action can be viewed as a legitimate component of the right of self-defense. I argue that it cannot. The right of self-defense has historically been grounded in a number of different theoretical justifications including those that invoke a conception of psychological necessity and those that invoke human rights. On neither of these theories, however, can preventive self-defense be justified. . . .

From David Rodin, "The Problem of Preventive War," in *Preemption: Military Action and Moral Justification*, H. Shue and D. Rodin, eds. Oxford: Oxford University Press, pp. 143–153; 160–166.

PREVENTION AND PREEMPTION

First, however, I want to address an important issue of terminology. In the National Security Strategy and in the speeches of the Bush and Blair administrations, the policy that is to be our concern is referred to as 'preemptive' rather 'preventive' war. But this is a rhetorical sleight of hand. According to well-established legal usage, preemption consists in a first strike against an enemy who has not yet attacked but whose attack is clearly imminent. It involves 'anticipating' an aggressor who is literally poised to attack. Prevention, on the other hand, involves a first strike against a potential future aggressor who does not yet pose an imminent threat. In Michael Walzer's words it is ' . . . an attack that responds to a distant danger, a matter of foresight and free choice'.[5]

It is sometimes said that a right of preemptive self-defense is clearly and uncontroversialy recognized under international law.[6] This is simply not true. Many scholars believe that even a limited right of preemption against imminent attack is ruled out under international law. The UN Charter is very clear that the right of self-defense can only be invoked 'if an armed attacks occurs' (UN Charter, Article 51). Under traditional means of treaty interpretation this has been taken to unequivocally rule out a right to preemption. On the other hand there does exist older customary law, in the form of the famous Caroline doctrine (of which more later), which encompasses a limited right to engage in preemptive strikes against an imminent attack. Those who support a right of preemptive self-defense must argue that Article 51 does not replace, but merely supplements, this older customary law right. But this customary law argument is undermined by the fact that states have tended to avoid invoking a right of preemptive defense even in circumstances that might justify it (e.g. the right was not invoked by Israel to justify its first strike against Egypt in the Six Day War, which is often regarded as the *locus classicus* of justified preemptive action by the doctrine's supporters). Thus, while it is possible to argue that there exists a right of preemptive self-defense in international law, it is by no means a settled question.

On the other hand, there is no uncertainty as to the legality of undertaking unilateral military action against 'emerging threats before they are fully formed'. Such action against a nonimminent threat is properly referred to as 'prevention' rather than 'preemption', and it clearly contravenes international law as it currently stands.[7] The 'Bush doctrine' articulated in the National Security Strategy, while not historically unprecedented, does represent a genuine innovation in the grounds for war, one which would transform the moral and legal framework on the international use of force.

THE DISUTILITY OF CONSEQUENTIALISM

It is not difficult to construct a consequentialist argument for preventive war, particularly in light of the much-discussed potential nexus between international terrorism and WMD. *If* undertaking a particular preventive war is an effective way of averting a significant terrorist attack or act of future aggression from a hostile state, and *if* the war does not itself cause more harm than it prevents, and *if* there is no less costly way of achieving the same good, and *if* the opportunity costs of the expended blood and treasure do not outweigh the projected goods, then the war would be prima facie justified on consequentialist grounds.

These are all big ifs, and much of the plausibility of the consequentialist argument rests on its ability to fulfill the evidentiary burdens they impose. I argue that the consequentialist approach to war quite generally suffers from two traditional vulnerabilities of consequentialist theory. The first is its tendency to generate counterintuitive ethical conclusions and assessments. The second, and far more serious, is a severe epistemological weakness resulting from the radical indeterminacy of the historical judgments required to yield a meaningful consequentialist conclusion about the justification of war. This criticism is not new, it was made by Walzer in *Just and Unjust Wars*,[8] but I believe that the full force of the objection has not been fully appreciated by consequentialist writers on war.

Of course, we may expect the case of preventive war to generate special difficulties for any ethical theory. Let us begin, therefore, with what should be an easy case: the Allies' war against Nazi Germany, which many feel is the clearest modern example of a justified war. The first problem is that it is not clear that a consequentialist analysis supports this judgment. The Nazi regime was brutal and aggressive: it systematically murdered approximately six million innocent people, and subjected many millions more to a regime of extraordinary moral repugnance. But the costs of the war against Germany were in many ways more horrific still. Those who lost their lives to the war outnumber the victims of German murder and genocide, by approximately ten to one. This does not yet include the suffering of the approximately forty million persons displaced or made homeless by the war and the incalculable destruction to the world's cultural and material wealth. This was a horrific price to pay for stopping Nazi Germany. Even allowing for the expanded genocide that would certainly have taken place if the war had not been fought, it is not obvious that *on strict consequentialist grounds* it was a price worth paying.[9]

What is most striking about the assessment of war from a consequentialist perspective, however, is not that particular wars fail or pass the test in a counterintuitive way, but rather the near impossibility of accurately determining the long-term balance of consequences of engaging in war. To return to World War II, there is a very real sense in which we still do not know the long-term balance of consequences of this war six decades after its end. This is the case for a number of reasons. First, we do not, even now, know the actual casualty figures of the war with any degree of precision. Estimates of the Soviet War casualties alone have ranged from seven to forty million persons.[10] That is a margin of error of 470 per cent—an almost incomprehensible thirty three million human lives!

Chairman Zhou En-lai famously responded that 'its too early to tell' when asked about the impact of the French Revolution. In a similar way, it may be literally true that it is too early to tell what the ultimate balance sheet of World War II's costs and benefits is, because the war continues to have a profound and ongoing impact on the world today. This is true both on the macro and on the micro level. The war and its aftermath continue to shape patterns of political alliance and economic exchange within Europe and around the world (e.g. it continues to play a significant role in the development of the European Union). On a micro level the war continues to affect the lives and well-being of countless individuals in both subtle and profound ways. To take but one example, the trauma of experiencing the war has left legacies of mental illness and emotional abuse that continue to ripple down through the generations of many families.

Secondly and most damagingly, because consequentialist assessment requires a comparative judgment between the consequences of fighting and not fighting a given war, it always depends upon questions of counterfactual history that are intrinsically unknowable. For example, if the Allies had not chosen to fight Nazi Germany we can assume that it would have continued to expand its genocidal and aggressive policies—but by how much? Would the Nazi state have collapsed under the weight of its own inefficiency and inequity as the Soviet Union did 45 years later? Would National Socialism have survived the death or assassination of Hitler? There is simply no reliable way to answer these and countless other relevant counterfactual questions like them.

These profound epistemological difficulties arise even when conducting a retrospective analysis, with the benefit of hindsight and decades of painstaking academic research. But if consequentialism is to function as a guide to action for policymakers rather than simply as a form of backward-looking moral assessment, then it is necessary to undertake an immeasurably more difficult task still. That is an accurate prospective analysis of the likely long-term consequences of engaging in war before the conflict has even begun. To return to World War II, it is almost impossible to believe that any of the leaders in 1939 could have reliably foreseen the long-term consequences of the war that was about to begin. . . .

Moreover, World War II commenced with clear and unambiguous acts of aggression on the part of Germany. But the case of preventive war generates further difficulties still for consequentialism. This is because the feared act of aggression lies sometime in the future and indeed may never eventuate. In such a case, the problems of indeterminacy and the dependence on unknowable counterfactual judgments, present in all war, are magnified many times over.

Now, I certainly do not want to claim that we can never make an accurate and well-founded determination of whether the balance of consequences favors war or not. In fact it is often very easy to make this determination *in the negative*. Because initiating a war always has very significant moral costs, it is obvious that going to war to prevent a minor infringement or slight injury will not lead to better over all consequences.[11] This points to an important asymmetry in our ability to assess the consequences of war. In general, it is easier to fulfill the evidentiary burdens of the negative judgment that engaging in war will *not* lead to better overall consequences than it is to fulfill the burdens of the positive judgment that fighting *will* lead to better consequences.

There is a structural factor inherent to war that explains why a positive assessment of the likely consequences of war will always be more problematic and less reliable than the purely negative assessment. As Clausewitz observed, war is subject to an inherent tendency to escalate to levels of violence beyond those that combatants would rationally have chosen or indeed predicted at the outset: 'If one side uses force without compunction, undeterred by the bloodshed it involves, while the other side refrains, the first will gain the upper hand. That side will force the other to follow suit . . . '. 'Each side, therefore, compels its opponent to follow suit; a reciprocal action is started which must lead in theory to extremes'.[12]

Clausewitz's structural observation about the logic of escalation in war is, moreover, backed up by empirical evidence which shows that historically most war leaders have assumed, prior to conflict, that the war on which they were about to embark would be short and relatively easy. Sometimes they are correct. More often they are not, and the war proves to be more protracted, difficult and costly than generally expected. If this is correct, this points to a general and persistent tendency for leaders and war planners to underestimate the costs and overestimate the benefits of war.

Act-consequentialism appears to offer an obvious strategy for justifying preventive wars (or wars more generally). But the appearance is illusory. There are many straightforward cases in which a decision to go to war would unambiguously lead to morally worse consequences than other policy alternatives. But it is exceptionally difficult to meet the epistemological burdens for demonstrating that going to war would lead to *better* consequences than alternatives. Wars are events of enormous historical magnitude, and extreme unpredictability. Action in war is subject to a pervasive tendency toward escalation, that can make even the most careful and good-faith assessments of its projected costs wildly inaccurate. Consequentialist analysis necessarily involves issues of counterfactual history that are quite literally unknowable. In the case of preventive war, the relevant counterfactual questions include whether the feared attack would even have taken place without war—in other words whether a preventive war has 'prevented' anything at all.[13] For governments and citizens seeking to justify a preventive war, act-consequentialism has almost no use.[14]

Rule Consequentialism and the Impasse Problem

When philosophers talk of a consequentialist approach to war, they are often thinking about rule-consequentialism. Unfortunately, rule-consequentialism faces even greater difficulties than act-consequentialism as an ethical theory of war. This should not surprise us. Rule-consequentialism requires assessing the long-term consequences of iterated patterns of behavior, and hence it amplifies further the epistemological weaknesses inherent in act-consequentialism. I argue that rule-consequentialism suffers from two forms of epistemological weakness. First, we have no sufficient empirical data for assessing the truth of rule-consequentialist judgments. Second the rule-consequentialist arguments invoked by philosophers and International Relations theorists to support their conclusions persistently generate what I call the impasse problem: the existence of equally plausible rule-consequentialist arguments for countervailing conclusions.

The rule-consequentialist argument for preventive war is very old. It dates back at least to Cicero who argued in favor of preventive war against the internal threat of Marcus Antonius by observing that 'every evil is easily crushed at its birth; become inveterate it as a rule gathers strength.'[15] Alberico Gentili, the Oxford jurist of the sixteenth century echoed these sentiments: 'it is better to provide that men should not acquire too great power, than to be obliged to seek remedy later, when they have already become too powerful.'[16] Michael Walzer takes as the starting point for his discussion of prevention the argument of Edmond Burke, which develops this theme by invoking the notion of balance of power. According to Burke an effective balance of power between the main states of Europe preserves European liberty by preventing any one state from becoming too dominant, and secondly that fighting early, before the balance has become unstable, is less costly than waiting till the threat becomes imminent.[17]

As David Luban points out, the Bush doctrine as spelled out in the National Security Strategy turns this argument on its head, by claiming that the *imbalance* of power (i.e. US dominance) is worth preserving because it is necessary to protect *American* liberty. But Luban suggests that both variants of the argument can be assimilated to a more general argumentative scheme:

1. that some state of affairs X (balance of power, U.S. dominance, whatever) preserves some important value V (European liberty, U.S. liberty, whatever) and is therefore worth defending even at some cost; and
2. that to fight early, before X begins to unravel, greatly reduces the cost of the defense, while waiting doesn't mean avoiding war (unless one gives up V) but only fighting on a larger scale and at worse odds.[18]

This rule-consequentialist argument seems plausible. However as both Walzer and Luban point out, there is a rule-consequentialist rejoinder that is at least as plausible. The rejoinder is that even if (1) and (2) are true, it would be better on consequentialist grounds for states not to accept them because doing so would expand the grounds for going to war and thereby lead (in Burke's words) to 'innumerable and fruitless wars.' The ultimate consequences of a general rule permitting preventive war would therefore be worse than one that prohibited it.[19] What we are faced with

is what I call the impasse problem: two competing and apparently equally plausible rule-consequentialist interpretations of the preventive-war norm. One interpretation claims that a rule permitting preventive war would lead to better overall consequences because wars fought early would have less human cost, and would protect valuable goods such as national or international liberties. The other interpretation claims that a rule prohibiting preventive war would lead to better overall consequences because a more permissive doctrine would multiply the number of wars fought.

Which interpretation is correct? Luban has three rule-consequentialist arguments for why a general norm permitting preventive war should be rejected. I suggest that each can be matched by an equally plausible rule-consequentialist interpretation for the opposite conclusion, hence the impasse problem is not avoided. I want to stress that my intention is not to endorse these counterarguments as the correct rule-consequentialist assessment of prevention. Rather by showing the ease with which rule-consequentialist arguments can be matched by apparently equally plausible counterargument I wish to draw attention to the spurious character of these arguments' apparent plausibility.

Luban's first argument is that a general right of prevention would make war more likely because it would broaden the category of permissible war. In particular it would justify first strikes by both sides in all the world's most dangerous hotspots. For example, it would justify a first strike by both India and Pakistan, North Korea and Japan, Israel and Syria, and most frighteningly during the Cold War it would have justified preventive strikes by both the United States and the Soviet Union given a favorable opportunity.[20]

But the counterinterpretation of these cases runs as follows: the existence of such hotspots itself imposes substantial moral cost because of the risk and instability they bring to international affairs, and the way they impede valuable economic and cultural exchange. Over the long term, a rule permitting prevention would have positive consequences, by transforming the strategic environment itself in ways that make such dangerous strategic standoffs less likely. Thus, if a norm of prevention had permitted dominant states to hit early and hit hard when a potential rival emerged, many of the hotspots referred to by Luban might never have developed. For example, had the United States used its nuclear monopoly at the end of World War II to act preventively against the Soviet Union, there might never have been a Cold War with the associated risks of global nuclear annihilation. Similarly, one may argue, the other hotspots only pose a danger to the world because the emerging standoff was not nipped in the bud by early preventive action.

Luban's second argument is that a general doctrine of prevention introduces too much ambiguity into the rules of war, which will in turn make war more likely. The reason the doctrine introduces ambiguity is that the judgment as to whether a state constitutes a sufficient threat to justify preventive action necessarily involves what Rawls calls *burdens of judgment* [the inevitability that different (reasonable) people's judgment will diverge] and *infirmities of judgment* (the fact that people's judgment about matters of great moment and high risk is seldom rational).

But it is not clear that increased ambiguity in the rules of war would increase the incidence of war. Michael Byers has argued that ambiguous laws increase the latitude of action for strong states while having little effect on the ability of weak states to engage in military action. This is because ambiguity 'allow[s] power and influence to play a greater role in the application of the law to particular situations.'[21] Strong states can bring to bear various forms of political, economic, and military pressure to influence the assessments pertaining to the application of the law, while still retaining the law as a diplomatic tool to be deployed against weaker states. If this assessment is correct, then one can see how an ambiguous law could increase the overall stability of the international system, especially when (as is now the case) the international system is dominated by one powerful state. By freeing the hand of the strong state to take decisive measures against potential rivals and disruptive smaller states, the rule could have a strong deterrent effect that would mean fewer wars in the long run. Moreover, because the strong will disproportionately influence how the ambiguous criteria for the rule are applied, there is little risk of a general increase in violence among weaker states.

Luban's third argument is linked to the first two. The doctrine of prevention 'actually *makes* rival states into potential threats to each other by permitting preventive invasion of potential adversaries based on risk calculations whose indeterminacy makes them inherently unpredictable by the adversary—and then it licenses attacks by both of them, because now they are potential threats to each other.'[22]

But here we need to know much more about the specific incentive structures in play and how they would cash out in real strategic negotiations. According to standard assumptions of International Relations theory, the primary interest of states is to maintain their own security. Typically states will seek to achieve this through building up their military capability and developing alliances to deter neighbors or rivals from attacking them. This deterrence strategy can result in reasonably long periods of stability and security. But the strategy is not cost free. It can also contribute to the initiation of disastrous conflicts that diminish the security of all states involved, as for example the armament and alliance strategies of the major European powers did in the lead up to World War I.

Luban's argument suggests that a general doctrine of prevention would radically increase the costs of the deterrence strategy by making it much more difficult to develop and maintain a stable relationship of military deterrence. This conclusion contradicts the arguments I have just given which suggest that stabilizing deterrence effects could indeed be increased by recognizing a general doctrine of prevention. But suppose Luban's conclusion is correct. In this case, the effects of a doctrine of prevention could play out in other ways.

In essence, if Luban is correct then the deterrence strategy of military armament and alliance formation would cease to function as a rational strategy for states to maintain their security under a general doctrine of prevention. Given this, states would have to look to alternative strategies to maintain their security. Plausible alternatives would include strategies of mutual assurance and disarmament, for example through the implementation of strong nonaggression treaties and mutual disarmament initiatives backed up by independent inspections and monitoring. It is moreover plausible that the mutual assurance and disarmament strategy would results in less cost over-all than the deterrence strategy. Therefore by chang-ing the incentive structures so as to make the current deterrence and armament strategy untenable (if indeed this was the effect), a general doctrine of prevention could still lead to better overall consequences.

Once again we are faced with an impasse between differing and opposed rule-consequentialist inter-pretations of the doctrine of prevention. As I have said, certainly do not want to claim that my coun-terarguments should be accepted as the correct and authoritative rule-consequentialist interpretation of prevention. Nor, indeed, do I need to establish this for my argument to succeed. I simply need to show that they are as plausible as the countervailing inter-pretations given available information. The relevant question is of course: is there a conclusive empirical basis for ruling out one set of rule-consequentialist arguments or interpretations in favor of those that support their contradictory?

What is most striking in the rule-consequentialist literature on war is the general absence of reference to empirical evidence that could answer these ques-tions.[23] On reflection, it seems obvious why this is. There does not seem to be any empirical evidence capable of verifying rule-consequentialist interpreta-tions of the rules of war. It is certainly possible to sub-ject the historical record of war to statistical analysis (although it is interesting how little interest most rule-consequentialist philosophers show in sustained anal-ysis of the historical record). But at best this can tell us what the incidence of war *was* during periods when the rules of war were interpreted differently. It cannot tell us what the incidence of war *would have been*, had the rules of war been different. For we have no way to control for the effects that differing social, economic, technological, climatic, administrative, and institu-tional conditions have on the incidence of war. Not only do we not have the required empirical evidence to settle such rule-consequentialist questions, it is unclear even what could count as empirical evidence.

In light of this absence of empirical evidence, rule-consequentialists are compelled to resort to gen-eral arguments of the form Luban offers. It is not that these arguments seem implausible. On the contrary they seem very plausible. It is just that there are rule

consequentialist arguments for the countervailing position that are equally plausible. Once we recog-nize this, we can see that the apparent plausibility of these rule-consequentialist arguments is spurious. The arguments are a kind of armchair conjecture, conducted without empirical data or even a clear con-ception of what would count as empirical data.

Rule-consequentialist arguments, like their act-consequentialist counterparts, can provide no useful justification of preventive war. There is no empiri-cal evidence that could settle the question of which interpretation of the laws of war will lead to the best overall consequences, and the arguments that philoso-phers and legal theorists use to defend their preferred consequentialist interpretation of the rules of war can be matched, point for point, with equally plausible arguments for the exact opposite conclusion. . . .

PREVENTIVE WAR AND SELF-DEFENSE

I believe that the best way of investigating the jus-tice of preventive war, is to look at the question of whether preventive war can be justified as an act of legitimate self-defense. The notion of self-defense is fundamental to the way we think about the ethics of war, and the National Security Strategy itself casts the issue of prevention as one of self-defense. The right of self-defense is normally taken to require that three conditions be met.

1. Necessity: defensive action must be necessary in the sense that there is no less harmful way to avert the harm or attack.
2. Proportionality: harm inflicted in the course of defensive action must be proportionate to (or not disproportionately greater than) the harm or attack one is seeking to avert.
3. Imminence: the harm or attack one is defend-ing against cannot be a distant or remote one, but must be truly immanent.

The National Security Strategy addresses, at least implicitly, each of these conditions. The condition of immanence is explicitly acknowledged, but it is argued that 'we must adapt the concept of imminent threat to the capabilities and objectives of today's adversaries.'[24] This adapted conception of immanence is clearly meant to include more than the 'visible mobilization of armies, navies, and air forces preparing for attack'[25] and would permit action against 'emerging threats before they are fully formed'[26] and 'even if uncertainty remains as to the time and place of the enemies attack'.[27]

But this talk of 'adapting' the concept of imminence is, once again, mere rhetoric. Any doctrine which allows the use of force against potential threats that have not yet fully formed and where it is unclear when, or even if, an attack will occur has not adapted the traditional condition of imminence, but has abandoned it. The real challenge of the Bush doctrine, therefore, is not whether the concept of imminence needs reform but whether it needs to be abandoned entirely. To put the question another way: can we can make sense of the right of national self-defense, without the traditional condition of imminence? It is this question I propose to discuss and I hope to show that the notion of imminence lies very deep in the idea of self-defense. Correspondingly, it is very difficult to understand preventive war as a legitimate part of self-defense.

I used to believe otherwise: that the concept of immanence is not fundamental to the right of self-defense. I previously argued that the condition of immanence is subsidiary to the condition of necessity.[28] Imminence, I argued, is derived from necessity because of epistemic constraints on human action. The point is that one cannot *know* that defensive action is necessary, unless the attack one is defending against is really imminent. If on the other hand, one had superhuman knowledge and could foresee that the only way to prevent some future wrongful harm or attack was to engage in defensive measures, then one would not be required to wait till the attack was imminent: necessity would be enough.

If such an interpretation were correct, then it would open a way to allowing prevention as a legitimate form of self-defense. The view would certainly place an enormous, and probably unsustainable, burden on the intelligence used as a basis for going to war, for one would have to be certain that the defensive measures were really necessary to prevent the harm in question. But the idea of a preventive war of

self-defense against a nonimminent threat would not be ruled out at the level of moral theory.

I now think that this view is wrong, and that the condition of immanence is much more fundamental to the right of self-defense. To see this we must look into the theoretical underpinnings of the right of self-defense. The right of self-defense as we currently have it in law and moral theory, has been influenced by at least three distinct traditions of thought. The first is the consequentialist tradition. The second tradition views self-defense as action conditioned by a kind of psychological necessity. The third tradition views the aggressor as morally liable to harm by an act of legitimate self-defense and explains this liability on the basis of his fault or culpability for initiating the attack. As I have discussed consequentialism above, I will say no more about it here. But I do intend to examine the role played by imminence in the other two traditions, both of which have been influential on modern ideas of legitimate self-defense.

Self-Defense as Necessity

The connection between self-defense and necessity is an old and deep one. In fact, in some jurisdictions self-defense is referred to simply as 'necessary defense'. Necessity in this context is close to the legal concept of duress. It is a form of excuse stemming from the fact that a wrongful action is viewed as psychologically necessary or unavoidable in situations of extreme danger or pressure.[29] . . .

What underlies this necessity approach is a compassionate stance towards the frailty of human nature. Given the kinds of creature we are, there are some things (such as abstaining from taking action sufficient to save our own life) that we simply cannot be expected to do. As Aristotle says they 'strain human nature to breaking-point and no one would endure.'[30] If it is to be just and humane, the law must take account of this, and not hold us responsible for actions taken under the enormous psychological pressures of the shadow of death. This psychological necessity view of self-defense was reflected in the medieval law of *se defendendo*. According to this law one was not to be punished for killing in the course of a fight, if one quite literally 'had one's back against the wall', and taking the opponent's life was the only way of saving one's own.

Now one might think that such a conception of self-defense can have little connection with the laws of war, for states are not psychological entities that feel fear in the way that individual persons do. But it is precisely this account which is suggested by the most famous legal text on the right of national self-defense: the Caroline doctrine. This text states that a nation's right of self-defense is based on a' . . . necessity of self-defense, instant, overwhelming, leaving no choice of means, and no moment for deliberation'.[31] Although states do not experience the psychological fear of a real person, perhaps they can experience something analogous.

Viewing self-defense in this way, does however, have a number of significant and somewhat unpalatable consequences. The first is that contrary to modern legal theory, self-defense is viewed not as a justification but merely as an excuse. An act is justified if it is the right or permissible thing to do in the circumstances. An act is excused if it was the wrong thing to do, but the agent ought not in the circumstances be held fully responsible for the act . . .

The second consequence is that self-defense on this view takes a form which is rather peculiar to the modern eye. The modern right of self-defense encompasses, in most jurisdictions, the defense of others including strangers. But because on the psychological necessity view self-defense is grounded in the idea of action under extreme fear or pressure, the excuse is only available for defending certain kinds of person. The medieval claim of *se defendendo* was only available if one was defending one's own life or that of close friends or family. Only then were the psychological pressures considered sufficiently grave to provide an excuse for murder.

Thirdly, the necessity view makes no discriminations based on fault as to who can claim the excuse of self-defense. The excuse is available to anyone facing the extinction of their life, be they innocent victim or culpable aggressor of the original attack.

What is clear, however, is that the psychological necessity view of self-defense is quite incompatible with the idea of a preventive war. For on this view it is precisely the imminence of the potentially fatal attack and the extreme psychological pressure this imposes that makes defensive acts excusable. When the attack is remote and merely potential there is no psychological necessity of this form. What is required on the necessity view is precisely suggested by the language of the Caroline doctrine: ' . . . necessity of self-defense, instant, overwhelming, leaving no choice of means, and no moment for deliberation'.[32] In contrast (and almost in contradiction) to this the National Security Strategy explicitly states: 'We will always proceed deliberately, weighing the consequences of our actions.'[33] This brings out an important feature of preventive wars; they are wars of choice. Their function, strategically, is to engage the enemy at a time and on terms of one's own choosing. As such they are antithetical to the tradition of thought on self-defense which views that right as grounded in the overwhelming psychological necessity of facing an imminent lethal attacker.

If a doctrine of preventive war is to be integrated into self-defense then it must be on the basis of a very different theory of self-defense to that of psychological necessity. In fact, the most plausible theory of self-defense *is* very different to the necessity view. It is a theory which views self-defense as a justification grounded in a conception of human rights and concomitant notions of liability to harm.

Self-Defense and Rights

Here I do no more than sketch out the rights-based theory of self-defense which I have defended in detail elsewhere.[34] One starts with the observation that human beings have rights. Paramount among these is the right not to be killed or subject to significant bodily harm. But killing and harming another human is precisely what is done in acts of self-defense including the fighting of a defensive war. This raises a simple but profound question for the theory of self-defense: what is it that makes the person against whom one is using defensive force liable to be harmed in this way? Some part of our theory of self-defense must account for the fact that an aggressor has lost or forfeited or fails to possess the right to life when he is killed in defense.

The best way to account for this moral liability to harm on the part of aggressors is to point to the fact that they commit wrong by engaging in an act of aggression. One way to understand this is to observe that many rights are implicitly reciprocal in their nature. Thus on a plausible understanding of rights, one only has the right to life so long as one respects the right to life of others. At the moment one wrongfully attacks the life of another, one becomes morally vulnerable or liable to being killed in self-defense. This explains why we believe that it is permissible to kill an aggressor in self-defense but not to kill an innocent bystander even if this were the only way to save one's life. For an innocent bystander has done us no wrong and therefore has the right not to be killed by us, even if this were the only way to save our life.

If one accepts that the permission to kill in self-defense is tied to some wrongdoing on the part of the aggressor, then it is easy to see why there is a problem with preventive acts of self-defense. In a preventive war, one attacks and kills those who have not yet committed an act of wrongful aggression against you. Without the presence of active aggression it is difficult to see how there can exist the liability to harm which seems to be such a crucial part of the classic model of self-defense.

Against this, it might be objected that in cases of preventive self-defense one has good reason to believe that the persons one is using force against are *about to* engage in wrongful aggression. Is not this sufficient to establish their liability to be harmed? If you have good reason to believe that they will act aggressively, why must one wait till they actually engage in aggression before using defensive force?

To answer this question, we may consider an analogy with liability for punishment in criminal law. The analogy is not perfect because self-defense is not itself a form of punishment. Nonetheless there are sufficient similarities in the grounds of liability for punishment and self-defense to make the comparison instructive. In order for there to exist liability for punishment one must establish both a criminal intent and the existence of a criminal act—both *mens rea* and *actus reus*. Without criminal intent and the existence of a criminal act a person may not be punished even if we have good reason to think that he will commit a certain crime in the future.

In the movie 'Minority Report', magical clairvoyants have the ability to see infallibly into the future. Law enforcement agencies are able to use these predictions to arrest and punish those whom the clairvoyants had predicted will commit murder, before they ever have the chance to commit the crime. This procedure is viewed as efficient law enforcement in this imaginary future world. But most of us feel a deep moral repugnance toward such an idea (this indeed is the point of the movie), and this stems from the fact that it is unjust to punish someone who has not yet *done anything* to merit punishment (even if we grant some supernaturally reliable prediction that they *will* do it).

On the rights-based theory of self-defense a similar problem arises with preventive self-defense. A Minority Report style supernatural example is not required to see this. Imagine that I know you have a violently jealous nature and that if you ever discovered that I have been sleeping with your wife, you would almost certainly take your revenge by killing me. Suppose now that I see you reading through my private papers and that among those papers is a letter proving my infidelity. As soon as you read that letter you are almost certain to form and act upon a murderous intent. But it seems clear in this case that I would be justified in using defensive force only after this had happened. Until such time, there is nothing you have done that makes you liable to my defensive force. Preventive self-defense is therefore ruled out, because you retain your full rights not to be attacked or harmed.

Examples like these show us that the conditions of self-defense (necessity, proportionality, and imminence) function in a fundamentally different way within a forfeiture-of-right theory of self-defense than they do within a consequentialist theory of self-defense. Within a consequentialist theory, the conditions of self-defense are interpreted so as to ensure that the balance of harms in a self-defense situation is maximally conducive to overall welfare. It is therefore appropriate to construe the conditions in a way that is probabilistic. For example, a highly harmful potential attack with a low probability of occurring might yield the same defensive justification as a less harmful attack with a high probability of occurring. But within a forfeit of right account of self-defense, the function of the self-defense conditions is quite different. Although on this account the necessity, proportionality, and immanence conditions often function to reduce harm, they are not intended to reliably minimize overall harm, as on the consequentialist model (e.g. one is entitled to kill virtually any number of culpable aggressors if this is necessary to save one's own life). Instead their central function is to ensure that the person or persons against whom defensive force is used *are really morally liable* to the infliction of force, and that the level of harm inflicted on each aggressor is proportionate to his or her individual moral liability.

The imminence requirement, then, does more than simply bolster the necessity requirement in conditions of imperfect knowledge or ensure that the outcome of conflict situations are welfare maximizing. By requiring that self-defense cannot be undertaken until an unjust attack is imminent, the condition guarantees that those who are subject to defensive force are morally liable to it because they are currently engaged in an unjust aggressive attack. It would seem then, that the condition of imminence has an essential not derivative role in the theory of self-defense and that preventive self-defense is thereby ruled out at the level of moral theory.

NOTES

1. I am indebted to many people for careful and helpful criticism and comments particularly Henry Shue, Jeff McMahan, Alan Buchanan, Bob Goodin, members of the Princeton Center for Human Values research seminar especially Charles Beitz, Michael Smith, Stephen Macedo, Philip Pettit, and most especially all the other participants of the Changing Character of War workshop including the fellow contributors to this volume.

2. National Security Strategy of the United States of America, September 2002, p. 2.

3. The doctrine of preventive war was not the stated legal justification for the war, which instead invoked rights granted under earlier Security Council resolutions dating from the termination of the first Gulf War. Nonetheless, the doctrine of prevention and the reasoning behind it figured strongly in the debate over the war and its public justification.

4. David Luban, 'Preventive War', *Philosophy and Public Affairs,* vol. 32, no. 3, 2004, 207–48.

5. Michael Walzer, *Just and Unjust Wars,* Basic Books, 3rd edn, 2000, p. 75.

6. See, e.g. David Luban, 'Preventive War', *Philosophy and Public Affairs,* vol. 32, no. 3, 2004, 207–48, pp. 212–14.

7. Unilateral preventive action in this context refers to the use of force by a state or group of states without Security Council authorization. The Security Council is mandated to authorize preventive force in order to maintain international peace and security under Chapter VII of the UN Charter.

8. Michael Walzer, *Just and Unjust Wars,* Basic Books, 1977, p. 77.

9. Of course a sophisticated form of consequentialism will consider a range of morally relevant consequences beyond the crude metric of lives lost or saved. It would consider, for example, the moral disvalue of the potential subjection of many millions of people to a regime as deeply unjust as Nazism. It may also be the case that genocide is morally worse than the murder of an equivalent number of unrelated people. But even on a sophisticated form of consequentialism it is very difficult to see how a consequentialist could justify World War II given the magnitude of its actual moral costs. Consider how one of the ultimate consequences of the war was to usher in the Soviet Union's brutal half-century dominion over the states of Eastern Europe.

10. See Eric Hobsbawn, *The Age of Extremes,* Michael Joseph, London, 1994, pp. 43–4.

11. My argument concerns a consequentialist assessment of *war.* I make no claims about international use of force that falls below the threshold of war.

12. Clausewitz, Carl Von, *On War,* Michael Howard and Peter Paret (eds), Princeton University Press, Princeton, 1976, b. 1, ch. 1, §3 pp. 75–6 and 77.

13. As Walter Sinnott-Armstrong points out in this volume if the effects of war are as indeterminate and unpredictable as I have suggested, this raises the difficult question of how *any* rational military or political planning is possible. What precisely are planners doing when they assess that going to war would be, for instance, in the national interest? I think that much military planning is subject to similar difficulties, and many policymakers, if they are honest will say as much. But it is also important to note that the criteria according to which most policymakers assess military decisions are substantially narrower in scope than those proposed by consequentialism. For example, judging what is in the national interest is a much narrower (and hence easier) question than judging what will generate best overall long-term consequences (consider: what is in the national interest need not be in the interest of all or even the majority of the members of the nation). Often the consequences that matter to policymakers are more narrow still—the consequences of a given military action for their own political party, department, or career.

14. An alternative way of interpreting this argument is to view it not as a critique of consequentialism per se, but as a strong rule-consequentialist argument for pacifism, or at least a moral presumption against war close to pacifism. Walter Sinnott-Armstrong considers this possibility in his chapter in

[*Preemption*, Shue and Rodin, eds., p. 211], and I think that if the epistemological difficulties of consequentialism could be overcome, this would indeed be its likely conclusion.

15. Cicero, *Works,* XIV, Loeb Classical Library, London and Cambridge, MA, 1979, 16–17 (*Pro Milone,* 10–11).

16. Quoted in Richard Tuck, *The Rights of War and Peace: Political Thought and the International Order From Grotius to Kant,* Oxford University Press, Oxford, 1999, p. 18.

17. Michael Walzer, *Just and Unjust Wars,* Basic Books, 3rd edn, 2000, pp. 76–7.

18. David Luban, 'Preventive War', *Philosophy and Public Affairs,* vol. 32, no. 3, 2004, 207–48, p. 220.

19. Michael Walzer, *Just and Unjust Wars,* p. 77; David Luban, 'Preventive War', *Philosophy and Public Affairs,* vol. 32, no. 3, 2004, 207–48, pp. 223ff.

20. David Luban, 'Preventive War', *Philosophy and Public Affairs,* vol. 32, no. 3, 2004, 207–48, p. 226–7.

21. Michael Byers, 'preemptive Self-Defense: Hegemony, Equality and Strategies of Legal Change', *The Journal of Political Philosophy,* vol. 11, no. 2, 2003, 171–90, p. 182.

22. David Luban, 'Preventive War', *Philosophy and Public Affairs,* vol. 32, no. 3, 2004, 207–48, p. 227.

23. Luban does gesture at one point to what 'experience has taught us', without explaining either which experience he has in mind or how he supposes that it has taught us.

(David Luban, 'Preventive War', *Philosophy and Public Affairs,* vol. 32, no. 3, 2004, 207–48, p. 225.)

24. National Security Strategy of the United States of America, September 2002, p. 15

25. Ibid.

26. Ibid., v.

27. Ibid., 15.

28. See David Rodin, *War and Self-Defense,* Oxford University Press, Oxford, 2001, p. 41.

29. The term 'necessity' can have two meanings in moral and legal theory. The first is the excuse under discussion here. The second is the condition found *inter alia* within just war theory and the law of self-defense which requires that an action may only be undertaken if there is no less costly or harmful way of achieving the same result.

30. Aristotle, *Nicomachean Ethics,* Crisp, R. (tr.), Cambridge: Cambridge University Press, 2000, 1110a.

31. Quoted in Yoram Dinstein, *War, Aggression and Self-Defense,* 4th edn, Cambridge University Press, Cambridge, 1988, p. 249.

32. Quoted in Yoram Dinstein, *War, Aggression and Self-Defense,* p. 249.

33. National Security Strategy of the United States of America, September 2002, p. 16.

34. David Rodin, *War and Self-Defense,* Oxford, Oxford University Press, 2002, ch. 4.

READING QUESTIONS

1. How does Rodin argue that act consequentialist defenses of preventive war fail?
2. Explain the "impasse" problem that Rodin uses in criticizing rule consequentialist attempts to address the moral justification of preventive war.
3. Rodin claims that he used to hold that the concept of imminence is fundamental to the right of self-defense. Why does he now reject this view?
4. What objections does Rodin raise against self-defense understood as a psychological necessity as a basis for justifying preventive wars?
5. Why does Rodin think that rights-based defenses of preventive war are problematic?

DISCUSSION QUESTIONS

1. Discuss how might one respond to Rodin's epistemological objection to the act consequentialist approach to preventive war.
2. Rodin argues that appeal to the right of self-defense cannot be used to justify preventive wars. He bases his argument on claims about the conditions under which one is liable for criminal punishment. Discuss whether there are important disanalogies between conditions applying to the justification of criminal punishment and conditions under which (for reasons of self-defense) a preventive war would be morally justified.

WALTER SINNOTT-ARMSTRONG

Preventive War—What Is It Good For?

Approaching the issue of the moral justification from an act consequentialist perspective, Walter Sinnott-Armstrong defends this approach to preventive war against Rodin's charge of "uselessness" presented in the preceding selection. Sinnott-Armstrong then proceeds to critically consider the just war approach to preventive war, in particular, the "just cause" provision of *jus ad bellum* concerning the moral justification of going to war. He also critically evaluates appeals to imminence, which is used to distinguish preemptive from preventive wars, and argues that meeting this condition is not necessary for an anticipatory war to be morally justified. He concludes by considering the implications of consequentialism regarding preventive war.

   Recommended Reading: consequentialism, chap. 1, sec. 2A, and the presentation of just-war theory in this chapter's introduction.

After the horrific terrorist attack on September 11, 2001, US President George W. Bush announced a policy of preventive war. True to his word, Bush soon implemented his policy.[1]

   The first war occurred in Afghanistan. This war was aimed partly at punishing al-Qaeda terrorists and partly at helping the people of Afghanistan by liberating them from the Taliban and creating a democracy with greater freedom and prosperity. Hence, this war was not purely preventive. Still, one of its goals was to prevent attacks on the United States and its allies by terrorists from training camps in Afghanistan, and Bush admitted that no attacks by Afghanistan were imminent. To that extent the war in Afghanistan was preventive.[2]

   Bush's next war was in Iraq. The Iraq War had several announced aims, including the enforcement of UN resolutions and international law as well as helping the people in Iraq partly by removing Saddam Hussein and introducing democracy. Of course, critics charged that Bush's real aims were to control

Iraq's oil, to help his cronies make money, and to avenge or surpass his father, who had failed to subdue Iraq in 1991. In any case, both sides agreed that one of the main announced goals of the Iraq War was to prevent or reduce distant future terrorist attacks on the United States and its allies, especially attacks with WMD. If this announced goal really was Bush's goal, which has been questioned, then to that extent the Iraq War was a preventive war. That is how I will view the Iraq War here.[3]

   Many opponents of the Iraq War responded by denying that any preventive war is ever justified. This reaction goes too far in my opinion. Bush's preventive war in Iraq is morally wrong, and his policy is too broad, but some exceptional preventive wars can still be morally justified.

   To see which and why, we need to explore the general moral theories behind these opposing stances. Most of Bush's arguments for his policy and the Iraq War are about consequences. Bush usually emphasized consequences for the United

From Walter Sinnott-Armstrong, "Preventive War—What Is It Good For?" in *Preemption: Military Action and Moral Justification*, H. Shue and D. Rodin, eds. Oxford: Oxford University Press, pp. 202–221.

States, but sometimes he adds consequences for others, including allies in the coalition and Iraqis and others in the Middle East. Either way, Bush dwells on consequences. As his National Security Strategy announces, 'We will always proceed deliberately, weighing the consequences of our actions.'[4] In contrast, Bush's critics often argue that the Iraq War violates absolute rules against certain general kinds of acts that are defined independently of consequences. The most often-cited rule is a prohibition on preventive war. In their view, preventive wars are always morally wrong by their very nature, regardless of their consequences.

This practical debate mirrors a deep divide in philosophical moral theory. Consequentialists hold that what we morally ought to do depends on consequences alone. Nothing else counts, except insofar as it affects consequences. Deontologists claim that what we morally ought to do also depends on other factors (such as the agent's intention or the kind of action) that are independent of consequences. Some deontologists allow consequences to matter as well, but they still think that other factors sometimes make something morally wrong even when it has better consequences.

Although Bush's arguments recall the consequentialist approach, Bush is not a consistent consequentialist. He freely cites deontological rules against some actions he opposes, such as abortion and stem cell research. Even in the case of war, Bush alludes to a right to national defense, which can conflict with consequentialism. Nonetheless, it might seem that consequentialists would support Bush's war and policy if they agreed with him about the consequences of his war and policy, whereas deontologists could still oppose the war and policy on non-consequentialist grounds.

This appearance might lead Bush's critics away from consequentialism so that they would have something left to say against Bush if they reached an impasse in arguing about the consequences of the Iraq War. That retreat would be a mistake. The strongest arguments against Bush's war and policy are consequentialist, not deontological. To show why, I shall develop and defend a version of consequentialism about war. Then I shall criticize the relevant part

of the most common deontological alternative, just war theory. Finally, I shall apply all of this theory to preventive war in general and Bush's war and policy in particular.

DEEP MORALITY *VERSUS* PUBLIC RULES

My argument will hinge on a certain characterization of the issue. I will assume that both consequentialist and deontological theories are about objective moral wrongness. The question they address is whether certain wars really are morally wrong, not whether people think that they are morally wrong or even whether it is reasonable to think that they are morally wrong. Moreover, these competing theories concern what McMahan calls the deep morality of war.[5] These theories try to specify conditions that must be met for war not to be morally wrong. They do not claim that their conditions should be written directly into public laws of war that are or should be accepted by international groups or enforced by international courts.

Such public laws might need to be formulated differently from deep morality in order to be useful in practice. For example, as McMahan argues, many combatants are innocent and nonthreatening, whereas many noncombatants are guilty and threatening, so the deep morality of war should not distinguish combatants from noncombatants. It still might be too difficult in practice to tell who is innocent or threatening, so the public laws of war might need to forbid attacks on noncombatants but not combatants. In such ways, practical public laws of war can come apart from the deep morality of war. I will then be concerned mainly with the deep morality of war.[6]

A consequentialist theory of the deep morality of war can admit that public rules of war should be formulated in deontological terms. Such public rules might have better consequences because actual agents would make too many mistakes in applying public rules formulated directly in terms of consequences. Even if so, the deep morality of war still might be consequentialist because the public rules are justified only by their consequences. Thus, theorists who claim only that deontological rules should be publicly accepted and enforced do not deny what is claimed by a consequentialist theory of the deep morality of war. To disagree with consequentialism on that topic, deontologists need to argue that some factor independent of consequences determines which wars are really morally wrong.

Some just war theorists might not make any such claim. They might talk only about public rules and not consider deep morality at all. If so, consequentialists have no quarrel with them. That kind of just war theory is simply beside the point here. However, many other just war theorists and deontologists do claim that their rules determine which wars are morally wrong, and they deny that consequences alone determine moral wrongness. Those are the just war theorists whom consequentialists oppose and whom I will discuss here. . . .

CONSEQUENTIALIST MORAL THEORY

My consequentialist theory of the deep morality of war is an application of a more general approach to morality.[7] Consequentialism as a general moral theory claims that the moral status of an act depends only on consequences. I favor act-consequentialism which claims that an agent morally ought not to do an act if and only if that act has significantly worse consequences than any available alternative. Consequences are worse when they contain more death, pain, disability (including lack of freedom), and possibly injustice and rights violations, considering everyone equally.

This act-consequentialism contrasts with the rule-consequentialism adopted by other[s] . . . including David Luban.[8] Rule-consequentialism is the claim that whether a particular act is morally wrong depends on whether that act violates a general rule that is justified by its own consequences. Rule consequentialism is indirect in the sense that the moral status of

one thing (an act) depends on the consequences of a different thing (a rule). In contrast, act consequentialism is direct insofar as it morally judges one thing by the consequences of that thing itself.

The first problem for rule utilitarianism is its indirectness. Why should the moral status of one thing depend on the consequences of something else? More specifically, since a rule as an abstract entity cannot have consequences, what are called the consequences of the rule are really consequences of most or all people in a certain group endorsing, teaching, following, and/or enforcing that rule. Rule consequentialism, thus, makes the moral status of one particular act by one particular agent in one particular set of circumstances depend on consequences of separate acts by separate agents in separate circumstances. I see no adequate reason for such indirection.

Moreover, any particular act falls under many general rules. A war, for example, might violate a rule against preventive war while also being the only way to avoid violating another rule that requires protecting citizens. I see no non-arbitrary way to determine which rules are the ones whose consequences matter for judging an act that is distinct from all of those rules.

Rules are also used in many ways in many contexts. Rules might be used to teach children or to award damages in international courts. Different rules might be justified in different circumstances, often because of varying dangers of misuse. Act consequentialists can recognize this variety and say that it is morally right to use one rule for teaching children and a different rule for international courts. Rule consequentialists, however, need to pick one role for rules as the one and only central role that determines whether a particular act is or is not morally wrong. I see no good reason why one role would be decisive for all moral judgments, so rule consequentialists again cannot avoid arbitrariness.

Admittedly, moral theorists must allow some roles for rules, but act consequentialists can do so. Just as they assess acts directly by consequences of those acts, so they assess rules directly by consequences of using those rules. Act consequentialists can (and usually do) also admit that people normally ought to decide what to do not by calculating consequences but, instead, by consulting rules. This move does not turn act consequentialism into rule consequentialism, because act consequentialists can still insist that an act is morally wrong even when its agent used the best rules as a guide or decision procedure if the particular act fails their standard or criterion of the right, because it causes more harm than some alternative.

PROBLEMS FOR CONSEQUENTIALISM

Critics propose a slew of counterexamples to act consequentialism. A popular case involves transplanting organs from one healthy person to save five other people. This and most other alleged counterexamples, however, depend on secrecy. It would not make the world better if people knew it was going on. Thus, such counterexamples do not apply to consequentialism about war, since wars are hard to keep secret.[9]

Other critics of consequentialism cite commonsense principles that are supposed to be obvious and exceptionless, such as the claim that it is always morally wrong to intentionally kill an innocent person. However, wars are filled with emergencies that create exceptions. In the Vietnam War, the Vietcong sometimes tied explosives to the back of a young child and told the child that a certain group of American soldiers had candy. The child ran to the soldiers to get the candy. The soldiers sometimes had no way to save their lives except to shoot the child before the child got too close. They were killing (or at least harming) the child as a means to save their own and others' lives, even though they knew the child was totally innocent. Soldiers usually felt horrible about such acts, and their feelings are understandable, but their acts were not morally wrong. Thus, the commonsense principle is not exceptionless after all, and it cannot be used to refute consequentialism about war.

More generally, such principles and counterexamples depend on moral intuitions. Moral intuitions in contexts of war are particularly unreliable, because they are notoriously subject to disagreement as well as distortion by partiality, culture, and strong emotions, such as fear.[10] Our moral intuitions evolved to fit situations in everyday life that are very different from war. Hence, any objections that depend on such moral intuitions lose their force when applied to consequentialism about war.

Critics might respond that our moral intuitions are reliable and run counter to consequentialism outside war. I would be happy to defend consequentialism in general on another occasion. For now it is enough if consequentialism can be defended as a criterion of what is right in war.

The most serious remaining objection to consequentialism about war is epistemological. This objection arises elsewhere, but it is particularly pressing in war, because wars are so unpredictable.[11] It is hard to predict in advance how many people will die on either side of a war. This problem would not be serious if the point were only that we often cannot be sure that a war is justified on consequentialist terms. Everyone should agree that there are many cases where we do not know what is morally right.

Rodin thinks the point goes deeper, because consequentialism is 'useless' even in 'clear' cases. The Allies' war against Nazi Germany is often presented as the clearest example of a justified war. Rodin argues, however, that it is not clear whether even that war minimized bad consequences:

> The Nazi regime was brutal and aggressive: it systematically murdered approximately 6 million innocent people, and subjected many millions more to a regime of extraordinary moral repugnance. But the war itself cost somewhere in the region of 55 million lives. In addition it made 40 million persons homeless, caused incalculable destruction to the world's cultural and material wealth, and had the after-effect of initiating the Soviet Union's brutal half-century dominion over Eastern Europe. This was a horrific price to pay for stopping Nazi Germany. It is certainly not obvious on strict consequentialist grounds it was a price worth paying.[12]

The challenge seems simple: The war against the Nazis is clearly morally justified, but it would not be clearly morally justified if consequentialism were correct, so consequentialism is not correct.

Consequentialists can respond in several ways. One possibility is to deny that the war against the Nazis is 'an easy case'. Any act that causes so much death and destruction is at least questionable. Indeed, it was questioned by many opponents of US entry into the war and by many pacifists during World War II. And even if it does seem easy to assess this war, consequentialism might show us that it is not as easy as it seems. The fact that consequentialism raises serious doubts about cases that previously seemed easy might show how illuminating consequentialism is. That is a virtue, not a vice, of consequentialism.[13]

Consequentialists can add that, compared to other wars, it is relatively clear that war against the Nazis minimized bad consequences. The Nazis did not merely kill six million Jews. They also killed millions of non-Jews. They had aggressive plans to continue occupying more and more territory. Resistance was inevitable and would lead to more killing. If the Nazis took over Europe, then there would also be loss not only of life but also of freedom and other values. Europeans would have lived in constant fear of arbitrary execution or imprisonment. Their 'regime of extraordinary moral repugnance' would have continued for much longer than the war.[14] Moreover, if the Nazis had been allowed to rule Europe without opposition, they could have built up strength and continued their expansion. The larger wave of fascism that accompanied the rise of the Nazis would most likely have spread elsewhere, leading to more wars. When all these bad consequences are considered together, it seems relatively clear (or at least reasonable to conclude) that refusing to fight the Nazis would probably have cost far more than fifty-five million lives over the long run.

Consider also the perspective of a single country. The United States, for example, did not have a choice between war and no war. There was going to be a war as soon as Hitler invaded his neighbors. The only options for the United States were (a) a war between the Nazis and the Allies without the United States or (b) a war between the Nazis and the Allies with the United States. Option (a) had a higher probability of Hitler taking over Europe, including Britain, and then continuing to expand the Third Reich. Option (b) reduced that probability even though it increased the chances of US losses. I see little reason to doubt that option (b) has less bad consequences overall than option (a). That comparison is all that is needed for consequentialists to conclude that the United States was morally justified in entering the war. Similar comparisons for other countries could show why each of the Allies was justified in joining up.

We also need to ask why the costs of the war against the Nazis were so high. Many historians argue that part of the reason is that the United States took too long to get involved. If so, consequentialists can say that for the United States to join the war in 1941 was better than not joining the war ever or until later, but joining the war in 1941 was also not as good as joining the war sooner. This example might then suggest consequentialist reasons for preventive war, contrary to any blanket deontological prohibition.

Of course, we cannot be certain about any of this. It is possible that the war against the Nazis did more harm than good. However, that is unlikely, and we have to live with probabilities here as elsewhere. Consequentialists need to admit that they are often unsure about the right thing to do, especially with regard to war. Is this a problem? No, because we often are and should be unsure whether to enter into war.

This admission is not enough, according to Rodin, because it is unclear even what could count as empirical evidence for any conclusion that a war minimizes bad consequences.[15] However, the evidence is clear. Every bit of pain, death, and disability in a war is a bit of evidence for the moral wrongness of that war. Of course, every bit of pain, death, and disability that is prevented by a war is a bit of evidence against the moral wrongness of the war. The problem is not in finding evidence but in weighing all of the evidence together. It is not clear how to do that, but many people seem to focus on one or a small number of reasons that strike them as more likely and important, to discount possibilities that are unlikely or balanced by opposite possibilities, and to remain open to new considerations. The process is hardly mechanical, but it is still based on evidence. Anyway, however they do it, many people do somehow succeed in making decisions by weighing together many and varied long-term consequences (or, at least, by using defeasible heuristics). Military planners do it. So do everyday people who choose careers, get married, or decide to have children. Since we make such choices reasonably in everyday life, it is not clear why we cannot also make such choices reasonably in war.

Admittedly, as Rodin says, 'Consequentialism is frequently a deeply disappointing guide.'[16] Still, this does not make consequentialism 'useless'. Even if we could not weigh the consequences of any war as costly as the war against the Nazis, we still might be justified in believing that other less costly wars are not morally wrong. And even if we were never justified in believing that any war has good consequences overall, we still might be justified in believing that certain wars *are* morally wrong. We can know, for example, that it was morally wrong for Nazi Germany to invade Poland. Such negative judgments provide guidance insofar as they tell us what not to do. These suppositions might lead to the conclusion that we are never justified in believing that any war is morally right, but we can still be justified in believing that some wars are morally wrong. If so, consequentialism leads to an epistemic variation on pacifism. That conclusion is not obviously implausible, if the suppositions are granted.

Still, I am not as pessimistic about our epistemic abilities as Rodin is. It strikes me as reasonable to believe that the war against the Nazis prevented more harm than it caused. I admit uncertainty, but that need not force me to give up my belief or even my meta-belief that my belief is reasonable and justified. Admittedly, consequentialists still need some way to make decisions in the face of uncertainty. . . . I wish I could be more definitive, but I can only admit that I, along with all other moral philosophers (deontologists as well as consequentialists), need to develop better ways of dealing with the crucial and pervasive issue of uncertainty. Luckily, since my act consequentialism provides a criterion of the right instead of a decision procedure, I can set this issue of uncertainty aside for now.

Other consequentialists might try to avoid problems of uncertainty by claiming that moral wrongness depends not on actual consequences but, instead, on foreseen or reasonably foreseeable consequences. If so, consequentialists do not have to argue that the war against the Nazis actually did minimize bad consequences. All they have to claim is that the Allies believed or had reason to believe that this war would prevent more harm than it would cause. If they could not have expected, for example, the Soviet domination of Eastern Europe after World War II, then those bad consequences could not show that the war was morally wrong on their view.

However, consequentialists who count only expected or expectable consequences run into problems of their own. Such consequentialists have trouble answering, 'Foreseen or foreseeable *by whom?*' If an observer foresees horrific consequences that the agent cannot foresee, the observer should not say that the agent ought to do the act with horrific consequences.[17] Moreover, in a collective action, such as a war, different people would be able to foresee different consequences. Hence, if moral wrongness depended on foreseeable consequences, it would make no sense to ask whether the war was morally wrong without qualification. Finally, it is hard to understand why the true moral status of an act would depend on its agent's false beliefs, even if reasonable. When an act has overall bad consequences that its agent could not have reasonably foreseen, the agent should not be blamed or criticized morally as an agent, but the act itself can still be morally wrong. Every moral theory needs to distinguish agents and acts, and the most natural way to recognize this distinction is to let foreseeable consequences determine whether the agent is blameworthy and actual consequences determine whether the act ought to be done.

For such reasons, I am inclined to think that the moral rightness of wars depends on their actual consequences, including counterfactual consequences or what have happened if a different act had been actual. However, if I had to give up that position and count foreseeable consequences instead, I would not be terribly upset. What is important is that the moral status of a war depends only on consequences of that war rather than on any rule or factor that is independent of consequences.

JUST WAR THEORY

Despite its virtues, consequentialism is not as popular as its main rival, just war theory. It is difficult to discuss just war theory as a whole because it contains so many parts and comes in so many versions. . . .

Some just war theories propose only public rules of war. These versions might seem to conflict with consequentialism, because their public rules refer to deontological factors other than consequences. However, as I said, consequentialists can accept such public rules and even justify them by their consequences. Hence, just war theories that are only about public rules do not conflict with consequentialism. I am interested in versions of just war theory that challenge consequentialism. Thus, although just war theories about public rules might be correct and important, they are simply not my topic here.

Just war theories conflict with consequentialism only when they make claims about the deep morality of war. Just war theories of deep morality specify conditions that must be met for a war to be not merely just but morally justified overall. These conditions are normally divided into three parts: *jus ad bellum, jus in bello,* and *jus post bellum.*[18] What concerns us here is *jus ad bellum*—when it is or is not morally wrong to go to war. Within that subdivision, the condition that is most relevant to preventive war is just cause.

Just Cause

The condition of just cause says that it is morally wrong for anyone to wage war without a just cause. But that cannot be all there is to it. Even consequentialists grant that wars need some just cause in order to be morally justified, since wars have bad consequences, so they cannot make the world better overall unless they have compensating benefits. Consequentialists and just war theorists also agree that the just cause must be important enough to overcome the strong presumption against war. The conflict between consequentialism and just war theory arises only when just war theorists specify exactly which causes can justify war.

Which causes are just causes? Wars have been fought for many reasons: defense of self or allies or others against external attack, enforcement of international law or punishment for past aggression, to stop internal atrocities or defend human rights, to spread a religion or form of government, for economic gain or glory, out of hatred of the enemy or love of battle, and so on. Just war theorists need to specify which of these candidates are just causes and, hence, adequate to justify war given the other conditions in their theory. They also need to say why these candidates are just causes and why the others are not. This task will not be easy. Many of these candidates are controversial. Emotions, partiality, and culture are likely to distort intuitions. And just war theorists cannot specify just causes by reference to consequences without, in effect, giving in to consequentialism. So it is not clear how just war theorists can justify their claims.

Some just war theorists might think that they can avoid these problems by limiting their claims to the clearest case: self-defense.[19] However, even if everyone agreed that self-defense is sufficient to justify war given other conditions, its sufficiency would not show that it is necessary. Other causes might also be sufficient. Hence, just war theorists who talk only about self-defense cannot argue that any war lacks a just cause or that consequentialism justifies wars without just causes. To reach such a negative conclusion, just war theorists need to explain why selfdefense is the only just cause and nothing else on the above list is a just cause. It is hard to imagine any good argument for that claim.

Some just war theorists . . . seem to suggest an argument like this: Until you have been wronged, you have no good enough reason to use force. However, the reason for a preventive war is to prevent harmful attacks. That sure looks like a good reason. It simply begs the question to assume that this good reason is not good enough, at least when the prevented harms are much greater than the harms inflicted by the preventive war.

Just war theorists, including Crawford, might respond that too many countries will start wars if we tell them that wars might sometimes be permitted for humanitarian purposes, to enforce international law, or to spread democracy. This is far from obvious if other conditions limit such wars to clear and extreme cases, such as the rare cases where humanitarian wars meet consequentialist criteria. Moreover, even if publicly permitting such wars would lead to too much war, that is a reason not to build such permission into public rules of war. It shows nothing about the deep morality of war or about moral wrongness. That leaves no good reason to assume that self-defense is the only just cause that is adequate to justify war given other conditions.

In addition, the condition of self-defense needs to be interpreted carefully. Crawford, for example, claims that: 'A conception of the self that justifies legitimate preemption in self-defense must be narrowly confined to immediate risks to life and health within borders or to the life and health of citizens abroad.'[20]

A broader definition of the self might count war as self-defense when it is waged for the sake of 'economic well-being' and 'access to key markets and strategic resources.'[21] The Bush administration takes such a broad view of self-defense for the United States.

I grant that increasing the economic well-being of already prosperous nations, including the United States, is not true self-defense and could not justify war in any realistic scenario. However, if 'economic well-being' includes maintaining minimal economies for severely deprived people, then protecting economic wellbeing might count as self-defense. Perhaps such minimal economic well-being fits under 'life and health', but that just shows how economic well-being sometimes might be important enough to justify war.

It is also not clear why war could never be justified to protect 'strategic resources.' Strategic positions are ones that give an advantage, but resources are usually called strategic only when they are needed to be able to defend life and freedom. If we could not start a war to defend resources that are strategic in this narrower sense, then opponents who want to invade our country could cut off our strategic resources so as to make us unable to defend ourselves by the time they invaded.

By limiting self-defense to 'life and health', Crawford also implies that anticipatory war is never justified to protect our freedom at home or abroad. However, if it were morally wrong to start a war to defend our freedom, then it would be morally wrong to stop invaders who promised to keep us alive and healthy while taking over our government.

My most basic disagreement with Crawford and just war theory concerns method. Crawford announces that certain general kinds of values (life and health) are adequate and others (such as economic well-being) are not. However, particular instances of such general kinds vary along continua and are affected by circumstances. Freedom, health, and economic well-being come in endless degrees. The risk of attack can also vary from no chance to certainty. Whether a war is morally wrong depends on exactly where it falls along such continua. Most people's intuitions are not fine-grained enough for such complex questions. Hence, I see no reasonable alternative to the consequentialist position that whether a war is morally wrong depends on balance of probabilities of various values and disvalues among its consequences.

Imminence

We still need to ask whether prevention of future aggression is a just cause in the absence of any actual aggression at present. The traditional answer is that the future aggression must be imminent. This is the imminence condition. If the threat is imminent, the war is called preemptive. If it is not imminent, the war is called preventive. Traditional just war theory then forbids all preventive wars but not all preemptive wars.

A classic example of a preemptive war is Israel's Six Day War of 1967. Egypt was building up forces on its border with Israel, so it was credible that they would attack Israel very soon. Israel beat them to the punch by bombing Egyptian airfields while their planes were on the ground. Israel's attack was preemptive rather than preventive, because Egypt's attack was imminent. In contrast, a classic example of a preventive strike occurred when Israel bombed Iraq's Osirak nuclear reactor in 1981. The threatened attack was not imminent, because it would have been years before the reactor produced material for nuclear weapons.

When does an attack count as imminent? Some just war theorists specify a time period. Crawford, for example, answers that an attack is imminent when and only when it 'can be made manifest within hours or weeks.'[22] How many hours or weeks? Presumably, 'hours or weeks' must be shorter than a month. Crawford's formulation then suggests that Israel's bombing of Egyptian airfields at the start of the Six Day War met the condition of imminence, so it was not morally wrong, if the other conditions were met; but Israel's bombing of the Osirak reactor failed the condition of imminence, so it was morally wrong.

This condition makes moral wrongness depend on timing, but why does time matter? Several answers are common. First, by waiting until Egypt's attack was imminent, Israel gave Egypt an opportunity to forswear aggression. It might seem unfair to remove that chance to improve. Second, by waiting until Egypt's attack was imminent, Israel also waited until the probability of attack was high. Countries sometimes threaten aggression when they do not really mean it or at least will not really do it when push comes to shove. As time goes by, non-aggressive possibilities disappear and the preemptor gains more and stronger evidence (which increases the epistemic probability) of the feared attack. For such reasons, time is correlated with probability: When the attack is imminent, the probability of attack is usually higher than before it became imminent.

Consequentialists agree that probability can affect what is morally wrong, but usually they deny that time itself affects what is morally wrong. A test case would occur if time did not change probability (or did not change it enough to make a difference). Imagine that Israel had attacked Egypt in the same way as it did in 1967, but a month earlier. In this imaginary scenario, Israelis were just as certain about the impending attack by Egypt, and waiting a few weeks until the attack was imminent would not have made Israel more certain. Nevertheless, waiting would have made Israel's defense less likely to succeed and more costly in both Israeli and Egyptian lives. The imminence condition implies that this earlier anticipatory attack would have been morally

wrong, because the threatened attack was not imminent. I find this position hard to believe. If the level of certainty is high enough a week in advance, the same probability should be high enough a month in advance. If waiting will not decrease the probability of aggression and will increase the costs to both sides (in innocent Israeli as well as Egyptian lives), then I see no reason to wait. Time itself provides no reason. Temporal imminence is not necessary for guilt, since Egypt was conspiring to attack Israel more than a month in advance. It might seem unfair not to grant Egypt a last chance to mend its ways, but Egypt would have had many such opportunities long before Israel's attack, even if that attack had come a month earlier. If every last opportunity had to be provided, then Israel would not have been justified in bombing even one minute before the Egyptian planes took off (or entered Israeli airspace). Even just war theorists do not believe that. Hence, temporal imminence cannot really be necessary for an anticipatory war to avoid being morally wrong.

This point also applies to Israel's attack on the Osirak reactor. Israel argued that, if they had waited, the reactor would probably have been used to make nuclear weapons. If they had waited to bomb it when it was active, then very many people in Iraq would have been killed by the explosion and nuclear fallout, whereas only a few people were killed when they bombed the reactor before it was active. The same reasoning might also apply to Bush's attack on Iraq. Imagine that Bush had allowed Saddam Hussein to develop more chemical and biological weapons and then to begin loading them into missiles while expressing the intention to shoot those missiles at the United States or our allies, such as Israel. If we had bombed their missiles at that later time, then the chemical and biological agents might have spread widely throughout Iraq and neighboring countries. This would have caused even more devastation to innocent civilians than the current war. I am not claiming and do not believe that these facts are accurate or that this scenario motivated Bush. My point is only that certain types of weapons—nuclear as well as biological and chemical—change the equation . . . When threatened with weapons of these sorts, waiting can sometimes be much more dangerous for innocent people on both sides. I shall argue later that this affects what our public policies should be. For now the point is that it also affects whether preventive war can be morally justified.

My conclusion is that countries ought to wait when it is not too dangerous to wait, but sometimes waiting is too dangerous, and then preventive war might not be morally wrong. If so, time in itself makes no difference. What really matter are the likely benefits and costs of acting at one time as opposed to another, just as consequentialism suggests. . . .

A CONSEQUENTIALIST VIEW OF PREVENTIVE WAR

To determine whether preventive war is morally justified, just war theorists ask whether prevention of nonimminent aggression is a just cause. The answer is far from clear, partly because the question lumps together so many different circumstances. In contrast, consequentialism enables a more nuanced and insightful view of preventive war.

Because of its sensitivity to circumstances, consequentialism clearly implies that it is at least logically and physically possible for some preventive war to be morally justified. . . . A general rule against preventive war cannot hold in all possible cases if the moral wrongness of such wars depends on their consequences and the consequences of the available alternatives in the particular circumstances.

Preventive war still might never be justified in any actual case, according to consequentialism. However, we already saw a plausible example: Israel's preventive bombing of the Osirak reactor. Assuming that international negotiation and pressure would probably have failed, if Israel had waited for the reactor to start up, then they probably would have had to attack either an active reactor or a plant for building nuclear bombs. Either alternative would be likely to have spread nuclear radiation over a large area and harmed many more innocent people than the actual preventive bombing. On these facts, then,

consequentialism implies that this attack was morally justified.

The United Nations Security Council condemned Israel for bombing the Osirak reactor. However, that condemnation does not reveal any consensus that the bombing was immoral. It does not even show that the Security Council members shared that belief. They might have thought it useful to make such a public condemnation even though Israel's attack was justified. After all, the Security Council did nothing beyond making a statement. If they had really believed that the attack was morally wrong, then they should have done more than talk. Anyway, consequentialists can explain how public condemnation of Israel could be morally justified by the consequences of that public speech act, even if Israel's bombing was not morally wrong because of the beneficial consequences of that separate action.

I know of no actual case where a preventive war seems justified as defense against conventional weapons. An early preventive campaign against Hitler would have been a likely candidate, but Hitler had already attacked and was occupying several countries, so an early attack (say, in 1938) could have been justified as law enforcement or on humanitarian grounds rather than as prevention. That leaves no justified preventive war against conventional weapons. Why? Maybe because the cost of waiting until an attack is imminent is never actually too high with conventional weapons. It is possible that an early attack would prevent scattering of enemy weapons that would make a later attack less effective and more costly to both sides, and that these costs would outweigh the benefits of waiting; but this seems unlikely. The absence of actual cases supports this guess.

What about Bush's attack on Iraq? According to consequentialism, Bush's attack was morally wrong if any available alternative would have had better consequences overall for the world. The crucial question is not whether the attack was better than doing nothing at all to reduce terrorism. The critical question, instead, is whether any available alternative would have been better. One multipronged nonmilitary alternative has been proposed and supported forcefully by Bart Gruzalski:

Breaking up terrorist cells, arresting terrorists, putting terrorists on trial in a world court, negotiating with the Taliban, no longer propping up tyrannical Arab regimes, pulling U.S. troops out of Saudi Arabia, and even-handedly dealing with the Palestinian–Israeli conflict would have been a successful strategy both to protect Americans and to stop the spread of anti-American insurgents.[23]

More particularly,

> Instead of invading Iraq, one alternative approach would have let Hans Blitz and the U.N. inspectors finish their job. . . . In addition . . . , the U.S. could have insisted on overflights with high altitude surveillance planes to check for weapons and military activity. . . . Since there was no military threat from Iraq [under such circumstances], the U.S. and the rest of the world could have lifted sanctions against Iraq and brought Iraq into the world trading community. . . . Instead of turning Iraq into a recruitment poster for al-Qaeda, the nonmilitary approach would foreseeably undermine the support for terrorism in the Islamic world.[24]

If this alternative would have been better overall than Bush's attack on Iraq, as I believe, then Bush's war was morally wrong according to consequentialism.

Bush's defenders might respond that Gruzalski's proposal would not have reduced terrorism. After all, many members and leaders of al-Qaeda have been rounded up since the war began. That, however, is no reason to assume that they would not have been rounded up without the war. Even before the attack on Afghanistan, many countries were already taking significant steps to break up terrorist cells and arrest terrorists.[25] These steps would be likely to have produced many arrests of al-Qaeda members without any attack on Iraq. Indeed, the US attack on Iraq (as well as treatment of terrorists in Guantanamo) squandered good will after September 11, led to less international cooperation, and thereby hurt the previous efforts to round up terrorists. The attack on Iraq also increased hatred of the United States among Arabs and seemed to confirm Bin Laden's claim that he is defending Islam against US aggression. For these reasons, instead of decreasing terrorism, Bush's Iraq War seems likely to increase terrorism against the United States and its allies in the long run.

This point applies even if one appeals to a US right to self-defense or if one gives up impartiality and appeals to interests of the United States in particular. Neither of these justifications works if Gruzalski and I are correct, because Bush's Iraq War does not help to defend the United States or serve US interests. This point becomes even clearer when we add the costs of the war on the US economy and on US civil rights.

Bush still might justify his Iraq attack as the only way to maintain US preeminence. Preeminence by itself is never enough for a consequentialist. Still, if US preeminence is the best means to achieve or maintain peace, then the best means to United States preeminence might be justified. However, many people (and I among them) doubt that US preeminence is the best means to peace. Then Bush's attack cannot be justified as a means to US preeminence.

Finally, Bush might defend his war as a way to bring to justice those responsible for the terrorist attacks on September 11. Then the war was not preventive. It was also not justified. Al-Qaeda had already been attacked in Afghanistan, and there were no clear connections between al-Qaeda and Iraq (or at least none has been found yet). Other proposed justifications, such as to spread democracy or to enforce international law, also fail, because there were better ways to achieve those goals, as Gruzalski argues.

My conclusion is that Bush's war in Iraq is morally wrong on consequentialist grounds. Of course, I am not certain. However, given such uncertainty, there is at least no adequate reason to believe that Bush's war was morally justified.[26] This lack of any adequate reason plus the presumption against war based on long and painful experience together support my conclusion that it was morally wrong to go to war in Iraq.

What about Bush's general policy of preventive war? Bush announced that the United States will engage in preventive war whenever it sees that step as necessary to defend itself. I doubt that such an unfettered policy is defensible. Politicians in the heat of the moment are too likely to err. However, as I argued, some preventive wars might not be morally wrong, although the only realistic cases are preventive wars against nuclear, chemical, biological, and possibly other unconventional threats. I also agree with Luban (2004) that the only realistic examples are rogue states. If that is correct, then we might benefit by acknowledging it. The United States could publicly renounce any preventive war against conventional threats but still reserve the right to use preventive attacks against threats by rogue states with unconventional WMD, though only when there is strong enough evidence that no other option will be less costly overall.

This policy could even be written into some enforceable international law. It would be very tricky to specify details, such as which states are rogue states, which weapons are conventional, when destruction is mass destruction, and when the evidence is strong enough. But partial solutions can be developed. The problem of inadequate evidence, for example, could be reduced (though not removed) if countries agreed not to engage in preventive war unless an impartial body agrees (unanimously or by a supermajority) that the evidence that the attacked country both has weapons of mass destruction and also is a rogue state are strong enough to justify preventive war. Reluctance to invoke the permission and engage in preventive war could be induced by agreeing to impose penalties (such as forced reparations) on countries that engage in preventive wars on the basis of evidence that is later discovered to be faulty, such as when it turns out that there were no weapons of mass destruction. Countries that want to start a preventive war will then have to decide whether they really believe that their evidence is strong enough for them to take the chance that they will be forced to pay reparations later.

This plan is admittedly idealistic, because many countries will be unwilling to accept or enforce such international laws. There are also bound to be significant disagreements about which policy would be best if adopted. Still, if some such policy could be worked out (and written into international law, applied by impartial courts, and enforced by some group of nations), then it might help to slow the spread of unconventional WMD and also deter the acts that get countries classified as rogue states. This kind of policy might then satisfy some of the Bush administration's legitimate concerns without being as dangerous as the current Bush policy.[27]

NOTES

1. I shall often refer to Bush as shorthand for his administration or troops carrying out his plans.

2. Some commentators suggest that whether an attack is preventive depends not on the attacker's goal but only on the nature of the capability, threat, or attack to which the attack responds. However, an attack does not respond in the relevant sense to a threat if the attacker's goal is not even partly to prevent that threat The attacker's goal, thus, determines what it is that the attacker responds to.

3. When a war has several purposes, we can ask whether a particular reason is good enough by itself to justify the war. That is my question here. It is fair, because most defenders of the war claim that the Iraq War's role as a preventive war is enough to justify it apart from any other reasons for the war.

4. United States, White House, National Security Council, *National Security Strategy of the United States of America* (September 2002), 16. http://www.whitehouse.gov/nsc/nss/2002/nss.pdf.

5. Jeff(erson) McMahan, 'The Ethics of Killing in War', *Ethics*, 114:4 (2004), 693–733. . . .

6. McMahan's phrase 'deep morality' does not refer to fundamental as opposed to derived principles. Instead, the point is that public rules need to use easily accessible markers in place of obscure factors that really determine what is morally wrong. The depth of deep morality is more like the depth of chemistry (which looks at the deep structure of chemicals instead of their superficial perceivable properties) than like the depth of axioms as opposed to theorems.

7. On consequentialism in general, see Walter Sinnott-Armstrong, 'Consequentialism,' in E. N. Zalta (ed), *The Stanford Encyclopedia of Philosophy* (2006). http://plato.stanford.edu/entries/consequentialism/. Consequentialist views of war have also been defended by Richard Brandt, 'Utilitarianism and the Rules of War', *Philosophy & Public Affairs,* 1: 2 (1971), 145–65; and Douglas Lackey, *The Ethics of War and Peace* (Englewood Cliffs, NJ: Prentice-Hall, 1989).

8. David Luban, 'Preventive War', *Philosophy & Public Affairs*, 32: 3 (2004), 207–48.

9. Isolated strikes can be kept secret, at least in some cases, but isolated strikes by themselves do not make a war.

10. See Walter Sinnott-Armstrong, 'Moral Intuitionism Meets Empirical Psychology,' in T. Horgan and M. Timmons (eds), *Metaethics After Moore* (New York: Oxford University Press, 2005).

11. See Walter Sinnott-Armstrong, 'Gert Contra Consequentialism,' in W. Sinnott-Armstrong and R. Audi (eds), *Rationality, Rules, and Ideals: Critical Essays on Bernard Gert's Moral Theory* (Lanham, MD: Rowman and Littlefield, 2002).

12. David Rodin, *War and Self-Defense* (Oxford: Clarendon Press, 2002), 11; compare his chapter 6 [Shue and Rodin (eds), *Preemption*, 143–70.]

13. I grant Rodin's methodological point that moral theories should explain not only what is immoral and why but also why certain cases seem obvious and others do not. My point is only that this consideration is only one among others and can be overridden in some cases, including this one.

14. Rodin, *War and Self-Defense,* 11.

15. See Rodin in this volume, p. 579.

16. Rodin, *War and Self-Defense,* 10.

17. Sinnott-Armstrong, 'Gert Contra Consequentialism,' 152–3.

18. Brian Orend, 'War', in E. N. Zalta (ed) *The Stanford Encyclopedia of Philosophy* (2003).

19. Neta Crawford, 'The Justice of Preemption and Preventive War Doctrines', in Mark Evans (ed.), *Just War Theory Revisited* (Edinburgh: University of Edinburgh Press, 2005).

20. Neta Crawford, 'The Slippery Slope to Preventive War', *Ethics and International Affairs*, 17: 1 (2003), 30–6.

21. See "The False Promise of Preventive War" in *Preemption,* Shue and Rodin, eds, pp. 89–125. by Crawford . . . quoting US government documents.

22. See Crawford, ibid., 119.

23. Bart Gruzalski, 'Some Implications of Utilitarianism for Practical Ethics: The Case Against the Military Response to Terrorism', in Henry West (ed), *Blackwell's Guide to Mill's Utilitarianism* (Oxford: Blackwell, 2005), pp. 249–69.

24. Ibid.

25. Ibid.

26. The way in which the war was conducted was also morally wrong in many ways. The initial strategy of Shock and Awe, e.g. violated just war theory and, more importantly, produced unnecessary bad effects.

27. For helpful discussion and comments on drafts, I thank Sue Uniacke, David Rodin, Henry Shue, Frances Kamm, Jeff McMahan, Bart Gruzalski, Peter Singer, Bernard Gert, Julia Driver, Nir Eyal, Anne Eaton, John Oberdick, Philip Pettit, Nan Keohane, Kim Scheppele, Steve Macedo, and others in audiences at the University of Oxford, the International Society of Utilitarian Studies, and the Princeton Center for Human Values. I would also like to thank the Oxford Leverhulme Program on the Changing Character of War and the Princeton University Center for Human Values for financial support while writing this chapter.

READING QUESTIONS

1. What does Sinnott-Armstrong mean in claiming that consequentialism represents a "deep" theory about the morality of war?
2. How does Sinnott-Armstrong reply to Rodin's claim that consequentialism is useless in addressing preventive war?
3. What objections does Sinnott-Armstrong raise against just war theory appeals to just cause in addressing preventive wars?
4. Why does Sinnott-Armstrong claim that appeal to temporal imminence is problematic in distinguishing morally justified from unjustified anticipatory wars?

DISCUSSION QUESTIONS

1. Discuss whether Sinnott-Armstrong's responses to Rodin's objections to the act consequentialist approach to war are convincing.
2. Sinnott-Armstrong is critical of nonconsequentialist appeals to self-defense in objecting to preventive wars that define "self-defense" narrowly to rule out such considerations as economic well-being as part of a nation's self-defense. Discuss whether his objections to this conception of self-defense are plausible.

3. Sinnott-Armstrong claims that the imminence standard for distinguishing preventive from preemptive wars—a standard that relies on timing—is problematic. Discuss how a proponent of this standard might defend against Sinnott-Armstrong's objections.

MICHAEL WALZER

Terrorism: A Critique of Excuses

After explaining the particular evil of terrorism and why it cannot be morally justified, Michael Walzer criticizes the typical "excuses" that are offered in defense of terrorist acts. The excuses include (1) terrorism is a last resort, (2) terrorist activities are needed because of weakness or other inability to mobilize a movement or nation, (3) terrorism is effective on behalf of oppressed groups, and (4) terrorism is a proper response to oppression. He then proceeds to consider ways of best responding to terrorism and concludes by examining the link between terrorism and oppression.

No one these days advocates terrorism, not even those who regularly practice it. The practice is indefensible now that it has been recognized, like rape and murder, as an attack upon the innocent. In a sense, indeed, terrorism is worse than rape and murder commonly are, for in the latter cases the victim has been chosen for a purpose; he or she is the direct object of attack, and the attack has some reason, however twisted or ugly it may be. The victims of a terrorist attack are third parties, innocent bystanders; there is no special reason for attacking them; anyone else within a large class of (unrelated) people will do as well. The attack is directed indiscriminately against the entire class. Terrorists are like killers on a rampage, except that their rampage is not just expressive of rage or madness; the rage is purposeful and programmatic. It aims at a general vulnerability: Kill these people in order to terrify those. A relatively small number of dead victims makes for a very large number of living and frightened hostages.

This, then, is the peculiar evil of terrorism—not only the killing of innocent people but also the intrusion of fear into everyday life, the violation of private purposes, the insecurity of public spaces, the endless coerciveness of precaution. A crime wave might, I suppose, produce similar effects, but no one plans a crime wave; it is the work of a thousand individual

From "Terrorism: A Critique of Excuses" by Michael Walzer in *Problems of International Justice*, ed. Steven Luper-Foy (Boulder, CO: Westview Press, 1988), pp. 237–247. Reprinted by permission of the author.

decisionmakers, each one independent of the others, brought together only by the invisible hand. Terrorism is the work of visible hands; it is an organizational project, a strategic choice, a conspiracy to murder and intimidate . . . you and me. No wonder the conspirators have difficulty defending, in public, the strategy they have chosen.

The moral difficulty is the same, obviously, when the conspiracy is directed not against you and me but against *them*—Protestants, say, not Catholics; Israelis, not Italians or Germans; blacks, not whites. These "limits" rarely hold for long; the logic of terrorism steadily expands the range of vulnerability. The more hostages they hold, the stronger the terrorists are. No one is safe once whole populations have been put at risk. Even if the risk were contained, however, the evil would be no different. So far as individual Protestants or Israelis or blacks are concerned, terrorism is random, degrading, and frightening. That is its hallmark, and that, again, is why it cannot be defended.

But when moral justification is ruled out, the way is opened for ideological excuse and apology. We live today in a political culture of excuses. This is far better than a political culture in which terrorism is openly defended and justified, for the excuse at least acknowledges the evil. But the improvement is precarious, hard won, and difficult to sustain. It is not the case, even in this better world, that terrorist organizations are without supporters. The support is indirect but by no means ineffective. It takes the form of apologetic descriptions and explanations, a litany of excuses that steadily undercuts our knowledge of the evil. Today that knowledge is insufficient unless it is supplemented and reinforced by a systematic critique of excuses. That is my purpose [here]. I take the principle for granted: that every act of terrorism is a wrongful act. The wrongfulness of the excuses, however, cannot be taken for granted; it has to be argued. The excuses themselves are familiar enough, the stuff of contemporary political debate. I shall state them in stereotypical form. There is no need to attribute them to this or that writer, publicist, or commentator; my readers can make their own attributions.[1]

THE EXCUSES FOR TERRORISM

The most common excuse for terrorism is that it is a last resort, chosen only when all else fails. The image is of people who have literally run out of options. One by one, they have tried every legitimate form of political and military action, exhausted every possibility, failed everywhere, until no alternative remains but the evil of terrorism. They must be terrorists or do nothing at all. The easy response is to insist that, given this description of their case, they should do nothing at all; they have indeed exhausted their possibilities. But this response simply reaffirms the principle, ignores the excuse; this response does not attend to the terrorists' desperation. Whatever the cause to which they are committed, we have to recognize that, given the commitment, the one thing they cannot do is "nothing at all."

But the case is badly described. It is not so easy to reach the "last resort." To get there, one must indeed try everything (which is a lot of things) and not just once, as if a political party might organize a single demonstration, fail to win immediate victory, and claim that it was now justified in moving on to murder. Politics is an art of repetition. Activists and citizens learn from experience, that is, by doing the same thing over and over again. He is by no means clear when they run out of options, but even under conditions of oppression and war, citizens have a good run short of that. The same argument applies to state officials who claim that they have tried "everything" and are now compelled to kill hostages or bomb peasant villages. Imagine such people called before a judicial tribunal and required to answer the question, What exactly did you try? Does anyone believe that they could come up with a plausible list? "Last resort" has only a notional finality; the resort to terror is ideologically last, not last in an actual series of actions, just last for the sake of the excuse. In fact, most state officials and movements militants who recommend a policy of terrorism recommend it as a first resort; they are for it from the beginning, although they may not get their way at the beginning. If they are honest, then, they must make other excuses and give up the pretense of the last resort.

The second excuse is designed for national liberation movements struggling against established and powerful states. Now the claim is that nothing else is possible, that no other strategy is available except terrorism. This is different from the first excuse because it does not require would-be terrorists to run through all the available options. Or, the second excuse requires terrorist to run through all the options in their heads, not in the world; notional finality is enough. Movement strategists consider their options and conclude that they have no alternative to terrorism. They think that they do not have the political strength to try anything else, and thus they do not try anything else. Weakness is their excuse.

But two very different kinds of weakness are commonly confused here: the weakness of the movement vis-à-vis the opposing state and the movement's weakness vis-à-vis its own people. This second kind of weakness, the inability of the movement to mobilize the nation, makes terrorism the "only" option because it effectively rules out all the others: nonviolent resistance, general strikes, mass demonstrations, unconventional warfare, and so on.

These options are only rarely ruled out by the sheer power of the state, by the pervasiveness and intensity of oppression. Totalitarian states may be immune to nonviolent or guerrilla resistance, but all the evidence suggests that they are also immune to terrorism. Or, more exactly, in totalitarian states state terror dominates every other sort. Where terrorism is a possible strategy for the oppositional movement (in liberal and democratic states, most obviously), other strategies are also possible if the movement has some significant degree of popular support. In the absence of popular support, terrorism may indeed be the one available strategy, but it is hard to see how its evils can then be excused. For it is not weakness alone that makes the excuse, but the claim of the terrorists to represent the weak; and the particular form of weakness that makes terrorism the only option calls that claim into question.

One might avoid this difficulty with a stronger insistence on the actual effectiveness of terrorism. The third excuse is simply that terrorism works (and nothing else does); it achieves the ends of the oppressed even without their participation. "When

the act accuses, the result excuses."[2] This is a consequential argument, and given a strict understanding of consequentialism, this argument amounts to a justification rather than an excuse. In practice, however, the argument is rarely pushed so far. More often, the argument begins with an acknowledgment of the terrorists' wrongdoing. Their hands are dirty, but we must make a kind of peace with them because they have acted effectively for the sake of people who could not act for themselves. But, in fact, have the terrorists' actions been effective? I doubt that terrorism has ever achieved national liberation—no nation that I know of owes its freedom to a campaign of random murder—although terrorism undoubtedly increases the power of the terrorists within the national liberation movement. Perhaps terrorism is also conducive to the survival and notoriety (the two go together) of the movement, which is now dominated by terrorists. But even if we were to grant some means-end relationship between terror and national liberation, the third excuse does not work unless it can meet the further requirements of a consequentialist argument. It must be possible to say that the desired end could not have been achieved through any other, less wrongful, means. The third excuse depends, then, on the success of the first or second, and neither of these look likely to be successful.

The fourth excuse avoids this crippling dependency. This excuse does not require the apologist to defend either of the improbable claims that terrorism is the last resort or that it is the only possible resort. The fourth excuse is simply that terrorism is the universal resort. All politics is (really) terrorism. The appearance of innocence and decency is always a piece of deception, more or less convincing in accordance with the relative power of the deceivers. The terrorist who does not bother with appearances is only doing openly what everyone else does secretly.

This argument has the same form as the maxim "All's fair in love and war." Love is always fraudulent, war is always brutal, and political action is always terrorist in character. Political action works (as Thomas Hobbes long ago argued) only by generating fear in innocent men and women. Terrorism is the politics of state officials and movement militants alike. This argument does not justify either the officials or the militants, but it does excuse them all. We hardly can be harsh with people who act the way everyone else acts. Only saints are likely to act differently, and sainthood in politics is supererogatory, a matter of grace, not obligation.

But this fourth excuse relies too heavily on our cynicism about political life, and cynicism only sometimes answers well to experience. In fact, legitimate states do not need to terrorize their citizens, and strongly based movements do not need to terrorize their opponents. Officials and militants who live, as it were, on the margins of legitimacy and strength sometimes choose terrorism and sometimes do not. Living in terror is not a universal experience. The world the terrorists create has its entrances and exits.

If we want to understand the choice of terror, the choice that forces the rest of us through the door, we have to imagine what in fact always occurs, although we often have no satisfactory record of the occurrence: A group of men arid women, officials or militants, sits around a table and argues about whether or not to adopt a terrorist strategy. Later on, the litany of excuses obscures the argument. But at the time, around the table, it would have been no use for defenders of terrorism to say, "Everybody does it," because there they would be face to face with people proposing to do something else. Nor is it historically the case that the members of this last group, the opponents of terrorism, always lose the argument. They can win, however, and still not be able to prevent a terrorist campaign; the would-be terrorists (it does not take very many) can always split the movement and go their own way. Or, they can split the bureaucracy or the police or officer corps and act in the shadow of state power. Indeed, terrorism often has its origin in such splits. The first victims are the terrorists' former comrades or colleagues. What reason can we possibly have, then, for equating the two? If we value the politics of the men and women who oppose terrorism, we must reject the excuses of their murderers. Cynicism at such a time is unfair to the victims.

The fourth excuse can also take, often does take, a more restricted form. Oppression, rather than political rule more generally, is always terroristic in character, and thus, we must always excuse the opponents of oppression. When they choose terrorism, they are only reacting to someone else's previous choice, repaying in kind the treatment they have long received. Of course, their terrorism repeats the evil—innocent people are killed, who were never themselves oppressors—but repetition is not the same as initiation. The oppressors set the terms of the struggle. But if the struggle is fought on the oppressors' terms, then the oppressors are likely to win. Or, at least, oppression is likely to win, even if it takes on a new face. The whole point of a liberation movement or a popular mobilization is to change the terms. We have no reason to excuse the terrorism reactively adopted by opponents of oppression unless we are confident of the sincerity of their opposition, the seriousness of their commitment to a nonoppressive politics. But the choice of terrorism undermines that confidence.

We are often asked to distinguish the terrorism of the oppressed from the terrorism of the oppressors. What is it, however, that makes the difference? The message of the terrorist is the same in both cases: a denial of the peoplehood and humanity of the groups among whom he or she finds victims. Terrorism anticipates, when it does not actually enforce, political domination. Does it matter if one dominated group is replaced by another? Imagine a slave revolt whose protagonists dream only of enslaving in their turn the children of their masters. The dream is understandable, but the fervent desire of the children that the revolt be repressed is equally understandable. In neither case does understanding make for excuse—not, at least, after a politics of universal freedom has become possible. Nor does an understanding of oppression excuse the terrorism of the oppressed, once we have grasped the meaning of "liberation."

These are the four general excuses for terror, and each of them fails. They depend upon statements about the world that are false, historical arguments for which there is no evidence, moral claims that turn out to be hollow or dishonest. This is not to say that there might not be more particular excuses that have greater plausibility, extenuating circumstances in particular cases that we would feel compelled to recognize. As with murder, we can tell a story (like the story that Richard Wright tells in *Native Son*, for example) that might lead us, not to justify terrorism, but to excuse this or that individual terrorist. We can provide a personal history, a psychological study, of compassion destroyed by fear, moral reason by hatred and rage, social inhibition by unending violence—the product, an individual driven to kill or readily set on a killing course by his or her political leaders.[3] But the force of this story will not depend on any of the four general excuses, all of which grant what the storyteller will have to deny: that terrorism is the deliberate choice of rational men and women. Whether they conceive it to be one option among others or the only one available, they nevertheless argue and choose. Whether they are acting or reacting, they have made a decision. The human instruments they subsequently find to plant the bomb or shoot the gun may act under some psychological compulsion, but the men and women who choose terror as a policy act "freely." They could not act in any other way, or accept any other description of their action, and still pretend to be the leaders of the movement or the state. We ought never to excuse such leaders.

THE RESPONSE TO TERRORISM

What follows from the critique of excuses? There is still a great deal of room for argument about the best way of responding to terrorism. Certainly, terrorists should be resisted, and it is not likely that a purely defensive resistance will ever be sufficient. In this sort of struggle, the offense is always ahead. The technology of terror is simple; the weapons are readily produced and easy to deliver. It is virtually impossible to protect people against random and indiscriminate attack. Thus, resistance will have to be supplemented by some combination of repression and retaliation. This is a dangerous business because repression and retaliation so often take terroristic forms and there are a host of apologists ready with excuses that sound remarkably like those of the terrorists themselves. It should be clear by now, however, that counterterrorism cannot be excused merely because it is reactive. Every new actor, terrorist or counterterrorist, claims to be reacting to someone else, standing in a circle

and just passing the evil along. But the circle is ideological in character; in fact, every actor is a moral agent and makes an independent decision.

Therefore, repression and retaliation must not repeat the wrongs of terrorism, which is to say that repression and retaliation must be aimed systematically at the terrorists themselves, never at the people for whom the terrorists claim to be acting. That claim is in any case doubtful, even when it is honestly made. The people do not authorize the terrorists to act in their name. Only a tiny number actually participate in terrorist activities; they are far more likely to suffer than to benefit from the terrorist program. Even if they supported the program and hoped to benefit from it, however, they would still be immune from attack—exactly as civilians in time of war who support the war effort but are not themselves part of it are subject to the same immunity. Civilians may be put at risk by attacks on military targets, as by attacks on terrorist targets, but the risk must be kept to a minimum, even at some cost to the attackers. The refusal to make ordinary people into targets, whatever their nationality or even their politics, is the only way to say no to terrorism. Every act of repression and retaliation has to be measured by this standard.

But what if the "only way" to defeat the terrorists is to intimidate their actual or potential supporters? It is important to deny the premise of this question: that terrorism is a politics dependent on mass support. In fact, it is always the politics of an elite, whose members are dedicated and fanatical and more than ready to endure, or to watch others endure, the devastations of a counterterrorist campaign. Indeed, terrorists will welcome counterterrorism; it makes the terrorists' excuses more plausible and is sure to bring them, however many people are killed or wounded, however many are terrorized, the small number of recruits needed to sustain the terrorist activities.

Repression and retaliation are legitimate responses to terrorism only when they are constrained by the same moral principles that rule out terrorism itself. But there is an alternative response that seeks to avoid the violence that these two entail. The alternative is to address directly, ourselves, the oppression the terrorists claim to oppose. Oppression, they say, is the cause of terrorism. But that is merely one more excuse. The real cause of terrorism is the decision to launch a terrorist campaign, a decision made by that group of people sitting around a table whose deliberations I have already described. However, terrorists do exploit oppression, injustice, and human misery generally and look to these at least for their excuses. There can hardly be any doubt that oppression strengthens their hand. Is that a reason for us to come to the defense of the oppressed? It seems to me that we have our own reasons to do that, and do not need this one, or should not, to prod us into action. We might imitate those movement militants who argue against the adoption of a terrorist strategy—although not, as the terrorists say, because these militants are prepared to tolerate oppression. They already are opposed to oppression and now add to that opposition, perhaps for the same reasons, a refusal of terror. So should we have been opposed before, and we should now make the same addition.

But there is an argument, put with some insistence these days, that we should refuse to acknowledge any link at all between terrorism and oppression—as if any defense of oppressed men and women, once a terrorist campaign has been launched, would concede the effectiveness of the campaign. Or, at least, a defense of oppression would give terrorism the appearance of effectiveness and so increase the likelihood of terrorist campaigns in the future. Here we have the reverse side of the litany of excuses; we have turned over the record. First oppression is made into an excuse for terrorism, and then terrorism is made into an excuse for oppression. The first is the excuse of the far left; the second is the excuse of the neo-conservative right.[4] I doubt that genuine conservatives would think it a good reason for defending the status quo that it is under terrorist attack; they would have independent reasons and would be prepared to defend the status quo against any attack. Similarly, those of us who think that the status quo urgently requires change have our own reasons for thinking so and need not be intimidated by terrorists or, for that matter, antiterrorists.

If one criticizes the first excuse, one should not neglect the second. But I need to state the second more

precisely. It is not so much an excuse for oppression as an excuse for doing nothing (now) about oppression. The claim is that the campaign against terrorism has priority over every other political activity. If the people who take the lead in this campaign are the old oppressors, then we must make a kind of peace with them—temporarily, of course, until the terrorists have been beaten. This is a strategy that denies the possibility of a two-front war. So long as the men and women who pretend to lead the fight against oppression are terrorists, we can concede nothing to their demands. Nor can we oppose their opponents.

But why not? It is not likely in any case that terrorists would claim victory in the face of a serious effort to deal with the oppression of the people they claim to be defending. The effort would merely expose the hollowness of their claim, and the nearer it came to success, the more they would escalate their terrorism. They would still have to be defeated, for what they are after is not a solution to the problem but rather the power to impose their own solution. No decent end to the conflict in Ireland, say, or in Lebanon, or in the Middle East generally, is going to look like a victory for terrorism—if only because the different groups of terrorists are each committed, by the strategy they have adopted, to an indecent end.[5] By working for our own ends, we expose the indecency.

OPPRESSION AND TERRORISM

It is worth considering at greater length the link between oppression and terror. To pretend that there is no link at all is to ignore the historical record, but the record is more complex than any of the excuses acknowledge. The first thing to be read out of it, however, is simple enough: Oppression is not so much the cause of terrorism as terrorism is one of the primary means of oppression. This was true in ancient times, as Aristotle recognized, and it is still true today. Tyrants rule by terrorizing their subjects; unjust and illegitimate regimes are upheld through a combination of carefully aimed and random violence.[6] If this method works in the state, there is no reason to think that it will not work, or that it does not work, in the liberation movement. Wherever we see terrorism, we should look for tyranny and oppression. Authoritarian states, especially in the moment of their founding, need a terrorist apparatus—secret police with unlimited power, secret prisons into which citizens disappear, death squads in unmarked cars. Even democracies may use terror, not against their own citizens, but at the margins, in their colonies, for example, where colonizers also are likely to rule tyrannically. Oppression is sometimes maintained by a steady and discriminate pressure, sometimes by intermittent and random violence—what we might think of as terrorist melodrama—designed to render the subject population fearful and passive.

This latter policy, especially if it seems successful, invites imitation by opponents of the state. But terrorism does not spread only when it is imitated. If it can be invented by state officials, it can also be invented by movement militants. Neither one need take lessons from the other; the circle has no single or necessary starting point. Wherever it starts, terrorism in the movement is tyrannical and oppressive in exactly the same way as is terrorism in the state. The terrorists aim to rule, and murder is their method. They have their own internal police, death squads, disappearances. They begin by killing or intimidating those comrades who stand in their way, and they proceed to do the same, if they can, among the people they claim to represent. If terrorists are successful, they rule tyrannically, and their people bear, without consent, the costs of the terrorists' rule. (If the terrorists are only partly successful, the costs to the people may be even greater: What they have to bear now is a war between rival terrorist gangs.) But terrorists cannot win the ultimate victory they seek without challenging the established regime or colonial power and the people it claims to represent, and when terrorists do that, they themselves invite imitation. The regime may then respond with its own campaign of aimed and random violence. Terrorist tracks terrorist, each claiming the other as an excuse.

The same violence can also spread to countries where it has not yet been experienced; now terror is reproduced not through temporal succession but

through ideological adaptation. State terrorists wage bloody wars against largely imaginary enemies: army colonels, say, hunting down the representatives of "international communism." Or movement terrorists wage bloody wars against enemies with whom, but for the ideology, they could readily negotiate and compromise: nationalist fanatics committed to a permanent irredentism. These wars, even if they are without precedents, are likely enough to become precedents, to start the circle of terror and counterterror, which is endlessly oppressive for the ordinary men and women whom the state calls its citizens and the movement its "people."

The only way to break out of the circle is to refuse to play the terrorist game. Terrorists in the state and the movement warn us, with equal vehemence, that any such refusal is a sign of softness and naiveté. The self-portrait of the terrorists is always the same. They are tough-minded and realistic; they know their enemies (or privately invent them for ideological purposes); and they are ready to do what must be done for victory. Why then do terrorists turn around and around in the same circle? It is true: Movement terrorists win support because they pretend to deal energetically and effectively with the brutality of the state. It also is true: State terrorists win support because they pretend to deal energetically and effectively with the brutality of the movement. Both feed on the fears of brutalized and oppressed people. But there is no way of overcoming brutality with terror. At most, the burden is shifted from these people to those; more likely, new burdens are added for everyone. Genuine liberation can come only through a politics that mobilizes the victims of brutality and takes careful aim at its agents, or by a politics that surrenders the hope of victory and domination and deliberately seeks a compromise settlement. In either case, once tyranny is repudiated, terrorism is no longer an option. For what lies behind all the excuses, of officials and militants alike, is the predilection for a tyrannical politics.

NOTES

1. I cannot resist a few examples: Edward Said, "The Terrorism Scam," *The Nation*, June 14, 1986; and (more

intelligent and circumspect) Richard Falk, "Thinking About Terrorism," *The Nation,* June 28, 1986.

2. Machiavelli, *The Discourses* I:ix. As yet, however, there have been no results that would constitute a Machiavellian excuse.

3. See, for example, Daniel Goleman, "The Roots of Terrorism Are Found in Brutality of Shattered Childhood," *New York Times,* September 2, 1986, pp. C1, 8. Goleman discusses the psychic and social history of particular terrorists, not the roots of terrorism.

4. The neoconservative position is represented, although not as explicitly as I have stated it here, in

Benjamin Netanyahu, ed., *Terrorism: How the West Can Win* (New York: Farrar, Straus & Giroux, 1986).

5. The reason the terrorist strategy, however indecent in itself, cannot be instrumental to some decent political purpose is because any decent purpose must somehow accommodate the people against whom the terrorism is aimed, and what terrorism expresses is precisely the refusal of such an accommodation, the radical devaluing of the Other. See my argument in *Just and Unjust Wars* (New York: Basic Books, 1977), pp. 197–206, especially 203.

6. Aristotle, *The Politics* 1313–1314a.

READING QUESTIONS

1. Walzer examines excuses for terrorism while granting that terrorism cannot be morally justified. What is the distinction between a justification and an excuse?
2. Why does Walzer think that the third excuse depends on the success of the first or second?
3. What is the significance of Walzer's claim that an act of terror is a deliberate, free, and rational choice of a moral agent?
4. Why does Walzer think that the last-resort excuse is a pretense for both state officials and movement militants who recommend a policy of terrorism?

DISCUSSION QUESTIONS

1. Walzer's article was written prior to the 9/11 attacks. Do you think his critique of excuses is applicable to the type of terrorists involved in the 9/11 attacks? Why or why not?
2. Discuss the reasons one might give for claiming that all politics is a form of terrorism. Should terrorism be excused because terrorists are doing nothing different than what state officials sometimes do? Why or why not?
3. Do you agree with Walzer that the proper response to terrorism is to refuse to play the terrorists' game? Why or why not? If you agree, what alternative action do you propose? If you disagree, do you think counterterrorism can be morally justified or excused?

Andrew Valls

Can Terrorism Be Justified?

After defining "terrorism" so that by definition not all instances are necessarily morally wrong, Andrew Valls argues that "if just war theory can justify violence committed by states, then terrorism committed by nonstate actors can also, under certain circumstances, be justified by it as well." In defending this claim, Valls considers each of the provisions of just-war theory, with particular attention given to the provisions of just cause, legitimate authority, and discrimination.

Recommended Reading: the discussion of just-war theory in the introduction to this chapter.

[J]ust war theory, despite its ambiguities, provides a rich framework with which to assess the morality of war. But interstate war is only the most conventional form of political violence. The question arises, Is it the only form of political violence that may ever he justified? If not, how are we to assess the morality of other cases of political violence, particularly those involving nonstate actors? In short, does just war theory apply to terrorism, and, if so, can terrorism satisfy its criteria?

In the public and scholarly reactions to political violence, a double standard often is at work. When violence is committed by states, our assessment tends to be quite permissive, giving states a great benefit of the doubt about the propriety of their violent acts. However, when the violence is committed by nonstate actors, we often react with horror, and the condemnations cannot come fast enough. Hence, terrorism is almost universally condemned, whereas violence by states, even when war has not been declared, is seen as legitimate, if not always fully justified. This difference in assessments remains when innocent civilians

are killed in both cases and sometimes when such killing is deliberate. Even as thoughtful a commentator as Michael Walzer, for example, seems to employ this double standard. In his *Just and Unjust Wars*, Walzer considers whether "soldiers and statesmen [can] override the rights of innocent people for the sake of their own political community" and answers "affirmatively, though not without hesitation and worry" (1992, 254). Walzer goes on to discuss a case in point, the Allied bombing of German cities during World War II, arguing that, despite the many civilians who deliberately were killed, the bombing was justified. However, later in the book, Walzer rejects out of hand the possibility that terrorism might sometimes be justified, on the grounds that it involves the deliberate killing of innocents (1992, chapter 12). He never considers the possibility that stateless communities might confront the same "supreme emergency" that justified, in his view, the bombing of innocent German civilians. I will have more to say about Walzer's position below, but for now I wish to point out that, on the face of it at least, his position seems quite inconsistent.

From: "Can Terrorism Be Justified?" by Andrew Valls in *Ethics in International Affairs*, ed. A. Valls (Lanham, MD: Rowman and Littlefield), pp. 65–79.

From a philosophical point of view, this double standard cannot be sustained. As Coady (1985) argues, consistency requires that we apply the same standards to both kinds of political violence, state and nonstate. Of course, it may turn out that there are simply some criteria that states can satisfy that nonstate actors cannot, so that the same standard applied to both inevitably leads to different conclusions. There may be morally relevant features of states that make their use of violence legitimate and its use by others illegitimate. However, I will argue that this is not the case. I argue that, on the most plausible account of just war theory, taking into account the ultimate moral basis of its criteria, violence undertaken by nonstate actors can, in principle, satisfy the requirements of a just war.

To advance this view, I examine each criterion of just war theory in turn, arguing in each case that terrorism committed by nonstate actors can satisfy the criterion. The most controversial parts of my argument will no doubt be those regarding just cause, legitimate authority, and discrimination, so I devote more attention to these than to the others. I argue that, once we properly understand the moral basis for each of these criteria, it is clear that some nonstate groups may have the same right as states to commit violence and that they are just as capable of committing that violence within the constraints imposed by just war theory. My conclusion, then, is that if just war theory can justify violence committed by states, then terrorism committed by nonstate actors can also, under certain circumstances, be justified by it as well. But before commencing the substantive argument, I must attend to some preliminary matters concerning the definition of *terrorism*.

DEFINITIONAL ISSUES

There is little agreement on the question of how *terrorism* is best defined. In the political arena, of course, the word is used by political actors for political purposes, usually to paint their opponents as monsters. Scholars, on the other hand, have at least attempted to arrive at a more detached position, seeking a definition that captures the essence of terrorism. However, there is reason, in addition to the lack of consensus, to doubt whether much progress has been made.

Most definitions of terrorism suffer from at least one of two difficulties. First, they often define terrorism as murder or otherwise characterize it as intrinsically wrong and unjustifiable. The trouble with this approach is that it prejudges the substantive moral issue by a definitional consideration. I agree with Teichman, who writes that "we ought not to begin by *defining* terrorism as a bad thing" (1989, 507). Moral conclusions should follow from moral reasoning, grappling with the moral issues themselves. To decide a normative issue by definitional considerations, then, ends the discussion before it begins.

The second shortcoming that many definitions of terrorism exhibit is being too revisionist of its meaning in ordinary language. As I have noted, the word is often used as a political weapon, so ordinary language will not settle the issue. Teichman (1989, 505) again is correct that any definition will necessarily be stipulative to some extent. But ordinary language does, nevertheless, impose some constraints on the stipulative definition that we can accept. For example, Carl Wellman defines *terrorism* as "the use or attempted use of terror as a means of coercion" (1979, 251) and draws the conclusion that when he instills terror in his students with threats of grade penalties on late papers, he commits terrorism. Clearly this is not what most of us have in mind when we speak of terrorism, so Wellman's definition, even if taken as stipulative, is difficult to accept.

Some definitions of terrorism suffer from both of these shortcomings to some degree. For example, those that maintain that terrorism is necessarily random or indiscriminate seem both to depart markedly from ordinary usage—there are lots of acts we call terrorist that specifically target military facilities and personnel—and thereby to prejudice the moral issue. (I will argue below that terrorism need not be indiscriminate at all.) The same can be said of definitions that insist that the aim of terrorism must be to terrorize, that it targets some to threaten many more. . . . As Virginia Held has argued, "We should probably not construe either the intention to spread fear or the intention to kill noncombatants as necessary for an act of political violence to be an act of terrorism" (1991, 64). Annette Baier adds that "the terrorist may be ill named" because what she sometimes wants is not to terrorize but "the shocked attention of her audience population" (1994, 205).

With all of this disagreement, it would perhaps be desirable to avoid the use of the term *terrorism* altogether and simply to speak instead of political violence. I would be sympathetic to this position were it not for the fact that *terrorism* is already too much a part of our political vocabulary to be avoided. Still, we can with great plausibility simply define *terrorism* as a form of political violence, as Held does: "I [see] terrorism as a form of violence to achieve political goals, where creating fear is usually high among the intended effects" (1991, 64). This is a promising approach, though I would drop as nonessential the stipulation that terrorism is usually intended to spread fear. In addition, I would make two stipulations of my own. First, "violence" can include damage to property as well as harm to people. Blowing up a power plant can surely be an act of terrorism, even if no one is injured. Second, for the purposes of this chapter, I am interested in violence committed by nonstate actors. I do not thereby deny the existence of state terrorism. . . . However, for the purposes of my present argument, I assume that when a state commits terrorism against its own citizens, this is a matter for domestic justice, and that when it commits violence outside of its own borders, just war theory can, fairly easily, be extended to cover these cases. The problem for international ethics that I wish to address here is whether just war theory can be extended to nonstate actors. So my stipulative definition of *terrorism* in this chapter is simply that it is violence committed by nonstate actors against persons or property for political purposes. This definition appears to leave open the normative issues involved and to be reasonably consistent with ordinary language.

JUS AD BELLUM

It is somewhat misleading to speak of just war *theory,* for it is not a single theory but, rather, a tradition within which there is a range of interpretation. That is, just war theory is best thought of as providing a framework for discussion about whether a war is just, rather than as providing a set of unambiguous criteria that are easily applied. In what follows I rely on what I believe is the most plausible and normatively appealing version of just war theory, one that is essentially the same as the one articulated and developed by the preceding chapters. I begin with the *jus ad bellum* criteria, concerning the justice of going to war, and then turn to *jus in bello* criteria, which apply to the conduct of the war.

Just Cause

A just cause for a war is usually a defensive one. That is, a state is taken to have a just cause when it defends itself against aggression, where *aggression* means the violation or the imminent threat of the violation of its territorial integrity or political independence (Walzer 1992). So the just cause provision of just war theory holds, roughly, that the state has a right to defend itself against the aggression of other states.

But on what is this right of the state based? Most students of international ethics maintain that any right that a state enjoys is ultimately based on the rights of its citizens. States in and of themselves have value only to the extent that they serve some good for the latter. The moral status of the state is therefore derivative, not foundational, and it is derivative of the rights of the individuals within it. This, it seems, is the dominant (liberal) view, and only an exceedingly statist perspective would dispute it (Beitz 1979; Walzer 1992).

The right that is usually cited as being the ground for the state's right to defend itself is the right of self-determination. The state is the manifestation of, as well as the arena for, the right of a people to determine itself. It is because aggression threatens the common life of the people within a state, as well as threatening other goods they hold dear, that the state can defend its territory and independence. This is clear, for example, from Walzer's (1992, chapter 6) discussion of intervention. Drawing on John Stuart Mill (1984), Walzer argues that states generally ought not to intervene in the affairs of other states because to do so would be to violate the right of self-determination of the community within the state. However, once the right of self-determination is recognized, its implications go beyond a right against intervention or a right of defense. Walzer makes this clear as well, as his discussion of Mill's argument for nonintervention is followed immediately by exceptions to the rule, one of which is secession. When a secessionist movement has demonstrated that it represents the will of its people, other states may intervene to aid the secession because, in this case, secession reflects the self-determination of that people.

In the twenty years since Walzer presented this argument, a great deal of work has been done on nationalism, self-determination, and secession. Despite the range of views that has developed, it is fair to say that something of an overlapping consensus has formed, namely, that under certain circumstances, certain kinds of groups enjoy a right of self-determination that entitles them to their own state or at least to some autonomy in a federal arrangement within an existing state. The debate is mostly over what these circumstances are and what kinds of groups enjoy the right. For example, Allen Buchanan, in his important book *Secession* (1991), argues that the circumstances must include a historical injustice before a group is entitled to secede. Others are more permissive. Christopher Wellman (1995) and Daniel Philpott (1995) argue that past injustice is not required to entitle a group to secession and, indeed, that any group within a territory may secede, even if it is not plausibly seen as constituting a nation.

The modal position in the debate is, perhaps, somewhere between these positions, holding that certain groups, even absent a history of injustice, have a right to self-determination but that this applies not to just any group but only to "peoples" or "nations." This is essentially the position taken by Kymlicka (1995), Tamir (1993), Miller (1995), and Margalit and Raz (1990). There are, of course, important differences among these authors. Kymlicka argues that groups with "societal cultures" have a right to self-government but not necessarily secession. Margalit and Raz advance a similar argument, and their notion of an "encompassing group" is very close to Kymlicka's

"societal culture." Tamir emphasizes that, in her view, the right to self-determination is a cultural right, not a political one, and does not necessarily support a right to political independence. Miller does interpret the right of self-determination as a right to a state, but he hesitates to call it a right, for it may not always be achievable due to the legitimate claims of others. (His concern would perhaps be alleviated by following Philpott in speaking of a "prima facie" right.)

For the purposes of my present argument, I need not enter this important debate but only point out that any one of these views can support the weak claim I wish to make. The claim is that under some circumstances, some groups enjoy a right to self-determination. The circumstances may include—or, following Buchanan, even be limited to—cases of injustice toward the group, or, in a more permissive view, it may not. This right may be enjoyed only by nations or by any group within a territory. It may be that the right of self-determination does not automatically ground a right to political independence, but if some form of self-determination cannot be realized within an existing state, then it can, under these circumstances, ground such a right. For the sake of simplicity, in the discussion that follows I refer to nations or peoples as having a right of self-determination, but this does not commit me to the view that other kinds of groups do not enjoy this right. Similarly, I will sometimes fail to distinguish between a right of self-determination and a right to a state, despite realizing that the former does not necessarily entail the latter. I will assume that in some cases—say, when a federal arrangement cannot be worked out—one can ground the right to a state on the right to self-determination.

My conclusion about the just cause requirement is obvious. Groups other than those constituted by the state in which they live can have a just cause to defend their right of self-determination. While just war theory relies on the rights of the citizens to ground the right of a state to defend itself, other communities within a state may have that same right. When the communal life of a nation is seriously threatened by a state, that nation has a just cause to defend itself. In the case in which the whole nation is within a single state, this can justify secession. In a case in which the community is stateless, as with colonial rule, it is probably less accurate to speak of secession than national liberation.

This is not a radical conclusion. Indeed, it is recognized and endorsed by the United Nations, as Khatchadourian points out: "The UN definition of 'just cause' recognizes the rights of peoples as well as states," and in Article 7 of the definition of *aggression*, the United Nations refers to "the right to self-determination, freedom, and independence, as derived from the Charter, of *peoples* forcibly deprived of that right" (1998, 41). So both morally and legally, "peoples" or "nations" enjoy a right to self-determination. When that right is frustrated, such peoples, I have argued, have the same just cause that states have when the self-determination of their citizens is threatened.

Legitimate Authority

The legitimate authority requirement is usually interpreted to mean that only states can go to war justly. It rules out private groups waging private wars and claiming them to be just. The state has a monopoly on the legitimate use of force, so it is a necessary condition for a just war that it be undertaken by the entity that is uniquely authorized to wield the sword. To allow other entities, groups, or agencies to undertake violence would be to invite chaos. Such violence is seen as merely private violence, crime.

The equation of legitimate authority with states has, however, been criticized by a number of philosophers—and with good reason. Gilbert has argued that "the equation of proper authority with a lawful claim to it should be resisted" (1994, 29). Tony Coates (1997, chapter 5) has argued at some length and quite persuasively that to equate legitimate authority with state sovereignty is to rob the requirement of the moral force that it historically has had. The result is that the principle has become too permissive by assuming that any de facto state may wage war. This requirement, then, is too easily and quickly "checked off": If a war is waged by a state, this requirement is satisfied. This interpretation has meant that "the criterion of legitimate authority has become the most neglected of all the criteria that have been traditionally

employed in the moral assessment of war" (Coates 1997, 123). Contrary to this tendency in recent just war thinking, Coates argues that we must subject to close scrutiny a given state's claim to represent the interests and rights of its people.

When we reject the view that all states are legitimate authorities, we may also ask if some nonstates may be legitimate authorities. The considerations just adduced suggest that being a state is not sufficient for being a legitimate authority. Perhaps it is not necessary either. What matters is the plausibility of the claim to represent the interests and rights of a people. I would like to argue that some non-state entities or organizations may present a very plausible case for being a people's representative. Surely it is sufficient for this that the organization is widely seen as their representative by the members of the nation itself. If an organization claims to act on behalf of a people and is widely seen by that people as legitimately doing so, then the rest of us should look on that organization as the legitimate authority of the people for the purposes of assessing its entitlement to engage in violence on their behalf.

The alternative view, that only states may be legitimate authorities, "leads to political quietism [and is] conservative and uncritical" (Coates 1997, 128). Once we acknowledge that stateless peoples may have the right to self-determination, it would render that right otiose to deny that the right could be defended and vindicated by some nonstate entity. As Dugard (1982, 83) has pointed out, in the case of colonial domination, there is no victim state, though there is a victim people. If we are to grant that a colonized people has a right to self-determination, it seems that we must grant that a nonstate organization—a would-be state, perhaps—can act as a legitimate authority and justly engage in violence on behalf of the people. Examples are not difficult to find. Coates cites the Kurds and the Marsh Arabs in Iraq and asks, "Must such persecuted communities be denied the right of collective self-defense simply because, through some historical accident, they lack the formal character of states?" (1997, 128).

It must be emphasized that the position advocated here requires that the organization not only claim representative status but be perceived to enjoy that status by the people it claims to represent. This is a rather conservative requirement because it rules out "vanguard" organizations that claim representative status despite lack of support among the people themselves. The position defended here is also more stringent than that suggested by Wilkins, who writes that it might "be enough for a terrorist movement simply to claim to represent the aspirations or the moral rights of a people" (1992, 71). While I agree that "moral authority may be all that matters" (Wilkins 1992, 72), I would argue that moral authority requires not merely claiming to represent a people but also being seen by the people themselves as their representative.

How do we know whether this is the case? No single answer can be given here. Certainly the standard should not be higher than that used for states. In the case of states, for example, elections are not required for legitimacy, as understood in just war theory. There are many members of the international community in good standing that are not democratic regimes, authorized by elections. In the case of nonstate entities, no doubt a number of factors will weigh in, either for or against the claim to representativeness, and, in the absence of legal procedures (or public opinion polls), we may have to make an all-things-considered judgment. No doubt there will be some disagreement in particular cases, but all that is required for the present argument is that, in principle, nonstate organizations may enjoy the moral status of legitimate authorities.

Right Intention

If a national group can have a just cause, and if a non-state entity can be a legitimate authority to engage in violence on behalf of that group, it seems unproblematic that those engaging in violence can be rightly motivated by that just cause. Hence, if just cause and legitimate authority can be satisfied, there seems to be no reason to think that the requirement of right intention cannot be satisfied. This is not to say, of course, that if the first two are satisfied, the latter is as well, but only that if the first two requirements are met, the latter can be. All that it requires is that the relevant actors be motivated by the just cause and not some other end.

Last Resort

Can terrorist violence, undertaken by the representatives of a stateless nation to vindicate their right of self-determination, be a last resort? Some have doubted that it can. For example, Walzer refers to the claim of last resort as one of the "excuses" sometimes offered for terrorism. He suggests that terrorism is usually a first resort, not a last one, and that to truly be a last resort, "one must indeed try everything (which is a lot of things), and not just once. . . . Politics is an art of repetition" (1988, 239). Terrorists, according to Walzer, often claim that their resort to violence is a last resort but in fact it never is and never can be.

Two problems arise concerning Walzer's position. First, related to the definitional issues discussed above and taken up again below when discrimination is treated, Walzer takes terrorism to be "an attack upon the innocent," and he "take[s] the principle for granted: that every act of terrorism is a wrongful act" (1988, 238). Given the understanding of terrorism as murder, it can never be a justified last resort. But as Fullinwider (1988) argues in his response to Walzer, it is puzzling both that Walzer construes terrorism this way, for not all terrorism is random murder, and that Walzer simply takes it for granted that nothing can justify terrorism. Walzer's position is undermined by a prejudicial definition of *terrorism* that begs the substantive moral questions, reflected in the fact that he characterizes arguments in defense of terrorism as mere "excuses."

The second problem is that again Walzer appears to use a double standard. While he does not say so explicitly in the paper under discussion, Walzer elsewhere clearly endorses the resort to war by states. Here, however, he argues that, because "politics is an art of repetition," the last resort is never arrived at for nonstate actors contemplating violence. But why is it that the territorial integrity and political independence of, say, Britain, justify the resort to violence—even violence that targets civilians—but the right of self-determination of a stateless nation never does? Why can states arrive at last resort, while stateless nations cannot? Walzer never provides an answer to this question.

The fact is that judgment is called for by all political actors contemplating violence, and among the judgments that must be made is whether last resort has been. This is a judgment about whether all reasonable nonviolent measures have been tried, been tried a reasonable number of times, and been given a reasonable amount of time to work. There will always be room for argument about what *reasonable* means here, what it requires in a particular case, but I see no justification for employing a double standard for what it means, one for states, another for nonstate actors. If states may reach the point of deciding that all nonviolent measures have failed, then so too can nonstate actors.

Probability of Success

Whether terrorism ever has any probability of success, or enough probability of success to justify embarking on a terrorist campaign, depends on a number of factors, including the time horizon one has in mind. Whether one considers the case of state actors deciding to embark on a war or nonstate actors embarking on terrorism, a prospective judgment is required, and prospective judgments are liable to miscalculations and incorrect estimations of many factors. Still, one must make a judgment, and if one judges that the end has little chance of being achieved through violence, the probability of success criterion requires that the violence not be commenced.

Does terrorism ever have any probability of success? There are differing views of the historical record on this question. For example, Walzer thinks not. He writes, "No nation that I know of owes its freedom to a campaign of random murder" (1988, 240). Again, we find that Walzer's analysis is hindered by his conception of what terrorism is, and so it is of little help to us here. To those who have a less loaded notion of terrorism, the evidence appears more ambiguous. Held provides a brief, well-balanced discussion of the issue. She cites authors who have argued on both sides of the question, including one who uses the bombing of the U.S. Marines' barracks in Beirut in 1982 (which prompted an American withdrawal) as an example of a successful terrorist attack. Held concludes that "it may be impossible to predict whether an act of terrorism will in fact have its intended effect" but notes that in this it is no different from other prospective judgments (1991, 71). Similarly, Teichman concludes that

the historical evidence on the effectiveness of terrorism is "both ambiguous and incomplete" (1989, 517). And Baier suggests that, at the least, "the prospects for the success of a cause do not seem in the past to have been reduced by resort to unauthorized force, by violent demonstrations that cost some innocent lives" (1994, 208). Finally, Wilkins (1992, 39) believes that some terrorist campaigns have indeed accomplished their goal of national independence and cites Algeria and Kenya as examples.

I am not in a position to judge all of the historical evidence that may be relevant to this issue. However, it seems clear that we cannot say that it is never the case that terrorism has some prospect of success. Perhaps in most cases—the vast majority of them, even—there is little hope of success. Still, we cannot rule out that terrorism can satisfy the probability of success criterion.

Proportionality

The proportionality criterion within *jus ad bellum* also requires a prospective judgment—whether the overall costs of the violent conflict will be outweighed by the overall benefits. In addition to the difficulties inherent in prospective judgments, this criterion is problematic in that it seems to require us to measure the value of costs and benefits that may not be amenable to measurement and seems to assume that all goods are commensurable, that their value can be compared. As a result, there is probably no way to make these kinds of judgments with any great degree of precision.

Still, it seems clear that terrorism can satisfy this criterion at least as well as conventional war. Given the large scale of destruction that often characterizes modern warfare, and given that some very destructive wars are almost universally considered just, it appears that just war theory can countenance a great deal of violence if the end is of sufficient value. If modem warfare is sometimes justified, terrorism, in which the violence is usually on a far smaller scale, can be justified as well. This is especially clear if the end of the violence is the same or similar in both cases, such as when a nation wishes to vindicate its right to self-determination.

JUS IN BELLO

Even if terrorism can meet all the criteria of *jus ad bellum,* it may not be able to meet those of *jus in bello,* for terrorism is often condemned, not so much for who carries it out and why but for how it is carried out. Arguing that it can satisfy the requirements of *jus in bello,* then, may be the greatest challenge facing my argument.

Proportionality

The challenge, however, does not come from the proportionality requirement of *jus in bello.* Like its counterpart in *jus ad bellum,* the criterion requires proportionality between the costs of an action and the benefits to be achieved, but now the requirement is applied to particular acts within the war. It forbids, then, conducting the war in such a way that it involves inordinate costs, costs that are disproportionate to the gains.

Again, there seems to be no reason to believe that terrorist acts could not satisfy this requirement. Given that the scale of the death and destruction usually involved in terrorist acts pales in comparison with that involved in wars commonly thought to be just, it would seem that terrorism would satisfy this requirement more easily than war (assuming that the goods to be achieved are not dissimilar). So if the means of terrorism is what places it beyond the moral pale for many people, it is probably not because of its disproportionality.

Discrimination

The principle of discrimination holds that in waging a war we must distinguish between legitimate and illegitimate targets of attack. The usual way of making this distinction is to classify persons according to their status as combatants and noncombatants and to maintain that only combatants may be attacked. However, there is some disagreement as to the moral basis of this distinction, which creates disagreement as to where exactly this line should be drawn. While usually based on the notion of moral innocence, noncombatant status, it can

be argued, has little to do with innocence, for often combatants are conscripts, while those truly responsible for aggression are usually not liable (practically, not morally) to attack. Moreover, many who provide essential support to the war effort are not combatants.

For the moment, though, let us accept the conventional view that discrimination requires that violence be directed at military targets. Assuming the line can be clearly drawn, two points can be made about terrorism and discrimination. The first is that, a priori, it is possible for terrorism to discriminate and still be terrorism. This follows from the argument presented above that, as a matter of definition, it is implausible to define terrorism as intrinsically indiscriminate. Those who define terrorism as random or indiscriminate will disagree and maintain that "discriminate terrorism" is an oxymoron, a conceptual impossibility. Here I can only repeat that this position departs substantially from ordinary language and does so in a way that prejudges the moral issues involved. However, if my argument above does not convince on this question, there is little more to be said here.

Luckily, the issue is not a purely a priori one. The fact is that terrorists, or at least those called terrorists by almost everyone, in fact do often discriminate. One example, cited above, is the bombing of the barracks in Beirut, which killed some 240 American soldiers. Whatever one wants to say to condemn the attack, one cannot say that it was indiscriminate. Fullinwider cites the example of the kidnapping, trail, and killing of Aldo Moro by the Italian Red Brigades in 1978 and argues that, whatever else one might want to say about it, "there was nothing indiscriminate about the taking of Aldo Moro" (1988, 250). Coady (1985, 63) cites another example, that of an American diplomat in Uruguay who was targeted and killed in 1970 because of the assistance he was providing to the authoritarian regime. These may be the exceptions rather than the rule, but it clearly is not accurate to say that terrorists—and there was never any doubt that these were acts of terrorism—never discriminate.

It might be useful to look, one last time, at Walzer's position on this issue because, from the point of view I have developed, he errs on both the conceptual and the empirical question. Walzer maintains that "terrorism in the strict sense, the random murder of innocent people, emerged . . . only in the period after World War II" (1992, 198). Previously, non-state actors, especially revolutionaries, who committed violence did discriminate. Walzer gives several examples of this in which Russian revolutionaries, the Irish Republican Army, and the Stern Gang in the Middle East went to great lengths to not kill civilians. He also notes that these people were called terrorists. Yet he refuses to say that they *were* terrorists, insisting instead that they were not, really, and using scare quotes when he himself calls them terrorists. This is tortured analysis indeed. Why not simply acknowledge that these earlier terrorists were indeed terrorists while also maintaining, if evidence supports it, that today more terrorists are more indiscriminate than in the past? I suspect that Walzer and I would agree in our moral assessment of particular acts. Our main difference is that he believes that calling an act terrorism (without the scare quotes) settles the question.

All of this is consistent with the assumption that a clear line can be drawn between combatants and noncombatants. However, the more reasonable view may be that combatancy status, and therefore liability to attack, are matters of degree. This is suggested by Holmes (1989, 187), and though Holmes writes as a pacifist critic of just war theory, his suggestion is one that just war theorists may nevertheless want to endorse. Holmes conceives of a spectrum along which we can place classes of individuals, according to their degree of responsibility for an aggressive war. At one end he would place political leaders who undertake the aggression, followed by soldiers, contributors to the war, supporters, and, finally, at the other end of the spectrum, noncontributors and nonsupporters. This view does indeed better capture our moral intuitions about liability to attack and avoids debates (which are probably not resolvable) about where the absolute line between combatants and noncombatants is to be drawn.

If correct, this view further complicates the question of whether and when terrorism discriminates. It means we must speak of more and less discriminate violence, and it forces us to ask questions like, To what *extent* were the targets of violence implicated in unjust aggression? Children, for example,

would be clearly off-limits, but nonmilitary adults who actively take part in frustrating a people's right to self-determination may not be. With terrorism, as with war, the question to ask may not be, Was the act discriminate, yes or no? but, rather, How discriminate was the violence? Our judgment on this matter, and hence our moral appraisal of the violence, is likely to be more nuanced if we ask the latter question than if we assume that a simple yes or no settles the matter. After all, is our judgment really the same—and ought it be—when a school bus is attacked as when gun-toting citizens are attacked? Terrorism, it seems, can be more discriminate or less so, and our judgments ought to reflect the important matters of degree involved.

One final issue is worth mentioning, if only briefly. Even if one were to grant that terrorism necessarily involves the killing of innocents, this alone does not place it beyond the scope of just war theory, for innocents may be killed in a just war. All that just war theory requires is that innocents not be *targeted*. The basis for this position is the principle of double effect, which holds, roughly, that innocents may be killed as long as their deaths are not the intended effects of violence but, rather, the unintended (though perhaps fully foreseen) side effects of violence. So the most that can be said against my position, even granting that terrorism involves the killing of innocents, is that the difference between (just) war and terrorism is that in the former innocents are not targeted but (routinely) killed while in the latter they are targeted and killed. Whether this is a crucial distinction is a question that would require us to go too far afield at this point. Perhaps it is enough to say that if there are reasons to reject the principle of double effect, such as those offered by Holmes (1989, 193–200), there is all the more basis to think that terrorism and war are not so morally different from each other.

CONCLUSION

I have argued that terrorism, understood as political violence committed by nonstate actors, can be assessed from the point of view of just war theory and that terrorist acts can indeed satisfy the theory's criteria. Though stateless, some groups can nevertheless have a just cause when their right to self-determination is frustrated. Under such circumstances, a representative organization can be a morally legitimate authority to carry out violence as a last resort to defend the group's rights. Such violence must conform to the other criteria, especially discrimination, but terrorism, I have argued, can do so. . . .

It is important to be clear about what I have not argued here. I have not defended terrorism in general, nor certainly have I defended any particular act of violence. It follows from my argument not that terrorism can be justified but that if war can be justified, then terrorism can be as well. I wish to emphasize the conditional nature of the conclusion. I have not established just war theory as the best or the only framework within which to think about the moral issues raised by political violence. Instead I have relied on it because it is the most developed and widely used in thinking about violence carried out by states. I have done so because the double standard that is often used in assessing violence committed by states and nonstate actors seems indefensible. Applying just war theory to both, I believe, is a plausible way to bring both kinds of violence under one standard.

I have little doubt that most terrorist acts do not satisfy all of the criteria of just war theory and that many of them fall far short. In such cases we are well justified in condemning them. But the condemnation must follow, not precede, examination of the case and is not settled by calling the act terrorism and its perpetrators terrorists. I agree with Fullinwider that, while terrorism often fails to be morally justified, "this failure is contingent, not necessary. We cannot define terrorism into a moral corner where we do not have to worry any more about justification" (1988, 257). Furthermore, failure to satisfy the requirements of just war theory is not unique to acts of terrorism. The same could be said of wars themselves. How many wars, after all, are undertaken and waged within the constraints imposed by the theory?

The conditional nature of the conclusion, if the above argument is sound, forces a choice. Either both interstate war and terrorism can be justified or

neither can be. For my part, I must confess to being sorely tempted by the latter position, that neither war nor terrorism can be justified. This temptation is bolstered by pacifist arguments, such as that presented by Holmes (1989, chapter 6), that the killing of innocents is a perfectly predictable effect of modern warfare, the implication of which is that no modern war can be just. That is, even if we can imagine a modern just war, it is not a realistic possibility. Though the pacifist position is tempting, it also seems clear that some evils are great enough to require a response, even a violent response. And once we grant that states may respond violently, there seems no principled reason to deny that same right to certain nonstate groups that enjoy a right to self-determination.

REFERENCES

Baier, Annette. 1994. Violent Demonstrations. In *Moral Prejudices: Essays on Ethics.* Cambridge: Harvard University Press.

Beitz, Charles R. 1979. *Political Theory and International Relations.* Princeton: Princeton University Press.

Buchanan, Allen. 1991. *Secession: The Morality of Political Divorce from Fort Sumter to Lithuania and Quebec.* Boulder: Westview Press.

Coady, C. A. J. 1985. The Morality of Terrorism. *Philosophy* 60: 47–69.

Coates, Anthony J. 1997. *The Ethics of War.* Manchester: Manchester University Press.

Fullinwider, Robert K. 1988. Understanding Terrorism. In *Problems of International Justice,* ed. Steven Luper-Foy. Boulder: Westview Press.

Gilbert, Paul. 1994. *Terrorism, Security, and Nationality: An Introductory Study in Applied Political Philosophy.* New York: Routledge.

Held, Virginia. 1991. Terrorism, Rights, and Political Goals. In *Violence, Terrorism, and Justice,* ed. R. G. Frey and Christopher W. Morris. Cambridge: Cambridge University Press.

Holmes, Robert L. 1989. *On War and Morality.* Princeton: Princeton University Press.

Khatchadourian, Haig. 1998. *The Morality of Terrorism.* New York: Peter Lang.

Kymlicka, Will. 1995. *Multicultural Citizenship: A Liberal Theory of Minority Rights.* Oxford: Clarendon Press.

Margalit, Avishai, and Joseph Raz. 1990. National Self-Determination. *Journal of Philosophy* 87: 439–61.

Mill, John Stuart. 1984 [1859]. A Few Words on Non-Intervention. In *Essays on Equality, Law, and Education: Collected Works of John Stuart Mill,* Vol. 21, ed. John Robson. Toronto: University of Toronto Press.

Miller, David. 1995. *On Nationality.* Oxford: Oxford University Press.

Philpott, Daniel. 1995. In Defense of Self-Determination. *Ethics* 105: 352–85.

Tamir, Yael. 1993. *Liberal Nationalism.* Princeton: Princeton University Press.

Teichman, Jenny. 1989. How to Define Terrorism. *Philosophy* 64: 505–17.

Walzer, Michael. 1988. Terrorism: A Critique of Excuses. In *Problems of International Justice,* ed. Steven Luper-Foy. Boulder: Westview Press.

———. 1992 [1979]. *Just and Unjust Wars: A Moral Argument with Historical Illustrations.* 2nd edition. New York: Basic Books.

Wellman, Carl. 1979. On Terrorism Itself. *Journal of Value Inquiry* 13: 250–58.

Wellman, Christopher H. 1995. A Defense of Secession and Political Self-Determination. *Philosophy and Public Affairs* 24: 142–71.

Wilkins, Burleigh Taylor. 1992. *Terrorism and Collective Responsibility.* New York: Routledge.

READING QUESTIONS

1. According to Valls, what are the two difficulties that arise when one is trying to define "terrorism"? What final definition of the term does Valls stipulate that he will use in his arguments?

2. Valls' weak claim for just cause is that some groups enjoy a right to self-determination. Which groups, according to Valls, might enjoy such a right?

3. Valls argues that the legitimate authority requirement can be met by a nonstate organization under two conditions. First, the organization must claim to represent the rights and interests of a people. What is the second condition?

4. If the first two requirements of jus ad bellum are met, is entailment of the right intention requirement necessarily entailed? How does Valls answer that question?

5. Valls argues that there are two problems arising from Walzer's claim that terrorism never can be a last resort. What are those problems?

6. What is the difference in context between the proportionality requirement of jus ad bellum and the proportionality requirement of jus in bello?

7. Valls suggests that the question of discrimination between combatants and noncombatants be replaced with a question about the extent to which a violent act discriminates among targets along a continuum. What reasons does he give for this view?

DISCUSSION QUESTIONS

1. Various commentators claim that acts of violence need not be indiscriminate, or directed toward innocents, or intended to spread fear in order to be classed as acts of "terror." Discuss whether you think that each of these is or is not a necessary condition of "terrorism."

2. Someone might argue that although certain acts of terrorism may satisfy the criteria of jus ad bellum, they do not satisfy the criteria of jus in bello. Give an example (real or fictional) of such a case.

3. Valls claims that the decision to commit violence as a last resort is justified when all reasonable nonviolent measures have been tried, and there is always room for argument about what "reasonable" means. Think of an example of an act of state or nonstate violence and discuss whether and to what extent "reasonable" nonviolent measures were tried.

ALAN M. DERSHOWITZ

Should the Ticking Bomb Terrorist Be Tortured?

The "ticking bomb" case refers to a hypothetical situation in which only by torturing a terrorist who knows the whereabouts of a ticking bomb can the bomb be found and defused before it detonates and kills many innocent people. Should the ticking bomb terrorist be tortured? Dershowitz argues from an act utilitarian moral perspective for an affirmative answer to this question. He then argues that a democratic society governed by the rule of law should never declare some action to be absolutely wrong, yet knowingly allow the military or other public officials to engage in that activity "off the books." But if torture is morally permissible in extreme "necessity" cases such as the ticking bomb case, democratic governments ought to change existing law to accommodate this practice. Dershowitz proposes that a system of judicial "torture warrants" be instituted as part of a legal system regulating the practice.

Recommended Reading: consequentialism, chap. 1, sec. 2A, particularly act utilitarianism.

HOW I BEGAN THINKING ABOUT TORTURE

In the late 1980s I traveled to Israel to conduct some research and teach a class at Hebrew University on civil liberties during times of crisis. In the course of my research I learned that the Israeli security services were employing what they euphemistically called "moderate physical pressure" on suspected terrorists to obtain information deemed necessary to prevent future terrorist attacks. The method employed by the security services fell somewhere between what many would regard as very rough interrogation (as practiced by the British in Northern Ireland) and outright torture (as practiced by the French in Algeria and by Egypt, the Philippines, and Jordan today). In most cases the suspect would be placed in a dark room with a smelly sack over his head. Loud, unpleasant music or other noise would blare from speakers. The suspect would be seated in an extremely uncomfortable position and then shaken vigorously until he disclosed the information. Statements made under this kind of nonlethal pressure could not be introduced in any court of law, both because they were involuntarily secured and because they were deemed potentially untrustworthy—at least without corroboration. But they were used as leads in the prevention of terrorist acts. Sometimes the leads proved false, other times they proved true. There is little doubt that some acts of terrorism—which would have killed many civilians—were prevented. There is also little doubt that the cost of saving these lives—measured in terms of basic human rights—was extraordinarily high.

In my classes and public lectures in Israel, I strongly condemned these methods as a violation of core civil liberties and human rights. The response that people gave, across the political spectrum from

From Alan M. Dershowitz, *Why Terrorism Works: Understanding the Threat, Responding to the Challenge* (New Haven and London: Yale University Press, 2002). Reprinted by permission.

civil libertarians to law-and-order advocates, was essentially the same: but what about the "ticking bomb" case?

The ticking bomb case refers to a scenario that has been discussed by many philosophers, including Michael Walzer, Jean-Paul Sartre, and Jeremy Bentham. Walzer described such a hypothetical case in an article titled "Political Action: The Problem of Dirty Hands." In this case, a decent leader of a nation plagued with terrorism is asked "to authorize the torture of a captured rebel leader who knows or probably knows the location of a number of bombs hidden in apartment buildings across the city, set to go off within the next twenty-four hours. He orders the man tortured, convinced that he must do so for the sake of the people who might otherwise die in the explosions—even though he believes that torture is wrong, indeed abominable, not just sometimes, but always."[1]

In Israel, the use of torture to prevent terrorism was not hypothetical; it was very real and recurring. I soon discovered that virtually no one was willing to take the "purist" position against torture in the ticking bomb case: namely, that the ticking bomb must be permitted to explode and kill dozens of civilians, even if this disaster could be prevented by subjecting the captured terrorist to nonlethal torture and forcing him to disclose its location. I realized that the extraordinarily rare situation of the hypothetical ticking bomb terrorist was serving as a moral, intellectual, and legal justification for a pervasive *system* of coercive interrogation, which, though not the paradigm of torture, certainly bordered on it. It was then that I decided to challenge this system by directly confronting the ticking bomb case. I presented the following challenge to my Israeli audience: If the reason you permit nonlethal torture is based on the ticking bomb case, why not limit it exclusively to that compelling but rare situation? Moreover, if you believe that nonlethal torture is justifiable in the ticking bomb case, why not require advance judicial approval—a "torture warrant"? That was the origin of a controversial proposal that has received much attention, largely critical, from the media. Its goal was, and remains, to reduce the use of torture to the smallest amount and degree possible, while creating public accountability

for its rare use. I saw it not as a compromise with civil liberties but rather as an effort to maximize civil liberties in the face of a realistic likelihood that torture would, in fact, take place below the radar screen of accountability. . . .

THE CASE FOR TORTURING THE TICKING BOMB TERRORIST

The arguments in favor of using torture as a last resort to prevent a ticking bomb from exploding and killing many people are both simple and simple-minded. Bentham constructed a compelling hypothetical case to support his utilitarian argument against an absolute prohibition on torture:

> Suppose an occasion were to arise, in which a suspicion is entertained, as strong as that which would be received as a sufficient ground for arrest and commitment as for felony—a suspicion that at this very time a considerable number of individuals are actually suffering, by illegal violence inflictions equal in intensity to those which if inflicted by the hand of justice, would universally be spoken of under the name of torture. For the purpose of rescuing from torture these hundred innocents, should any scruple be made of applying equal or superior torture, to extract the requisite information from the mouth of one criminal, who having it in his power to make known the place where at this time the enormity was practising or about to be practised, should refuse to do so? To say nothing of wisdom, could any pretence be made so much as to the praise of blind and vulgar humanity, by the man who to save one criminal, should determine to abandon 100 innocent persons to the same fate?[2]

If the torture of one guilty person would be justified to prevent the torture of a hundred innocent persons, it would seem to follow—certainly to Bentham—that it would also be justified to prevent the murder of thousands of innocent civilians in the ticking bomb case. Consider two hypothetical situations that are not, unfortunately, beyond the realm of possibility. In fact, they are both extrapolations on actual situations we have faced.

Several weeks before September 11, 2001, the Immigration and Naturalization Service detained Zacarias Moussaoui after flight instructors reported suspicious statements he had made while taking flying lessons and paying for them with large amounts of cash.[3] The government decided not to seek a warrant to search his computer. Now imagine that they had, and that they discovered he was part of a plan to destroy large occupied buildings, but without any further details. They interrogated him, gave him immunity from prosecution, and offered him large cash rewards and a new identity. He refused to talk. They then threatened him, tried to trick him, and employed every lawful technique available. He still refused. They even injected him with sodium pentothal and other truth serums, but to no avail. The attack now appeared to be imminent, but the FBI still had no idea what the target was or what means would be used to attack it. We could not simply evacuate all buildings indefinitely. An FBI agent proposes the use of nonlethal torture—say, a sterilized needle inserted under the fingernails to produce unbearable pain without any threat to health or life, or the method used in the film *Marathon Man,* a dental drill through an unanesthetized tooth.

The simple cost-benefit analysis for employing such nonlethal torture seems overwhelming: it is surely better to inflict nonlethal pain on one guilty terrorist who is illegally withholding information needed to prevent an act of terrorism than to permit a large number of innocent victims to die. Pain is a lesser and more remediable harm than death; and the lives of a thousand innocent people should be valued more than the bodily integrity of one guilty person. If the variation on the Moussaoui case is not sufficiently compelling to make this point, we can always raise the stakes. Several weeks after September 11, our government received reports that a ten-kiloton nuclear weapon may have been stolen from Russia and was on its way to New York City, where it would be detonated and kill hundreds of thousands of people. The reliability of the source, code named Dragonfire, was uncertain, but assume for purposes of this hypothetical extension of the actual case that the source was a captured terrorist—like the one tortured by the Philippine authorities—who knew precisely how and where the weapon was being brought into New York and was to be detonated. Again, everything short of torture is tried, but to no avail. It is not absolutely certain torture will work, but it is our last, best hope for preventing a cataclysmic nuclear devastation in a city too large to evacuate in time. Should nonlethal torture be tried? Bentham would certainly have said yes.

The strongest argument against any resort to torture, even in the ticking bomb case, also derives from Bentham's utilitarian calculus. Experience has shown that if torture, which has been deemed illegitimate by the civilized world for more than a century, were now to be legitimated—even for limited use in one extraordinary type of situation—such legitimation would constitute an important symbolic setback in the worldwide campaign against human rights abuses. Inevitably, the legitimation of torture by the world's leading democracy would provide a welcome justification for its more widespread use in other parts of the world. Two Bentham scholars, W. L. Twining and P. E. Twining, have argued that torture is unacceptable even if it is restricted to an extremely limited category of cases:

> There is at least one good practical reason for drawing a distinction between justifying an isolated act of torture in an extreme emergency of the kind postulated above and justifying the *institutionalisation* of torture as a regular practice. The circumstances are so extreme in which most of us would be prepared to justify resort to torture, if at all, the conditions we would impose would be so stringent, the practical problems of devising and enforcing adequate safeguards so difficult and the risks of abuse so great that it would be unwise and dangerous to entrust any government, however enlightened, with such a power. Even an out-and-out utilitarian can support an absolute prohibition against institutionalised torture on the ground that no government in the world can be trusted not to abuse the power and to satisfy in practice the conditions he would impose.[4]

Bentham's own justification was based on *case* or *act* utilitarianism—a demonstration that in a *particular case,* the benefits that would flow from the limited use of torture would outweigh its costs. The argument against any use of torture would derive from *rule* utilitarianism—which considers the implications of establishing a precedent that would inevitably be extended beyond its limited case utilitarian justification to other possible evils of lesser magnitude. Even terrorism itself could be justified by a case utilitarian approach. Surely one could come up with a singular situation in which the targeting of a small number of civilians could be thought necessary to save thousands of other civilians—blowing up a German kindergarten by the relatives of inmates in a Nazi death camp, for example, and threatening to repeat the targeting of German children unless the death camps were shut down.

The reason this kind of single-case utilitarian justification is simple-minded is that it has no inherent limiting principle. If nonlethal torture of one person is justified to prevent the killing of many important people, then what if it were necessary to use lethal torture—or at least torture that posed a substantial risk of death? What if it were necessary to torture the suspect's mother or children to get him to divulge the information? What if it took threatening to kill his family, his friends, his entire village? Under a simple-minded quantitative case utilitarianism, anything goes as long as the number of people tortured or killed does not exceed the number that would be saved. This is morality by numbers, unless there are other constraints on what we can properly do. These other constraints can come from rule utilitarianisms or other principles of morality, such as the prohibition against deliberately punishing the innocent. Unless we are prepared to impose some limits on the use of torture or other barbaric tactics that might be of some use in preventing terrorism, we risk hurtling down a slippery slope into the abyss of amorality and ultimately tyranny. Dostoevsky captured the complexity of this dilemma in *The Brothers Karamazov* when he had Ivan pose the following question to Alyosha: "Imagine that you are creating a fabric of human destiny with the object of making men happy in the end, giving them peace at least, but that it was essential and inevitable to torture to death only one tiny creature—that baby beating its breast with its fist, for instance—and to found that edifice on its unavenged tears, would you consent to be the architect on those conditions? Tell me the truth."

A willingness to kill an innocent child suggests a willingness to do anything to achieve a necessary result. Hence the slippery slope.

It does not necessarily follow from this understandable fear of the slippery slope that we can never consider the use of nonlethal infliction of pain, if its use were to be limited by acceptable principles of morality. After all, imprisoning a witness who refuses to testify after being given immunity is designed to be punitive—that is painful. Such imprisonment can, on occasion, produce more pain and greater risk of death than nonlethal torture. Yet we continue to threaten and use the pain of imprisonment to loosen the tongues of reluctant witnesses.

It is commonplace for police and prosecutors to threaten recalcitrant suspects with prison rape. As one prosecutor put it: "You're going to be the boyfriend of a very bad man." The slippery slope is an argument of caution, not a debate stopper, since virtually every compromise with an absolutist approach to rights carries the risk of slipping further. An appropriate response to the slippery slope is to build in a principled break. For example, if nonlethal torture were legally limited to convicted terrorists who had knowledge of future massive terrorist acts, were given immunity, and still refused to provide the information, there might still be objections to the use of torture, but they would have to go beyond the slippery slope argument.

The case utilitarian argument for torturing a ticking bomb terrorist is bolstered by an argument from analogy—an a fortiori argument. What moral principle could justify the death penalty for past individual murders and at the same time condemn nonlethal torture to prevent future mass murders? Bentham posed this rhetorical question as support for his argument. The death penalty is, of course, reserved for convicted murderers. But again, what if torture was limited to convicted terrorists who refused to divulge information about future terrorism? Consider as well the analogy to the use of deadly force against suspects fleeing from arrest for dangerous felonies of which they have not yet been convicted. Or military retaliations that produce the predictable and inevitable collateral killing of some innocent civilians. The case against torture, if made by a Quaker who opposes the death penalty, war, self-defense, and the use of lethal force against fleeing felons, is understandable. But for anyone who justifies killing on the basis of a cost-benefit analysis, the case against the use of nonlethal torture to save multiple lives is more difficult to make. In the end, absolute opposition to torture—even nonlethal torture in the ticking bomb case—may rest more on historical and aesthetic considerations than on moral or logical ones.

In debating the issue of torture, the first question I am often asked is, "Do you want to take us back to the Middle Ages?" The association between any form of torture and gruesome death is powerful in the minds of most people knowledgeable of the history of its abuses. This understandable association makes it difficult for many people to think about nonlethal torture as a technique for *saving* lives.

The second question I am asked is, "What kind of torture do you have in mind?" When I respond by describing the sterilized needle being shoved under the fingernails, the reaction is visceral and often visible—a shudder coupled with a facial gesture of disgust. Discussions of the death penalty on the other hand can be conducted without these kinds of reactions, especially now that we literally put the condemned prisoner "to sleep" by laying him out on a gurney and injecting a lethal substance into his body. There is no breaking of the neck, burning of the brain, bursting of internal organs, or gasping for breath that used to accompany hanging, electrocution, shooting, and gassing. The executioner has been replaced by a paramedical technician, as the aesthetics of death have become more acceptable. All this tends to cover up the reality that death is forever while nonlethal pain is temporary. In our modern age death is underrated, while pain is overrated.

I observed a similar phenomenon several years ago during the debate over corporal punishment that was generated by the decision of a court in Singapore to sentence a young American to medically supervised lashing with a cane. Americans who support the death penalty and who express little concern about inner-city prison conditions were outraged by the specter of a few welts on the buttocks of an American. It was an utterly irrational display of hypocrisy and double standards. Given a choice

between a medically administrated whipping and one month in a typical state lockup or prison, any rational and knowledgeable person would choose the lash. No one dies of welts or pain, but many inmates are raped, beaten, knifed, and otherwise mutilated and tortured in American prisons. The difference is that we don't see—and we don't want to see—what goes on behind their high walls. Nor do we want to think about it. Raising the issue of torture makes Americans think about a brutalizing and unaesthetic phenomenon that has been out of our consciousness for many years.[5]

THE THREE—OR FOUR—WAYS

The debate over the use of torture goes back many years, with Bentham supporting it in a limited category of cases, Kant opposing it as part of his categorical imperative against improperly using people as means for achieving noble ends, and Voltaire's views on the matter being "hopelessly confused."[6] The modern resort to terrorism has renewed the debate over how a rights-based society should respond to the prospect of using nonlethal torture in the ticking bomb situation. In the late 1980s the Israeli government appointed a commission headed by a retired Supreme Court justice to look into precisely that situation. The commission concluded that there are "three ways for solving this grave dilemma between the vital need to preserve the very existence of the state and its citizens, and maintain its character as a law-abiding state." The first is to allow the security services to continue to fight terrorism in "a twilight zone which is outside the realm of law." The second is "the way of the hypocrites: they declare that they abide by the rule of law, but turn a blind eye to what goes on beneath the surface." And the third, "the truthful road of the rule of law," is that the "law itself must insure a proper framework for the activity" of the security services in seeking to prevent terrorist acts.

There is of course a fourth road: namely to forgo any use of torture and simply allow the preventable terrorist act to occur.[7] After the Supreme Court of Israel outlawed the use of physical pressure, the Israeli security services claimed that, as a result of the Supreme Court's decision, at least one preventable act of terrorism had been allowed to take place, one that killed several people when a bus was bombed. Whether this claim is true, false, or somewhere in between is difficult to assess.[8] But it is clear that if the preventable act of terrorism was of the magnitude of the attacks of September 11, there would be a great outcry in any democracy that had deliberately refused to take available preventive action, even if it required the use of torture. During numerous public appearances since September 11, 2001, I have asked audiences for a show of hands as to how many would support the use of nonlethal torture in a ticking bomb case. Virtually every hand is raised. The few that remain down go up when I ask how many believe that torture would actually be used in such a case.

Law enforcement personnel give similar responses. This can be seen in reports of physical abuse directed against some suspects that have been detained following September 11, reports that have been taken quite seriously by at least one federal judge. It is confirmed by the willingness of U.S. law enforcement officials to facilitate the torture of terrorist suspects by repressive regimes allied with our intelligence agencies. As one former CIA operative with thirty years of experience reported: "A lot of people are saying we need someone at the agency who can pull fingernails out. Others are saying, 'Let others use interrogation methods that we don't use.' The only question then is, do you want to have CIA people in the room?" The real issue, therefore, is not whether some torture would or would not be used in the ticking bomb case—it would. The question is whether it would be done openly, pursuant to a previously established legal procedure, or whether it would be done secretly, in violation of existing law.

Several important values are pitted against each other in this conflict. The first is the safety and security of a nation's citizens. Under the ticking bomb scenario this value may require the use of torture, if that is the only way to prevent the bomb from exploding and killing large numbers of civilians. The second value is the preservation of civil liberties and human rights. This value requires that we

not accept torture as a legitimate part of our legal system. In my debates with two prominent civil libertarians, Floyd Abrams and Harvey Silverglate, both have acknowledged that they would want nonlethal torture to be used if it could prevent thousands of deaths, but they did not want torture to be officially recognized by our legal system. As Abrams put it: "In a democracy sometimes it is necessary to do things off the books and below the radar screen." Former presidential candidate Alan Keyes took the position that although torture might be *necessary* in a given situation it could never be *right*. He suggested that a president *should* authorize the torturing of a ticking bomb terrorist, but that this act should not be legitimated by the courts or incorporated into our legal system. He argued that wrongful and indeed unlawful acts might sometimes be necessary to preserve the nation, but that no aura of legitimacy should be placed on these actions by judicial imprimatur.

This understandable approach is in conflict with the third important value: namely, open accountability and visibility in a democracy. "Off-the-book actions below the radar screen" are antithetical to the theory and practice of democracy. Citizens cannot approve or disapprove of governmental actions of which they are unaware. We have learned the lesson of history that off-the-book actions can produce terrible consequences. Richard Nixon's creation of a group of "plumbers" led to Watergate, and Ronald Reagan's authorization of an off-the-books foreign policy in Central America led to the Iran-Contra scandal. And these are only the ones we know about!

Perhaps the most extreme example of such a hypocritical approach to torture comes—not surprisingly—from the French experience in Algeria. The French army used torture extensively in seeking to prevent terrorism during a brutal colonial war from 1955 to 1957. An officer who supervised this torture, General Paul Aussaresses, wrote a book recounting what he had done and seen, including the torture of dozens of Algerians. "The best way to make a terrorist talk when he refused to say what he knew was to torture him," he boasted. Although the book was published decades after the war was over, the general was prosecuted—but not for what he had done to the

Algerians. Instead, he was prosecuted for *revealing* what he had done, and seeking to justify it.

In a democracy governed by the rule of law, we should never want our soldiers or our president to take any action that we deem wrong or illegal. A good test of whether an action should or should not be done is whether we are prepared to have it disclosed—perhaps not immediately, but certainly after some time has passed. No legal system operating under the rule of law should ever tolerate an "off-the-books" approach to necessity. Even the defense of necessity must be justified lawfully. The road to tyranny has always been paved with claims of necessity made by those responsible for the security of a nation. Our system of checks and balances requires that all presidential actions, like all legislative or military actions, be consistent with governing law. If it is necessary to torture in the ticking bomb case, then our governing laws must accommodate this practice. If we refuse to change our law to accommodate any particular action, then our government should not take that action.

Only in a democracy committed to civil liberties would a triangular conflict of this kind exist. Totalitarian and authoritarian regimes experience no such conflict, because they subscribe to neither the civil libertarian nor the democratic values that come in conflict with the value of security. The hard question is: which value is to be preferred when an inevitable clash occurs? One or more of these values must inevitably be compromised in making the tragic choice presented by the ticking bomb case. If we do not torture, we compromise the security and safety of our citizens. If we tolerate torture, but keep it off the books and below the radar screen, we compromise principles of democratic accountability. If we create a legal structure for limiting and controlling torture, we compromise our principled opposition to torture in all circumstances and create a potentially dangerous and expandable situation.

In 1678, the French writer François de La Rochefoucauld said that "hypocrisy is the homage that vice renders to virtue." In this case we have two vices: terrorism and torture. We also have two virtues: civil liberties and democratic accountability. Most civil libertarians I know prefer hypocrisy, precisely because it appears to avoid the conflict between security and civil liberties, but by choosing the way of the hypocrite these civil libertarians compromise the value of democratic accountability. Such is the nature of tragic choices in a complex world. As Bentham put it more than two centuries ago: "Government throughout is but a choice of evils." In a democracy, such choices must be made, whenever possible, with openness and democratic accountability, and subject to the rule of law.[9]

Consider another terrible choice of evils that could easily have been presented on September 11, 2001—and may well be presented in the future: a hijacked passenger jet is on a collision course with a densely occupied office building; the only way to prevent the destruction of the building and the killing of its occupants is to shoot down the jet, thereby killing its innocent passengers. This choice now seems easy, because the passengers are certain to die anyway and their somewhat earlier deaths will save numerous lives. The passenger jet must be shot down. But what if it were only *probable,* not certain, that the jet would crash into the building? Say, for example, we know from cell phone transmissions that passengers are struggling to regain control of the hijacked jet, but it is unlikely they will succeed in time. Or say we have no communication with the jet and all we know is that it is off course and heading toward Washington, D.C., or some other densely populated city. Under these more questionable circumstances, the question becomes *who* should make this life and death choice between evils—a decision that may turn out tragically wrong?

No reasonable person would allocate this decision to a fighter jet pilot who happened to be in the area or to a local airbase commander—unless of course there was no time for the matter to be passed up the chain of command to the president or the secretary of defense. A decision of this kind should be made at the highest level possible, with visibility and accountability.

Why is this not also true of the decision to torture a ticking bomb terrorist? Why should that choice of evils be relegated to a local policeman, FBI agent, or CIA operative, rather than to a judge, the attorney general, or the president?

There are, of course, important differences between the decision to shoot down the plane and the decision to torture the ticking bomb terrorist. Having to shoot down an airplane, though tragic, is not likely to be a recurring issue. There is no slope down which to slip. Moreover, the jet to be shot down is filled with our fellow citizens—people with whom we can identify. The suspected terrorist we may choose to torture is a "they"—an enemy with whom we do not identify but with whose potential victims we do identify. The risk of making the wrong decision, or of overdoing the torture, is far greater, since we do not care as much what happens to "them" as to "us." Finally, there is something different about torture—even nonlethal torture—that sets it apart from a quick death. In addition to the horrible history associated with torture, there is also the aesthetic of torture. The very idea of deliberately subjecting a captive human being to excruciating pain violates our sense of what is acceptable. On a purely rational basis, it is far worse to shoot a fleeing felon in the back and kill him, yet every civilized society authorizes shooting such a suspect who poses dangers of committing violent crimes against the police or others. In the United States we execute convicted murderers, despite compelling evidence of the unfairness and ineffectiveness of capital punishment. Yet many of us recoil at the prospect of shoving a sterilized needle under the finger of a suspect who is refusing to divulge information that might prevent multiple deaths. Despite the irrationality of these distinctions, they are understandable, especially in light of the sordid history of torture.

We associate torture with the Inquisition, the Gestapo, the Stalinist purges, and the Argentine colonels responsible for the "dirty war." We recall it as a prelude to death, an integral part of a regime of gratuitous pain leading to a painful demise. We find it difficult to imagine a benign use of nonlethal torture to save lives.

Yet there was a time in the history of Anglo-Saxon law when torture was used to save life, rather than to take it, and when the limited administration of nonlethal torture was supervised by judges, including some who are well remembered in history. This fascinating story has been recounted by Professor John Langbein of Yale Law School, and it is worth summarizing here

because it helps inform the debate over whether, if torture would in fact be used in a ticking bomb case, it would be worse to make it part of the legal system, or worse to have it done off the books and below the radar screen.

In his book on legalized torture during the sixteenth and seventeenth centuries, *Torture and the Law of Proof,* Langbein demonstrates the trade-off between torture and other important values. Torture was employed for several purposes. First, it was used to secure the evidence necessary to obtain a guilty verdict under the rigorous criteria for conviction required at the time—either the testimony of two eyewitnesses or the confession of the accused himself. Circumstantial evidence, no matter how compelling, would not do. As Langbein concludes, "no society will long tolerate a legal system in which there is no prospect in convicting unrepentant persons who commit clandestine crimes. Something had to be done to extend the system to those cases. The two-eyewitness rule was hard to compromise or evade, but the confession invited 'subterfuge.'" The subterfuge that was adopted permitted the use of torture to obtain confessions from suspects against whom there was compelling circumstantial evidence of guilt. The circumstantial evidence, alone, could not be used to convict, but it was used to obtain a torture warrant. That torture warrant was in turn used to obtain a confession, which then had to be independently corroborated—at least in most cases (witchcraft and other such cases were exempted from the requirement of corroboration).[10]

Torture was also used against persons already convicted of capital crimes, such as high treason, who were thought to have information necessary to prevent attacks on the state.

Langbein studied eighty-one torture warrants, issued between 1540 and 1640, and found that in many of them, especially in "the higher cases of treasons, torture is used for discovery, and not for evidence." Torture was "used to protect the state" and "mostly that meant preventive torture to identify and forestall plots and plotters." It was only when the legal system loosened its requirement of proof (or introduced the "black box" of the jury system) and when perceived threats against the state diminished that torture was no longer deemed necessary to convict guilty defendants against whom there had previously been insufficient evidence, or to secure preventive information.[11] . . .

Every society has insisted on the incapacitation of dangerous criminals regardless of strictures in the formal legal rules. Some use torture, others use informal sanctions, while yet others create the black box of a jury, which need not explain its common-sense verdicts. Similarly, every society insists that, if there are steps that can be taken to prevent effective acts of terrorism, these steps should be taken, even if they require some compromise with other important principles.

. . . In deciding whether the ticking bomb terrorist should be tortured, one important question is whether there would be less torture if it were done as part of the legal system, as it was in sixteenth- and seventeenth-century England, or off the books, as it is in many countries today. The Langbein study does not definitively answer this question, but it does provide some suggestive insights. The English system of torture was more visible and thus more subject to public accountability, and it is likely that torture was employed less frequently in England than in France. "During these years when it appears that torture might have become routinized in English criminal procedure, the Privy Council kept the torture power under careful control and never allowed it to fall into the hands of the regular law enforcement officers," as it had in France. In England "no law enforcement officer . . . acquired the power to use torture without special warrant." Moreover, when torture warrants were abolished, "the English experiment with torture left no traces." Because it was under centralized control, it was easier to abolish than it was in France, where it persisted for many years.[12]

It is always difficult to extrapolate from history, but it seems logical that a formal, visible, accountable, and centralized system is somewhat easier to control than an ad hoc, off-the-books, and under-the-radar-screen nonsystem. I believe, though I certainly cannot prove, that a formal requirement of a judicial warrant as a prerequisite to nonlethal torture would decrease the amount of physical violence directed against suspects. At the most obvious level, a double check is always more protective than a single check. In every instance in which a warrant is requested, a field officer has already decided that torture is justified and, in the absence of a warrant requirement, would simply proceed with the torture. Requiring that decision to be approved by a judicial officer will result in fewer instances of torture even if the judge rarely turns down a request. Moreover, I believe that most judges would require compelling evidence before they would authorize so extraordinary a departure from our constitutional norms, and law enforcement officials would be reluctant to seek a warrant unless they had compelling evidence that the suspect had information needed to prevent an imminent terrorist attack. A record would be kept of every warrant granted, and although it is certainly possible that some individual agents might torture without a warrant, they would have no excuse, since a warrant procedure would be available. They could not claim "necessity," because the decision as to whether the torture is indeed necessary has been taken out of their hands and placed in the hands of a judge. In addition, even if torture were deemed totally illegal without any exception, it would still occur, though the public would be less aware of its existence.

I also believe that the rights of the suspect would be better protected with a warrant requirement. He would be granted immunity, told that he was now compelled to testify, threatened with imprisonment if he refused to do so, and given the option of providing the requested information. Only if he refused to do what he was legally compelled to do—provide necessary information, which could not incriminate him because of the immunity—would he be threatened with torture. Knowing that such a threat was authorized by the law, he might well provide the information.[13] If he still refused to, he would be subjected to judicially monitored physical measures designed to cause excruciating pain without leaving any lasting damage.

Let me cite two examples to demonstrate why I think there would be less torture with a warrant requirement than without one. Recall the case of the alleged national security wiretap placed on the phones of Martin Luther King by the Kennedy administration in the early 1960s. This was in the days when the attorney general could authorize a national security wiretap without a warrant. Today no judge would issue a warrant in a case as flimsy as that one. When Zacarias Moussaoui was detained after raising suspicions while trying to learn how to fly an airplane, the government did not even seek a national security wiretap because its lawyers believed that a judge would not have granted one. If Moussaoui's computer could have been searched without a warrant, it almost certainly would have been.

It should be recalled that in the context of searches, our Supreme Court opted for a judicial check on the discretion of the police, by requiring a search warrant in most cases. The Court has explained the reason for the warrant requirement as follows: "The informed and deliberate determinations of magistrates . . . are to be preferred over the hurried action of officers."[14] Justice Robert Jackson elaborated:

> The point of the Fourth Amendment, which often is not grasped by zealous officers, is not that it denies law enforcement the support of the usual inferences which reasonable men draw from evidence. Its protection consists in requiring that those inferences be drawn by a neutral and detached magistrate instead of being judged by the officer engaged in the often competitive enterprise of ferreting out crime. Any assumption that evidence sufficient to support a magistrate's disinterested determination to issue a search warrant will justify the officers in making a search without a warrant would reduce the Amendment to nullity and leave the people's homes secure only in the discretion of police officers.[15]

Although torture is very different from a search, the policies underlying the warrant requirement are relevant to the question whether there is likely to be more torture or less if the decision is left entirely to field officers, or if a judicial officer has to approve a request for a torture warrant. As Abraham Maslow once observed, to a man with a hammer, everything looks like a nail. If the man with the hammer must get judicial approval before he can use it, he will probably use it less often and more carefully.

There are other, somewhat more subtle, considerations that should be factored into any decision regarding torture. There are some who see silence as a virtue when it comes to the choice among such horrible evils as torture and terrorism. It is far better,

they argue, not to discuss or write about issues of this sort, lest they become legitimated. And legitimation is an appropriate concern. Justice Jackson, in his opinion in one of the cases concerning the detention of Japanese-Americans during World War II, made the following relevant observation:

> Much is said of the danger to liberty from the Army program for deporting and detaining these citizens of Japanese extraction. But a judicial construction of the due process clause that will sustain this order is a far more subtle blow to liberty than the promulgation of the order itself. A military order, however unconstitutional, is not apt to last longer than the military emergency. Even during that period a succeeding commander may revoke it all. But once a judicial opinion rationalizes such an order to show that it conforms to the Constitution, or rather rationalizes the Constitution to show that the Constitution sanctions such an order, the Court for all time has validated the principle of racial discrimination in criminal procedure and of transplanting American citizens. The principle then lies about like a loaded weapon ready for the hand of any authority that can bring forward a plausible claim of an urgent need. Every repetition imbeds that principle more deeply in our law and thinking and expands it to new purposes. All who observe the work of courts are familiar with what Judge Cardozo described as "the tendency of a principle to expand itself to the limit of its logic." A military commander may overstep the bounds of constitutionality, and it is an incident. But if we review and approve, that passing incident becomes the doctrine of the Constitution. There it has a generative power of its own, and all that it creates will be in its own image.[16]

A similar argument can be made regarding torture: if an agent tortures, that is "an incident," but if the courts authorize it, it becomes a precedent. There is, however, an important difference between the detention of Japanese-American citizens and torture. The detentions were done openly and with presidential accountability; torture would be done secretly, with official deniability. Tolerating an off-the-book system of secret torture can also establish a dangerous precedent.

A variation on this "legitimation" argument would postpone consideration of the choice between authorizing torture and forgoing a possible tactic necessary to prevent an imminent act of terrorism until after the choice—presumably the choice to torture—has been made. In that way, the discussion would not, in itself, encourage the use of torture. If it were employed, then we could decide whether it was justified, excusable, condemnable, or something in between. The problem with that argument is that no FBI agent who tortured a suspect into disclosing information that prevented an act of mass terrorism would be prosecuted—as the policemen who tortured the kidnapper into disclosing the whereabouts of his victim were not prosecuted. In the absence of a prosecution, there would be no occasion to judge the appropriateness of the torture.

I disagree with these more passive approaches and believe that in a democracy it is always preferable to decide controversial issues in advance, rather than in the heat of battle. I would apply this rule to other tragic choices as well, including the possible use of a nuclear first strike, or retaliatory strikes—so long as the discussion was sufficiently general to avoid giving our potential enemies a strategic advantage by their knowledge of our policy.

Even if government officials decline to discuss such issues, academics have a duty to raise them and submit them to the marketplace of ideas. There may be danger in open discussion, but there is far greater danger in actions based on secret discussion, or no discussion at all.

NOTES

1. Michael Walzer, "Political Action: The Problem of Dirty Hands," *Philosophy and Public Affairs,* 1973.

2. Quoted in W. L. Twining and P. E. Twining, "Bentham on Torture," *Northern Ireland Legal Quarterly,* Autumn 1973, p. 347. Bentham's hypothetical question

does not distinguish between torture inflicted by private persons and by governments.

3. David Johnston and Philip Shenon, "F.B.I. Curbed Scrutiny of Man Now a Suspect in the Attacks," *New York Times,* 10/6/2001.

4. Twining and Twining, "Bentham on Torture," pp. 348–49. The argument for the limited use of torture in the ticking bomb case falls into a category of argument known as "argument from the extreme case," which is a useful heuristic to counter arguments for absolute principles.

5. On conditions in American prisons, see Alan M. Dershowitz, "Supreme Court Acknowledges Country's Other Rape Epidemic," *Boston Herald,* 6/12/1994. . . .

6. John Langbein, *Torture and the Law of Proof* (Chicago: University of Chicago Press, 1977), p. 68. Voltaire generally opposed torture but favored it in some cases.

7. A fifth approach would be simply to never discuss the issue of torture—or to postpone any such discussion until after we actually experience a ticking bomb case—but I have always believed that it is preferable to consider and discuss tragic choices before we confront them, so that the issue can be debated without recriminatory emotions and after-the-fact finger-pointing.

8. Charles M. Sennott, "Israeli High Court Bans Torture in Questioning; 10,000 Palestinians Subjected to Tactics," *Boston Globe,* 9/7/1999.

9. Quoted in Twining and Twining, "Bentham on Torture," p. 345.

10. Langbein, *Torture and the Law of Proof,* p. 7.

11. Ibid., p. 90, quoting Bacon.

12. Langbein, *Torture and the Law of Proof,* pp.136–37, 139.

13. When it is known that torture is a possible option, terrorists sometimes provide the information and then claim they have been tortured, in order to be able to justify their complicity to their colleagues.

14. *U.S. v. Lefkowitz,* 285 U.S. 452, 464 (1932).

15. *Johnson v. U.S.* 333 U.S. 10, 13–14 (1948).

16. *Korematsu v. U.S.* 323 U.S. 214, 245–46 (1944) (Jackson, J., dissenting).

READING QUESTIONS

1. Explain the case for why the ticking bomb terrorist should be tortured according to Dershowitz. How did his visit to Israel impact his views on this matter?
2. What is the strongest argument against the view that the ticking bomb terrorist should be tortured? Explain how the distinction between act and rule utilitarianism is relevant to this argument.

3. What is the biggest problem for an act utilitarian justification of torture according to Dershowitz? What is a "torture warrant" and how does Dershowitz believe torture warrants could be implemented in order to overcome the relevant problem?

4. What are the four ways that Dershowitz considers for how we can resolve the dilemma between the conflicting values of security and abiding by the law? Why are accountability and visibility in democracy important according to Dershowitz? Consider in particular the possible consequences of a lack of accountability in a democracy.

DISCUSSION QUESTIONS

1. Should we agree with Dershowitz that the introduction of torture warrants would result in fewer terrorist attacks as well as allow for more government accountability? Why or why not? Consider and discuss some of the potential problems that might arise with the introduction of such warrants. Are there any better or additional alternatives that could be implemented in order to prevent terrorist attacks that would also result in greater accountability in a democracy?

2. Consider and discuss whether the act utilitarian argument that Dershowitz gives for the justification of torture fails to provide adequate reasons to support his view. Is Bentham's hypothetical case different in any morally relevant ways from the case of the ticking bomb terrorist that Dershowitz considers? If so, how?

MARCIA BARON

The Ticking Bomb Hypothetical

In her essay, Marcia Baron (like others) claims that using the case of the ticking bomb terrorist to reject an absolute prohibition on torture is problematic. She asks why this is. Baron rejects the claim that such a ban is problematic just because the case is artificial. Artificial cases as used by philosophers doing ethics, she argues, can sometimes help one untangle moral complexities in order to focus on some particular moral issue; their artificiality does not matter. But, she claims, the ticking bomb hypothetical is different—its artificiality does matter—because it is intended to weaken a commitment to the absolutist position that torture should be banned in all circumstances. She defends this claim by examining in detail versions of the ticking bomb hypothetical, explaining why their artificiality is seriously misleading and should not be employed to justify torture in special circumstances.

Recent literature arguing for, or reaffirming, the impermissibility of torture has deplored the ticking bomb hypothetical and its frequent invocation. I have in mind in particular the work of David Luban and Henry Shue.[1] I share their views, by and large, but at the same time think that just what is so problematic about the hypothetical remains somewhat unclear.[2] This essay, while very much indebted to their work, aims to bring out more sharply how the focus on the ticking bomb hypothetical in the revived torture debates has led us astray.[3] I take issue not only with those who rely on the hypothetical to defend the use of interrogational torture,[4] but also with those who, while taking a much more nuanced view, insist on "the relevance and significance of the catastrophic case."[5] Oren Gross writes that "there are two perspectives from which we ought to approach the question of the use of preventive interrogational torture, namely, the general policy perspective and the perspective of the catastrophic case . . . . We can only focus on one to the exclusion of the other at our peril."[6] I see no peril in ceasing to take "the perspective of the catastrophic case."

When I presented a version of this paper at a conference, some expressed perplexity at my attention to empirical facts. Perhaps the expectation, given my strong Kantian leanings, was that I would focus on moral principles, and offer a Kantian argument against torture. But arguing against torture on Kantian grounds is unlikely to budge those who believe that moral opposition to torture needs to be tempered by (as they see it) realism. Indeed, one often comes across such phrases as "all but unabashed Kantians recognize" in discussions of torture, as in this: "the fact that all but unabashed Kantians recognize the difficulties presented by extreme cases to any absolutist position is taken as further evidence that an absolutist position with respect to a ban on torture is untenable."[7] To engage those who defend torture, or who believe that the ticking bomb hypothetical forces us to reconsider the ban on torture, it is crucial to meet them on their turf rather than invite them to consider the issue from a Kantian perspective.

2

I begin by quoting two versions of the ticking bomb hypothetical, the first by an opponent of torture, and the second by authors who defend it. Henry Shue presents it as follows in his classic 1978 article, "Torture":

> There is a standard philosopher's example which someone always invokes: suppose a fanatic, perfectly willing to die rather than collaborate in the thwarting of his own scheme, has set a hidden nuclear device to explode in the heart of Paris. There is no time to evacuate . . . the only hope of preventing tragedy is to torture the perpetrator, find the device, and deactivate it.[8]

Mirko Bagaric and Julie Clarke offer the following version:

> A terrorist network has activated a large bomb on one of hundreds of commercial planes carrying more than three hundred passengers that are flying somewhere in the world at any point in time. The bomb is set to explode in thirty minutes. The leader of the terrorist organization announces this via a statement on the Internet. He states that the bomb was planted by one of his colleagues at one of the major airports in the world in the past few hours. No details are provided regarding the location of the plane where the bomb is located. Unbeknownst to him, he was under police surveillance and is immediately apprehended by police. The terrorist leader refuses to answer any police questions, declaring that the passengers must die and will shortly.[9]

The conclusion, as Bagaric and Clarke see it, is clear. "Who would deny that all possible means should be used to extract the details of the plane and the location of the bomb?"[10]

So, just what is problematic about the hypothetical? Doesn't it test our intuitions, getting us to question our commitment to a principle that torture is always wrong? The idea in putting forward the example, David Luban writes, is to "force the liberal prohibitionist to admit that yes, even . . . she would agree to torture in at least this one situation. Once [she . . .] admits that, then she has conceded that her opposition to torture is not based on principle. Now that [she] has admitted that her moral principles can be breached, all that is left is haggling about the price."[11] Luban goes on to say that the ticking bomb example "bewitches" us, and I think he is right, though just how it bewitches us is somewhat elusive. But I can also see that this would sound pretty lame to those who defend torture, as if when confronted by an example that clinches their case (as they see it) we protest that there is some unfairness, some trickery, that we are being bewitched. We seem to be dodging the problem. Shouldn't we have to answer their question and say whether or not we think that torture in such a situation is permissible?

I don't think we should have to. I also don't think that granting that torture might be permissible in extraordinary circumstances would weaken the prohibitionist's case in the way Luban's remarks suggest. But before we get to that, and before I explain in what ways the hypothetical has misled us, we need to be clear on what the problem isn't.

Those who take the ticking bomb hypothetical very seriously sometimes suppose that opposition to it is merely opposition to "artificial cases" or "fantastic examples" in general.[12] This is not entirely surprising. Although both Shue and Luban provide excellent reasons for seeing the ticking bomb hypothetical as problematic in a way that distinguishes it from most "fantastic examples," some of their remarks, at least if read out of context, may leave the impression that the ticking bomb example is of the same ilk as other "artificial cases." Luban remarks that "artificial cases" such as those of "fat men thrown in front of runaway trolleys, blown out of mineshafts with bazookas, or impaled on pitchforks as they fall from windows" are "deeply cartoonish."[13] Shue writes that "There is a saying in jurisprudence that hard cases make bad law, and there might well be one in philosophy that artificial cases make bad ethics."[14]

Artificial cases are not all of a kind. Some help us focus on key issues, while others distract us from the real issues or distort a reality they purport to depict (or both). The ticking bomb hypothetical is artificial and dangerously misleading in a way that the examples Luban refers to are not.[15] There may be reasons for objecting to them, but the problem I wish to bring out is not a problem they share.[16]

Just as it is not the sheer "cartoonishness" or "artificiality" of the examples that is the problem, the objection to the reliance on the hypothetical is not that ticking bomb scenarios are so rare that it is unwise to let them shape our general policy regarding the use of torture (though that is closer).

3

So what is the problem? Partly this: as Shue has explained, it is almost impossible to be in the position depicted in ticking bomb hypotheticals and also to know that one is in such a position. But once again it may sound as if the claim is only that the hypothetical is unrealistic, and why does that matter, when many hypotheticals are unrealistic? To understand why it matters in this case yet not in general and to see in what way this hypothetical is aptly said to "bewitch" us, we need to reflect on the role of hypotheticals in philosophical discussion, and then examine how this hypothetical differs from others.

Normally when we are presented with a hypothetical, we accept it as a hypothetical and focus attention on whatever the person presenting the hypothetical asks us to consider. It is bad form to ask "Does it really work that way?" We are expected to accept the hypothetical as such. But if we do so, granting it for the sake of discussion, we may be granting assumptions that are highly implausible. Often in philosophy it doesn't matter that we are granting highly implausible assumptions for the sake of discussion; we bracket one thing in order to focus on another. With many hypotheticals, it is fruitful to do so. There is something to be gained by thinking about the issue without worrying about the details that we are agreeing not to question. The fantastic examples may provide (as they do in Thomson's "A Defense of Abortion")[17] a way to disentangle the various arguments against a particular practice or policy or individual choice and examine them more clearheadedly. In the case of the ticking bomb hypothetical, however, it is hard to see why it would be helpful to set aside relevant facts about torture, since the matter under discussion is the moral permissibility of the practice of interrogational torture.

In many discussions involving an implausible hypothetical, the person proffering it is not claiming or assuming that this is in fact something that happens (or that we had better be prepared to see happen or, if it is something we might want to see happen, that we can bring about). With the ticking bomb hypothetical, things are different; yet we may, if we treat the hypothetical as one normally treats a hypothetical, fail to recognize this. We may, in effect, be tricked by the ticking bomb hypothetical into thinking that we are only accepting it as a hypothetical, when in fact we are being led to view torture in a wholly inaccurate way.

It should now be somewhat clearer why the ticking bomb hypothetical is problematic in a way that other "artificial cases" are not, but more needs to be said to bring out how the former differs from the latter. Recall the runaway trolley, the fat man wedged in the mouth of a cave, the kidnapped violinist, and the people seeds that can drift into homes and take root in the upholstery. Or consider the cases involving killing someone—or, in another case, helping a starving person to die—so that his body can be used for medical research, or for "spare parts," or for making a serum from his dead body that will save several lives. Imagine someone objecting to one of the medical examples by saying, "Wait a minute, is it really possible to make a serum from someone's dead body that would then save several lives?" We would reply, "Don't worry about that; it doesn't matter whether it is possible," and we would then explain (supposing that we are discussing Philippa Foot's "Abortion and the Doctrine of Double Effect"[18]) that Foot's point was to contrast (a) our view that killing or allowing someone to die in order to save several people is clearly wrong to (b) our reaction to a case where a decision is made to withhold a life-saving drug that is in short supply from a patient who requires a massive dose, and instead to give it to several people who also require the drug, but for whom a much smaller dose will suffice. Note that her point in doing this was not to convince us of the wrongness or rightness of one medical policy or another, so her use of "fantastic examples" is strikingly different from the use

to which the ticking bomb hypothetical is put. Her aim, rather, was to consider whether the doctrine of double effect or a different principle better accounts for our judgments about such cases.

In the essays from which I've drawn these examples—Foot's "Abortion and the Doctrine of Double Effect" and Thomson's "A Defense of Abortion"—there is a distance between the example and the point in support of which the example is put forward, a distance that we don't have between the ticking bomb hypothetical and the claim it is intended to support. The relation between the example and the intended point is such that it makes no difference at all that the example is artificial, or unrealistic. But because the ticking bomb hypothetical is intended to weaken our commitment to prohibitions on torture and lend support to a (possibly very limited) practice of torture, it indeed does matter whether the hypothetical is realistic. Yet, perhaps because normally we do not question the realism of a hypothetical, many people pay little attention to whether the ticking bomb hypothetical is at all plausible.

4

Let's look more closely at a couple of versions of the ticking bomb hypothetical—versions put forward by those who believe the hypothetical should be taken seriously—to see in what way it is unrealistic, and in what way its being unrealistic leads us astray.

Recall the Bagaric and Clarke example. There we are asked to envision a situation where a leader of a terrorist organization has announced that a bomb has been placed on a passenger jet. The jet is now in flight, and the bomb is set to go off in thirty minutes. The terrorist leader was already under surveillance; we are asked to imagine that he is therefore apprehended quickly. We are to accept that he knows where the bomb is, that by torturing him (but by no other means[19]) we can extract the necessary information, that the pilots can then be contacted, and that it will be possible either to quickly land and evacuate the plane, or to locate the bomb on the plane and defuse it— all in less than thirty minutes. We are to accept, in short, that torture is the solution, and that the only thing standing in the way of saving the lives of over three hundred people is our moral scruples.

Or consider a version of the ticking bomb hypothetical put forward by Jean Bethke Elshtain. In her version, a bomb has been planted in one of several hundred elementary schools in a particular city. We don't know which school (though we know which city), but we are virtually certain that we have apprehended someone who is not only part of the plot, but who also knows in which school the bomb has been placed. The bomb is to go off within the hour. Officials know, Elshtain writes, that "they cannot evacuate all of the schools."[20] Curiously, it is considered a much surer thing to torture the suspect, extract the information, and then evacuate the school in question. If there is time to evacuate the school in question after the torture has extracted the information, why not skip the torture and immediately evacuate all the several hundred schools? That would be a much surer way to prevent loss of life.

These versions of the hypothetical stand in stark contrast to such cases as the runaway trolley and the drifting people seeds. To make sense of the hypothetical we accept, perhaps without fully realizing we are doing so, assumptions that in effect give the game away: that torture works, works very quickly, in some situations is the only thing that will work,[21] and moreover, that we can know when we are in a situation where torture, and only torture, will prevent a disaster. If we do not accept these assumptions, we will find the hypothetical baffling; if we accept it as a hypothetical and do not question the assumptions, most of the important issues about the moral permissibility of the practice of torture have been taken off the table. The only thing that has not been taken off the table is moral principles condemning torture; concern about these, however, is dismissed as a sort of prissiness, or moral narcissism.[22]

The ticking bomb hypothetical asks us to forget about the fact that we do not know that our prisoner actually has the information we need, and to ignore all the evidence that even if we do have the right person, torture is generally ineffective—certainly unreliable—as a way of obtaining the information we need.[23] It invites us to conceive of torture as in effect a truth serum. Indirectly, it also prods us to ignore the evidence that torture is very difficult to contain. I'll say more about this shortly.

5

The ticking bomb hypothetical is marred by the very feature that is supposed to make it so compelling: that there is no time to lose. Torture is particularly unlikely to work when the bomb will go off within thirty minutes, or even a couple of hours. A determined terrorist is likely to be able to withstand the torture until the bomb goes off, and even this isn't necessary, since naming the wrong flight or school is as likely to end the torture as is naming the correct one.

A defender of torture might concede this, and put forward a different hypothetical, where there is more time. But when there *is* time for torture to have a somewhat better chance of working,[24] there is also time to try to gain the captive's trust; when one does, one generally learns far more than when one tortures. Some defenders of torture (e.g., Charles Krauthammer) find such suggestions preposterous; one would almost think from their scoffing that intelligence is generally obtained only via torture.[25]

Readers accustomed to such scoffing might find it helpful to hear something about how interrogators can successfully interrogate without relying on violence, humiliation, degradation, and in general breaking the person down so fully that (if he survives intact enough to be able to remember the information and communicate it) he blurts out whatever the interrogator wants to hear (which defenders of torture assume will be something true). Given space limitations, a brief summary drawn from Ali Soufan's Senate testimony will have to do.[26] The "Informed Interrogation Approach" is based on the following, Soufan explains: the interrogator turns "the fear that the detainee feels as a result of his capture and isolation from his support base" and the fact that people "crave human contact" to his advantage, "becoming the one person the detainee can talk to and who listens to what he has to say, and uses this to encourage the detainee to open up"; in addition, the kindness he shows the detainee takes the detainee by surprise, as the detainee (if a member of Al Qaeda, anyway) is trained to resist torture, but not to resist kindness. (Soufan's offer of sugar-free cookies to Abu Jandal, whom he knew to be diabetic, is but one example of the many ways he established the rapport that quickly led Jandal to share with him extensive information, just after 9/11, on the 9/11 hijackers and the structure of Al Qaeda.) The interrogator also takes into account "the need the detainee feels to sustain a position of respect and value to interrogator." In addition, "there is the impression the detainee has of the evidence against him. The interrogator has to do his or her homework and become an expert in every detail known to the intelligence community about the detainee." This serves both "to impress upon the detainee that everything about him is known and that any lie will be easily caught" and to establish rapport.[27] Such expertise of course is also important in other ways: without it, the interrogator is less likely to ask the right questions and to pick up on details that might otherwise not seem significant.[28]

6
_____

I mentioned that the ticking bomb hypothetical encourages us to view torture as something easily contained. It suggests that torture can happen just once, just for this particular emergency, without there being a practice of torture, and without torture ever being used again. But it is seriously misleading to speak of a single instance of torture, necessary only for this one emergency.

There are two reasons for this. To have any prospect of even occasional success, torture requires, *inter alia*, training, manuals, equipment, practice at torturing, personnel to assist in torturing, and medical personnel to revive the detainee as needed and to advise on limits that need to be observed lest the torture result in death or another state that precludes

extracting the needed information. So although it would be an exaggeration to say that torture is impossible except as part of a practice of torture, we have to assume that torture defended on the grounds that it may be necessary, albeit only in rare circumstances, for obtaining information needed to prevent a ticking bomb from detonating, will be not a "one time" use of torture, but part of a practice. Any attempt to justify interrogational torture for use only in rare circumstances will also either be, or require, a justification of torture as a practice.

The second reason torture needs to be viewed as a practice concerns not what must have preceded it if the contemplated torture is going to have any chance of being effective, but what follows in its train. As Rejali has meticulously documented and Shue, Luban, and others have elaborated, it is virtually impossible for torture to be limited to just one instance. Even when the plan is to allow it in only very rare instances, soon other situations arise where a catastrophe looms, even if not quite as huge a catastrophe, and torture is deemed necessary there, too; and then, as we have seen in the conduct of the United States in recent years, it is pointed out that we cannot afford to wait until there is a ticking bomb, and need to uncover terrorist plots before they are executed (a sound thought so far!), and to that end—given the seriousness of the calamity if we do not prevent it—we must employ "enhanced techniques" of interrogation as an ongoing part of our war on terror.

Torture spreads. History shows that soldiers bring it home, where it is used in police interrogations and by prison guards.[29] Torture intended only for very limited use (e.g., in Guantánamo) soon shows up in U.S.-run prisons in Iraq and Afghanistan.[30] It spreads not only geographically, but also from one accepted purpose to a purpose that initially was not seen as justifying it. As the torture equipment, training, and personnel expand, and reports of the use of torture spread, torture becomes "normalized," and the range of instances where torture is deemed necessary (or even just "worth a try") expands. The more torture is viewed as the best way to get crucial intelligence, the more the truly valuable techniques languish, and intelligence-gathering skills deteriorate; torture is then relied on all the more.[31] In addition, torture initially justified only for intelligence gathering is soon used to express a sense of mastery, to humiliate . . . and to get the captive to say what one wants to hear (possibly to provide a pretext for some military action,[32] or to justify action already taken).

7
_____

It might be objected that I have chosen to examine versions of the ticking bomb hypothetical that are stunningly stupid. It is true that they are—especially the one about the school. But that itself tells us something. It is very telling that those who take the hypothetical so seriously do not even notice that in the scenario they draw up, either the time frame is such that torture hardly stands a chance of working in time (as in the example of the bomb on the plane) or that there is another, far better solution, not involving torture (as in the case of the schools, where immediate evacuation of all the schools would be a much surer way of saving lives than torturing first, and then, relying on whatever one elicited from the captive, evacuating only the school in question). It is evidence of how mesmerized people are by the idea of a ticking bomb scenario that people with JDs or PhDs and a record of excellent scholarship, can commit such a blunder. More specifically, it is evidence of the readiness on the part of many intelligent people to see torture as the best solution (if moral issues are set to one side), the most effective way (at least when time is of the essence) to deal with terrorism. The mindless way the topic of torture is discussed itself deserves our attention, and is part of the reason for the aptness of Luban's hyperbolic claim that the ticking bomb hypothetical has bewitched us.

Still, we might ask if these are just poor versions of the ticking bomb hypothetical. Will a better version avoid the problems I have noted? Shue's version fares somewhat better than those put forward by supporters of torture. In his version, it is an entire city that will be blown up, not just a school, so evacuation is not a very serious option (depending on the

time frame, which is not indicated). Still, it is hard to imagine—even if we somehow know we have the (or a) perpetrator, and that the perpetrator knows where the bomb is—that we know with a reasonable degree of certainty that torture will extract the information and will do so in time for the bomb to be located and deactivated. If the terrorist is determined that the bomb go off, he is more likely to hold out or lie or otherwise gain time than to tell the truth.[33] This and other points made earlier apply to thoughtfully crafted ticking bomb hypotheticals, not only to Elshtain's and to Bagaric and Clarke's.

It may be countered that torture has worked—that there have been real ticking bomb scenarios, where torture succeeded in extracting the necessary information in time, where the bomb really would have gone off had the information not been extracted, and where there is very good reason to believe that nothing else would have worked. Those who have scrutinized the cases report that in fact it wasn't like that. In a case defenders of torture often cite, that of Abdul Hakim Murad, the torture—67 days of it!—may possibly have played a role in gleaning the information, though the information was provided not under torture, but only afterward, when the interrogators threatened to turn Murad over to the Israelis. But in fact, all the information that Murad eventually provided was on his laptop, which the interrogators had in their possession the entire time they were busy torturing Murad. Not only was torture unnecessary, but the information could have been obtained much more quickly if proper intelligence-gathering procedures were used. Rejali describes that interrogation as a textbook case of "how a police force is progressively deskilled by torture."[34] In another case often cited to show that torture does indeed work, Abu Zubaydah in fact revealed valuable information[35] only when the interrogators quit torturing and a new interrogator persuaded the captive that it was his religious duty to reveal the requested information.[36]

Rather than discuss further the question of whether there have been any authentic ticking bomb scenarios—where torture thwarted a major disaster that could not have been thwarted otherwise, and where those deciding to use torture believed on good evidence that torture and only torture would do the trick—I want to shift my focus and ask this question: Suppose there really have been authentic ticking bomb scenarios. Or, even if there haven't been such cases, suppose there can be. What would that show?

I raise this question in part because I note in some of the literature with which I sympathize an eagerness to deny that a ticking bomb scenario could ever happen. The worry is that if we concede that it could, we'll be asked whether it is permissible to torture in such circumstances. And then, it is thought, we are in trouble. Luban writes (as noted earlier) that the idea in putting forward the ticking bomb hypothetical is to "force the liberal prohibitionist to admit that yes, even . . . she would agree to torture in at least this one situation. Once the prohibitionist admits that, then she has conceded that her opposition to torture is not based on principle. Now that [she] has admitted that her moral principles can be breached, all that is left is haggling about the price."[37] In the article from which I am quoting, it is not entirely clear whether Luban is agreeing that the concession really is this significant or simply explaining a strategy. But in his "Unthinking the Ticking Bomb," he makes it clear that he does think it quite significant: "After making the initial concession, any prohibition on torture faces significant dialectical pressure toward balancing tests and the unwelcome . . . conclusion that interrogational torture can be justified whenever the expected benefits outweigh the expected costs."[38]

But the problem is not as serious as that suggests. Switch for a moment from torture to rape. Suppose that in some very weird scenario, perhaps involving a demented character like Jack D. Ripper from *Dr. Strangelove*, a horrible catastrophe—the detonation of nuclear bombs—could be prevented only by raping or abetting a rape. (If it helps, add to the example that one has to rape a child, and has to do so in front of the child's family and one's own family.) We do not in any way deny that rape is impermissible—nor do we deny that our objection to it is based on principle—if we do not rule out the possibility that were this absolutely the only way to prevent a horrific catastrophe, and we knew it would prevent it, choosing to do so would not be wrong in those circumstances. The categories countenanced by Luban are too limited. It is not as if believing that X is wrong on principle—even horribly wrong—entails denying that there could be a scenario in which X would be a permissible choice. That we allow this does not mean that X can be permitted any time the benefits of permitting it outweigh the costs.[39]

We are expected to be prepared to answer questions about whether we would torture, or want others to torture, in a ticking bomb scenario, yet are not expected to answer questions about whether we would be willing to rape someone, or order or abet a rape, if that were necessary to prevent a catastrophe of massive proportions. Both scenarios are very unlikely, but torture is treated differently. I believe it is treated differently only because we are still bedeviled into thinking that torture is generally effective and that therefore in a ticking bomb scenario, or perhaps even in a situation where we think there may be plans to bomb a city, torture is—from a strictly pragmatic standpoint—our best bet for obtaining the crucial information. We have not fully abandoned the idea that torture will work when nothing else will. Despite the fact that most of us really do know better, torture retains its status as the method of choice—as what you'll do if you really want to get the job done.

8

I have tried in my paper to bring out what is so misleading about the ticking bomb hypothetical, in the context of a discussion of the practice of interrogational torture, and to show that it is problematic in a way that other hypotheticals—the runaway trolley, etc.—are not. The latter in no way rely for their effectiveness on the case being realistic, whereas the ticking bomb hypothetical does. Relatedly, the ticking bomb hypothetical takes off the table most of the objections to torture, in effect asking us to ignore such facts as that torture is a very unreliable way to gather intelligence and that torture is both very difficult to contain and particularly unlikely to succeed if it is not part of an ongoing practice, involving assistants, equipment, and extensive training. It is thus not well suited to a "one time" or very occasional usc that those who think it justifiable in ticking bomb scenarios envision.

I realize that some may find there to be something chilling about my attention to these pragmatic considerations, and in closing I want to emphasize that nothing I say should be construed as an indication that I think torture would be morally defensible if only it did work. As I noted at the outset, arguing against torture by focusing on its moral wrongness is very unlikely to budge those I hope to engage. Some defenders of torture believe that morality requires that we use torture in such a ticking bomb scenario; others do not, but hold that moral principles—or "scruples"—are a luxury that we cannot afford in an emergency. What is needed to convince those inclined to either position is to show how very misleading the ticking bomb hypothetical is.[40]

NOTES

1. David Luban, "Liberalism, Torture, and the Ticking Bomb," *Virginia Law Review* 91 (2005): 1425–61, and "Unthinking the Ticking Bomb," in *Global Basic Rights*, ed. Charles R. Beitz and Robert E. Goodin (New York: Oxford University Press, 2009), 181–206; and Henry Shue, "Torture in Dreamland: Disposing of the Ticking Bomb," *Case Western Reserve Journal of International Law* 37 (2005): 231–39. See also Bob Brecher, *Torture and the Ticking Bomb* (Malden, MA: Blackwell, 2007); Claudia Card, "Ticking Bombs and Interrogations," *Criminal Law and Philosophy* 2 (2008): 1–15; Elaine Scarry, "Five Errors in the Reasoning of Alan Dershowitz," in *Torture: A Collection* (revised ed.), ed. Sanford Levinson (New York: Oxford University Press, 2005): 281–98; Kim Lane Scheppele, "Hypothetical Torture in the 'War on Terrorism,'" *Journal of National Security Law and Policy* 1 (2005): 285–340; and Yuval Ginbar, *Why Not Torture Terrorists?* (Oxford: Oxford University Press, 2010).

2. This much, however, is very clear: employing the hypothetical to try to justify the use of torture by the United States during the administration of George W. Bush is deplorable. There torture was used (among other reasons, such as to humiliate, and to avenge killings) as a fishing expedition to uncover plots, *not* to prevent a ticking bomb from detonating. For more on the singular inappropriateness of trying to justify via the ticking bomb hypothetical the use of torture in the "war on terror," see Scheppele, "Hypothetical Torture."

3. That there is some confusion about just what the point is in dismissing ticking bomb hypotheticals as "artificial" is evident from Oren Gross, "The Prohibition on Torture and the Limits of Law," in Levinson, *Torture*, 229–55 at 234.

4. My focus throughout this paper is on interrogational torture (i.e., torture aimed at acquiring information crucial to preventing, or limiting the scope of, a catastrophe). I do not in this paper address instances of torture in direct self-defense or defense of others, where, say, someone is torturing my child and threatening to kill her, and for some reason the only way to get him to stop is to torture him (or his confederate . . . or his child). For discussion of such cases, see Sherry F. Colb, "Why Is Torture 'Different' and How 'Different' Is It?" *Cardozo Law Review* 30 (2009): 1411–73. Nor do I consider in this paper torture for purposes of obtaining information that could then be used to convict someone; I assume that readers of this volume would not regard that to be worth considering. Even those who think that torture might very occasionally be permissible presumably would not want the criminal justice system to rely on information obtained by torture. Indeed torture other than preventive interrogational torture or torture in direct self-defense (e.g., torture to extract confessions, exorcise demons, intimidate rebels, get revenge, or relieve boredom) I assume all readers of this volume, indeed all even moderately reasonable persons, agree is absolutely impermissible.

5. Gross, "Prohibition on Torture," 239.

6. *Ibid.*, 239–40.

7. *Ibid.*, 231.

8. Henry Shue,"Torture," *Philosophy and Public Affairs* 7 (1978): 124–43 at 141.

9. Mirko Bagaric and Julie Clarke, *Torture: When the Unthinkable Is Morally Permissible* (Albany: SUNY Press, 2007), 2.

10. *Ibid.*, 3.

11. Luban, "Liberalism," 1440.

12. See, e.g., Bagaric and Clarke, *Torture*, 3, where they write that "fantastic examples cannot be dismissed summarily merely because they are 'simply' hypothetical." I agree (though not with the implication that some opponents of torture dismiss the ticking bomb hypothetical solely on those grounds).

13. Luban, "Unthinking," 206.

14. Shue, "Torture," 141.

15. Clarification is in order concerning the content of the hypothetical. It is part of the content not only that a bomb will detonate soon unless we disable it and that we don't know where it is, but also that (a) we cannot find out in time except by torturing someone we have in captivity,

(b) torturing him or her will indeed enable us to prevent the catastrophe, and (c) we know this. The clarification is needed because some respond to claims that the hypothetical is extremely implausible by saying there is no doubt that ticking bomb scenarios do occur, pointing in support of their claim to a case where a suicide bombing was averted but where (not only was the bomb not yet ticking, but more importantly) there is no indication that torture was used in the interrogation that led to the disclosure of the planned bombing, let alone that torture was needed (and, moreover, known to be needed). See e.g., Stephen de Wijze's review of Karen Greenberg, ed., *The Torture Debate in America*, in *Democratiya* 7 (2006): 10–36, especially 21.

16. As this paper goes to press, Allen Wood points out to me ways in which some of the problems I single out as particularly problems with ticking bomb hypotheticals also afflict trolley examples. See, his excellent "Humanity as End in Itself," in Samuel Scheffler (ed.), Derek Parfit, *On What Matters*, Volume 2 (Oxford: Oxford University Press, 2011), pp. 58–82.

17. Judith Jarvis Thomson, "A Defense of Abortion," *Philosophy and Public Affairs* 1 (1971): 47–66.

18. Philippa Foot, *Virtues and Vices* (Berkeley: University of California Press, 1978), Ch. 2.

19. Bagaric and Clarke do not specify that no other means will be effective, though "the terrorist leader refuses to answer any police questions" (*Torture*, 2) seems intended to indicate this. It is possible that they think that we should use an assortment of techniques, torture included, with the idea that by using "all means" we increase our chances of extracting information. But success is not increased by increasing the number of means used. Using torture seriously undermines the effectiveness of Army Field Manual techniques, since these are based on establishing some rapport. See Jane Mayer, *The Dark Side* (New York: Doubleday, 2008); Darius Rejali, *Torture and Democracy* (Princeton, NJ: Princeton University Press, 2007); and Sherwood Moran, "Suggestions for Japanese Interpreters Based on Work in the Field," excerpted in William F. Schulz, ed., *The Phenomenon of Torture: Readings and Commentary* (Philadelphia: University of Pennsylvania Press, 2007), 249–54. Someone might hold that torture can be justifiable other than as a last resort, but I do not think that view worth discussing, and so do not take it up here. See also note 20.

20. Jean Bethke Elshtain, "Reflection on the Problem of 'Dirty Hands'," in Levinson, ed. *Torture*, 78.

21. This assumes that we regard torture as something to be avoided if at all possible. Of course if one thinks that terrorists deserve to be tortured, it may not seem necessary, to justify torture, that it be the only way to prevent a catastrophe; it will matter more that we not make mistakes and torture someone who (whether or not he or she has the information we need to prevent the catastrophe) is not a terrorist.

22. Elshtain asks us who we would want in a position of judgment in her hypothetical. Would we prefer a "person of such stringent moral and legal rectitude that he or she would not consider torture because violating his or her own conscience is the most morally serious thing a person can do? Or a person, aware of the stakes and the possible deaths of hundreds of children, who acts in the light of harsh necessity and orders the prisoner tortured? This second leader," Elshtain adds, "does not rank his or her 'purity' above human lives." Elshtain, "Reflection," 80–81.

23. See, among other sources, Rejali, *Torture and Democracy*, especially chaps. 21 and 22; the Senate testimony of former FBI agent Ali Soufan (who obtained extremely important information without using "enhanced" techniques and saw effective interrogations ruined when another agent insisted on torturing the detainee), Committee on the Judiciary, U.S. Senate, May 13, 2009. (Available at <http://www.judiciary.senate.gov/hearings/testimony.cfm?id=e655f9e2809e5476862f735da14945e6&wit_id=e655f9e2809e5476862f735da14945e6–1-2>, accessed February 1, 2012; hereafter Soufan, "Testimony"), and his *New York Times* op-eds, in particular, "My Tortured Decision," (April 22, 2009), and "What Torture Never Told Us" (September 5, 2009); Mayer, *The Dark Side*; Jean Maria Arrigo, "A Utilitarian Argument against Torture Interrogation of Terrorists," *Science and Engineering Ethics* 10 (2004): 1–30; and the Army Field Manual.

24. Only somewhat, however, and only at enormous cost. It has a better chance of working in part because time provides an opportunity to interrogate many other people, and thereby confirm or disconfirm the information obtained. But once the notion that torture is the most effective way of obtaining information has taken hold, there is now an incentive for torturing an ever increasing number of people, and over a long period of time. As torture becomes an ongoing activity, torturing those whom one has no good reason to think have valuable information becomes increasingly common. For a vivid picture, see the literature on the use of torture by the French in Algeria (e.g., Rejali, *Torture and Democracy*, chap. 22, part of which is published, with some modification, as "Does Torture Work?" in Schulz, *Phenomenon of Torture*, 256–65).

Worth noting, too, is that it is not as if detainees will have reason to figure that any misinformation they provide will be easily detected; some misinformation will be hard to detect, particularly by agents focused on torturing rather than on understanding the political situation. A tactic when one is pressed for names of those plotting terrorist attacks is to name members of a rival, more moderate group. The effect is that those who might have helped to develop a compromise and end the violence are themselves destroyed or radicalized by torture; support for the more extremist, more violent group thus increases. This strategy was employed by the Algerian Front de Libération Nationale (FLN). As Rejali writes, the French soldiers, knowing little about the subtleties of Algerian nationalism, "helped the FLN liquidate the infrastructure of the more cooperative organization and tortured members of the Movement National Algérien (MNA), driving them into extreme opposition" (Rejali, "Does Torture Work?" 256).

The other reason that prolonged torture is more likely to work than brief torture is that it is more likely to "break" the captive. Not to be forgotten, though, is that the captive may well not have the information sought, and if she does, may be so damaged by the torture as to be unable to recall or articulate the information. The particular horrors of prolonged torture need to be borne in mind here; they are hard to fathom, but we can get some sense of them from the film "Taxi to the Dark Side" (2007) and from memoirs of those who survived torture.

25. Charles Krauthammer, "Torture? No. Except . . . " op-ed, *Washington Post*, May 1, 2009.

26. Readers wanting more detail might read the full text of his statement in Soufan, "Testimony." See also Michael Isikoff, " 'We Could Have Done This the Right Way': How Ali Soufan, FBI Agent, Got Abu Zubaydah to Talk without Torture," *Newsweek* (April 25, 2009); the film *The Oath* (Laura Poitras, 2010); Sherwood Moran, "Suggestions for Japanese Interpreters" 249–54; Scott Pelley's interview with George Piro about his interrogations of Saddam Hussein, "60 Minutes," January 27, 2008, available at <http://www.cbsnews.com/video/watch/?id=4758713n&tag=mncol;lst;3>, accessed November 27, 2012; and Rejali, *Torture and Democracy*.

27. In his first interrogation of Zubaydah, Soufan asked him his name; Zubaydah replied with his alias, and Soufan responded, "How about if I call you 'Hani'?" 'Hani' being the name Zubaydah's mother nicknamed him as a child. "He looked at me in shock, said 'ok,' and we started talking," Soufan recounts. Soufan, "Testimony."

28. The need for interrogators to be very knowledgeable is put more starkly by an unnamed former CIA operative. Lamenting the interrogations in Afghanistan by people with "no understanding of Al Qaeda or the Arab World," the operative said that "the key to interrogation

is knowledge, not techniques. We didn't know anything. And if you don't know anything, you can't get anything." Mayer, *The Dark Side*, 144.

29. See Rejali, *Torture and Democracy*, 436 and 178–80.

30. For details, see Scheppele, "Hypothetical Torture," and Mayer, *The Dark Side*, among others.

31. A further factor, difficult to assess, is that torture—it is reported by some who have taken part in torturing or in exercises designed to fortify soldiers in case they become victims of torture—is often quite intoxicating. See Jane Mayer, "The Experiment," *The New Yorker* (July 11, 2005); see also Rejali, *Torture and Democracy*, pp. 486–87.

32. See Mayer, *The Dark Side*, chaps. 6 and 7, and in particular her discussion of the interrogation of Ibn al-Shaykh al-Libi, who was speaking freely with FBI agents interviewing him in the traditional "rapport" based way, but then was forcibly removed by the CIA and taken to Egypt. There, under torture, he said what he gathered they wanted him to say, and thus provided the "intelligence" [CIA director George] Tenet relied on when he told [Secretary of State Colin] Powell that Al Qaeda and Hussein's secret police trained together in Baghdad, and that chemical and biological weapons were involved (137). See also the discussion of al-Libi in Rejali, *Torture and Democracy*, 504–505.

33. And if he does cave in and release the information, chances are that it is no longer accurate, since when terrorists suspect that a member of their cohort is in custody, they generally alter their plans and their own locations. This is a consideration worth bearing in mind in assessing claims one often hears along the following lines (paraphrased and quoted from Jeff McMahan's "Torture, Morality, and Law," *Case Western Reserve Journal of International Law* 37 (2006): 241–48 at 244): in some instances in which Israeli security forces captured persons in the process of making or transporting such bombs, those captured were then "tortured in order to force them to divulge information about other attacks . . . planned for the future." The information thereby obtained "then enabled the security forces to take preemptive action to thwart the planned attacks." This may be just what happened; it is hard to say because no specifics are provided. But given the standard practice of altering plans when a member of their cohort cannot be reached and is presumed to be in custody, one wonders if what thwarted the planned attacks was perhaps simply the capture of someone involved in, and informed about, the plan, rather than the intelligence gleaned through the torture.

34. Rejali, *Torture and Democracy*, 507. Another instructive example is that of an Algerian locksmith

arrested by the French and tortured for three days. He had in his pocket "bomb blueprints with the address of an FLN bomb factory in Algiers." The "locksmith bought time, the bombers relocated, and the French raid three days later fell on open air." "Had the soldiers been able to read Arabic, they would have found the bomb factory days earlier," and had they not been focused on torturing, they could have sought help with the Arabic. Ibid., 486.

35. Such as it was; the value of the information Abu Zubaydah provided is a matter of dispute. See Luban, "Unthinking," 189–90.

36. See details in ibid., 189. See also Ali Soufan, "My Tortured Decision." Soufan was one of Zubaydah's interrogators.

37. Luban, "Liberalism," 1440.

38. Luban, "Unthinking," 198.

39. It is worth noting here that Kant, despite his position that suicide is impermissible, raised the following question, to which he did not offer an answer: "A man who had been bitten by a mad dog already felt hydrophobia coming on. He explained, in a letter he left, that, since as far as he knew the disease was incurable, he was taking his life lest he harm others as well in his madness (the onset of which he already felt). Did he do wrong?" Immanuel Kant, *The Metaphysics of Morals*, Mary Gregor, ed. and trans. (New York: Cambridge University Press, 1996), 178 (AK 6: 423–24).

40. I am grateful to Scott Anderson and Sandra Shapshay for helpful comments, and to discussants at conferences at the University of Chicago Law School (2008) and at Washington University (2008) for stimulating discussion of earlier drafts of this paper.

READING QUESTIONS

1. In section 4, how does Baron object to the ticking bomb hypotheticals as described by Bagaric and Clarke and by Elshtain?
2. What is the "Informed Interrogation Approach" to interrogation?
3. What reasons does Baron give for rejecting the idea that interrogational torture can be limited in its use?
4. What point is Baron making in section 7 with the example of rape?

DISCUSSION QUESTIONS

1. Would Dershowitz's proposal involving torture warrants adequately address Baron's worries about limiting the use of interrogational torture?
2. Can interrogational torture in a ticking bomb terrorist case ever be justified by Kant's Humanity formulation of the categorical imperative?

ADDITIONAL RESOURCES

Web Resources

Amnesty International, <www.amnesty.org>. International organization that campaigns for recognition of human rights. A source of up-to-date news on torture.

The World Organization Against Torture, <www.omct.org>. Information about and opposition to torture and other human rights violations.

CIA website, <www.cia.gov>. See "CIA & the War on Terrorism" link for the CIA's perspective on terrorism.

Anti-War.Com, <www.antiwar.com>. Site devoted to opposition to war. Critical of current and past U.S. administration positions on wars.

Fiala, Andrew, "Pacifism," *Stanford Encyclopedia of Philosophy*, <http://plato.stanford.edu/entries/pacifism>. An overview of types of pacifism with discussion of consequentialist, deontological, and religious approaches to the topic.

Miller, Seamus, "Torture," *Stanford Encyclopedia of Philosophy*, <http://plato.stanford.edu/entries/torture/>. An overview of the torture debate.

Orend, Brian, "War," *Stanford Encyclopedia of Philosophy*, <http://plato.stanford.edu/entries/war/>. An overview of the ethics of war and peace. Includes an extended treatment of the provisions of just war theory.

Authored Books and Articles

Allhoff, Fritz, "Terrorism and Torture," *International Journal of Applied Philosophy* 17 (2003): 105–18. A defense of torture for certain purposes only, including obtaining information regarding significant threats.

Davis, Michael, "The Moral Justification of Torture," *International Journal of Applied Philosophy* 19 (2005): 161–78. Critical of using ticking bomb scenarios in arguments over torture.

Dershowitz, Alan M., *Why Terrorism Works: Understanding the Threat, Responding to the Challenge*. (New Haven and London: Yale University Press, 2002). A lively exploration of the causes of and recommended responses to recent state-sponsored terrorism.

Holmes, Robert L., *On War and Morality* (Princeton, N.J.: Princeton University Press, 1989). Holmes defends a historically informed version of anti-war pacifism.

May, Larry, "Torturing Detainees During Interrogation," *International Journal of Applied Philosophy* 19 (2005): 193–208. Argues against the torture of captured suspected terrorists.

Miller, Seamus, "Is Torture Ever Morally Justified?" *International Journal of Applied Philosophy* 19 (2005): 179–92. Defense of the moral justification but not legalization of torture.

Waldron, Jeremy, "Torture and Positive Law," *Columbia Law Review* 105 (2005): 1681–750. Argues against the legalization of torture.

Walzer, Michael, *Just and Unjust Wars*, 2nd ed. (New York: Basic Books, 1992). An important book defending a just-war approach.

Walzer, Michael, *Arguing about War* (New Haven and London: Yale University Press, 2004). A collection of Walzer's essays in which he appeals to a version of just war theory in examining a variety of issues including nuclear deterrence, humanitarian intervention, the recent wars in Afghanistan and Iraq, and terrorism.

Edited Collections

Cole, David (ed.), *The Torture Memos: Rationalizing the Unthinkable* (New York: The New Press, 2009). A collection of memos released by the U.S. Department of Justice describing interrogation techniques used by the CIA under the Bush administration.

Greenberg, Karen (ed.), *The Torture Debate in America* (Cambridge: Cambridge University Press, 2006). A collection of twenty essays, organized into four parts: "Democracy, Terror and Torture," "The Geneva Conventions and International Law," "On Torture," and "Looking Forward."

Levinson, Sanford (ed.), *Torture: A Collection* (New York: Oxford University Press, 2004). A collection of essays by different authors organized into four parts: (1) Philosophical Considerations, (2) Torture as Practiced, (3) Contemporary Attempts to Abolish Torture through Law, and (4) Reflections on the Post-September 11 Debate about Legalizing Torture. Part 4 includes articles by Elaine Scarry and Richard A. Posner that are critical of Dershowitz's views on the morality of torture.

Shue, Henry, and Rodin, David (eds.), *Preemption: Military Action and Moral Justification* (Oxford and New York: Oxford University Press, 2009). A collection of nine essays by scholars from the fields of history, law, political science, and philosophy debating the justifiability of preemptive war.

Sterba, James P. (ed.), *Terrorism and International Justice* (New York: Oxford University Press, 2003). A collection of essays by various authors covering basic questions about the natural causes and morality of terrorism.

14 World Hunger and Poverty

The devastation caused by the Indian Ocean tsunami disaster in December 2004 prompted massive relief efforts by many nations including generous donations from many individuals. In 2005, parts of Alabama, Louisiana, and Mississippi were devastated by Hurricane Katrina, leaving many people without food, water, electricity, and shelter. More recently, in October 2012, Hurricane Sandy devastated portions of the Caribbean, as well as the mid-Atlantic, and northeastern United States, causing many deaths, destroying homes and businesses, and again leaving survivors without basic necessities. According to a 2008 report by the World Bank, 1.4 billion of the world's population lives in extreme poverty, which it defines as not having enough income to meet one's most basic needs. These disasters and the World Bank's statistics call attention to the fact that disease, famine, poverty, and displacement are widespread evils that especially afflict the economically disadvantaged and may afflict those who live in relatively wealthy countries. Moral reflection on hunger, poverty, and other such evils prompts the following questions about the obligations of those more affluent countries and their citizens:

- Are economically advantaged people morally required to participate in a scheme of redistribution so that some of their wealth goes to people who are severely economically disadvantaged?
- If so, what best explains this obligation?

One way in which we can think about these questions is by focusing on the widely recognized duty of **beneficence** or charity, which is roughly the duty to help those in dire need.

1. THE DUTY OF BENEFICENCE

Let us assume there is a duty of beneficence, and let us assume further that this duty is a requirement only for those who are in a position to help others. There are three questions we can raise about this duty. First, there is the question of *scope*—to whom is this duty owed? Assuming for the sake of simplicity that we are concerned just with members of the current world population who are in need of help, does this obligation extend to distant strangers? The second question is about the duty's *content*—for those who can afford to do so, how much are they morally required to sacrifice? The third question is about *strength*—how strong is one's obligation to help those in need when doing so conflicts with other moral duties (such as educating one's own children) and with various nonmoral reasons for action including the pursuit of, say, expensive hobbies or various artistic endeavors? One can imagine a very strong duty of beneficence according to which the economically advantaged have an obligation to all disadvantaged individuals worldwide, which requires not only that they sacrifice a great amount of what they now have in an effort to help those in need, but also that this obligation to help is as strong as any conflicting duty they might have. On the other hand, one can easily imagine a moral code that includes a much weaker duty of beneficence along one or more of the three dimensions just described.

2. THEORY MEETS PRACTICE

Three main theoretical approaches to the moral issues of hunger and poverty are represented in this chapter's selections: consequentialism, the ethics of prima facie duty, and Kantian moral theory. Let us consider them in order.

Consequentialism

A purely consequentialist moral theory of the sort described in chapter 1, section 2A, is going to imply that one's moral obligation to help those in need will depend on the likely consequences of doing so compared to not doing so. Consequentialists can and do disagree about likely consequences, because they often disagree about the root causes of hunger and poverty. Thomas Robert Malthus (1766–1834) claimed that population necessarily outruns economic growth, which in turn necessarily leads to famine. Neo-Malthusians, as they are called, follow Malthus in claiming that the level of economic growth needed to sustain increases in population cannot be maintained, and that eventually unchecked population growth will lead to massive poverty and famine. This analysis of famine and poverty, together with a commitment to consequentialism, is the basis for Garrett Hardin's view that affluent countries and individuals have a moral obligation to *not* help those in overpopulated countries by giving food and other forms of aid. His claim is that doing so will in the long run likely be worse for humanity generally (including those who now have their basic needs met) than will be the likely consequences of refusing to help the needy in overpopulated countries. We can express Hardin's view on the morality of helping those in need by saying that for him, the scope, content, and strength of any such obligation depend entirely on the likely consequences on overall human welfare of engaging in such aid. Since the overall human welfare would likely be decreased by such aid, we have no obligation to help those in overpopulated countries; indeed, we have an obligation to not help.

   Peter Singer also approaches the issue of helping those in need from a broadly consequentialist perspective—one that emphasizes one's moral obligation to reduce the level of human misery. On this basis, Singer reaches a different moral conclusion about giving aid from the one Hardin reaches. He argues that given the great evils of poverty and starvation, those who now enjoy an affluent life and who, by helping, would sacrifice nothing of genuine moral significance have a moral obligation to help those in need. As Singer points out, the scope, content, and strength of the duty to help would require a radical revision in how most people currently think about their obligations to others in need.

Another broadly consequentialist approach to moral questions about world hunger and poverty allows for the idea that rights in general and property rights in particular have intrinsic and not just instrumental value. (The idea that rights have only instrumental value is perhaps the most common view of rights held by consequentialists.) But, as Amartya Sen points out in one of our selections, recognizing the intrinsic value of a right does not rule out considering the consequences of adhering to the right. Sen's idea is that in thinking about our obligations to help those in need, we need to consider both the intrinsic value of holding some property right as well as the overall value of the consequences of adhering to that right. On this basis, Sen makes a case for the moral justification of redistribution of wealth in preventing famine.

Ethics of Prima Facie Duty

According to an ethics of prima facie duty, thinking about world hunger and poverty requires that we consider various competing prima facie duties. Suppose we grant that those living in affluence have a duty to help alleviate the evils of poverty and starvation. (Arguably, we might have this duty even if those to whom it is owed have no moral right against those who are in a position to help.) From this theoretical perspective, we have all sorts of prima facie duties—negative duties not to injure, lie, and break promises, as well as such positive duties as self-improvement and beneficence. When two or more of these prima facie duties conflict in some circumstance, we have to decide which of them is overriding and thus which of them is one's all-things-considered duty in that circumstance. This in turn requires that we think in detail about our circumstances and carefully weigh the relevant strengths of our prima facie obligations.

Kantian Moral Theory

Kant defended the claim that we have a duty of beneficence—a duty to help at least some of those in need on at least some occasions. Because it is up to those who are in a position to help to decide when and how to fulfill this duty—its fulfillment involves a good deal of latitude—Kant claimed that our duty of beneficence is a wide duty. (By contrast, duties to others to not inflict harm and duties to ourselves to not commit suicide are among the narrow duties—duties that do not involve the kind of latitude for choice that is characteristic of our wide obligations.)[1] What is the basis in Kant's theory for the wide duty of beneficence? In her article, Onora O'Neill explains that the Humanity formulation of Kant's fundamental moral principle—the categorical imperative—requires that we not treat others as mere means to our own ends and that we positively treat others as ends in themselves. It is this second, positive part of the categorical imperative that, according to O'Neill, is the basis for our wide duty of beneficence, which she explains and defends.

NOTE

1. For more on the distinction between wide and narrow duty in Kantian moral theory, see chapter 1, section 2C.

GARRETT HARDIN

Lifeboat Ethics

According to Hardin, in thinking about hunger and poverty as moral issues, it is useful to think of them in terms of the metaphor of a lifeboat. Each rich nation is to be thought of as occupying a lifeboat full of comparatively rich people, whereas each poor nation is thought of as a lifeboat containing mostly relatively poor people. Put in these terms, the question is what obligations do rich passengers in one boat have to their poorer counterparts in the less fortunate boats? Hardin rejects essentially Christian and Marxist approaches that would require rich nations to help poor ones, because he thinks that their ultimately unrealistic approaches to solving problems of hunger and poverty—problems of overpopulation—will lead to what he calls "the tragedy of the commons." Taking an essentially consequentialist perspective, Hardin argues that given the likely disastrous overall consequences of rich countries aiding poor countries, the moral implication is that the affluent ought not to help people in countries where overpopulation cannot realistically be brought under control.

Recommended Reading: consequentialism, chap. 1, sec. 2A.

No generation has viewed the problem of the survival of the human species as seriously as we have. Inevitably, we have entered this world of concern through the door of metaphor. Environmentalists have emphasized the image of the earth as a spaceship—Spaceship Earth. Kenneth Boulding (1966) is the principal architect of this metaphor. It is time, he says, that we replace the wasteful "cowboy economy" of the past with the frugal "spaceship economy" required for continued survival in the limited world we now see ours to be. The metaphor is notably useful in justifying pollution control measures.

Unfortunately, the image of a spaceship is also used to promote measures that are suicidal. One of these is a generous immigration policy, which is only a particular instance of a class of policies that are in error because they lead to the tragedy of the commons (Hardin 1968). These suicidal policies are attractive because they mesh with what we unthinkingly take

to be the ideals of "the best people." What is missing in the idealistic view is an insistence that rights and responsibilities must go together. The "generous" attitude of all too many people results in asserting inalienable rights while ignoring or denying matching responsibilities.

For the metaphor of a spaceship to be correct the aggregate of people on board would have to be under unitary sovereign control (Ophuls 1974). A true ship always has a captain. It is conceivable that a ship could be run by a committee. But it could not possibly survive if its course were determined by bickering tribes that claimed rights without responsibilities.

What about Spaceship Earth? It certainly has no captain, and no executive committee. The United Nations is a toothless tiger, because the signatories of its charter wanted it that way. The spaceship metaphor is used only to justify spaceship demands on common

From Garrett Hardin, "Living on a Lifeboat," *Science* 24 (1974). Reprinted by permission.

resources without acknowledging corresponding spaceship responsibilities.

An understandable fear of decisive action leads people to embrace "incrementalism"—moving toward reform in tiny stages. As we shall see, this strategy is counterproductive in the area discussed here if it means accepting rights before responsibilities. Where human survival is at stake, the acceptance of responsibilities is a precondition to the acceptance of rights, if the two cannot be introduced simultaneously.

LIFEBOAT ETHICS

Before taking up certain substantive issues let us look at an alternative metaphor, that of a lifeboat. In developing some relevant examples the following numerical values are assumed. Approximately two-thirds of the world is desperately poor, and only one-third is comparatively rich. The people in poor countries have an average per capita GNP (Gross National Product) of about $200 per year; the rich, of about $3,000. (For the United States it is nearly $5,000 per year.) Metaphorically, each rich nation amounts to a lifeboat full of comparatively rich people. The poor of the world are in other, much more crowded lifeboats. Continuously, so to speak, the poor fall out of their lifeboats and swim for a while in the water outside, hoping to be admitted to a rich lifeboat, or in some other way to benefit from the "goodies" on board. What should the passengers on a rich lifeboat do? This is the central problem of "the ethics of a lifeboat."

First we must acknowledge that each lifeboat is effectively limited in capacity. The land of every nation has a limited carrying capacity. The exact limit is a matter for argument, but the energy crunch is convincing more people every day that we have already exceeded the carrying capacity of the land. We have been living on "capital"—stored petroleum and coal—and soon we must live on income alone.

Let us look at only one lifeboat—ours. The ethical problem is the same for all, and is as follows. Here we sit, say 50 people in a lifeboat. To be generous, let us assume our boat has a capacity of 10 more, making 60. (This, however, is to violate the engineering principle of the "safety factor." A new plant disease or a bad change in the weather may decimate our population if we don't preserve some excess capacity as a safety factor.)

The 50 of us in the lifeboat see 100 others swimming in the water outside, asking for admission to the boat, or for handouts. How shall we respond to their calls? There are several possibilities.

One. We may be tempted to try to live by the Christian ideal of being "our brother's keeper," or by the Marxian ideal (Marx 1875) of "from each according to his abilities, to each according to his needs." Since the needs of all are the same, we take all the needy into our boat, making a total of 150 in a boat with a capacity of 60. The boat is swamped, and everyone drowns. Complete justice, complete catastrophe.

Two. Since the boat has an unused excess capacity of 10, we admit just 10 more to it. This has the disadvantage of getting rid of the safety factor, for which action we will sooner or later pay dearly. Moreover, *which* 10 do we let in? "First come, first served"? The best 10? The neediest 10? How do we *discriminate?* And what do we say to the 90 who are excluded?

Three. Admit no more to the boat and preserve the small safety factor. Survival of the people in the lifeboat is then possible (though we shall have to be on our guard against boarding parties).

The last solution is abhorrent to many people. It is unjust, they say. Let us grant that it is.

"I feel guilty about my good luck," say some. The reply to this is simple: *Get out and yield your place to others.* Such a selfless action might satisfy the conscience of those who are addicted to guilt but it would not change the ethics of the lifeboat. The needy person to whom a guilt-addict yields his place will not himself feel guilty about his sudden good luck. (If he did he would not climb aboard.) The net result of conscience-stricken people relinquishing their unjustly held positions is the elimination of their kind of conscience from the lifeboat. The lifeboat, as it were, purifies itself of guilt. The ethics of the lifeboat persist, unchanged by such momentary aberrations.

This then is the basic metaphor within which we must work out our solutions. Let us enrich the image step by step with substantive additions from the real world.

REPRODUCTION

The harsh characteristics of lifeboat ethics are heightened by reproduction, particularly by reproductive differences. The people inside the lifeboats of the wealthy nations are doubling in numbers every 87 years; those outside are doubling every 35 years, on the average. And the relative difference in prosperity is becoming greater.

Let us, for a while, think primarily of the U.S. lifeboat. As of 1973 the United States had a population of 210 million people, who were increasing by 0.8% per year, that is, doubling in number every 87 years.

Although the citizens of rich nations are outnumbered two to one by the poor, let us imagine an equal number of poor people outside our lifeboat—a mere 210 million poor people reproducing at a quite different rate. If we imagine these to be the combined populations of Colombia, Venezuela, Ecuador, Morocco, Thailand, Pakistan, and the Philippines, the average rate of increase of the people "outside" is 3.3% per year. The doubling time of this population is 21 years.

Suppose that all these countries, and the United States, agreed to live by the Marxian ideal, "to each according to his needs," the ideal of most Christians as well. Needs, of course, are determined by population size, which is affected by reproduction. Every nation regards its rate of reproduction as a sovereign right. If our lifeboat were big enough in the beginning it might be possible to live *for a while* by Christian-Marxian ideals. *Might.*

Initially, in the model given, the ratio of non-Americans to Americans would be one to one. But consider what the ratio would be 87 years later. By this time Americans would have doubled to a population of 420 million. The other group (doubling every 21 years) would now have swollen to 3,540 million.

Each American would have more than eight people to share with. How could the lifeboat possibly keep afloat?

All this involves extrapolation of current trends into the future, and is consequently suspect. Trends may change. Granted: but the change will not necessarily be favorable. If—as seems likely—the rate of population increase falls faster in the ethnic group presently inside the lifeboat than it does among those now outside, the future will turn out to be even worse than mathematics predicts, and sharing will be even more suicidal.

RUIN IN THE COMMONS

The fundamental error of the sharing ethics is that it leads to the tragedy of the commons. Under a system of private property the man (or group of men) who own property recognize their responsibility to care for it, for if they don't they will eventually suffer. A farmer, for instance, if he is intelligent, will allow no more cattle in a pasture than its carrying capacity justifies. If he overloads the pasture, weeds take over, erosion sets in, and the owner loses in the long run.

But if a pasture is run as a commons open to all, the right of each to use it is not matched by an operational responsibility to take care of it. It is no use asking independent herdsmen in a commons to act responsibly, for they dare not. The considerate herdsman who refrains from overloading the commons suffers more than a selfish one who says his needs are greater. (As Leo Durocher says, "Nice guys finish last.") Christian-Marxian idealism is counterproductive. That it *sounds* nice is no excuse. With distribution systems, as with individual morality, good intentions are no substitute for good performance.

A social system is stable only if it is insensitive to errors. To the Christian-Marxian idealist a selfish person is a sort of "error." Prosperity in the system of the commons cannot survive errors. If *everyone* would only restrain himself, all would be well; but it takes *only one less than everyone* to ruin a system of voluntary restraint. In a crowded world of less than perfect human beings—and we will never know any other—mutual ruin is inevitable in the commons. This is the core of the tragedy of the commons....

WORLD FOOD BANKS

In the international arena we have recently heard a proposal to create a new commons, namely an international depository of food reserves to which nations will contribute according to their abilities, and from which nations may draw according to their needs. Nobel laureate Norman Borlaug has lent the prestige of his name to this proposal.

A world food bank appeals powerfully to our humanitarian impulses. We remember John Donne's celebrated line, "Any man's death diminishes me." But before we rush out to see for whom the bell tolls let us recognize where the greatest political push for international granaries comes from, lest we be disillusioned later. Our experience with Public Law 480 clearly reveals the answer. This was the law that moved billions of dollars worth of U.S. grain to food-short, population-long countries during the past two decades. When P.L. 480 first came into being, a headline in the business magazine *Forbes* (Paddock 1970) revealed the power behind it: "Feeding the World's Hungry Millions: How it will mean billions for U.S. business."

And indeed it did. In the years 1960 to 1970 a total of $7.9 billion was spent on the "Food for Peace" program, as P.L. 480 was called. During the years of 1948 to 1970 an additional $49.9 billion were extracted from American taxpayers to pay for other economic aid programs, some of which went for food and food-producing machinery. (This figure does *not* include military aid.) That P.L. 480 was a give-away program was concealed. Recipient countries went through the motions of paying for P.L. 480 food—with IOU's. In December 1973 the charade was brought to an end as far as India was concerned when the United States "forgave" India's $3.2 billion debt (Anonymous 1974). Public announcement of the cancellation of the debt was delayed for two months: one wonders why....

What happens if some organizations budget for emergencies and others do not? If each organization is solely responsible for its own well-being, poorly managed ones will suffer. But they should be able to learn from experience. They have a chance to mend their ways and learn to budget for infrequent but certain emergencies. The weather, for instance, always varies and periodic crop failures are certain. A wise and competent government saves out of the production of the good years in anticipation of bad years that are sure to come. This is not a new idea. The Bible tells us that Joseph taught this policy to Pharaoh in Egypt more than 2,000 years ago. Yet it is literally true that the vast majority of the governments of the world today have no such policy. They lack either the wisdom or the competence, or both. Far more difficult than the transfer of wealth from one country to another is the transfer of wisdom between sovereign powers or between generations.

"But it isn't their fault! How can we blame the poor people who are caught in an emergency? Why must we punish them?" The concepts of blame and punishment are irrelevant. The question is, what are the operational consequences of establishing a world food bank? If it is open to every country every time a need develops, slovenly rulers will not be motivated to take Joseph's advice. Why should they? Others will bail them out whenever they are in trouble.

Some countries will make deposits in the world food bank and others will withdraw from it: there will be almost no overlap. Calling such a depository-transfer unit a "bank" is stretching the metaphor of *bank* beyond its elastic limits. The proposers, of course, never call attention to the metaphorical nature of the word they use.

THE RATCHET EFFECT

An "international food bank" is really, then, not a true bank but a disguised one-way transfer device for moving wealth from rich countries to poor. In the absence of such a bank, in a world inhabited by individually responsible sovereign nations, the population

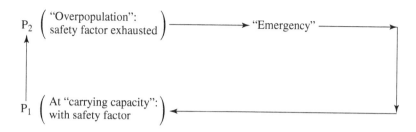

FIGURE 14.1

of each nation would repeatedly go through a cycle of the sort shown in Figure 14.1. P_2 is greater than P_1, either in absolute numbers or because a deterioration of the food supply has removed the safety factor and produced a dangerously low ratio of resources to population. P_2 may be said to represent a state of overpopulation, which becomes obvious upon the appearance of an "accident," e.g., a crop failure. If the "emergency" is not met by outside help, the population drops back to the "normal" level—the "carrying capacity" of the environment—or even below. In the absence of population control by a sovereign, sooner or later the population grows to P_2 again and the cycle repeats. The long-term population curve (Hardin 1966) is an irregularly fluctuating one, equilibrating more or less about the carrying capacity.

A demographic cycle of this sort obviously involves great suffering in the restrictive phase, but such a cycle is normal to any independent country with inadequate population control. The third century theologian Tertullian (Hardin 1969) expressed what must have been the recognition of many wise men when he wrote: "The scourges of pestilence, famine, wars, and earthquakes have come to be regarded as a blessing to overcrowded nations, since they serve to prune away the luxuriant growth of the human race."

Only under a strong and farsighted sovereign—which theoretically could be the people themselves, democratically organized—can a population equilibrate at some set point below the carrying capacity, thus avoiding the pains normally caused by periodic and unavoidable disasters. For this happy state to be achieved it is necessary that those in power be able to contemplate with equanimity the "waste" of surplus food in times of bountiful harvests. It is essential that those in power resist the temptation to convert extra food into extra babies. On the public relations level it is necessary that the phrase "surplus food" be replaced by "safety factor."

But wise sovereigns seem not to exist in the poor world today. The most anguishing problems are created by poor countries that are governed by rulers insufficiently wise and powerful. If such countries can draw on a world food bank in times of "emergency," the population *cycle* of Figure 14.1 will be replaced by the population *escalator* of Figure 14.2. The input of food from a food bank acts as the pawl of a ratchet, preventing the population from retracing its steps to a lower level. Reproduction pushes the population upward, inputs from the world bank prevent its moving downward. Population size escalates, as does the absolute magnitude of "accidents" and "emergencies." The process is brought to an end only by the total collapse of the whole system, producing a catastrophe of scarcely imaginable proportions.

Such are the implications of the well-meant sharing of food in a world of irresponsible reproduction....

To be generous with one's own possessions is one thing; to be generous with posterity's is quite another. This, I think, is the point that must be gotten across to those who would, from a commendable love of distributive justice, institute a ruinous system of the commons....

If the argument of this essay is correct, so long as there is no true world government to control reproduction everywhere it is impossible to survive in dignity if we are to be guided by Spaceship ethics. Without

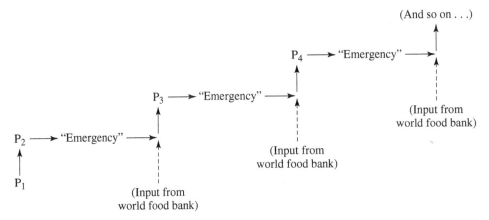

FIGURE 14.2

a world government that is sovereign in reproductive matters mankind lives, in fact, on a number of sovereign lifeboats. For the foreseeable future survival demands that we govern our actions by the ethics of a lifeboat. Posterity will be ill served if we do not.

REFERENCES

Anonymous. 1974. *Wall Street Journal,* 19 Feb.

Boulding, K. 1966. The economics of the coming spaceship earth. In H. Jarrett, ed. *Environmental Quality in a Growing Economy.* Johns Hopkins Press, Baltimore.

Hardin, G. 1966. Chap. 9 in *Biology: Its Principles and Implications,* 2nd ed. Freeman, San Francisco.

———. 1968. The tragedy of the commons. *Science* 162: 1243–1248.

———. 1969. Page 18 in *Population, Evolution, and Birth Control,* 2nd ed. Freeman, San Francisco.

Marx, K. 1875. *Critique of the Gotha program.* Page 388 in R. C. Tucker, ed. *The Marx-Engels Reader,* Norton, N.Y., 1972.

Ophuls, W. 1974. The scarcity society. *Harper's* 248 (1487): 47–52.

Paddock, W. C. 1970. How green is the green revolution? *Bioscience* 20: 897–902.

READING QUESTIONS

1. What are the problems with the metaphor of Earth as a spaceship according to Hardin?
2. Explain Hardin's lifeboat metaphor and the three possible responses that we might take toward the ethical problems it suggests.
3. Why does Hardin reject the first response to the ethical lifeboat problem? How does he respond to those who claim that the third possibility is unjust?
4. Why does Hardin think that an international food bank is an implausible solution to the problem of world hunger and poverty? What is the "ratchet effect" and how does it figure into his objections and proposed solution to the problem?

DISCUSSION QUESTIONS

1. Consider whether Hardin's lifeboat metaphor represents a plausible understanding of the way the nations of the world can or do operate. Are there any ways in which the metaphor could or should be modified?

2. Is Hardin correct to assume that the implementation of something like an international food bank would result in a vicious cycle of overpopulation accompanied by emergency scenarios? Consider some ways that a world food bank could operate more successfully in order to prevent such disasters.

PETER SINGER

The Life You Can Save

In this excerpt from his 2009 book, *The Life You Can Save*, Singer presents a basic argument for the claim that in not donating to human aid organizations, those in a financial position to do so are acting immorally—an argument he originally advanced in his influential 1972 article, "Famine, Affluence, and Morality." In the following selection, Singer presents recent empirical data about poverty and affluence, and he also responds to various objections to his basic argument that he has encountered over the years.

Recommended Reading: consequentialism, chap. 1, sec. 2A.

1. SAVING A CHILD

On your way to work, you pass a small pond. On hot days, children sometimes play in the pond, which is only about knee-deep. The weather's cool today, though, and the hour is early, so you are surprised to see a child splashing about in the pond. As you get closer, you see that it is a very young child, just a toddler, who is flailing about, unable to stay upright or walk out of the pond. You look for the parents or babysitter, but there is no one else around. The child is unable to keep his head above the water for more than a few seconds at a time. If you don't wade in and pull him out, he seems likely to drown. Wading in is easy and safe, but you will ruin the new shoes you bought only a few days ago, and get your suit wet and muddy. By the time you hand the child

over to someone responsible for him, and change your clothes, you'll be late for work. What should you do?

I teach a course called Practical Ethics. When we start talking about global poverty, I ask my students what they think you should do in this situation. Predictably, they respond that you should save the child. "What about your shoes? And being late for work?" I ask them. They brush that aside. How could anyone consider a pair of shoes, or missing an hour or two at work, a good reason for not saving a child's life?

In 2007, something resembling this hypothetical situation actually occurred near Manchester, England. Jordon Lyon, a ten-year-old boy, leaped into a pond after his stepsister Bethany slipped in. He struggled to support her but went under himself.

From Peter Singer, *The Life You Can Save* (New York: Random House, 2009). Reprinted with permission of the author.

Anglers managed to pull Bethany out, but by then Jordon could no longer be seen. They raised the alarm, and two police community support officers soon arrived; they refused to enter the pond to find Jordon. He was later pulled out, but attempts at resuscitation failed. At the inquest on Jordon's death, the officers' inaction was defended on the grounds that they had not been trained to deal with such situations. The mother responded: "If you're walking down the street and you see a child drowning you automatically go in that water... You don't have to be trained to jump in after a drowning child."[1]

I think it's safe to assume that most people would agree with the mother's statement. But consider that, according to UNICEF, nearly 10 million children under five years old die each year from causes related to poverty. Here is just one case, described by a man in Ghana to a researcher from the World Bank:

> Take the death of this small boy this morning, for example. The boy died of measles. We all know he could have been cured at the hospital. But the parents had no money and so the boy died a slow and painful death, not of measles but out of poverty.[2]

Think about something like that happening 27,000 times every day. Some children die because they don't have enough to eat. More die, like that small boy in Ghana, from measles, malaria, and diarrhea, conditions that either don't exist in developed nations, or, if they do, are almost never fatal. The children are vulnerable to these diseases because they have no safe drinking water, or no sanitation, and because when they do fall ill, their parents can't afford any medical treatment. UNICEF, Oxfam, and many other organizations are working to reduce poverty and provide clean water and basic health care, and these efforts are reducing the toll. If the relief organizations had more money, they could do more, and more lives would be saved.

Now think about your own situation. By donating a relatively small amount of money, you could save a child's life. Maybe it takes more than the amount needed to buy a pair of shoes—but we all spend money on things we don't really need, whether on drinks, meals out, clothing, movies, concerts, vacations, new cars, or house renovation. Is it possible that by choosing to spend your money on such things rather than contributing to an aid agency, you are leaving a child to die, a child you could have saved?

Poverty Today

A few years ago, the World Bank asked researchers to listen to what the poor are saying. They were able to document the experiences of 60,000 women and men in seventy-three countries. Over and over, in different languages and on different continents, poor people said that poverty meant these things:

- You are short of food for all or part of the year, often eating only one meal per day, sometimes having to choose between stilling your child's hunger or your own, and sometimes being able to do neither.
- You can't save money. If a family member falls ill and you need money to see a doctor, or if the crop fails and you have nothing to eat, you have to borrow from a local moneylender and he will charge you so much interest as the debt continues to mount and you may never be free of it.
- You can't afford to send your children to school, or if they do start school, you have to take them out again if the harvest is poor.
- You live in an unstable house, made with mud or thatch that you need to rebuild every two or three years, or after severe weather.
- You have no nearby source of safe drinking water. You have to carry your water a long way, and even then, it can make you ill unless you boil it.

But extreme poverty is not only a condition of unsatisfied material needs. It is often accompanied by a degrading state of powerlessness. Even in countries that are democracies and are relatively well governed, respondents to the World Bank survey described a range of situations in which they had to accept humiliation without protest. If someone takes what little you have, and you complain to the police, they may not listen to you. Nor will the law necessarily protect you from rape or sexual harassment. You have a pervading sense of shame and failure because you cannot provide for your children. Your poverty traps you, and you lose hope of ever escaping from a life of hard work for which, at the end, you will have nothing to show beyond bare survival.[3]

The World Bank defines extreme poverty as not having enough income to meet the most basic human needs for adequate food, water, shelter, clothing, sanitation, health care, and education. Many people are familiar with the statistic that 1 billion people are living on less than one dollar per day. That was the World Bank's poverty line until 2008, when better data on international price comparisons enabled it to make a more accurate calculation of the amount people need to meet their basic needs. On the basis of this calculation, the World Bank set the poverty line at $1.25 per day. The number of people whose income puts them under this line is not 1 billion but 1.4 billion. That there are more people living in extreme poverty than we thought is, of course, bad news, but the news is not all bad. On the same basis, in 1981 there were 1.9 billion people living in extreme poverty. That was about four in every ten people on the planet, whereas now fewer than one in four are extremely poor.

South Asia is still the region with the largest number of people living in extreme poverty, a total of 600 million, including 455 million in India. Economic growth has, however, reduced the proportion of South Asians living in extreme poverty from 60 percent in 1981 to 42 percent in 2005. There are another 380 million extremely poor people in sub-Saharan Africa, where half the population is extremely poor—and that is the same percentage as in 1981. The most dramatic reduction in poverty has been in East Asia, although there are still more than 200 million extremely poor Chinese, and smaller numbers elsewhere in the region. The remaining extremely poor people are distributed around the world, in Latin America and the Caribbean, the Pacific, the Middle East, North Africa, Eastern Europe, and Central Asia.[4]

In response to the "$1.25 a day" figure, the thought may cross your mind that in many developing countries, it is possible to live much more cheaply than in the industrialized nations. Perhaps you have even done it yourself, backpacking around the world, living on less than you would have believed possible. So you may imagine that this level of poverty is less extreme than it would be if you had to live on that amount of money in the United States, or any industrialized nation. If such thoughts did occur to you, you should banish them now, because the World Bank has already made the adjustment in purchasing power: Its figures refer to the number of people existing on a daily total consumption of goods and services—whether earned or home-grown—comparable to the amount of goods and services that can be bought in the United States for $1.25.

In wealthy societies, most poverty is relative. People feel poor because many of the good things they see advertised on television are beyond their budget—but they do have a television. In the United States, 97 percent of those classified by the Census Bureau as poor own a color TV. Three quarters of them own a car. Three quarters of them have air-conditioning. Three quarters of them have a VCR or DVD player. All have access to health care.[5] I am not quoting these figures in order to deny that the poor in the United States face genuine difficulties. Nevertheless, for most, these difficulties are of a different order than those of the world's poorest people. The 1.4 billion people living in extreme poverty are poor by an absolute standard tied to the most basic human needs. They are likely to be hungry for at least part of each year. Even if they can get enough food to fill their stomachs, they will probably be malnourished because their diet lacks essential nutrients. In children, malnutrition stunts growth and can cause permanent brain damage. The poor may not be able to afford to send their children to school. Even minimal health care services are usually beyond their means.

This kind of poverty kills. Life expectancy in rich nations averages seventy-eight years; in the poorest nations, those officially classified as "least developed," it is below fifty.[6] In rich countries, fewer than one in a hundred children die before the age of five; in the poorest countries, one in five does. And to the UNICEF figure of nearly 10 million young children dying every year from avoidable, poverty-related causes, we must add at least another 8 million older children and adults.[7]

Affluence Today

Roughly matching the 1.4 billion people living in extreme poverty, there are about a billion living at a level of affluence never previously known except in the courts of kings and nobles. As king of France, Louis XIV, the "Sun King," could afford to build the most magnificent palace Europe had ever seen, but he could not keep it cool in summer as effectively as most middle-class people in industrialized nations can keep their homes cool today. His gardeners, for all their skill, were unable to produce the variety of fresh fruits and vegetables that we can buy all year-round. If he developed a toothache or fell ill, the best his dentists and doctors could do for him would make us shudder.

But we're not just better off than a French king who lived centuries ago. We are also much better off than our own greatgrandparents. For a start, we can expect to live about thirty years longer. A century ago, one child in ten died in infancy. Now, in most rich nations, that figure is less than one in two hundred.[8] Another telling indicator of how wealthy we are today is the modest number of hours we must work in order to meet our basic dietary needs. Today Americans spend, on average, only 6 percent of their income on buying food. If they work a forty-hour week, it takes them barely two hours to earn enough to feed themselves for the week. That leaves far more to spend on consumer goods, entertainment, and vacations.

And then we have the superrich, people who spend their money on palatial homes, ridiculously large and luxurious boats, and private planes. Before the 2008 stock market crash trimmed the numbers, there were more than 1,100 billionaires in the world, with a combined net worth of $4.4 trillion.[9] To cater to such people, Lufthansa Technik unveiled its plans for a private configuration of Boeing's new 787 Dreamliner. In commercial service, this plane will seat up to 330 passengers. The private version will carry 35, at a price of $150 million. Cost aside, there's nothing like owning a really big airplane carrying a small number of people to maximize your personal contribution to global warming. Apparently, there are already several billionaires who fly around in private commercial-sized airliners, from 747s down. Larry Page and Sergey Brin, the Google cofounders, reportedly bought a Boeing 767 and spent millions fitting it out for their private use.[10] But for conspicuous waste of money and resources it is hard to beat Anousheh Ansari, an Iranian-American telecommunications entrepreneur who paid a reported $20 million for eleven days in space. Comedian Lewis Black said on Jon Stewart's *The Daily Show* that Ansari did it because it was "the only way she could achieve her life's goal of flying over every single starving person on earth and yelling 'Hey, look what I'm spending my money on!'"

While I was working on this book, a special advertising supplement fell out of my Sunday edition of *The New York Times*: a sixty-eight-page glossy magazine filled with advertising for watches by Rolex, Patek Philippe, Breitling, and other luxury brands. The ads didn't carry price tags, but a puff piece about the revival of the mechanical watch gave guidance about the lower end of the range. After admitting that inexpensive quartz watches are extremely accurate and functional, the article opined that there is "something engaging about a mechanical movement." Right, but how much will it cost you to have this engaging something on your wrist? "You might think that getting into mechanical watches is an expensive proposition, but there are plenty of choices in the $500–$5000 range." Admittedly, "these opening-price-point models are pretty simple: basic movement, basic time display, simple decoration and so on." From which we can gather that most of the watches advertised are priced upward of $5,000, or more than one hundred times what anyone needs to pay for a reliable, accurate quartz watch. That there is a market for such products—and one worth advertising at such expense to the wide readership of *The New York Times*—is another indication of the affluence of our society.[11]

If you're shaking your head at the excesses of the superrich, though, don't shake too hard. Think again about some of the ways Americans with average incomes spend their money. In most places in the

United States, you can get your recommended eight glasses of water a day out of the tap for less than a penny, while a bottle of water will set you back $1.50 or more.[12] And in spite of the environmental concerns raised by the waste of energy that goes into producing and transporting it, Americans are still buying bottled water, to the tune of more than 31 billion liters in 2006.[13] Think, too, of the way many of us get our caffeine fix: You can make coffee at home for pennies rather than spending three dollars or more on a latte. Or have you ever casually said yes to a waiter's prompt to order a second soda or glass of wine that you didn't even finish? When Dr. Timothy Jones, an archaeologist, led a U.S. government–funded study of food waste, he found that 14 percent of household garbage is perfectly good food that was in its original packaging and not out of date. More than half of this food was drypackaged or canned goods that keep for a long time. According to Jones, $100 billion of food is wasted in the United States every year.[14] Fashion designer Deborah Lindquist claims that the average woman owns more than $600 worth of clothing that she has not worn in the last year.[15] Whatever the actual figure may be, it is fair to say that almost all of us, men and women alike, buy things we don't need, some of which we never even use.

Most of us are absolutely certain that we wouldn't hesitate to save a drowning child, and that we would do it at considerable cost to ourselves. Yet while thousands of children die each day, we spend money on things we take for granted and would hardly notice if they were not there. Is that wrong? If so, how far does our obligation to the poor go?

2. IS IT WRONG NOT TO HELP?

Bob is close to retirement. He has invested most of his savings in a very rare and valuable old car, a Bugatti, which he has not been able to insure. The Bugatti is his pride and joy. Not only does Bob get pleasure from driving and caring for his car, he also knows that its rising market value means that he will be able to sell it and live comfortably after retirement. One day when Bob is out for a drive, he parks the Bugatti near the end of a railway siding and goes for a walk up the track. As he does so, he sees that a runaway train, with no one aboard, is rolling down the railway track. Looking farther down the track, he sees the small figure of a child who appears to be absorbed in playing on the tracks. Oblivious to the runaway train, the child is in great danger. Bob can't stop the train, and the child is too far away to hear his warning shout, but Bob can throw a switch that will divert the train down the siding where his Bugatti is parked. If he does so, nobody will be killed, but the train will crash through the decaying barrier at the end of the siding and destroy his Bugatti. Thinking of his joy in owning the car and the financial security it represents, Bob decides not to throw the switch.

The Car or the Child?

Philosopher Peter Unger developed this variation on the story of the drowning child to challenge us to think further about how much we believe we should sacrifice in order to save the life of a child. Unger's story adds a factor often crucial to our thinking about real-world poverty: uncertainty about the outcome of our sacrifice. Bob cannot be certain that the child will die if he does nothing and saves his car. Perhaps at the last moment the child will hear the train and leap to safety. In the same way, most of us can summon doubts about whether the money we give to a charity is really helping the people it's intended to help.

In my experience, people almost always respond that Bob acted badly when he did not throw the switch and destroy his most cherished and valuable possession, thereby sacrificing his hope of a financially secure retirement. We can't take a serious risk with a child's life, they say, merely to save a car, no matter how rare and valuable the car may be. By implication, we should also believe that with the simple act of saving money for retirement, we are acting as badly as Bob. For in saving money for retirement, we are effectively refusing to use that money to help save lives. This is a difficult implication to confront. How can it be wrong to save for a comfortable retirement? There is, at the very least, something puzzling here.

Another example devised by Unger tests the level of sacrifice we think people should make to alleviate suffering in cases when a life is not at stake:

> You are driving your vintage sedan down a country lane when you are stopped by a hiker who has seriously injured his leg. He asks you to take him to the nearest hospital. If you refuse, there is a good chance that he will lose his leg. On the other hand, if you agree to take him to hospital, he is likely to bleed onto the seats, which you have recently, and expensively, restored in soft white leather.

Again, most people respond that you should drive the hiker to the hospital. This suggests that when prompted to think in concrete terms, about real individuals, most of us consider it obligatory to lessen the serious suffering of innocent others, even at some cost (even a high cost) to ourselves.[16]

The Basic Argument

The above examples reveal our intuitive belief that we ought to help others in need, at least when we can see them and when we are the only person in a position to save them. But our moral intuitions are not always reliable, as we can see from variations in what people in different times and places find intuitively acceptable or objectionable. The case for helping those in extreme poverty will be stronger if it does not rest solely on our intuitions. Here is a logical argument from plausible premises to the same conclusion.

First premise: Suffering and death from lack of food, shelter, and medical care are bad.

Second premise: If it is in your power to prevent something bad from happening, without sacrificing anything nearly as important, it is wrong not to do so.

Third premise: By donating to aid agencies, you can prevent suffering and death from lack of food, shelter, and medical care, without sacrificing anything nearly as important.

Conclusion: Therefore, if you do not donate to aid agencies, you are doing something wrong.

The drowning-child story is an application of this argument for aid, since ruining your shoes and being late for work aren't nearly as important as the life of a child. Similarly, reupholstering a car is not nearly as big a deal as losing a leg. Even in the case of Bob and the Bugatti, it would be a big stretch to suggest that the loss of the Bugatti would come close to rivaling the significance of the death of an innocent person.

Ask yourself if you can deny the premises of the argument. How could suffering and death from lack of food, shelter, and medical care not be really, really bad? Think of that small boy in Ghana who died of measles. How you would feel if you were his mother or father, watching helplessly as your son suffers and grows weaker? You know that children often die from this condition. You also know that it would be curable, if only you could afford to take your child to a hospital. In those circumstances you would give up almost anything for some way of ensuring your child's survival.

Putting yourself in the place of others, like the parents of that boy, or the child himself, is what thinking ethically is all about. It is encapsulated in the Golden Rule, "Do unto others as you would have them do unto you." Though the Golden Rule is best known to most westerners from the words of Jesus as reported by Matthew and Luke, it is remarkably universal, being found in Buddhism, Confucianism, Hinduism, Islam, and Jainism, and in Judaism, where it is found in Leviticus, and later emphasized by the sage Hillel[17] The Golden Rule requires us to accept that the desires of others ought to count as if they were our own. If the desires of the parents of the dying child were our own, we would have no doubt that their suffering and the death of their child are about as bad as anything can be. So if we think ethically, then those desires must count as if they were our own, and we cannot deny that the suffering and death are bad.

The second premise is also very difficult to reject, because it leaves us some wiggle room when it comes to situations in which, to prevent something bad, we would have to risk something *nearly* as important as the bad thing we are preventing. Consider, for example, a situation in which you can only prevent the deaths of other children by neglecting your own children. This standard does not require you to prevent the deaths of the other children.

"Nearly as important" is a vague term. That's deliberate, because I'm confident that you can do without plenty of things that are clearly and inarguably not as valuable as saving a child's life. I don't know what *you* might think is as important, or nearly as important, as saving a life. By leaving it up to you to decide what those things are, I can avoid the need to find out. I'll trust you to be honest with yourself about it.

Analogies and stories can be pushed too far. Rescuing a child drowning in front of you, and throwing a switch on a railroad track to save the life of a child you can see in the distance, where you are the only one who can save the child, are both different from giving aid to people who are far away. The argument I have just presented complements the drowning-child case, because instead of pulling at your heartstrings by focusing on a single child in need, it appeals to your reason and seeks your assent to an abstract but compelling moral principle. That means that to reject it, you need to find a flaw in the reasoning....

3. COMMON OBJECTIONS TO GIVING

Charity begins at home, the saying goes, and I've found that friends, colleagues, students, and lecture audiences express that resistance in various ways. I've seen it in columns, letters, and blogs too. Particularly interesting, because they reflect a line of thought prevalent in affluent America, were comments made by students taking an elective called Literature and Justice at Glennview High (that's not its real name), a school in a wealthy Boston suburb. As part of the reading for the course, teachers gave students an article that I wrote for *The New York Times* in 1999, laying out a version of the argument you have just read, and asked them to write papers in response.[18] Scott Seider, then a graduate student at Harvard University researching how adolescents think about obligations to others, interviewed thirty-eight students in two sections of the course and read their papers.[19]

Let's look at some of the objections raised by these varied sources. Perhaps the most fundamental objection comes from Kathryn, a Glennview student who believes we shouldn't judge people who refuse to give:

> There is no black and white universal code for everyone. It is better to accept that everyone has a different view on the issue, and all people are entitled to follow their own beliefs.

Kathryn leaves it to the individual to determine his or her moral obligation to the poor. But while circumstances do make a difference, and we should avoid being too black-and-white in our judgments, this doesn't mean we should accept that everyone is entitled to follow his or her own beliefs. That is moral relativism, a position that many find attractive only until they are faced with someone who is doing something really, really wrong. If we see a person holding a cat's paws on an electric grill that is gradually heating up, and when we vigorously object he says, "But it's fun, see how the cat squeals," we don't just say, "Oh, well, you are entitled to follow your own beliefs," and leave him alone. We can and do try to stop people who are cruel to animals, just as we stop rapists, racists, and terrorists. I'm not saying that failing to give is like committing these acts of violence, but if we reject moral relativism in some situations, then we should reject it everywhere.

After reading my essay, Douglas, another Glennview student, objected that I "should not have the right to tell people what to do." In one sense, he's correct about that. I've no right to tell you or anyone else what to do with your money, in the sense that that would imply that you *have* to do as I say. I've no authority over Douglas or over you. On the other hand, I do have the right of free speech, which I'm exercising right now by offering you some arguments you might consider before you decide what to do with your money. I hope that you will want to listen to a variety of views before making up your mind about such an important issue. If I'm wrong about that, though, you are free to shut the book now, and there's nothing I can do about it.

It's possible, of course, to think that morality is not relative, and that we should talk about it, but that the right view is that we aren't under any obligation to give anything at all. Lucy, another Glennview High student, wrote as follows:

> If someone wants to buy a new car, they should. If someone wants to redecorate their house, they should, and if they need a suit, get it. They work for their money and they have the right to spend it on themselves. . . .

Lucy said that people have a right to spend the money they earn on themselves. Even if we agree with that, having a *right* to do something doesn't settle the question of what you *should* do. If you have a right to do something, I can't justifiably force you not to do it, but I can still tell you that you would be a fool to do it, or that it would be a horrible thing to do, or that you would be wrong to do it. You may have a right to spend your weekend surfing, but it can still be true that you ought to visit your sick mother. Similarly, we might say that the rich have a right to spend their money on lavish parties, Patek Philippe watches, private jets, luxury yachts, and space travel, or, for that matter, to flush wads of it down the toilet. Or that those of us with more modest means shouldn't be forced to forgo any of the less-expensive pleasures that offer us some relief from all the time we spend working. But we could still think that to choose to do these things rather than use the money to save human lives is wrong, shows a deplorable lack of empathy, and means that you are not a good person. . . .

Libertarians resist the idea that we have a duty to help others. Canadian philosopher Jan Narveson articulates that point of view:

> We are certainly responsible for evils we inflict on others, no matter where, and we owe those people compensation. . . Nevertheless, I have seen no plausible argument that we owe something, as a matter of general duty, to those to whom we have done nothing wrong.[20]

There is, at first glance, something attractive about the political philosophy that says: "You leave me alone, and I'll leave you alone, and we'll get along just fine." It appeals to the frontier mentality, to an ideal of life in the wide-open spaces where each of us can carve out our own territory and live undisturbed by the neighbors. At first glance, it seems perfectly reasonable. Yet there is a callous side to a philosophy that denies that we have any responsibilities to those who, through no fault of their own, are in need. Taking libertarianism seriously would require us to abolish all state-supported welfare schemes for those who can't get a job or are ill or disabled, and all state-funded health care for the aged and for those who are too poor to pay for their own health insurance. Few people really support such extreme views. Most think that we do have obligations to those we can help with relatively little sacrifice—certainly to those living in our own country, and I would argue that we can't justifiably draw the boundary there. But if I have not persuaded you of that, there is another line of argument to consider: If we have, in fact, been at least in part a cause of the poverty of the world's poorest people—if we are harming the poor—then even libertarians like Narveson will have to agree that we ought to compensate them. . . . There are many ways in which it is clear, however, that the rich *have* harmed the poor. Ale Nodye knows about one of them. He grew up in a village by the sea, in Senegal, in West Africa. His father and grandfather were fishermen, and he tried to be one too. But after six years in which he barely caught enough fish to pay for the fuel for his boat, he set out by canoe for the Canary Islands, from where he hoped to become another of Europe's many illegal immigrants. Instead, he was arrested and deported. But he says he will try again, even though the voyage is dangerous and one of his cousins died on a similar trip. He has no choice, he says, because "there are no fish in the sea here anymore." A European Commission report shows that Nodye is right: The fish stocks from which Nodye's father and grandfather took their catch and fed their families have been destroyed by industrial fishing fleets that come from Europe, China, and Russia and sell their fish to well-fed Europeans who can afford to pay high prices. The industrial fleets drag vast nets across the seabed, damaging the coral reefs where fish breed. As a result, a major protein source for poor people has vanished, the boats are idle, and people who used to make a living fishing or building boats are unemployed. The story is repeated in many other coastal areas around the world.[21]

Or consider how we citizens of rich countries obtain our oil and minerals. Teodoro Obiang, the dictator of tiny Equatorial Guinea, sells most of his country's oil to American corporations, among them Exxon Mobil, Marathon, and Hess. Although his official salary is a modest $60,000, this ruler of a country of 550,000 people is richer than Queen Elizabeth II. He owns six private jets and a $35 million house in Malibu, as well as other houses in Maryland and Cape Town and a fleet of Lamborghinis, Ferraris, and Bentleys. Most of the people over whom he rules live in extreme poverty, with a life expectancy of forty-nine and an infant mortality of eighty-seven per one thousand (this means that more than one child in twelve dies before its first birthday).[22] Equatorial Guinea is an extreme case, but other examples are almost as bad. In 2005, the Democratic Republic of the Congo exported minerals worth $200 million. From this, its total tax revenues were $86,000. Someone was surely making money from these dealings, but not the people of the Congo.[23] In 2006, Angola made more than $30 billion in oil revenue, about $2,500 for each of its 12 million citizens. Yet the majority of Angolans have no access to basic health care; life expectancy is forty-one years; and one child in four dies before reaching the age of five. On Transparency International's corruption perception index, Angola is currently ranked 147th among 180 countries.

In their dealings with corrupt dictators in developing countries, international corporations are akin to people who knowingly buy stolen goods, with the difference that the international legal and political order recognizes the corporations not as criminals in possession of stolen goods but as the legal owners of the goods they have bought. This situation is, of course, profitable for corporations that do deals with dictators, and for us, since we use the oil, minerals, and other raw materials we need to maintain our prosperity. But for resource-rich developing countries, it is a disaster. The problem is not only the loss of immense wealth that, used wisely, could build the prosperity of the nation. Paradoxically, developing nations with rich deposits of oil or minerals are often worse off than otherwise comparable nations without those resources. One reason is that the revenue from the sale of the resources provides a huge financial incentive for anyone tempted to overthrow the government and seize power. Successful rebels know that if they

succeed, they will be rewarded with immense personal wealth. They can also reward those who backed their coup, and they can buy enough arms to keep themselves in power no matter how badly they rule. Unless, of course, some of those to whom they give the arms are themselves tempted by the prospect of controlling all that wealth... Thus the resources that should benefit developing nations instead become a curse that brings corruption, coups, and civil wars.[24] If we use goods made from raw materials obtained by these unethical dealings from resource-rich but money-poor nations, we are harming those who live in these countries.

One other way in which we in the rich nations are harming the poor has become increasingly clear over the past decade or two. President Yoweri Museveni of Uganda put it plainly, addressing the developed world at a 2007 meeting of the African Union: "You are causing aggression to us by causing global warming....Alaska will probably become good for agriculture, Siberia will probably become good for agriculture, but where does that leave Africa?"[25]

Strong language, but the accusation is difficult to deny. Two-thirds of the greenhouse gases now in the atmosphere have come from the United States and Europe. Without those gases, there would be no human-induced global warming problem. Africa's contribution is, by comparison, extremely modest: less than 3 percent of the global emissions from burning fuel since 1900, somewhat more if land clearing and methane emissions from livestock production are included, but still a small fraction of what has been contributed by the industrialized nations. And while every nation will have some problems in adjusting to climate change, the hardship will, as Museveni suggests, fall disproportionately on the poor in the regions of the world closer to the equator. Some scientists believe that precipitation will decrease nearer the equator and increase nearer the poles. In any case, the rainfall upon which hundreds of millions rely to grow their food will become less reliable. Moreover, the poor nations depend on agriculture to a far greater degree than the rich. In the United States, agriculture represents only 4 percent of the economy; in Malawi it is 40 percent, and 90 percent of the population are subsistence farmers, virtually all of whom are dependent on rainfall. Nor will drought be the only problem climate change brings to the poor. Rising sea levels will inundate fertile, densely settled delta regions that are home to tens of millions of people in Egypt, Bangladesh, India, and Vietnam. Small Pacific Island nations that consist of low-lying coral atolls, like Kiribati and Tuvalu, are in similar danger, and it seems inevitable that in a few decades they will be submerged.[26]

The evidence is overwhelming that the greenhouse gas emissions of the industrialized nations have harmed, and are continuing to harm, many of the world's poorest people—along with many richer ones, too. If we accept that those who harm others must compensate them, we cannot deny that the industrialized nations owe compensation to many of the world's poorest people. Giving them adequate aid to mitigate the consequences of climate change would be one way of paying that compensation.

In a world that has no more capacity to absorb greenhouse gases without the consequence of damaging climate change, the philosophy of "You leave me alone, and I'll leave you alone" has become almost impossible to live by, for it requires ceasing to put any more greenhouse gases into the atmosphere. Otherwise, we simply are not leaving others alone.

America is a generous nation. As Americans, we are already giving more than our share of foreign aid through our taxes. Isn't that sufficient?

Asked whether the United States gives more, less, or about the same amount of aid, as a percentage of its income, as other wealthy countries, only one in twenty Americans gave the correct answer. When my students suggest that America is generous in this regard, I show them figures from the website of the OECD, on the amounts given by all the organization's donor members. They are astonished to find that the United States has, for many years, been at or near the bottom of the list of industrialized countries in terms of the proportion of national income given as foreign aid. In 2006, the United States fell behind Portugal and Italy, leaving Greece as the only industrialized country to give a smaller percentage of its national income in foreign aid. The average nation's effort in that year came to 46 cents of every $100 of gross national income, while the United States gave only 18 cents of every $100 it earned.

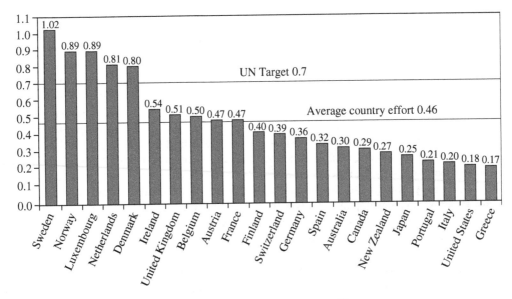

FIGURE 14.3 Official Aid as a Percentage of Gross National Income (2006)[27]

Philanthropic responses undermine real political change.

If those on the right fear that I am encouraging the state to seize their money and give it to the world's poor, some on the left worry that encouraging the rich to donate to aid organizations enables them to salve their consciences while they continue to benefit from a global economic system that makes them rich and keeps billions poor.[28] Philanthropy, philosopher Paul Gomberg believes, promotes "political quietism," deflecting attention from the institutional causes of poverty—essentially, in his view, capitalism—and from the need to find radical alternatives to these institutions.[29]

Although I believe we ought to give a larger portion of our income to organizations combating poverty, I am open-minded about the best way to combat poverty.[30] Some aid agencies, Oxfam for example, are engaged in emergency relief, development aid, *and* advocacy work for a fairer global economic order. If, after investigating the causes of global poverty and considering what approach is most likely to reduce it, you really believe that a more revolutionary change is needed, then it would make sense to put your time, energy, and money into organizations promoting that revolution in the global economic system. But this is a practical question, and if there is little chance of achieving the kind of revolution you are seeking, then you need to look around for a strategy with better prospects of actually helping some poor people.

Giving people money or food breeds dependency.

I agree that we should not be giving money or food directly to the poor, except in emergencies like a drought, earthquake, or flood, where food may need to be brought in to stop people from starving in the short term. In less dire situations, providing food can make people dependent. If the food is shipped in from a developed nation, for example the United States, it can destroy local markets and reduce incentives for local farmers to produce a surplus to sell. We need to make it possible for people to earn their own money, or to produce their own food and meet their other needs in a sustainable manner and by their own

work. Giving them money or food won't achieve that. Finding a form of aid that will really help people is crucial, and not a simple task, but as we'll see, it can be done.[31]

Cash is the seed corn of capitalism. Giving it away will reduce future growth.

Gaetano Cipriano contacted me after reading one of my articles because he thought that as an entrepreneurial capitalist, he could offer a helpful perspective. The grandson of immigrants to America, he owns and runs EI Associates, an engineering and construction firm based in Cedar Knolls, New Jersey, that has assets of around $80 million. "Cash is the seed corn of capitalism" is his phrase. Gaetano told me that he deploys his capital to the best of his ability to promote profits and enduring growth, and that giving more of it away would be "cutting my own throat." But he does not spend extravagantly. "I do not live in a splendid house," he told me. "I have no second home. I drive a 2001 Ford Explorer with 73,000 miles. I belong to a nice squash club, and have four suits and two pairs of black shoes. When I take vacations they are short and local. I do not own a boat or a plane." While he does give to charity, he does it "at a level which is prudent and balanced with sustainable growth." If he were to give much more money away, it would have to come out of sums that he now reinvests in his business. That, in turn, would reduce his future earnings and perhaps the number of people he is able to employ, or how well he can pay them. It would also leave him with less to give if, later in life, he decides that he wants to give more.

For similar reasons, we can agree that it's a good thing Warren Buffett did not give away the first million dollars he earned. Had he done so, he would not have had the investment capital he needed to develop his business, and would never have been able to give away the $31 billion that he has now pledged to give. If you are as skilled as Buffett in investing your money, I urge you to keep it until late in life, too, and then give away most of it, as he has done. But people with less-spectacular investment abilities might do better to give it away sooner....

What if you took every penny you ever had and gave it to the poor of Africa...? What we would have is no economy, no ability to generate new wealth or help anybody.

This objection comes from Colin McGinn, a professor of philosophy at the University of Miami.[32] It isn't clear whether McGinn's "you" is you, the individual reader, or the group an American Southerner might refer to as "y'all." If you [insert your name], took every penny you ever had and gave it to the poor of Africa, our national economy would not notice. Even if every reader of this book did that, the economy would barely hiccup (unless the book's sales exceed my wildest dreams). If *everyone* in America did it, the national economy would be ruined. But, at the moment, there is no cause for worry about the last possibility: there is no sign of it happening, and I am not advocating it.

Because so few people give significant amounts, the need for more to be given is great, and the more each one of us gives, the more lives we can save. If everyone gave significantly more than they now give, however, we would be in a totally different situation. The huge gulf between rich and poor means that if everyone were giving, there would be no need for them to take every penny they ever had and give it all to Africa. As you'll see before the end of this book, quite a modest contribution from everyone who has enough to live comfortably, eat out occasionally, and buy bottled water, would suffice to achieve the goal of lifting most of the world's extremely poor people above the poverty line of $1.25 per day. If that modest contribution were given, we would no longer be in a situation in which 10 million children were dying from poverty every year. So whether a small number of people give a lot, or a large number of people give a little, ending large-scale extreme poverty wouldn't cripple our national economy. It leaves plenty of scope for entrepreneurial activity and individual wealth. In the long run, the global economy would be enhanced, rather than diminished, by bringing into it the 1.4 billion people now outside it, creating new markets and new opportunities for trade and investment.

People do have special relationships with their families, their communities, and their countries.

This is the standard equipment of humanity, and most people, in all of human history, have seen nothing wrong with it.[33]
—*Alan Ryan, philosopher and warden of New College, Oxford*

It is true that most of us care more about our family and friends than we do about strangers. That's natural, and there is nothing wrong with it. But how far should preference for family and friends go? Brendan, a Glennview High student, thought that instead of going to aid for the poor, money "can be better spent helping your family and friends who need the money as well." If family and friends really *need* the money, in anything remotely like the way those living in extreme poverty need it, it would be going too much against the grain of human nature to object to giving to them before giving to strangers. Fortunately, most middle-class people in rich nations don't have to make this choice. They can take care of their families in an entirely sufficient way on much less than they are now spending, and thus have money left over that can be used to help those in extreme poverty. Admittedly, saying just where the balance should be struck is difficult....

Kiernan, another Glennview High School student, made a point similar to Alan Ryan's:

[*Giving what we don't need to the poor*] *would make the world a better, more equal place. But it is like a little kid buying a pack of candy, keeping one piece, and giving the rest away. It just doesn't happen.*

The issue raised by all these remarks is the link between what we humans are (mostly) like, and what we *ought* to do. When Brendan O'Grady, a philosophy student at Queen's University in Ontario, posted a blog about this issue, he got the following response from another Canadian philosophy student Thomas Simmons:

Of course I do not want people to die, but I just feel generally unattached to them. I have no doubt that if I were to take a trip to places where people are starving then I might think differently, but as it stands now they are just too far removed. In not making these donations, I am implicitly valuing the affluence of my own life over the basic sustenance of many others. And, well, I guess I do. Am I immoral for doing so? Maybe.[34]

When O'Grady queried this, Simmons clarified his position: "I don't intend to make a moral defense, but rather just reveal my personal feelings—that is, just to explain how I feel." The distinction between describing how things are and saying how they ought to be is also relevant to what Kiernan and Alan Ryan are saying. The fact that we tend to favor our families, communities, and countries may explain our failure to save the lives of the poor beyond those boundaries, but it does not justify that failure from an ethical perspective, no matter how many generations of our ancestors have seen nothing wrong with it.

NOTES

1. BBC News, September 21, 2007, http://news.bbc.co.uk/2/hi/uk_news/england/manchester/7006412.stm.

2. Deepa Narayan with Raj Patel, Kai Schafft, Anne Rademacher, and Sarah Koch-Schulte. *Voices of the Poor: Can Anyone Hear Us?* Published for the World Bank by Oxford University Press (New York, 2000), p. 36.

3. This is a compilation of things said by the poor, cited in ibid., p. 28.

4. World Bank Press Release, "New Data Show 1.4 Billion Live on Less Than US$1.25 a Day, But Progress Against Poverty Remains Strong," August 26, 2008, http://go.worldbank.org/ T0TEVOV4E0. The estimate is based on price data from 2005, and does not reflect increases in food prices in 2008, which are likely to have increased the number below the poverty line. For the research on which the press release is based, see Shaohua Chen and Martin Ravallion, "The Developing World Is Poorer Than We Thought, But No Less Successful in the Fight Against Poverty," Policy Research Working Paper 4073, World Bank Development Research Group, August 2008, www.wds.worldbank.org/external/default/WDSContentServer/IW3P/IB/2008/08/26/000158349_2008082611323 9/Rendered/PDF/WPS4703.pdf.

For further discussion of World Bank statistics, see Sanjay Reddy and Thomas Pogge, "How *Not* to Count the Poor," www.columbia.edu/-sr793/count.pdf, and Martin Ravallion, "How *Not* to Count the Poor: A Reply to Reddy and Pogge," www.columbia.edu/-sr793/wbreply.pdf.

5. Robert Rector and Kirk Anderson, "Understanding Poverty in America," Heritage Foundation Backgrounder #1713 (2004), www.heritage.org/Research/Welfare/bg1713.

cfm. Rector and Anderson draw on data available from the 2003 U.S. Census Bureau report on poverty and on various other government reports.

6. United Nations, Office of the High Representative for the Least Developed Countries, Landlocked Developing Countries and the Small Island Developing States, and World Bank, World Bank Development Data Group, "Measuring Progress in Least Developed Countries: A Statistical Profile" (2006), tables 2 and 3, pp. 14–15. Available at www.un.org/ohrlls/.

7. United Nations Development Program, *Human Development Report 2000* (Oxford University Press, New York, 2000) p. 30; *Human Development Report 2001* (Oxford University Press, New York, 2001) pp. 9–12, p. 22; and World Bank, *World Development Report 2000/2001*, overview, p. 3, www.worldbank.org/poverty/wdrpoverty/report/overview.pdf, for the other figures. The *Human Development Reports* are available at http://hdr.undp.org.

8. James Riley, *Rising Life Expectancy: A Global History* (New York: Cambridge University Press, 2001); Jeremy Laurance, "Thirty Years: Difference in Life Expectancy Between the World's Rich and Poor Peoples," *The Independent* (UK), September 7, 2007.

9. "Billionaires 2008," *Forbes*, March 24, 2008, www.forbes.com/forbes/2008/0324/080.html.

10. Joe Sharkey, "For the Super-Rich, It's Time to Upgrade the Old Jumbo," *The New York Times,* October 17, 2006.

11. "Watch Your Time," Special Advertising Supplement to *The New York Times,* October 14, 2007. The passage quoted is on p. 40.

12. Bill Marsh, "A Battle Between the Bottle and the Faucet," *The New York Times,* July 15, 2007.

13. Pacific Institute, "Bottled Water and Energy: A Fact Sheet," www.pacinst.org/topics/water_and_sustainability/bottled_water/bottled_water_and_energy.html.

14. Lance Gay, "Food Waste Costing Economy $100 Billion, Study Finds," Scripps Howard News Service, August 10, 2005, www.knoxstudio.com/shns/story.cfm?pk=GARBAGE-08-10-05.

15. Deborah Lindquist, "How to Look Good Naked," Lifetime Network, Season 2, Episode 2, July 29, 2009. As relayed by Courtney Moran.

16. Peter Unger, *Living High and Letting Die* (New York: Oxford University Press, 1996).

17. For further discussion see Peter Singer, *The Expanding Circle* (Oxford: Clarendon Press, 1981), pp. 136, 183. For futher examples, see www.unification.net/ws/theme015.htm.

18. Peter Singer, "The Singer Solution to World Poverty," *The New York Times Sunday Magazine,* September 5, 1999.

19. Glennview High School is Seider's fictional name for the school, and the names of the students are also pseudonyms.

20. Jan Narveson, " 'We Don't Owe Them a Thing!' A Tough-minded but Soft-hearted View of Aid to the Faraway Needy," *The Monist,* 86:3 (2003), p. 419.

21. Sharon Lafraniere, "Europe Takes Africa's Fish, and Boatloads of Migrants Follow," *The New York Times,* January 14, 2008, and Elizabeth Rosenthal, "Europe's Appetite for Seafood Propels Illegal Trade," *The New York Times,* January 15, 2008.

22. See Leif Wenar, "Property Rights and the Resource Curse," *Philosophy & Public Affairs* 36:1 (2008), pp. 2–32. A more detailed version is available on Wenar's website: www.wenar.staff.shef.ac.uk/PRRCwebpage.html.

23. Paul Collier, *The Bottom Billion* (New York: Oxford University Press, 2007).

24. See Leonard Wantchekon, "Why Do Resource Dependent Countries Have Authoritarian Governments?" *Journal of African Finance and Economic Development* 5:2 (2002), pp. 57–77; an earlier version is available at www.yale.edu/leitner/pdf/1999-11.pdf. See also Nathan Jensen and Leonard Wantchekon, "Resource Wealth and Political Regimes in Africa," *Comparative Political Studies,* 37 (2004), pp. 816–841.

25. President Museveni was speaking at the African Union summit, Addis Ababa, Ethiopia, February 2007, and the speech was reported in Andrew Revkin, "Poor Nations to Bear Brunt as World Warms," *The New York Times,* April 1, 2007.

26. Andrew Revkin, op. cit., and "Reports from Four Fronts in the War on Warming," *The New York Times,* April 3, 2007; Kathy Marks, "Rising Tide of Global Warming Threatens Pacific Island States," *The Independent* (UK), October 25, 2006.

27. Organisation for Economic Co-operation and Development *(OECD), OECD Journal on Development: Development Co-operation Report 2007,* p. 134, www.oecd.org/dac/dcr. The table is reproduced by kind permission of OECD. See also *Statistical Annex of the 2007 Development Co-operation Report,* www.oecd.org/dataoecd/52/9/1893143.xls, Fig. 1e.

28. See, for example, Anthony Langlois, "Charity and Justice in the Singer Solution," in Raymond Younis (ed) *On the Ethical Life* (Newcastle upon Tyne: Cambridge Scholars, forthcoming); Paul Gomberg, "The Fallacy of Philanthropy," *Canadian Journal of Philosophy* 32:1 (2002), pp. 29–66.

29. Gomberg, *op. cit.,* pp. 30, 63–64.

30. See Andy Lamey's response to Anthony Langlois's paper in the volume referred to in n. 28, above.

31. Singer addresses the question of finding a form of aid that really works in chapter 7 of *The Life You Can Save,* "Improving Aid."

32. Colin McGinn, as quoted by Michael Specter in "The Dangerous Philosopher," *The New Yorker,* September 6, 1999.

33. Alan Ryan, as quoted by Michael Specter in "The Dangerous Philosopher," *The New Yorker,* September 6, 1999.

34. http://www.muzakandpotatoes.com/2008/02/peter-singer-on-affluence.html.

READING QUESTIONS

1. Explain what poverty and affluence are like today according to the information provided by Singer. Include in your explanation the World Bank's definition of "extreme poverty."

2. Describe the two main thought experiments utilized by Singer. Explain the differences between them.

3. What is Singer's basic argument for why failing to donate to aid organizations such as UNICEF is wrong? Why does Singer think that it is hard to reject each of the premises?

4. Describe a few of the common objections raised against the basic argument by high school students. How does Singer respond to each of these objections?

5. Explain the Libertarian view with respect to whether we have a duty to help others. How does Singer argue that wealthy nations and their citizens have caused harm to developing nations and their people?

DISCUSSION QUESTIONS

1. Are there any objections Singer fails to consider in response to his basic argument? Consider responses on his behalf to any further objections.
2. What do people spend money on what they either don't need or rarely use other than those things mentioned by Singer? What things might people be most easily convinced to do without?
3. How would you respond in the cases of the drowning child and the child on the train tracks? Consider and discuss differing reactions to these two thought experiments.

JOHN ARTHUR

World Hunger and Moral Obligation

One of the premises in Peter Singer's basic argument from the previous selection states: *If it is in your power to prevent something bad from happening, without sacrificing anything nearly as important, it is wrong not to do so.* Arthur labels this premise Singer's "greater moral evil rule," pointing out that it is meant to capture the idea that morality involves giving equal consideration to the interests of all, which is part of our moral code. However, as Arthur observes, such equality is only one part, and Singer's rule ignores other elements of our moral code including considerations of entitlement which involve both rights and desert. On the basis of considerations of entitlement, Arthur argues that our present moral code allows such considerations to qualify considerations of equality of interests. For example, our moral rights to life and to property represent entitlements that we can invoke as a moral justification for not helping strangers when the cost to us is substantial.

Of course, the fact that our current moral code includes such entitlements does not show that such entitlements are justified. Perhaps there is good reason to move to a new moral code that drops the sorts of entitlements mentioned above and includes Singer's greater moral evil rule. In the final section of his paper, Arthur considers this proposal and argues that an ideal moral code that is genuinely workable would include entitlements that justify the sort of rights to property that one can invoke as a moral justification for not helping strangers when the cost is substantial.

Recommended Reading: consequentialism, chap. 1, sec. 2A, see especially the discussion of rule consequentialism. Also relevant, the discussion of moral rights in chap. 1, sec. 2D, and Rawls's principles of justice in chap. 1, sec 2G.

INTRODUCTION

My guess is that everyone who reads these words is wealthy by comparison with the poorest millions of people on our planet. Not only do we have plenty of money for food, clothing, housing, and other necessities, but a fair amount is left over for far less important purchases like phonograph records, fancy clothes, trips, intoxicants, movies, and so on. And what's more we don't usually give a thought to whether or not we ought to spend our money on such luxuries rather than to give it to those who need it more; we just assume it's ours to do with as we please.

Peter Singer, in "Famine, Affluence, and Morality," argues that our assumption is wrong, that we should not buy luxuries when others are in severe need. But [is he] correct? . . .

He first argues that two general moral principles are widely accepted, and then that those principles imply an obligation to eliminate starvation.

The first principle is simply that "suffering and death from lack of food, shelter and medical care are bad." Some may be inclined to think that the mere existence of such an evil in itself places an obligation on others, but that is, of course, the problem which Singer addresses. I take it that he is not begging the question in this obvious way and will argue from the existence of evil to the obligation of others to eliminate it. But how, exactly, does he establish this? The second principle, he thinks, shows the connection, but it is here that controversy arises.

This principle, which I will call the greater moral evil rule, is as follows:

> If it is in our power to prevent something bad from happening, without thereby sacrificing anything of comparable moral importance, we ought, morally, to do it.[1]

In other words, people are entitled to keep their earnings only if there is no way for them to prevent a greater evil by giving them away. Providing others with food, clothing, and housing would generally be of more importance than buying luxuries, so the greater moral evil rule now requires substantial redistribution of wealth.

Certainly there are few, if any, of us who live by that rule, although that hardly shows we are *justified* in our way of life; we often fail to live up to our own standards. Why does Singer think our shared morality requires that we follow the greater moral evil rule? What arguments does he give for it?

He begins with an analogy. Suppose you came across a child drowning in a shallow pond. Certainly we feel it would be wrong not to help. Even if saving the child meant we must dirty our clothes, we would emphasize that those clothes are not of comparable significance to the child's life. The greater moral evil rule thus seems a natural way of capturing why we think it would be wrong not to help.

But the argument for the greater moral evil rule is not limited to Singer's claim that it explains our feelings about the drowning child or that it appears "uncontroversial." Moral equality also enters the picture. Besides the Jeffersonian idea that we share certain rights equally, most of us are also attracted to another type of equality, namely that like amounts of suffering (or happiness) are of equal significance, no matter who is experiencing them. I cannot reasonably say that, while my pain is no more severe than yours, I am somehow special and it's more important that mine be alleviated. Objectivity requires us to admit the opposite, that no one has a unique status which warrants such special pleading. So equality demands equal consideration of interests as well as respect for certain rights.

But if we fail to give to famine relief and instead purchase a new car when the old one will do, or buy fancy clothes for a friend when his or her old ones are perfectly good, are we not assuming that the relatively minor enjoyment we or our friends may get is as important as another person's life? And that is a form of prejudice; we are acting as if people were not equal in the sense that their interests deserve equal consideration. We are giving special consideration to ourselves or to our group, rather like a racist does. Equal consideration of interests thus leads naturally to the greater moral evil rule.

RIGHTS AND DESERT

Equality, in the sense of giving equal consideration to equally serious needs, is part of our moral code. And so we are led, quite rightly I think, to the conclusion that we should prevent harm to others if in doing so we do not sacrifice anything of comparable moral importance. But there is also another side to the coin, one which Singer ignore[s]. . . . This can be expressed rather awkwardly by the notion of entitlements. These fall into two broad categories, rights and desert. A few examples will show what I mean.

All of us could help others by giving away or allowing others to use our bodies. While your life may be shortened by the loss of a kidney or less enjoyable if lived with only one eye, those costs are probably not comparable to the loss experienced by a person who will die without any kidney or who is totally blind. We can even imagine persons who will actually be harmed in some way by your not granting sexual favors to them. Perhaps the absence of a sexual partner would cause psychological harm or even rape. Now suppose that you can prevent this evil without sacrificing anything of comparable importance. Obviously such relations may not be pleasant, but according to the greater moral evil rule that is not enough; to be justified in refusing, you must show that the unpleasantness you would experience is of equal importance to the harm you are preventing. Otherwise, the rule says you must consent.

If anything is clear, however, it is that our code does not *require* such heroism; you are entitled to keep your second eye and kidney and not bestow sexual favors on anyone who may be harmed without them. The reason for this is often expressed in terms of rights; it's your body, you have a right to it, and that weighs against whatever duty you have to help. To sacrifice a kidney for a stranger is to do more than is required, it's heroic.

Moral rights are normally divided into two categories. Negative rights are rights of noninterference. The right to life, for example, is a right not to be killed. Property rights, the right to privacy, and the right to exercise religious freedom are also negative, requiring only that people leave others alone and not interfere.

Positive rights, however, are rights of recipience. By not putting their children up for adoption, parents give them various positive rights, including rights to be fed, clothed, and housed. If I agree to share in a business venture, my promise creates a right of recipience, so that when I back out of the deal, I've violated your right.

Negative rights also differ from positive in that the former are natural; the ones you have depend on what you are. If lower animals lack rights to life or liberty it is because there is a relevant difference between them and us. But the positive rights you may have are not natural; they arise because others have promised, agreed, or contracted to give you something.

Normally, then, a duty to help a stranger in need is not the result of a right he has. Such a right would be positive, and since no contract or promise was made, no such right exists. An exception to this would be a lifeguard who contracts to watch out for someone's children. The parent whose child drowns would in this case be doubly wronged. First, the lifeguard should not have cruelly or thoughtlessly ignored the child's interests, and second, he ought not to have violated the rights of the parents that he helped. Here, unlike Singer's case, we can say there are rights at stake. Other bystanders also act wrongly by cruelly ignoring the child, but unlike the lifeguard they do not violate anybody's rights. Moral rights are one factor to be weighed, but we also have other obligations; I am not claiming that rights are all we need to consider. That view, like the greater moral evil rule, trades simplicity for accuracy. In fact, our code expects us to help people in need as well as to respect negative and positive rights. But we are also entitled to invoke our own rights as justification for not giving to distant strangers or when the cost to us is substantial, as when we give up an eye or kidney. . . .

Desert is a second form of entitlement. Suppose, for example, an industrious farmer manages through hard work to produce a surplus of food for the winter while a lazy neighbor spends his summer fishing. Must our industrious farmer ignore his hard work and give the surplus away because his neighbor or his family will suffer? What again seems clear is that we have more than one factor to weigh. Not only should we compare the consequences of his keeping it with his giving it away; we also should weigh the fact that one farmer deserves the food, he earned it through his hard work. Perhaps his deserving the product of his labor is outweighed by the greater need of his lazy neighbor, or perhaps it isn't, but being outweighed is in any case not the same as weighing nothing!

Desert can be negative, too. The fact that the Nazi war criminal did what he did means he deserves punishment, that we have a reason to send him to jail. Other considerations, for example the fact that nobody will be deterred by his suffering, or that he is old and harmless, may weigh against punishment and so we may let him go; but again that does not mean he doesn't still deserve to be punished.

Our moral code gives weight to both the greater moral evil principle and entitlements. The former emphasizes equality, claiming that from an objective point of view all comparable suffering, whoever its victim, is equally significant. It encourages us to take an impartial look at all the various effects of our actions; it is thus forward-looking. When we consider matters of entitlement, however, our attention is directed to the past. Whether we have rights to money, property, eyes, or whatever, depends on how we came to possess them. If they were acquired by theft rather than from birth or through gift exchange, then the right is suspect. Desert, like rights, is also backward-looking, emphasizing past effort or past transgressions which now warrant reward or punishment.

Our commonly shared morality thus requires that we ignore neither consequences nor entitlements, neither the future results of our action nor relevant events in the past. It encourages people to help others in need, especially when it's a friend or someone we are close to geographically, and when the cost is not significant. But it also gives weight to rights and desert, so that we are not usually obligated to give to strangers....

But unless we are moral relativists, the mere fact that entitlements are an important part of our moral code does not in itself justify such a role. Singer ... can perhaps best be seen as a moral reformer advocating the rejection of rules which provide for distribution according to rights and desert. Certainly the fact that in the past our moral code condemned

suicide and racial mixing while condoning slavery should not convince us that a more enlightened moral code, one which we would want to support, would take such positions. Rules which define acceptable behavior are continually changing, and we must allow for the replacement of inferior ones.

Why should we not view entitlements as examples of inferior rules we are better off without? What could justify our practice of evaluating actions by looking backward to rights and desert instead of just to their consequences? One answer is that more fundamental values than rights and desert are at stake, namely fairness, justice, and respect. Failure to reward those who earn good grades or promotions is wrong because it's *unfair;* ignoring past guilt shows a lack of regard for *justice;* and failure to respect rights to life, privacy, or religious choice suggests a lack of *respect for other persons.*

Some people may be persuaded by those remarks, feeling that entitlements are now on an acceptably firm foundation. But an advocate of equality may well want to question why fairness, justice, and respect for persons should matter. But since it is no more obvious that preventing suffering matters than that fairness, respect, and justice do, we again seem to have reached an impasse....

ENTITLEMENTS AND THE IDEAL MORAL CODE

The idea I want now to consider is that part of our code should be dropped, so that people could no longer invoke rights and desert as justification for not making large sacrifices for strangers. In place of entitlements would be a rule regarding that any time we can prevent something bad without sacrificing anything of comparable moral significance we ought to do it. Our current code, however, allows people to say that while they would do more good with their earnings, still they have rights to the earnings, the earnings are deserved, and so need not be given away.

The crucial question is whether we want to have such entitlement rules in our code, or whether we should reject them in favor of the greater moral evil rule....

I believe that our best procedure is not to think about this or that specific rule, drawing analogies, refining it, and giving counterexamples, but to focus instead on the nature of morality as a whole. What is a moral code? What do we want it to do? What type of code do we want to support? These questions will give us a fresh perspective from which to consider the merits of rules which allow people to appeal to rights and desert and to weigh the issue of whether our present code should be reformed.

We can begin with the obvious: A moral code is a system of rules designed to guide people's conduct. As such, it has characteristics in common with other systems of rules. Virtually every organization has rules which govern the conduct of members; clubs, baseball leagues, corporations, bureaucracies, professional associations, even *The* Organization all have rules. Another obvious point is this: What the rules are depends on why the organization exists. Rules function to enable people to accomplish goals which lead them to organize in the first place. Some rules, for example, "Don't snitch on fellow mafiosi," "Pay dues to the fraternity," and "Don't give away trade secrets to competing companies," serve in obvious ways. Other times the real purposes of rules are controversial, as when doctors do not allow advertising by fellow members of the AMA.

Frequently rules reach beyond members of a specific organization, obligating everyone who is capable of following them to do so. These include costs of civil and criminal law, etiquette, custom, and morality. But before discussing the specific purposes of moral rules, it will be helpful to look briefly at some of the similarities and differences between these more universal codes.

First, the sanctions imposed on rule violators vary among different types of codes. While in our legal code, transgressions are punished by fines, jail, or repayment of damages, informal sanctions of praise, blame, or guilt encourage conformity to the rules of morality and etiquette. Another difference is that while violation of a moral rule is always a serious affair, this need not be so for legal rules of etiquette and custom. Many of us think it unimportant whether a fork is on the left side of a plate or whether an outmoded and widely ignored Sunday closing law is violated, but violation of a moral rule is not ignored. Indeed, that a moral rule has lost its importance is often shown by its demotion to status of mere custom.

A third difference is that legal rules, unlike rules of morality, custom, and etiquette, provide for a specific person or procedure that is empowered to alter the rules. If Congress acts to change the tax laws, then as of the date stated in the statute the rules are changed. Similarly for the governing rules of social clubs, government bureaucracies, and the AMA. Rules of custom, morals, and etiquette also change, of course, but they do so in a less precise and much more gradual fashion, with no person or group specifically empowered to make changes.

This fact, that moral rules are *in a sense* beyond the power of individuals to change, does not show that rules of morality, any more than those of etiquette, are objective in the same sense that scientific laws are. All that needs to happen for etiquette or morality to change is for people to change certain practices, namely the character traits they praise and blame, or the actions they approve and disapprove. Scientific laws, however, are discovered, not invented by society, and so are beyond human control. The law that the boiling point of water increases as its pressure increases cannot be changed by humans, either individually or collectively. Such laws are a part of the fabric of nature.

But the fact that moral rules, like legal ones, are not objective in the same sense as scientific ones does not mean that there is no objective standard of right or wrong, that one code is as good as another, or even that the "right thing to do" is just what the moral code currently followed in our society teaches is right. Like the rules of a fraternity or corporation, legal and moral rules can serve their purposes either well or poorly, and whether they do is a matter of objective fact. Further, if a moral code doesn't serve its purpose, we have good reason to think of a way to change it, just as its serving us well provides a good reason to obey. In important respects morality is not at all subjective.

345

Take, for example, a rule which prohibits homosexual behavior. Suppose it serves no useful purpose, but only increases the burdens of guilt, shame, and social rejection borne by 10% of our population. If this is so, we have good reason to ignore the rule. On the other hand, if rules against killing and lying help us to accomplish what we want from a moral code, we have good reason to support those rules. Morality is created, and as with other systems of rules which we devise, a particular rule may or may not further the shared human goals and interests which motivated its creation. There is thus a connection between what we ought to do and how well a code serves its purposes. If a rule serves well the general purposes of a moral code, then we have reason to support it, and if we have reason to support it, we also have reason to obey it. But if, on the other hand, a rule is useless, or if it frustrates the purposes of morality, we have reason neither to support nor to follow it. All of this suggests the following conception of a right action: Any action is right which is approved by an ideal moral code, one which it is rational for us to support. Which code we would want to support would depend, of course, on which one is able to accomplish the purposes of morality.

If we are to judge actions in this way, by reference to what an ideal moral code would require, we must first have a clear notion of just what purposes morality is meant to service. And here again the comparison between legal and moral rules is instructive. Both systems discourage certain types of behavior—killing, robbing, and beating—while encouraging others—repaying debts, keeping important agreements, and providing for one's children. The purpose which both have in discouraging various behaviors is obvious. Such negative rules help keep people from causing harm. Think, for example, of how we are first taught it is wrong to hit a baby brother or sister. Parents explain the rule by emphasizing that it hurts the infant when we hit him. Promoting the welfare of ourselves, our friends and family, and to a lesser degree all who have the capacity to be harmed is the primary purpose of negative moral rules. It's how we learn them as children and why we support them as adults.

The same can be said of positive rules, rules which encourage various types of behavior. Our own welfare, as well as that of friends, family, and others, depends on general acceptance of rules which encourage keeping promises, fulfilling contracts, and meeting the needs of our children. Just try to imagine a society in which promises or agreements mean nothing, or where family members took no concern for one another. A life without positive or negative rights would be as Thomas Hobbes long ago observed: nasty, brutish, and short.

Moral rules thus serve two purposes. They promote our own welfare by discouraging acts of violence and promoting social conventions like promising and paying debts, and second, they perform the same service for our family, friends, and others. We have reason to support a moral code because we care about our own welfare, and because we care about the well-being of others. For most of us the ideal moral code, the one we would support because it best fulfills these purposes, is the code which is most effective in promoting general welfare.

But can everyone be counted on to share these concerns? Think, for example, of an egoist, who only desires that *he* be happy. Such a person, if he existed, would obviously like a code which maximizes his own welfare. How can we hope to get agreement about which code it is rational to support, if different people expect different things from moral rules?...

There is also a line of reasoning which suggests that disagreement about which moral code to support need not be as deep as is often thought. What sort of code in fact *would* a rational egoist support? He would first think of proposing one which allows him to do anything whatsoever that he desires, while requiring that others ignore their own happiness and do what is in his interests. But here enters a family of considerations which will bring us back to the merits of entitlements versus the greater moral evil rule. Our egoist is contemplating what code to *support*, which means going before the public and trying to win general acceptance of his proposed rules. Caring for nobody else, he might secretly prefer the code I mentioned, yet it would hardly make sense for him to work for its public adoption since others are unlikely to put his welfare above the happiness of themselves and their families. So it looks as if the code an egoist would actually support might not be all that different from the ideal (welfare maximizing) code; he would be wasting his time to advocate rules that serve only his own interests because they have no chance of public acceptance.

The lesson to be learned here is a general one: The moral code it is rational for us to support must be practical; it must actually work. This means, among other things, that it must be able to gain the support of almost everyone.

But the code must be practical in other respects as well. I have emphasized that it is wrong to ignore the possibilities of altruism, but it is also important that a code not assume people are more unselfish than they are. Rules that would work only for angels are not the ones it is rational to support for humans. Second, an ideal code cannot assume we are more objective than we are; we often tend to rationalize when our own interests are at stake, and a rational person will also keep that in mind when choosing a moral code. Finally, it is not rational to support a code which assumes we have perfect knowledge. We are often mistaken about the consequences of what we do, and a workable code must take that into account as well.

I want now to bring these various considerations together in order to decide whether or not to reject entitlements in favor of the greater moral evil rule. I will assume that the egoist is not a serious obstacle to acceptance of a welfare maximizing code, either because egoists are, like angels, merely imaginary, or because a practical egoist would only support a code which can be expected to gain wide support. We still have to ask whether entitlements would be included in a welfare maximizing code. The initial temptation is to substitute the greater moral evil rule for entitlements, requiring people to prevent something bad whenever the cost to them is less significant than the benefit to another. Surely, we might think, total welfare would be increased by a code requiring people to give up their savings if a greater evil can be prevented.

I think, however, that this is wrong, and that an ideal code would provide for rights and would

encourage rewarding according to desert. My reasons for thinking this stem from the importance of insuring that a moral code really does, in fact, work. Each of the three practical considerations mentioned above now enters the picture. First, it will be quite difficult to get people to accept a code which requires that they give away their savings, extra organs, or anything else merely because they can avoid a greater evil for a stranger. Many people simply wouldn't do it: they aren't that altruistic. If the code attempts to require it anyway, two results would likely follow. First, because many would not live up to the rules, there would be a tendency to create feelings of guilt in those who keep their savings in spite of having been taught it is wrong, as well as conflict between those who meet their obligations and those who do not. And, second, a more realistic code, one which doesn't expect more than can be accomplished, may actually result in more giving. It's a bit like trying to influence how children spend their money. Often they will buy less candy if rules allow them to do so occasionally but they are praised for spending on other things than if its purchase is prohibited. We cannot assume that making a charitable act a requirement will always encourage such behavior. Impractical rules not only create guilt and social conflict, they often tend to encourage the opposite of the desired result. By giving people the right to use their savings for themselves, yet praising those who do not exercise the right but help others instead, we have struck a good balance; the rules are at once practical yet reasonably effective.

Similar practical considerations would also influence our decision to support rules that allow people to keep what they deserve. For most people, working is not their favorite activity. If we are to prosper, however, goods and services must be produced. Incentives are therefore an important motivation, and one such incentive for work is income. Our code encourages work by allowing people to keep a large part of what they earn, indeed that's much the point of entitlements. "I worked hard for it, so I can keep it" is an oft-heard expression. If we eliminate this rule from our code and ask people to follow the greater moral evil rule instead, the result would likely be less work done and so less total production. Given a choice between not working and continuing to work knowing the efforts should go to benefit others, many would choose not to work.

Moral rules should be practical in a third sense, too. They cannot assume people are either more unbiased or more knowledgeable than they are. This fact has many implications for the sorts of rules we would want to include in a welfare maximizing code. For example, we may be tempted to avoid slavish conformity to counterproductive rules by allowing people to break promises whenever they think doing so would increase total welfare. But again we must not ignore human nature, in this case our tendency to give special weight to our own welfare and our inability to be always objective in tracing the effects of our actions. While we would not want to teach that promises must never be broken no matter what the consequences, we also would not want to encourage breaking promises any time a person can convince himself the results of doing so would be better than if he kept his word.

Similar considerations apply to the greater moral evil rule. Imagine a situation where someone feels he can prevent an evil befalling himself by taking what he needs from a large store. The idea that he's preventing something bad from happening (to himself) without sacrificing anything of comparable moral significance (the store won't miss the goods) would justify robbery. Although sometimes a particular act of theft really is welfare maximizing, it does not follow that we should support a *rule* which allows theft whenever the robber is preventing a greater evil. Such a rule, to work, would require more objectivity and more knowledge of long-term consequences than we have. Here again, including rights in our moral code serves a useful role, discouraging the tendency to rationalize our behavior by underestimating the harm we may cause to others or exaggerating the benefits that may accrue to ourselves.

The first sections of this paper attempted to show that our moral code is a bit schizophrenic. It seems to pull us in opposite directions, sometimes toward helping people who are in need, other times toward the view that rights and desert justify keeping things we have even if greater evil could be avoided were we to give away our extra eye or our savings account. This apparent inconsistency led us to a further question: Is the emphasis on entitlements really defensible, or should we try to resolve the tension in our own code by adopting the greater moral evil rule and ignoring entitlements? In this section I considered the idea that we might choose between entitlements and the greater moral evil rule by paying attention to the general nature of a moral code; and in particular to the sort of code we might want to support. I argued that all of us, including egoists, have reason to support a code which promotes the welfare of everyone who lives under it. That idea, of an ideal moral code which it is rational for everyone to support, provides a criterion for deciding which rules are sound and which ones we should support.

My conclusion is a conservative one: Concern that our moral code encourages production and not fail because it unrealistically assumes people are more altruistic or objective than they are means that our rules giving people rights to their possessions and encouraging distribution according to desert should be part of an ideal moral code. And since this is so, it is not always wrong to invoke rights or claim that money is deserved as justification for not giving aid, even when something worse could be prevented by offering help. The welfare maximizing moral code would not require us to maximize welfare in each individual case.

I have not yet discussed just how much weight should be given to entitlements, only that they are important and should not be ignored...Certainly an ideal moral code would not allow people to overlook those in desperate need by making entitlements absolute, any more than it would ignore entitlements. But where would it draw the line?

It's hard to know, of course, but the following seems to me to be a sensible stab at an answer. Concerns about discouraging production and the general adherence to the code argue strongly against expecting too much; yet on the other hand, to allow extreme wealth in the face of grinding poverty would seem to put too much weight on entitlements. It seems to me, then, that a reasonable code would require people to help when there is no substantial cost to themselves, that is, when what they are sacrificing would not mean *significant* reduction in their own or their families' level of happiness. Since most people's savings accounts and nearly everybody's second kidney are not insignificant, entitlements would in those cases outweigh another's need. But if what is at stake is trivial, as dirtying one's clothes would normally be, then an ideal moral code would not allow rights to override the greater evil that can be prevented. Despite our code's unclear and sometimes schizophrenic posture, it seems to me that these judgments are not that different from our current moral attitudes. We tend to blame people who waste money on trivia when they could help others in need, yet not to expect people to make large sacrifices to distant strangers. An ideal moral code thus might not be a great deal different from our own.

NOTE

1. Singer also offers a "weak" version of this principle which, it seems to me, is *too* weak. It requires giving aid only if the gift is of *no* moral significance to the giver. But since even minor embarrassment or small amounts of happiness are not completely without moral importance, this weak principle implies little or no obligation to aid, even to the drowning child.

READING QUESTIONS

1. What part of our moral code does Arthur think is being ignored by Peter Singer?
2. Explain Arthur's argument for why our moral code does not require the sort of heroism involved in actions such as giving up one's kidney or eye.
3. Explain the distinction between negative and positive moral rights according to Arthur. Give examples of each.
4. How does Arthur explain the difference between positive and negative forms of desert?
5. What two purposes do moral rules serve, according to Arthur?
6. Arthur mentions three ways in which a moral code must be practical. State those three ways.

DISCUSSION QUESTIONS

1. Does Peter Singer's greatest moral evil rule require that persons act in heroic ways or go above and beyond the call of duty as Arthur suggests?
2. How might Peter Singer respond to Arthur's claim that he has ignored the notion of entitlements in his argument for why we should give to charity?
3. In the final paragraph of his article, Arthur suggests that "to allow extreme wealth in the face of grinding poverty would seem to put too much weight on entitlements. It seems to me, then, that a reasonable code would require people to help when there is no substantial cost to themselves, that is, when what they are sacrificing would not mean *significant* reduction in their own or their families' level of happiness." How might one go about determining what counts as a "significant" reduction in one's level of happiness?

Amartya Sen

Property and Hunger

According to Sen, starvation and famine result from failures of entitlements to property that would otherwise provide the resources for the starving to afford life's necessities including food. This "entitlement" analysis suggests a redistributive economic policy to deal with famine that would increase the entitlements of severely deprived groups while reducing the entitlements of those in economically advantaged groups. Would such redistributive intervention represent a morally wrongful violation of the property rights of the advantaged? Does one's entitlement right to one's own property justify refusing to contribute to the alleviation of poverty and hunger of strangers? One might suppose that if rights have intrinsic value, then such redistribution is not justified. However, Sen proposes a moral system which, unlike a purely consequentialist view of rights, recognizes their intrinsic value, but like consequentialism insists that an overall moral assessment of any right must include a consideration of its likely consequences. If the value of the consequences of limiting or abridging a right are of very great benefit in helping to fulfill morally important goals, such limits are morally justified. The importance of avoiding starvation and famine is the basis for a moral claim or right not to be hungry, which can justify limiting the property entitlements of the economically advantaged. Sen concludes by exploring the likely practical implications of recognizing this right.

Recommended Reading: rights-focused approach to moral issues, chap. 1, sec. 2D. Also relevant is consequentialism, chap. 1, sec. 2A.

...[T]he claims of property rights, which some would defend and some...would dispute, are not just matters of basic moral belief that could not possibly be influenced one way or the other by any empirical arguments. They call for sensitive moral analysis responsive to empirical realities, including economic ones.

Moral claims based on intrinsically valuable rights are often used in political and social arguments. Rights related to ownership have been invoked for ages. But there are also other types of rights which have been seen as "inherent and inalienable," and the American Declaration of Independence refers to "certain unalienable rights," among which are "life, liberty and the pursuit of happiness." The Indian constitution talks even of "the right to an adequate means of livelihood."[1] The "right not to be hungry" has often been invoked in recent discussions on the obligation to help the famished.

RIGHTS: INSTRUMENTS, CONSTRAINTS, OR GOALS?

Rights can be taken to be morally important in three different ways. First, they can be considered to be valuable *instruments* to achieve other goals. This is

From Amartya Sen, "Property and Hunger," *Economics and Philosophy* 4 (1988): 57–68. Reprinted by permission of Cambridge University Press.

the "instrumental view," and is well illustrated by the utilitarian approach to rights. Rights are, in that view, of no intrinsic importance. Violation of rights is not in itself a bad thing, nor fulfillment intrinsically good. But the acceptance of rights promotes, in this view, things that are ultimately important, to wit, utility. Jeremy Bentham rejected "natural rights" as "simple nonsense," and "natural and imprescriptible rights" as "rhetorical nonsense, nonsense upon stilts." But he attached great importance to rights as instruments valuable to the promotion of a good society, and devoted much energy to the attempt to reform appropriately the actual system of rights.

The second view may be called the "constraint view," and it takes the form of seeing rights as *constraints* on what others can or cannot do. In this view rights *are* intrinsically important. However, they don't figure in moral accounting as goals to be generally promoted, but only as constraints that others must obey. As Robert Nozick has put it in a powerful exposition of this "constraint view": "Individuals have rights, and there are things no person or group may do to them (without violating their rights)." Rights "set the constraints within which a social choice is to be made, by excluding certain alternatives, fixing others, and so on."[2]

The third approach is to see fulfillments of rights as goals to be pursued. This "goal view" differs from the instrumental view in regarding rights to be intrinsically important, and it differs from the constraint view in seeing the fulfillment of rights as goals to be generally promoted, rather than taking them as demanding only (and exactly) that we refrain from violating the rights of others. In the "constraint view" there is no duty to help anyone with his or her rights (merely not to hinder), and also in the "instrumental view" there is no duty, in fact, to help unless the right fulfillment will also promote some other goal such as utility. The "goal view" integrates the valuation of rights—their fulfillment and violation—in overall moral accounting, and yields a wider sphere of influence of rights in morality.

I have argued elsewhere that the goal view has advantages that the other two approaches do not share, in particular, the ability to accommodate integrated moral accounting including inter alia the intrinsic importance of a class of fundamental rights. I shall not repeat that argument here. But there is an interesting question of dual roles of rights in the sense that some rights may be *both* intrinsically important and instrumentally valuable. For example, the right to be free from hunger could—not implausibly—be regarded as being valuable in itself as well as serving as a good instrument to promote other goals such as security, longevity or utility. If so, both the goal view and the instrumental view would have to be simultaneously deployed to get a comprehensive assessment of such a right....

The instrumental aspect is an inescapable feature of every right, since irrespective of whether a certain right is intrinsically valuable or not, its acceptance will certainly have other consequences as well, and these, too, have to be assessed along with the intrinsic value of rights (if any). A right that is regarded as quite valuable in itself may nevertheless be judged to be morally rejectable if it leads to disastrous consequences. This is a case of the rights playing a *negative* instrumental role. It is, of course, also possible that the instrumental argument will *bolster* the intrinsic claims of a right to be taken seriously....

There are two general conclusions to draw, at this stage, from this very preliminary discussion. First, we must distinguish between (1) the intrinsic value of a right, and (2) the overall value of a right taking note inter alia of its intrinsic importance (if any). The acceptance of the intrinsic importance of any right is no guarantee that its overall moral valuation must be favorable. Second, no moral assessment of a right can be independent of its likely consequences. The need for empirical assessment of the effects of accepting any right cannot be escaped. Empirical arguments are quite central to moral philosophy.

PROPERTY AND DEPRIVATION

The right to hold, use and bequeath property that one has legitimately acquired is often taken to be inherently valuable. In fact, however, many of its defenses seem to be actually of the instrumental type, e.g., arguing that property rights make people more free to choose one kind of a life rather than another. But even if we do accept that property rights may have some intrinsic value, this does not in any way amount to an overall justification of property rights, since property rights may have consequences which themselves will require assessment. Indeed, the causation of hunger as well as its prevention may materially depend on how property rights are structured. If a set of property rights leads, say, to starvation, as it well might, then the moral approval of these rights would certainly be compromised severely. In general, the need for consequential analysis of property rights is inescapable whether or not such rights are seen as having any intrinsic value....

...I have tried to argue elsewhere...that famines are, in fact, best explained in terms of failures of entitlement systems. The entitlements here refer, of course, to legal rights and to practical possibilities, rather than to moral status, but the laws and actual operation of private ownership economies have many features in common with the moral system of entitlements analyzed by Nozick and others.

The entitlement approach to famines need not, of course, be confined to private ownership economies, and entitlement failures of other systems can also be fruitfully studied to examine famines and hunger. In the specific context of private ownership economies, the entitlements are substantially analyzable in terms, respectively, of what may be called "endowments" and "exchange entitlements." A person's endowment refers to what he or she initially owns (including the person's own labor power), and the exchange entitlement mapping tells us what the person can obtain through exchanging what he or she owns, either by production (exchange with nature), or by trade (exchange with others), or a mixture of the two. A person has to starve if neither the endowments, nor what can be obtained through exchange, yields an adequate amount of food.

If starvation and hunger are seen in terms of failures of entitlements, then it becomes immediately clear that the total availability of food in a country is only one of several variables that are relevant. Many famines occur without any decline in the availability of food. For example, in the Great Bengal famine

of 1943, the total food availability in Bengal was not particularly bad (considerably higher than two years earlier when there was no famine), and yet three million people died, in a famine mainly affecting the rural areas, through rather violent shifts in the relative purchasing powers of different groups, hitting the rural laborers the hardest. The Ethiopian famine of 1973 took place in a year of average per capita food availability, but the cultivators and other occupation groups in the province of Wollo had lost their means of subsistence (through loss of crops and a decline of economic activity, related to a local drought) and had no means of commanding food from elsewhere in the country. Indeed, some food moved *out* of Wollo to more prosperous people in other parts of Ethiopia, repeating a pattern of contrary movement of food that was widely observed during the Irish famines of the 1840s (with food moving out of famine-stricken Ireland to prosperous England which had greater power in the battle for entitlements). The Bangladesh famine of 1974 took place in a year of *peak* food availability, but several occupation groups had lost their entitlement to food through loss of employment and other economic changes (including inflationary pressures causing prices to outrun wages). Other examples of famines without significant (or any) decline in food availability can be found, and there is nothing particularly surprising about this fact once it is recognized that the availability of food is only one influence among many on the entitlement of each occupation group. Even when a famine *is* associated with a decline of food availability, the entitlement changes have to be studied to understand the particular nature of the famine, e.g., why one occupation group is hit but not another. The causation of starvation can be sensibly sought in failures of entitlements of the respective groups.

The causal analysis of famines in terms of entitlements also points to possible public policies of prevention. The main economic strategy would have to take the form of increasing the entitlements of the deprived groups, and in general, of guaranteeing minimum entitlements for everyone, paying particular attention to the vulnerable groups. This can, in the long run, be done in many different ways, involving both economic growth (including growth of food output) and distributional adjustments. Some of these policies may, however, require that the property rights and the corresponding entitlements of the more prosperous groups be violated. The problem, in fact, is particularly acute in the short run, since it may not be possible to engineer rapid economic growth instantly. Then the burden of raising entitlements of the groups in distress would largely have to fall on reducing the entitlements of others more favorably placed. Transfers of income or commodities through various public policies may well be effective in quashing a famine (as the experience of famine relief in different countries has shown), but it may require substantial government intervention in the entitlements of the more prosperous groups.

There is, however, no great moral dilemma in this if property rights are treated as purely *instrumental*. If the goals of relief of hunger and poverty are sufficiently powerful, then it would be just right to violate whatever property rights come in the way, since—in this view—property rights have no intrinsic status. On the other hand, if property rights are taken to be morally inviolable irrespective of their consequences, then it will follow that these policies cannot be morally acceptable even though they might save thousands, or even millions, from dying. The inflexible moral "constraint" of respecting people's legitimately acquired entitlements would rule out such policies.

In fact this type of problem presents a reductio ad absurdum of the moral validity of constraint-based entitlement systems. However, while the conclusions to be derived from that approach might well be "absurd," the situation postulated is not an imaginary one at all. It is based on studies of actual famines and the role of entitlement failures in the causation of mass starvation. If there is an embarrassment here, it belongs solidly to the consequence-independent way of seeing rights.

I should add that this dilemma does not arise from regarding property rights to be of intrinsic value, which can be criticized on other grounds, but not this one. Even if property rights *are* of intrinsic value, their violation may be justified on grounds of the favorable consequences of that violation. A right, as was mentioned earlier, may be intrinsically valuable and still be justly violated taking everything into account. The "absurdum" does not belong to attaching intrinsic value to property rights, but to regarding these rights as simply acceptable, regardless of their consequences. A moral system that values both property rights and other goals—such as avoiding famines and starvation, or fulfilling people's right not to be hungry—can, on the one hand, give property rights intrinsic importance, and on the other, recommend the violation of property rights when that leads to better overall consequences (*including* the disvalue of rights violation).

The issue here is not the valuing of property rights, but their alleged inviolability. There is no dilemma here either for the purely instrumental view of property rights or for treating the fulfillment of property rights as one goal among many, but specifically for consequence-independent assertions of property rights and for the corresponding constraint-based approaches to moral entitlement of ownership.

That property and hunger are closely related cannot possibly come as a great surprise. Hunger is primarily associated with not owning enough food and thus property rights over food are immediately and directly involved. Fights over that property right can be a major part of the reality of a poor country, and any system of moral assessment has to take note of that phenomenon. The tendency to see hunger in purely technocratic terms of food output and availability may help to hide the crucial role of entitlements in the genesis of hunger, but a fuller economic analysis cannot overlook that crucial role. Since property rights over food are derived from property rights over other goods and resources (through production and trade), the entire system of rights of acquisition and transfer is implicated in the emergence and survival of hunger and starvation.

THE RIGHT NOT TO BE HUNGRY

Property rights have been championed for a long time. In contrast, the assertion of "the right not to be hungry" is a comparatively recent phenomenon. While this right is much invoked in political debates, there is a good deal of skepticism about treating this as truly a right in any substantial way. It is often asserted that this concept of "right not to be hungry" stands essentially for nothing at all ("simple nonsense," as Bentham called "natural rights" in general). That piece of sophisticated cynicism reveals not so much a penetrating insight into the practical affairs of the world, but a refusal to investigate what people mean when they assert the existence of rights that, for the bulk of humanity, are not in fact guaranteed by the existing institutional arrangements.

The right not to be hungry is not asserted as a recognition of an institutional right that already exists, as the right to property typically is. The assertion is primarily a moral claim as to what should be valued, and what institutional structure we should aim for, and try to guarantee if feasible. It can also be seen in terms of Ronald Dworkin's category of "background rights—rights that provide a justification for political decisions by society in abstract."[3] This interpretation serves as the basis for a reason to change the existing institutional structure and state policy.

It is broadly in this form that the right to "an adequate means of livelihood" is referred to in the Constitution of India: "The state shall, in particular, direct its policy towards securing . . . that the citizens, men and women equally, have the right to an adequate means of livelihood." This does not, of course, offer to each citizen a guaranteed right to an adequate livelihood, but the state is asked to take steps such that this right could become realizable for all.

In fact, this right has often been invoked in political debates in India. The electoral politics of India does indeed give particular scope for such use of what are seen as background rights. It is, of course, not altogether clear whether the reference to this right in the Indian constitution has in fact materially influenced the political debates. The constitutional statement is often cited, but very likely this issue would have figured in any case in these debates, given the nature of the moral and political concern. But whatever the constitutional contribution, it is interesting to ask whether the implicit acceptance of the value of the right to freedom from hunger makes any difference to actual policy.

It can be argued that the general acceptance of the right of freedom from acute hunger as a major goal has played quite a substantial role in preventing famines in India. The last real famine in India was in 1943, and while food availability per head in India has risen only rather slowly (even now the food availability per head is no higher than in many sub-Saharan countries stricken by recurrent famines), the country has not experienced any famine since independence in 1947. The main cause of that success is a policy of public intervention. Whenever a famine has threatened, a public policy of intervention and relief has offered minimum entitlements to the potential famine victims, and thus have the threatening famines been averted. It can be argued that the quickness of the response of the respective governments (both state and central) reflects a political necessity, given the Indian electoral system and the importance attached by the public to the prevention of starvation. Political pressures from opposition groups and the news media have kept the respective governments on their toes, and the right to be free from acute hunger and starvation has been achieved largely because it has been seen as a valuable right. Thus the recognition of the intrinsic moral importance of this right, which has been widely invoked in public discussions, has served as a powerful political instrument as well.

On the other hand, this process has been far from effective in tackling pervasive and persistent undernourishment in India. There has been no famine in post-independence India, but perhaps a third of India's rural population is perennially undernourished. So long as hunger remains non-acute and starvation deaths are avoided (even though morbidity and mortality rates are enhanced by undernourishment), the need for a policy response is neither much discussed by the news media, nor forcefully demanded even by opposition parties. The elimination of famines coexists with the survival of widespread "regular hunger." The right to "adequate means" of *nourishment* does not at all seem to arouse political concern in a way that the right to "adequate means" to *avoid starvation* does.

The contrast can be due to one of several different reasons. It could, of course, simply be that the ability to avoid undernourishment is not socially accepted as very important. This could be so, though what is socially accepted and what is not is also partly a matter of how clearly the questions are posed. It is, in fact, quite possible that the freedom in question would be regarded as a morally important right if the question were posed in a transparent way, but this does not happen because of the nature of Indian electoral politics and that of news coverage. The issue is certainly not "dramatic" in the way in which starvation deaths and threatening famines are. Continued low-key misery may be too familiar a phenomenon to make it worthwhile for political leaders to get some mileage out of it in practical politics. The news media may also find little profit in emphasizing a non-spectacular phenomenon—the quiet survival of disciplined, non-acute hunger.

If this is indeed the case, then the implications for action of the goal of eliminating hunger, or guaranteeing to all the means for achieving this, may be quite complex. The political case for making the quiet hunger less quiet and more troublesome for governments in power is certainly relevant. Aggressive political journalism might prove to have an instrumental moral value if it were able to go beyond reporting the horrors of visible starvation and to portray the pervasive, non-acute hunger in a more dramatic and telling way. This is obviously not the place to discuss the instrumentalities of practical politics, but the endorsement of the moral right to be free from hunger—both acute and non-acute—would in fact raise pointed questions about the means which might be used to pursue such a goal....

NOTES

1. This is presented as a "Directive Principle of State Policy." It does not have a direct operational role in the working of the Indian legal system, but it has considerable political force.

2. Robert Nozick, *Anarchy, State, and Utopia* (New York: Basic, 1974), pp. ix, 166.

3. Ronald Dworkin, *Taking Rights Seriously* (Cambridge, Mass.: Harvard University Press, 1977), p. 93.

READING QUESTIONS

1. Explain how rights can be instruments, constraints, or goals according to Sen. What does he think the advantages of the goal view of rights are?
2. What are the two conclusions about rights that he draws from the distinction among the three different views? How does he distinguish between the intrinsic value of a right and the overall value of a right?
3. What is the best explanation for the cause of famines according to Sen? Explain the difference between endowments and entitlements.
4. Explain what Sen means when he talks about the right not be hungry. How does he use the notion of background rights to argue for his view?

DISCUSSION QUESTIONS

1. How does Sen's solution to the problem of world hunger compare to the others proposed in this chapter? Discuss whether there are any potential problems with his view that he fails to consider.
2. What are some of the ways that private citizens could work to implement the sort of strategies suggested by Sen?

ONORA O'NEILL

A Kantian Approach to World Hunger

O'Neill approaches questions about our obligations to the hungry and poor through Kant's Humanity formulation of his fundamental moral principle, the categorical imperative: *So act that you use humanity, whether in your own person or that of another, always at the same time as an end, never merely as a means.* In requiring that we never treat others merely as means, the principle in question imposes requirements of justice. But in requiring that we treat humanity as an end, it goes further and imposes requirements of beneficence. After explaining the rudiments of Kant's Humanity principle, O'Neill proceeds to explore the implications of Kantian justice and beneficence regarding obligations to help those in need.

Recommended Reading: Kantian moral theory, chap. 1, sec. 2C, particularly the Humanity formulation of the categorical imperative.

We use others as *mere means* if what we do reflects some maxim *to which they could not in principle consent.* Kant does not suggest that there is anything wrong about using someone as a means. Evidently every cooperative scheme of action does this. A government that agrees to provide free or subsidized food to famine-relief agencies both uses and is used by the agencies; a peasant who sells food in a local market both uses and is used by those who buy it. In such examples each party to the transaction can and does consent to take part in that transaction. Kant would say that the parties to such transactions use one another but do not use one another as *mere* means. Each party assumes that the other has its own maxims of action and is not just a thing or prop to be used or manipulated.

But there are other cases where one party to an arrangement or transaction not only uses the other but does so in ways that could only be done on the basis of a fundamental principle or maxim to which the other could not in principle consent. If a false promise is given, the party that accepts the promise is not just used but used as a mere means, because it is *impossible* for consent to be given to the fundamental principle or project of deception that must guide every false promise, whatever its surface character. Those who accept false promises *must* be kept ignorant of the underlying principle or maxim on which the "undertaking" is based. If this isn't kept concealed, the attempted promise will either be rejected or will not be a *false* promise at all. In false promising the deceived party becomes, as it were, a prop or tool—a *mere* means—in the false promisor's scheme. Action based on any such maxim of deception would be wrong in Kantian terms, whether it is a matter of a breach of treaty obligations, of contractual undertakings, or of accepted and relied upon modes of interaction. Maxims of deception *standardly* use others as mere means, and acts that could only be based on such maxims are unjust.

From Onora O'Neill, "The Moral Perplexities of Famine and World Hunger," in Tom Regan, ed., *Matters of Life and Death,* 2nd edition, New York, Random House, 1986, pp. 322–329.

Another standard way of using others as mere means is by coercing them. Coercers, like deceivers, standardly don't give others the possibility of dissenting from what they propose to do. In deception, "consent" is spurious because it is given to a principle that couldn't be the underlying principle of *that* act at all; but the principle governing coercion may be brutally plain. Here any "consent" given is spurious because there was no option *but* to consent. If a rich or powerful landowner or nation threatens a poorer or more vulnerable person, group, or nation with some intolerable difficulty unless a concession is made, the more vulnerable party is denied a genuine choice between consent and dissent. While the boundary that divides coercion from mere bargaining and negotiation varies and is therefore often hard to discern, we have no doubt about the clearer cases. Maxims of coercion may threaten physical force, seizure of possessions, destruction of opportunities, or any other harm that the coerced party is thought to be unable to absorb without grave injury or danger. A moneylender in a Third World village who threatens not to make or renew an indispensable loan, without which survival until the next harvest would be impossible, uses the peasant as mere means. The peasant does not have the possibility of genuinely consenting to the "offer he can't refuse." The outward form of some coercive transactions may *look* like ordinary commercial dealings: but we know very well that some action that is superficially of this sort is based on maxims of coercion. To avoid coercion, action must be governed by maxims that the other party can choose to refuse and is not bound to accept. The more vulnerable the other party in any transaction or negotiation, the less their scope for refusal, and the more demanding it is likely to be to ensure that action is noncoercive.

In Kant's view, acts done on maxims that coerce or deceive others, so therefore cannot in principle have the consent of those others, are wrong. When individuals or institutions, or nation states act in ways that can only be based on such maxims they fail in their duty. They treat the parties who are either deceived or coerced unjustly. To avoid unjust action it is not enough to observe the outward forms of free agreement and cooperation; it is also essential to see that the weaker party to any arrangement has a genuine option to refuse the fundamental character of the proposal.

TREATING OTHERS AS ENDS IN THEMSELVES

For Kant, as for utilitarians, justice is only one part of duty. We may fail in our duty, even when we don't use anyone as mere means (by deception or coercion), if we fail to treat others as "ends in themselves." To treat others as "Ends in Themselves" we must not only avoid using them as mere means but also treat them as rational and autonomous beings with their own maxims. If human beings were *wholly* rational and autonomous then, on a Kantian view, duty would require only that they not use one another as mere means. But, as Kant repeatedly stressed, but later Kantians have often forgotten, human beings are *finite* rational beings. They are finite in several ways.

First, human beings are not ideal rational calculators. We *standardly* have neither a complete list of the actions possible in a given situation nor more than a partial view of their likely consequences. In addition, abilities to assess and to use available information are usually quite limited.

Second, these cognitive limitations are *standardly* complemented by limited autonomy. Human action is limited not only by various sorts of physical barrier and inability but by further sorts of (mutual or asymmetrical) dependence. To treat one another as ends in themselves such beings have to base their action on principles that do not undermine but rather sustain and extend one another's capacities for autonomous action. A central requirement for doing so is to share and support one another's ends and activities at least to some extent. Since finite rational beings cannot generally achieve their aims without some help and support from others, a general refusal of help and support amounts to failure to treat others as rational and autonomous beings, that is as ends in themselves. Hence Kantian principles require us not only to act justly, that is in accordance with maxims that don't coerce or deceive others, but also to avoid manipulation and to lend some support to others' plans and activities. Since famine, great poverty and powerlessness all undercut the possibility of autonomous action, and the requirement of treating others as ends in themselves demands that Kantians standardly act to support the possibility of autonomous action where it is most vulnerable, Kantians are required to do what they can to avert, reduce, and remedy famine. On a Kantian view, beneficence is as indispensable as justice in human lives.

JUSTICE AND BENEFICENCE IN KANT'S THOUGHT

Kant is often thought to hold that justice is morally required, but beneficence is morally less important. He does indeed, like Mill, speak of justice as a *perfect duty* and of beneficence as an *imperfect duty*. But he does not mean by this that beneficence is any less a duty; rather, he holds that it has (unlike justice) to be selective. We cannot share or even support *all* others' maxims *all* of the time. Hence support for others' autonomy is always selective. By contrast we can make all action and institutions conform fundamentally to standards of nondeception and noncoercion. Kant's understanding of the distinction between perfect and imperfect duties differs from Mill's. In a Kantian perspective justice isn't a matter of the core requirements for beneficence, as in Mill's theory, and beneficence isn't just an attractive but optional moral embellishment of just arrangements (as tends to be assumed in most theories that take human rights as fundamental).

JUSTICE TO THE VULNERABLE IN KANTIAN THINKING

For Kantians, justice requires action that conforms (at least outwardly) to what could be done in a given situation while acting on maxims neither of deception nor of coercion. Since anyone hungry or destitute is more than usually vulnerable to deception and coercion, the possibilities and temptations to injustice are then especially strong.

Examples are easily suggested. I shall begin with some situations that might arise for somebody who happened to be part of a famine-stricken population. Where shortage of food is being dealt with by a reasonably fair rationing scheme, any mode of cheating to get more than one's allocated share involves using some others and is unjust. Equally, taking advantage of others' desperation to profiteer—for example, selling food at colossal prices or making loans on the security of others' future livelihood, when these are "offers they can't refuse"—constitutes coercion and so uses others as mere means and is unjust. Transactions that have the outward form of normal commercial dealing may be coercive when one party is desperate. Equally, forms of corruption that work by deception—such as bribing officials to gain special benefits from development schemes, or deceiving others about their entitlements—use others unjustly. Such requirements are far from trivial and frequently violated in hard times; acting justly in such conditions may involve risking one's own life and livelihood and require the greatest courage.

It is not so immediately obvious what justice, Kantianly conceived, requires of agents and agencies who are remote from destitution. Might it not be sufficient to argue that those of us fortunate enough to live in the developed world are far from famine and destitution, so if we do nothing but go about our usual business will successfully avoid injustice to the destitute? This conclusion has often been reached by those who take an abstract view of rationality and forget the limits of human rationality and autonomy. In such perspectives it can seem that there is nothing more to just action than meeting the formal requirements of nondeception and noncoercion in our dealings with one another. But once we remember the limitations of human rationality and autonomy, and the particular ways in which they are limited for those living close to the margins of subsistence, we can see that mere conformity to ordinary standards of commercial honesty and political bargaining is not enough for justice toward the destitute. If international agreements themselves can constitute "offers that cannot be refused" by the government of a poor country, or if the concessions required for investment by a transnational corporation or a development project reflect the desperation of recipients rather than an appropriate contribution to the project, then (however benevolent the motives of some parties) the weaker party to such agreements is used by the stronger.

In the earlier days of European colonial penetration of the now underdeveloped world it was evident enough that some of the ways in which "agreements" were made with native peoples were in fact deceptive or coercive or both. "Sales" of land by those who had no grasp of market practices and "cession of sovereignty" by those whose forms of life were prepolitical constitute only spurious consent to the agreements struck. But it is not only in these original forms of bargaining between powerful and powerless that injustice is frequent. There are many contemporary examples. For example, if capital investment (private or governmental) in a poorer country requires the receiving country to contribute disproportionately to the maintenance of a developed, urban "enclave" economy that offers little local employment but lavish standards of life for a small number of (possibly expatriate) "experts," while guaranteeing long-term exemption from local taxation for the investors, then we may doubt that the agreement could have been struck without the element of coercion provided by the desperation of the weaker party. Or if a trade agreement extracts political advantages (such as military bases) that are incompatible with the fundamental political interests of the country concerned, we may judge that at least some leaders of that country have been "bought" in a sense that is not consonant with ordinary commercial practice.

Even when the actions of those who are party to an agreement don't reflect a fundamental principle of coercion or deception, the agreement may alter the life circumstances and prospects of third parties in ways to which they patently could not have not consented. For example, a system of food aid and imports agreed upon by the government of a Third World country and certain developed countries or international agencies may give the elite of that Third World country access

to subsidized grain. If that grain is then used to control the urban population and also produces destitution among peasants (who used to grow food for that urban population), then those who are newly destitute probably have not been offered any opening or possibility of refusing their new and worsened conditions of life. If a policy is imposed, those affected *cannot* have been given a chance to refuse it: had the chance been there, they would either have assented (and so the policy would not have been *imposed*) or refused (and so proceeding with the policy would have been evidently coercive).

BENEFICENCE TO THE VULNERABLE IN KANTIAN THINKING

In Kantian moral reasoning, the basis for beneficent action is that we cannot, without it, treat others of limited rationality and autonomy as ends in themselves. This is not to say that Kantian beneficence won't make others happier, for it will do so whenever they would be happier if (more) capable of autonomous action, but that happiness secured by purely paternalistic means, or at the cost (for example) of manipulating others' desires, will not count as beneficent in the Kantian picture. Clearly the vulnerable position of those who lack the very means of life, and their severely curtailed possibilities for autonomous action, offer many different ways in which it might be possible for others to act beneficently. Where the means of life are meager, almost any material or organizational advance may help extend possibilities for autonomy. Individual or institutional action that aims to advance economic or social development can proceed on many routes. The provision of clean water, of improved agricultural techniques, of better grain storage systems, or of adequate means of local transport may all help transform material prospects. Equally, help in the development of new forms of social organization—whether peasant self-help groups, urban cooperatives, medical and contraceptive services, or improvements in education or in the position of women—may help to extend possibilities for autonomous action. Kantian thinking docs not provide a means by which all possible projects of this sort could be listed and ranked. But where some activity helps secure possibilities for autonomous action for more people, or is likely to achieve a permanent improvement in the position of the most vulnerable, or is one that can be done with more reliable success, this provides reason for furthering that project rather than alternatives.

Clearly the alleviation of need must rank far ahead of the furthering of happiness in the Kantian picture. I might make my friends very happy by throwing extravagant parties: but this would probably not increase anybody's possibility for autonomous action to any great extent. But the sorts of development-oriented changes that have just been mentioned may *transform* the possibilities for action of some. Since famine and the risk of famine are always and evidently highly damaging to human autonomy, any action that helps avoid or reduce famine must have a strong claim on any Kantian who is thinking through what beneficence requires. Depending on circumstances, such action may have to take the form of individual contribution to famine relief and development organizations, of individual or collective effort to influence the trade and aid policies of developed countries, or of attempts to influence the activities of those Third World elites for whom development does not seem to be an urgent priority. Some activities can best be undertaken by private citizens of developed countries; others are best approached by those who work for governments, international agencies, or transnational corporations. Perhaps the most dramatic possibilities to act for a just or an unjust, a beneficent or selfish future belong to those who hold positions of influence within the Third World. But wherever we find ourselves, our duties are not, on the Kantian picture, limited to those close at hand. Duties of justice arise whenever there is some involvement between parties—and in the modern world this is never lacking. Duties of beneficence arise whenever destitution puts the possibility of autonomous action in question for the more vulnerable. When famines were not only far away, but nothing could be done to relieve them, beneficence or charity may well have begun—and stayed—at home. In a global village, the moral significance of distance has shrunk, and we may be able to affect the capacities for autonomous action of those who are far away.

THE SCOPE OF KANTIAN DELIBERATIONS ABOUT FAMINE AND HUNGER

In many ways Kantian moral reasoning is less ambitious than utilitarian moral reasoning. It does not propose a process of moral reasoning that can (in principle) rank *all* possible actions or all possible institutional arrangements from the happiness-maximizing "right" action or institution downward. It aims rather to offer a pattern of reasoning by which we can identify whether *proposed action or institutional arrangements* would be just or unjust, beneficent or lacking in beneficence. While *some* knowledge of causal connections is needed for Kantian reasoning, it is far less sensitive than is utilitarian reasoning to gaps in our causal knowledge. The conclusions reached about particular proposals for action or about institutional arrangements will not hold for all time, but be relevant for the contexts for which action is proposed. For example, if it is judged that some institution—say the World Bank—provides, under present circumstances, a just approach to certain development problems, it will not follow that under all other circumstances such an institution would be part of a just approach. There may be other institutional arrangements that are also just; and there may be other circumstances under which the institutional structure of the World Bank would be shown to be in some ways deceptive or coercive and so unjust.

These points show us that Kantian deliberations about famine and hunger can lead only to conclusions that are useful in determinate contexts. This, however, is standardly what we need to know for action, whether individual or institutional. We do not need to be able to generate a complete list of available actions in order to determine whether proposed lines of action are not unjust and whether any are beneficent. Kantian patterns of moral reasoning cannot be guaranteed to identify the optimal course of action in a situation. They provide methods neither for listing nor for ranking all possible proposals for action. But any line of action that is considered can be checked.

The reason this pattern of reasoning will not show any action or arrangement the most beneficent one available is that the Kantian picture of beneficence is less mathematically structured than the utilitarian one. It judges beneficence by its overall contribution to the prospects for human autonomy and not by the quantity of happiness expected to result. To the extent that the autonomous pursuit of goals is what Mill called "one of the principal ingredients of human happiness" (but only to that extent), the requirements of Kantian and of utilitarian beneficence will coincide. But whenever expected happiness is not a function of the scope for autonomous action, the two accounts of beneficent action diverge. For utilitarians, paternalistic imposition of, for example, certain forms of aid and development assistance need not be wrong and may even be required. But for Kantians, whose beneficence should secure others' possibilities for autonomous action, the case for paternalistic imposition of aid or development projects without the recipients' involvement must always be questionable.

In terms of some categories in which development projects are discussed, utilitarian reasoning may well endorse "top-down" aid and development projects which override whatever capacities for autonomous choice and action the poor of a certain area now have in the hopes of securing a happier future. If the calculations work out in a certain way, utilitarians may even think a "generation of sacrifice"—or of forced labor or of imposed population-control policies not only permissible but mandated. In their darkest Malthusian moments some utilitarians have thought that average happiness might best be maximized not by improving the lot of the poor but by minimizing their numbers, and so have advocated policies of "benign neglect" of the poorest and most desperate. Kantian patterns of reasoning are likely to endorse less global and less autonomy-overriding aid and development projects; they are not likely to endorse neglect or abandoning of those who are most vulnerable and lacking in autonomy. If the aim of beneficence is to keep or put others in a position to act for themselves, then emphasis must be placed on "bottom-up" projects, which from the start draw on, foster, and establish indigenous capacities and practices of self-help and local action....

READING QUESTIONS

1. Under what circumstances does one individual use another as a means according to O'Neill? Explain why false promises and coercion involve using someone as a means.
2. How can we treat others as ends in themselves according to O'Neill? In what ways are human beings limited by their finitude?
3. Explain the role of justice and beneficence in Kant's thought. Why do justice and beneficence require helping the vulnerable?
4. What reasons does O'Neill give for thinking that a Kantian approach to the problem of hunger is less ambitious but more successful than the utilitarian approach?

DISCUSSION QUESTIONS

1. Is O'Neill right to claim that the Kantian approach does not face the same sorts of difficulties as the utilitarian approach to the problem of world hunger? Why or why not? What sorts of problems might the Kantian approach face that the utilitarian approach does not?
2. Consider and discuss whether the Kantian argument for helping the vulnerable is more or less convincing than the traditional utilitarian arguments. What kinds of arguments would be the most likely to persuade people to help those in need?

361

ADDITIONAL RESOURCES

Web Resources

Hunger Notes, <www.worldhunger.org>. Established in 1976 by the World Hunger Education Services features information about world hunger.

The World Food Programme, <www.wfp.org>. A branch of the United Nations whose objectives include reducing hunger.

OXFAM, <http://www.oxfam.org/>. An international organization devoted to helping the world's poor.

Beauchamp, Tom, "The Principle of Beneficence in Applied Ethics," *Stanford Encyclopedia of Philosophy*, <http://plato.stanford.edu/entries/principle-beneficence>. A useful discussion of the place of a principle of beneficence in various ethical theories including those of Kant, Mill, and Hume, as well as how considerations of beneficence figures in discussions of applied ethics.

Authored Books and Articles

Cullity, Garrett, *The Moral Demands of Affluence* (Oxford: Oxford University Press, 2004). Cullity argues that the obligations of the affluent to help those in desperate need are modestly demanding.

O'Neill, Onora, *Faces of Hunger: An Essay on Poverty, Justice, and Development* (London and Boston: Unwin Hyman, 1986).

Pogge, Thomas, *World Poverty and Human Rights: Cosmopolitan Responsibilities and Reforms* (Cambridge: Polity Press, 2002). Pogge argues that our current economic order is morally indefensible and that those who are relatively economically well off are responsible for serious global injustices.

Murdoch, William W. and Oaten, Allan, "Population and Food: Metaphors and the Reality," *Bioscience* 25 (1975). A reply to Hardin's "lifeboat ethics."

Sen, Amartya, *Poverty and Famines: An Essay on Entitlement and Deprivation* (Oxford: Oxford University Press, 1984). A penetrating analysis of the causes of poverty and famine.

Unger, Peter, *Living High and Letting Die: Our Illusion of Innocence* (Oxford: Oxford University Press, 1996). An examination of the incongruity between basic moral principles most people do accept and their attitudes toward those in need.

Edited Collections

Aiken, William and LaFollette, Hugh, eds., *World Hunger and Moral Obligation*, 2nd ed. (Englewood Cliffs, NJ: Prentice Hall, 1996). An extensive and important collection of essays.

Crocker, David, A. and Toby Linden (eds.), *Ethics of Consumption: The Good Life, Justice, and Global Stewardship* (Lanham, MD: Rowman & Littlefield, 1997). A collection of essays from renowned scholars from many disciplines that cover many aspects of morality and consumption.

15 The Environment, Consumption, and Climate Change

On March 15, 2005, the U.S. Senate voted (51–49) to approve a measure that would allow oil companies to drill for oil beneath the coastal plain of the Arctic National Wildlife Refuge (ANWR) in the northeastern region of Alaska. But in December 2005, the Senate voted to strip language from a defense appropriations bill that would have allowed drilling for gas and oil in the ANWR. Legal battles between pro-drilling interests and environmentalists over this refuge are likely to continue. Environmentalists opposed to this measure argue that drilling and laying pipelines would harm various forms of wildlife and the wilderness of the region generally. This is but one of a long list of environmental concerns that raise both legal and ethical issues.

One reason one might take up environmental causes is purely instrumental, namely, that human life depends crucially on the environment and so, out of concern for human welfare, we ought to preserve what we need to survive. But many environmentally concerned individuals think there is more to an ethical concern for the environment than how the welfare of human beings might be affected. Their thought is that at least some so-called lower forms of life (nonhuman and non-higher-animal life) have intrinsic value and thus some degree of **direct moral standing**. Their moral concern for the environment thus goes beyond a concern for how changing the environment might impact human beings. The moral claims of such environmentalists raise a number of fundamental ethical questions, including the following:

- Do biological entities other than humans and higher nonhuman animals have at least some degree of direct moral standing?
- What about nonliving things such as mountains and streams? What sort of direct moral standing (if any) do they have?
- If either some nonhuman biological creatures or nonliving things have direct moral standing, what does this imply about how human beings ought to treat such things?

1. EXPANDING THE SCOPE OF DIRECT MORAL STANDING?

As in the chapter on the ethical treatment of animals, the main philosophical issue in this chapter concerns what we are calling the scope of *direct* moral standing. You may recall that

363

for something to be within the scope of direct moral standing is for it itself to count morally because of its own nature and not merely because it is of instrumental value to human beings or any other creature. If anything is clear in the realm of disputed moral issues it is that human beings have direct moral standing—each of us possesses a kind of standing that imposes requirements on others and how they treat us. We can put the point in terms of reasons: that your action would cause me serious injury is a reason for you not to do that action. Granted, there may be cases in which this reason is overridden by an even more important moral reason. But still, because of the fact that I am the sort of creature I am, I am of direct (not just indirect) moral concern.

Those who would ascribe moral rights to (at least some) nonhuman animals, or who would claim that human beings have obligations *to* nonhuman animals, advocate expanding the sphere of direct moral standing beyond the realm of human beings to include some nonhuman animals. As we shall see in this chapter, some philosophers propose that we expand the scope of direct moral standing even further and include a wider range of entities. These "expansionists" differ among themselves as to how inclusive this scope should be. In order to get a sense of the issues and arguments featured in some discussions about ethics and the environment, let us first introduce some terminology that is often used to pick out different positions one might take on this issue of scope, and then consider some of the arguments featured in debates over environmental ethics.

2. FOUR APPROACHES

Here, then, are four general approaches to questions about the scope of direct moral standing, organized from least to most inclusive:

- **Anthropocentrism:** The only beings who possess direct moral standing are human beings. All other beings (living and nonliving) are of mere indirect moral concern.
- **Sentientism:** All and only sentient creatures—creatures who have the capacity to experience pleasure and pain—have direct moral standing. Thus, morality includes requirements that include direct moral concern for all sentient beings.
- **Biocentrism:** All living beings *because they are living* possess direct moral standing. Thus, morality includes requirements that include direct moral concern for all living beings.
- **Ecocentrism:** The primary bearers of direct moral standing are ecosystems in virtue of their functional integrity. An **ecosystem** is a whole composed of both living and nonliving things including animals, plants, bodies of water, sunlight, and other geological factors. Hence, morality involves moral obligations to maintain the functional integrity of ecosystems and because, according to this view, ecosystems are *primary* bearers of direct moral standing, their preservation takes moral precedence over concern for individual things and creatures that compose the system.

One basic difference between the first three approaches and ecocentrism is the contrast between **atomism** and **holism** regarding the primary bearers of direct moral standing—a distinction implicit in the previous characterizations. Atomism in this context is the view that the primary items of moral appraisal are individuals—only individuals can be properly judged as intrinsically valuable, or rights holders, or as having obligations. By contrast, holism maintains that wholes or collectives are bearers of value, or of rights, or of obligations. Of course, the view that wholes are bearers of direct moral standing is compatible with the atomistic view that individual members of a whole also have direct moral standing. Thus, one view, sometimes called **ecoholism,** maintains that both ecosystems and at least some individual items that make up an ecosystem have direct moral standing. But notice that the eco*centrist* makes a stronger holistic claim: the *only* bearers of direct moral standing are wholes, and not the individual items of which they are composed.

3. THE VERY IDEA OF AN ENVIRONMENTAL ETHIC

Having described four basic positions about the scope of moral concern, we are now in a position to clarify the very idea of an environmental ethic. Here it is important to distinguish between an ethic *of* the environment and an ethic *for the use of* the environment. The latter kind of "management ethic" for the environment is consistent with anthropocentrism, and so it does not count as an environmental ethic. Thus, an environmental ethic must accord direct moral standing to beings other than humans. But this minimum necessary condition is not enough—not sufficient—for an ethic to be an environmental ethic. After all, an ethical theory that accorded some direct moral standing to humans and to apes, but nothing else, would not, strictly speaking, count as an **environmental ethic.** So, with some modification, let us follow philosopher Tom Regan's characterization of an environmental ethic:

1. An environmental ethic must hold that there are nonhuman beings that have direct moral standing.
2. An environmental ethic must hold that the class of beings that have direct moral standing is larger than the class of conscious beings—that is, this sort of ethic must ascribe direct moral standing to nonconscious beings.[1]

This characterization of an environmental ethic, while perhaps not airtight, does at least properly categorize the three basic approaches we discussed in the previous section. Clearly, anthropocentric and sentientist accounts of direct moral standing ethic are ruled out by Regan's definition, even if they allow for a management ethic in dealing with environmental issues. However, both biocentric and ecocentric views do count as versions of an environmental ethic. So, on this way of understanding ethical issues concerning treatment of the environment, the fundamental issue is over the scope of those beings (including living, nonliving, individuals, and collectives) that possess direct moral standing. And this issue brings us in direct contact with one of the most fundamental questions of ethical theory: *in virtue of what does something have direct moral standing?*

4. CONSUMPTION AND CLIMATE CHANGE

Perhaps the most publicized contemporary ethical issue associated with the environment is that of climate change and, in particular, global warming. Many have recently argued that excessive human consumption that produces emissions of greenhouse gases (GHGs), including in particular high emission levels of carbon dioxide (CO_2),[2] has brought about certain undesirable climactic changes: global warming, severe weather, and changes in ocean currents. For instance, according to a 2007 report by the Intergovernmental Panel on Climate Change (IPCC).[3]

> Global atmospheric concentrations of CO_2, CH_4 and N_2O have increased markedly as a result of human activities since 1750 and now far exceed pre-industrial values determined from ice cores spanning many thousands of years. The atmospheric concentrations of CO_2 and CH_4 in 2005 exceed by far the natural range over the last 650,000 years. Global increases in CO_2 concentrations are due primarily to fossil fuel use, with land-use change providing another significant but smaller contribution. It is very likely that the observed increase in CH_4 concentration is predominantly due to agriculture and fossil fuel use. The increase in N_2O concentration is primarily due to agriculture.[4]

The IPCC report contains projections for the 21st century about the likely effects of climate change and global warming in particular on four categories of concern: (1) agriculture, forestry, and ecosystems; (2) water resources; (3) human health; and (4) industry, settlement, and society. These projections are based on the assumption that GHGs will continue to be emitted at the same rate or higher than 2007 emission levels. Figure 15.1 presents the 2007 IPCC report that summarizes their projections.[5] (Note: Reference to SRES scenarios [Special Report on Emissions Scenarios] in the top row of the second column refers to various possible projections regarding demographic, economic, and technological changes on the basis of which predictions about climate change are projected. For example, one of the four basic scenarios "assumes a world of very rapid economic growth, a global population that peaks in mid-century and rapid introduction of new and more efficient technologies."[6])

Two comments are in order here. First, notice that not all of the predicted effects mentioned in this table are negative. For instance, one likely human health benefit from warmer temperatures is a decrease in mortality rates from exposure to cold. Also, reduced energy demand for purposes of heating homes and increased yields in agricultural products in areas whose temperatures will increase are among the projected positive effects of global warming. However, when put side to side with the number of projected negative effects (some of them, e.g., increased energy demand for cooling), the likely positive effects seem to be seriously outweighed by the likely negative effects.

Second, although most experts seem to agree that climate change is a genuine phenomenon, questions have been raised about the accuracy of the predictions featured in the IPCC report. Some have argued that the projections are faulty or misleading. Such critics include those who argue that the severity of the projected negative effects are exaggerated, while others have argued that such projections are too conservative, that the IPCC report underestimates the harm that will likely result from global warming.[7] Questions have also been raised about the extent to which climate change is due to human activities and how much is due to other, naturally occurring factors.

Examples of major projected impacts by sector

Phenomena and direction of trend	Likelihood of future trends based on projections for 21st century using SRES scenarios	Agriculture, forestry, and ecosystems	Water resources	Human health	Industry, settlement, and society
Over most land areas, warmer and fewer cold days and nights, warmer and more frequent hot days and nights.	Virtually certain	Increased yields in colder environments; decreased yields in warmer environments; increased insect outbreaks.	Effects on water resources relying on snowmelt; effects on some water supplies.	Reduced human mortality from decreased cold exposure.	Reduced energy demand for heating; increased demand for cooling; declining air quality in cities; reduced disruption to transport due to snow, ice; effects on winter tourism.
Warm spells/heat waves. Frequency increases over most land areas.	Very likely	Reduced yields in warmer regions due to heat stress; increased danger of wildfire.	Increased water demand; water quality problems, e.g., algal blooms.	Increased risk of heat-related mortality, especially for the elderly, chronically sick, very young, and socially isolated.	Reduced in quality of life for people in warm areas without appropriate housing; impacts on elderly, very young, and poor.
Heavy precipitation events. Frequency increases over most areas.	Very likely	Damage to crops; soil erosion, inability to cultivate land due to waterlogging of soils.	Adverse effects on quality of surface and groundwater; contamination of water supply; water scarcity may be relieved.	Increased risk of deaths, injuries, and infectious respiratory and skin diseases.	Disruption of settlements, commerce, transport and societies due to flooding: pressures on urban and rural infra-structures; loss of property.
Area affected by drought increases.	Likely	Land degradation; lower yields/crop damage and failure; increased livestock deaths; increased risk of wildfire.	More widespread water stress.	Increased risk of food and water shortage; increased risk of malnutrition; increased risk of water- and food-borne diseases.	Water shortage for settlements, industry and societies; reduced hydropower generation potentials; potential for population migration.
Intense tropical cyclone activity increases.	Likely	Damage to crops; windthrow (uprooting) of trees; damage to coral reefs.	Power outages causing disruption of public water supply.	Increased risk of deaths, injuries, water- and food-borne diseases; post–traumatic stress disorders.	Disruption by flood and high winds; withdrawal of risk coverage in vulnerable areas by private insurers; potential for population migrations; loss of property.
Increased incidence of extreme high sea level (excludes tsunamis).	Likely	Salinization of irrigation water, estuaries, and fresh-water systems.	Decreased fresh-water availability due to saltwater intrusion.	Increased risk of deaths and injuries by drowning in floods; migration-related health effects.	Costs of coastal protection versus costs of land-use relocation; potential for movement of populations and infrastructure.

FIGURE 15.1 Examples of possible impacts of climate change due to changes in extreme weather and climate events, based on projections to the mid- to late 21st century. These do not take into account any changes or developments in adaptive capacity. The likelihood estimates in column 2 relate to the phenomena listed in column 1.

But assuming that climate change is a genuine phenomenon and assuming, too, that much of it is due to human activity including, for instance, the use of fossil fuels that emit high levels of CO_2 into the atmosphere, the main ethical questions are these:

- What ethical implications does climate change have for individuals who live in a consumer society?
- What ethical implications does climate change have for governments, particularly those such as the United States whose consumer population apparently contributes a high percentage of the greenhouse gases that contribute to the phenomenon of global warming?

These questions receive attention from Peter Wenz, Walter Sinnott-Armstrong, and Bjørn Lomborg in their contributions to this chapter.

5. THEORY MEETS PRACTICE

Kantian moral theory extended

Many defenders of an environmental ethic base their view (whether biocentric or ecocentric) on the claim that intrinsic value is possessed by such things as nonsentient life forms, features of the environment, perhaps whole species, and the ecosystem itself. Thus, on their view, some or all of these items have direct moral standing. If we now add the idea that creatures and things having direct moral standing require that they be treated with an appropriate kind and level of respect, we arrive at a Kantian ethical theory, extended in scope.

Consequentialism

A consequentialist might go a number of ways with regard to an environmental ethic. If she follows the utilitarian tradition and accords direct moral standing only to sentient creatures—creatures who have the developed capacity to have experiences of pleasure and pain—then she is going to deny that nonsentient creatures and nonliving things have direct moral standing. This view will thus deny that there is or can be a genuine environmental ethic as we defined it earlier.

However, recall that the main consequentialist idea is that the rightness or wrongness of an action depends entirely on the net intrinsic value of the likely consequences of the various alternative actions or policies under consideration. It is open to a nonutilitarian consequentialist to hold that nonsentient creatures and perhaps nonliving things have intrinsic value and thus embrace the central tenets of an environmental ethic. If a consequentialist goes this route, there is still a difference between consequentialism so extended and a Kantian environmental ethic: the consequentialist maintains that what has intrinsic value is something *to be promoted*, while the Kantian holds that respecting what has intrinsic value is not simply a matter of promoting more of it. For instance, it is open to a Kantian to claim that proper respect for the environment requires of us that we *appreciate* and *preserve* it (or certain of its elements) where doing so is not a matter of (but may sometime include) promoting in the sense of increasing the items having intrinsic value.

Thus, consequentialists as such need not reject the main tenets of an environmental ethic, and those who do embrace such an ethic need not worry about collapsing their view into an essentially Kantian view.

Virtue Ethics

Suppose one is skeptical of the idea that nonsentient creatures and/or nonliving things have direct moral standing, and thus skeptical of the idea of an environmental ethic. And suppose one rejects any form of consequentialism, including utilitarianism. What sense might one make of the idea that responsible moral agents morally ought to have a certain noninstrumental regard for the environment? One answer is provided by a virtue-centered approach to ethics, according to which to fail to have a proper noninstrumental regard for the environment might involve one or more failures of character. This is the approach taken by Thomas E. Hill Jr. in his article included in this chapter. Virtue ethics is also the basis of Peter Wenz's approach to environmental issues related to human consumption in his essay "Synergistic Environmental Virtues: Consumerism and Human Flourishing," also included here.

Social Contract Theory

According to T. M. Scanlon's version of social contract theory (which he labels "contractualism"), one has a moral obligation to refrain from performing an action whenever it violates a general principle or rule that no one (suitably motivated) could reasonably reject as a public principle governing behavior of people in a society. In the selection "It's Not *My* Fault: Global Warming and Individual Moral Obligation," Walter Sinnott-Armstrong considers a variety of moral principles that one might attempt to use as a basis for arguing that it is morally wrong to, say, drive a gas-guzzling vehicle just for fun. He argues that neither the contractualist principle nor any of the other moral principles featured in leading moral theories can ground a plausible argument for wrongness of such an action.

NOTES

1. See Tom Regan, "The Nature and Possibility of an Environmental Ethic," *Environmental Ethics* 3 (1981): 19–34. I have broadened Regan's conception by not requiring that an environmental ethic attribute direct moral standing to conscious beings. Clearly, a holistic ethic of the sort described earlier counts as an environmental ethic, but it *need not* attribute any direct moral standing to the individuals (both living and nonliving) that compose a whole ecosystem. It should also be noted that Regan's conception of an environmental ethic excludes both anthropocentrism and sentientism from counting as environmental ethics. But other writers define "environmental ethics" more generally as the study of the ethics of human interactions with, and impact upon, the natural environment. On this broader definition, neither anthropocentrist nor sentientist views are excluded.

2. In addition to CO_2, other greenhouse gases include methane (CH_4), nitrous oxide (N_2O) and halocarbons (a group that includes hydrocarbons containing fluorine, chlorine, or bromine).

3. Established in 1988, the IPCC is a scientific intergovernmental body whose main task is to study the effects of human activity on climate.

4. From IPCC, *Climate Change 2007: Synthesis Report*, p. 15.

5. IPCC, *Climate Change 2007: Synthesis Report*, p. 31.

6. IPCC, *Climate Change 2007: Synthesis Report*, p. 44.

7. See, for instance, ch. 7 of the Wikipedia entry on the IPCC, "Criticisms of IPCC," <http://en.wikipedia.org/wiki/Intergovernmental_Panel_on_Climate_Change>.

WILLIAM F. BAXTER

People or Penguins: The Case for Optimal Pollution

Baxter defends an anthropocentric approach to ethical issues concerning the environment by specifying four goals that are to serve as criteria for determining solutions to problems of human organization. On the basis of these "people-oriented" criteria, Baxter argues that we should view our treatment of the environment as a matter of various trade-offs whose aim is to promote human welfare. Two of Baxter's criteria appeal to the Kantian idea that all persons are to be treated as ends in themselves, and so his view represents one way in which Kant's ethics can be extended to environmental concerns.

    Recommended Reading: Kantian moral theory, chap. 1, sec. 2C, particularly the Humanity formulation of the categorical imperative.

I start with the modest proposition that, in dealing with pollution, or indeed with any problem, it is helpful to know what one is attempting to accomplish. Agreement on how and whether to pursue a particular objective, such as pollution control, is not possible unless some more general objective has been identified and stated with reasonable precision. We talk loosely of having clean air and clean water, of preserving our wilderness areas, and so forth. But none of these is a sufficiently general objective: each is more accurately viewed as a means rather than as an end.

With regard to clean air, for example, one may ask, "how clean?" and "what does clean mean?" It is even reasonable to ask, "why have clean air?" Each of these questions is an implicit demand that a more general community goal be stated—a goal sufficiently general in its scope and enjoying sufficiently general assent among the community of actors that such "why" questions no longer seem admissible with respect to that goal.

If, for example, one states as a goal the proposition that "every person should be free to do whatever he wishes in contexts where his actions do not interfere with the interests of other human beings," the speaker is unlikely to be met with a response of "why." The goal may be criticized as uncertain in its implications or difficult to implement, but it is so basic a tenet of our civilization—it reflects a cultural value so broadly shared, at least in the abstract—that the question "why" is seen as impertinent or imponderable or both.

I do not mean to suggest that everyone would agree with the "spheres of freedom" objective just stated. Still less do I mean to suggest that a society could subscribe to four or five such general objectives that would be adequate in their coverage to serve as testing criteria by which all other disagreements might be measured. One difficulty in the attempt to construct such a list is that each new goal added will conflict, in certain applications, with each prior goal listed; and thus each goal serves as a limited qualification on prior goals.

Without any expectation of obtaining unanimous consent to them, let me set forth four goals that I generally use as ultimate testing criteria in attempting to frame solutions to problems of human organization.

From William F. Baxter, *People or Penguins: The Case for Optimal Pollution*, Columbia University Press, 1974, pp. 1–13. Reprinted with permission of the publisher.

My position regarding pollution stems from these four criteria. If the criteria appeal to you and any part of what appears hereafter does not, our disagreement will have a helpful focus: which of us is correct, analytically, in supposing that his position on pollution would better serve these general goals. If the criteria do not seem acceptable to you, then it is to be expected that our more particular judgments will differ, and the task will then be yours to identify the basic set of criteria upon which your particular judgments rest.

My criteria are as follows:

1. The spheres of freedom criterion stated above.
2. Waste is a bad thing. The dominant feature of human existence is scarcity—our available resources, our aggregate labors, and our skill in employing both have always been, and will continue for some time to be, inadequate to yield to every man all the tangible and intangible satisfactions he would like to have. Hence, none of those resources, or labors, or skills, should be wasted—that is, employed so as to yield less than they might yield in human satisfactions.
3. Every human being should be regarded as an end rather than as a means to be used for the betterment of another. Each should be afforded dignity and regarded as having an absolute claim to an evenhanded application of such rules as the community may adopt for its governance.
4. Both the incentive and the opportunity to improve his share of satisfactions should be preserved to every individual. Preservation of incentive is dictated by the "no-waste" criterion and enjoins against the continuous, totally egalitarian redistribution of satisfactions, or wealth; but subject to that constraint, everyone should receive, by continuous redistribution if necessary, some minimal share of aggregate wealth so as to avoid a level of privation from which the opportunity to improve his situation becomes illusory.

The relationship of these highly general goals to the more specific environmental issues at hand may not be readily apparent, and I am not yet ready to demonstrate their pervasive implications. But let me give one indication of their implications. Recently scientists have informed us that use of DDT in food production is causing damage to the penguin population. For the present purposes let us accept that assertion as an indisputable scientific fact. The scientific fact is often asserted as if the correct implication—that we must stop agricultural use of DDT—followed from the mere statement of the fact of penguin damage. But plainly it does not follow if my criteria are employed.

My criteria are oriented to people, not penguins. Damage to penguins, or sugar pines, or geological marvels is, without more, simply irrelevant. One must go further, by my criteria, and say: Penguins are important because people enjoy seeing them walk about rocks; and furthermore, the well-being of people would be less impaired by halting use of DDT than by giving up penguins. In short, my observations about environmental problems will be people-oriented, as are my criteria. I have no interest in preserving penguins for their own sake.

It may be said by way of objection to this position, that it is very selfish of people to act as if each person represented one unit of importance and nothing else was of any importance. It is undeniably selfish. Nevertheless I think it is the only tenable starting place for analysis for several reasons. First, no other position corresponds to the way most people really think and act—i.e., corresponds to reality.

Second, this attitude does not portend any massive destruction of nonhuman flora and fauna, for people depend on them in many obvious ways, and they will be preserved because and to the degree that humans do depend on them.

Third, what is good for humans is, in many respects, good for penguins and pine trees—clean air for example. So that humans are, in these respects, surrogates for plant and animal life.

Fourth, I do not know how we could administer any other system. Our decisions are either private or collective. Insofar as Mr. Jones is free to act privately, he may give such preferences as he wishes to other forms of life: he may feed birds in winter and do with less himself, and he may even decline to resist an advancing polar bear on the ground that the bear's appetite is more important than those portions of himself that the bear may choose to eat. In short my basic premise does not rule out private altruism to competing life-forms. It does rule out, however, Mr. Jones' inclination to feed Mr. Smith to the bear, however hungry the bear, however despicable Mr. Smith.

Insofar as we act collectively on the other hand, only humans can be afforded an opportunity to participate in the collective decisions. Penguins cannot vote now and are unlikely subjects for the franchise—pine trees more unlikely still. Again each individual is free to cast his vote so as to benefit sugar pines if that is his inclination. But many of the more extreme assertions that one hears from some conservationists amount to tacit assertions that they are specially appointed representatives of sugar pines, and hence that their preferences should be weighted more heavily than the preferences of other humans who do not enjoy equal rapport with "nature." The simplistic assertion that agricultural use of DDT must stop at once because it is harmful to penguins is of that type.

Fifth, if polar bears or pine trees or penguins, like men, are to be regarded as ends rather than means, if they are to count in our calculus of social organization, someone must tell me how much each one counts, and someone must tell me how these life-forms are to be permitted to express their preferences, for I do not know either answer. If the answer is that certain people are to hold their proxies, then I want to know how those proxy-holders are to be selected: self-appointment does not seem workable to me.

Sixth, and by way of summary of all the foregoing, let me point out that the set of environmental issues under discussion—although they raise very complex technical questions of how to achieve any objective—ultimately raise a normative question: what *ought* we to do? Questions of *ought* are unique to the human mind and world—they are meaningless as applied to a nonhuman situation.

I reject the proposition that we *ought* to respect the "balance of nature" or to "preserve the environment" unless the reason for doing so, express or implied, is the benefit of man.

I reject the idea that there is a "right" or "morally correct" state of nature to which we should return. The word "nature" has no normative connotation. Was it "right" or "wrong" for the earth's crust to heave in contortion and create mountains and seas?

Was it "right" for the first amphibian to crawl up out of the primordial ooze? Was it "wrong" for plants to reproduce themselves and alter the atmospheric composition in favor of oxygen? For animals to alter the atmosphere in favor of carbon dioxide both by breathing oxygen and eating plants? No answers can be given to these questions because they are meaningless questions.

All this may seem obvious to the point of being tedious, but much of the present controversy over environment and pollution rests on tacit normative assumptions about just such nonnormative phenomena: that it is "wrong" to impair penguins with DDT, but not to slaughter cattle for prime rib roasts. That it is wrong to kill stands of sugar pines with industrial fumes, but not to cut sugar pines and build housing for the poor. Every man is entitled to his own preferred definition of Walden Pond, but there is no definition that has any moral superiority over another, except by reference to the selfish needs of the human race.

From the fact that there is no normative definition of the natural state, it follows that there is no normative definition of clean air or pure water—hence no definition of polluted air—or of pollution—except by reference to the needs of man. The "right" composition of the atmosphere is one which has some dust in it and some lead in it and some hydrogen sulfide in it—just those amounts that attend a sensibly organized society thoughtfully and knowledgeably pursuing the greatest possible satisfaction for its human members.

The first and most fundamental step toward solution of our environmental problems is a clear recognition that our objective is not pure air or water but rather some optimal state of pollution. That step immediately suggests the question: How do we define and attain the level of pollution that will yield the maximum possible amount of human satisfaction?

Low levels of pollution contribute to human satisfaction but so do food and shelter and education and music. To attain ever lower levels of pollution, we must pay the cost of having less of these other things. I contrast that view of the cost of pollution control with the more popular statement that pollution control will "cost" very large numbers of dollars.

The popular statement is true in some senses, false in others; sorting out the true and false senses is of some importance. The first step in that sorting process is to achieve a clear understanding of the difference between dollars and resources. Resources are the wealth of our nation; dollars are merely claim checks upon those resources. Resources are of vital importance; dollars are comparatively trivial.

Four categories of resources are sufficient for our purposes: At any given time a nation, or a planet if you prefer, has a stock of labor, of technological skill, of capital goods, and of natural resources (such as mineral deposits, timber, water, land, etc.). These resources can be used in various combinations to yield goods and services of all kinds—in some limited quantity. The quantity will be larger if they are combined efficiently, smaller if combined inefficiently. But in either event the resource stock is limited, the goods and services that they can be made to yield are limited; even the most efficient use of them will yield less than our population, in the aggregate, would like to have.

If one considers building a new dam, it is appropriate to say that it will be costly in the sense that it will require x hours of labor, y tons of steel and concrete, and z amount of capital goods. If these resources are devoted to the dam, then they cannot be used to build hospitals, fishing rods, schools, or electric can openers. That is the meaningful sense in which the dam is costly.

Quite apart from the very important question of how wisely we can combine our resources to produce goods and services, is the very different question of how they get distributed—who gets how many goods? Dollars constitute the claim checks which are distributed among people and which control their share of national output. Dollars are nearly valueless pieces of paper except to the extent that they do represent claim checks to some fraction of the output of goods and services. Viewed as claim checks, all the dollars outstanding during any period of time are worth, in the aggregate, the goods and services that are available to be claimed with them during that period—neither more nor less.

It is far easier to increase the supply of dollars than to increase the production of goods and services—printing dollars is easy. But printing more dollars doesn't help because each dollar then simply becomes a claim to fewer goods, i.e., becomes worth less.

The point is this: many people fall into error upon hearing the statement that the decision to build a dam, or to clean up a river, will cost $X million. It is regrettably easy to say: "It's only money. This is a wealthy country, and we have lots of money." But you cannot build a dam or clean a river with $X million—unless you also have a match, you can't even make a fire. One builds a dam or cleans a river by diverting labor and steel and trucks and factories from making one kind of goods to making another. The cost in dollars is merely a shorthand way of describing the extent of the diversion necessary. If we build a dam for $X million, then we must recognize that we will have $X million less housing and food and medical care and electric can openers as a result.

Similarly, the costs of controlling pollution are best expressed in terms of the other goods we will have to give up to do the job. This is not to say the job should not be done. Badly as we need more housing, more medical care, more can openers, and more symphony orchestras, we could do with somewhat less of them, in my judgment at least, in exchange for somewhat cleaner air and rivers. But that is the nature of the trade-off, and analysis of the problem is advanced if that unpleasant reality is kept in mind. Once the trade-off relationship is clearly perceived, it is possible to state in a very general way what the optimal level of pollution is. I would state it as follows:

People enjoy watching penguins. They enjoy relatively clean air and smog-free vistas. Their health is improved by relatively clean water and air. Each of these benefits is a type of good or service. As a society we would be well advised to give up one washing machine if the resources that would have gone into that washing machine can yield greater human satisfaction when diverted into pollution control. We should give up one hospital if the resources thereby freed would yield more human satisfaction when devoted to elimination of noise in our cities. And so on, trade-off by trade-off, we should divert our productive capacities from the production of existing goods and services to the production of a cleaner, quieter, more pastoral nation up to—and no further than—the point at which we value more highly the next washing machine or hospital that we would have to do without than we value the next unit of environmental improvement that the diverted resources would create.

Now this proposition seems to me unassailable but so general and abstract as to be unhelpful—at least unadministerable in the form stated. It assumes we can measure in some way the incremental units of human satisfaction yielded by very different types of goods. . . . But I insist that the proposition stated describes the result for which we should be striving—and again, that it is always useful to know what your target is even if your weapons are too crude to score a bull's eye.

READING QUESTIONS

1. What are the four goals Baxter proposes in order to develop a solution to the problems of human organization?
2. How does Baxter respond to the objection that it is selfish to act as if one person counts as one unit of importance? Mention at least four of the six reasons he gives in defense of his starting position.
3. What are the four categories of resources mentioned by Baxter? What is the difference between resources and dollars according to Baxter?
4. Explain Baxter's argument for why there is no "morally correct" state of nature to which we should return.
5. What is the ultimate goal toward which we should be striving according to Baxter?

DISCUSSION QUESTIONS

1. Should we go along with Baxter and reject the idea that we should not strive to protect and preserve nature and the environment unless doing so is a benefit to humans?
2. Is there such a thing as an optimal state of pollution? Is Baxter right to claim that part of our goal should be to achieve some optimal state of pollution?
3. What should our goals be regarding nature and the environment other than the one Baxter mentions here?

ALDO LEOPOLD

The Land Ethic

This essay is from the final chapter of Aldo Leopold's classic in environmentalism, *A Sand County Almanac*. Leopold proposes an ecocentric ethic whose basic principle is "A thing is right when it tends to preserve the integrity, stability, and beauty of the biotic community [including soils, waters, plants, animals]. It is wrong when it tends otherwise."

When god-like Odysseus returned from the wars in Troy, he hanged all on one rope a dozen slave-girls of his household whom he suspected of misbehavior during his absence.

This hanging involved no question of propriety. The girls were property. The disposal of property was then, as now, a matter of expediency, not of right and wrong.

Concepts of right and wrong were not lacking from Odysseus' Greece: witness the fidelity of his wife through the long years before at last his black-prowed galleys clove the wine-dark seas for home. The ethical structure of that day covered wives, but had not yet been extended to human chattels. During the three thousand years which have since elapsed, ethical criteria have been extended to many fields of conduct, with corresponding shrinkages in those judged by expediency only.

THE ETHICAL SEQUENCE

This extension of ethics, so far studied only by philosophers, is actually a process in ecological evolution. Its sequences may be described in ecological as well as in philosophical terms. An ethic, ecologically, is a limitation on freedom of action in the struggle for existence. An ethic, philosophically, is a differentiation of social from antisocial conduct. These are two definitions of one thing. The thing has its origin in the tendency of interdependent individuals or groups to evolve modes of co-operation. The ecologist calls these symbioses. Politics and economics are advanced symbioses in which the original free-for-all competition has been replaced, in part, by co-operative mechanisms with an ethical content.

The complexity of co-operative mechanisms has increased with population density, and with the efficiency of tools. It was simpler, for example, to define the antisocial uses of sticks and stones in the days of the mastodons than of bullets and billboards in the age of motors.

The first ethics dealt with the relation between individuals; the Mosaic Decalogue is an example. Later accretions dealt with the relation between the individual and society. The Golden Rule tries to integrate the individual to society; democracy to integrate social organization to the individual.

There is as yet no ethic dealing with man's relation to land and to the animals and plants which grow upon it. Land, like Odysseus' slave-girls, is still property. The land-relation is still strictly economic, entailing privileges but not obligations.

From *A Sand County Almanac, with Other Essays on Conservation from Round River*, Aldo Leopold, Oxford: Oxford University Press (1949, reprinted in 1981). Reprinted by permission of Oxford University Press, Inc.

The extension of ethics to this third element in human environment is, if I read the evidence correctly, an evolutionary possibility and an ecological necessity. It is the third step in a sequence. The first two have already been taken. Individual thinkers since the days of Ezekiel and Isaiah have asserted that the despoliation of land is not only inexpedient but wrong. Society, however, has not yet affirmed their belief. I regard the present conservation movement as the embryo of such an affirmation.

An ethic may be regarded as a mode of guidance for meeting ecological situations so new or intricate, or involving such deferred reactions, that the path of social expediency is not discernible to the average individual. Animal instincts are modes of guidance for the individual in meeting such situations. Ethics are possibly a kind of community instinct in-the-making.

THE COMMUNITY CONCEPT

All ethics so far evolved rest upon a single premise: that the individual is a member of a community of interdependent parts. His instincts prompt him to compete for his place in that community, but his ethics prompt him also to co-operate (perhaps in order that there may be a place to compete for).

The land ethic simply enlarges the boundaries of the community to include soils, waters, plants, and animals, or collectively, the land.

This sounds simple: do we not already sing our love for and obligation to the land of the free and the home of the brave? Yes, but just what and whom do we love? Certainly not the soil, which we are sending helter-skelter downriver. Certainly not the waters, which we assume have no function except to turn turbines, float barges, and carry off sewage. Certainly not the plants, of which we exterminate whole communities without batting an eye. Certainly not the animals, of which we have already extirpated many of the largest and most beautiful species. A land ethic of course cannot prevent the alteration, management, and use of these "resources," but it does affirm their

right to continued existence, and, at least in spots, their continued existence in a natural state.

In short, a land ethic changes the role of *Homo sapiens* from conqueror of the land-community to plain member and citizen of it. It implies respect for his fellow-members, and also respect for the community as such.

In human history, we have learned (I hope) that the conqueror role is eventually self-defeating. Why? Because it is implicit in such a role that the conqueror knows, ex cathedra, just what makes the community clock tick, and just what and who is valuable, and what and who is worthless, in community life. It always turns out that he knows neither, and this is why his conquests eventually defeat themselves.

In the biotic community, a parallel situation exists. Abraham knew exactly what the land was for: it was to drip milk and honey into Abraham's mouth. At the present moment, the assurance with which we regard this assumption is inverse to the degree of our education.

The ordinary citizen today assumes that science knows what makes the community clock tick; the scientist is equally sure that he does not. He knows that the biotic mechanism is so complex that its workings may never be fully understood. . . .

SUBSTITUTES FOR A LAND ETHIC

When the logic of history hungers for bread and we hand out a stone, we are at pains to explain how much the stone resembles bread. I now describe some of the stones which serve in lieu of a land ethic.

One basic weakness in a conservation system based wholly on economic motives is that most members of the land community have no economic value. Wildflowers and songbirds are examples. Of the 22,000 higher plants and animals native to Wisconsin, it is doubtful whether more than 5 percent can be sold, fed, eaten, or otherwise put to economic use. Yet these creatures are members of the biotic community, and if (as I believe) its stability depends on its integrity, they are entitled to continuance.

When one of these non-economic categories is threatened, and if we happen to love it, we invent subterfuges to give it economic importance. At the beginning of the century songbirds were supposed to be disappearing. Ornithologists jumped to the rescue with some distinctly shaky evidence to the effect that insects would eat us up if birds failed to control them. The evidence had to be economic in order to be valid.

It is painful to read these circumlocutions today. We have no land ethic yet, but we have at least drawn nearer the point of admitting that birds should continue as a matter of biotic right, regardless of the presence or absence of economic advantage to us.

A parallel situation exists in respect of predatory mammals, raptorial birds, and fish-eating birds. Time was when biologists somewhat overworked the evidence that these creatures preserve the health of game by killing weaklings, or that they control rodents for the farmer, or that they prey only on "worthless" species. Here again, the evidence had to be economic in order to be valid. It is only in recent years that we hear the more honest argument that predators are members of the community, and that no special interest has the right to exterminate them for the sake of a benefit, real or fancied, to itself. . . .

Some species of trees have been "read out of the party" by economics-minded foresters because they grow too slowly, or have too low a sale value to pay as timber crops: white cedar, tamarack, cypress, beech, and hemlock are examples. In Europe, where forestry is ecologically more advanced, the non-commercial tree species are recognized as members of the native forest community, to be preserved as such, within reason. Moreover, some (like beech) have been found to have a valuable function in building up soil fertility. The interdependence of the forest and its constituent tree species, ground flora, and fauna is taken for granted.

Lack of economic value is sometimes a character not only of species or groups, but of entire biotic communities: marshes, bogs, dunes, and "deserts" are examples. Our formula in such cases is to relegate their conservation to government as refuges, monuments, or parks. The difficulty is that these communities are usually interspersed with more valuable private lands; the government cannot possibly own or control such scattered parcels. The net effect is that we have relegated some of them to ultimate extinction over large areas. . . .

To sum up: a system of conservation based solely on economic self-interest is hopelessly lopsided. It tends to ignore, and thus eventually to eliminate, many elements in the land community that lack commercial value, but that are (as far as we know) essential to its healthy functioning. It assumes, falsely, I think, that the economic parts of the biotic clock will function without the uneconomic parts. . . .

THE LAND PYRAMID

An ethic to supplement and guide the economic relation to land presupposes the existence of some mental image of land as a biotic mechanism. We can be ethical only in relation to something we can see, feel, understand, love, or otherwise have faith in.

The image commonly employed in conservation education is "the balance of nature." For reasons too lengthy to detail here, this figure of speech fails to describe accurately what little we know about the land mechanism. A much truer image is the one employed in ecology: the biotic pyramid. I shall first sketch the pyramid as a symbol of land. . . .

Plants absorb energy from the sun. This energy flows through a circuit called the biota, which may be represented by a pyramid consisting of layers. The bottom layer is the soil. A plant layer rests on the soil, an insect layer on the plants, a bird and rodent layer on the insects, and so on up through various animal groups to the apex layer, which consists of the larger carnivores.

The species of a layer are alike not in where they came from, or in what they look like, but rather in what they eat. Each successive layer depends on those below it for food and often for other services, and each in turn furnishes food and services to those above. Proceeding upward, each successive layer decreases in numerical abundance. Thus, for every carnivore there are hundreds of his prey, thousands of their prey, millions of insects, uncountable plants. The pyramidal form of the system reflects this numerical progression from apex to base. Man shares an intermediate layer with the bears, raccoons, and squirrels which eat both meat and vegetables.

The lines of dependency for food and other services are called food chains. Thus soil-oak-deer-Indian is a chain that has now been largely converted to soil-corn-cow-farmer. Each species, including ourselves, is a link in many chains. The deer eats a hundred plants other than oak, and the cow a hundred plants other than corn. Both, then, are links in a hundred chains. The pyramid is a tangle of chains so complex as to seem disorderly, yet the stability of the system proves it to be a highly organized structure. Its functioning depends on the co-operation and competition of its diverse parts.

In the beginning, the pyramid of life was low and squat, the food chains short and simple. Evolution has added layer after layer, link after link. Man is one of thousands of accretions to the height and complexity of the pyramid. Science has given us many doubts, but it has given us at least one certainty: the trend of evolution is to elaborate and diversify the biota.

Land, then, is not merely soil; it is a fountain of energy flowing through a circuit of soils, plants, and animals. Food chains are the living channels which conduct energy upward; death and decay return it to the soil. The circuit is not closed; some energy is dissipated in decay, some is added by absorption from the air, some is stored in soils, peats, and long-lived forests; but it is a sustained circuit, like a slowly augmented revolving fund of life. There is always a net loss by downhill wash, but this is normally small and offset by the decay of rocks. It is deposited in the ocean and, in the course of geological time, raised to form new lands and new pyramids.

The velocity and character of the upward flow of energy depend on the complex structure of the plant and animal community, much as the upward flow of sap in a tree depends on its complex cellular organization. Without this complexity, normal circulation would presumably not occur. Structure means the characteristic numbers, as well as the characteristic

kinds and functions, of the component species. This interdependence between the complex structure of the land and its smooth functioning as an energy unit is one of its basic attributes.

When a change occurs in one part of the circuit, many other parts must adjust themselves to it. Change does not necessarily obstruct or divert the flow of energy; evolution is a long series of self-induced changes, the net result of which has been to elaborate the flow mechanism and to lengthen the circuit. Evolutionary changes, however, are usually slow and local. Man's invention of tools has enabled him to make changes of unprecedented violence, rapidity, and scope. . . .

THE OUTLOOK

It is inconceivable to me that an ethical relation to land can exist without love, respect, and admiration for land, and a high regard for its value. By value, I of course mean something far broader than mere economic value; I mean value in the philosophical sense. . . .

The "key-log" which must be moved to release the evolutionary process for an ethic is simply this: quit thinking about decent land-use as solely an economic problem. Examine each question in terms of what is ethically and esthetically right, as well as what is economically expedient. A thing is right when it tends to preserve the integrity, stability, and beauty of the biotic community. It is wrong when it tends otherwise.

It of course goes without saying that economic feasibility limits the tether of what can or cannot be done for land. It always has and it always will. The fallacy the economic determinists have tied around our collective neck, and which we now need to cast off, is the belief that economics determines *all* land-use. This is simply not true. An innumerable host of actions and attitudes, comprising perhaps the bulk of all land relations, is determined by the land-users' tastes and predilections, rather than by his purse. The bulk of all land relations hinges on investments of time, forethought, skill, and faith rather than on investments of cash. As a land-user thinketh, so is he.

I have purposely presented the land ethic as a product of social evolution because nothing so important as an ethic is ever "written." Only the most superficial student of history supposes that Moses "wrote" the Decalogue; it evolved in the minds of a thinking community, and Moses wrote a tentative summary of it for a "seminar." I say tentative because evolution never stops.

The evolution of a land ethic is an intellectual as well as emotional process. Conservation is paved with good intentions which prove to be futile, or even

dangerous, because they are devoid of critical understanding either of the land, or of economic land-use. I think it is a truism that as the ethical frontier advances from the individual to the community, its intellectual content increases.

The mechanism of operation is the same for any ethic: social approbation for right actions; social disapproval for wrong actions.

By and large, our present problem is one of attitudes and implements. We are remodeling the Alhambra with a steamshovel, and we are proud of our yardage. We shall hardly relinquish the shovel, which after all has many good points, but we are in need of gentler and more objective criteria for its successful use.

READING QUESTIONS

1. How does Leopold distinguish an ethic from a philosophical ethic? Explain the ethical sequence in terms of ecological evolution.
2. How does Leopold characterize the idea of a land ethic? What is the main substitute for a land ethic and what are its weaknesses according to Leopold?
3. Explain the land pyramid structure characterized by Leopold. What role does evolution play in this system?
4. How does Leopold suggest we change the way we think about land use?
5. When is an action considered right in Leopold's view?

DISCUSSION QUESTIONS

1. Leopold suggests that economics should not be our only concern when it comes to the use of land. To what extent should economic considerations play a part in our treatment of nature and the environment? Are there any situations in which economic concerns might trump environmental ones?
2. Should we adopt the land ethic suggested by Leopold? What sorts of difficulties might arise if we consider things like soil, water, and plants as members of the same moral community to which we belong?

THOMAS E. HILL JR.

Ideals of Human Excellence and Preserving the Natural Environment

Hill rejects those attempts to explain proper environmental concern that appeal either to rights, to intrinsic value, or to religious considerations. Rather, Hill advocates an alternative to such views that focuses on ideals of human excellence as a basis for understanding proper moral concern for the natural world. In particular, Hill claims that insensitivity to the environment reflects either ignorance, exaggerated self-importance, or a lack of self-acceptance that are crucial for achieving the human excellence of proper humility. Hill's approach to environmental issues can be understood through the lens of a virtue ethics approach.

Recommended Reading: virtue ethics, chap. 1, sec. 2E. Also relevant are consequentialism, chap. 1, sec. 2A, and rights-based moral theory, chap. 1, sec. 2D.

I

A wealthy eccentric bought a house in a neighborhood I know. The house was surrounded by a beautiful display of grass, plants, and flowers, and it was shaded by a huge old avocado tree. But the grass required cutting, the flowers needed tending, and the man wanted more sun. So he cut the whole lot down and covered the yard with asphalt. After all it was his property and he was not fond of plants.

It was a small operation, but it reminded me of the strip mining of large sections of the Appalachians. In both cases, of course, there were reasons for the destruction, and property rights could be cited as justification. But I could not help but wonder, "What sort of person would do a thing like that?"

Many Californians had a similar reaction when a recent governor defended the leveling of ancient redwood groves, reportedly saying, "If you have seen one redwood, you have seen them all."

Incidents like these arouse the indignation of ardent environmentalists and leave even apolitical observers with some degree of moral discomfort. The reasons for these reactions are mostly obvious. Uprooting the natural environment robs both present and future generations of much potential use and enjoyment. Animals too depend on the environment; and even if one does not value animals for their own sakes, their potential utility for us is incalculable. Plants are needed, of course, to replenish the atmosphere quite aside from their aesthetic value. These reasons for hesitating to destroy forests and gardens are not only the most obvious ones, but also the most persuasive for practical purposes. But, one wonders, is there nothing more behind our discomfort? Are we concerned solely about the potential use and enjoyment of the forests, etc., for ourselves, later generations, and perhaps animals? Is there not something else which disturbs us when we witness the destruction or even listen to those who would defend it in terms of cost/benefit analysis?

From Thomas E. Hill Jr., "Ideals of Human Excellence and Preserving the Natural Environment," *Environmental Ethics* 5 (1998). Reprinted by permission.

Imagine that in each of our examples those who would destroy the environment argue elaborately that, even considering future generations of human beings and animals, there are benefits in "replacing" the natural environment which outweigh the negative utilities which environmentalists cite.[1] No doubt we could press the argument on the facts, trying to show that the destruction is shortsighted and that its defenders have underestimated its potential harm or ignored some pertinent rights or interests. But is this all we could say? Suppose we grant, for a moment, that the utility of destroying the redwoods, forests, and gardens is equal to their potential for use and enjoyment by nature lovers and animals. Suppose, further, that we even grant that the pertinent human rights and animal rights, if any, are evenly divided for and against destruction. Imagine that we also concede, for argument's sake, that the forests contain no potentially useful endangered species of animals and plants. Must we then conclude that there is no further cause for moral concern? Should we then feel morally indifferent when we see the natural environment uprooted? . . .

II

The problem, then, is this. We want to understand what underlies our moral uneasiness at the destruction of the redwoods, forests, etc., even apart from the loss of these as resources for human beings and animals. But I find no adequate answer by pursuing the questions, "Are rights or interests of plants neglected,?" "What is God's will on the matter?" and "What is the intrinsic value of the existence of a tree or forest?" My suggestion, which is in fact the main point of this paper, is that we look at the problem from a different perspective. That is, let us turn for a while from the effort to find reasons why certain *acts* destructive of natural environments are morally wrong to the ancient task of articulating our ideals of human excellence. Rather than argue directly with destroyers of the environment who say, "Show me why what I am doing is *immoral*," I want to ask,

"What sort of person would want to do what they propose?" The point is not to skirt the issue with an ad hominem, but to raise a different moral question, for even if there is no convincing way to show that the destructive acts are wrong (independently of human and animal use and enjoyment), we may find that the willingness to indulge in them reflects the absence of human traits that we admire and regard morally important.

This strategy of shifting questions may seem more promising if one reflects on certain analogous situations. Consider, for example, the Nazi who asks, in all seriousness. "Why is it wrong for me to make lampshades out of human skin—provided, of course, I did not myself kill the victims to get the skins?" We would react more with shock and disgust than with indignation, I suspect, because it is even more evident that the question reveals a defect in the questioner than that the proposed act is itself immoral. Sometimes we may not regard an act wrong at all though we see it as reflecting something objectionable about the person who does it. Imagine, for example, one who laughs spontaneously to himself when he reads a newspaper account of a plane crash that kills hundreds. Or, again, consider an obsequious grandson who, having waited for his grandmother's inheritance with mock devotion, then secretly spits on her grave when at last she dies. Spitting on the grave may have no adverse consequences and perhaps it violates no rights. The moral uneasiness which it arouses is explained more by our view of the agent than by any conviction that what he did was immoral. Had he hesitated and asked, "Why shouldn't I spit on her grave?" it seems more fitting to ask him to reflect on the sort of person he is than to try to offer reasons why he should refrain from spitting.

III

What sort of person, then, would cover his garden with asphalt, strip mine a wooded mountain, or level an irreplaceable redwood grove? Two sorts of answers, though initially appealing, must be ruled out. The first is that persons who would destroy the environment in these ways are either shortsighted, underestimating the harm they do, or else are too little concerned for the well-being of other people. Perhaps too they have insufficient regard for animal life. But these considerations have been set aside in order to refine the controversy. Another tempting response might be that we count it a moral virtue, or at least a human ideal, to love nature. Those who value the environment only for its utility must not really love nature and so in this way fall short of an ideal. But such an answer is hardly satisfying in the present context, for what is at issue is *why* we feel moral discomfort at the activities of those who admittedly value nature only for its utility. That it is ideal to care for nonsentient nature beyond its possible use is really just another way of expressing the general point which is under controversy.

What is needed is some way of showing that this ideal is connected with other virtues, or human excellences, not in question. To do so is difficult and my suggestions, accordingly, will be tentative and subject to qualification.

The main idea is that, though indifference to nonsentient nature does not *necessarily* reflect the absence of virtues, it often signals the absence of certain traits which we want to encourage because they are, in most cases, a natural basis for the development of certain virtues. It is often thought, for example, that those who would destroy the natural environment must lack a proper appreciation of their place in the natural order, and so must either be ignorant or have too little humility. Though I would argue that this is not necessarily so, I suggest that, given certain plausible empirical assumptions, their attitude may well be rooted in ignorance, a narrow perspective, inability to see things as important apart from themselves and the limited groups they associate with, or reluctance to accept themselves as natural beings. Overcoming these deficiencies will not guarantee a proper moral humility, but for most of us it is probably an important psychological preliminary. . . .

Consider first the suggestion that destroyers of the environment lack an appreciation of their place in the universe. Their attention, it seems, must be focused on parochial matters, on what is, relatively speaking,

close in space and time. They seem not to understand that we are a speck on the cosmic scene, a brief stage in the evolutionary process, only one among millions of species on Earth, and an episode in the course of human history. Of course, they know that there are stars, fossils, insects, and ancient ruins; but do they have any idea of the complexity of the processes that led to the natural world as we find it? Are they aware how much the forces at work within their own bodies are like those which govern all living things and even how much they have in common with inanimate bodies? Admittedly scientific knowledge is limited and no one can master it all; but could one who had a broad and deep understanding of his place in nature really be indifferent to the destruction of the natural environment?

This first suggestion, however, may well provoke a protest from a sophisticated anti-environmentalist. "Perhaps *some* may be indifferent to nature from ignorance," the critic may object, "but *I* have studied astronomy, geology, biology, and biochemistry, and I still unashamedly regard the nonsentient environment as simply a resource for our use. It should not be wasted, of course, but what should be preserved is decidable by weighing long-term costs and benefits." "Besides," our critic may continue, "as philosophers you should know the old Humean formula, 'You cannot derive an *ought* from an *is*.' All the facts of biology, biochemistry, etc., do not entail that I ought to love nature or want to preserve it. What one understands is one thing; what one values is something else. Just as nature lovers are not necessarily scientists, those indifferent to nature are not necessarily ignorant."

Although the environmentalist may concede the critic's logical point, he may well argue that, as a matter of fact, increased understanding of nature tends to heighten people's concern for its preservation. If so, despite the objection, the suspicion that the destroyers of the environment lack deep understanding of nature is not, in most cases, unwarranted, but the argument need not rest here.

The environmentalist might amplify his original idea as follows: "When I said that the destroyers of nature do not appreciate their place in the universe, I was not speaking of intellectual understanding alone, for, after all, a person can *know* a catalog of facts without ever putting them together and seeing vividly the whole picture which they form. To see oneself as just one part of nature is to look at oneself and the world from a certain perspective which is quite different from being able to recite detailed information from the natural sciences. What the destroyers of nature lack is this perspective, not particular information."

Again our critic may object, though only after making some concessions: "All right," he may say, "*some* who are indifferent to nature may lack the cosmic perspective of which you speak, but again there is no *necessary* connection between this failing, if it is one, and any particular evaluative attitude toward nature. In fact, different people respond quite differently when they move to a wider perspective. When *I* try to picture myself vividly as a brief, transitory episode in the course of nature, I simply get depressed. Far from inspiring me with a love of nature, the exercise makes me sad and hostile. You romantics think only of poets like Wordsworth and artists like Turner, but you should consider how differently Omar Khayyám responded when he took your wider perspective. His reaction, when looking at his life from a cosmic viewpoint, was 'Drink up, for tomorrow we die.' Others respond in an almost opposite manner with a joyless Stoic resignation, exemplified by the poet who pictures the wise man, at the height of personal triumph, being served a magnificent banquet, and then consummating his marriage to his beloved, all the while reminding himself, 'Even this shall pass away.'"[2] In sum, the critic may object, "Even if one should try to see oneself as one small transitory part of nature, doing so does not dictate any particular normative attitude. Some may come to love nature, but others are moved to live for the moment; some sink into sad resignation; others get depressed or angry. So indifference to nature is not necessarily a sign that a person fails to look at himself from the larger perspective."

The environmentalist might respond to this objection in several ways. He might, for example, argue that even though some people who see themselves as part of the natural order remain indifferent to nonsentient nature, this is not a common reaction. Typically, it may be argued, as we become more and more aware that we are parts of the larger whole we come to value the whole independently of its effect on ourselves. Thus, despite the possibilities the critic raises, indifference to nonsentient nature is still in most cases a sign that a person fails to see himself as part of the natural order.

If someone challenges the empirical assumption here, the environmentalist might develop the argument along a quite different line. The initial idea, he may remind us, was that those who would destroy the natural environment fail to *appreciate* their place in the natural order. "Appreciating one's place" is not simply an intellectual appreciation. It is also an attitude, reflecting what one values as well as what one knows. When we say, for example, that both the servile and the arrogant person fail to *appreciate* their place in a society of equals, we do not mean simply that they are ignorant of certain empirical facts, but rather that they have certain objectionable attitudes about their importance relative to other people. Similarly, to fail to appreciate one's place in nature is not merely to lack knowledge or breadth of perspective, but to take a certain attitude about what matters. A person who *understands* his place in nature but still views nonsentient nature merely as a resource takes the attitude that nothing is *important* but human beings and animals. Despite first appearances, he is not so much like the pre-Copernican astronomers who made the intellectual error of treating the Earth as the "center of the universe" when they made their calculations. He is more like the racist who, though well aware of other races, treats all races but his own as insignificant.

So construed, the argument appeals to the common idea that awareness of nature typically has, and should have, a humbling effect. The Alps, a storm at sea, the Grand Canyon, towering redwoods, and "the starry heavens above" move many a person to remark on the comparative insignificance of our daily concerns and even of our species, and this is generally taken to be a quite fitting response.[3] What seems to be missing, then, in those who understand nature but remain unmoved is a proper humility.[4] Absence of proper humility is not the same as selfishness or egoism, for one can be devoted to self-interest while still viewing one's own pleasures and projects as trivial and unimportant. And one can have an exaggerated view of one's own importance while grandly sacrificing for those one views as inferior. Nor is the lack of humility identical with belief that one has power and influence, for a person can be quite puffed up about himself while believing that the foolish world will never acknowledge him. The humility we miss seems not so much a belief about one's relative effectiveness and recognition as an attitude which measures the importance of things independently of their relation to oneself or to some narrow group with which one identifies. A paradigm of a person who lacks humility is the self-important emperor who grants status to his family because it is *his,* to his subordinates because *he* appointed them, and to his country because *he* chooses to glorify it. Less extreme but still lacking proper humility is the elitist who counts events significant solely in proportion to how they affect his class. The suspicion about those who would destroy the environment, then, is that what they count important is too narrowly confined insofar as it encompasses only what affects beings who, like us, are capable of feeling.

This idea that proper humility requires recognition of the importance of nonsentient nature is similar to the thought of those who charge meat eaters with "speciesism." In both cases it is felt that people too narrowly confine their concerns to the sorts of beings that are most like them. But, however intuitively appealing, the idea will surely arouse objections from our nonenvironmentalist critic. "Why," he will ask, "do you suppose that the sort of humility I *should* have requires me to acknowledge the importance of nonsentient nature aside from its utility? You cannot, by your own admission, argue that nonsentient nature *is* important, appealing to religious or intuitionist grounds. And simply to assert, without further argument, that an ideal humility requires us to view nonsentient nature as important for its own sake begs the question at issue. If proper humility is acknowledging the relative importance of things as one should, then to show that I must lack this you must first establish that one *should* acknowledge the importance of nonsentient nature."

Though some may wish to accept this challenge, there are other ways to pursue the connection between humility and response to nonsentient nature. For example, suppose we grant that proper humility requires only acknowledging a due status to sentient beings. We must admit, then, that it is logically possible for a person to be properly humble even though he viewed all nonsentient nature simply as a resource. But this logical possibility may be a psychological rarity.

It may be that, given the sort of beings we are, we would never learn humility before persons without developing the general capacity to cherish, and regard important, many things for their own sakes. The major obstacle to humility before persons is self-importance, a tendency to measure the significance of everything by its relation to oneself and those with whom one identifies. The processes by which we overcome self-importance are doubtless many and complex, but it seems unlikely that they are exclusively concerned with how we relate to other people and animals. Learning humility requires learning to feel that something matters besides what will affect oneself and one's circle of associates. What leads a child to care about what happens to a lost hamster or a stray dog he will not see again is likely also to generate concern for a lost toy or a favorite tree where he used to live. Learning to value things for their own sake, and to count what affects them important aside from their utility, is not the same as judging them to have some intuited objective property, but it is necessary to the development of humility and it seems likely to take place in experiences with nonsentient nature as well as with people and animals. If a person views all nonsentient nature merely as a resource, then it seems unlikely that he has developed the capacity needed to overcome self-importance.

IV

This last argument, unfortunately, has its limits. It presupposes an empirical connection between experiencing nature and overcoming self-importance, and this may be challenged. Even if experiencing nature promotes humility before others, there may be other ways people can develop such humility in a world of concrete, glass, and plastic. If not, perhaps all that is needed is limited experience of nature in one's early, developing years; mature adults, having overcome youthful self-importance, may live well enough in artificial surroundings. More importantly, the argument does not fully capture the spirit of the intuition that an ideal person stands humbly before nature. That idea is not simply that experiencing nature tends to foster proper humility before other people; it is, in part, that natural surroundings encourage and are appropriate to an ideal sense of oneself as part of the natural world. Standing alone in the forest, after months in the city, is not merely good as a means of curbing one's arrogance before others; it reinforces and fittingly expresses one's acceptance of oneself as a natural being.

Previously we considered only one aspect of proper humility, namely, a sense of one's relative importance with respect to other human beings. Another aspect, I think, is a kind of *self-acceptance.* This involves acknowledging, in more than a merely intellectual way, that we are the sort of creatures that we are. Whether one is self-accepting is not so much a matter of how one attributes *importance* comparatively to oneself, other people, animals, plants, and other things as it is a matter of understanding, facing squarely, and responding appropriately to who and what one is, e.g., one's powers and limits, one's affinities with other beings and differences from them, one's unalterable nature and one's freedom to change. Self-acceptance is not merely intellectual awareness, for one can be intellectually aware that one is growing old and will eventually die while nevertheless behaving in a thousand foolish ways that reflect a refusal to acknowledge these facts. On the other hand, self-acceptance is not passive resignation, for refusal to pursue what one truly wants within one's limits is a failure to accept the freedom and power one has. Particular behaviors, like dyeing one's gray hair and dressing like those 20 years younger, do not *necessarily* imply lack of self-acceptance, for there could be reasons for acting in these ways other than the wish to hide from oneself what one really is. One fails to accept oneself when the patterns of behavior and emotion are rooted in a desire to disown and deny features of oneself, to pretend to oneself that they are not there. This is not to say that a self-accepting person makes no value judgments about himself, that he likes all facts about himself, wants equally to develop and display them; he can, and should feel remorse for his past misdeeds and strive to change his current vices. The point is that he does not disown them, pretend that they do not exist or are facts about something other than himself. Such pretense is incompatible with proper humility because it is seeing oneself as better than one is.

Self-acceptance of this sort has long been considered a human excellence, under various names, but what has it to do with preserving nature? There is, I think, the following connection. As human beings we are part of nature, living, growing, declining, and dying by natural laws similar to those governing other living beings; despite our awesomely distinctive human powers, we share many of the needs, limits, and liabilities of animals and plants. These facts are neither good nor bad in themselves, aside from personal preference and varying conventional values. To say this is to utter a truism which few will deny, but to accept these facts, as facts about oneself, is not so easy—or so common. Much of what naturalists deplore about our increasingly artificial world reflects, and encourages, a denial of these facts, an unwillingness to avow them with equanimity.

Like the Victorian lady who refuses to look at her own nude body, some would like to create a world of less transitory stuff, reminding us only of our intellectual and social nature, never calling to mind our affinities with "lower" living creatures. The "denial of death," to which psychiatrists call attention, reveals an attitude incompatible with the sort of self-acceptance which philosophers, from the ancients to Spinoza and on, have admired as a human excellence. My suggestion is not merely that experiencing nature causally promotes such self-acceptance, but also that those who fully accept themselves as part of the natural world lack the common drive to disassociate themselves from nature by replacing natural environments with artificial ones. A storm in the wilds helps us to appreciate our animal vulnerability, but, equally important, the reluctance to experience it may *reflect* an unwillingness to accept this aspect of ourselves. The person who is too ready to destroy the ancient redwoods may lack humility, not so much in the sense that he exaggerates his importance relative to others, but rather in the sense that he tries to avoid seeing himself as one among many natural creatures. . . .

NOTES

I thank Gregory Kavka, Catherine Harlow, the participants at a colloquium at the University of Utah, and the referees for *Environmental Ethics*, Dale Jamieson and Donald Scherer, for helpful comments on earlier drafts of this paper.

1. When I use the expression "the natural environment," I have in mind the sort of examples with which I began. There is also a broad sense, as Hume and Mill noted, in which all that occurs, miracles aside, is "natural." As will be evident, I shall use "natural" in a narrower, more familiar sense.

2. T. Tildon, "Even This Shall Pass Away," in *The Best Loved Poems of the American People,* ed. Hazel Felleman (Garden City, New York: Doubleday, 1936).

3. An exception, apparently, was Kant, who thought "the starry heavens" sublime and compared them with "the moral law within," but did not for all that see our species as comparatively insignificant.

4. By "proper humility" I mean that sort and degree of humility that is a morally admirable character trait. How precisely to define this is, of course, a controversial matter; but the point for present purposes is just to set aside obsequiousness, false modesty, underestimation of one's abilities, and the like.

READING QUESTIONS

1. What is Hill's "strategy," mentioned in section II, for addressing cases that involve problematic treatment of the environment?
2. Why does Hill think that pointing to the shortsightedness or lack of proper concern with other people and animals does not really help explain what is morally problematic about the person who would cover his garden with asphalt, strip mine a wooded mountain, or level an irreplaceable redwood grove?
3. How does Hill understand the attitude of humility? What role does proper humility play in the case Hill makes for acknowledging the importance of nonsentient nature? How, according to Hill, does one learn to become humble?
4. Another theme in Hill's essay is the importance of self-acceptance. What does Hill mean by self-acceptance? How does he connect self-acceptance with preserving nature?

DISCUSSION QUESTIONS

1. Should we agree with Hill that considerations of self-acceptance are important in thinking about how we ought to treat the environment?
2. How might a utilitarian respond to Hill's appeals to humility and self-acceptance in explaining what is wrong with the person who would pave over his front yard in asphalt? Can a utilitarian appeal to these same sorts of considerations (humility and self-acceptance) in explaining on utilitarian grounds what is wrong with the person who paves over his garden? If so, would there be any significant difference between the views of Hill and the utilitarian with regard to how they would explain what is morally problematic about destroying (within one's rights) some part of the environment?

PETER WENZ

Synergistic Environmental Virtues: Consumerism and Human Flourishing

Wenz argues that consumerism—the ideology of maximizing consumption without limit— leads to various social harms affecting not only residents of Third World countries, but people who live in industrialized countries as well. He then proceeds to argue that consumerism promotes the traditional vices of greed, avarice, envy, and gluttony, while such traditional virtues as frugality and temperance oppose this ideology and promote human flourishing. He further argues that both anthropocentric and nonanthropocentric approaches to environmental ethics offer, in their own distinctive ways, complementary support to the traditional virtues as well as opposition to the traditional vices.

Recommended Reading: virtue ethics, chap. 1, sec. 2E.

There is no conflict at this time between anthropocentric and nonanthropocentric goals in the moral development of people in industrial countries. Exercising the traditional virtues of frugality, appreciation, temperance, self-development, dedication, benevolence, generosity, empathy, and justice fosters human flourishing around the world and protects nature. Traditional vices, on the other hand, including six of the seven deadly sins—greed, avarice, gluttony, envy, luxury, and pride—as well as intemperance, selfishness, and indifference, foster lifestyles among current industrial people that diminish human well-being and harm the environment. The linchpin is consumerism, as currently understood and practiced in industrial countries, because it relies on vices that harm both people and nature. Traditional virtues oppose such consumerism.

I begin by defining consumerism and illustrating its harmful environmental effects. I argue next that consumerism harms poor people in the Third World.

I then contend that it harms industrial people. Finally, I argue that consumerism promotes and relies on the cultivation of traditional vices whereas traditional virtues foster human flourishing and environmental protection.

If I am correct about consumerism, then nonanthropocentric environmentalists have reasons to favor traditional virtues because their exercise tends to protect the nonhuman environment. Anthropocentrists have reason to support the same virtues because their exercise promotes human flourishing. Nonanthropocentric and anthropocentric considerations regarding human virtue and vice are thus mutually reinforcing. Each is stronger in combination with the other than alone, a relationship I define as synergistic.[1] In addition, if I am correct, defenders of traditional virtues have reason to embrace nonanthropocentric environmentalism because it supports many traditional virtues. I conclude by suggesting how synergistic environmental virtues should be manifest in practice.

CONSUMERISM HARMS THE ENVIRONMENT

Current environmental problems stem largely from consumerism in industrial countries, such as the United States. Consuming goods and services is not the problem. Human beings, like all living systems, require material throughput. We need food, clothing, shelter, and, because we are culture-oriented primates, education. Many products of modern technology make life easier or more fun, such as washing machines, CD players, trains, and cars. Consumerism differs from the consumption of such items, however, in treating consumption as good in itself. Consumerism is the ideology that society should maximize consumption, pursue consumption without limit.

Consumerism dominates American politics. No candidate for national office ever suggests maintaining or reducing the American economy. Everyone supports economic growth. The economy is never large enough. Life would be better if more people had more jobs producing more goods and services and earning more money to spend on consumption. "Enough" is politically subversive in a consumerism-dominated culture.

Attempts at unlimited consumption, pursued as an end in itself, degrade the environment. Global warming, for example, threatens species with extinction because of rapid climate change.[2] The warming results primarily from increased emissions of greenhouse gases, such as carbon dioxide. The United States, with less than 5 percent of the world's population, emits 24 percent of carbon into the atmosphere, caused significantly by consumer preference for gas-guzzling light trucks and sport utility vehicles (SUVs).[3] Such vehicles promote economic growth more than efficient alternatives—fuel-efficient cars and public transportation—through increased gasoline sales and required expansion of parking facilities. Commitment to unlimited economic growth favors inefficient transportation that threatens biodiversity through global warming.

Consumerism harms nonhumans in other ways as well: "Aquatic songbirds, called dippers, for example, disappear from stream waters acidified by pine plantations and acid rain."[4] Pine plantations are monocultures created to serve a growing market for wood pulp and building materials. The size of the average American home increased more than 50 percent between the 1960s and the 1990s, adding to economic growth and to the demand for building materials from pine plantations.[5] Acid rain results primarily from burning fossil fuels rich in sulfur, most often to generate electricity to run increasing numbers of electric appliances and air conditioners. The economy grows when people build larger houses, buy and use more appliances, and use more air conditioning. But pine plantations and acid rain harm the environment and endanger many species.

Development economist David Korten explains why environmental decline tends to accompany the rise in production required by increasing consumption: "About 70 percent of this productivity growth has been in…economic activity accounted for by the petroleum, petrochemical, and metal industries; chemical-intensive agriculture; public utilities; road building; transportation; and mining—specifically, the industries that are most rapidly drawing down natural capital, generating the bulk of our most toxic waste, and consuming a substantial portion of our nonrenewable energy."[6] Environmental researcher Alan Durning agrees that consumer-oriented societies are most responsible for impairing environmental quality: "Industrial countries' factories generate most of the world's hazardous chemical wastes….The fossil fuels that power the consumer society are its most ruinous input. Wresting coal, oil, and natural gas from the earth permanently disrupts countless habitats; burning them causes an overwhelming share of the world's air pollution; and refining them generates huge quantities of toxic wastes."[7]

CONSUMERISM HARMS POOR PEOPLE IN THE THIRD WORLD

Anthropocentrists would not care that environmental decline accompanies consumerism so long as people flourish. Advocates of global free market capitalism, such as Thomas Friedman, believe that growing economies will help all people in the long run, so consumerism, the engine of economic growth in capitalist societies, is good for people. He writes: "When it comes to the question of which system today is the most effective at generating rising standards of living, the historical debate is over. The answer is free-market capitalism....In the end, if you want higher standards of living in a world without walls, the free market is the only ideological alternative left."[8] And all people can share in the cornucopia, according to Friedman:

> Countries...can now increasingly choose to be prosperous. They don't have to be prisoners of their natural resources, geography or history. In a world where a country can plug into the Internet and import knowledge, in a world where a country can find shareholders from any other country to invest in its infrastructure..., where a country can import the technology to be an auto producer or computer maker even if it has no raw materials, a country can more than ever before opt for prosperity or poverty, depending on the policies it pursues.[9]

Unfortunately, Friedman is wrong. The whole world cannot consume at the level of citizens of industrial nations. Friedman seems to have missed the difference between *anyone* being able to do something and *everyone* being able to do it. If I order twenty texts for a class of twenty-five students, anyone could have bought the book at the university store, but everyone could not. Similarly, even if Friedman were correct that any country may become rich like industrial countries (which is already problematic), environmental limits preclude most of the world's people living consumer lifestyles. David Korten writes: "If the earth's sustainable natural output were shared equally among the earth's present population, the needs of all could be met. But it is...clear that it is a physical impossibility, even with the most optimistic assumptions about the potential of new technologies, for the world to consume at levels even approximating those in North America, Europe, and Japan."[10] According to environmental researchers Mia MacDonald and Danielle Nierenberg, "If every person alive today consumed at the rate of an average person in the United States, three more planets would be required to fulfill these demands."[11]

Korten cites a study by William Rees, an urban planner at the University of British Columbia: "Rees estimates that four to six hectares of land are required to maintain the consumption of the average person living in a high-income country—including the land required to maintain current levels of energy consumption using renewable sources. Yet in 1990, the total available ecologically productive land area (land capable of generating consequential biomass) in the world was only an estimated 1.7 hectares per capita."[12] What is worse, the world's human population is expected to increase more than 50 percent over its 1990 level by 2050, whereas Earth remains stubbornly resistant to growth.[13]

This environmental analysis suggests what international economists actually observe: economic globalization, intended to increase world economic growth so that everyone can be prosperous consumers, impoverishes many people in the Third World. Some examples illustrate how this occurs. One goal of consumer society is to grow food efficiently so that more resources are available for optional consumer items. The United States often claims to have the world's most efficient agriculture because less than 2 percent of the population is engaged directly in farming.[14] Agricultural research to improve efficiency resulted in the high-yield varieties (HYVs) of wheat and rice behind the Green Revolution of the 1960s and 1970s.

Agriculture and food security are central to many Third World countries. HYVs were marketed to the Third World partly out of humanitarian concern for human nutrition and partly to make a profit from the sale of agricultural inputs. Such sales help the economy grow. The unintended result, however, was to impoverish many people in the Third World, explains Vandana Shiva, a physicist and the director of the Research Foundation for Science, Technology and Natural Resource Policy in India. HYVs yielded substantially more cash crops of wheat and rice per hectare than traditional varieties, which helped the economy to grow. But HYVs require much more water per bushel. Unfortunately, many poor countries, including India, suffer from water shortage. So

HYVs required deeper wells, which only relatively wealthy farmers could afford. With more water being pumped, water tables lowered beyond the reach of poor farmers, who could no longer get enough water even for traditional varieties. Many farmers lost their farms and became landless peasants seeking work.

HYVs also need more artificial fertilizer than traditional varieties. This again helped the economy grow but limited access to poorer farmers who could not afford such fertilizer. Worse yet, the fertilizer made *bathau*, a wild plant freely harvested for its vitamin A, a weed that threatened cash crops. Herbicides, another bought input that spurs economic growth, became necessary. Not only could poor farmers ill afford herbicides, but the intended result of their application, killing *bathau*, deprived many poor people of a free source of vitamin A. As a result, tens of thousands of children in India go blind each year for lack of vitamin A.

Dependence on free sources of food and materials is common in the Third World. Equally common is their reduction by globalization efforts aimed at turning traditional societies into "emerging markets." Worldwatch researcher Aaron Sachs compares rural Thailand with areas in the Amazon rain forest:

Many of the villagers, like the peoples of the Amazon rainforest, used to derive their income from forest products—charcoal, bamboo shoots, wild mushrooms, squirrels, even edible toads. Small-scale subsistence farmers also depended on the forests to provide breaks against soil erosion and to regulate natural irrigation systems.

Because they get much of what they need free, traditional peasants add little to the GDP of Thailand. In addition, they are too poor to buy goods produced in industrial countries, so they add little to the economic growth that consumerism requires. Thailand is better integrated into a consumer-oriented world economy when its land is taken from peasants, its trees are sold to logging interests, and its agriculture produces goods for export.

But logging projects...have laid waste to the area's hillsides over the last three decades. Economists often point to Thailand as a clear success—and the country's lucrative exports, consisting mostly of agricultural products grown on previously forested land, have certainly helped boost the Thai economy....However..., the poorest people...lost...their livelihoods.[15]

Shiva similarly criticizes monocultural commercial forestry in India for depriving poor people of free forest products:

An important biomass output of trees that is never assessed by foresters who look for timber and wood is the yield of seeds and fruits. Fruit trees such as jack, jaman, mango, tamarind etc. have been important components of indigenous forms of social forestry as practiced over the centuries in India.... Other trees, such as neem, pongamia and sal provide annual harvests of seeds which yield non-edible oils....The coconut,...besides providing fruits and oil, provides leaves used in thatching huts and supports the large coir industry.[16]

David Korten gives examples of Third World industrialization that fosters economic growth as measured in purely monetary terms, ties poor countries ever closer to global consumerism, and is supposed to help the world's poor. In each case, however, such development harms poor people more than it helps them. Japan, for instance, wanting to avoid domestic pollution from smelting copper, financed the Philippine Associated Smelting and Refining Corporation:

The plant occupies 400 acres of land expropriated by the Philippine government from local residents at give-away prices. Gas and wastewater emissions from the plant contain high concentrations of boron, arsenic, heavy metals, and sulfur compounds that have contaminated local water supplies, reduced fishing and rice yields, damaged the forest, and increased the occurrence of upper-respiratory diseases among local residents. Local people...are now largely dependent on the occasional part-time or contractual employment they are offered to do the plant's most dangerous and dirtiest jobs.

The company has prospered. The local economy has grown....The Philippine government is repaying the foreign aid loan from Japan that financed the construction of supporting infrastructure for the plant. And the Japanese are congratulating themselves for...their generous assistance to the poor of the Philippines.[17]

Korten claims that this case is typical of Third World industrialization:

Rapid economic growth in low-income countries brings modern airports, television, express highways, and air-conditioned shopping malls...for the fortunate few. It rarely improves living conditions for the many. This kind of growth requires gearing the economy toward exports to earn the foreign exchange to buy the things that wealthy people desire. Thus, the lands of the poor are appropriated for export crops. The former tillers of these lands find themselves subsisting in urban slums on starvation wages paid by sweatshops producing for export. Families are broken up, the social fabric is strained to the breaking point, and violence becomes endemic.[18]

And Aaron Sachs discusses one effect of desperate poverty and social disruption brought on by integrating traditional societies into the consumer-oriented global economy—child prostitution:

> Brazil alone has between 250,000 and 500,000 children involved in the sex trade, and a recent study conducted by the Bogota Chamber of Commerce concluded that the number of child prostitutes in the Colombian capital had nearly trebled over the past three years.... But the center of the child sex industry is Asia: children's advocacy groups assert that there are about 60,000 child prostitutes in the Philippines, about 400,000 in India, and about 800,000 in Thailand.[19]

Income and nutrition statistics also indicate that integrating Third World countries into the economic system that supports First World consumerism hurts the world's poor:

> In 1960, the per capita gross domestic product (GDP) in the 20 richest countries was 18 times that in the 20 poorest countries, according to the World Bank. By 1995 the gap between the richest and poorest nations had more than doubled—to 37 times.
>
> To a large extent, these vast income gaps drive global consumption patterns. Disproportionate consumption by the world's rich often creates pollution, waste, and environmental damage that harm the world's poor. For example, growing demand for fish for non-food uses, mainly animal feed and oils, is diminishing the source of low-cost, high-protein nutrition for a billion of the world's poor people.[20]

In the year 2000, at least 1.2 billion people were hungry, and roughly half the human population lacked sufficient vitamins and minerals.[21] The World Health Organization reports that six million people die each year as a result of hunger and malnutrition.[22]

Environmental change brought on by consumerism could exacerbate this problem. Although global warming is not yet responsible for hunger and malnutrition, a one-meter rise in sea level, which such warming may cause, would inundate much cropland used by poor people for subsistence.[23] Global warming is also expected to lower soil moisture during the growing season in the world's breadbaskets—the U.S. Great Plains, Western Europe, northern Canada, and Siberia—reducing yields and increasing the price of grain in world markets beyond the means of many people in the Third World.[24]

In sum, First World consumerism tends to harm people in the Third World, except for local elites. The environment could never support industrial lifestyles for all humanity, so the promise of currently poor people living consumer lifestyles is chimerical. Second, the pattern of development in Third World countries that ties those lands to consumerism in industrial countries tends to benefit only local elites and leave the vast majority much worse off than before, both materially and socially. Finally, gross statistics show that on balance consumerism increases income gaps between the world's rich and poor and jeopardizes food supplies for the poor.

CONSUMERISM HARMS INDUSTRIAL PEOPLE

Industrial people suffer from consumerism because it fosters perpetual discontent, social isolation, and depression. Here is how. A consumer society must have a growing economy to provide jobs and incomes needed for more consumption. Advertising whets people's appetites for consumption. Radio talk show host Dave Ramsey writes in his 1999 book *More Than Enough* that these ads work largely by sowing discontent: "Professional marketers and advertisers understand that they have to point out a need to you so you will recognize a need you didn't know you had. When you recognize that need, [a] process...has started [that] will end in frustration and finally purchase.... If you are a good marketer or advertiser your job is to bring dissonance or a disturbance to the person receiving your message.... That is the essence of marketing, to create an emotional disturbance."[25] ...

Discontent also motivates consumers to work more hours to earn the money needed for desired purchases. One result is social isolation because people have less time for leisure, friends, and family. As a social species, people flourish only when they have close personal relationships, but the work time that consumerism demands interferes with such relationships. Ramsey writes:

A workaholic gerbil in a wheel invented the stupid phrase "quality time." There is no question that quantity time is what is needed to develop strong fruitful relationships. We are failing miserably in this culture by not slowing down enough to enjoy each other. ...

When I was growing up in the sixties, my mom would often be at a neighbor's kitchen table having a cup of coffee at midmorning while the kids played. ... The evenings would find half the neighborhood gathered on a deck or patio to enjoy a night of interaction. We camped together, the men fished together, and as a kid you could get your butt busted by any adult in the neighborhood. There was a real sense of community.

What has stolen our ability to find those luxurious hours to invest in family and friends? Several things have stolen that time. We are so marketed to that we have started to believe that more stuff will make us happy. But in this country, more stuff has resulted in more debt. What debt means is that we end up spending our every waking hour working to pay off our bills.[26]

Vicki Robin and Joe Dominguez, authors of the bestseller *Your Money or Your Life* concur: "It would seem that the primary 'thing' many people have sacrificed in 'going for the gold' is their relationships with other people. Whether you think of that as a happy marriage, time with the children, neighborliness, a close circle of friends, shopkeepers who know you, civic involvement, community spirit, or just living in a place where you can walk to work and the beat cop is your friend, it's disappearing across the country."[27] ...

Consumer items can also impair the sense of community. Air conditioning is one example. Older homes had porches, which were the coolest spots on hot summer days. Neighbors talked or visited porch to porch while avoiding indoor heat. Now people remain in their houses, isolated from neighbors, to avoid the heat. Air conditioning is wonderful and a lifesaver for some, but it does detract from a sense of community.

The car is [an] example. Cars are here to stay, but that does not tell us how many we should have or how best to use them. Cars have enabled people to move to suburbs where they live farther from neighbors and where neighbors commute in different directions to their respective jobs. The economy grows because more production is needed per capita when each person has his and her own car. "By 1990," [Robert] Putman notes, "America had more cars than drivers." What is more, "the fraction of us who travel to work in a private vehicle rose from 61 percent in 1960 to 91 percent in 1995, while all other forms of commuting ... declined."[28] Unlike private vehicle commuting, public transportation and walking foster the kind of community involvement that people need to flourish. As Putnam found:

The car and the commute ... are demonstrably bad for community life. In round numbers the evidence suggests that *each additional ten minutes in daily commuting time cuts involvement in community affairs by 10 percent*—fewer public meetings attended, fewer committees chaired, fewer petitions signed, fewer church services attended, less volunteering, and so on. ...

Strikingly, increased commuting time among the residents of a community lowers average levels of civic involvement even among noncommuters.[29]

Gary Gardner, the director of research for the Worldwatch Institute, cites research showing that consumerism does not foster human flourishing. He notes

the failure of advanced industrial societies to deliver widely their most hyped product: well-being, or happiness. Studies of societal happiness show that income growth and happiness, which once marched upward together, have been uncoupled. In the United States, for example, the share of people describing themselves as "very happy" declined from 35 percent in 1957 to 30 percent today [2001], despite a more than doubling of income per person. For many of us, it seems, the more we ask consumption to fill our lives, the emptier we feel.[30]

Increasing rates of depression also show that the social isolation that consumerism fosters interferes with human flourishing: "Today, a quarter of Americans live alone, up from 8 percent in 1940, and at least 20 percent of the population is estimated to have poor mental health. By contrast, the Old Order Amish people of…Pennsylvania, who have a strong community life made possible in part by their car-free, electricity-free lifestyles, suffer depression at less than one-fifth the rate of people in nearby Baltimore."[31]… So in sum, consumerism degrades the environment, further impoverishes poor people in the Third World, and impairs the ability of industrial people to lead fulfilling lives.

CONSUMERISM PROMOTES RECOGNIZED VICES

In 1956 Lewis Mumford pointed out a transformation in accepted virtues and vices that accompanies industrial civilization: "Observe what happened to the seven deadly sins of Christian theology. All but one of these sins, sloth, was transformed into a positive virtue. Greed, avarice, envy, gluttony, luxury and pride were the driving forces of the new economy: if once they were mainly the vices of the rich, they now under the doctrine of expanding wants embrace every class in [industrial] society."[32] Consumer society cultivates *greed*, the unlimited desire for more. Without greed consumer demand would flag, the economy would slump, and people would lose their jobs. *Avarice*, an inordinate desire for wealth, is implied by greed. People who want more and more of what money can buy desire unlimited amounts of money.

Gluttony is excessive food consumption. It seems that immoderate consumerism spawns overeating Worldwatch researchers Gary Gardner and Brian Halweil report:

Today [2000] it is more common than not for American adults to be overweight: 55 percent.…Moreover, the share of American adults who are obese has climbed from 15 to 23 percent just since 1980. And one out of five American children are now overweight or obese, a 50 percent increase in the last two decades.

Treating the effects of obesity in the United States…costs more than $100 billion annually—more than 10 percent of the nation's bill for healthcare.[33]

In England adult obesity doubled during the 1990s to 16 percent.[34]

Envy is essential in a consumer society. Advertisers portray people with a product as having a better life than those without it. Consumers must envy the life of those with the product, or they would not buy it. Envy must often be strong enough to motivate hard work or long working hours to afford the product.

Pride is a factor in such motivation. Advertisers invite consumers to take pride in their ability to afford expensive or attractive goods and services. Ads often show others admiring a new car, window treatment, or hair color. If the item is a true *luxury*, then pride is enhanced. Luxury is no vice in a consumer society because, after all, you are worth it.…

Sloth is the only one of the seven deadly sins that is not considered a virtue in a consumer society, perhaps because people must work more and more hours to produce the increasing volume of goods and services that consumerism requires. In addition to making virtues of what medieval Christians considered vices, consumerism fosters character traits that most people consider vices today. These include intemperance, selfishness, and indifference.

Intemperance is a lack of moderation or restraint. Consumerism cultivates and relies on intemperate consumers when economic growth rests in part on rich people creating jobs for others by, for example, building $2 million houses with six bedrooms for only two people. Even more consumers buy SUVs that are far larger than they need, cars with "performance" designed for professional racing, and mountain-climbing all-terrain vehicles to use in the flat Midwest. (Whose corn or soybean field do they imagine driving through?)

Selfishness is insufficient regard for the welfare of others. Consumerism fosters selfishness along with envy and greed. Envious people want the jobs, income, luxuries, recognition, and so forth that others have. They habitually compare themselves with those who have more and lament or resent their inferior position. This catalyzes greed. Such people have little mental energy to compare themselves with those who have less, so they tend selfishly to ignore occasions for helping the poor: hence the continuing appeal of middle-class tax cuts that reduce government programs needed by poor people.

As the tax cut example suggests, *indifference* follows selfishness. As people become more preoccupied with themselves, they pay less attention to other people's needs. Dramatic evidence comes from First World consumer indifference to the plight of poor people in the Third World who increasingly produce what we wear. According to David Korten, the footwear company Nike, for example,

> leaves production [of its shoes] in the hands of some 75,000 workers hired by independent contractors. Most of the outsourced production takes place in Indonesia, where a pair of Nikes that sells in the United States or Europe for $73 to $135 is produced for about $5.60 by girls and young women paid as little as fifteen cents an hour. The workers are housed in company barracks, there are no unions, overtime is often mandatory, and if there is a strike, the military may be called to break it up. The $20 million that basketball star Michael Jordan reportedly received in 1992 for promoting Nike shoes exceeded the entire annual payroll of the Indonesian factories that made them.[35]

This is typical, yet American consumers are so preoccupied with "stuff" that they ignore information about the near slave conditions of production that keep prices low. At the same time, however, our culture condemns the indifference of Germans during World War II who failed to help Jews. This is perverse. Opposing Nazi policies could be harmful to your health; buying domestically manufactured clothing is perfectly safe.

TRADITIONAL VIRTUES OPPOSE CONSUMERISM AND PROMOTE HUMAN FLOURISHING

Traditional virtues inhibit the consumerism that impairs human flourishing and degrades the environment. Consider *frugality*, which is, write Robin and Dominguez, "getting good *value* for every minute of your life energy and from everything you *have the use of*.... Waste lies not in the number of possessions but in the failure to enjoy them.... To be frugal means to have a high joy-to-stuff ratio. If you get one unit of joy for each material possession, that's frugal. But if you need ten possessions to even begin registering on the joy meter, you're missing the point of being alive."[36] Such frugality is closely allied to *appreciation*, the ability to appreciate and enjoy what you have. People who joyfully appreciate what they have are less likely to envy people who have more. They avoid the frustration and anger characteristic of envy and live happily without the compulsive consumption inherent in consumerism. Without compulsive consumption, they have fewer worries about money and more time to spend in meaningful relationships with family and friends. It is a win–win–win–win thing.

Temperance is another traditional virtue that opposes consumerism. When people have a sense of what is enough, they are more rational consumers. They have houses that are big enough but not so big as to waste space, money, and natural resources. Temperate consumers know when to stop eating, when they have enough clothing, and when a fancy wine is just too expensive. Advertisers and neoclassical economists oppose temperance. According to the economic theory dominant in consumer societies, people's wants are infinite, and there is no distinction between wants and needs, so any want can be considered a need. Hence, people are continually frustrated because they cannot have all that they are induced to think they need.

Practicing frugality, appreciation, and temperance creates opportunities to exercise another traditional virtue, *self-development*. At least some of the time saved from working to afford items that give little joy can be used to develop hobbies and skills. People can learn to play tennis, play the guitar, speak a foreign language, or knit. The sense of accomplishment from personal improvement in such pursuits cannot be bought. Of course, these pursuits also require some consumption, but it is not compulsive consumption. Practicing most sports and hobbies is much less expensive than acquiring material goods without sense or limit, especially when self-development is combined with frugality, appreciation, and temperance.

394

Dedication is another traditional virtue that stands between self-development and overconsumption. People who go quickly from one activity to another without the dedication needed for a reasonable chance of improvement or success may become major consumers of equipment, books, materials, and training. Embarking on a new activity often requires many purchases. On the other hand, those who, after some trial and error, dedicate themselves for years to one or more projects of self-development find long-term joy in the same books, equipment, and instruction. Such people tend to avoid overconsumption, especially, again, when their dedication is combined with frugality, appreciation, and temperance so that they avoid dedication to inherently wasteful or environmentally destructive pursuits, such as off-road racing.

People who avoid compulsive consumption find it easier to practice the virtue of *generosity* because they are not living on the edge of bankruptcy and can more easily live without the money and possessions that compete with generosity for personal resources. The possibility of generosity, in turn, promotes *empathy* with the plight of less fortunate people. Overspent and overworked Americans find empathy difficult because, lacking the means to be helpful (money and time), their insight into other people's troubles, which can be painful for anyone, is unrelieved by the joy of participating in improvement. Frugal, appreciative, and temperate people, by contrast, have the resources to be helpful and therefore the incentive to empathize with and help those less fortunate than themselves. The virtue of dedication can be used in projects of *benevolence* motivated by empathy.

Dedicated, empathic people engaged in projects of benevolence avoid the twin vices of indifference and injustice. Empathy itself opposes indifference. Injustice often results from people taking advantage of others, directly or indirectly, knowingly or unknowingly, as when Americans buy inexpensive clothing produced by child or near-slave labor. People whose sense of self-worth is tied to the amount of "stuff" they own resist paying the higher prices needed if workers are to receive just wages. By contrast, frugal, appreciative, temperate consumers can make justice a condition of purchase. Working conditions will improve in the Third World if enough consumers exercise these virtues.

TRADITIONAL VIRTUES AND ENVIRONMENTALISM ARE MUTUALLY REINFORCING

I have argued that traditional virtues oppose consumerism and that consumerism is a major impediment to human flourishing and a major cause of environmental degradation. This makes traditional virtues an ally of both anthropocentrism and nonanthropocentric environmentalism. It means that anthropocentrism and nonanthropocentrism are mutually supporting through their different but complementary support for many traditional virtues and their different but complementary opposition to many traditional vices.

Imagine an anthropocentrist who is most interested in human flourishing. If the arguments given above are correct, such a person should promote traditional virtues as a means to human flourishing. At the same time, the exercise of these virtues will reduce human consumption and associated environmental degradation, a result favored on other grounds by nonanthropocentrists (who consider nature valuable in itself).

Now imagine a nonanthropocentric environmentalist who values nature for itself. She can argue that nonanthropocentrism among industrial people at this time calls for reduced consumption and therefore opposition to consumerism. If the arguments given above are correct, then consumerism is effectively opposed by traditional virtues, so the environmentalist has a nonanthropocentrically based argument for traditional virtues. These arguments reinforce anthropocentrically based arguments for these virtues. There is synergy here because the two sets of arguments for environment-friendly traditional virtues are stronger together than either set is alone.

An illustration may help to clarify the point. Consider nonanthropocentrists opposed to people driving gas-guzzling SUVs because such vehicles contribute greatly to rapid climate change that threatens many species with extinction. Such nonanthropocentrists have reason to oppose the vices of envy, pride, luxury, indifference, and selfishness because these vices are implicated in decisions to own SUVs. Advertisements for SUVs induce envy. Drivers take pride in owning a vehicle larger and more expensive than most others on the road. SUV owners seek the luxury of extra room in the vehicle and are selfishly indifferent to the effects of its greenhouse gas emissions on nature. So nonanthropocentrists oppose the traditional vices of envy, pride, luxury, indifference, and selfishness and support the traditional virtues of appreciation, frugality, and temperance, which incline people to reject SUVs in favor of more modest vehicles.

Anthropocentrists also have reasons to oppose SUVs on the ground that they promote climate change, which is likely to harm many poor people around the world by increasing vector-born diseases and reducing food availability.[37] Domestically, SUVs endanger people in smaller cars. SUVs also exacerbate dependence on foreign sources of oil, which motivates attempts to control oil-rich areas of the world, resulting in conflicts that take human lives. Finally, people trying to find happiness and fulfillment in the kind of car they drive are doomed to frustration because human flourishing cannot rest on any such basis. So anthropocentrists have their own reasons to oppose vices that promote SUV ownership and to favor virtues that discourage the purchase of an SUV.

The two sets of reasons against SUV ownership are compatible, complementary, and additive, as they are mediated by opposition to the same vices and promotion of the same virtues. Together these two sets of reasons are stronger than either set is by itself. Thus, there is synergy between them. . . .

PRACTICAL IMPLICATIONS

In light of the arguments above, the following questions must be addressed: How should we expect people with the traditional virtues discussed above to act differently from most other people in society? How thoroughly should we expect them to reject consumerism? Must a virtuous person abjure automobile ownership? Must a virtuous person be a vegetarian? What are the practical implications of synergistic environmental virtues?

If virtue is to promote human flourishing, it cannot often require lifestyles so out of harmony with mainstream social expectations that virtuous people lack the companionship and camaraderie that flourishing as a social animal requires. To promote human flourishing, virtue must also avoid prescribing behavior that is impractical in the human-built environment, such as life without a car in many American communities.

I suggest addressing such matters with what I call the Principle of Anticipatory Cooperation (PAC). The PAC calls for actions that deviate from the social norm in the direction of the ideal that virtuous people aspire to for themselves and others but which do not deviate so much that virtue impairs instead of fosters flourishing. Consider, for example, car ownership and use. If life without a car is nearly crippling, the PAC does not require that virtuous people abjure car ownership and use. It requires only that they try to arrange their lives so that their car use and its adverse impacts are substantially less than is common in that society at that time. If most cars get twenty miles to the gallon, but good cars are available at reasonable cost that get thirty miles to the gallon, the virtuous person will, other things being equal, choose the more fuel-efficient car. She will also use public transportation and carpool more than is common when she can do so without bending her life out of shape. Her behavior anticipates more widespread participation in such practices and therefore helps to move society in a desirable direction.

If behavior like this becomes more common in society—average fuel efficiency approaches thirty miles to the gallon, for example, and car makers come out with reasonably priced cars that are even more fuel efficient—the virtuous person should, when finances permit, choose a car that is again considerably more fuel efficient than average. Absent some special need or problem, the virtuous person buying a new car today would choose a gas/electric hybrid that gets at least forty-five miles to the gallon. Similarly, if the transportation infrastructure changes to make public transportation more convenient and popular, the virtuous person will increase her use of public transportation so that it still exceeds the norm for people with similar transportation needs. A virtuous couple would likely be among the first to get by with only one car. . . .

The spirit of compromise in the PAC stems from two considerations. One, already mentioned, is that virtue should promote human flourishing; it would not if it required heroic sacrifice. The second consideration is justice. There is no justice in virtuous people trying to be perfect in social circumstances that make such attempts nearly self-destructive. Of course, the virtues considered here may require some short-term sacrifice. If my arguments are correct, however, the long-term result will be a better life. People who reject consumerism (without becoming utterly at odds with society) will flourish better than people whose lives are dominated by envy, greed, work, money worries, and separation from family and friends. People who reject consumerism in favor of traditional virtues will also lead more environmentally friendly lives.

In conclusion, people in industrial, consumer-oriented societies should cultivate traditional virtues to benefit themselves, other human beings, and the nonhuman environment. Anthropocentric and nonanthropocentric arguments for cultivating and exercising these virtues are mutually reinforcing, and their combination is synergistic. However, because the arguments for this conclusion depend on the baleful effects of consumerism, I draw no conclusions about virtue in nonconsumer-oriented societies.

NOTES

1. For a more complete exposition of environmental synergism, see Peter S. Wenz, "Environmental Synergism," *Environmental Ethics* 24 (2002): 389–408.

2. Linda Starke, ed., *Vital Signs 2003* (New York: W. W. Norton, 2003), 84.

3. Starke, *Vital Signs 2003*, 40.

4. Starke, *Vital Signs 2003*, 82.

5. Dave Ramsey, *More Than Enough* (New York: Viking Penguin, 1999), 24.

6. David C. Korten, *When Corporations Rule the World* (West Hartford, CT: Kumarian Press, 1995), 37–38.

7. Alan Thein Durning, *How Much Is Enough?* (New York: W. W. Norton, 1992), 51–52.

8. Thomas L. Friedman, *The Lexus and the Olive Tree* (New York: Farrar, Straus and Giroux, 1999), 85–86.

9. Friedman, *The Lexus and the Olive Tree*, 167.

10. Korten, *When Corporations Rule the World*, 35.

11. Mia MacDonald with Danielle Nierenberg, "Linking Population, Women, and Biodiversity," in *State of the World 2003*, ed. Linda Starke (New York: W. W. Norton, 2003), 43.

12. Korten, *When Corporations Rule the World*, 33.

13. MacDonald with Nierenberg, "Linking Population, Women, and Biodiversity," 40.

14. For a critique of this view, see Peter S. Wenz, "Pragmatism in Practice: The Efficiency of Sustainable Agriculture," *Environmental Ethics* 21 (1999): 391–410.

15. Aaron Sachs, "The Last Commodity: Child Prostitution in the Developing World," *WorldWatch* 7, no. 4 (July–August 1994): 26–27.

16. Vandana Shiva, *Monocultures of the Mind* (London: Zed Books, 1993), 36.

17. Korten, *When Corporations Rule the World*, 31–32.

18. Korten, *When Corporations Rule the World*, 42.

19. Sachs, "The Last Commodity," 26.

20. Starke, *Vital Signs 2003*, 88.

21. Gary Gardner and Brian Halweil, "Overfed and Underfed: The Global Epidemic of Malnutrition," in *Worldwatch Paper 150* (Washington, DC: Worldwatch Institure, 2000), 7.

22. World Health Organization, *World Health Report 1998*, in Lester R. Brown, "Challenges of the New Century," *State of the World 2000*, ed. Linda Starke (New York: W. W. Norton, 2000), 7.

23. Grover Foley, "The Threat of Rising Seas," *The Ecologist* 29, no. 2 (March–April 1999): 77.

24. Peter Bunyard, "A Hungrier World," *The Ecologist* 29, no. 2 (March–April 1999): 87.

25. Ramsey, *More Than Enough*, 234.

26. Ramsey, *More Than Enough,* 22–23.

27. Vicki Robin and Joe Dominguez, *Your Money or Your Life* (New York: Penguin Books, 1992), 142.

28. Robert D. Putnam, *Bowling Alone* (New York: Penguin Books, 2000), 212.

29. Putnam, *Bowling Alone*, 213.

30. Gary Gardner, "The Virtue of Restraint," *WorldWatch* 14, no. 2 (March–April 2001): 14.

31. Gardner, "The Virtue of Restraint," 15.

32. Lewis Mumford, *The Transformation of Man* (New York: Harper and Row, 1956), 104–5.

33. Gardner and Halweil, "Overfed and Underfed," 14, 8.

34. Gardner and Halweil, "Overfed and Underfed," 14.

35. Korten, *When Corporations Rule the World*, 111.

36. Robin and Dominguez, *Your Money or Your Life*, 167–68.

37. See Paul Kingsnorth, "Human Health on the Line," *The Ecologist* 29, no. 2 (March–April 1999): 92–94; Bunyard, "A Hungrier World"; and Korten, *When Corporations Rule the World*, 31–32.

READING QUESTIONS

1. How does Wenz define "consumerism"? How does he believe that consumerism harms the environment?
2. How does consumerism harm people in the Third World according to Wenz? How does it harm people in the industrialized world?
3. What vices are promoted by consumerism according to Wenz? Explain the three other bad character traits that Wenz believes are promoted by consumerism.
4. Explain the seven traditional virtues that oppose consumerism and promote human flourishing according to Wenz. What reasons does Wenz offer for thinking that traditional virtues and environmentalism are mutually reinforcing?
5. Explain Wenz's Principle of Anticipatory Cooperation. What are the two major consequences of this principle's application according to Wenz?

DISCUSSION QUESTIONS

1. Discuss which of the traditional virtues opposed to consumerism are the most important and useful ones to develop. Are there any other virtues that are in opposition to consumerism not considered by Wenz? Consider and discuss some of the practical ways in which any of these virtues can work to oppose the vices promoted by consumerism? Are there any other vices promoted by consumerism that Wenz fails to mention?
2. Suppose that individuals start working together to apply the Principle of Anticipatory Cooperation in their daily lives. How successful do you think such a project would be? Consider and discuss the sorts of practical and theoretical problems that might arise and how we might overcome such problems in order to increase the chances of a successful implementation of the principle.

WALTER SINNOTT-ARMSTRONG

It's Not *My* Fault: Global Warming and Individual Moral Obligations

Sinnott-Armstrong addresses the question: Given the enormity of the problem of global warming, what moral obligations does an *individual* (living in relative affluence) have in light of all this? To focus his question, he considers whether it is morally wrong for him to take a Sunday drive in a gas-guzzling car just for fun. In answering this question,

This article was published in *Perspectives on Climate Change*, Walter Sinnott-Armstrong and Richard B. Howarth, "It's Not *My* Fault: Global Warming and Individual Moral Obligations," 295–315. Copyright Elsevier (2006).

Sinnott-Armstrong appeals to a wide range of moral principles, including principles familiar from consequentialist, natural law (double effect), Kantian, virtue ethics, and social contract traditions. He argues that applying the various principles does not imply that he (or similarly situated individuals) has a *moral obligation* to refrain from taking the Sunday drive, though he admits that it is still "morally better or ideal" for individuals not to engage in such activities. Governments, however, do have a moral obligation to address the problem of global warming partly because only they are in a position to help fix the problem.

Recommended Reading: consequentialism, natural law theory, Kantian moral theory, virtue ethics, and social contract theory chap. 1, secs. 2A, 2B, 2C, 2E, and 2G.

Previous chapters in *Perspectives on Climate Change* have focused on scientific research, economic projections, and government policies. However, even if scientists establish that global warming is occurring, even if economists confirm that its costs will be staggering, and even if political theorists agree that governments must do something about it, it is still not clear what moral obligations regarding global warming devolve upon individuals like you and me. That is the question to be addressed in this essay.

1. ASSUMPTIONS

To make the issue stark, let us begin with a few assumptions. I believe that these assumptions are probably roughly accurate, but none is certain, and I will not try to justify them here. Instead, I will simply take them for granted for the sake of argument.[1]

First, global warming has begun and is likely to increase over the next century. We cannot be sure exactly how much or how fast, but hot times are coming.[2]

Second, a significant amount of global warming is due to human activities. The main culprit is fossil fuels.

Third, global warming will create serious problems for many people over the long term by causing climate changes, including violent storms, floods from sea level rises, droughts, heat waves, and so on. Millions of people will probably be displaced or die.

Fourth, the poor will be hurt most of all. The rich countries are causing most of the global warming, but they will be able to adapt to climate changes more easily.[3] Poor countries that are close to sea level might be devastated.

Fifth, governments, especially the biggest and richest ones, are able to mitigate global warming.[4] They can impose limits on emissions. They can require or give incentives for increased energy efficiency. They can stop deforestation and fund reforestation. They can develop ways to sequester carbon dioxide in oceans or underground. These steps will help, but the only long-run solution lies in alternatives to fossil fuels. These alternatives can be found soon if governments start massive research projects now.[5]

Sixth, it is too late to stop global warming. Because there is so much carbon dioxide in the atmosphere already, because carbon dioxide remains in the atmosphere for so long, and because we will remain dependent on fossil fuels in the near future, governments can slow down global warming or reduce its severity, but they cannot prevent it. Hence, governments need to adapt. They need to build seawalls. They need to reinforce houses that cannot withstand storms. They need to move populations from low-lying areas.[6]

Seventh, these steps will be costly. Increased energy efficiency can reduce expenses, adaptation will create some jobs, and money will be made in the research and production of alternatives to fossil fuels. Still, any steps that mitigate or adapt to global warming will slow down our economies, at least in the short run.[7] That will hurt many people, especially many poor people.

Eighth, despite these costs, the major governments throughout the world still morally ought to take some of these steps. The clearest moral obligation falls on the United States. The United States caused and continues to cause more of the problem than any other country. The United States can spend more resources on a solution without sacrificing basic necessities. This country has the scientific expertise to solve technical problems. Other countries follow its lead (sometimes!). So the United States has a special moral obligation to help mitigate and adapt to global warming.[8]

2. THE PROBLEM

Even assuming all of this, it is still not clear what I as an individual morally ought to do about global warming. That issue is not as simple as many people assume. I want to bring out some of its complications.

It should be clear from the start that "individual" moral obligations do not always follow directly from "collective" moral obligations. The fact that your government morally ought to do something does not prove that "you" ought to do it, even if your government fails. Suppose that a bridge is dangerous because so much traffic has gone over it and continues to go over it. The government has a moral obligation to make the bridge safe. If the government fails to do its duty, it does not follow that I personally have a moral obligation to fix the bridge. It does not even follow that I have a moral obligation to fill in one crack in the bridge, even if the bridge would be fixed if everyone filled in one crack, even if I drove over the bridge many times, and even if I still drive over it every day. Fixing the bridge is the government's job, not mine. While I ought to encourage the government to fulfill its obligations,[9] I do not have to take on those obligations myself.

All that this shows is that government obligations do not "always" imply parallel individual obligations. Still, maybe "sometimes" they do. My government has a moral obligation to teach arithmetic to the children in my town, including my own children.

If the government fails in this obligation, then I do take on a moral obligation to teach arithmetic to my children.[10] Thus, when the government fails in its obligations, sometimes I have to fill in, and sometimes I do not.

What about global warming? If the government fails to do anything about global warming, what am I supposed to do about it? There are lots of ways for me as an individual to fight global warming. I can protest against bad government policies and vote for candidates who will make the government fulfill its moral obligations. I can support private organizations that fight global warming, such as the Pew Foundation,[11] or boycott companies that contribute too much to global warming, such as most oil companies. Each of these cases is interesting, but they all differ. To simplify our discussion, we need to pick one act as our focus.

My example will be wasteful driving. Some people drive to their jobs or to the store because they have no other reasonable way to work and eat. I want to avoid issues about whether these goals justify driving, so I will focus on a case where nothing so important is gained. I will consider driving for fun on a beautiful Sunday afternoon. My drive is not necessary to cure depression or calm aggressive impulses. All that is gained is pleasure: Ah, the feel of wind in your hair! The views! How spectacular! Of course, you could drive a fuel-efficient hybrid car. But fuel-efficient cars have less "get up and go." So let us consider a gas-guzzling sport utility vehicle. Ah, the feeling of power! The excitement! Maybe you do not like to go for drives in sport utility vehicles on sunny Sunday afternoons, but many people do.

Do we have a moral obligation not to drive in such circumstances? This question concerns driving, not "buying" cars. To make this clear, let us assume that I borrow the gas-guzzler from a friend. This question is also not about "legal" obligations. So let us assume that it is perfectly legal to go for such drives. Perhaps it ought to be illegal, but it is not. Note also that my question is not about what would be "best." Maybe it would be better, even morally better, for me not to drive a gas-guzzler just for fun. But that is not the issue I want to address here. My question is whether I have a "moral" obligation not to drive a gas-guzzler just for fun on this particular sunny Sunday afternoon.

One final complication must be removed. I am interested in global warming, but there might be other moral reasons not to drive unnecessarily. I risk causing an accident, since I am not a perfect driver. I also will likely spew exhaust into the breathing space of pedestrians, bicyclists, or animals on the side of the road as I drive by. Perhaps these harms and risks give me a moral obligation not to go for my joyride. That is not clear. After all, these reasons also apply if I drive the most efficient car available, and even if I am driving to work with no other way to keep my job. Indeed, I might scare or injure bystanders even if my car gave off no greenhouse gases or pollution. In any case, I want to focus on global warming. So my real question is whether the facts about global warming give me any moral obligation not to drive a gas-guzzler just for fun on this sunny Sunday afternoon.

I admit that I am "inclined" to answer, "Yes." To me, global warming does "seem" to make such wasteful driving morally wrong.

Still, I do not feel confident in this judgment. I know that other people disagree (even though they are also concerned about the environment). I would probably have different moral intuitions about this case if I had been raised differently or if I now lived in a different culture. My moral intuition might be distorted by overgeneralization from the other cases where I think that other entities (large governments) do have moral obligations to fight global warming. I also worry that my moral intuition might be distorted by my desire to avoid conflicts with my environmentalist friends.[12] The issue of global warming generates strong emotions because of its political implications and because of how scary its effects are. It is also a peculiarly modern case, especially because it operates on a much grander scale than my moral intuitions evolved to handle long ago when acts did not have such long-term effects on future generations (or at least people were not aware of such effects). In such circumstances, I doubt that we are justified in trusting our moral intuitions alone. We need some kind of confirmation.[13]

One way to confirm the truth of my moral intuitions would be to derive them from a general moral principle. A principle could tell us why wasteful driving is morally wrong, so we would not have to depend on bare assertion. And a principle might be supported by more trustworthy moral beliefs. The problem is "which" principle?

3. ACTUAL ACT PRINCIPLES

One plausible principle refers to causing harm. If one person had to inhale all of the exhaust from my car, this would harm him and give me a moral obligation not to drive my car just for fun. Such cases suggest:

The harm principle: We have a moral obligation not to perform an act that causes harm to others.

This principle implies that I have a moral obligation not to drive my gas-guzzler just for fun "if" such driving causes harm.

The problem is that such driving does "not" cause harm in normal cases. If one person were in a position to inhale all of my exhaust, then he would get sick if I did drive, and he would not get sick if I did not drive (under normal circumstances). In contrast, global warming will still occur even if I do not drive just for fun. Moreover, even if I do drive a gas-guzzler just for fun for a long time, global warming will not occur unless lots of other people also expel greenhouse gases. So my individual act is neither necessary nor sufficient for global warming.

There are, admittedly, special circumstances in which an act causes harm without being either necessary or sufficient for that harm. Imagine that it takes three people to push a car off a cliff with a passenger locked inside, and five people are already pushing. If I join and help them push, then my act of pushing is neither necessary nor sufficient to make the car go off the cliff. Nonetheless, my act of pushing is a cause (or part of the cause) of the harm to the passenger. Why? Because I intend to cause harm to the passenger, and because my act is unusual. When I intend a harm to occur, my intention provides a reason to pick my act out of all the other background circumstances and identify it as a cause. Similarly, when my act is unusual in the sense that most people would not act that way, that also provides a reason to pick out my act and call it a cause.

Why does it matter what is usual? Compare matches. For a match to light up, we need to strike it so as to create friction. There also has to be oxygen. We do not call the oxygen the cause of the fire, since oxygen is usually present. Instead, we say that the friction causes the match to light, since it is unusual for that friction to occur. It happens only once in the life of each match. Thus, what is usual affects ascriptions of causation even in purely physical cases.

In moral cases, there are additional reasons not to call something a cause when it is usual. Labeling an act a cause of harm and, on this basis, holding its agent responsible for that harm by blaming the agent or condemning his act is normally counterproductive when that agent is acting no worse than most other people. If people who are doing "no" worse than average are condemned, then people who are doing "much" worse than average will suspect that they will still be subject to condemnation even if they start doing better, and even if they improve enough to bring themselves up to the average. We should distribute blame (and praise) so as to give incentives for the worst offenders to get better. The most efficient and effective way to do this is to reserve our condemnation for those who are well below average. This means that we should not hold people responsible for harms by calling their acts causes of harms when their acts are not at all unusual, assuming that they did not intend the harm.

The application to global warming should be clear. It is not unusual to go for joyrides. Such drivers do not intend any harm. Hence, we should not see my act of driving on a sunny Sunday afternoon as a cause of global warming or its harms.

Another argument leads to the same conclusion: the harms of global warming result from the massive quantities of greenhouse gases in the atmosphere. Greenhouse gases (such as carbon dioxide and water vapor) are perfectly fine in small quantities. They help plants grow. The problem emerges only when there is too much of them. But my joyride by itself does not cause the massive quantities that are harmful.

Contrast someone who pours cyanide poison into a river. Later someone drinking from the river downstream ingests some molecules of the poison. Those molecules cause the person to get ill and die. This is very different from the causal chain in global warming, because no particular molecules from my car cause global warming in the direct way that particular molecules of the poison do cause the drinker's death. Global warming is more like a river that is going to flood downstream because of torrential rains. I pour a quart of water into the river upstream (maybe just because I do not want to carry it). My act of pouring the quart into the river is not a cause of the flood. Analogously, my act of driving for fun is not a cause of global warming.

Contrast also another large-scale moral problem: famine relief. Some people say that I have no moral obligation to contribute to famine relief because the famine will continue and people will die whether or not I donate my money to a relief agency. However, I could help a certain individual if I gave my donation directly to that individual. In contrast, if I refrain from driving for fun on this one Sunday, there is no individual who will be helped in the least.[14] I cannot help anyone by depriving myself of this joyride.

The point becomes clearer if we distinguish global warming from climate change. You might think that my driving on Sunday raises the temperature of the globe by an infinitesimal amount. I doubt that, but, even if it does, my exhaust on that Sunday does not cause any climate change at all. No storms or floods or droughts or heat waves can be traced to my individual act of driving. It is these climate changes that cause harms to people. Global warming by itself causes no harm without climate change. Hence, since my individual act of driving on that one Sunday does not cause any climate change, it causes no harm to anyone.

The point is not that harms do not occur from global warming. I have already admitted that they do. The point is also not that my exhaust is overkill, like poisoning someone who is already dying from poison. My exhaust is not sufficient for the harms of global warming, and I do not intend those harms. Nor is it the point that the harms from global warming occur much later in time. If I place a time bomb in a building, I can cause harm many years later. And the point is not that the harm I cause is imperceptible. I admit that some harms can be imperceptible because they are too small or for other reasons.[15] Instead, the point is simply that my individual joyride does not cause global warming, climate change, or any of their resulting harms, at least directly.

Admittedly, my acts can lead to other acts by me or by other people. Maybe one case of wasteful driving creates a bad habit that will lead me to do it again and again. Or maybe a lot of other people look up to me and would follow my example of wasteful driving. Or maybe my wasteful driving will undermine my commitment to environmentalism and lead me to stop supporting important green causes or to harm the environment in more serious ways. If so, we could apply:

The indirect harm principle: We have a moral obligation not to perform an act that causes harm to others indirectly by causing someone to carry out acts that cause harm to others.

This principle would explain why it is morally wrong to drive a gas-guzzler just for fun if this act led to other harmful acts.

One problem here is that my acts are not that influential. People like to see themselves as more influential than they really are. On a realistic view, however, it is unlikely that anyone would drive wastefully if I did and would not if I did not. Moreover, wasteful driving is not that habit forming. My act of driving this Sunday does not make me drive next Sunday. I do not get addicted. Driving the next Sunday is a separate decision.[16] And my wasteful driving will not undermine my devotion to environmentalism. If my argument in this chapter is correct, then my belief that the government has a moral obligation to fight global warming is perfectly compatible with a belief that I as an individual have no moral obligation not to drive a gas-guzzler for fun. If I keep this compatibility in mind, then my driving my gas-guzzler for fun will not undermine my devotion to the cause of getting the government to do something about global warming.

Besides, the indirect harm principle is misleading. To see why, consider David. David is no environmentalist. He already has a habit of driving his gas-guzzler for fun on Sundays. Nobody likes him, so nobody follows his example. But David still has a moral obligation not to drive his gas-guzzler just for fun this Sunday, and his obligation has the same basis as mine, if I have one. So my moral obligation cannot depend on the factors cited by the indirect harm principle.

The most important problem for supposed indirect harms is the same as for direct harms: even if I create a bad habit and undermine my personal environmentalism and set a bad example that others follow, all of this would still not be enough to cause climate change if other people stopped expelling greenhouse gases. So, as long as I neither intend harm nor do anything unusual, my act cannot cause climate change even if I do create bad habits and followers. The scale of climate change is just too big for me to cause it, even "with a little help from my friends."

Of course, even if I do not cause climate change, I still might seem to contribute to climate change in the sense that I make it worse. If so, another principle applies:

The contribution principle: We have a moral obligation not to make problems worse.

This principle applies if climate change will be worse if I drive than it will be if I do not drive.

The problem with this argument is that my act of driving does not even make climate change worse. Climate change would be just as bad if I did not drive. The reason is that climate change becomes worse only if more people (and animals) are hurt or if they are hurt worse. There is nothing bad about global warming or climate change in itself if no people (or animals) are harmed. But there is no individual person or animal who will be worse off if I drive than if I do not drive my gas-guzzler just for fun. Global warming and climate change occur on such a massive scale that my individual driving makes no difference to the welfare of anyone.

Some might complain that this is not what they mean by "contribute." All it takes for me to contribute to global warming in their view is for me to expel greenhouse gases into the atmosphere. I do "that" when I drive, so we can apply:

The gas principle: We have a moral obligation not to expel greenhouse gases into the atmosphere.

If this principle were true, it would explain why I have a moral obligation not to drive my gas-guzzler just for fun.

Unfortunately, it is hard to see any reason to accept this principle. There is nothing immoral about greenhouse gases in themselves when they cause no harm. Greenhouse gases include carbon dioxide and water vapor, which occur naturally and help plants grow. The problem of global warming occurs because of the high quantities of greenhouse gases, not because of anything bad about smaller quantities of the same gases. So it is hard to see why I would have a moral obligation not to expel harmless quantities of greenhouse gases. And that is all I do by myself.

Furthermore, if the gas principle were true, it would be unbelievably restrictive. It implies that I have a moral obligation not to boil water (since water vapor is a greenhouse gas) or to exercise (since I expel carbon dioxide when I breathe heavily). When you think it through, an amazing array of seemingly morally acceptable activities would be ruled out by the gas principle. These implications suggest that we had better look elsewhere for a reason why I have a moral obligation not to drive a gas-guzzler just for fun.

Maybe the reason is risk. It is sometimes morally wrong to create a risk of a harm even if that harm does not occur. I grant that drunk driving is immoral, because it risks harm to others, even if the drunk driver gets home safely without hurting anyone. Thus, we get another principle:

The risk principle: We have a moral obligation not to increase the risk of harms to other people.[17]

The problem here is that global warming is not like drunk driving. When drunk driving causes harm, it is easy to identify the victim of this particular drunk

driver. There is no way to identify any particular victim of my wasteful driving in normal circumstances.

In addition, my earlier point applies here again. If the risk principle were true, it would be unbelievably restrictive. Exercising and boiling water also expel greenhouse gases, so they also increase the risk of global warming if my driving does. This principle implies that almost everything we do violates a moral obligation.

Defenders of such principles sometimes respond by distinguishing significant from insignificant risks or increases in risks. That distinction is problematic, at least here. A risk is called significant when it is "too" much. But then we need to ask what makes this risk too much when other risks are not too much. The reasons for counting a risk as significant are then the real reasons for thinking that there is a moral obligation not to drive wastefully. So we need to specify those reasons directly instead of hiding them under a waffle-term like "significant."

4. INTERNAL PRINCIPLES

None of the principles discussed so far is both defensible and strong enough to yield a moral obligation not to drive a gas-guzzler just for fun. Maybe we can do better by looking inward.

Kantians claim that the moral status of acts depends on their agents' maxims or "subjective principles of volition"[18]—roughly what we would call motives or intentions or plans. This internal focus is evident in Kant's first formulation of the categorical imperative:

The universalizability principle: We have a moral obligation not to act on any maxim that we cannot will to be a universal law.

The idea is not that universally acting on that maxim would have bad consequences. (We will consider that kind of principle below.) Instead, the claim is that some maxims "cannot even be thought as a universal law of nature without contradiction."[19] However, my maxim when I drive a gas-guzzler just for fun on this sunny Sunday afternoon is simply to have harmless fun. There is no way to derive a contradiction from a universal law that people do or may have harmless fun. Kantians might respond that my maxim is, instead, to expel greenhouse gases. I still see no way to derive a literal contradiction from a universal law that people do or may expel greenhouse gases. There would be bad consequences, but that is not a contradiction, as Kant requires. In any case, my maxim (or intention or motive) is not to expel greenhouse gases. My goals would be reached completely if I went for my drive and had my fun without expelling any greenhouse gases. This leaves no ground for claiming that my driving violates Kant's first formula of the categorical imperative.

Kant does supply a second formulation, which is really a different principle:

The means principle: We have a moral obligation not to treat any other person as a means only.[20]

It is not clear exactly how to understand this formulation, but the most natural interpretation is that for me to treat someone as a means implies my using harm to that person as part of my plan to achieve my goals. Driving for fun does not do that. I would have just as much fun if nobody were ever harmed by global warming. Harm to others is no part of my plans. So Kant's principle cannot explain why I have a moral obligation not to drive just for fun on this sunny Sunday afternoon.

A similar point applies to a traditional principle that focuses on intention:

The doctrine of double effect: We have a moral obligation not to harm anyone intentionally (either as an end or as a means).

This principle fails to apply to my Sunday driving both because my driving does not cause harm to anyone and because I do not intend harm to anyone. I would succeed in doing everything I intended to do if I enjoyed my drive but magically my car gave

off no greenhouse gases and no global warming occurred.

Another inner-directed theory is virtue ethics. This approach focuses on general character traits rather than particular acts or intentions. It is not clear how to derive a principle regarding obligations from virtue ethics, but here is a common attempt:

The virtue principle: We have a moral obligation not to perform an act that expresses a vice or is contrary to virtue.

This principle solves our problem if driving a gas-guzzler expresses a vice, or if no virtuous person would drive a gas-guzzler just for fun.

How can we tell whether this principle applies? How can we tell whether driving a gas-guzzler for fun "expresses a vice"? On the face of it, it expresses a desire for fun. There is nothing vicious about having fun. Having fun becomes vicious only if it is harmful or risky. But I have already responded to the principles of harm and risk. Moreover, driving a gas-guzzler for fun does not always express a vice. If other people did not produce so much greenhouse gas, I could drive my gas-guzzler just for fun without anyone being harmed by global warming. Then I could do it without being vicious. This situation is not realistic, but it does show that wasteful driving is not essentially vicious or contrary to virtue.

Some will disagree. Maybe your notions of virtue and vice make it essentially vicious to drive wastefully. But why? To apply this principle, we need some antecedent test of when an act expresses a vice. You cannot just say, "I know vice when I see it," because other people look at the same act and do not see vice, just fun. It begs the question to appeal to what you see when others do not see it, and you have no reason to believe that your vision is any clearer than theirs. But that means that this virtue principle cannot be applied without begging the question. We need to find some reason why such driving is vicious. Once we have this reason, we can appeal to it directly as a reason why I have a moral obligation not to drive wastefully. The side step through virtue does not help and only obscures the issue.

Some virtue theorists might respond that life would be better if more people were to focus on general character traits, including green virtues, such as moderation and love of nature.[21] One reason is that it is so hard to determine obligations in particular cases. Another reason is that focusing on particular obligations leaves no way to escape problems like global warming. This might be correct. Maybe we should spend more time thinking about whether we have green virtues rather than about whether we have specific obligations. But that does not show that we do have a moral obligation not to drive gas-guzzlers just for fun. Changing our focus will not bring any moral obligation into existence. There are other important moral issues besides moral obligation, but this does not show that moral obligations are not important as well.

5. COLLECTIVE PRINCIPLES

Maybe our mistake is to focus on individual persons. We could, instead, focus on institutions. One institution is the legal system, so we might adopt.

The ideal law principle: We have a moral obligation not to perform an action if it ought to be illegal.

I already said that the government ought to fight global warming. One way to do so is to make it illegal to drive wastefully or to buy (or sell) inefficient gas-guzzlers. If the government ought to pass such laws, then, even before such laws are passed, I have a moral obligation not to drive a gas-guzzler just for fun, according to the ideal law principle.

The first weakness in this argument lies in its assumption that wasteful driving or gas-guzzlers ought to be illegal. That is dubious. The enforcement costs of a law against joyrides would be enormous. A law against gas-guzzlers would be easier to enforce, but inducements to efficiency (such as higher taxes on gas and gas-guzzlers, or tax breaks for buying fuel-efficient cars) might accomplish the same goals with less loss of individual freedom. Governments ought to accomplish their goals with less loss of freedom, if they can. Note the "if." I do not claim that these other laws would work as well as an outright prohibition of gas-guzzlers. I do not know. Still, the point is that such alternative laws would not make it illegal (only expensive) to drive a gas-guzzler for fun. If those alternative laws are better than outright prohibitions (because they allow more freedom), then the ideal law principle cannot yield a moral obligation not to drive a gas-guzzler now.

Moreover, the connection between law and morality cannot be so simple. Suppose that the government morally ought to raise taxes on fossil fuels in order to reduce usage and to help pay for adaptation to global warming. It still seems morally permissible for me and for you not to pay that tax now. We do not have any moral obligation to send a check to the government for the amount that we would have to pay if taxes were raised to the ideal level. One reason is that our checks would not help to solve the problem, since others would continue to conduct business as usual. What would help to solve the problem is for the taxes to be increased. Maybe we all have moral obligations to try to get the taxes increased. Still, until they are increased, we as individuals have no moral obligations to abide by the ideal tax law instead of the actual tax law.

Analogously, it is actually legal to buy and drive gas-guzzlers. Maybe these vehicles should be illegal. I am not sure. If gas-guzzlers morally ought to be illegal, then maybe we morally ought to work to get them outlawed. But that still would not show that now, while they are legal, we have a moral obligation not to drive them just for fun on a sunny Sunday afternoon.

Which laws are best depends on side effects of formal institutions, such as enforcement costs and loss of freedom (resulting from the coercion of laws). Maybe we can do better by looking at informal groups.

Different groups involve different relations between members. Orchestras and political parties, for example, plan to do what they do and adjust their actions to other members of the group in order to achieve a common goal. Such groups can be held responsible for their joint acts, even when no individual alone performs those acts. However, gas-guzzler drivers do not form this kind of group.

Gas-guzzler drivers do not share goals, do not make plans together, and do not adjust their acts to each other (at least usually).

There is an abstract set of gas-guzzler drivers, but membership in a set is too arbitrary to create moral responsibility. I am also in a set of all terrorists plus me, but my membership in that abstract set does not make me responsible for the harms that terrorists cause.

The only feature that holds together the group of people who drive gas-guzzlers is simply that they all perform the same kind of act. The fact that so many people carry out acts of that kind does create or worsen global warming. That collective bad effect is supposed to make it morally wrong to perform any act of that kind, according to the following:

The group principle: We have a moral obligation not to perform an action if this action makes us a member of a group whose actions together cause harm.

Why? It begs the question here merely to assume that, if it is bad for everyone in a group to perform acts of a kind, then it is morally wrong for an individual to perform an act of that kind. Besides, this principle is implausible or at least questionable in many cases. Suppose that everyone in an airport is talking loudly. If only a few people were talking, there would be no problem. But the collective effect of so many people talking makes it hard to hear announcements, so some people miss their flights. Suppose, in these circumstances, I say loudly (but not too loudly), "I wish everyone would be quiet." My speech does not seem immoral, since it alone does not harm anyone. Maybe there should be a rule (or law) against such loud speech in this setting (as in a library), but if there is not (as I am assuming), then it does not seem immoral to do what others do, as long as they are going to do it anyway, so the harm is going to occur anyway.[22]

Again, suppose that the president sends everyone (or at least most taxpayers) a check for $600. If all recipients cash their checks, the government deficit will grow, government programs will have to be slashed, and severe economic and social problems will result. You know that enough other people will cash their checks to make these results to a great degree inevitable. You also know that it is perfectly legal to cash your check, although you think it should be illegal, because the checks should not have been issued in the first place. In these circumstances, is it morally wrong for you to cash your check? I doubt it. Your act of cashing your check causes no harm by itself, and you have no intention to cause harm. Your act of cashing your check does make you a member of a group that collectively causes harm, but that still does not seem to give you a moral obligation not to join the group by cashing your check, since you cannot change what the group does. It might be morally good or ideal to protest by tearing up your check, but it does not seem morally obligatory.

Thus, the group principle fails. Perhaps it might be saved by adding some kind of qualification, but I do not see how.[23]

6. COUNTERFACTUAL PRINCIPLES

Maybe our mistake is to focus on actual circumstances. So let us try some counterfactuals about what would happen in possible worlds that are not actual. Different counterfactuals are used by different versions of rule-consequentialism.[24]

One counterfactual is built into the common question, "What would happen if everybody did that?" This question suggests a principle:

The general action principle: I have a moral obligation not to perform an act when it would be worse for everyone to perform an act of the same kind.[25]

It does seem likely that, if everyone in the world drove a gas-guzzler often enough, global warming would increase intolerably. We would also quickly run out of fossil fuels. The general action principle is, thus, supposed to explain why it is morally wrong to drive a gas-guzzler.

Unfortunately, that popular principle is indefensible. It would be disastrous if every human had no children. But that does not make it morally wrong for a particular individual to choose to have no children. There is no moral obligation to have at least one child.

The reason is that so few people "want" to remain childless. Most people would not go without children even if they were allowed to. This suggests a different principle:

The general permission principle: I have a moral obligation not to perform an act whenever it would be worse for everyone to be permitted to perform an act of that kind.

This principle seems better because it would not be disastrous for everyone to be permitted to remain childless. This principle is supposed to be able to explain why it is morally wrong to steal (or lie, cheat, rape, or murder), because it would be disastrous for everyone to be permitted to steal (or lie, cheat, rape, or murder) whenever (if ever) they wanted to.

Not quite. An agent is permitted or allowed in the relevant sense when she will not be liable to punishment, condemnation (by others), or feelings of guilt for carrying out the act. It is possible for someone to be permitted in this sense without knowing that she is permitted and, indeed, without anyone knowing that she is permitted. But it would not be disastrous for everyone to be permitted to steal if nobody knew that they were permitted to steal, since then they would still be deterred by fear of punishment, condemnation, or guilt. Similarly for lying, rape, and so on. So the general permission principle cannot quite explain why such acts are morally wrong.

Still, it would be disastrous if everyone knew that they were permitted to steal (or lie, rape, etc.). So we simply need to add one qualification:

The public permission principle: I have a moral obligation not to perform an act whenever it would be worse for everyone to know that everyone is permitted to perform an act of that kind.[26]

Now this principle seems to explain the moral wrongness of many of the acts we take to be morally wrong, since it would be disastrous if everyone knew that everyone was permitted to steal, lie, cheat, and so on.

Unfortunately, this revised principle runs into trouble in other cases. Imagine that 1,000 people want to take Flight 38 to Amsterdam on October 13, 2003, but the plane is not large enough to carry that many people. If all 1,000 took that particular flight, then it would crash. But these people are all stupid and stubborn enough that, if they knew that they were all allowed to take the flight, they all would pack themselves in, despite warnings, and the flight would crash. Luckily, this counterfactual does not reflect what actually happens. In the actual world, the airline is not stupid. Since the plane can safely carry only 300 people, the airline sells only 300 tickets and does not allow anyone on the flight without a ticket. If I have a ticket for that flight, then there is nothing morally wrong with me taking the flight along with the other 299 who have tickets. This shows that an act is not always morally wrong when it would (counterfactually) be disastrous for everyone to know that everyone is allowed to do it.[27]

The lesson of this example applies directly to my case of driving a gas-guzzler. Disaster occurs in the airplane case when too many people do what is harmless by itself. Similarly, disaster occurs when too many people burn too much fossil fuel. But that does not make it wrong in either case for one individual to perform an individual act that is harmless by itself. It only creates an obligation on the part of the government (or airline) to pass regulations to keep too many people from acting that way.

Another example brings out another weakness in the public permission principle. Consider open marriage. Max and Minnie get married because each loves the other and values the other person's love. Still, they think of sexual intercourse as a fun activity that they separate from love. After careful discussion before they got married, each happily agreed that each may have sex after marriage with whomever he or she wants. They value honesty, so they did add one condition: every sexual encounter must be reported to the other spouse. As long as they keep no secrets from each other and still love each other, they see no problem with their having sex with other people. They do not broadcast this feature of their marriage, but they do know (after years of experience) that it works for them.

Nonetheless, the society in which Max and Minnie live might be filled with people who are very different from them. If everyone knew that everyone is permitted to have sex during marriage with other people as long as the other spouse is informed and agreed to the arrangement, then various problems would arise. Merely asking a spouse whether he or she would be willing to enter into such an agreement would be enough to create suspicions and doubts in the other spouse's mind that would undermine many marriages or keep many couples from getting married, when they would have gotten or remained happily married if they had not been offered such an agreement. As a result, the society will have less love, fewer stable marriages, and more unhappy children of unnecessary divorce. Things would be much better if everyone believed that such agreements were not permitted in the first place, so they condemned them and felt guilty for even considering them. I think that this result is not unrealistic, but here I am merely postulating these facts in my example.

The point is that, even if other people are like this, so that it would be worse for everyone to know that everyone is permitted to have sex outside of marriage with spousal knowledge and consent, Max and Minnie are not like this, and they know that they are not like this, so it is hard to believe that they as individuals have a moral obligation to abide by a restriction that is justified by other people's dispositions. If Max and Minnie have a joint agreement that works for them, but they keep it secret from others, then there is nothing immoral about them having sex outside of their marriage (whether or not this counts as adultery). If this is correct, then the general permission principle fails again.

As before, the lesson of this example applies directly to my case of driving a gas-guzzler. The reason why Max and Minnie are not immoral is that they

have a right to their own private relationship as long as they do not harm others (such as by spreading disease or discord). But I have already argued that my driving a gas-guzzler on this Sunday afternoon does not cause harm. I seem to have a right to have fun in the way I want as long as I do not hurt anybody else, just like Max and Minnie. So the public permission principle cannot explain why it is morally wrong to drive a gas-guzzler for fun on this sunny Sunday afternoon.[28]

One final counterfactual approach is contractualism, whose most forceful recent proponent is Tim Scanlon.[29] Scanlon proposes:

The contractualist principle: I have a moral obligation not to perform an act whenever it violates a general rule that nobody could reasonably reject as a public rule for governing action in society.

Let us try to apply this principle to the case of Max and Minnie. Consider a general rule against adultery, that is, against voluntary sex between a married person and someone other than his or her spouse, even if the spouse knows and consents. It might seem that Max and Minnie could not reasonably reject this rule as a public social rule, because they want to avoid problems for their own society. If so, Scanlon's principle leads to the same questionable results as the public permission principle. If Scanlon replies that Max and Minnie "can" reasonably reject the anti-adultery rule, then why? The most plausible answer is that it is their own business how they have fun as long as they do not hurt anybody. But this answer is available also to people who drive gas-guzzlers just for fun. So this principle cannot explain why that act is morally wrong.

More generally, the test of what can be rejected "reasonably" depends on moral intuitions. Environmentalists might think it unreasonable to reject a principle that prohibits me from driving my gas-guzzler just for fun, but others will think it reasonable to reject such a principle, because it restricts my freedom to perform an act that harms nobody. The appeal to reasonable rejection itself begs the question in the absence of an account of why such rejection is unreasonable. Environmentalists might be able to specify reasons why it is unreasonable, but then it is those reasons that explain why this act is morally wrong. The framework of reasonable rejection becomes a distracting and unnecessary side step.[30]

7. WHAT IS LEFT?

We are left with no defensible principle to support the claim that I have a moral obligation not to drive a gas-guzzler just for fun. Does this result show that this claim is false? Not necessarily.

Some audiences[31] have suggested that my journey through various principles teaches us that we should not look for general moral principles to back up our moral intuitions. They see my arguments as a "reductio ad absurdum" of principlism, which is the view that moral obligations (or our beliefs in them) depend on principles. Principles are unavailable, so we should focus instead on particular cases, according to the opposing view called particularism.[32]

However, the fact that we cannot find any principle does not show that we do not need one. I already gave my reasons why we need a moral principle to back up our intuitions in this case. This case is controversial, emotional, peculiarly modern, and likely to be distorted by overgeneralization and partiality. These factors suggest that we need confirmation for our moral intuitions at least in this case, even if we do not need any confirmation in other cases.

For such reasons, we seem to need a moral principle, but we have none. This fact still does not show that such wasteful driving is not morally wrong. It only shows that we do not "know" whether it is morally wrong. Our ignorance might be temporary. If someone comes up with a defensible principle that does rule out wasteful driving, then I will be happy to listen and happy if it works. However, until some such principle is found, we cannot claim to know that it is morally wrong to drive a gas-guzzler just for fun.

The demand for a principle in this case does not lead to general moral skepticism. We still might know that acts and omissions that cause harm are morally

wrong because of the harm principle. Still, since that principle and others do not apply to my wasteful driving, and since moral intuitions are unreliable in cases like this, we cannot know that my wasteful driving is morally wrong.

This conclusion will still upset many environmentalists. They think that they know that wasteful driving is immoral. They want to be able to condemn those who drive gas-guzzlers just for fun on sunny Sunday afternoons.

My conclusion should not be so disappointing. Even if individuals have no such moral obligations, it is still morally better or morally ideal for individuals not to waste gas. We can and should praise those who save fuel. We can express our personal dislike for wasting gas and for people who do it. We might even be justified in publicly condemning wasteful driving and drivers who waste a lot, in circumstances where such public rebuke is appropriate. Perhaps people who drive wastefully should feel guilty for their acts and ashamed of themselves, at least if they perform such acts regularly; and we should bring up our children so that they will feel these emotions. All of these reactions are available even if we cannot truthfully say that such driving violates a moral "obligation." And these approaches might be more constructive in the long run than accusing someone of violating a moral obligation.

Moreover, even if individuals have no moral obligations not to waste gas by taking unnecessary Sunday drives just for fun, governments still have moral obligations to fight global warming, because they can make a difference. My fundamental point has been that global warming is such a large problem that it is not individuals who cause it or who need to fix it. Instead, governments need to fix it, and quickly. Finding and implementing a real solution is the task of governments. Environmentalists should focus their efforts on those who are not doing their job rather than on those who take Sunday afternoon drives just for fun.

This focus will also avoid a common mistake. Some environmentalists keep their hands clean by withdrawing into a simple life where they use very little fossil fuels. That is great. I encourage it. But some of these escapees then think that they have done their duty, so they rarely come down out of the hills to work for political candidates who could and would change government policies. This attitude helps nobody. We should not think that we can do enough simply by buying fuel-efficient cars, insulating our houses, and setting up a windmill to make our own electricity. That is all wonderful, but it does little or nothing to stop global warming, nor does this focus fulfill our real moral obligations, which are to get governments to do their job to prevent the disaster of excessive global warming. It is better to enjoy your Sunday driving while working to change the law so as to make it illegal for you to enjoy your Sunday driving.

NOTES

1. For skeptics, see Lomborg (1998, chapter 24) and Singer (1997). A more reliable partial skeptic is Richard S. Lindzen, but his papers are quite technical. If you do not share my bleak view of global warming, treat the rest of this essay as conditional. The issue of how individual moral obligations are related to collective moral obligations is interesting and important in its own right, even if my assumptions about global warming turn out to be inaccurate.

2. See the chapters by Mahlman, Schlesinger, and Weatherly in Sinnott-Armstrong and Howarth (eds.), *Perspectives on Climate Change.*

3. See the chapter by Shukla in Sinnott-Armstrong and Howarth (eds.), *Perspectives on Climate Change.*

4. See the chapter by Bodansky in Sinnott-Armstrong and Howarth (eds.), *Perspectives on Climate Change.*

5. See the chapter by Shuc in Sinnott-Armstrong and Howarth (eds.), *Perspectives on Climate Change.*

6. See the chapter by Jamieson in Sinnott-Armstrong and Howarth (eds.), *Perspectives on Climate Change.*

7. See the chapter by Toman in Sinnott-Armstrong and Howarth (eds.), *Perspectives on Climate Change.*

8. See the chapter by Driver in Sinnott-Armstrong and Howarth (eds.), *Perspectives on Climate Change.*

9. If I have an obligation to encourage the government to fulfill its obligation, then the government's obligation does impose some obligation on me. Still, I do not have an obligation to do what the government has an obligation to do. In short, I have no parallel moral obligation. That is what is at issue here.

10. I do not seem to have the same moral obligation to teach my neighbors' children when our government fails to teach them. Why not? The natural answer is that I have a special relation to my children that I do not have to their children. I also do not have such a special relation to future people who will be harmed by global warming.

11. See the chapter by Claussen in Sinnott-Armstrong and Howarth (eds.), *Perspectives on Climate Change.*

12. Indeed, I am worried about how my environmentalist friends will react to this essay, but I cannot let fear stop me from following where arguments lead.

13. For more on why moral intuitions need confirmation, see Sinnott-Armstrong (2005).

14. Another difference between these cases is that my failure to donate to famine relief is an inaction, whereas my driving is an action. As Bob Fogelin put it in conversation, one is a sin of omission, but the other is a sin of emission. But I assume that omissions can be causes. The real question is whether my measly emissions of greenhouse gases can be causes of global warming.

15. Cf. Parfit (1984, pp. 75–82).

16. If my act this Sunday does not cause me to drive next Sunday, then effects of my driving next Sunday are not consequences of my driving this Sunday. Some still might say that I can affect global warming by driving wastefully many times over the course of years. I doubt this, but I do not need to deny it. The fact that it is morally wrong for me to do all of a hundred acts together does not imply that it is morally wrong for me to do one of those hundred acts. Even if it would be morally wrong for me to pick all of the flowers in a park, it need not be morally wrong for me to pick one flower in that park.

17. The importance of risks in environmental ethics is a recurrent theme in the writings of Kristin Shrader-Frechette.

18. Kant (1785/1959, p. 400, n. 1).

19. *Ibid.*, 424. According to Kant, a weaker kind of contradiction in the will signals an imperfect duty. However, imperfect duties permit "exception in the interest of inclination" (421), so an imperfect obligation not to drive a gas-guzzler would permit me to drive it this Sunday when I am so inclined. Thus, I assume that a moral obligation not to drive a gas-guzzler for fun on a particular occasion would have to be a perfect obligation in Kant's view.

20. *Ibid.*, 429. I omit Kant's clause regarding treating others as ends because that clause captures imperfect duties, which are not my concern here (for reasons given in the preceding note).

21. Jamieson (n.d.).

22. Compare also standing up to see the athletes in a sporting event, when others do so. Such examples obviously involve much less harm than global warming. I use trivial examples to diminish emotional interference. The point is only that such examples share a structure that defenders of the group principle would claim to be sufficient for a moral obligation.

23. Parfit (1984, pp. 67–86) is famous for arguing that an individual act is immoral if it falls in a group of acts that collectively cause harm. To support his claim Parfit uses examples like the Harmless Torturers (p. 80). But torturers intend to cause harm. That's what makes them torturers. Hence, Parfit's cases cannot show anything wrong with wasteful driving, where there is no intention to cause any harm. For criticisms of Parfit's claims, see Jackson (1997).

24. Cf. Sinnott-Armstrong (2003) and Hooker (2003).

25. Cf. Singer (1971).

26. Cf. Gert (2005). Gert does add details that I will not discuss here. For a more complete response, see Sinnott-Armstrong (2002).

27. The point, of course, depends on how you describe the act. It would not be disastrous to allow everyone "with a ticket" to take the flight (as long as there are not too many tickets). What is disastrous is to allow everyone (without qualification) to take the flight. Still, that case shows that it is not always morally wrong to do X when it would be disastrous to allow everyone to do X. To solve these problems, we need to put some limits on the kinds of descriptions that can replace the variable X. But any limit needs to be justified, and it is not at all clear how to justify such limits without begging the question.

28. The examples in the text show why violating a justified public rule is not sufficient for private immorality. It is also not necessary, since it might not be disastrous if all parents were permitted to kill their children, if no parent ever wanted to kill his or her children. The failure of this approach to give a necessary condition is another reason to doubt that it captures the essence of morality.

29. Scanlon (1998).

30. Scanlon's framework still might be useful as a heuristic, for overcoming partiality, as a pedagogical tool, or as a vivid way to display coherence among moral intuitions at different levels. My point is that it cannot be used to justify moral judgments or to show what makes acts morally wrong. For more, see Sinnott-Armstrong (2006, chap. 8).

31. Such as Bill Pollard in Edinburgh.

32. Developed by Dancy (1993, 2004). For criticisms, see Sinnott-Armstrong (1999).

ACKNOWLEDGMENTS

For helpful comments, I would like to thank Kier Olsen DeVries, Julia Driver, Bob Fogelin, Bernard Gert, Rich Howarth, Bill Pollard, Mike Ridge, David Rodin, Peter Singer, and audiences at the University of Edinburgh, the International Society for Business, Economics, and Ethics, and the Center for Applied Philosophy and Public Ethics in Melbourne.

REFERENCES

Dancy, J. (1993). *Moral reasons.* Oxford: Blackwell.

Dancy. J. (2004). *Ethics without principles.* New York: Oxford University Press.

Gert, B. (2005). *Morality: Its nature and justification* (Revised ed.). New York: Oxford University Press.

Hooker, B. (2003). Rule consequentialism. In: *The Stanford Encyclopedia of Philosophy.* Available at: http://plato.stanford.edu/entrics/consequentialism-rule

Jackson, F. (1997). Which effects? In: J. Dancy (Ed.), *Reading Parfit* (pp. 42–53). Oxford: Blackwell.

Jamieson, D. (n.d.). When utilitarians should be virtue theorists. Unpublished manuscript.

Kant, I. (1959). *Foundations of the metaphysics of morals* (L. W. Beck, Trans.). Indianapolis. IN: Bobbs-Merrill. (Original work published in 1785).

Lomborg, B. (1998). *The skeptical environmentalist.* New York: Cambridge University Press.

Parfit, D. (1984). *Reasons and persons.* Oxford: Clarendon Press.

Scanlon, T. (1998). *What we owe to each other.* Cambridge, MA: Harvard University Press.

Singer, M. (1971). *Generalization in ethics.* New York: Atheneum.

Singer, S. F. (1997). *Hot talk, cold science.* Oakland, CA: The Independent Institute.

Sinnott-Armstrong, W. (1999). Some varieties of particularism. *Metaphilosophy, 30,* 1–12.

———. (2002). Gert contra consequentialism. In: W. Sinnott-Armstrong and R. Audi (Eds.), *Rationality, rules, and ideals: Critical essays on Bernard Gert's moral theory* (pp. 145–163). Lanham, MD: Rowman and Littlefield.

———. (2003). Consequentialism. In: *The Stanford Encyclopedia of Philosophy.* Available at: http://plato.stanford.edu/entries/consequentialism.

———. (2005). Moral intuitionism and empirical psychology. In: T. Horgan and M. Timmons (Eds.), *Metaethics after Moore* (pp. 339–365). New York: Oxford University Press.

———. (2006). *Moral skepticisms.* New York: Oxford University Press.

READING QUESTIONS

1. How does Sinnott-Armstrong argue that individual moral obligations do not always follow directly from collective moral obligations (e.g., obligations of the government)?
2. What is the harm principle, and how does Sinnott-Armstrong argue that it does not imply that he has a moral obligation not to drive his gas-guzzler just for fun? Why does he think the principle implies this only if his driving the gas-guzzler is both unusual and done with the intent to harm?
3. One of Sinnott-Armstrong's objections to the risk principle is that it is too restrictive, and one possible response to this objection involves distinguishing significant from insignificant risks. What is the risk principle, and what does Sinnott-Armstrong believe is wrong with this response to his objection?
4. How does Sinnott-Armstrong interpret Kant's means principle, and why does he think the principle cannot explain why he has no moral obligation not to drive his gas-guzzler just for fun?
5. In his discussion of the group principle, Sinnott-Armstrong presents a hypothetical case where the president sends everyone a $600 check. What is the group principle, and how is Sinnott-Armstrong's case supposed to show that the group principle fails?
6. What is the contractualist principle, and how does Sinnott-Armstrong use the case of Max and Minnie to show that the principle cannot explain why driving gas-guzzlers just for fun is wrong?
7. How does Sinnott-Armstrong argue that we cannot know whether driving gas-guzzlers just for fun is wrong unless we can provide a defensible general moral principle that implies that it is wrong?

DISCUSSION QUESTIONS

1. Is Sinnott-Armstrong right that the virtue principle "cannot be applied without begging the question"? How might one argue, without begging the question, that driving gas-guzzlers just for fun is contrary to virtue?
2. Sinnott-Armstrong suggests that there is no contradiction in claiming that (i) people who drive wastefully should feel guilty and ashamed for doing so and that (ii) there is no moral obligation not to drive wastefully. But how could it be the case that one *should* feel guilty and ashamed for doing something even when what one did violates no moral obligation?

BJØRN LOMBORG

Let's Keep Our Cool about Global Warming

Lomborg argues that the drastic reductions in CO_2 emissions that some have proposed as a way of curbing global warming are not politically realistic. Instead he advocates a balanced approach to the problem that involves economically feasible taxing of CO_2 emissions along with expenditures on the research and development of noncarbon emitting technologies.
Recommended Reading: consequentialism, chap. 1, sec. 2A.

There is a kind of choreographed screaming about climate change from both sides of the debate. Discussion would be on much firmer ground if we could actually hear the arguments and the facts and then sensibly debate long-term solutions.

Man-made climate change is certainly a problem, but it is categorically not the end of the world. Take the rise in sea levels as one example of how the volume of the screaming is unmatched by the facts. In its 2007 report, the United Nations estimates that sea levels will rise about a foot over the remainder of the century.[1] While this is not a trivial amount, it is also important to realize that it is not unknown to mankind: since 1860, we have experienced a sea level rise of about a foot without major disruptions.[2] It is also important to realize that the new prediction is lower than previous Intergovernmental Panel on Climate Change (IPCC) estimates and much lower than the expectations from the 1990s of more than two feet and the 1980s, when the Environmental Protection Agency projected more than six feet.[3]

We dealt with rising sea levels in the past century, and we will continue to do so in this century. It will be problematic, but it is incorrect to posit the rise as the end of civilization. We will actually lose very little dry land to the rise in sea levels. It is estimated that almost all nations in the world will establish maximal coastal protection almost everywhere, simply because doing so is fairly cheap. For more than 180 of the world's 192 nations, coastal protection will cost less than 0.1 percent GDP and approach 100 percent protection.[4]

The rise in sea level will be a much bigger problem for poor countries. The most affected nation will be Micronesia, a federation of 607 small islands in the West Pacific with a total land area only four times larger than Washington, D.C.[5] If nothing were done, Micronesia would lose some 21 percent of its area by the end of the century (Tol 2004, 5). With coastal protection, it will lose just 0.18 percent of its land area. However, if we instead opt for cuts in carbon emissions and thus reduce both the sea level rise and the economic growth, Micronesia will end up losing a larger land area. The increase in wealth for poor nations is more important than sea levels: poorer nations will be less able to defend themselves against rising waters, even if they rise more slowly. This is the same for other vulnerable nations: Tuvalu, the Maldives, Vietnam, and Bangladesh. The point is that we cannot just talk about CO_2 when we talk about climate change. The dialogue needs to include both considerations about carbon emissions and economics for the benefit of humans and the environment. Presumably, our goal is not just to cut carbon emissions, but to do the best we can for people and the environment.

We should take action on climate change, but we need to be realistic. The UK has arguably engaged in the most aggressive rhetoric about climate change. Since the Labour government promised in 1997 to cut emissions by a further 15 percent by 2010, emissions have *increased* 3 percent.[6] American emissions during the Clinton/Gore administration increased 28 percent. Look at our past behavior: at the Earth Summit in Rio in 1992, nations promised to cut emissions back to 1990 levels by 2000 (UNFCCC 1992, 4.2a). The member countries of the Organisation for Economic Cooperation and Development (OECD) overshot their target in 2000 by more than 12 percent.

Many believe that dramatic political action will follow if people only knew better and elected better politicians.[7] Despite the European Union's enthusiasm for the Kyoto Protocol on Climate Change—and a greater awareness and concern over global warming in Europe than in the United States—emissions per person since 1990 have remained stable in the U.S. while E.U. emissions have increased 4 percent (EIA 2006). Even if the wealthy nations managed to rein in their emissions, the majority of this century's emissions will come from developing countries—which are responsible for about 40 percent of annual carbon emissions; this is likely to increase to 75 percent by the end of the century.[8]

In a surprisingly candid statement from Tony Blair at the Clinton Global Initiative, he pointed out:

> I think if we are going to get action on this, we have got to start from the brutal honesty about the politics of how we deal with it. The truth is no country is going to cut its growth or consumption substantially in the light of a long-term environmental problem. What countries are prepared to do is to try to work together cooperatively to deal with this problem in a way that allows us to develop the science and technology in a beneficial way. (Clinton Global Initiative 2005, 15)

Similarly, one of the top economic researchers tells us: "Deep cuts in emissions will only be achieved if alternative energy technologies become available at reasonable prices" (Tol 2007, 430). We need to engage in a sensible debate about how to tax CO_2. If we set the tax too low, we emit too much. If we set it too high, we end up much poorer without doing enough to reduce warming.

In the largest review of all of the literature's 103 estimates, climate economist Richard Tol makes two important points. First, the really scary, high estimates typically have not been subjected to peer review and published. In his words: "studies with better methods yield lower estimates with smaller uncertainties." Second, with reasonable assumptions, the cost is very unlikely to be higher than $14 per ton of CO_2 and likely to be much smaller (Tol 2005).[9] When I specifically asked him for his best guess, he wasn't too enthusiastic about shedding his cautiousness—as few true researchers . . . are—but gave the estimate of $2 per ton of CO_2.[10]

Therefore, I believe that we should tax CO_2 at the economically feasible level of about $2/ton, or maximally $14/ton. Yet, let us not expect this will make any major difference. Such a tax would cut emissions by 5 percent and reduce temperatures by 0.16°F. And before we scoff at 5 percent, let us remember that the Kyoto Protocol, at the cost of 10 years of political and economic toil, will reduce emissions by just 0.4 percent by 2010.[11]

Neither a tax nor Kyoto nor draconian proposals for future cuts move us closer toward finding better options for the future. Research and development in renewable energy and energy efficiency is at its lowest for twenty-five years. Instead, we need to find a way that allows us to "develop the science and technology in a beneficial way," a way that enables us to provide alternative energy technologies at reasonable prices. It will take the better part of a century and will need a political will spanning parties, continents, and generations. We need to be in for the long haul and develop cost-effective strategies that won't splinter regardless of overarching ambitions or false directions.

This is why one of our generational challenges should be for *all nations to commit themselves to spending 0.05 percent of GDP in research and development of noncarbon emitting energy technologies*. This is a tenfold increase on current expenditures yet would cost a relatively minor $25 billion per year (seven times cheaper than Kyoto and many more times cheaper than Kyoto II). Such a commitment could include all nations, with wealthier nations paying the larger share, and would let each country focus on its own future vision of energy needs, whether that means concentrating on renewable sources, nuclear energy, fusion, carbon storage, conservation, or searching for new and more exotic opportunities.

Funding research and development globally would create a momentum that could recapture the vision of delivering both a low-carbon and high-income world. Lower energy costs and high spin-off innovation are potential benefits that possibly avoid ever stronger temptations to free-riding and the ever tougher negotiations over increasingly restrictive Kyoto Protocol-style treaties. A global financial commitment makes it plausible to envision stabilizing climate changes at reasonable levels.

I believe it would be the way to bridge a century of parties, continents, and generations, creating a sustainable, low-cost opportunity to create the alternative energy technologies that will power the future.

To move toward this goal we need to create sensible policy dialogue. This requires us to talk openly about priorities. Often there is strong sentiment in any public discussion that we should do *anything* required to make a situation better. But clearly we don't actually do that. When we talk about schools, we know that more teachers would likely provide our children with a better education.[12] Yet we do not hire more teachers simply because we also have to spend money in other areas. When we talk about hospitals, we know that access to better equipment is likely to provide better treatment, yet we don't supply an infinite amount of resources.[13] When we talk about the environment, we know tougher restrictions will mean better protection, but this also comes with higher costs.

Consider traffic fatalities, which are one of the ten leading causes of deaths in the world. In the U.S., 42,600 people die in traffic accidents and 2.8 million people are injured each year (USCB, 2006, 672). Globally, it is estimated that 1.2 million people die from traffic accidents and 50 million are injured every year (Lopez, Mathers, Ezzati, Jamison, and Murray 2006, 1751; WHO 2002, 72; 2004, 3, 172).

About 2 percent of all deaths in the world are traffic-related and about 90 percent of the traffic deaths occur in third world countries (WHO 2004, 172). The total cost is a phenomenal $512 billion

a year (WHO 2004, 5). Due to increasing traffic (especially in the third world) and due to ever better health conditions, the World Heath Organization estimates that by 2020, traffic fatalities will be the second leading cause of death in the world, after heart disease.[14]

Amazingly, we have the technology to make all of this go away. We could instantly save 1.2 million humans and eliminate $500 billion worth of damage. We would particularly help the third world. The answer is simply lowering speed limits to 5 mph. We could avoid almost all of the 50 million injuries each year. But of course we will not do this. Why? The simple answer that almost all of us would offer is that the benefits from driving moderately fast far outweigh the costs. While the cost is obvious in terms of those killed and maimed, the benefits are much more prosaic and dispersed but nonetheless important—traffic interconnects our society by bringing goods at competitive prices to where we live and bringing people together to where we work, and lets us live where we like while allowing us to visit and meet with many others. A world moving only at 5 mph is a world gone medieval.

This is not meant to be flippant. We really could solve one of the world's top problems if we wanted. We know traffic deaths are almost entirely caused by man. We have the technology to reduce deaths to zero. Yet we persist in exacerbating the problem each year, making traffic an ever-bigger killer.

I suggest that the comparison with global warming is insightful; we have the technology to reduce it to zero, yet we seem to persist in going ahead and exacerbating the problem each year, causing temperatures to continue to increase to new heights by 2020. Why? Because the benefits from moderately using fossil fuels far outweigh the costs. Yes, the costs are obvious in the "fear, terror, and disaster" we read about in the papers every day.

But the benefits of fossil fuels, though much more prosaic, are nonetheless important. Fossil fuels provide us with low-cost electricity, heat, food, communication, and travel.[15] Electrical air conditioning means that people in the U.S. no longer die in droves during heat waves (Davis, Knappenberger, Michaels, and Novicoff 2003). Cheaper fuels would have avoided a significant number of the 150,000 [deaths] in the UK since 2000 due to cold winters.[16]

Because of fossil fuels, food can be grown cheaply, giving us access to fruits and vegetables year round, which has probably reduced cancer rates by at least 25 percent.[17] Cars allow us to commute to city centers for work while living in areas that provide us with space and nature around our homes, whereas communication and cheap flights have given ever more people the opportunity to experience other cultures and forge friendships globally (Schäfer 2006).

In the third world, access to fossil fuels is crucial. About 1.6 billion people don't have access to electricity, which seriously impedes human development (IEA 2004, 338–40). Worldwide, about 2.5 billion people rely on biomass such as wood and waste (including dung) to cook and keep warm (IEA 2006, 419ff). For many Indian women, searching for wood takes about three hours each day, and sometimes they walk more than 10 kilometers a day. All of this causes excessive deforestation (IEA 2006, 428; Kammen 1995; Kelkar 2006). About 1.3 million people—mostly women and children—die each year due to heavy indoor air pollution. A switch from biomass to fossil fuels would dramatically improve 2.5 billion lives; the cost of $1.5 billion annually would be greatly superseded by benefits of about $90 billion.[18] Both for the developed and the developing world, a world without fossil fuels—in the short or medium term—is, again, a lot like reverting back to the middle ages.

This does not mean that we should not talk about how to reduce the impact of traffic and global warming. Most countries have strict regulation on speed limits—if they didn't, fatalities would be much higher. Yet, studies also show that lowering the average speed in Western Europe by just 5 kilometers per hour could reduce fatalities by 25 percent—with about 10,000 fewer people killed each year (WHO, 2002, 72; 2004, 172). Apparently, democracies in Europe are not willing to give up on the extra benefits from faster driving to save 10,000 people.

This is parallel to the debate we are having about global warming. We can realistically talk about $2 or even a $14 CO_2 tax. But suggesting a $140 tax, as Al Gore does, seems to be far outside the envelope.

Suggesting a 96 percent carbon reduction for the OECD by 2030 seems a bit like suggesting a 5 mph speed limit in the traffic debate. It is technically doable, but it is very unlikely to happen.

One of the most important issues when it comes to climate change is that we cool our dialogue and consider the arguments for and against different policies. In the heat of a loud and obnoxious debate, facts and reason lose out.

NOTES

1. (IPCC, 2007b:10.6.5). Notice that the available report (IPCC 2007a) has a midpoint of 38.5 cm.
2. Using (Jevrejeva, Grinsted, Moore, and Holgate 2006), 11.4 inches since 1860.
3. 1996: 38–35 cm (IPCC and Houghton 1996:364), 1992 and 1983 EPA from Yohe and Neumann 1997, 243; 250.
4. (Nicholls and Tol 2006, 1088), estimated for 2085. Notice low-lying undeveloped coasts in places such as Arctic Russia, Canada and Alaska are expected to be undefended. Notice that the numbers presented are for loss of dry land, whereas up to 18 percent of global wetlands will be lost.
5. "Micronesia" (CIA 2006).
6. Labour has urged a 20 percent CO_2 emission cut from 1990 in 2010 in three election manifestos (BBC Anon. 2006a); this translates into a 14.6 percent reduction from 1997 levels. From 1997 to 2004, CO_2 emissions increased 3.4 percent (EIA 2006).
7. Take, for instance, both Gore's "we have to find a way to communicate the direness of the situation" and Hansen's "scientists have not done a good job communicating with the public" (Fischer 2006).
8. Developing countries emitted 10.171 Gt of the global 26 Gt in 2004 (IEA, 2006, 513, 493) (OECD countries 51 percent in 2003 (OECD 2006, 148), Weyant estimates 29 percent from industrialized countries (1998, 2286), IPCC emission scenarios from 23 in the business-as-usual A1 to 36 percent (Nakicenovic and IPCC WG III 2000).
9. Based on a cost of $50 per ton of carbon (Tol 2005:2071).
10. From the Environmental Assessment Institute we asked him in July 2005: "Would you still stick by the conclusion that $15/tC seems justified or would you rather only present an upper limit of the estimate?" He answered: "I'd prefer not to present a central estimate, but if you put a gun to my head I would say $7/tC, the median estimate

with a 3 percent pure rate of time preference" ($7/tC = $1.9/tCO$_2$). This is comparable with Pearce's estimate of $1–2.5/tCO$_2$ ($4–9/tC) (2003:369).

11. There are many advantages to taxes over emission caps, mainly that with taxes, authorities have an interest in collecting them (because it funds the government), whereas with caps, individual countries have much less interest in achieving goals with such an effort, because the benefits are dispersed (global) and the damages localized (to local industries).

12. (Akerhielm 1995; Angrist and Lavy 1999; Graddy and Stevens 2005). Of course, this could be modified in many ways, such as by focusing on paying teachers better, more resources for books, computers, etc. It is also important that we should be saying "more teachers will at least not make schools worse and will likely make them better," as most studies show some or no effect from extra resources but very few show negative results.

13. E.g., (Fleitas et al. 2006; Gebhardt and Norris 2006). On the other hand, it is less clear that (after a certain limit) more doctors and bed space is the answer, since they may just make for more visits and increase the possibility of infections and harm (Weinberger, Oddone, and Henderson 1996; Wennberg et al. 2004).

14. (WHO 2002, 129) puts it second, whereas (WHO 2004, 5) puts it third.

15. This only looks at the marginal benefit of fossil fuels—which is the relevant one for our discussion. On a basic level, though, it is important to remember that they have fundamentally changed our lives. Before fossil fuels, we would spend hours gathering wood, contributing to deforestation and soil erosion—as billions in the third world still do today (Kammen 1995). We have electric washing machines that have cut domestic work dramatically. The historical economist Stanley Lebergott wrote only semi-jokingly: "From 1620 to 1920 the American washing machine was a housewife" (Lebergott 1993, 112). In 1900, a housewife spent seven hours a week laundering, carrying 200 gallons of water into the house and using a scrub board. Today, she spends 84 minutes with much less strain (Robinson and Godbey 1997, 327). We have a fridge that has both given us more spare time and allowed us to avoid rotten food and eat a more healthy diet of fruit and vegetables (Lebergott 1995, 155). By the end of the nineteenth century human labor made up 94 percent of all industrial work in the U.S. Today, it constitutes only 8 percent (Berry, Conkling, Ray, and Berry 1993, 131). If we think for a moment of the energy we use in terms of "servants," each with the same work power as a human being,

each person in Western Europe has access to 150 servants, in the U.S. about 300, and even in India each person has 15 servants to help (Craig, Vaughan, and Skinner 1996:103).

16. Steve Jones, "Help the Aged," said: "Many pensioners still agonize about whether or not to heat their homes in the cold weather. In the world's fourth richest country, this is simply shameful" (BBC Anon. 2006b).

17. The World Cancer Research Fund study estimates that increasing the intake of fruit and vegetables from an average of about 250 g/day to 400 g/day would reduce the overall frequency of cancer by around 23 percent (WCRF 1997:540).

18. Mainly from fewer deaths and less time use.

REFERENCES

Akerhielm, K. 1995. "Does class size matter?" *Economics of Education Review* 14(3), 229–41.

Angrist, J. D., and V. Lavy. 1999. "Using Maimonides' rule to estimate the effect of class size on scholastic achievement." *Quarterly Journal of Economics* 114(2), 533–75.

BBC Anon. 2006a, March 28. UK to miss CO$_2$ emissions target. BBC. Available at http://news.bbc.co.uk/2/hi/science/nature/4849672.stm. Accessed January 29, 2007.

———. 2006b, October 27. "Winter death toll" drops by 19%: Deaths in England and Wales fell to 25,700 last winter, a decline of 19% on the previous year. BBC Web site. Available at http://news.bbc.co.uk/2/hi/uk_news/6090492.stm. Accessed November 13, 2006.

Berry, B. J. L., E. C. Conkling, and D. M. Ray. 1993. *The Global Economy: Resource Use, Locational Choice, and International Trade.* Englewood Cliffs, N.J.: Prentice Hall.

CIA. 2006. *CIA World Fact Book.* Central Intelligence Agency, December 12.

Clinton Global Initiative. 2005, September 15. Special Opening Plenary Session: Perspectives on the Global Challenges of Our Time. Available at http://attend.clintonglobalinitiative.org/pdf/transcripts/plenary/cgi_09_15_05_plenary_1.pdf. Accessed January 29, 2007.

Craig, J. R., D. J. Vaughan, and B. J. Skinner. 1996. *Resources of the Earth: Origin, Use and Environmental Impact.* Upper Saddle River, N.J.: Prentice Hall.

Davis, R. E., P. C. Knappenberger, P. J. Michaels, and W. M. Novicoff. 2003. "Changing heat-related mortality in the United States." *Environmental Health Perspectives* 111(14), 1712–18.

EIA. 2006. International Energy Annual 2004. Energy Information Agency. Available at http://www.eia.doe.gov/iea/. Accessed November 30, 2006.

Fischer, D. 2006, December 15. Gore urges scientists to speak up. *Contra Costa Times*. Available at http://www.truthout.org/cgi-bin/artman/exec/view.cgi/67/24524. Accessed January 29, 2007.

Fleitas, I., et al. 2006. The quality of radiology services in five Latin American countries. *Revista Panamericana de Salud Publica-Pan American. Journal of Public Health* 20(2–3), 113–24.

Gebhardt, J. G., and T. E. Norris 2006. Acute stroke care at rural hospitals in Idaho: Challenges in expediting stroke care. *Journal of Rural Health* 22, 88–91.

Graddy, K., and M. Stevens. 2005. The impact of school resources on student performance: A study of private schools in the United Kingdom. *Industrial & Labor Relations Review* 58(3), 435–51.

IEA. 2004. World Energy Outlook 2004: IEA Publications.

———. 2006. World Energy Outlook 2006: IEA Publications.

IPCC. 2007a. Climate Change 2007: WGI: Summary for Policymakers.

———. 2007b. Climate Change 2007: WGI: The Physical Science Basis. Cambridge (UK): Cambridge University Press.

IPCC and J. T. Houghton. 1996. Climate Change 1995: The Science of Climate Change. Cambridge and New York: Cambridge University Press.

Jevrejeva, S., A. Grinsted, J. C. Moore, and S. Holgate. 2006. Nonlinear trends and multiyear cycles in sea level records. *Journal of Geophysical Research-Oceans* 111(C9).

Kammen, D. M. 1995. Cookstoves for the Developing-World. *Scientific American* 273(1), 72–75.

Kelkar, G. 2006, May 8. The Gender Face of Energy. Presentation at CSD 14 Learning Centre, United Nations. Available at http://www.un.org/esa/sustdev/csd/csd14/lc/presentation/gender2.pdf. Accessed January 30, 2007.

Lebergott, S. 1993. Pursuing Happiness: American Consumers in the Twentieth Century. Princeton, N.J.: Princeton University Press.

———. 1995. Long-term trends in the US standard of living. In J. Simon (Ed.), State of Humanity (pp. 149–60). Oxford: Blackwell.

Lopez, A. D., C. D. Mathers, M. Ezzati, D. T. Jamison, and C. J. L. Murray. 2006. Global and regional burden of disease and risk factors, 2001: systematic analysis of population health data. *Lancet* 367(9524), 1747–57.

Nakicenovic, N., and IPCC WG III. 2000. Special Report on Emissions Scenarios: A Special Report of Working Group III of the Intergovernmental Panel on Climate Change. Cambridge and New York: Cambridge University Press.

Nicholls, R. J., and R. S. J. Tol. 2006. "Impacts and responses to sea-level rise: a global analysis of the SRES scenarios over the twenty-first century." *Philosophical Transactions of the Royal Society A—Mathematical Physical and Engineering Sciences* 364(1841), 1073–95.

OECD. 2006. *OECD Factbook* 2006 (p. v.). Paris: Organization for Economic Co-operation and Development.

Pearce, D. 2003. "The social cost of carbon and its policy implications." *Oxford Review of Economic Policy* 19(3), 362–84.

Robinson, J. P., and G. Godbey. 1997. *Time for Life: The Surprising Ways Americans Use Their Time.* University Park, PA.: Pennsylvania State University Press.

Schäfer, A. 2006. "Long-term trends in global passenger mobility." *Bridge* 36(4), 24–32.

Tol, R. S. J. 2004. The double trade-off between adaptation and mitigation for sea level rise: an application of FUND. Hamburg University and Centre for Marine and Atmospheric Science, Hamburg.

———. 2005. "The marginal damage costs of carbon dioxide emissions: An assessment of the uncertainties." *Energy Policy* 33(16), 2064–74.

———. 2007. "Europe's long-term climate target: A critical evaluation." *Energy Policy* 35(1), 424–32.

UNFCCC. 1992. United Nations Framework Convention on Climate Change.

USCB. 2006. Statistical Abstract of the United States: 2007. U.S. Census Bureau. Available at http://www.census.gov/prod/www/statistical-abstract.html. Accessed January 30, 2007.

WCRF. 1997. *Food, Nutrition and the Prevention of Cancer: A Global Perspective.* Washington, D.C.: World Cancer Research Fund & American Institute for Cancer Research.

Weinberger, M., E. Z. Oddone, and W. G. Henderson. 1996. "Does increased access to primary care reduce hospital readmissions?" *New England Journal of Medicine* 334(22), 1441–47.

Wennberg, J. E., et al. 2004. "Use of hospitals, physician visits, and hospice care during last six months of life among cohorts loyal to highly respected hospitals in the United States." *British Medical Journal* 328(7440), 607–610A.

WHO. 2002. The world health report 2002—reducing risk, promoting healthy life. World Health Organization.

———. 2004. World report on road traffic injury prevention: World Health Organization.

Wigley, T. M. L. 1998. "The Kyoto Protocol: CO_2, CH_4 and climate implications." *Geophysical Research Letters* 25(13), 2285–88.

Yohe, G., and J. Neumann. 1997. "Planning for sea level rise and shore protection under climate uncertainty." *Climatic Change* 37, 243–70.

READING QUESTIONS

1. How will climate change affect the poorest countries like Micronesia? How will it affect the richest countries? Where should our focus be regarding climate change according to Lomborg?
2. Why does Lomborg think we need to be more realistic about climate change? How have current governments failed with respect to their past promises to reduce emissions?
3. What two points does Lomborg raise for the statistical research that has been done so far on the costs of reducing CO_2 emissions? What should the goal of each nation be according to Lomborg? How does he think the nations of the world can achieve this goal?
4. Explain the traffic analogy considered by Lomborg. How does this case illustrate why it is unlikely that the nations and people of the world will be able to meet the reduced emissions goals set by Al Gore?

DISCUSSION QUESTIONS

1. Lomborg claims that climate change is not the end of the world but that it will be bad for some people. How realistic is this claim? What reasons could be offered in support of the view that climate change does pose a significant threat to the majority of people in the world?
2. Lomborg suggests that we need to consider arguments for and against different policies in order to combat the effects of climate change successfully. Is he right to suggest that the nations of the world are not currently engaged in this type of project? Why or why not? Are there any sorts of policies that deserve more consideration than others? What kinds of policies should be rejected?

ADDITIONAL RESOURCES

Web Resources

Global Issues, <www.globalissues.org/>. Site featuring many articles on global ethical issues (most of them written by the site's creator, Anup Shah).

The World Watch Institute, <www.worldwatch.org>. Features independent research on the environment and its protection.

Wikipedia, <http://en.wikipedia.org/wiki/Main Page>. Contains useful entries on global warming and on the International Panel of Climate Change (IPCC).

Brennan, Andrew and Yeuk-Sze Lo, "Environmental Ethics," *Stanford Encyclopedia of Philosophy*, <http://plato.stanford.edu/entries/ethics-environmental/>. An overview of the topic including a discussion of traditional ethical theories and environmental ethics.

Authored Books and Articles

Attfield, Robin, *Environmental Ethics: An Overview for the Twenty-First Century* (Cambridge: Polity Press, 2003). An introduction to environmental ethics that usefully surveys major positions and defends what the author calls "biocentric consequentialism."

Brown, Donald, *Climate Change Ethics: Navigating the Perfect Storm* (London: Routledge, 2012). The author examines why ethical principles have not had much effect on policy formation and makes proposals for ensuring that climate change policies do respond to ethical concerns.

Gardiner, Stephen M., "Ethics and Global Climate Change," *Ethics* 114 (2004): 555–600. A critical evaluation of the arguments by Lomborg and other like-minded skeptics.

Gore, Al, *An Inconvenient Truth* (Emmaus, PA: Rodale Books, 2006). Former U.S. vice president's book version of his documentary film of the same name about the dangers of global warming.

Houghton, John, *Global Warming: The Complete Briefing*, 4th ed. (Cambridge: Cambridge University Press, 2009). An undergraduate textbook that provides a comprehensive scientific guide to global warming.

Lomborg, Bjørn, *Cool It: The Skeptical Environmentalist's Guide to Global Warming* (New York: Random House, 2007, reprinted: Vintage, 2008). An overview by an economist and statistician of the problems produced by global warming and how best to address them. This book and Lomborg's previous books on global warming have stirred much controversy.

Anthologies

Hayward, Tim and Carol Gould (eds.), *The Journal of Social Philosophy* 40 (2009), special issue: The Global Environment, Climate Change, and Justice. Eight articles exploring ethical and political implications of global climate change, including issues of intra- and intergenerational justice.

Jamieson, Dale (ed.), *A Companion to Environmental Philosophy* (Oxford: Blackwell Publishing, 2003). Contains thirty-six articles written for this volume, which covers a wide variety of cultural, legal, political, and ethical issues relating to the environment.

Kaufman, Frederick, A. (ed.), *Foundations of Environmental Philosophy* (New York: McGraw-Hill, 2003). Combines text written for students with selected readings covering a wide range of topics, including biocentrism, ecocentric ethics, anthropomorphism, deep ecology, and ecofeminism.

Light, Andrew and Rolston Holmes III (eds.), *Environmental Ethics: An Anthology* (London: Blackwell, 2002). Classical and contemporary selections covering a wide range of topics organized into six parts: (1) What Is Environmental Ethics?, (2) Who Counts in Environmental Ethics?, (3) Is Nature Intrinsically Valuable?, (4) Is There One Environmental Ethics?, (5) Focusing on General Issues, and (6) What on Earth Do We Want? Human Social Issues and Environmental Values.

Pojman, Louis P., *Environmental Ethics: Readings in Theory and Application,* 4th ed. (Belmont, CA: Wadsworth, 2004). A collection of eighty-two articles debating most every aspect of ethical concern for the environment including new articles for this edition on ecorealism, world hunger, population, and city life.

Sandler, Ronald and Philip Cafaro (eds.), *Environmental Virtue Ethics* (Lanham, MD: Rowman & Littlefield, 2005). Thirteen essays organized into four parts: (1) Recognizing Environmental Virtue Ethics, (2) Environmental Virtue Ethics Theory, (3) Environmental Virtues and Vices, and (4) Applying Environmental Virtue Ethics.

Schmidtz, David and Elizabeth Willott (eds.), *Environmental Ethics: What Really Matters, What Really Works* (New York: Oxford University Press, 2001). This comprehensive anthology features sixty-two selections organized into two major parts: (1) What Really Matters: Essays on Value in Nature, and (2) What Really Works: Essays on Human Ecology.

GLOSSARY

Each entry in the glossary indicates the chapter and section in which the term is first introduced and, in some cases, additional places where the term occurs. Cross-references are in italics.

Abolitionist   Someone who is opposed to the death penalty and advocates its abolition. (chap. 12, intro.)

Abortion   Cases in which a pregnancy is intentionally interrupted and involves (as part of the process or aim of interruption) the intentional killing of the fetus. (chap. 10, sec. 2)

Acceptance value   The value of the consequences that would likely be brought about through the acceptance of some rule. (chap. 10, sec. 7) See *rule consequentialism*. (chap. 1, sec. 2; chap. 13, sec. 4)

Act consequentialism   Any version of *consequentialism* according to which it is the net intrinsic value of the consequences of particular alternative actions open to an agent in some situation that determines the rightness or wrongness of those alternative actions. See *rule consequentialism*. (chap. 1, sec. 2A)

Active euthanasia   Cases of euthanasia in which one party actively intervenes to bring about the death of another. See *euthanasia, passive euthanasia*. (chap. 8, sec. 1)

Addiction   A type of compulsive behavior involving dependence on some substance or activity that is undesirable. It is common to distinguish between physical and psychological addiction. (chap. 5, sec. 2)

Adult stem cell   Stem cell of a fully formed individual. See *stem cell*. (chap. 11, sec. 1)

Adultery   The act of voluntary sexual intercourse between a married person and someone other than his or her legal spouse. (chap. 3, sec. 3)

Anthropocentrism   The view that the only beings who possess *direct moral standing* are human beings. All other beings (living and nonliving) are of mere indirect moral concern. (chap. 15, sec. 2)

Anticosmopolitanism   The denial of cosmopolitanism. See *cosmopolitanism*. (chap. 7, sec. 2)

Antiwar pacifism   The view that wars are always or nearly always morally wrong. (chap. 13, sec. 4)

Assisted suicide   A suicide in which another party helps an individual commit suicide by providing either the information or the means, or by directly helping the person who commits the act. See *suicide*. (chap. 8, sec. 2)

Atomism   The view according to which the primary items of moral appraisal are individuals—it is only individuals that can be properly judged as intrinsically valuable, or rights holders, or as having obligations. (chap. 15, sec. 2)

Basic right   Any right of particular importance within the realm of rights. So, for instance, the right to life is a basic right. (chap. 1, sec. 2D)

Beneficence, duty of   The duty to help those in dire need. (chap. 14, intro. and sec. 1)

Biocentrism   The view that all living beings, because they are living, possess *direct moral standing*. Thus, morality includes requirements of direct moral concern for all living beings. (chap. 15, sec. 2)

Categorical imperative   The fundamental moral principle in the moral theory of Immanuel Kant. As this principle is employed in reasoning about moral issues, it takes two forms: the *Universal Law* and the *Humanity* formulations. (chap. 1, sec. 2C)

Civil unions   A legal category that grants some rights to same-sex couples. (chap. 3, sec. 3)

Clone   An individual that comes about as a result of cloning. Also referred to as an *SCNT individual*. (chap. 11, sec. 1)

Cloning   The process of "asexually" producing a biological organism that is virtually genetically identical to another organism. (chap. 11, sec. 1)

Cold war   A conflict over ideological differences carried on by methods short of sustained overt military action and usually without breaking off diplomatic relations. (chap 13, sec. 1)

Consequentialism (C)   A type of moral theory according to which the rightness and wrongness of actions is to be explained entirely in terms of the intrinsic value of the consequences associated with either individual concrete actions or rules associated with actions. See *act consequentialism, rule consequentialism, intrinsic value, utilitarianism, perfectionist consequentialism*. (chap. 1, sec. 2A)

Consequentialist theory of punishment   A theory of punishment according to which (C1) punishment as a response to crime is morally justified if and only if this practice, compared to any other response to crime, will likely produce as much overall intrinsic value as would any other response, and (C2) a specific punishment for a certain crime is morally justified if and only if it would likely produce at least as much overall intrinsic value as would any other alternative punishment. See *retributive theory of punishment*. (chap 12, sec. 2)

Conservatism   A political ideology that maintains that it is proper for a government to advocate and sometimes enforce a particular conception of the good life. This ideology tends to attach great importance to various cultural traditions, in contrast to Liberal ideology. See *Liberalism*. (chap. 4, sec. 2)

Conservative position on some issue   A moral position on some issue which, in contrast to moderate and liberal positions, is restrictive in what it holds to be morally permissible behavior with regard to the issue. For example, with regard to issues of sexual morality, a typical conservative position holds that sexual intercourse is morally wrong except between married couples of the opposite sex. (chap. 3, sec. 1; chap. 10, sec. 5) See *liberal position, moderate position.* (chap. 10, sec. 5)

Cosmopolitanism   The idea that all human beings, regardless of political affiliation, are part of a single human community, which should be cultivated. (chap. 7, sec. 2)

Deterrence   Someone is deterred from committing murder by the threat of the death penalty only if his recognition of the death penalty as a possible consequence of committing murder explains why he does not commit it. (chap. 12, sec. 2)

Direct moral standing   For something to have direct moral standing is for it to possess features in virtue of which it deserves to be given moral consideration by agents who are capable of making moral choice. See *indirect moral standing.* (chap. 9, sec. 1; chap. 10, sec. 3; chap. 15, sec. 1)

Doctrine of double effect (DDE)   This doctrine is composed of a set of provisions under which it is morally permissible to knowingly bring about evil in the pursuit of the good. DDE is associated with *natural law theory.* (chap. 1, sec. 2B; chap. 13, sec. 4)

DOMA   An abbreviation for the 1997 U.S. Defense of Marriage Act which, for purposes of U.S. Federal law, defines "marriage" as a legal union between one man and one woman. (chap. 3, sec. 3)

Domestic partnerships   A legal category comprising unmarried couples, including same-sex couples, to whom some rights are granted. (chap. 3, sec. 3)

Drug   Any chemical substance that affects the functioning of living organisms. See also *psychotropic drug.* (chap. 5, sec. 1)

Drug abuse   Excessive nonmedical use of a drug that may cause harm to oneself or to others. (chap. 5, sec. 2)

Drug criminalization/decriminalization The former refers to having legal penalties for the use and possession of small quantities of drugs; the latter refers to not having such legal penalties. (chap. 5, sec. 4)

Drug prohibition/legalization The former refers to having legal penalties for the manufacture, sale, and distribution of large quantities of drugs; the latter refers to lack of such penalties. (chap. 5, sec. 4)

Duty-based moral theory   Any moral theory that takes the concept of duty to be basic and so characterizes or defines right action independently of considerations of intrinsic value and independently of considerations of moral rights. Examples include the ethics of prima facie duty and Kantian moral theory. Duty-based moral theories contrast with *value-based moral theories* and with *rights-based moral theories.* (chap. 1, sec.1)

Ecocentrism   The view according to which the primary bearers of *direct moral standing* are ecosystems in virtue of their functional integrity. Hence, morality involves moral obligations to maintain the functional integrity of ecosystems, and because, according to this view, ecosystems are primary bearers of direct moral standing, their preservation takes moral precedence over concern for individual things and creatures that compose the system. See *ecosystem, ecoholism.* (chap. 15, sec. 2)

Ecoholism   The view that both ecosystems and at least some individual items that make up an ecosystem have direct moral standing. (chap. 15, sec. 2)

Ecosystem   A whole composed of both living and nonliving things including animals, plants, bodies of water, sunlight, and other environmental factors. See *ecocentrism*. (chap. 15, sec. 2)

Embryo   The term used to refer to a stage in prenatal development which in humans begins at roughly the second week of pregnancy and lasts until roughly the eighth week. See *zygote, fetus*. (chap. 10, sec. 1; chap. 11, sec. 1)

Embryonic stem cell   Stem cells found in an embryo. See *stem cell*. (chap. 11, sec. 1)

Environmenal ethics   The view that (1) there are nonhuman beings that have direct moral standing, and (2) the class of such beings is larger than the class of conscious beings. (chap. 15, sec. 3)

Erotica   The depiction of erotic behavior (as in pictures or writing) intended to cause sexual excitement, but that either does not describe or portray sexual behavior that is degrading or does not endorse such degrading behavior. See *pornography*. (chap. 4, sec. 1)

Ethics of prima facie duty   A moral theory, originally developed by W. D. Ross, that features a plurality of moral principles that express *prima facie duties*. (chap. 1, sec. 2F)

Eugenics, human   The aim of improving the human race through genetic manipulation. (chap. 11, sec. 3)

Euthanasia   The act or practice of killing or allowing someone to die on grounds of mercy. (chap. 8, sec. 1)

Explanatory power, principle of   A principle for evaluating how well a moral theory does at satisfying the *theoretical aim* of such theories. According to this principle, a moral theory should feature principles that explain our more specific considered moral beliefs, thus helping us to understand why actions and other items of evaluation have the moral status they have. See *theoretical aim*. (chap. 1, sec. 3)

Extrinsic value   Something has extrinsic value when its value (good or bad) depends on how it is related to something having *intrinsic value*. (chap. 1, sec. 1)

Fetus   Used in a strict biological sense, a fetus is an unborn vertebrate animal that has developed to the point of having the basic structure that is characteristic of its kind. This stage is characterized by growth and full development of its organs. Also spelled "foetus." See *zygote, embryo*. (chap. 10, sec. 1)

Genetic enhancement   The process of manipulating genetic material in order to enhance the talents and capacities of living creatures. See *cloning*. (chap. 11, sec. 3)

Golden rule   Do unto others as you would have them do unto you. (chap. 1, sec. 2C)

Harm principle   A liberty-limiting principle according to which a government may justifiably pass laws to limit the liberty of its citizens in order to prohibit individuals from causing harm to other individuals or to society. See *liberty-limiting* principle. (chap. 4, sec. 2; chap. 5, sec. 3)

Hate speech   Language (oral or written) that expresses strong hatred, contempt, or intolerance for some social group, particularly social groups classified according to race, ethnicity, gender, sexual orientation, religion, disability, or nationality. (chap. 4, sec. 4)

Hedonistic utilitarianism (HU)   A version of *utilitarianism* featuring a hedonistic theory of intrinsic value. See *value hedonism.* (chap. 1, sec. 2A)

Holism   The view that wholes or collectives are bearers of value, or of rights, or of obligations. (chap. 15, sec. 2)

Homosexuality   Sexual activity, particularly intercourse, between members of the same sex. (chap. 3, sec. 3)

Hot war   A conflict involving actual fighting. (chap. 13, sec. 1)

Humanity formulation   A particular formulation of Kant's categorical imperative according to which an action is morally permissible if and only if (and because) the action treats humanity (whether in oneself or others) never as a mere means but as an end in itself. (chap. 1, sec. 2C)

Human rights   Moral rights that are universally shared by all human beings, including rights to life, liberty, and well-being. (chap. 1, sec. 2D).

In vitro fertilization (IVF)   The process through which a sperm fertilizes an egg outside a woman's body and is later implanted in a woman's uterus. (chap. 11, intro.)

Indirect moral standing   For something to have indirect moral standing is for it to deserve moral consideration only because it is related to something with direct moral standing. See *direct moral standing.* (chap. 9, sec. 1; chap. 10, sec. 3; chap. 15, sec. 1)

Induced pluripotent stem cells (iPSC)   Adult stem cells that have been genetically reprogrammed so as to have the capacity to develop into cells of most any type. (chap. 11, notes)

Interrogational torture   Torture whose aim is to gain information from the victim. See *torture.* (chap. 13, sec. 3)

Intrinsic value   To say that something has intrinsic positive value—that it is intrinsically good—is to say that its goodness is grounded in features that are inherent in that thing. Similarly for intrinsic negative value. See *extrinsic value.* (chap. 1, sec. 1)

Involuntary euthanasia   Euthanasia in which the individual has expressed a desire not to be the subject of euthanasia, but others act in violation of that desire, that is, *against* the individual's consent. See *euthanasia, voluntary euthanasia, nonvoluntary euthanasia.* (chap. 8, sec. 1)

Jus in bello   That part of *just-war theory* that sets forth moral requirements for military activities within a war. (chap. 13, sec. 4)

Jus ad bellum   That part of *just-war theory* that sets forth moral requirements for going to war. (chap. 13, sec. 4)

Just-war theory   A moral theory about the conditions under which a government is morally justified in going to war (*jus ad bellum*) and what military activities are morally permissible within a war (*jus in bello*). (chap. 13, sec. 4)

Just-war pacifism   The moral view that all or nearly all wars fail to meet the demands of just-war theory and are therefore morally wrong. (chap. 13, sec. 4)

Kantian moral theory   A type of moral theory first developed by German philosopher Immanuel Kant (1724–1804) that features the notions of respect for persons and universality. These two guiding ideas are expressed in Kant's *Humanity formulation* of his fundamental moral principle—*the categorical imperative*—and in the *Universal Law formulation,* respectively. (chap 1, sec. 2C)

Legal moralism principle   A liberty-limiting principle according to which a government may justifiably pass laws to limit the liberty of its citizens in order to protect common moral standards, independently of whether the activities in question are harmful to others or to oneself. See *liberty-limiting principle.* (chap. 4, sec. 2; chap. 5, sec. 3)

Legal paternalism principle   A liberty-limiting principle according to which a government may justifiably pass laws to limit the liberty of its citizens in order to prohibit individuals from causing harm to themselves. See *liberty-limiting principle.* (chap. 4, sec. 2; chap. 5, sec. 3)

Legal punishment   Punishment administered by a legal authority. (chap. 12, sec. 1)

Legal rights   Rights that result or come into existence as the result of the activities of a legal statute or some other form governmental activity. To be contrasted with *moral rights.* (chap. 1, sec. 2D)

Lex talionis (law of retribution)   A principle of punishment for specific offenses according to which the appropriate punishment for a crime involves doing to the wrongdoer the same kind of action that he or she did to his or her victim(s). See *retributive theory of punishment.* (chap. 12, sec. 2)

Liberal position on some issue   A moral position on some issue which, in contrast to conservative and moderate positions, is not as restrictive in what it holds to be morally permissible behavior with regard to the issue. For example, on issues of sexual morality, a typical liberal position holds that sexual intercourse is morally permissible so long as those involved do not violate any general moral rules such as rules against deception and coercion. See *conservative position, moderate position.* (chap. 3, sec. 1; chap. 10, sec. 5)

Liberalism   A political ideology that puts strong emphasis on liberty and equality of individuals, maintaining in particular that proper respect for the liberty and equality of individuals requires that governments remain as neutral as possible over conceptions of the good life. See *conservatism.* (chap. 4, sec. 2)

Liberty-limiting principle   A principle that purports to set forth conditions under which a government may be morally justified in passing laws that limit the liberty of its citizens. (chap. 4, sec. 2; chap. 5, sec. 3)

Moderate position on some issue   A moral position on some issue which is less restrictive than a conservative position and more restrictive than a liberal position. For example, with regard to issues of sexual morality, a typical moderate, in contrast to a typical conservative, will hold that marriage is not a necessary condition for morally permissible sexual intercourse. In contrast to a typical liberal, a moderate will hold that there are such requirements as being committed to a relationship with one's sexual partner that must be observed in order for sexual intercourse to be morally permissible. See *conservative position, liberal position.* (chap. 3, sec. 1; chap. 10, sec. 5)

Moral criteria   Features of an action or other item of evaluation in virtue of which the action or item is morally right or wrong, good or bad. Moral criteria for an action's rightness or wrongness are often expressed in *principles of right conduct,* while criteria for something's being intrinsically good or bad are often expressed in *principles of value.* (chap. 1, sec. 1)

Moral judgment   An acquired skill at discerning what matters the most morally speaking and coming to an all-things-considered moral verdict, where this skill cannot be entirely captured by a set of rules. (chap. 1, secs. 2D and 2F)

Moral nihilism (regarding war)   The view that morality does not apply to war. (chap. 13, sec. 4)

Moral principle   A general statement that purports to set forth conditions under which an action or other item of evaluation is right or wrong, good or bad, virtuous or vicious. (chap. 1, sec. 1)

Moral rights   Rights that an individual or group has independently of any legal system or other conventions. Such rights have also been called "natural rights." To be contrasted with *legal rights*. (chap. 1, sec. 2D)

Moral standing   See *direct moral standing, indirect moral standing*.

Moral theory   An attempt to provide well-argued-for answers to general moral questions about the nature of right action and value. Typically, answers to such questions are expressed as *moral principles*. See *theory of right conduct, theory of value*. (chap. 1, intro. and sec. 1)

Natural law theory   A type of nonconsequentialist moral theory that attempts to ground morality on objective facts about human nature. See *doctrine of double effect, consequentialism*. (chap. 1, sec. 2B)

Natural right   See *moral right*. (chap. 1, sec. 2D)

Negative right   A right corresponding to a negative duty on the part of rights addressees to refrain from certain actions that would violate the right in question. For instance, the right to free speech is a negative right demanding that others not interfere with one's attempt to express oneself in speech. (chap. 1, sec. 2D)

Nonvoluntary euthanasia   Euthanasia in which the individual has not given his consent to be subject to euthanasia because he has not expressed a view about what others may do in case, for example, he goes into a persistent vegetative state. See *euthanasia, voluntary euthanasia, involuntary euthanasia*. (chap. 8, sec. 1)

Offense principle   A liberty-limiting principle according to which a government may justifiably pass laws to limit the liberty of its citizens in order to prohibit individuals from offending others. See *liberty-limiting principle*. (chap. 4, sec. 2; chap. 5, sec. 3)

Oocyte   An unfertilized egg whose fertilization results in a *zygote*. (chap. 11, sec. 1)

Pacifism (regarding war)   See *antiwar pacifism*.

Passive euthanasia   Euthanasia in which the death of the individual in question resulted from (or was hastened by) withholding or withdrawing some form of treatment which, had it been administered, would likely have prolonged the life of that individual. See *euthanasia, active euthanasia*. (chap. 8, sec. 1)

Perfectionist consequentialism   A version of *consequentialism* that accepts a perfectionist theory of value. See *value perfectionism*. (chap. 1, sec. 2A)

Pornography   The depiction of erotic behavior (as in pictures or writing) intended to cause sexual excitement. See *erotica*. (chap. 4, sec. 1)

Positive right   A right corresponding to a positive duty on the part of rights addressees to perform certain actions called for by the right in question. For instance, the right to an education corresponds to an obligation, presumably of a state, to engage in certain activities to help ensure that its citizens receive (or have the opportunity to receive) an education. (chap. 1, sec. 2D)

Practical aim (of a moral theory)   To offer *practical guidance* for how we might arrive at correct or justified moral verdicts about matters of moral concern. See *theoretical aim.* (chap. 1, sec. 1)

Practical guidance, principle of   A principle for evaluating how well a moral theory does at satisfying the practical aim of such theories. According to this principle, a moral theory should feature principles that are useful in guiding moral deliberation toward correct or justified moral verdicts about particular cases which can in turn be used to help guide choice. See *practical aim.* (chap. 1, sec. 3)

Prevention   For example, someone is prevented by execution from committing a particular murder only if, had the individual not been executed, he or she would have committed the murder. (chap. 12, sec. 2)

Preemptive war   A war initiated by a state as a response to a clear imminent threat of attack by another state. (chap. 13, sec. 1)

Preventive war   A war initiated by one state as a response to an action of a potential aggressor who does not yet pose an imminent threat. (chap. 13, sec. 1)

Prima facie duty   An action which (1) possesses a duty-relevant feature where (2) this feature is a defeasibly sufficient condition for the action being an all-things-considered duty. (chap. 1, sec. 2F)

Principle of proportionality   A principle of punishment according to which the appropriate moral measure of specific punishments requires that they be in "proportion" to the crime: that the severity of the punishment should "be commensurate" with the gravity of the offense. See *retributive theory of punishment, lex talionis.* (chap. 12, sec. 2)

Principle of right conduct   A general moral statement that purports to set forth conditions under which an action or a practice is morally right and, by implication, when an action is morally wrong. (chap. 1, sec. 1)

Principle of utility   The fundamental moral principle of the utilitarian moral theory, according to which (in its "act" version) an action is morally right (not wrong) if and only if (and because) it would likely produce as high a utility as would any available alternative action open to the agent. See *utility.* (chap. 1, sec. 2A)

Principle of value   A general statement that purports to set forth conditions under which some item of evaluation (a person, experience, or state of affairs) is intrinsically good and, by implication, when any such item is intrinsically bad (or evil). See *intrinsic value, moral theory.* (chap. 1, sec. 1)

Psychotropic drug   A drug that produces changes in mood, feeling, and perception, including opiates, hallucinogens, stimulants, cannabis, and depressants. (chap. 5, sec. 1)

Racism   Racial prejudice or discrimination based on a belief that race is the primary determinant of human traits and capacities and that racial differences produce an inherent superiority of a particular race. (chap. 6, sec. 1)

Reparation   Activities involved in making up for past wrongs. (chap. 6, sec. 2)

Reproductive cloning   Cloning whose main purpose is to produce an individual member of the species. Human reproductive cloning has as its aim the production of a child. See *cloning, therapeutic cloning.* (chap. 11, intro.)

Retentionist   Someone who favors the death penalty and wants states that have it to retain it. (chap. 12, intro.)

Retributive theory of punishment   A theory of punishment according to which (R1) what morally justifies punishment of wrongdoers is that those who break the law (and are properly judged to have done so) *deserve* to be punished, and (R2) the punishment for a particular offense against the law should "fit" the crime. See *lex talionis, principle of proportionality.* (chap. 12, sec. 2)

Right   An entitlement (either moral or legal) to be free to engage in some activity or exercise some power or to be given something. See *legal rights, moral rights, negative rights, positive rights, rights addressee, rights content, rights holder.* (chap. 1, sec. 2D)

Rights   See *moral rights.*

Rights-based moral theory (R)   A type of moral theory according to which moral rights (claims) are the basis for explaining the rightness and wrongness of actions. See *moral rights, rights-focused approach.* (chap. 1, sec. 2D)

Rights-focused approach   An approach to moral issues that focuses primarily on moral rights. Such an approach need not be committed to a rights-based moral theory. See *moral rights, rights-based moral theory.* (chap. 1, sec. 2D)

Rights addressee   The individual or group against whom a right is held and who thus has an obligation toward the holder of the right. (chap. 1, sec. 2D)

Rights content   What a moral or legal right is a right to. (chap. 1, sec. 2D)

Rights holder   The individual or group that possesses rights. (chap. 1, sec. 2D)

Rights infringement   An action that goes against the rights of a rights holder but which in the circumstances is justified. A moral rights infringement is morally justified, a legal rights infringement is legally justified. (chap. 1, sec. 2D)

Rights, strength of   The strength of a right corresponds to how strong the moral or legal justification must be in order for the right to be justifiably overridden. The stronger the right, the stronger the justification must be in order to override the right. See *rights infringement.* (chap. 1, sec. 2D)

Rights violation   An action that goes against the rights of a rights holder and which is either not morally justified (and hence a moral wrong) or not legally justified (and hence illegal). (chap. 1, sec. 2D)

Rule consequentialism (RC)   Any version of consequentialism according to which the rightness or wrongness of some particular action that is (or might be) performed in some situation depends on the *acceptance value* of the rule corresponding to the action in question. A right action is one falling under a rule with at least as high an acceptance value as any other rule governing the situation in question. See *act consequentialism.* (chap. 1, sec. 2A)

Same-sex marriage   A marriage between members of the same sex recognized as legal by a state. (chap. 3, sec. 3)

SCNT individual   An individual produced through the process of *somatic cell nuclear transfer.* (chap. 11, sec. 1)

Sentience   The developed capacity to have experiences of pleasure and pain. (chap. 10, sec. 1)

Sentientism   The view that all and only sentient creatures—creatures who have the capacity to experience pleasure and pain—have *direct moral standing.* Thus, morality includes requirements of direct moral concern for all sentient beings. (chap. 15, sec. 2)

Sexism   Prejudice or discrimination based on sex, especially prejudice and discrimination against women. (chap. 6, sec. 1)

Social contract theory of morality   A species of moral theory according to which (roughly) correct or justified moral rules or principles are ones that result from some sort of social agreement—whether the agreement in question is conceived of as having actually taken place or (more likely) is hypothetical. (chap. 1, sec. 2G)

Somatic cell Any cell other than an egg or sperm (gametes). (chap. 11, notes)

Somatic cell nuclear transfer (SCNT)   Process of asexually producing an individual in which the nucleus of an unfertilized egg (oocyte) is replaced by the nucleus of a donor cell. This is the process involved in cloning. See *cloning.* (chap. 11, sec. 1)

Speciesism   The systematic discrimination against the members of some species by the members of another species. (chap. 9, sec. 2)

Stem cell   A cell found throughout the body that is significant because of its capability of developing into any kind of cell or tissue in the body. See *adult stem cell.* (chap. 11, sec. 1)

Suicide   Intentionally and thus voluntarily ending one's own life. (chap. 8, sec. 2)

Terrorism   The use of threat or violence against innocent people to elicit terror in them, or in some other group of people, in order to further a political objective. See *interrogational torture, terrorist torture.* (chap. 13, sec. 2)

Terrorist torture   Torture whose aim is to punish, coerce, or derive sadistic satisfaction. See *terrorism, torture.* (chap. 13, sec. 3)

Theoretical aim (of a moral theory)   To discover those underlying features of actions, persons, and other items of moral evaluation that *make* them right or wrong, good or bad, and thus *explain why* such items have the moral properties they have. Features of this sort serve as *moral criteria* of the right and the good. See *practical aim.* (chap. 1, sec. 1)

Therapeutic cloning   Cloning that aims only at producing an embryo which might then be used for medical purposes. See *cloning, reproductive cloning.* (chap. 11, intro.)

Torture   Activities involving the infliction of intense pain (either physical, psychological, or both) on a victim with the aim of punishing, coercing, or deriving sadistic satisfaction. See *terrorist torture* (chap. 13, sec. 3)

Universal Law formulation   A formulation of Kant's *categorical imperative* which states that an action is morally permissible if and only if the maxim associated with the action is universalizable. (chap. 1, sec. 2C)

Utilitarianism   A consequentialist moral theory according to which happiness has positive intrinsic value in terms of which actions are right or wrong. See *consequentialism, hedonistic utilitarianism, act consequentialism, rule consequentialism.* (chap. 1, sec. 2A)

Utility   A technical term introduced in connection with *utilitarianism* to refer to the net intrinsic value (positive or negative) of the consequences of some action or rule, where what has intrinsic positive value for the utilitarian is happiness and what has intrinsic negative value is unhappiness. (chap. 1, sec. 2A)

Value hedonism   A theory of intrinsic value according to which only states of pleasure possess positive intrinsic value (are intrinsically good) and only states of pain possess negative intrinsic value (are intrinsically bad or evil). This theory of value is featured in *hedonistic utilitarianism*. (chap. 1, sec. 2A)

Value perfectionism   The view that certain forms of human perfection have intrinsic value, the most general being knowledge and achievement. See *perfectionist consequentialism*. (chap. 1, sec. 2A)

Value-based moral theory   Any moral theory according to which the concept of intrinsic value is more basic than the concept of right action, and so right action is characterized or defined in terms of intrinsic value. Value-based theories are contrasted with *duty-based moral theories* and with *rights-based moral theories. Consequentialism* is one clear example of a value-based moral theory. (chap. 1, sec. 1)

Viability   The stage in fetal development wherein it is possible for the fetus to survive outside the uterus. (chap. 10, sec. 2)

Vice   A trait of character or mind that involves dispositions to act, feel, and think in certain ways, and is central in the negative evaluation of persons. See *virtue, virtue ethics*. (chap. 1, sec. 2E)

Virtue   A trait of character or mind that involves dispositions to act, feel, and think in certain ways, and is central in the positive evaluation of persons. See *vice, virtue ethics*. (chap. 1, sec. 2E)

Virtue ethics (VE)   A type of moral theory that makes considerations of virtue and vice the basis for explaining the rightness and wrongness of actions. See *virtue, vice*. (chap. 1, sec. 2E)

Voluntary euthanasia   Euthanasia in which the party has consented to the active bringing about of her death or to some means of passively allowing her to die. See *euthanasia, nonvoluntary euthanasia, involuntary euthanasia*. (chap. 8, sec. 1)

War   A state of usually open and declared armed hostile conflict between states or nations. (chap. 13, sec. 1)

Zygote   A fertilized ovum. Also called a "conceptus." See *embryo, fetus*. (chap. 10, sec. 1; chap. 11, sec. 1)